REAL ESTATE PRINCIPLES AND PRACTICES

REAL ESTATE PRINCIPLES AND PRACTICES

FIFTH EDITION

Edmund F. Ficek
Illinois State University

Thomas P. Henderson
Richland College

Ross H. Johnson
James Madison University

MERRILL PUBLISHING COMPANY
Columbus Toronto London Melbourne

Cover Photo: Larry Hamill

Published by Merrill Publishing Company
Columbus, Ohio 43216

This book was set in Garamond.

Administrative Editor: John Stout
Developmental Editor: Sally B. MacGregor
Production Editor: Mary M. Irvin
Art Coordinator: Vincent A. Smith
Cover Designer: Russ Maselli
Text Designer: Connie Young

Library of Congress Catalog Card Number: 89–62522
International Standard Book Number: 0–675–21129–8
Printed in the United States of America
1 2 3 4 5 6 7 8 9—94 93 92 91 90

PREFACE

This book is designed to provide a thorough understanding of the nature and practice of real estate from the practical viewpoint. It deals with a broad span of topics, and provides an in-depth coverage of appropriate subjects. This broad coverage gives the reader the background needed in everyday life and in various careers, and at the same time provides a basis for more specialized courses required for a real estate professional position. The book that also deals with contemporary and emerging issues related to real estate may affect a person purchasing or selling a home or considering real estate as an investment.

RATIONALE

This text assumes that the student has no prior educational or business background in real estate, and the topics are written accordingly. We have presented the concepts and practices in an understandable fashion, while retaining an appropriate depth of coverage needed by real estate professionals. Initially we introduce the basic principles and concepts of real estate, and then we explain their application to real estate practices. This text and its supplementary materials are intended for use in any of the following:

1. Basic courses in real estate at the university or community college level
2. Introductory college level courses to prepare students for more specialized courses such as real estate finance, investments, law and appraisal
3. Adult education courses designed primarily for investors, homeowners, and others seeking an understanding of the principles and practices of real estate
4. Courses directed primarily toward persons preparing for state real estate licensing examinations
5. As a reference for persons seeking to increase their professional skills as practicing brokers or salespersons, loan officers, mortgage bankers, trust officers, or farm managers

TEXT ORGANIZATION

The chapters in the text were sequenced to provide steps in a learning process so that chapters build upon one another. The first five chapters provide basic legal information the student needs for later topics. Chapters 6 through 12 proceed into the practical topics of real estate practices, including leasing and financing. Chapters 13 through 15 cover brokerage, marketing, and licensing. Chapters 16 and 17 summarize the closing of a residential transaction. The instructor can choose from the remaining chapters, placing preferred degrees of emphasis on these topics, possibly omitting chapters or portions of chapters.

NEW TO THIS EDITION

Real estate is a dynamic and exciting field. The changes in practice, legislation, and theory require constant attention. In this fifth edition, we have thoroughly revised every chapter. Some of the more important changes and new coverage include:

1. Updates in the finance chapters to cover current HUD rules and current practices in the secondary market. This includes coverage of the new FAMC (Farmer Mac).
2. New government assistance corporations established to help bail out FCS and FSLIC and other developments in the Savings and Loan industry.
3. New types of mortgages such as price level adjusted mortgage (PLAM), as well as REMTS and REMICS.
4. Recent developments related to buyer brokerage and new state requirements for disclosures by agents to potential buyers, as well as degrees of protection given to agents through errors and omissions insurance.
5. New developments related to home inspection, radon inspection, and steel fabrication in single family residential construction, along with changes in the 1974 manufactured housing act.
6. Risks placed on buyers by new environmental lien laws.
7. New cases related to downzoning and laws prohibiting spot zoning. Other recent court cases are cited where they affect rights of buyers, sellers, agents, property owners, and the public.
8. Revisions to Chapters 11 and 21, reflecting the impact of tax law changes on home ownership and investments.
9. New problems causing increased FHA foreclosures. HUD's trial plan to support reverse mortgages.
10. New rules to help alleviate abuses in property tax and insurance escrow accounts.
11. Fair Housing Amendment Act of 1988.

TEACHING PACKAGE

We have developed comprehensive supplementary materials to facilitate the learning process.

- The Instructor's Manual contains in-depth answers to the end-of-chapter problems in the text, and provides numerous multiple choice questions and selected case problems (with answers) for use by the instructor in preparing examinations.
- A computerized test bank is available to facilitate accurate preparation of examinations, giving the instructor a choice of questions.
- A set of over 150 updated transparency masters is also available to adopters.

QUALITY FIRST

This edition of *Real Estate Principles and Practices* was prepared under the Merrill Quality First concept. As professors, we are assured by this program that the publisher has expended extra effort, time, and resources to assure that Merrill books uniquely meet the needs of students and faculty.

ACKNOWLEDGEMENTS

We would like to thank our students and colleagues at Illinois State University, Richland College, and James Madison University for their input and observations. Important ideas and suggestions were provided by the reviewers of this edition: Charles Lafollette, University of Wisconsin at Stevens Point; Mike Owen, Western Kentucky University; Virgil O'Connor, Lindenwood College, Missouri; Michel Glower, The Ohio State University; and Carl Hemmeler, Columbus State Community College.

Thanks also to the production and design staff at Merrill Publishing Company for their professional treatment of our manuscript, and especially Sally MacGregor, developmental editor, who supported our progress throughout the project.

BRIEF CONTENTS

CONTENTS

CHAPTER 8
Instruments of Finance

CHAPTER 9
Taxes and Liens

CHAPTER 10
Land Use Planning and Zoning

CHAPTER 11
Home Ownership

CHAPTER 12
Real Property Insurance

277

CHAPTER 13
Brokerage

291

CHAPTER 14
Marketing Real Estate

311

CHAPTER 15
Federal Regulations, State Licensing, and Ethics

329

CHAPTER 20
Property Management

CHAPTER 21
Real Estate Investments

APPENDIXES

REAL ESTATE PRINCIPLES
AND PRACTICES

CHAPTER 1
The Real Estate Business

Real estate includes land and the structures built upon the land. We encounter real estate every day in our home living, our occupations, and our outside activities, and it makes up a substantial portion of the wealth of this or any nation. Land is a valuable asset that we must learn to conserve and to utilize effectively.

WHY WE STUDY REAL ESTATE

Each one of us owns or rents real estate to meet our basic housing needs, and the money we pay for housing represents a significant portion of our personal income. If we purchase a home, we are making a significant investment. Therefore, when we make a decision to rent or buy, or when we select between buying alternatives, we are making an important life decision. Although we might first think of real estate as a possible career when we begin to study this subject, knowledge of real estate is also very helpful in our personal lives. Real estate ownership has been a sound investment over the past fifty years. An understanding of real property, what gives it value, and the risks involved are important to each of us.

By recent estimates, the value of taxable real estate in the United States is especially impressive when we compare it to the value of stocks on the three major stock exchanges and to the value of savings and currency in circulation (see Figure 1–1).

The differences become more significant when we realize what a large amount of nontaxable real estate—not included in these figures—is owned by the federal and state governments and by tax-exempt organizations. These figures tend to highlight the importance of real estate in our economy.

A study of real estate also provides an opportunity to consider the many real estate career opportunities. These careers provide rewarding and interesting fields of work. In addition to the careers directly involving real estate sales and brokerage, every business is actually involved with real estate. Each business needs an office or building in which to operate. The selection of location and type of structure on the site can have a serious impact on the success of the business. Real estate also provides opportunities for investment, either personally or from a business standpoint. Knowledge of real estate will help us in evaluating investment opportunities. Thus, we see that the study of real estate provides an opportunity to evaluate a variety of career possibilities and gives us knowledge useful in our personal or business affairs.

PROPERTY RESOURCES

Before proceeding into the legal, economic, and business aspects of real estate, we will discuss several types of properties. Raw land has a wide variety of uses—food production; recreation; development into residential housing, factories, or commercial establishments. Land containing structures is called *improved property* and can be classified as residential, farm, commercial, industrial, or recreational. These cat-

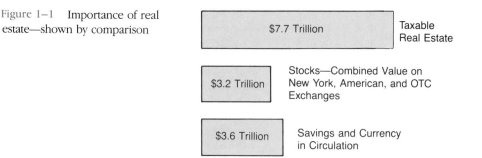

Figure 1–1 Importance of real estate—shown by comparison

$7.7 Trillion — Taxable Real Estate

$3.2 Trillion — Stocks—Combined Value on New York, American, and OTC Exchanges

$3.6 Trillion — Savings and Currency in Circulation

egories are based on the use or intended use of the property with its improvements. Urban areas require some of each of these property types. Urban planners usually designate a proper mix of these types to support the area's industry, commerce, and population.

Residential

The United States has become a nation of homeowners. The availability of financing has enabled a substantial percentage of families to own their own homes. Concurrently, many find it necessary to change their place of residence, either to improve their standard of living or to accept a job opportunity that requires a move to a different locality. These pressures create the need for more residential construction and for a system of marketing new and existing properties.

A recent census shows that approximately 68 percent of housing units were single-family homes, 28 percent were multiunit structures, and the remaining 4 percent were mobile units. About two-thirds of the units were owner occupied, leaving about one-third in rental status. In a typical community, about 3 to 10 percent of the units were vacant or for sale at any one time.

Single- and Multifamily Units

Residential property includes not only the single-family dwelling, but almost any type of structure designed for personal living. In addition to the single-family dwelling, other types of residence include the duplex, triplex, and four-family homes. Sometimes owners live in one of the units while renting out the others. Additional forms of residential dwellings are the town house, row house, and garden apartments.

Apartments

Apartments comprise a category of residential real estate defined officially as having five or more living units. Often they have several hundred units. They have become very popular with both older and younger persons. Many in these age groups do not want to be tied to one place, or do not have the substantial investment required to own a home, or prefer not to have the considerable responsibilities associated with home care.

Life insurance companies and investment trusts frequently invest in apartments because these investments often produce a relatively high rate of return. Although most apartments in the past have been located in urban centers, there is an increasing trend to construct new apartments in suburban areas. Apartments may be either high-, medium-, or low-rise or of the garden type. In any case, the success of an apartment as an investment depends to a large extent upon the skill of the property manager, who is responsible for maintaining adequate occupancy rates and for efficiently handling property maintenance. Although some hotels and motels have also been converted into residential housing, they are more suitably classified as commercial properties that cater to transient persons.

Condominiums and Cooperatives

Condominiums and cooperatives have become an increasingly important element in the real estate business, and their construction has increased considerably in the past twenty years. Both the condominium and the cooperative allow people who prefer an apartment-like environment to enjoy some of the financial advantages of home ownership. Although condominiums and cooperatives both provide a means for a person to invest in his own place of residence, there are important differences between the two.

In a *cooperative,* the title to the building and property is held by a corporation. The person who resides in a unit of the cooperative owns stock in the corporation and also has a proprietary lease on his apartment. Property taxes are levied against the corporation, and if there is any mortgage, the corporation is the mortgagor.

The *condominium,* in contrast, provides a means whereby each person residing in the building owns his own apartment, just as a home owner owns his own home. The owner of an individual unit in the condominium can sell his unit to someone else, he receives his own individual tax bill, and he can obtain a mortgage on his single unit. The number of condominiums in the United States has increased substantially since 1970, with couples over age forty-five whose children have left home representing the dominant buyers. In urban areas, many apartments as well as other buildings are being converted to condominiums.

Mobile Homes

From a legal viewpoint, mobile homes are usually considered personal property and not real property. They are mentioned here, however, because of their impact on the real estate business and because some states have special laws that consider mobile homes that are fixed in position much the same as real property.

Mobile homes consist of movable or portable year-round dwellings constructed without a permanent foundation. They can be towed on their own chassis and connected to utilities. Sometimes a mobile home consists of two or more sections that are towed separately and later combined. A mobile home may be comprised of units that can be telescoped for towing. Mobile homes make up a substantial portion of the housing that can be purchased for under $50,000. Frequently, the units contain many of the conveniences of regular homes. Most mobile homes are situated in mobile home parks where suitable utility connections are available.

Since, legally, mobile homes are considered personal property, they are not normally subject to real property taxes. In California, mobile homes without wheels are taxed as homes, however, and similar taxation is under consideration in other states. Mobile homes are subject to annual license fees. By paying rent for the space they occupy, their owners contribute indirectly to the taxing communities. It is often argued, however, that the mobile home owners' share of taxes is not in proportion to their use of schools and other services financed by real estate taxes.

Manufactured Housing

Prior to the 1970s the term *mobile home* referred to movable year-round dwellings constructed with or without permanent foundations. Most states considered them to be personal property, so that normal homeowner privileges and taxes did not apply.

The term *manufactured housing* now includes all housing constructed off the building site. Homes of this type are more widespread in the Sun Belt states. Previous restrictions prohibiting manufactured housing are being gradually abolished by state and municipal laws.

Commercial

Commercial properties include those that house retail and wholesale services, banking or other financial services, office space, and shopping centers. In general, the category includes most improved property acquired for investment purposes, except apartment houses and similar residential units. The trend to locate commercial property in suburban areas has increased as the population moves away from urban centers.

Central Business Districts (CBDs)

Through the 1940s, a central business district included an area's largest department stores, hotels, banks, office buildings, and other retail establishments. These facilities were grouped together for the convenience of pedestrian customers. This central business area also usually served as the center for culture and entertainment. Frequently the state, federal, and municipal government offices were located in this same general area. The central business district served further as the converging point for metropolitan transportation as well as intercity bus and rail transportation and highways. This high concentration of activities resulted in the need for substantial parking facilities in the area, and land in central business areas has tended to have a high per-square-foot value relative to other land. Changing neighborhoods have led to the demise of some central business districts. Some cities, however, have incorporated cultural centers, condominiums, or other more attractive land uses into their rejuvenated central business districts.

Shopping Centers and Malls

The increase in number and size of suburban shopping centers and malls has gone hand-in-hand with the expansion of residential housing in suburban areas. Malls and large shopping centers have come to be a focal point of suburban living by including not only retail establishments, but also theaters, post offices, churches, and recreational facilities. Other services include branch banking, insurance, real estate brokerage, fast foods, law offices, and amusement centers. The shopping center's popularity is due primarily to the convenience of having many facilities in one location. Shopping center development provides attractive opportunities for real estate investors because of the high ratio of building-to-land value. Tenants can either rent, buy, or purchase and lease back the store facilities. Developers emphasize the attractiveness of the facility design and the convenience of parking. The placement of a shopping center or mall enhances the expansion of the nearby urban area and the development of residential housing in nearby suburbs.

Cultural Centers

In some urban areas, the center of cultural activities is separate from the more congested central business district. The cultural center may group around a university or park. It can include a hospital, stadium, music hall, museum, botanical garden, zoo, and other activities. Secondary urban centers often develop around airports also. There is an increasing trend for these centers to have many facilities formerly found only in a central business district.

Industrial Property

Industrial properties are used for the manufacture and warehousing of industrial and consumer products. This category includes factories, utility companies, research laboratories, warehouses, and mining or lumbering operations. Industry has been following the general trend of moving into suburban areas where land is more abundant and parking space is more readily available. The trend has been toward industrial parks, which have one- or two-story buildings rather than the older style multistory structures. Industrial parks provide such advantages as readily available utilities and sewage facilities, maintenance, police protection, fencing, and existing streets. They are also usually situated close to transportation facilities. The trend toward greater use of truck rather than rail transportation has increased the suitability of outlying areas for industrial usage.

Industrial properties can be divided into *light* and *heavy* manufacturing. Heavy manufacturing generally creates more noise, air pollution, and other problems requiring that the plant be located at a greater distance from residential and cultural areas of the community.

Farm and Rural Property

Farm property is used for a variety of agricultural purposes such as crops, dairyland, ranches, pasture, orchards, and timber. In the past, farms were often small and were operated by the owner. Today, some farmland near urban areas has been taken over by industrial plants and urban residential expansion. Many other small farms have been consolidated into larger farms to spread costs and permit purchase of mechanized equipment and use of scientific methods to increase yields per acre. Some farmers have sold their property to neighbors, while others act as absentee landlords, with the land being farmed by a tenant. Recently, many farms have been purchased by investors and then leased back to the farmer to operate.

Recreation Property

Land and improvements used principally for leisure activities or vacations are classified as recreational property. This category includes lakeside properties, mountain and seaside resort property, golf courses, and amusement areas, as well as city parks. As people and the society become more affluent, they seek recreation areas with facilities for boating, fishing, swimming, skiing, hunting, camping, and other leisure activities. Most urban complexes of residential areas and commercial areas have recreation areas set aside.

Government Surplus Lands

The government, through its many agencies, owns approximately one-third of all the land in the United States, primarily in eleven western states and Alaska. Much of the land is designated as public areas. Other lands are turned over to public or private agencies for park or recreational use. Still other lands have been sold outright or leased to private citizens or local governments, which helps local governments broaden their tax base to support greater services for their citizens.

There are over 2.5 billion acres of land in the United States and trillions of dollars invested in buildings and other improvements on the land. Persons who select a career in real estate have the opportunity to influence the wise use of this resource. They also have the opportunity to participate in a field where growth is generated by increases in the population and in the gross national product. Residential housing, as well as commercial and industrial needs, provides an ever-increasing demand for real estate. As in most challenging and interesting careers, the practitioner must be willing to prepare for a position of responsibility by learning the technical, legal, economic, and business aspects of real estate.

The real estate business includes many, many career opportunities—including entrepreneurial opportunities for a person to run his own business, positions in large corporations or institutions, and opportunities for independent professional work. Real estate careers offer personal satisfaction because they offer interesting and challenging work and provide sufficient rewards in terms of prestige and salary to ensure a good standard of living. These careers relate to developing, marketing, financing, and managing real estate. These functional occupations tend to offer more independence than do positions in many other lines of business.

Land developers and builders may be thought of as performing the *production* function in real estate. They use the land by converting it into improved resources. Real estate brokers can be compared to the *marketing* function, since they provide the services needed for buyers and sellers to transfer ownership of property. The third functional area is *finance,* which is handled by banks, savings and loan associations, and investment companies.

In addition to these three functions, a variety of other professionals are involved in real estate transactions. As legal considerations are very important in every real estate transaction, attorneys become involved. Land planners and architects have the skills needed in development, construction, and urban planning. Property managers, appraisers, and consultants comprise other important professional groups. Each of these performs a highly specialized, important function.

Brokerage

The real estate brokerage operation is similar to the marketing function of other businesses. Brokerage involves buying and selling property by using marketing approaches such as promotion, advertising, and sales. From another viewpoint, the real estate broker is an agent. With professional knowledge and an established business as a background, the broker brings together people who wish to buy, sell, lease, or exchange real estate.

Brokerage is the largest branch of the real estate industry, with annual sales in the billions of dollars. Since everyone is a user of real estate, the broker works within a large market and is in a position to help many people satisfy their housing needs.

Real estate brokerages vary in size from one-person operations to large companies. Some are national firms, whereas others are local. Some brokers specialize, such as in commercial or farm properties, whereas others handle all kinds of real estate. Some concentrate in a specific part of a city, but others have multiple offices in the same city. Some brokers are on multiple listing services, whereas others are not. Finally, some brokerages deal with property management, appraisal, subdividing, construction, investments, or insurance. A person considering real estate as a career can select from a number of choices.

The Broker

The real estate *broker* needs professional as well as managerial capabilities to run a brokerage operation. He must have the technical knowledge to carry out the agency function in real estate, as well as the business knowledge to establish a business and manage other people. Many brokers belong to national or local professional real estate associations. The best-known of these is the NATIONAL ASSOCIATION OF REALTORS®, which has established professional and ethical standards for its members. Most states also require that real estate brokers pass examinations and meet other requirements in order to obtain a license.

The most important aspect of real estate brokerage is arranging the buying and selling of real estate. Brokers usually are compensated for their services in the form of a fee based on a percentage of the value of the property sold. The brokerage business depends to a large extent on public realization that the broker performs an important service. The success or failure of the individual broker depends to a great extent upon his ability to provide good service to his clients and upon his technical knowledge. As a manager, the broker is responsible for operating his business, which includes setting up an office, hiring people, directing advertising and promotion, and carrying transactions through to completion. The broker is also responsible for office personnel as well as salespeople. Sometimes, too, a broker will manage property for clients, perform appraisals where qualified, and handle other functions. The practice of management has become more scientific during the past two decades, and the broker can often take advantage of newly developed management concepts. He can use computers, market analyses, motivation concepts, studies of consumer behavior, and other techniques to improve his business performance and competitive edge. Many brokers earn very substantial incomes and direct large staffs of people.

The Salesperson

The real estate broker hires salespeople to sell real estate under his direction. A salesperson is usually paid on a commission basis. Most states require that salespeople be licensed only after having passed examinations showing technical competence in the legal, ethical, economic, and business aspects of real estate. Each salesperson must work for a licensed broker and cannot sell independently. As with brokers, much of the success of a salesperson depends on technical competence and the ability to provide services desired by buyers and sellers. Much of this success depends upon the reputation the salesperson builds up in the community. High earnings are available to the salesperson who works hard and is successful.

In any real estate transaction, the salesperson acts for the broker. State regulations require that the broker supervise the salespeople and assume responsibility for their actions. A salesperson can work for only one broker at any one time, usually under a contractual or employment agreement. As in most occupations, the real estate salesperson who enjoys the work and approaches it with a good attitude is often the one who is most successful.

Land Subdividers and Developers

This category of real estate professional buys land for subdividing and possible development and manages land development for other owners. Some developers are involved in long-term speculation, whereas others are involved in shorter-term improvements. The work may include the purchase of older properties for renovation, alteration, or modernization.

Land may be developed for residential, commercial, industrial, recreational, or other use. The developer is usually required to adhere to applicable urban master plans and local zoning regulations. Compliance with these requirements will also help ensure the compatibility and success of the projects. Frequently, the developer will subdivide a tract of land and improve it in steps. This method helps to reduce the initial financing required and allows the value of the land to increase as the development proceeds.

Builders

The construction of buildings represents an important part of the real estate business. The design of the structure by an architect is usually the initial step in the process. Architects consider the contemplated use of the building, its surroundings, and any other available land in designing a building. From the architect's plans and specifications, the owner will normally seek competitive bids from several contractors before selecting one. The contractor will then work for the owner in accordance with a signed contract agreement. The size of a contractor's operation varies from one who works alone in constructing a house to a multimillion dollar contractor such as U.S. Homes, the largest on-site residential builder in the United States. Usually the contractor will subcontract portions of the job such as the electrical work or plumbing.

Financing

Real estate has a long life over which it tends to retain its value. Since it requires substantial initial investment, outside financing is often necessary. Both private and government sources may be involved in financing real estate. These sources provide funding for everything from small residential properties all the way to very large hotels, office buildings, shopping centers, and entire housing developments. Banks, savings and loan associations, insurance companies, investment brokers, and the federal government are all involved. All of these institutions employ professionals knowledgeable in real estate to handle their part of the transactions.

Usually the financing institution receives a pledge of the property as security for a loan. In other words, the financial institution holds a mortgage on the property. This system lets the institution obtain an acceptable return on its money and also have good security. At the same time, the real estate developer or individual property owner obtains the funding needed for new construction. The financing of real estate involves the analysis of risk, appraisal, and extending credit, plus the servicing of the mortgage.

Investments

Some institutions, such as insurance companies, invest in real estate with the objective of securing a satisfactory return on the investment. Small investors also invest

9

or speculate in property with their own funds. Investment firms where real estate investment activity comprises an important part of the company effort seek persons knowledgeable in real estate and investments to fill challenging positions.

Consulting and Research

A number of companies, such as the Real Estate Research Corporation in Chicago, have research specialists in the various aspects of real estate. Typical consulting tasks include selecting a location for a company, managing property for a company, disposing of real estate, evaluating investment alternatives, and planning energy conservation. Independent consultants or counselors offer professional services just as do lawyers or other professionals. Counselors in real estate may belong to the American Society of Real Estate Counselors. Some real estate research centers—such as those at Texas A&M University and The University of Illinois—are funded from licensing fees.

Teaching

Courses in real estate are offered by universities, community colleges, and private organizations. Some universities offer bachelor's, master's, or doctoral degree programs in real estate. Most states require at least one course for a license to sell and additional courses for a brokerage license. Some states also require that licensees take courses periodically to maintain their licenses. All of these factors have increased the need for qualified persons to teach real estate courses.

Appraisal

Appraisers estimate the value of real estate. Buyers or sellers often want property evaluated before sales transactions. Those who estimate for tax purposes are called *assessors.* Financial institutions depend upon appraisers for estimates of value before mortgage loans are made. Appraisers who work independently charge a fee for each appraisal. Other appraisers are employed by banks, savings and loan institutions, or other companies. Extensive experience and training are required to achieve the professional appraisal designations offered by appraisal societies.

Property Management

Office buildings, hotels, apartments, resorts, and country clubs represent large investments in real estate and require professional property managers. The responsibilities of a property manager include securing and retaining tenants, service, public relations, maintenance, security, and financial management. Frequently property managers specialize in one category of real estate. The property manager carries considerable responsibility and is compensated accordingly. Some owners of income-producing real estate manage their own properties.

Legal

The many legal aspects of real estate transactions and ownership are carried out by an attorney at law. Many attorneys, banks, or other institutions have paralegals to assist in the increasingly complex aspects of these real estate transactions. Schools have responded by offering degrees in paralegal and related areas.

Real estate has many unique characteristics that make it different from other types of products. The characteristics can be divided into physical and economic features.

Physical Characteristics

Immobility

Buildings, soil, gravel, and other items considered part of real estate might be moved by the actions of nature or people; however, the piece of land itself is immobile and can never be changed from its geographical location. Because of its fixed position, land has become a primary source of taxation to support local government. The immobility allows the government to use a lien to force the sale of the land in order to collect unpaid taxes. Being immobile, the land is subject to control of the state and local governments under whose jurisdiction it exists.

Lack of Standardization

Another characteristic of real estate is its lack of standardization. No two properties are exactly the same. Homes of identical configuration can be different in value because of location, upkeep, paint color, exterior condition, interior decoration or furnishing, and many other factors. Even if the physical features of two homes were almost identical, zoning, deed restrictions, or title encumbrances could make their values considerably different.

Long Life

Most manufactured products change in style over the years, and real estate does also. Automobiles and electric appliances have a shorter life span, however, and may be discarded after two to ten years. Real property may have a life span of 10 to 200 or more years. Consequently, the real estate market may contain properties of considerably varying age at any one time.

Indestructibility

Indestructibility, the fourth physical characteristic of land, causes real estate to be a durable and relatively stable investment. Except for economic factors, land does not depreciate. In fact, it more often appreciates with time. This does not mean that property value cannot be destroyed; for instance, topsoil removal or strip mining might reduce the value or usability of land for agricultural purposes. The value of the property can also be reduced by lack of care or maintenance or other deterioration of improvements on the property or its surroundings.

Economic Characteristics

In addition to the physical characteristics, land also has its particular economic characteristics: scarcity, fixed investment, location, and improvements. These economic characteristics also have an impact on the manner in which real estate business is carried out.

Scarcity

Although there is a large amount of land that can be purchased at a low price, land in other, more desirable locations is *scarce* or very valuable. There is no scarcity of land as such; however, land for specific uses in specific locations is frequently insufficient to meet demand. As population increases, a scarcity of land to produce food might develop; however, in the recent past, the increase in productivity of the land due to fertilizers, better seed, and better crop management has resulted in a decrease in the total demand for land for food production. In many cases, however, prices of the best agricultural land have increased substantially.

In urban areas, the ability to construct higher buildings, combined with expressway construction, which gives greater access to more land, has also reduced the scarcity of land. Further expected improvements in land use may reduce this scarcity in the future; concurrently, however, new uses for land drive values up. Feelings that all land was scarce sometimes caused land booms in the past that were followed by price collapses when it became evident that there was not a real demand for the land.

Fixed Investment

A second economic characteristic of land is the fixed nature of the investment, or *fixity*. Most modifications or improvements to the land cannot be moved, and it may take twenty or thirty years to repay the investment; thus, the investment is long lasting. Buildings and associated facilities, once installed, become part of the real estate. This characteristic makes the value of a land investment highly dependent on the economic changes in a specific location or on changes in people's preferences. The property improvements are tied to the neighborhood in which the land is located. Therefore, before purchasing or improving land, an investor must consider how long the land's usefulness will last.

Location

Location, or *situs,* is the third economic characteristic of land. Similar pieces of real property may have extremely different values just because of the difference in location. This difference can be caused by people's preference for natural attributes, such as weather, good soil, scenery, or for human-made factors, such as schools, cultural attractions, or places of employment. Both affect the quality of the land, and, thus, the value. Changing conditions such as population shifts or industrial build-up or decline frequently cause some land to increase substantially in value and other land to deteriorate in value.

Improvements

The fourth economic characteristic of land is its ability to be modified or improved, with the associated impact upon the value. *Improvements on* the land include buildings, fences, or other things that then become part of the real estate. In contrast, *improvements to* the land include access roads, nearby schools, construction of recreational facilities and industries, and other factors that make the real estate more valuable, often without modifying the site itself. Land in its natural state is called *raw land*. Real estate having its value enhanced by improvements is called *improved land*.

THE REAL ESTATE MARKET

All businesses must *market* their products or services. Marketing any product involves the buying, selling, or exchanging of the product. The concept of a *market,* therefore, includes the buyer and seller and the places or means whereby they get together and transact business. Thus, the real estate market relates to the buying and selling of real estate, the people involved, and the places where the business is conducted. In real estate, however, the terms *buying* and *selling* must be extended to include renting and leasing to a much greater extent than with most other products. Renting and leasing, along with other services, form a large segment of the real estate market.

Market Characteristics

Local Markets

Because the product is immobile, the real estate market is made up of a large number of local markets, each isolated to some degree from other local markets. With other commodities, such as automobiles or food, a high demand or short supply in one area can be offset by moving products from other areas where there is an oversupply. This movement is not possible in real estate; therefore, home prices in one city may be considerably higher than they are for similar property in a city only fifty miles away. An oversupply of homes in one area cannot satisfy a shortage in another area. Thus, real estate prices are highly vulnerable to local events such as plant layoffs or declines in local industries.

Unorganized Markets

We saw that the immobility of real estate results in local markets. This, in turn, causes the real estate business to be highly decentralized and, to some extent, unorganized.

A person wanting to purchase or sell stocks or bonds can immediately determine the market price. Other items such as autos or refrigerators sell through retail establishments. Real estate does not have such an organized market. Buying and selling is a matter for negotiation for each transaction. Sale prices are private in nature and seldom publicized. Deeds of record do not usually specify prices but rather may state a phrase such as "for five dollars and other valuable consideration." Sale prices are of importance to persons in the real estate business, however, and they do attempt to compile sales price data.

Unbalanced Supply and Demand

The local nature of the market results in an uneven supply and demand in different cities. There may be a strong demand in some cities where economic conditions are good and, at the same time, a weak market in other cities where employment is low or industries are deteriorating. The lack of flexibility to adjust to this shifting demand results in a wide variance in prices, even between towns as close as fifty miles apart. This rigidity makes it difficult to adjust to sudden changes in demand caused by changing economic factors.

Private Transactions

A large percentage of real estate transactions are between individual buyers and sellers where neither party is in the real estate business. As an example, a person moving away may sell his home to another person moving into the area. This is unlike other products, such as automobiles, furniture, and so forth, where the purchase is made from a dealer. This difference concerning real estate results in differences in the marketing of the product.

Other Factors Affecting the Market

Other factors also affect the strength or weakness of the real estate market. Population trends certainly affect the need for residential housing. The population age grouping in an area also affects the market, since couples with young children will have different housing requirements from those of older people. Marriage rates, divorce rates, and family size also affect the residential units that are in demand. A shift in any, or all, of these factors has a substantial effect on the demand for each category of residential unit.

The types of employment available in a community also affect the level of income and, thus, the demand and supply of available housing. The rate of unemployment will affect the demand for housing at any particular time. Both of these factors are subject to change within a short time and can lead to a shift in demand.

Other important economic factors include inflation, building costs, labor wage rates, and the availability of money for investments and mortgages. A short supply of money for mortgages drives the interest rates up, with resulting buyer resistance to purchasing real estate.

Rental Market

About one-third of the existing housing is in rental units; however, recent trends to convert rental apartments to condominium units in urban centers have caused some changes in this market. The rental housing market satisfies the needs of a segment of the housing market that might be defined as follows:

1. Persons with less secure or lower incomes, including mobile or seasonal workers
2. Newly married couples without sufficient assets or income to meet the down payment, closing cost, or monthly payments needed to buy a home
3. Single persons
4. Some professionals or executives who prefer the luxury and convenience of urban centers

The rental market continues to be a significant proportion of the total real estate market.

Factors Related to Market Demand

The complicated nature of the real estate market makes it difficult to predict demand or to correlate it to other factors in the economy. Authorities, however, tend to believe that demand for housing is related to eight factors:

1. *Per capita disposable income.* Families or individuals with insufficient income tend to live with parents or relatives and postpone formation of new households.
2. *Price of housing.* When prices are higher, some families are unable to purchase homes or to improve their living arrangements.

3. *Formation of new households.* Rates of marriage influence demand.
4. *Construction, demolition, and conversion to condominium units.* Construction of highways and other building projects cause demolition of existing units. Conversion to condominiums takes rental units off the market.
5. *Movement of families.* Moving to different locations because of job changes or other reasons.
6. *Personal savings.* The purchase of real estate requires a substantial down payment.
7. *Living style requirements.* Family size, changes in availability of labor-saving appliances, and number of employed persons in the family affect the demand for varied sizes of homes.
8. *Mortgage money availability and cost.* High interest rates and high down payments make purchases more difficult.

Measures of Market Conditions

The complex factors involved in the real estate business make it difficult to measure market conditions or predict future market conditions. The following are some of the more frequently used indicators of real estate market conditions.

1. *Vacancy rates.* High vacancy rates indicate a poorer market. Although normal vacancy rates vary from one locality to another, a rate of 5 percent is often used as a norm.
2. *Deed transfers.* The number of transactions is a good measure of the real estate market and can be tabulated by counting records of deed transfers.
3. *Mortgage foreclosures.* An increase in the rate of mortgage foreclosures tends to correspond to a decline in real estate market activity.
4. *Construction rates.* The number of new units built and the inventory of unsold homes indicate real estate market activity. Records of housing starts and building permits are both good sources of information. Sometimes, however, demand may shift up or down, but construction does not respond very quickly. Figure 1–2 shows housing starts over a recent period.
5. *Farmland prices.* Considerable publicity has spotlighted the plight of some farmers in the 1980s. There was a relatively stable price period in the 1960s, large increases in the 1970s, and then falling prices in the 1980s. A farmer who mortgaged his farm when prices were high found the land value dropping below the mortgage balance by 1983–84—a time of unfavorable prices for farm products.
6. *Inflation.* Figure 1–3 shows the increase in median price of a home in the United States from 1980 to 1988. In some locations, such as San Francisco, Boston, and New York, the median was about twice the national median.

Other indexes of economic activity, such as employment and gross national product, correlate with real estate market activity. These indexes are published in business periodicals such as *National Market Letter,*[1] a real estate newsletter that publishes data by region of the United States.

---

[1]*National Market Letter* (Chicago: Real Estate Research Corporation). Published monthly.

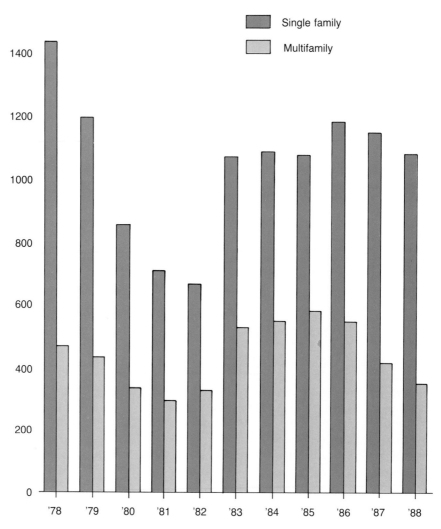

Figure 1–2   Housing starts, 1978–1988 (thousands of units)

Source: U.S. Bureau of the Census

SUMMARY

Land and improvements on the land provide the resources with which the real estate business works. Improved land can be classified as *residential, commercial, industrial, farm,* or *recreation.*

The development, construction, marketing, and financing of real estate provide a wide variety of interesting and challenging careers. Many of these occupations require a substantial amount of formal education.

The real estate market provides the means for handling the transactions required for all the categories of real property.

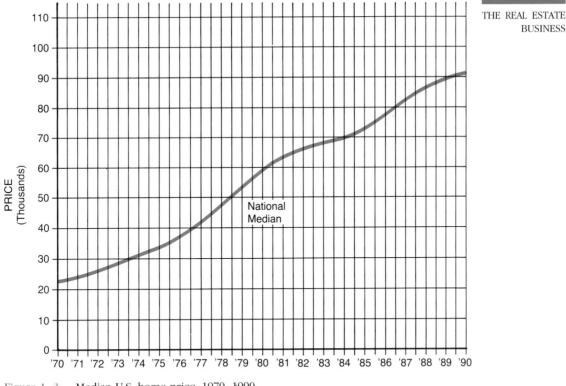

Figure 1–3   Median U.S. home price, 1970–1990

Source: U.S. Department of Commerce

Real estate itself is different from other products: real property is immobile, and each parcel of real estate is different in one way or another from any other parcel. Therefore, the real estate market is local in nature; prices, problems, and demand differ from one place to another.

Although there are published data and indexes purporting to measure the real estate market, in actuality, the large number of contributing factors makes it difficult to measure the real estate market accurately.

TERMS AND CONCEPTS

You can check your understanding of these terms against the glossary or by review in this chapter.

Apartment	Cooperative	Manufactured housing
Appraiser	Finance	Marketing
Assessor	Fixity	Production
Broker	Improved property	Raw land
Commercial property	Improvement	Residential property
Condominium	Industrial property	Situs

1-1. What aspects of real estate careers do you personally find most attractive? Which aspects are not attractive to you?

1-2. Review the real estate ads in the classified section of your local newspaper, and identify agents who tend to specialize in certain types of real estate.

1-3. In the area where you are living, how would you describe the geographical limits of the local real estate market?

1-4. What types of real estate would tend *not* to be part of a local market?

1-5. Identify an area of your community where most of the houses are rental units. Identify another area where most are owner-occupied. Explain the differences between the two areas.

1-6. Do you think mobile homes should be considered *real estate* for tax purposes?

1-7. List the factors that cause both a good and a poor real estate market. What other factors are a market influence in your particular area?

1-8. List the factors that authorities feel are correlated to the real estate market. What action by each of these factors would tend to indicate a *good* real estate market?

1-9. List the physical and economic characteristics of land.

■■■■ ■ **SUPPLEMENTARY READINGS**

Crean, Michael J. *Principles of Real Estate Analysis.* New York: Van Nostrand, 1979. Chapters 1 and 2.

Downs, James C. *Principles of Real Estate Management,* 12th ed. Chicago: Institute of Real Estate Management, 1980. Chapters 1–6.

Goulet, Peter G. *Real Estate.* Encino, Ca.: Glencoe, 1979. Chapters 1 and 10.

Lee, Steven J. *Buyers Handbook for Cooperatives and Condominiums.* New York: Van Nostrand Reinhold, 1982.

Mannheim, Uriel. *How to Do Housing Market Research: A Handbook for Local Home Builders Associations.* Washington, D.C.: National Association of Home Builders, 1973.

Reilly, John W. *The Language of Real Estate,* 3rd ed. Chicago: Real Estate Education Company, 1989.

Ring, Alfred A., and Dasso, Jerome. *Real Estate Principles and Practices,* 11th ed. Englewood Cliffs, N.J.: Prentice-Hall, 1989. Chapters 1, 2, 27, 28.

Unger, Maurice A., and Karvel, George R. *Real Estate Principles and Practices,* 8th ed. Cincinnati: South-Western, 1987. Chapters 1 and 2.

Wofford, L. E. *Real Estate,* 2nd ed. New York: Wiley, 1986.

■■■■ ■ **SOURCES OF CURRENT BUSINESS DATA**

"Construction Cost Index." American Appraisal Company, 525 E. Michigan St., Milwaukee, Wis.

"Construction Review." U.S. Department of Commerce/Bureau of Industrial Economics.

"Dodge Reports." F. W. Dodge Corporation, 119 W. 40th St., New York, N.Y.

Herman, George D. "Real Estate Data." Chicago: REALTORS® National Marketing Institute, 1980.

"The Housing Letter." The Housing Institute, 350 Fifth Ave., New York, N.Y. (biweekly)

"Monthly Construction Report Series." Bureau of the Census, U.S. Department of Commerce, Series C-40 and C-42.

"Monthly Vital Statistics Report." U.S. Department of Health, Education and Welfare.

"National Market Letter." Real Estate Research Corporation, Chicago. (monthly)

"Real Estate Analyst." Roy Wenzlich and Company, 706 Chestnut St., St. Louis. (monthly)

"Real Estate Today." NATIONAL ASSOCIATION OF REALTORS®, Chicago. (monthly)

"Realtor News.®" NATIONAL ASSOCIATION OF REALTORS®, Chicago. (weekly)

"Savings & Loan News." United States League of Savings Associations. (monthly)

CHAPTER 2
Land and Its Legal Descriptions

The surface of the earth is often referred to as *land,* but a true definition of land includes the earth below the surface and the air space above the land. *Land,* by legal definition, also includes permanent natural things such as trees and water, as well as minerals or other elements below the surface of the earth. ***Real estate,*** by definition, includes not only the land as defined above, but also improvements to the land and certain rights to its use. Purchasers of land have the right to assume that they are buying not only the land itself, but also any structures thereon. They also have the right to assume that they can use and maintain the structures and the land substantially as it has been used in the past. Some writers use the term *real estate* to refer to the physical land and structures, whereas they use the term ***real property*** to refer to property rights. These possible differences in definitions should be recognized by the reader; however, this text uses *real estate* and *real property* interchangeably.

LEGAL DESCRIPTIONS

The process of conveying real property from one party to another requires a positive method of property identification and description. These legal descriptions are used in contracts and deeds that convey real property from one person to another. It is necessary that any piece of real property can be unquestionably differentiated from any other piece and the exact boundaries determined. In some instances, an estate has been adequately described and conveyed by a name such as "The Highmark Estate"; however, the instances where property can be so identified are rare and sometimes open to question. Any lapse of time must not interfere with this ability to be able to clearly define the property and any improvements on it. If one person owns a parcel of property for thirty or forty years, many things can change. In the intervening period, street and road names may be changed, or neighboring properties might change ownership. If it is raw land, it may be subdivided or pieces sold from the main parcel. Houses can be torn down and replaced by apartments, or other factors may make the simple street address insufficient to identify the property clearly.

The legal description for real property provides this positive legal identification and the means to identify the exact same parcel clearly at a later date. Several methods are available to assure the identification of land so that there is no question as to the property involved or of its exact boundaries. The technical capabilities of land surveyors and the accuracy of their instruments are necessary to provide these exacting methods.

The three primary means for legally describing real estate are (a) *rectangular survey,* sometimes called *government survey,* (b) *metes and bounds,* and (c) *subdivision and lot,* sometimes called a *plat.* Two secondary methods are (d) monuments and (e) street and number. These secondary methods are often used to supplement the primary methods. Legal descriptions use one or more of these methods, and it is not unusual for a parcel of real property to be described by a combination of methods.

RECTANGULAR SURVEY

The rectangular survey system, or government survey system, was adopted by Congress in 1785. At that time the United States was expanding rapidly to the west, and it became evident that a simple and accurate method for identifying land was needed. Vast new land areas were being opened, and the government wanted to encourage settlement by assuring ownership rights to settlers. The rectangular survey system is based upon lines running north and south called *meridians,* which intersect with *baselines* running east and west. Certain of these meridians are called *principal meridians* or *prime meridians.* The map in Figure 2–1 shows the principal meridians in the United States and the baseline associated with each principal meridian.

As shown on the map, the rectangular system applies to most of the United States except for the white areas, which include Texas, the area covered by the original colonies, and a portion of Ohio. The original colonies included the first thirteen states—New Hampshire, Massachusetts, Connecticut, Rhode Island, New York, New Jersey, Pennsylvania, Maryland, Delaware, Virginia, North Carolina, South Carolina,

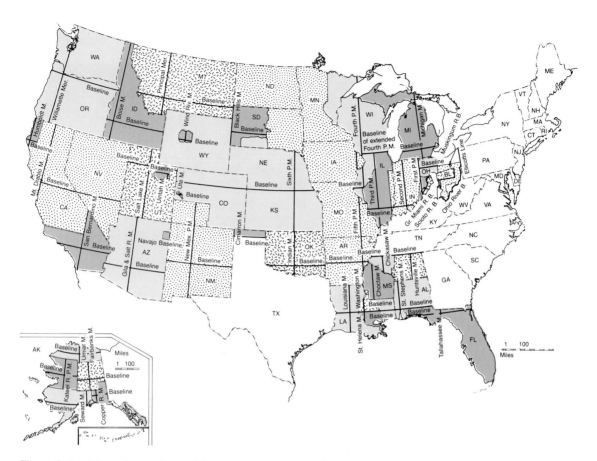

Figure 2–1   Principal meridians of the government rectangular survey system

Source: U.S. Department of the Interior, Bureau of Land Management. "Public Land Statistics, 1970."

and Georgia—and the states of Kentucky, Tennessee, Vermont, Maine, and West Virginia, which were admitted as states later.

In the area covered by the rectangular survey system, any piece of property is officially located relative to one particular meridian and its baseline. A parcel of land is not necessarily identified from the closest principal meridian; however, the location of any one parcel of land is never described from more than one principal meridian and the single baseline associated with that principal meridian.

The portion of the United States to which the rectangular grid system applies is divided into areas such that each area relates to a single principal meridian. As an example, Figure 2–2 shows a group of midwestern states and the specific areas associated with each meridian. These areas do not necessarily follow state lines. For example, there are two principal meridians actually in Illinois—the Third and Fourth Principal Meridians; however, an eastern piece of Illinois is related to the Second Principal Meridian, which is located in Indiana. Each piece of land in Illinois is associated with one of these three meridians. These principal meridians are numbered, whereas others have names, such as the Tallahassee Meridian or Michigan Meridian (shown in Figures 2–1 and 2–2).

Figure 2–2   Some principal meridians and associated baselines

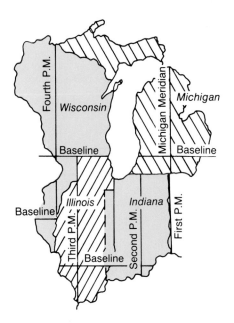

Township

The rectangular grid system subdivides land into smaller and smaller squares as necessary to describe precise locations of real property. The basic unit is the **township**, which is a square six miles on each side. Starting at the baseline in Figure 2–3, township lines run parallel to the baseline at each six-mile interval both north and south of the baseline. Those townships in the first tier are identified as T1N, or "township-one-north." The second tier is T2N, and so on. This system extends as far as necessary to cover the area related to the principal meridian and baseline. Townships numbered T30N or T40N are not unusual, since there is no limit on the numbers. Every fourth **township line** is also called a **parallel** or *standard parallel* or is sometimes called a **correction line**.

Range lines run every six miles east and west of the principal meridian to form the east and west boundaries of the township. Every fourth **range line** is called a **guide meridian** or just a *meridian*. Guide meridians run true north, but they are not exactly parallel to each other since they meet at the poles. This results in the need for a correction as shown in Figure 2–3a. The term **check** or **quadrangle** is used to describe a block of sixteen townships bounded by a parallel and a meridian, but it is seldom used in a legal description.

A particular township is designated, for example, as T9N, meaning the ninth tier of townships above the baseline, and as R3E to designate the third tier of townships east of the principal meridian (Figure 2–3b).

Section

The next smaller unit in the rectangular system is the **section,** which is 1 mile square. Two of the townships in Figure 2–3 are divided into sections, and Figure 2–4 shows the numbering of sections within a township, beginning with one at the upper right corner and sweeping left and right back and forth toward the bottom. In a few old surveys in Ohio, for example, the section numbering system is different,

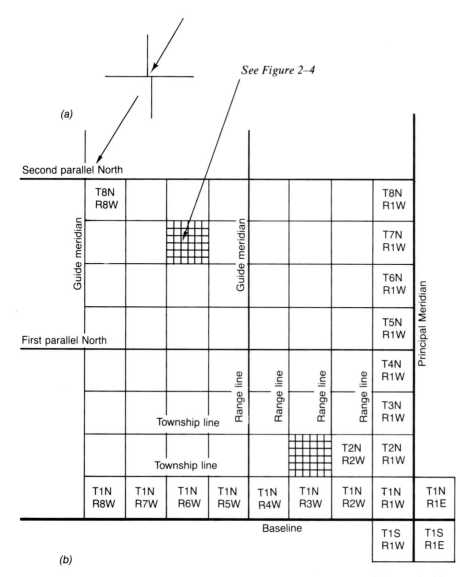

(a)

See Figure 2–4

Second parallel North

Guide meridian

T8N R8W

First parallel North

Township line

Range line

Range line

Range line

Range line

Township line

Guide meridian

Principal Meridian

T8N R1W

T7N R1W

T6N R1W

T5N R1W

T4N R1W

T3N R1W

T2N R2W

T2N R1W

| T1N R8W | T1N R7W | T1N R6W | T1N R5W | T1N R4W | T1N R3W | T1N R2W | T1N R1W | T1N R1E |

Baseline

| | T1S R1W | T1S R1E |

(b)

Figure 2–3   *(a)* Detail of intersection of parallel and guide meridian. *(b)* A grid of four checks (or quadrangles); each check 24 miles by 24 miles, divided into 16 townships.

6	5	4	3	2	1
7	8	9	10	11	12
18	17	16$_s$	15	14	13
19	20	21	22	23	24
30	29	28	27	26	25
31	32	33	34	35	36

Figure 2–4   A township of 36 square miles contains 36 sections, each 1 mile square

starting at the lower right and proceeding upward. Section 16 in any township was designated as a *school section* in the original survey to assure adequate land for schools within each township.

To locate smaller tracts of land within a section adequately, the section is subdivided into halves, quarters, or other fractions until a small enough part is defined to identify the parcel of land involved clearly. Figure 2–5 shows examples of portions of sections and the identifying description. A parcel of land might be defined as the NW¼ of the SE¼ of the SW¼ (NW¼ SE¼ SW¼) of Section 10. In relating a verbal description to the corresponding diagram, it is easier to start with the last item (i.e., SW¼) and work backward. This approach breaks the section into smaller and smaller parts.

Try to locate NW¼ of SE¼ of SW¼ in Figure 2–5. Working backward, the SW¼ is the lower left quarter of Figure 2–5. This verbal description then defines the cross-hatched area. A whole section is 640 acres, so the SW¼ would be 160 acres. The SE¼ of that would be forty acres, and the cross-hatched area would then be ten acres. Notice that the odd-sized pieces can be described by using *and* to replace *of* in the description, as illustrated by N½ of NW¼ of NE¼ and NE¼ of NE¼, giving the sixty-acre tract in the upper right corner. The "and" indicates there are two pieces making up the total parcel.

The concepts around which the rectangular (or governmental) survey system is laid out permit their use in describing a piece of property very clearly. A complete legal description for a piece of land could then be the NW¼ of the SE¼ of the SW¼ of Section 10 in T9N, R3E of the Third Principal Meridian. To locate a lot from a description, work backwards; in this example start with SW¼.

Land Measures

The following land measures are important in the use of the rectangular system and other legal description methods:

1 mile = 5,280 feet = 1.61 kilometers
1 acre = 43,560 square feet = 160 square rods = 4,050 square meters
1 square acre = 208,713 feet on each side
1 rod = 16½ feet = 5.03 meters
1 section = 1 square mile = 640 acres = 259 hectares
1 circle = 360 degrees (360°)
1 degree = 60 minutes (60′)
1 minute = 60 seconds (60″)
1 hectare = 2.471 acres = 10,000 square meters
1 yard = 3 feet = 0.91 meters

Corrections

Theoretically, each township is exactly six miles square and contains thirty-six square miles. Due to the shape of the earth, however, meridians eventually converge at the poles, so that in the northern hemisphere the north side of a township will be about fifty feet shorter than the south side. The rectangular survey system tries to compensate by establishing every fourth township line as a correction line, while leaving intervening townships a full six miles wide at top and bottom.

The detail would then appear as in Figure 2–3a, where a guide meridian is drawn

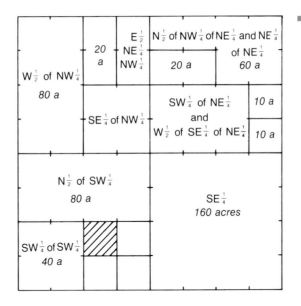

Figure 2–5 The section divided into various size parcels of land. The section contains 640 acres.

parallel to the principal meridian starting twenty-four miles away. Thus the square of sixteen townships is slightly narrower at the north than at the south. In practice, all townships are made square except those with their left sides along a guide meridian or their north boundaries along a parallel. In Figure 2–3b, all townships with a R4W, R8W, T4N, or T8N would have a correction and would not be absolutely square. Inaccuracies in survey, however, can also result in a township being unintentionally different from the exact six-mile by six-mile size. Since many townships contain less than the thirty-six square miles, rules have been established for making the adjustments. The rules provide that any shortage is taken from sections on the north and west boundary of a township, so that all other sections are surveyed to exactly one mile square.

The physical layout of the land may also cause sections not to be exact squares. Part of a section being under a lake could cause this situation. Other irregularly shaped sections occur where gaps were left in the original survey, which was carried out by survey teams. Gaps often occurred at junctions of areas surveyed by different teams. When the original government survey was completed, the survey results were recorded in U.S. district land offices. This recorded survey is the basis for describing land in that area.

Government Lots

In the original survey, lakes, streams, or other land features were sometimes encountered that created fractional pieces of land less than a quarter section in size. These pieces were designated in the original survey as *government lots.* These government lots were identified by number, and the lot number given to a piece of land in the original survey is the legal description of that piece of land.

A typical use of government lot numbers is illustrated in Figure 2–6, where the dotted lines represent one-sixteenth of a section. A piece of land might then be completely described as Government Lot 4 in Section 22, T3N, R4W of the Fourth Principal Meridian.

Figure 2–6 Designation of government lots

Reprinted by permission from *Farm Appraisal and Valuation,* by William G. Murray, fifth edition, © 1979 by Iowa State University Press, Ames, Iowa.

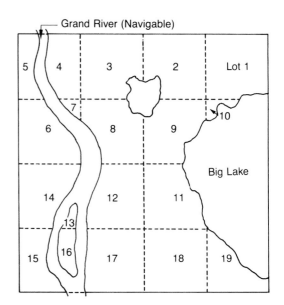

METES AND BOUNDS

The oldest method of describing land is by "metes and bounds." The method of metes and bounds can be likened to a walk around the edges of the property. *Metes* refers to distance measures using feet, inches, rods, meters, or other measure. *Bounds* refers to directions or landmarks used to locate the boundaries of the property. Bounds can refer to natural monuments such as trees or rocks; to artificial monuments such as stakes, walls, or posts; or to boundaries such as roads or streams on which the method may rely. The system can also use distances and directions only, as computed from a survey.

In the states equivalent to the original thirteen colonies and a few others, the method of metes and bounds is very significant since the states were not surveyed in the rectangular system.

Each "metes and bounds" description must have a starting point or *point of beginning (p.o.b.).* This point is usually identified relative to a road, stream, or some natural or artificial monument. Care must be taken in selecting the point of beginning since destruction of the item used can invalidate a property description. Starting at the p.o.b., the description proceeds clockwise around the property. It returns to the p.o.b. to form the enclosed parcel of land. The following example is a metes and bounds description of the property shown in Figure 2–7.

Commencing at a monument set at the SE point of the intersection of Manchester Avenue and Northpoint Road, proceed 240 ft directly East along Manchester Avenue to the point of beginning (p.o.b.); then 90 ft further directly East along Manchester Avenue; then S11°20'E for 184.3 ft; then directly West 141.2 ft; then 180.75 ft directly North to the point of beginning.

Note that once the p.o.b. is located, the complete parcel can be identified by only distance measurements and directions, which can be readily accomplished by a surveyor with a transit and tape.

Sometimes a metes and bounds description includes reference to natural monu-

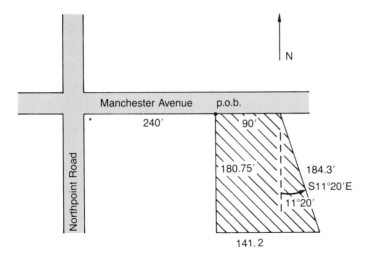

Figure 2–7 Property with metes and bounds description

ments such as a tree or large rock. It could also refer to artificial monuments such as a concrete post, edge of a road, stake, or corner of a building. In Figure 2–7, assume that the description reads "then S11°20′E for 184.3 ft, more or less, to the center of a concrete fence post." The only difference from the first description is that the concrete post has been introduced as an additional artificial monument. Frequently a long pipe is driven into the ground at the corner of a lot to serve as this monument. It is against the law to remove stakes inserted for property identification purposes. What if a later survey found the distance to be different from that in a property description? Distances and directions in a deed always give way to monuments if there is any discrepancy. The words "more or less" in the description allow for clarification of any apparent discrepancy and, therefore, actually strengthen the description. If the property were in a rural area with no street or other clearly recognizable bounds, it could be important to carry measures to the hundredths of a foot and express direction in degrees, minutes, and seconds. For a parcel of land, the distance along the road or along a lake is often used to determine value or to assess taxes. In Figure 2–7, this *front footage* is 90 feet.

Directions or bearings can be measured from magnetic north and south, usually called *magnetic bearings,* or from a meridian, usually called *true bearings.* Figure 2–8 shows magnetic bearings along with some examples of directional bearings.

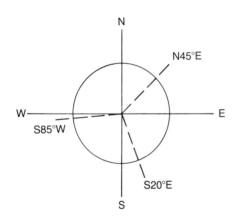

Figure 2–8 Direction measurements used in surveys

The bearing is the direction in which the surveyor is heading as he leaves a corner while walking around the property clockwise. Figure 2–8 shows that a bearing can deviate not more than 90 degrees from either north or south. A direction such as N95°E would more properly be expressed as S85°E.

SUBDIVISION AND LOT

The construction of new homes in an urban area usually involves breaking up a tract of land into lots as sites for building houses. Most municipalities require a careful survey of the subdivision tract showing blocks, lots, and streets. Each lot is assigned a lot number. Most local governments apply stringent regulations over the subdivision of land either for residential or industrial development. Prior to proceeding with any work, the developer must have the land surveyed and laid out in a *plat map*, showing lots, their exact sizes, streets, utility easements, and any areas dedicated to park use. Maps showing size, location, and shape of buildings are referred to as *spot surveys*.

Frequently, portions of the subdivision are set aside for parks or shopping centers. The process of setting aside a parcel of land for public use is called *dedication*. If Figure 2–7 were expanded to include other lots, it would look much like a plat. The plat is part of the material submitted to the government department having responsibility to review and approve the plan. Sometimes the review may involve a public hearing. When approved, the survey is recorded in the office of the Recorder of Deeds; the plat is maintained in the county Deed Registry Office. In any later conveyance of these lots from the developer to a buyer, or from the original purchaser to a new buyer, the lot number and plat reference form a legal description. Once a plat is approved and recorded, lots cannot be resubdivided without approval of the appropriate city or county board.

SECONDARY METHODS USED IN LEGAL DESCRIPTIONS

The three primary methods used in legal descriptions are rectangular survey, metes and bounds, and subdivision and lot. Other methods are monuments, tract, and street address. Most legal descriptions use more than one of these methods. The objective is to use as much description as necessary to establish an unquestionable identity for the land. There are many natural and artificial features of land that affect the ease or difficulty of property description and identification. The impact of natural features such as lakes and streams or of artificial features such as fences becomes important in legal descriptions. They can serve as easily observable boundaries; however, a body of water may interfere with the ability to survey accurately, or the route of a stream or shoreline may change. A statement of quantity (e.g., 5.4 acres) is usually considered supplementary information. If inconsistencies occur in a legal description, the usual order of precedence is (a) natural monuments or landmarks, (b) artificial monuments, (c) adjacent boundaries or adjoining tracts, (d) courses (directions) and distances, and (e) quantity.

Monuments

Monuments provide a means of land description, usually used in conjunction with metes and bounds, rectangular survey, or plat; however, in a few situations, they might be used alone. **Monuments** are points on the surface of the earth that serve as relatively permanent reference points from which to identify land. They can be either tangible or intangible. Tangible monuments such as trees, rocks, streams, posts, and streets, can be seen visibly. An example of an intangible monument would be the corner of a section in the rectangular survey system. It can be accurately located by survey, but it is not visibly identifiable unless a stake has been placed there.

In a remote area where land is relatively cheap, a parcel of property might be described solely by monuments. A forested plot used for hunting or camping would be an example. In these situations, possible small errors in the property line would not be significant enough to justify the expense of a survey. The familiarity of the land to both buyer and seller could be sufficient to assure that each has the same tract in mind, and actual acreage or distances are of less importance. A metes and bounds description for the property illustrated in Figure 2–9, using recognizable features only, would read in this way:

> Commencing at the bridge where Haletown Road crosses Lime Creek, proceed in a general southwest direction along Lime Creek about one-half mile to the fence separating the Pierce property from the property of Jameson. Then follow this fence to where it intersects Haletown Road, and along Haletown Road to the point of beginning.

Street and Number

The property identification familiar to almost everyone is the street address. Over a period of years, however, street names sometimes change and new subdivisions or streets are constructed. The construction of houses or apartments on previously

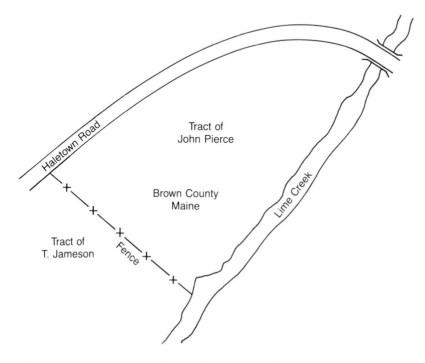

Figure 2–9   Property described by features of the land

vacant lots or the destruction of older buildings and new construction may result in the renumbering of property. Sometimes streets are permanently closed and the signs removed. These and other factors make the use of street name and house number an unreliable means for permanent and unquestionable identification of real estate. In a deed or contract, however, a legal description will usually be followed by a phrase such as this:

. . . known as 815 Manchester Road, Jonesville, Illinois

This statement assures the parties of the transaction that both have the same property in mind.

Tracts

Well-known names of tracts of land have been held to be sufficient legal description in some cases. A deed might convey "The Mt. Pleasant Estate" and be held a valid conveyance. A parcel of property might also be described by reference to neighboring tracts, sometimes showing the name of the owner of the adjacent tract.

In addition to one or more of the formal methods of description, deeds sometimes contain a so-called *"being" clause.* For example, the clause might state,

Being the same property as conveyed to the grantor by Jack and Martha Jones by deed dated June 24, 1971.

Roads and Fences

When land is conveyed from a seller (grantor) to a buyer (grantee) using reference to a road, the grantee secures title to the middle of the road, providing of course that the grantor held such title. This established precedent is valid unless the contract clearly states otherwise. The public right prevails, however, for use of the road. If a public road is abandoned at some time, the property owner again assumes ownership of land to the center of the old road.

Fences can be built either on a property line or entirely on either of the adjacent properties. If the fence is completely on one property, over a number of years the fence often becomes recognized by both parties as the boundary. In this case, the fence can become the actual legal boundary whether or not it is on the original property line, if it is used as a boundary for a set number of years.

Streams and Lakes

Streams frequently form the natural boundary for real property. Where these bodies of water form the property boundary, the grantee takes title to property to the center of nonnavigable streams. For *navigable* waterways, the high-water mark is the common-law boundary; however, in some states the low-water mark is the boundary by statute. A natural question is the definition of a navigable stream, since a raft can be used on almost any depth water. Navigable streams are those identified as navigable on a federal survey map. The land between the high- and low-water marks of navigable streams or rivers is known as *flat land,* and the rights of the property owner are subservient to the public use of the river or stream for navigation purposes.

Owners of land edging on navigable lakes are considered to own to the high- or low-water mark (depending on the state law) of the lake, and the submerged portion of the navigable body of the water is considered to be held in title by the state.

The owner of property bordering a stream has the rights of uninterrupted flow of that stream as well as nonpollution of the water. Obviously, the value of a piece of land can depend upon the availability of usable water for humans, livestock, or irrigation. Artificial changes in the flow of natural bodies of water are not permitted if they injure the rights of another owner. Gradual changes in the bed of a nonnavigable stream due to deposit of soil *(accretion)* or shrinking of the water course *(dereliction)* will change a boundary. A sudden change (such as that following a torrential rain), however, does not affect the boundary if the original course of the stream can be located and the stream is restored to its previous course.

State Plane Coordinate System

Since the methods described so far depend heavily on physical landmarks, those methods are sometimes supplemented by reference to points in the state plane coordinate system. Points have been specified in each state that were located in latitude and longitude in a project initiated by the U.S. Coast and Geodetic Survey in 1933. Although not readily understood by lay persons, the coordinates are often used, particularly in laying out highways and utility lines.

OTHER PHYSICAL ELEMENTS

The ancient doctrine of common law held that ownership of land extends from the depths of the earth to the reaches of heavens. Ownership of land includes rights not only on the surface of the earth, but also to an indefinite distance upward and downward, subject of course to limitations by law, such as the rights of air travel. Unless specified otherwise in the deed, an owner of land obtains rights to the minerals below the surface of the land and usage of the space above the surface of land.

Minerals

Solid minerals such as coal and metal ore are real property and remain as such until removed from their natural position in the earth. Once mined, however, the minerals become personal property. When real property is transferred, the rights to minerals beneath the ground go with the land, unless specified otherwise; a pile of coal, though, would not go with the land unless specified otherwise. A property owner could retain the surface land and sell the mineral rights alone; or she could sell the surface land to one party and separately sell the mineral rights to a different buyer. In other cases, an owner might sell the surface land and withhold the mineral rights for herself.

Once sold, the mineral rights to a property would be useless without means of extraction. If the document of conveyance is silent as to the right of access, the person receiving the mineral rights acquires the right of extraction by implication. It is important for the document to describe the access rights, since the manner of entrance to the subsurface can affect the appearance and value of the land. In an alternative kind of agreement, a party may be sold the ***right to extract*** minerals for a set period of time, such as two years. If the right of surface entry were expressly denied in the deed, the person owning the mineral rights would need access from an adjacent property. In any case, only a limited amount of minerals can be extracted without injury to the surface or affecting the support or stability of the adjacent properties. In most states, sand, gravel, and limestone are not considered to be minerals.

Oil and gas are different from solid minerals since a well drilled on one piece of property can extract oil or gas from a surrounding area. Many states, therefore, say that a property owner has the *right to drill* on her land for oil or gas. This right passes with the conveyance of real property and can be sold separately, just as mineral rights. This right to drill can also be leased to another party. A number of the petroleum-producing states apply the "ownership in place" theory to gas and oil; however, they also apply the *rule of capture,* which states that a landowner takes ownership to gas and oil from wells on her land even though part of it could have migrated from adjoining land.

Airspace

In common law it was understood that the landowner owned the airspace above her or his land to the heavens. Following a series of court challenges to this concept, the U.S. Supreme Court in 1946 decided that the landowner owns as much space above the ground as can be occupied or used. (It is not necessary that the space be occupied in a physical sense, so a person does not own a fixed distance into the air.) Federal and state law have declared sovereignty over the navigable airspace. Many court cases still arise involving litigation related to take-off and landing in places where aircraft fly at low altitude, causing noise that can disturb the landowner. Sometimes these rights are purchased by the airport authority.

A landowner may sell or lease the airspace over her land. The Prudential tower in Boston was built over the Massachusetts Turnpike. The Merchandise Mart in Chicago is built over the Chicago and Northwestern railroad tracks, leaving space for the trains to operate. In some multistory condominiums, the airspace is theoretically subdivided into blocks *(air lots)* that are owned by the individual condominium owners.

Datum

Air rights and condominium interests create the need for a method to identify property clearly in terms of its height. Systems for measuring property elevation have been in effect for over a hundred years. The mean sea level at New York harbor is defined as U.S.G.S. (United States Geological Survey) *datum* and serves as a base point from which to determine elevations. Most cities also have their own official datum so that the elevation of any local point can be readily measured and specified. In a larger city, however, it is not practical to start a survey from the official datum; therefore, benchmarks are established at many points throughout a city. Each benchmark has its recognized official elevation with respect to the official datum. A surveyor can begin at any benchmark to perform a property survey where elevation needs to be measured.

There are also many U.S.G.S. benchmarks throughout the United States, so that elevations can be established by a surveyor with respect to datum at New York harbor. Condominium property laws enacted by most states rely upon datum for the determination of elevation of floor and ceiling surfaces. These are important boundaries between condominium properties, since they define the boundaries of ownership.

Water Rights

Water is considered by common law to be part of real property, whether above or below the surface. Underground waters, except those flowing in underground streams, are called *percolating waters.* Different states specify either ownership of underground water or the right to use subsurface or ground waters. In some ways, these rights to use water below the surface are similar to the rights to extract oil or gas. In some localities, restrictions have been placed on use of water to that which is "reasonable and necessary." These restrictions are brought about by scarcity of water or the need to avoid pollution. The right to use underground water is sometimes referred to as an *overlying right,* which gives the right to extract and use these waters for the benefit of land owners.

The owner of land adjacent to a stream, lake, or ocean acquires certain rights and obligations. If the body of water is in movement (such as a stream or river), the rights are called *riparian rights* and the owner is referred to as a *riparian owner.* The term *littoral rights* is used where the property is adjacent to a lake, pond, or ocean where the water is not flowing, and the owner is called a *littoral owner.* These rights include swimming, boating, and fishing, as well as the right to take water from the body. The doctrine of *correlative rights* in some states provides that during periods when water is short and insufficient to meet the demands of all regular users, each user can use only a reasonable share.

In some of the western states where water is scarce, the doctrine of *prior appropriation* applies. In order to secure rights to use water, a person applies for a permit. As long as there is plenty of water in the stream or river, all persons with permits can use water from it. When the supply of water becomes insufficient, such as in a drought period, the persons with the permits issued earliest would have priority in using the water. The water right is attached to the land of the permit holder.

A property owner has the right to collect and use—or to protect her property against—surface waters such as those caused by storms or the flooding of a stream. *Surface water* is defined as water that does not flow in a well-defined channel and is not confined to a well-defined basin. Surface waters are governed by two rules: (a) the *common enemy* rule applies in most states and means that surface water can be warded off by a landowner as long as it is not done maliciously or through negligence; (b) the *natural flow rule* says that water should be allowed to flow in its natural path, and a landowner can be liable for altering the natural conditions. Many recent decisions apply the *reasonable conduct rule* stating that a landowner cannot be held liable if the flow change resulted from reasonable use of the land.

APPURTENANCES

Certain rights or easements pass from the grantor to the grantee along with the real property. These are called *appurtenances.* A right of way through property is a common type of easement. Following the legal description in any deed, the following clause will usually appear:

> . . . together with the appurtenances and all the estate and rights of the party of the first part in and to said premises.

SUMMARY

Legal descriptions are important in the preparation of contracts and deeds when conveying real property from one party to another. The three primary types of legal description are rectangular survey, metes and bounds, and subdivision and lot (plat map). The rectangular survey system is used in all states except the original colonies and Texas.

The ownership of land includes not only the surface of the land itself, but also rights to minerals beneath the ground, air rights above the ground, and rights to surface and underground water. These rights ordinarily go along with the land, but they can be sold or leased separately from the land surface area.

TERMS AND CONCEPTS

You can check your understanding of these terms against the glossary or by review of this chapter.

Accretion	Meridian	Range line
Appurtenances	Metes and bounds	Real estate
Baseline	Monuments	Real property
"Being" clause	Natural flow rule	Reasonable conduct rule
Check	Navigable	Rectangular survey
Common enemy	Overlying right	Right to drill
Correction line	Parallel	Right to extract
Correlative rights	Percolating waters	Riparian rights
Datum	Plat	Rule of capture
Dedication	Plat map	School section
Dereliction	Point of beginning	Section
Flat land	(p.o.b.)	Subdivision and lot
Front footage	Prime meridian	Surface water
Government lot	Principal meridian	Township
Guide meridian	Prior appropriation	Township line
Littoral rights	Quadrangle	True bearings
Magnetic bearings		

What are the differences or relationships, if any, between the following? Check your responses against the chapter text.

Artificial monument and Natural monument	Mineral rights and Oil rights	Range line and Township line
Common enemy rule and Natural flow rule	Mineral rights and Right to extract minerals	Real estate and Real property
Correlative rights and Prior appropriation	Parallel and Baseline	Right to extract and Right to drill
Magnetic bearings and True bearings	Prime meridian and Guide meridian	Riparian rights and Littoral rights
	Principal meridian and Prime meridian	Surface water and Percolating water

2-1. What types of legal description are used in your state?

2-2. What limitations are placed on rights to the airspace over a person's land?

2-3. On the grid of Figure 2–3, locate the following townships:
   (a) T3N, R3W
   (b) T5N, R1E
   (c) T1S, R7W
   (d) Township 5 north, Range 5 west
   (e) Section 14 T2N, R3W
   (f) Section 23 T7N, R6W
   (g) The school section of T2N, R3W

2-4. Draw a sketch similar to Figure 2–5. Then draw in and identify the following parcels of land. Determine the acreage of each:
   (a) NW¼ of NW¼
   (b) N½ of NE¼ of NE¼
   (c) S½ of SW¼ of SE¼
   (d) N½ and SW¼ of SW¼

2-5. Describe each of the parcels of land in Figure 2–10 by the rectangular system and determine the acreage:

Figure 2–10

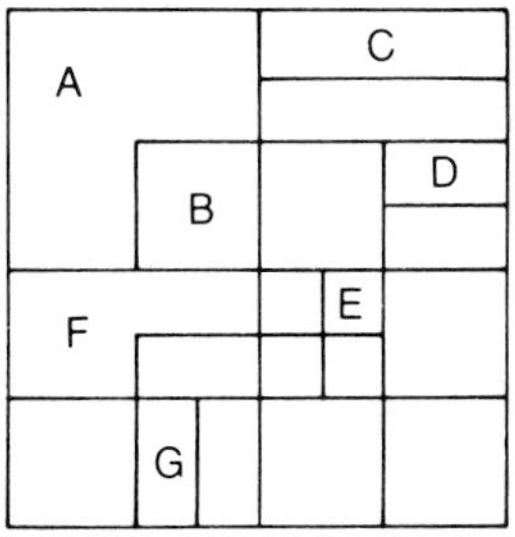

2-6. Sketch the property defined by the following metes and bounds description:

Commencing at a monument at the NE corner of Arce Street and Barnes Avenue, proceed 600 ft North along Arce Street to the point of beginning where a stake is placed; then 186 ft further along Arce Street; then 214 ft 7 in. more or less N87°6″E to a concrete fence post; then 190 ft S8°14″E; then 219 ft more or less to the point of beginning.

2-7. Sketch a check bounded on the south by a baseline and on the west by a principal meridian. Indicate the following:
   (a) T3N, R3E
   (b) T1N, R4E
   (c) T5N, R4E

2-8. Sketch a township and identify sections 8, 19, and 32.

2-9. A parcel of land along the seashore is 80 feet on the shoreline by 260 feet deep. Land sells for $150 per front foot. What is the price of the property?

2-10. Land sells for $1,200 per acre. What is the price of the N½ of the NE¼ of the SW¼?

2-11. Rental of warehouse space was specified as "$1.20 per sq ft per yr." What would be the monthly rental for a space 8 feet by 12 feet?

2-12. Storage space rents for $0.20 per cubic foot per year. What is the yearly rental for a space 10 feet by 20 feet by 8 feet high?

2-13. Due to drought, a stream provides sufficient water for only half of the regular users. What are the differences in rights of riparian owners where prior appropriation applies as opposed to owners where the doctrine of correlative rights applies?

2-14. Discuss whether you think that a town could take airspace by eminent domain. Use examples to illustrate your answer.

2-15. Assume that you are leasing mineral rights to your property. What provisions should you place in the agreement?

2-16. During a heavy rainstorm, a stream changed its course and left about 100 square feet of your former land on the opposite side of the stream. What could you do?

2-17. A neighboring property owner B was excavating for his basement. He did not touch A's land, but the excavating caused A's garage to collapse when the soil gave way. Give your opinions on the responsibilities of A and B by applying some of the concepts developed in this chapter.

SUPPLEMENTARY READINGS

Berger, Curtis J. *Land Ownership and Use*. Boston: Little, Brown, 1983.

Bergfield, Philip B. *Real Estate Law*. New York: McGraw-Hill, 1979. Chapters 2 and 3.

Bruce, Jon W. *Modern Property Law Cases and Materials.* St. Paul, Minn.: West, 1984.

Burby, William E. *Real Property.* St. Paul, Minn.: West, 1965. Chapter 6.

Casner, A. James, and Leach, W. Barton. *Cases and Text on Property.* Boston: Little, Brown, 1984.

Davis, Raymond E., and Foote, Francis S. *Surveying—Theory and Practice,* 6th ed. New York: McGraw-Hill, 1981. Chapters 22 and 23.

Faber, Stuart J. *Handbook of Real Estate Law,* 3rd ed. Los Angeles: Lega Books, 1985.

Galaty, Fillmore W.; Allway, Wellington J.; and Kyle, Robert C. *Modern Real Estate Practice,* 10th ed. Chicago: Real Estate Education Corporation, 1985. Chapters 2 and 9.

Henszey, Benjamin N., and Friedman, Ronald M. *Real Estate Law,* 2nd ed. New York: Wiley, 1984.

Herubin, Charles A. *Principles of Surveying,* 3rd ed. Reston, Va.: Reston Publishing Company, 1982.

Jennings, Marianne M. *Real Estate Law.* Boston: Kent, 1985.

Kratovil, Robert, and Werner, Raymond J. *Real Estate Law,* 8th ed. Englewood Cliffs, N.J.: Prentice-Hall, 1983. Chapter 5.

McEntyre, John G. *Land Survey Systems.* New York: John Wiley & Sons, 1986. Chapter 10.

Murray, William G. *Farm Appraisal and Valuation,* 6th ed. Ames, Ia.: Iowa State University Press, 1983. Chapter 4.

U.S. Department of the Interior. "Public Land Statistics, 1970." Washington, D.C.: Bureau of Land Management, 1970.

CHAPTER 3
Rights and Interests in Real Estate

The term *real estate* in its broader and perhaps most accurate definition includes land, every interest or estate in land, and the permanent improvements on the land. As mentioned earlier, in the real estate business the terms *real property* and *real estate* are frequently used synonymously. However, these terms are also used to mean either the land itself or an interest or estate in the land. Either meaning is technically correct, in that *real estate* is composed of a physical element as well as an ownership element. The physical element is the land and things of a permanent nature contained in it or affixed to it. The ownership element refers to the nature, duration, quantity, and quality of rights that one or more persons may possess in land.

Personal property includes everything that is subject to ownership other than land and anything permanently annexed to land (i.e., fixtures). Personal property is frequently referred to as *personalty* whenever real estate is called *realty.*

Land includes the earth, the area above the surface, the area beneath the surface, and anything permanently added to it or formed therein by nature or human beings.

The physical extent of land includes all things that are of a permanent nature, whether they be found on or affixed to the land or embedded beneath its surface. The term, therefore, includes growing things such as trees, natural ponds, and lakes found upon the earth's surface, and minerals and other matter found within the earth.

Air Rights

Before airplanes, spaceships, and orbiting satellites, it was almost universally accepted that not only did the boundaries of a parcel of land extend downward to the center of the earth, but also they extended upward to infinity. Now the landowner's right to space above the land is somewhat restricted. The courts permit such space to be entered by aircraft for purposes of legitimate air travel so long as the owner's rights to exclusive use and possession are not unreasonably interfered with. If an unreasonable interference occurs, the owner is entitled to recover any actual damages suffered as a result of the trespass. Rights to the space above the surface of land are commonly referred to as ***air rights***. Air rights can be freely transferred by gift, sale, or lease without a concurrent transfer of the physical property itself.

As the population density in our urban areas increases, air rights become even more important and valuable. In several large cities, the railroads have sold their air rights, together with small physical portions of their land, to buyers who have subsequently constructed multiple story commercial and office buildings in the air space above the railroad tracks. The buildings are attached to and rest upon foundations embedded in small sections of land along the railroad tracks. Airports frequently acquire air rights over properties adjacent to an airport to establish landing and takeoff paths for airplanes.

Fixtures

Land also includes permanent *improvements* made by people. Objects of personal property may be so attached to or used with land that they are legally considered part of the land. The personal property is said to become a *fixture*. Once personal property becomes a fixture, it becomes the property of the owner of the land to which it is attached.

Whether an article of personal property can be considered a fixture is governed by the intention of the person who attaches or uses the personal property with the land. This intention is rarely expressed. Consequently, the courts must look to all the facts and circumstances surrounding the use or the attachment to determine whether or not it was intended to become a fixture.

Where parties expressly agree as to whether or not an item of personal property is to be a fixture, the courts are generally willing to enforce their expressed intention. For example, a landlord and tenant agree that the tenant may build an automobile garage on the land and remove it prior to the expiration of the lease. The garage, even though attached to the land, is considered personal property and may be removed by the tenant. A well-established exception to this rule is when the article of personal property is permanently added into a building and its removal would substantially destroy the structure or the fixture itself (e.g., plumbing, electrical wiring, beams, or bricks). Regardless of the expressed agreement of the parties, such articles of personal property are fixtures.

If the parties have not expressly indicated their intention, the courts use the following guidelines:

1. *The method by which the personal property is attached to the land.* Attachment may be by gravity, by physical connection, or by incorporation. The personal property becomes a fixture if it is so attached to the land or building that it cannot be removed without materially damaging the land or building or destroying the personal property itself (e.g., masonry blocks in a wall, a heating system consisting of pipes and coils, structural steel or wood girders, railroad tracks, or a house trailer bolted on a concrete foundation).

2. *How the personal property relates to the existing use of the land.* Personal property designed for and used in the "normal use" of a specific parcel of land may be classified as a fixture. As a general rule, personal property that is reasonably necessary to the use of the land or building thereon need not be physically attached to the land or buildings to be classified as a fixture. As an example, window screens, storm windows and doors, industrial machinery placed upon the land by its owner, and hot sheds located on a hog farm are fixtures.

3. *The nature of the annexor's interest in the land.* In some cases, the legal interest of the annexor of personal property will be considered by a court in determining his intention. An owner of land who attaches personal property that relates to the existing use of the land clearly intends to install a fixture. However, personal property may be attached to land by persons having no legal interest in the land whatsoever, such as an intentional or mistaken trespasser or a person having only a temporary legal interest, such as a lessee or a licensee.

4. *Wrongful or mistaken annexation.* As a general rule, the owner of the land is entitled to all fixtures attached to his land by a trespasser, whether intentionally or by mistake. Some courts offer relief to the mistaken improver either in the form of a lien to the extent of the value of the improvement or permission to remove the fixture on the condition that he reimburse the owner for any damage caused by the removal.

Trade Fixtures

Personal property that is attached to leased land or buildings by a lessee for use in his business is generally held to be a **trade fixture.** The trade fixture principle has been interpreted to apply to fixtures for trade and business (e.g., bowling alleys, overhead crane, restaurant equipment), agriculture (e.g., tool sheds and chicken houses), and domestic use (e.g., bookshelves, carpeting, mirrors). A lessee is entitled to remove trade fixtures at any time prior to the expiration of the lease, unless the fixture has become an integral part of the land or building and its removal would materially damage the land, building, or the fixture itself. If they are not removed before the lease expires, the property becomes a fixture and legally belongs to the owner of the land or building to which it was attached.

Regardless of the method of **annexation,** if *expressly* agreed upon by the lessor and lessee, the lessee has the right to remove trade fixtures. The lessee's obligation is to reimburse the owner of the land for any physical damage caused by the removal. The lessee is not liable for any decrease in the market value of the land.

CONCEPT OF PRIVATE OWNERSHIP

Ownership is a creature of law. It cannot exist unless recognized and enforced by a sovereign power. When a sovereign power does recognize and enforce certain rights in property, the person who possesses them is said to be its owner and possess *title* to it. **Ownership** is thus defined as the *right* to control, possess, enjoy, and dispose of property in such manner as is not contrary to law. These rights are further broken down into the right to use, to sell, to make a gift of, to destroy, to improve, to profit from, to remove objects from, and to pass title to by a will upon the owner's death. It includes rights over contiguous and surrounding areas affecting the use of land, such as the right to lateral support of soil, to light and air, to ingress to and egress from the property, and to be free of nuisances on adjoining properties. One or more persons may possess some or all rights in land recognized by law. When two or more persons own rights in land, they are said to be **concurrent owners.**

Rights to land are not absolute and unrestricted. They are limited by rights possessed by other persons and by powers of government, as shown in Figure 3–1. An owner of land may not exercise personal rights thereon so as to cause wrongful injury to the person or property of another. In addition, rights are subject to the powers of government, such as (a) **eminent domain** (power to acquire title to private real estate for a public purpose in exchange for just compensation), (b) **police power** (power to regulate the use of land for the public welfare), (c) **power of taxation** (to raise revenue), and (d) **escheat** (the power to take title to land owned by a person who died without a will and heirs).

ESTATES AND OTHER INTERESTS IN REAL ESTATE

The law recognizes certain rights in land and refers to them as estates; however, not all rights in land constitute estates. Estates are classified according to the quality, quantity, and extent of the rights held by one or more persons. Each estate is identified by the types of rights and privileges a person possesses and may exercise toward his land and adjacent land owned by others.

In order for a right that relates to land to be an *estate,* it must be presently possessory or become possessory in the future (nonpossessory). Possessory and nonpossessory rights may be owned simultaneously by two or more different persons in the same parcel of land. The nonpossessory estate is known as a *future interest.* A future interest does not become possessory until a preceding possessory estate terminates and any existing condition precedents have been fulfilled. Examples of future interests are the vested and contingent remainders discussed later in this chapter. Figure 3–2 identifies the various estates in land.

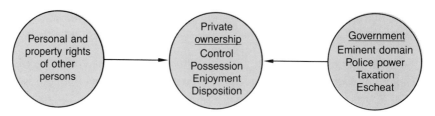

Figure 3–1   Rights to land and restrictions on private ownership

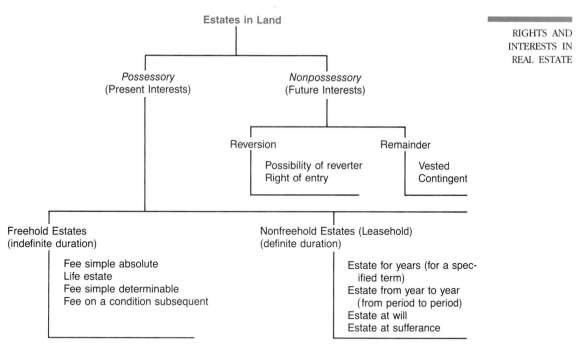

Figure 3–2   Estates in land

Possessory Estates

Possessory estates are classified on the basis of their duration, that is, *freehold estates* and *nonfreehold estates* (leasehold estates). Freehold estates exist for an indefinite length of time. Nonfreehold estates (leasehold estates) exist for a determinable length of time. Figure 3–2 identifies the various freehold and nonfreehold estates.

Freehold Estates

Fee simple absolute.   The owner of a *fee simple absolute estate* possesses all of the rights an individual can have in land. It is restricted only by the rights of other individuals and the powers of government. The fee simple absolute estate has the following characteristics:

1. It is freely transferable during the lifetime of the owner, by either gift or sale.
2. It is inheritable either by a will executed by the owner or by intestate succession (by state statute) if the owner dies without a will.
3. It has no time limit on its existence.
4. As qualified above, the owner possesses unrestricted control, possession, use, and enjoyment of the land. (See Figure 3–3.)

Life estate.   The *life tenant* is entitled to possession and use of the land and the income from it. He may mortgage, lease, sell, or give away the estate, but the duration of the estate remains governed by the life of the person or persons originally designated.

Figure 3–3   Fee simple absolute

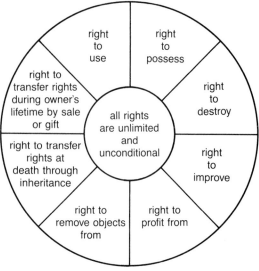

The life tenant's possession and use of the land is restricted by the duty not to commit waste. **Waste** occurs whenever the life tenant acts or fails to act in relationship to the land, causing the interests of the reversioner or remainderman (i.e., the person designated to receive the estate after the termination of the life estate) to be injured. Examples would be failure to pay taxes or mortgage payments or material change of the original use of the property, such as converting it from farming to industrial.

Life estates are created either by a conveyance by an owner of the estate or by operation of law. A life estate created by conveyance is known as a *conventional life estate*. A *legal life estate* is one created by law without the consent of the owner.

Conventional life estates are usually created by means of deeds, wills, and trusts. Legal life estates are created by state law. **Dower, curtesy,** and **homestead** are examples of legal life estates. These estates do not exist in all states; and where they do exist, the quantity and quality of rights created in the life tenant vary widely from state to state. Curtesy, dower, and homestead laws apply only to land located within the state.

The duration of a life estate is measured by the life or lives of one or more persons. Its duration can be measured by the life of its owner (life tenant), for example, "to A for his life." It can also be measured by the life of a person other than the life tenant, for example, "to A for the life of Z." Where the duration of the life estate is measured by the life of someone other than the life tenant, it is called a life estate *pur autre vie* (for the life of another). An ordinary life estate (whose duration is measured by the life of the life tenant) is not inheritable, and it terminates upon the death of the life tenant. However, a life estate *pur autre vie* does not terminate upon the death of the life tenant, and the life tenant's ownership interest continues until the death of the person by whose life the estate is measured. If the life tenant should die before the person by whose life the estate is measured dies, the ownership interest of the life tenant will pass to the life tenant's heirs. The ownership interest received by the heirs will remain in existence until the death of the person by whose life the interest is measured.

Upon termination of any life estate, the estate either reverts back to its original owner or the owner's heirs (*reversion*), or it is vested in any person (*remainderman*) who is designated to receive it upon termination. Reversionary and remainder interests will be discussed later in this chapter.

Fee simple determinable (qualified fee or base fee). A *fee simple determinable* is a fee simple subject to a condition. For example, A, by deed, conveys fee simple to B "so long as" the premises are used for residential purposes only. When the condition no longer holds, ownership *automatically* reverts back (reversion) to the person (reversioner) who created the estate or his heirs in fee simple. The interest retained by a grantor of a fee simple determinable is referred to as a *possibility of reverter.*

Fee simple on a condition subsequent. A fee simple subject to a condition subsequent is a fee simple that may be ended by the person who created the estate or that person's heirs upon the happening of a contingency. For example, A, by deed, conveys a fee simple in a parcel of farmland to B and provides that A retains the right to terminate the estate if it ceases to be used for farming purposes by exercising the *right of entry* (to sue for possession). The feature that distinguishes this estate from the fee simple determinable discussed above is that the *fee simple on a condition subsequent* does not terminate and revert back automatically when the stated event happens. The right of entry must be exercised to terminate the estate and cause its reversion.

At common law, owners of possibilities of reverter or rights of entry are allowed to freely transfer their legal interests during their lifetimes (i.e., *inter vivos*). Upon their deaths, their legal interests pass by will (i.e., testate succession) or, if they die without leaving a will, by law (i.e., intestate succession). Most states have changed the common law by enacting statutes that provide for one or more of the following: (1) outlawing the creation of such future interests, (2) prohibiting the transfer or inheritance of existing valid future interests, or (3) placing a time limitation on their legal existence. In many states, the maximum time limit is 40 years.

Nonfreehold Estates (Leasehold Estates)

A *lease* is both a contract and a conveyance of an interest in land. It is a transfer by one person named the *lessor* (landlord) of the right of exclusive possession of land for a limited period of time to a second party named the *lessee* (tenant) in consideration of the payment of rent. The lessor retains a reversionary right; that is, the lessor is entitled to a return of the legal interest upon the expiration of the lease.

Leasehold estates are classified and identified according to their duration. The four common leasehold estates are:

1. Estate for years (for a specified term)
2. Estate from year to year (from period to period)
3. Estate at will
4. Estate at sufferance

A detailed discussion of leases is provided in Chapter 6.

Nonpossessory Estates (Future Interests)

A *future interest* is a presently existing estate, but it does not entitle its owner to immediate use and possession of land in which the estate is held. Use and possession are postponed until the termination of a preceding estate or the occurrence of a condition, or both. The estate can take the form of a reversion or a remainder.

Reversion

Reversion is an estate remaining with a grantor or that grantor's heirs or assigns after the conveyance of a lesser estate to a grantee for a temporary or potentially temporary period of time under an express or implied reservation of a right to have the estate conveyed revert to the grantor or his heirs or assigns (i.e., transferees) after the expiration of such period of time. A *lesser estate* is conveyed whenever a person conveys one or more but not all rights in the property. The following estates are accompanied by a reversion:

1. A life estate where the estate returns to the grantor after the death of the person by whose life the estate is measured.
2. Leasehold estates.
3. A life estate with a contingent remainder. If the contingency does not occur, the estate will automatically revert back to the grantor or the grantor's heirs upon the death of the life tenant.
4. Fee simple determinable (qualified fee). The reversionary interest created by the conveyance of this estate is called a *possibility of reverter.*
5. Fee simple on a condition subsequent. Upon such a conveyance, the grantor retains a *right of entry,* exercisable only upon the happening of the condition.

As a general rule, reversions are inheritable and freely transferable during the life of the person who owns the reversionary estate. However, some state statutes prohibit the creation of the possibility of reverter and right of entry and also forbid transfer or inheritance of any such existing estates.

Remainder

A *remainder* is a presently existing estate in land where the actual use and possession of the land is postponed until the termination of a preceding estate and/or the happening of a specified future event that may or may not occur. A remainder comes into existence whenever a grantor conveys a lesser estate to a grantee for a temporary or potentially temporary period of time and at the same time conveys all remaining rights in the property to a third person. The third person is said to own a remainder. Remainders are classified as being either *vested* or *contingent.*

A *vested remainder* is an estate in land whereby the right to immediate use and possession of land depends *only* upon the termination of a preceding estate (e.g., A deeds a parcel of land to B for life with remainder to C and C's heirs). In this case, C is called the *remainderman.* A vested remainder is an inheritable estate. Therefore, upon the remainderman's death prior to the death of the life tenant, the remainder will pass to the remainderman's heirs. It is also transferable either by sale or gift, and it may be mortgaged as security for a debt or other obligation.

A *contingent remainder* is an estate in land whereby a person's right to the use and possession of the land depends *not only* upon the termination of a preceding estate *but also* upon the happening of some event that may or may not take place.

As an example, A deeds a parcel of land to B for life with remainder to C and her heirs, if C retains her maiden name. As a general rule, contingent remainders are transferable either by will, intestate succession, or by a conveyance during the remainderman's lifetime.

Easements

Legal Nature of an Easement

An *easement* is not an estate in land. It is a nonpossessory *right to use* or enjoy the land owned by another person for a specific purpose and in a specific manner. It does not include the right to possess or remove any part of the land, below or on its surface.

Easements may be *appurtenant* or *in gross* (Fig. 3–4). An easement appurtenant cannot be created without two parcels of land. The parcels of land need not be adjacent. Land that is subjected to use and enjoyment is referred to as the **servient estate.** The **dominant estate** is the land for whose benefit the easement was created. If the easement is created for use in connection with another specific parcel of land, it is said to be an **easement appurtenant.** However, if it is *not* intended to benefit another parcel of land, it is an **easement in gross.** As a general rule, an easement in gross is personal to the person to whom it was granted and, therefore, is not trans-

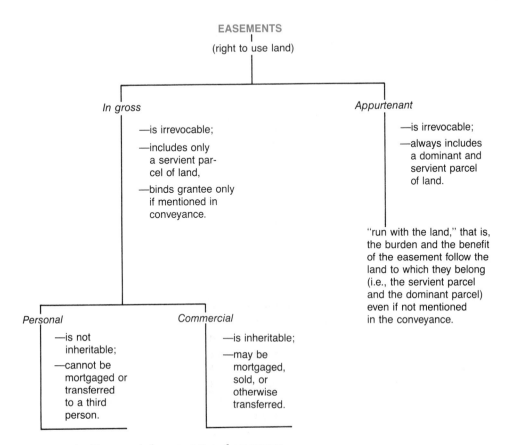

Figure 3–4   Types and characteristics of easements

45

ferable. It terminates upon its owner's death. However, some states have provided that easements in gross are freely transferable. This is especially true if the easement is commercial in nature. However, an easement in gross can always be made freely transferable by agreement of the parties in the contract who originally created the easement. Easements appurtenant are said to *"run with the land"*; that is, the benefits to the dominant estate and the burdens of the servient estate continue regardless of any change of the ownership of either estate, even if not mentioned in the conveyance. Easements in gross do not "run with the land" because they do not benefit or attach to a dominant estate. Both easements appurtenant and easements in gross are irrevocable. The following exemplify easements appurtenant:

1. A common driveway on a boundary line between two lots, each lot owned by a different person
2. A right of one owner of a tract of land to use water from an adjoining tract for irrigation purposes
3. A right to cross another person's adjoining tract at a specified place for the purpose of ingress or egress
4. The right to free flow of light and air across adjoining land owned by another person

The following exemplify easements in gross:

1. Utility easements for electric power lines, water mains, or sewers
2. Easements for railroads
3. Right to use a lake owned by another for swimming purposes
4. Cable television (CATV)
5. The right to install and maintain a billboard or advertisement sign on another's land

Creation of Easements

An easement is a legal interest in real estate; therefore, a contract, grant, or reservation creating an easement must be in writing to satisfy the Statute of Frauds. Easements are created in a number of different ways:

1. By agreement
2. By grant or reservation
3. By implication
4. By reference to plat
5. By prescription
6. By necessity

Easement by agreement.   Easements may be created **by agreement** wherein the parties make clear their intention to create the interest. A party wall, party driveway, a right to continued and unobstructed sunlight for solar energy purposes, and water rights are possible easements by agreement.

Easement by grant or reservation.   An owner of land may create an easement by executing and delivering a deed wherein title to the land is transferred to another party and either an easement is **granted** in favor of the tract conveyed or an easement is **reserved** for the benefit of the land retained.

Easement by implication. An easement that is created by operation of law rather than the express intention of the parties is called an **easement by implication.** The requisite elements for creation of an easement by implication are that:

1. One person owns two tracts of land
2. He subjects the use of one tract to the benefit of the other tract
3. The use is apparent and obvious
4. The use is continuous
5. The use is necessary
6. At some time thereafter, the owner transfers title to one of the tracts of land to another person without mentioning easements

Some examples of easements by implication are:

● Jones owns Lots A and B. Sewage from his house on Lot B drains through an underground pipe running across Lot A. There is a visible catch basin on the surface of Lot A. If Peters buys Lot A, she will own it subject to an implied easement for sewage drainage across her lot.
● Amos owns two adjacent parcels of land. Both parcels are improved with homes. Amos resides in the home on Lot A and leases Lot B with its improvements to Hendricks. A driveway runs down the boundary line of the adjacent lots and is used for ingress and egress purposes for both lots. Amos subsequently conveys Lot B to James. A party driveway easement was created by implication.

Easement by reference to subdivision plat. Each person who purchases a lot in a subdivision automatically acquires an easement for use of the streets, alleys, picnic areas, or swimming beach shown on the recorded plat as public areas.

Easement by prescription. An **easement by prescription** (by adverse use) arises when an unauthorized private person or the public uses another's property adversely to the owner's interest, visibly, openly, notoriously, and continuously for a period of time established by state statutes. The time period varies in different states up to a period of twenty years. Some states have passed laws that enable a landowner to prevent the creation of an easement by prescription by posting signs prohibiting use of the land (i.e., no trespassing).

Easement by necessity. An **easement by necessity** arises when an owner of land conveys a parcel of the land to another under such circumstances that the buyer has no access to the land except through the land of strangers or that of the seller. The buyer is entitled to a reasonable right of way over the seller's land.

Use of the Easement

The owner of the easement has the right to use the servient estate only for the purpose for which the easement exists. For example, if X has right of way easement across the land of Y, X has no right to lay water pipes in the servient estate or to use the right of way to benefit a parcel of land other than the dominant estate.

Maintenance and Repair of the Easement

Unless otherwise agreed, the owner of the servient estate has no duty to make the easement parcel ready for use, to repair it, or to do any other act for the benefit of the easement owner. On the other hand, the easement owner has the right to take any measures necessary to make the easement reasonably usable. For example, an owner of an easement for ingress and egress by a railroad would have the right to improve the existing track and track bed, lay down new track, and rebuild bridges. In the case of the shared driveway, however, each party would share equally the obligation to repair and maintain the driveway.

Termination of Easements

An easement is terminated under any of the following circumstances:

1. *By the fulfillment of the purpose for which it was created.* For example, a grant of right of way is made for so long as the dominant estate is used as a stable. Thereafter, the dominant estate was used for the purposes of a laundry and ceased to be used as a stable. The easement terminated. As another example, a right-of-way easement is granted in order to construct a nuclear power plant. The easement will end at the time the plant is completed.
2. *By written release by the owner of the dominant estate.*
3. *By an intentional abandonment of the easement.* For example, a manufacturing corporation owned a railroad right of way as a means to transport ore to its processing plant. The corporation removed the rails and ties and tore down its processing plant. The easement was extinguished.
4. *By destruction of the servient estate.* For example, a party wall is totally destroyed by fire.
5. *By prescription.* For example, the owner of the servient estate prevents the use of an easement for a statutory period of time. The period of time is usually the same as that necessary to acquire an easement by prescription.
6. *By merger.* The dominant and servient estates become owned by one person.

License

A *license* is the permission (not the right) to use land that is in the possession of someone other than the licensee. It is not an estate in land. It does not entitle the licensee to the exclusive possession or enjoyment of the land. A license differs from an easement in that it can be created orally and be terminated at the will of either party. It is personal in nature and consequently is not transferable or inheritable (e.g., permission to swim in a private lake or to harvest strawberries).

Profits à Prendre

A *profit à prendre* (or profit) is a nonpossessory interest in land that carries with it the right to remove the soil or the produce of soil belonging to another. Examples are the right to take minerals, to dig coal, or to cut timber. It may be created by agreement, grant, or prescription and can be classified as either a profit appurtenant or a profit in gross. If the right to remove may be exercised only for the benefit of a dominant estate, the right is a *profit appurtenant.* Where the right to remove is not restricted for the benefit of a dominant estate, it is a *profit in gross.* A profit appurtenant automatically is attached and belongs to any subsequent owner of the dominant estate (i.e., it "runs with the land") even though it was not mentioned in the conveyance. A profit in gross does not automatically follow ownership of the dominant estate; however, it is freely transferable. Profits are terminated in much the same manner as are easements: by fulfillment of purpose, by release, by abandonment, by merger, by destruction of the servient estate, or by prescription.

CONCURRENT OWNERSHIP OF REAL ESTATE

Rights to a specific parcel of land may be owned by one individual (i.e., ownership in *severalty*) or simultaneously by two or more persons as *co-owners*. Each co-owner simultaneously possesses an undivided interest in the entire estate and does not possess an unrestricted claim against any specific portion of the physical property itself. The interests of the co-owners need not be identical or equal.

One or more persons may possess *different simultaneous estates* in the same parcel of land. Each person is said to be a co-owner; however, the respective rights of each in the land are not identical. For example, A has a life estate and B and C have a remainder interest in the same parcel of land. As a second example, A has a fee on a condition subsequent and B has a right of entry. They each own a separate and distinct estate.

Frequently, one or more persons possess *identical and simultaneously existing* legal interests in the same freehold or nonfreehold estate. For example, A and B are granted the same interest in a remainder, or C and D receive a life estate in a farm. Persons may possess identical legal interests in the same property even though each person's fractional share may differ.

Concurrent ownership as discussed here is synonymous with cotenancy. The parties who are co-owners are called *cotenants*.

Joint Tenancy

A *joint tenancy* exists whenever two or more persons own an entire estate and also an undivided part thereof. Their ownership consists of the unities of time, title, interest, and possession and carries with it the *right of survivorship*. Upon the death of one joint tenant, the surviving joint tenant or tenants continue as co-owners of the estate in joint tenancy until the last survivor. The last survivor acquires sole ownership in fee simple. Joint tenancy is not an inheritable interest.

Under common law a joint tenancy could not be created unless the unities of time, title, interest, and possession were conveyed to the co-owners simultaneously. Therefore, an owner of fee simple could not create a joint tenancy by a conveyance to himself and another person. To avoid the common law rule, owners can utilize a "straw man." The fee simple owner conveys title to a disinterested party under an agreement that he reconvey the estate to the original owner and others as joint tenants. Many states have made this procedure unnecessary by enacting a statute that provides that the unities need not be acquired simultaneously. They allow a joint tenancy to be created by a conveyance from the owner of the estate to himself (the owner) and others as joint tenants.

A joint tenancy cannot be created by operation of law. The law will not imply a joint tenancy. When the intent to create a joint tenancy is not clearly expressed, the courts hold that the conveyance created is a *tenancy in common*. A grantor who wishes to create a joint tenancy must make the intention clear by indicating that the co-ownership created carries with it the right of survivorship; for example, conveying the estate "to A and B as joint tenants, not as tenants in common, with the right of survivorship" or "to A and B as joint tenants, with right of survivorship."

A joint tenant may arbitrarily sever his undivided legal interest by conveying or mortgaging the interest. Upon doing so, the conveyed or mortgaged interest becomes an interest held in tenancy in common. Where two or more joint tenants remain after severance, they own the remaining undivided interest in joint tenancy as between each other. For example, A, B, and C own in joint tenancy. A conveys his interest to D. D owns one-third in tenancy in common; B and C own two-thirds in joint tenancy.

Tenancy in Common

A *tenancy in common* exists whenever two or more persons own only an undivided fractional interest in an estate. It is created by a grant or devise to two or more persons where it is clearly indicated that a tenancy in common was intended or where the character of the estate conveyed cannot be established with certainty.

Tenants in common need not own equal undivided interests. Their estates are freely transferable during each tenant's lifetime and are inheritable by will or intestate succession.

Tenancy by the Entirety

A *tenancy by the entirety* is essentially a joint tenancy. However, it differs from a joint tenancy in the following three ways:

1. The tenants by entireties must be husband and wife.
2. Neither tenant by the entirety can sever his or her legal interest without the consent of the other.
3. The legal interest of either tenant cannot be reached by his or her creditors.

A tenancy by the entirety can be created only when allowed by state law.

Tenancy in Partnership

Under the Uniform Partnership Act, which has been adopted in most states, partners may own partnership real estate in their own names or in the name of the partnership itself. This act creates a special type of ownership called *tenancy in partnership*. It differs from both joint tenancy and tenancy in common as follows:

1. One partner alone cannot sell, assign, or mortgage any legal interest in the property without the consent of the other partners.
2. A partner's personal creditors cannot attach his legal interest in the partnership property.
3. A partner's legal interest in partnership property is not subject to dower or homestead and is not inheritable.

It is similar to joint tenancy in that, upon a partner's death, the partner's legal interest in specific partnership property goes to the surviving partners; however, it vests in the surviving partners only for partnership purposes. A partner's legal interest in specific partnership property should not be confused with a partner's "interest in the partnership," namely, his right to a share of profits, surplus, and goodwill; the return of any capital contribution; and the right to receive repayment of any loan the partner made to the partnership.

Community Property

The *community property* concept of ownership exists in conjunction with marital property rights and is followed in Arizona, California, Idaho, Louisiana, Nevada, New Mexico, Texas, Washington, and Wisconsin. The underlying theory is that a husband and wife should share equally any property acquired during their marriage and through their joint efforts. In these states, unless the spouses agree or a statute provides otherwise, each spouse owns one-half of the community property regardless of the spouse's name in which the legal title is held.

The laws in the community property states vary widely. However, each state does recognize two types of property that may be owned by the spouses: "separate property" and "community property." Separate property is solely owned by one spouse. It is owned by the spouse prior to marriage or subsequently acquired by one spouse alone during marriage by inheritance or by *inter vivos* (during the recipient's lifetime) gift. As a general rule, all other property acquired by one spouse during marriage by a joint effort with the other spouse is community property.

Another general rule is that the signatures of both spouses are required to effectively sell, convey, or mortgage all legal interests in community property.

As mentioned, each spouse owns one-half of their community property. For this reason, all community property states grant the spouse the right to transfer his or her share of community property by will. In the absence of a will, most states vest absolute title to the deceased spouse's share of community property in the surviving spouse.

Condominium Ownership

Most states have enacted statutes providing for creation and protection of condominium ownership.

For a *condominium* to come into existence legally—and before any individual units may be sold—the owner-developer must file both a condominium declaration and a three-dimensional subdivision plat that comply with the state condominium law, as well as any other applicable state law. In a condominium, each owner obtains a fee simple interest in the unit that he exclusively occupies and a tenancy in common interest in all other parts of the land and buildings shared and used in common with other owners. The condominium laws prohibit a unit owner from bringing an action to partition or otherwise divide the common elements. The property made subject to condominium law may be an apartment, a shopping center, or an office building. The areas shared by the owners are referred to as the *common elements*. Common elements include the foundation, roof, basement, stairway, elevators, swimming pools, parks, auto parking areas, and so forth.

The owner of an individual condominium unit possesses the following rights and duties:

Rights	Duties
1. To own the fee simple in the unit concurrently with others	1. To pay real estate taxes assessed against the unit
2. To mortgage the unit	2. To pay the proportionate share of any assessments for taxes and maintenance attributable to the common elements
3. To sell, lease, or make a gift of the unit	
4. To use the common elements	3. To make repairs and improvements to the unit at his own expense
5. To insure the unit	4. To observe the rules and regulations governing the use of the units as well as the common elements

Not all condominium laws provide for methods of termination of condominiums. Unless the condominium statute or the condominium declaration provides for a method of termination, termination cannot occur except by unanimous consent of the owners.

Time-share ownership is a unique method of obtaining the benefits of condominium ownership and, at the same time, sharing the use of residential units with other owners of the same condominium. This type of ownership is especially desirable in a recreational setting where the purchaser desires a vacation home for only that part of a year during which he plans to occupy the home. For example, high-rise buildings at an oceanside resort are declared condominium. The individual units are then sold to multiple buyers, granting each buyer the right to use the unit during a specified part of each year.

There are three types of time-share ownership.

1. *Tenancy in common (time-span ownership).* The purchasers of each unit are owners as tenants in common. Each owner's undivided legal interest is equal to the fraction of the year that he is to occupy the unit. The exclusive right to occupy the unit during a specified time period each year is acquired by virtue of an occupancy agreement signed by each tenant in common.

2. *Interval ownership.* In this situation, the purchasers receive a deed whereby they simultaneously receive title and the right to occupy. The deed to each owner creates a recurring estate for years (for a term) for the agreed-upon period of each year of the term and a remainder to all owners as tenants in common. The number of years designated as the term of the estate for years is an estimate of the useful life of the building.

3. *Vacation license.* Under a vacation license, the developer retains the fee simple ownership and transfers the right to occupy the units to the time-share purchasers for a specified period of time of each year for a stated number of years.

Cooperatives

In the *cooperative* form of ownership, all of the land and its improvements are owned and developed by a corporation. To finance its operation, the corporation relies on debt and equity capital. The corporation usually finances a portion of its acquisition costs by mortgaging the land and its improvements. It acquires the balance by selling stock to prospective tenants. Upon becoming a shareholder, each person is entitled to receive a long-term lease of an individual unit (apartment or office). The rent to be paid takes the form of an annual assessment by the board of directors of the corporation. The amount assessed each tenant is equal to that tenant's *pro rata* share of the total cash needed by the corporation to pay its obligations for taxes, mortgages, and operating expenses. Unlike condominium ownership, the tenant's interest in a cooperative is personal property. The cooperative owner may transfer ownership by an assignment of his stock, but the owner of a condominium interest must use the formalities of a deed in order to transfer the estate. (See Table 3–1.)

Table 3–1 Characteristics of condominiums and cooperatives

	Condominium	Cooperative
Owners of the real estate	Unit owners	Corporation
Funding of purchase of the real estate	a. Construction mortgage loan b. Conversion of existing apartment house into condominium	a. Sales of stock (equity capital) b. Mortgage loan
Legal status of residents	Owners	Owners of stock in the corporation and lessees of the units
Nature of the legal interest possessed by the owners	Real property	Personal property
Type of ownership	a. Fee simple absolute of each apartment unit b. Tenants in common in the common elements	a. Corporation is owner of the real estate in fee simple absolute b. Tenants own their stock and lease the units
Transfer of ownership interests	Unrestricted right to transfer title by deed	Stock and leases cannot be transferred without consent of the board of directors
Management of the complex	Board of managers	Board of directors
Funding of operational expenses	By assessments	Rent
Enforcement of assessments or rents	Foreclosable lien	Foreclosable lien
Termination of form of ownership	a. By unanimous consent of unit owners b. Destruction of the condominium without sufficient insurance proceeds to rebuild	Dissolution of the corporation

Syndicates

A *syndicate* is an association of a group of persons or entities or both under a contract for the express purpose of dealing in real estate and real estate transactions for profit.

Land Trusts

The land trust was developed in Illinois. In recent years, Virginia, North Dakota, Indiana, and Florida have authorized its use. A *land trust* by statute (a statutory trust) is that type of trust where, by deed, a trustee receives complete record title to real estate restricted by a concurrent agreement whereby the beneficiary retains full management and control (power of direction) over the real estate. The interest of the beneficiary is personal property. The beneficiary has the right of possession, the right of income, and the right to proceeds from a sale of the trust property. The trustee's duty is to execute deeds and mortgages and to deal otherwise with the real estate only at the written discretion of the beneficiaries. (See Figure 3–5.) The important advantages of a land trust are as follows:

1. The shares of the beneficiaries may be easily transferred by assignment of their interest.
2. The complexity and lack of flexibility of co-ownership of land is eliminated. A third party knows that he can deal safely with the trustee alone.
3. Identity of the beneficial owners is not disclosed in public records.
4. Mortgage loan financing is easily obtainable by use of the trust real estate as security and without pledging the personal credit of the beneficial owner.
5. Probate can be avoided by providing for succession of ownership upon the death of a beneficiary.
6. Dower, curtesy, and homestead do not attach to the trust real estate.
7. A lien of judgment against a land trust beneficiary does not attach to the trust real estate.
8. Beneficiaries do not have the right of partition.

These are the primary disadvantages of this type of trust:

1. The beneficiaries are liable for injuries caused by negligence in their possession, maintenance, and operation of the trust real estate.

Figure 3–5   Land trust

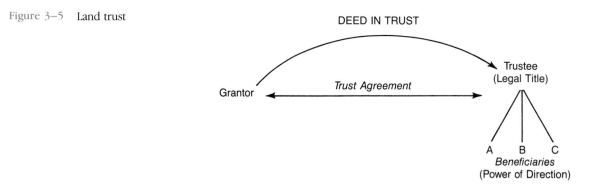

2. Where there is more than one beneficiary and they are unable to agree with respect to operation, lease, or sale of the trust real estate, the trust may be terminated upon petition, thereby frustrating the purpose of the trust.

Real Estate Investment Trust

A *real estate investment trust (REIT)* is a common law trust that is qualified for income tax exempt status under the provisions of the Real Estate Investment Trust Act. It is initially created by investors who transfer legal title and possession of real estate to a trustee (incorporated or unincorporated) under an agreement whereby the trustee agrees to manage the trust property for their benefit and profit. The ownership interests of investors are evidenced by certificates of ownership. Subsequent to its creation, investors purchase certificates of ownership from the trustee who, in turn, invests the money through purchases of additional real estate. The trustee is obligated to invest in real estate and to distribute trust income to certificate owners. If the trust is properly organized and operated pursuant to the provisions of the Real Estate Investment Trust Act (i.e., if it is an REIT), it is not treated as a legal entity for income tax purposes. Income earned by the trust and distributed to its beneficiaries is taxable only to the beneficiaries. To qualify its income for tax exempt status an REIT must meet the following requirements:

1. It must have a minimum of 100 owners of certificates of ownership.
2. No fewer than six may own 50 percent or more of all outstanding certificates.
3. The certificates of ownership must be freely transferable.
4. It cannot be a dealer in real estate. It must be a real estate investment trust. Its income must accrue primarily from rents, interest on mortgages, dividends, or other income from real estate rather than from capital gains on the sale or exchange of trust real estate.
5. It must distribute 95 percent or more of its earned income each year to its beneficiaries (i.e., owners of certificates).

PUBLIC RESTRICTIONS ON OWNERSHIP OF REAL ESTATE

Public limitations on ownership exist for the purpose of protecting the rights of the community as a whole as well as providing for the common welfare. To fulfill these purposes, the courts have consistently upheld the inherent power of the government to regulate the use of property and to deprive a private person of personal ownership of property for the public welfare. Public limitations and restrictions on private ownership are imposed by the right of eminent domain, police power, the right of taxation, and the escheat of land.

Eminent Domain

The right of *eminent domain* is the inherent power of the federal and state governments to acquire title to private property for public use without the owner's consent. This power can be and has been delegated to governmental subdivisions and quasi-public corporations, such as public utilities and railroads, but due process of law must be followed. A government's obligation is to pay *just compensation* for the value of the estate acquired. Examples of clear public use are public parks, roads, and buildings.

The only exception to the public use requirement lies in the area of condemnation and acquisition of title to real estate for urban renewal purposes. In such cases, the courts have held that the taking need only be for a public purpose. The real estate need not be subjected to a public use after the exercise of eminent domain. Under these holdings, the government may condemn a slum area and sell it to a private developer to be used for private purposes.

Police Power

Police power is the inherent power of government to regulate the use of real estate to provide for the public health, safety, morals, and general welfare of the community. State legislatures frequently delegate police power through enabling acts to political subdivisions, such as counties, cities, and villages. The most common types of exercise of police power are subdivision regulations, zoning, and building ordinances.

The U.S. Supreme Court has held that government regulation of use of property under its police power can be to such an extent that it amounts to a compensable "taking" under the law of eminent domain. For example, an ordinance that prohibited the construction or repair of any building in a flood protection area for a specified period of time was held to be a "taking."

Subdivision Regulations

A *subdivision* is a tract of land divided into lots suitable for residential purposes. Before a subdivider can legally begin selling lots in a subdivision, the sale must first be approved by the appropriate city or county. Approval will not be granted unless the subdivision complies with the criteria set forth in the subdivision regulations, which typically require (a) compliance with zoning ordinances; (b) posting of security by the developer to assure proper completion of improvements shown on the subdivision plat, such as roads, utilities, street signs, and recreation areas; (c) compliance with building codes when the subdivider is to construct buildings; and (d) dedication of land for public streets, schools, parks, and other recreational areas. (Subdivisions are covered in detail in Chapter 18.)

Zoning

Zoning ordinances are laws passed by local political units such as municipalities and counties to regulate and control the use of land. Land is usually zoned into classifications such as residential, agricultural, commercial, industrial, or special use (schools, churches, and hospitals). Most zoning ordinances provide regulation of more specific types of use, such as designated minimum lot size, building areas, square feet of living area, and building set-back lines. As long as the use imposed by the zoning ordinance is not discriminatory, unreasonable, or arbitrary, it is a valid and enforceable restriction on the use of private property. (Zoning is covered in detail in Chapter 10.)

Building Codes

A *building code* is an ordinance enacted by a local political unit (county or city) specifying detailed standards and requirements for remodeling existing structures and constructing new buildings. A typical building code may designate the types and quality of construction materials allowed to be used and provide a set of standards for electrical, heating, and plumbing installations. Most building codes prohibit remodeling, construction, or occupancy without a building or occupancy permit from the political unit having jurisdiction.

Local ordinances provide for a city or county officer to make periodic inspections to ensure that the landowner has complied with both the zoning ordinances and the provisions of any building code. Where a violation is found, the landowner is required to take appropriate action to comply with the law. Appropriate action may be as drastic as the complete removal and relocation of a part of a building to comply with set-back lines. Most ordinances also require a fine and, in some instances, imprisonment for flagrant violations. (Building codes are covered in detail in Chapter 10.)

Environmental Protection Laws

Both Congress and state legislatures have enacted statutes restricting the use of land for the purpose of protecting people and their environment. These laws deal primarily with air, water, and noise pollution. In most instances, the provisions of these statutes are enforced by governmental regulatory agencies. However, some statutes allow a private individual to bring a lawsuit for damages or to obtain an injunction against any person in violation of air, water, or noise pollution standards.

Some state antipollution statutes make it a crime to cause pollution wrongfully and provide for the payment of a fine for so doing. (Environmental protection laws are covered in Chapter 15 in more detail.)

Taxation and Tax Liens

Taxes are levied by various state and local political units to raise the revenue necessary to provide for the community welfare. One of the most controversial yet important taxes is that imposed upon real estate. Most tax laws consider real estate taxes as a *lien* upon land effective as of a specified date. A tax lien is an encumbrance that renders title to land unmarketable until the lien is discharged. The failure to discharge a real estate tax lien is legal cause for a landowner's title to be divested in legal proceedings initiated by the taxing unit. Such proceedings usually take the form of a court-ordered tax sale. (Taxation and tax liens are covered in detail in Chapter 9.)

Escheat

Escheat is a form of governmental restriction on private ownership of land. *Escheat* is the automatic vesting of title to real estate in a state or county upon the death of a landowner who died without a valid will and without leaving heirs or other lawful claimants to the property.

PRIVATE RESTRICTIONS ON OWNERSHIP OF REAL ESTATE

Private restrictions on ownership exist for the purpose of protecting the rights of other persons. Several examples follow.

Nuisance

An owner of real estate may not use his property so as to create a *nuisance* by interfering substantially with the use and enjoyment of real estate owned by another.

For example, acid from a nearby zinc-processing plant drifts onto and damages the fruit trees of a landowner; noise from incoming and outgoing airplanes at an airport causes a nearby landowner to be deprived of his peace of mind. Some courts have awarded damages or granted injunctions to landowners injured in their person or property by the nuisance.

Waste

Where one or more persons have rights in the same parcel of land, the person rightfully in possession has a duty to all co-owners not to commit any act that may impair the value of the land. Examples of this might be a life tenant failing to pay real estate taxes on the land, a joint tenant in possession failing to discharge a mortgage, a lessee removing minerals, or a life tenant changing the contemplated use of the land or failing to make necessary repairs.

Restrictive Covenants

Restrictive covenants are limitations imposed by private individuals on the use of land by provisions in a contract, plat, or deed. Restrictions may be of any type so long as they do not violate public policy. They may be imposed by any grantor, whether the land being sold is a single lot or multiple lots in a subdivision development. Since the purposes of restrictive covenants are basically the same as those for zoning laws, the uses restricted are generally similar. These restrictions include set-back lines, minimum living areas, residential use, style of architecture of buildings to be constructed, maximum height of buildings, prohibition on number of structures on a particular lot, and prohibition of mobile or prefabricated homes.

Restrictive covenants are enforceable by injunction issued by a court. Courts generally will not grant an injunction under the following circumstances:

1. A substantial or complete change in the characteristics of the neighborhood (e.g., area is restricted to residential, but over the years it has become predominantly commercial)
2. Abandonment, which results whenever the restrictions are voluntarily violated by owners throughout the neighborhood so as to indicate intent to disregard the original neighborhood plan
3. Where the person seeking the injunction has personally violated the restriction
4. Where a state statute has provided a time limit on a restriction and the time limit has expired
5. Where the deed agreement itself established a time limit on the restriction and the time limit has expired

Conditions

A *condition* is a restriction on use of land provided for in a deed that is accompanied by a possibility of reverter or a right of entry. The *possibility of reverter* provides for automatic reversion of title, if the condition is violated, to the grantor who created the condition or to the heirs. A *right of entry* allows the grantor who created the condition or the heirs of the grantor to enter the land and take possession. Upon taking possession, title reverts to the owner of the right of entry.

A properly recorded condition is enforceable against all subsequent grantees or others who may acquire an interest in the land subject to the condition.

Conditions are not generally looked upon favorably by the courts because they cause a forfeiture of title to land. Consequently, many states have enacted laws prohibiting the creation of conditions, voiding any attempted transfer of estates subject to conditions, and placing a time limit on the enforceability of already existing conditions.

Easements and Profits

As previously defined, easements and profits are interests in land owned by someone other than the owner of the land they burden. They are restrictions upon the use of land to which they attach because the owner of the land may not use the land so as to interfere with existing easements and profit rights. If properly recorded, all subsequent owners take the land subject to these restrictions.

Liens

A *lien* is the right of a creditor to subject property owned by his debtor to a forced sale and to use the proceeds for repayment of the debt. Examples of private liens are real estate mortgages, mechanic's liens, and judgment liens. The lien theory of mortgages is defined and discussed in Chapter 8.

Mechanic's liens are statutory liens granted to persons who provide labor or materials in the construction or improvement of land and buildings. Most state mechanic's lien statutes contain the following provisions:

1. Identification of those parties that may acquire the lien
2. Indication as to how and when the lien can be attached to the land
3. Identification of the extent of the lien
4. Method of protecting the lien against third parties who have or may acquire an interest in the land
5. Duration of the lien
6. Method of enforcement of the lien
7. Priority, if any, over existing liens
8. Identification of lienable labor and materials

In most states, a judgment that is rendered by a court of competent jurisdiction and recorded creates a *judgment lien* that attaches to all of the real estate owned by the judgment debtor that is located within the state.

A lien causes title to be "unmarketable" and is a deterrent to the debtor attempting to sell, mortgage, or convey his property. Until released, compromised, or satisfied, a lien remains an encumbrance upon title to real estate. (See Chapter 9.)

Tort Liability Arising Out of Use of Land

As a general rule, a landowner is under a duty to use, possess, and maintain properties so as not to injure the person or property of others intentionally or negligently. A violation of this duty is a private wrong called a *tort*. Some state statutes impose additional liability for damages upon a landowner for injuries caused while using the property *even* in a lawful, rightful, and nonnegligent manner. Examples are keeping dangerous animals on the land or carrying on blasting.

SUMMARY

Real estate includes land, every interest or estate in land, and any improvements to it. Personal property may become a part of the land by being permanently affixed to the land with the intent that its character change. Once personal property is attached, it is said to be a *fixture* and becomes the property of the owner of the land. The exception to this rule is trade fixtures, which remain the property of the annexor. A *trade fixture* is personal property that is attached to leased premises by a lessee for use in business, agricultural, or domestic activities conducted by the lessee on the premises.

Ownership is a creature of law. It cannot exist without being recognized and enforced by a sovereign power. Ownership consists of various rights a person possesses in a parcel of land. These rights have been identified as the right to control, possess, enjoy, and dispose of land. Ownership is not absolute and unrestricted. Rights in land are limited by the rights possessed by other persons and by the powers of government.

Rights in land may be classified as estates or as other interests that are something less than an estate. In order to be classified as an estate, a person's rights must be presently possessory or become possessory in the future. A nonpossessory estate is known as a *future interest*.

Possessory estates are classified as *freehold* and *nonfreehold* estates. Freehold estates exist for an indefinite period of time, while nonfreehold estates exist for a determinable length of time. The following estates are freehold: fee simple absolute, life estate, fee simple determinable, and fee on a condition subsequent. Nonfreehold estates are also known as *leasehold estates* and include an estate for a term, an estate from period to period, an estate at will, and an estate by sufferance.

A future interest (nonpossessory estate) does not entitle its owner to immediate use and possession of the land in which the estate is held. Use and possession are postponed until the termination of a preceding estate or the occurrence of a condition or both. Reversions and remainders are future interests.

Other interests, although not estates, consist of rights in real estate. These interests include *easements, licenses,* and *profits à prendre.* Easements are created by agreement, grant or reservation, implication, reference to plat, prescription, or necessity.

Rights to a specific parcel of land may be owned concurrently by two or more persons. These persons are called *cotenants.* They possess simultaneously undivided, equal or unequal, and similar or dissimilar interests in an estate. Types of concurrent ownership are joint tenancy, tenancy in common, tenancy by the entirety, tenancy in partnership, community property, condominium ownership, cooperative, syndicate, land trust, and real estate investment trust (REIT).

All private ownership is limited and restricted by the powers of government and private rights of other persons. Public limitations and restrictions on private ownership are imposed by the right of eminent domain, police power, the right of taxation, and escheat. Private restrictions on private ownership include the law of nuisance and waste, restrictive covenants, conditions, easements and profits, liens, and the law of torts (private wrongs).

You can check your understanding of these terms against the glossary or by review in this chapter.

Air rights
Annexation
Building code
Community property
Concurrent ownership
Condition
Condominium
Contingent remainder
Cooperative
Curtesy
Dominant estate
Dower
Easement
Easement appurtenant
Easement by agreement
Easement by grant or
   reservation
Easement by implication
Easement by necessity
Easement by
   prescription
Easement in gross
Eminent domain
Escheat
Estate
Fee simple absolute
   estate

Fee simple determinable
Fee simple on a
   condition subsequent
Fixture
Freehold estate
Future interest
Homestead
Joint tenancy
Judgment lien
Land
Land trust
Lease
License
Lien
Life estate
Life tenant
Mechanic's lien
Nonfreehold estate
Nuisance
Ownership
Personalty
Police power
Possibility of reverter
Power of taxation
Profit à prendre

Pur autre vie
Real estate
Real estate investment
   trust (REIT)
Realty
Remainder
Restrictive covenant
Reversion
Right of entry
Right of survivorship
Run with the land
Servient estate
Severalty
Subdivision
Syndicate
Tenancy by the entirety
Tenancy in common
Tenancy in partnership
Time-share ownership
Tort
Trade fixture
Vested remainder
Waste
Zoning

PROBLEMS ▬▬▬▬▬

3-1. T leased a factory building from L to be used in manufacturing machinery. To transport steel from one place in the factory to another, T installed an overhead moving crane weighing four tons. Installation of the crane required steel I-beams to be welded in place and to be set in concrete foundations. Prior to the expiration of the lease, T attempted to remove the crane but was prevented from doing so by L. L claimed that he was the owner of the crane. Is he correct? Explain.

3-2. L and T entered into a lease which provided that the lessee could remove all structures placed on the premises by her. T constructed a cabin on the leased premises. It rested on the land by means of posts and footings. Wiring and plumbing were

installed. Prior to the expiration of the lease, T sought to remove the cabin but was prevented from doing so by L. L claimed that the cabin was a fixture and therefore could not be removed. Is he correct? Explain.

3-3. Discuss and explain the concept of ownership.

3-4. Determine and explain the estate or estates existing after the following conveyances:
  (a) To A for life.
  (b) To A for the life of B.
  (c) To A for life, and after A's death to A's children.
  (d) To A for life, remainder to B and C, if B and C have attained age twenty-five at the time of A's death.

(e) To A and her heirs.

(f) To the city of Chicago in fee simple so long as the land is used as a park.

(g) To A in fee simple on the condition that liquor is never sold on the land.

(h) To A the use and possession of an apartment house until the completion of A's home which is presently under construction.

3-5. L orally gave X permission to graze his cattle upon L's land. X grazed his cattle on L's land for four years. During the four years, L sold his land to Y. A personal dispute arose between Y and X, and Y refused to allow X to graze his cattle any longer. X sued Y, claiming that he possessed an irrevocable right to graze his cattle on Y's land. Is he correct? Explain.

3-6. L, in writing, granted XYZ corporation the right to use water from a well upon her land and to lay a pipeline across the land to adjacent land owned by the XYZ corporation. XYZ corporation sold its land to T. L, who personally disliked T, ordered him to cease drawing water from the well and to remove the pipeline immediately. T sued L. Who wins? Explain.

3-7. L owned two adjoining lots. He constructed a driveway on the boundary line between the lots. L then sold one of the lots to T. Ten years later L asked T to share in the cost of providing a new surface for the driveway. T refused. L then sued T, asking the court for an order stopping T from using the driveway inasmuch as it involved a trespass on L's portion of the lot occupied by the driveway. What was the decision? Explain.

3-8. L and T owned land as "joint tenants with right of survivorship." L died, leaving a will wherein she devised all of her real estate to Z. Who is the owner of the land? Explain.

3-9. L, T, and Z owned land in joint tenancy with right of survivorship. L wanted to sell the land but T and Z refused to join in any conveyance. L executed and delivered a deed to the land to Y. Y died, leaving a will wherein he devised all his real estate to his son, S. What legal interests, if any, do L, T, Z, and S have in the land? Explain.

3-10. L and T, a married couple, lived in a community property state. During their marriage, L inherited a farm from his grandfather which was valued at $500,000. Shortly thereafter, T received a lifetime gift of 2,000 shares of General Motors stock from her father. L and T each claim community property interests in the property acquired by the other. Are their claims valid? Explain.

3-11. In 1980, Fontainebleau constructed a high-rise hotel facing the Atlantic Ocean in the Miami Beach area of Florida. Six years later the Eden Roc Hotel was built adjacent to and north of the Fontainebleau Hotel. The land upon which the Eden Roc Hotel was constructed had never been owned by Fontainebleau. Shortly after the construction of the Eden Roc Hotel was completed, Fontainebleau began construction of a fourteen-story addition to its hotel. Upon completion, the fourteen stories would cast a shadow on the swimming pool and sunbathing areas owned by the Eden Roc Hotel for the major part of each day during the winter tourist season. Eden Roc sued Fontainebleau for an injunction to stop construction of the addition. Eden Roc alleged that Fontainebleau had no right to interfere with its right to sunlight, air, and its use and enjoyment of its property. Is Eden Roc correct? Explain.

3-12. Assume that the facts are the same as stated in question 3-11 except as modified below:

In 1964, Fontainebleau purchased a large parcel of beachfront land on the Atlantic Ocean in Miami, Florida. Five years later it constructed the Fontainebleau Hotel on half of the parcel. The remaining one-half was used by the guests of the hotel for sunbathing, swimming, and other types of related recreational activities. In 1980, Fontainebleau sold the one-half of the parcel not occupied by its hotel to Eden Roc. In 1983, Eden Roc constructed a luxury hotel on the parcel it purchased from Fontainebleau. A year later, Fontainebleau began construction of a fourteen-story addition to its hotel. Eden Roc sued Fontainebleau for the same remedy and on the same basis as stated in question 3-11 above.

(a) What is the result? Explain.

(b) Could Eden Roc have avoided this legal problem at the time it purchased the parcel from Fontainebleau? Explain.

3-13. Vasquez executed her last will and testament wherein she devised all of her real estate "to my beloved husband Carlos, for all of his life, and thereafter to my daughters, Maria and Consuela, as joint tenants with right of survivorship." Vasquez died in an auto accident shortly after the execution of her will. She was survived by her husband, Carlos, her sons Juan and Edmundo, and her daughters, Maria and Consuela. Explain why each of the following statements is correct or incorrect as each relates to the facts stated above.

(a) Carlos cannot convey his interest in the real estate unless he obtains authority to do so from Maria and Consuela.

(b) The real estate must be included in Carlos's estate for inheritance purposes at the time of his death.

(c) Upon the death of Maria, Consuela will become the sole owner of the remainder.

3-14. Compare a profit with a license. How do they differ from an easement?

3-15. Compare a reversion with a remainder. Can a reversion exist simultaneously with a remainder with respect to ownership of the same parcel of real estate? Explain.

SUPPLEMENTARY READINGS

Burby, William E. *Real Property,* 3rd ed. St. Paul, Minn.: West, 1965.

Dasso, Jerome, and Ring, Alfred A. *Real Estate Principles and Practices,* 11th ed. Englewood Cliffs, N. J.: Prentice-Hall, 1989. Chapters 4 and 6.

Jennings, Marianne M. *Real Estate Law,* 2nd ed. Boston: PWS-Kent 1989. Chapters 2–6 and 15.

Kratovil, Robert, and Werner, Raymond J. *Real Estate Law,* 9th ed. Englewood Cliffs, N. J.: Prentice-Hall, 1988. Chapters 2–4, 6, 18, 32–34, 38 and 39.

Seidel, George. *Real Estate Law,* 2nd ed. St. Paul: West, 1989. Chapters 2–5 and 11–14.

CHAPTER 4
Contract Law and
Real Estate Contracts

The process of transferring a title to real estate from a seller to a buyer involves a number of stages over a considerable period of time. In the purchase of property other than real estate, the buyer usually assumes that the seller has good title, pays for the item, and takes possession of it immediately or has it delivered within a relatively short time. In contrast, in the sale or exchange of real estate, it is common to ascertain that the seller is the true owner and that no other person has adverse interests in the property prior to full payment of the purchase price and transfer of title.

To facilitate and to assure transfer of a title free of adverse interests, contracts are extensively used by brokers, sellers, and buyers. Two important and widely used contracts are the listing agreement between the broker and his client and the contract for sale of real estate entered into between the seller and buyer. Other important contracts are options, mortgages, leases, escrow agreements, and installment land contracts. A thorough understanding of the laws of contracts is important to the real estate broker. This chapter will cover basic elements of contract law as it applies to real estate transactions.

CHARACTERISTICS OF CONTRACTS

A contract can be express or implied in fact. An ***express contract*** is one in which the terms are stated in words, either orally or in writing. An ***implied in fact contract*** is one that is evidenced by the acts or conduct of the parties.

A contract can also have the characteristic of being bilateral or unilateral. A ***bilateral contract*** consists of a promise in exchange for a promise. For example, A promises to pay $100,000 if B promises to give A title to a farm. A ***unilateral contract*** is made up of a promise in exchange for an act or a forbearance. For example, Tedesco, a landowner, listed his land with Judd Realty. The listing contract provided that Tedesco promised to pay Judd Realty a commission of 8 percent of the price received from the sale of the land to any purchaser found by Judd Realty. Tedesco's promise is an offer for a unilateral contract that requires an act (i.e., finding a purchaser) on the part of Judd Realty to become a binding unilateral contract.

For any agreement between two or more parties to be enforceable in a court of law, it must contain the necessary elements of a contract. If all of these elements are present, the contract is said to be ***valid.*** Where one or more elements is missing, the agreement is either void or voidable by one or more of the parties to it. A ***void contract*** is an agreement whose subject matter or performance is against public policy. It is not a contract at all in the eyes of the law. An example is a contract for the purchase of an illegal distillery. A ***voidable contract*** remains in existence until the person who has the power to rescind it takes affirmative action to do so. As an example, a building contractor, while negotiating a contract for the sale of a newly constructed home, intentionally and falsely represented to the buyer that the home was not constructed on top of previously existing refuse landfill. This contract is voidable by the buyer on the grounds of fraud. The buyer may affirm or disaffirm the contract within a reasonable time after discovering the truth.

An ***unenforceable contract*** is neither void nor voidable, but is unenforceable because of the existence of a condition. For example, an oral contract for the sale of real estate is unenforceable because it is not in writing as required by the Statute of Frauds; likewise, if a lawsuit is not filed within prescribed time limits after a breach of contract occurs a contract is unenforceable because of the Statute of Limitations.

ELEMENTS OF AN ENFORCEABLE REAL ESTATE CONTRACT

An enforceable real estate contract has six necessary elements: agreement (mutual assent), consideration, reality of assent, legally competent parties, a legal objective and subject matter, and a document in writing if required by state statutes.

The Agreement (Mutual Assent)

An agreement can never be reached without an offer and an acceptance of the terms of the offer.

Offer

An ***offer*** is a promise made by one person called the ***offeror*** to another person known as the ***offeree*** that the offeror will act or refrain from acting on the condition that the offeree in turn will act or refrain from acting. As shown in Figure 4–1, to

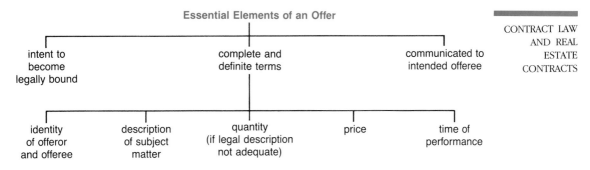

Figure 4–1   Essential elements of an offer

be a legal offer, the promise must meet the following three requirements. First, it must exhibit **contractual intent**; that is, the offeror, through words or conduct, must appear to intend to enter into a legal obligation with the intended offeree. *Test:* Under all of the circumstances, was the offeree justified in interpreting the promise as an offer? The test is objective rather than subjective. Therefore, promises obviously made in jest, rage, or extreme excitement; invitations to negotiate (such as circulars or advertisements); quotations of prices sent on request; and invitations to bid at auctions are not legal offers. In each of these situations, the offeree, as a reasonable person, should understand that the offeror did not intend the promise to have contractual intent.

Second, an offer must be **communicated** to the intended offeree. No person can accept an offer unless that person knew of its existence prior to her purported acceptance. Also, only the person or persons intended to be offerees can accept an offer. An offer made to John Javonsky cannot be accepted by Phillis Marcos.

Third, the promise must contain **complete and definite terms.** The offeror need not state the terms of the offer with absolute certainty. However, she must make them sufficiently definite to allow a court to determine the intention of the parties and thereupon assign their respective legal obligations. Most courts agree that the terms required to be included in a valid real estate contract are the identity of the parties, the time of performance, a description of the subject matter (the quantity), and the price to be paid. Absence of any one of the essential terms will prevent a promise from being a legal offer.

Termination of Offers

Once made, an offer does not last for an indefinite period. Figure 4–2 indicates that an offer terminates when, prior to acceptance, it lapses either by its own terms or, after a reasonable time if its duration is not stated, by revocation by the offeror, by a rejection of the offer by the offeree, or by the death or insanity of the offeror or offeree. An attempted acceptance after an offer is terminated is, in legal effect, a new offer to contract according to the terms of the original offer. If accepted, a contract is formed.

An offeror may state that the offer must be accepted within a specified period of time. The offeree does not have the right to accept after the expiration of the specified time. The offer is said to have *lapsed.*

If no definite period of time is specified in the offer, the offer *lapses* after the expiration of a reasonable time. What constitutes a "reasonable" length of time de-

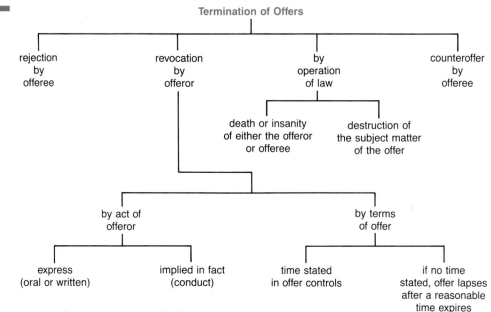

Figure 4–2   Termination of offers

pends on the circumstances surrounding the transaction and the custom in the community wherein the real estate is located.

The offeror may either expressly or impliedly **revoke** the offer prior to its acceptance. Every offer to sell, purchase, or lease real estate is revocable prior to its acceptance unless "consideration" is given in exchange for it by the offeree to the offeror. The legal meaning and examples of "consideration" are discussed subsequently in this chapter. Such offers are revocable by the offeror even though the offeror had expressly promised that the offer was to be irrevocable or that it was to remain open for a specified period of time. An example of an irrevocable offer (i.e., one supported by consideration) is one that is included in an **option.** The promise made in the option to hold the offer open for a stated time is binding on the offeror because it is part of an actual contract. The offeree (i.e., *optionee*) has the legal right to accept the offeror's (i.e., *optionor's*) offer during the time specified. Options are discussed more fully later in this chapter.

An offeror's revocation is effective at the time it is communicated to the offeree or the offeree's agent. An example of an express revocation is when an offeror telephones or writes to the offeree and states that the offer is revoked. An implied revocation occurs when the offeree receives information indicating that the offeror has taken such action as to make it impossible to perform the promise in the offer. For example, an offeror offered to sell a certain parcel of land to X. Thereafter, the offeror sold the same parcel to Y. Y informed X of the sale. The offer has been impliedly revoked.

An express or implied manifestation by the offeree that she is not willing to be bound by the terms of the offer constitutes a **rejection.** It is effective when it is communicated to the offeror or the offeror's agent. An offer may be rejected either expressly, or by a counteroffer, or by a conditional acceptance. A **counteroffer** results whenever the offeree's acceptance modifies one or more of the terms of the offer (e.g., X offers to sell to Y with possession and delivery of deed to be on July 1, 1990. Y accepts the offer but states that she must have possession and delivery of deed on June 1, 1990). However, a mere inquiry as to whether the offeror would be willing to change the terms of an offer is not a rejection or a counteroffer. A conditional acceptance is a statement by the offeree that she will accept the offer only if a specified event occurs (e.g., X offers to sell land to Y; Y accepts but states that her acceptance is subject to her successful negotiation of a loan and mortgage for part of the purchase price). If conditional acceptance or counteroffer is accepted by the original offeror, a contract is formed composed of the original terms modified by the new terms and conditions.

Offers can terminate also by **operation of law,** regardless of the intention of the parties. If the specified subject matter of the offer is destroyed, the offer is terminated automatically. Death or insanity of either the offeror or offeree will also terminate an offer. No notice of death, insanity, or destruction of the subject matter is necessary for termination of an offer by operation of law. (See Figure 4–2.)

Acceptance

An **acceptance** is an offeree's express or implied indication of willingness to be bound by all terms of an existing offer. It must comply exactly with the terms of the offer and any requests made by the offeror. It must be absolute and unconditional. As in determining whether or not a valid offer exists, the objective test is used in determining the intention of the offeree, that is, what a reasonable person would be justified in believing as to the intentions of the offeree under the circumstances surrounding the transaction. The acceptance may be by words or conduct. For example, X writes a letter to Y offering to sell real estate to Y on specified terms. Y replies by letter, stating that he accepts the offer. A contract is formed. As another example, X writes a letter to Y offering to sell her farm on specified terms and states that the unoccupied farm is available for possession at any time. Y takes possession and plants corn. A contract is again formed. Silence (as a general rule) does not result in an acceptance, even though the offer so indicates.

As with the rejection, an acceptance is effective when it is communicated to the offeror or her agent, according to the express and implied stipulations of the offeror. Where the offeror specifies the time, place, or method of communication, the offeree must comply. If she does not, her purported acceptance is not effective and no contract is formed. Communication of an acceptance may be actual or constructive. **Actual communication** occurs when the offeror or her agent receives an oral or written notification of the acceptance. **Constructive communication** is effective at the time it is sent. It is communication by operation of law, and the offeror need not ever receive actual communication of the acceptance in order to be bound. Constructive communication occurs whenever the offeror expressly or impliedly specifies the manner in which the acceptance is to be communicated (i.e., by mail, by telephone, by telegraph, by messenger, etc.) and the offeree forwards her acceptance by the method specified. Where no means of communication is specified in the offer, the offeror is held to have impliedly authorized a reply by customary, usual, or reasonable means of communication. For example, X sends Y an offer to sell her home by mail. Y accepts the offer by mail. A valid contract exists at the time Y properly posted her letter of acceptance. As another example, X writes to Y and offers to sell her farm. In the offer she requests Y to reply by telegraph. Y sends his telegram of acceptance; however, it is lost and never received by X. A contract exists at the time the telegraph message was given to the telegraph office.

The elements of a valid acceptance are illustrated in Figure 4–3.

Consideration

In order for a promise to be binding, it must be supported by legally sufficient consideration. *Legally sufficient consideration* consists of two elements: a presently bargained-for exchange and a legal detriment to the promisee. A promisee incurs a legal detriment when, in exchange for a promise, she does or promises to do something she is not legally obligated to do or she refrains or promises to refrain from doing something she has a legal right to do. As an example, X promises to sell her home to Y, and Y in exchange promises to transfer ownership of 500 shares of General Motors stock to X. Consideration is present. Since neither X nor Y was under a preexisting legal duty to make these promises, by doing so, they each incurred a legal detriment. As a second example, X promises to convey a parcel of land to Y in exchange for Y's promise not to construct a hog-feeding complex on Y's property that adjoins X's property. Consideration is present. X incurred a legal detriment by promising to do something she had no previous legal duty to do. Y incurred a legal detriment by promising to refrain from doing something she had a legal right to do.

The consideration must be presently bargained for as the exchange for the promise. For example, X saves Y from drowning. Y thereafter promises to convey title to her farm to X as a reward to X for saving Y's life. Y's promise is *not* supported by consideration, because X did not save Y's life in exchange for Y's promise.

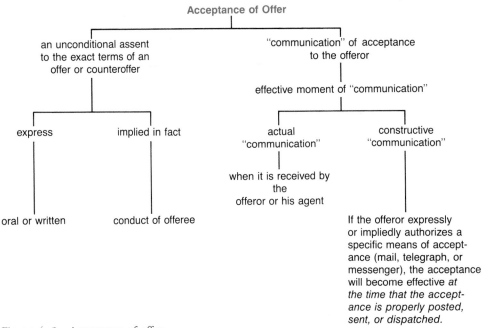

Figure 4–3   Acceptance of offer

The value of the consideration exchanged need not be equal or adequate. A promise to sell one's home in exchange for an amount $5,000 below its market value would be supported by legally sufficient consideration.

A few state statutes remove the requirement of consideration where the promise is made under seal. A promise is made under seal when a promisor's signature is accompanied by the word "Seal," or the letters "LS" (*locus sigilli,* Latin, meaning the place of the seal), or the phrase "Witness my hand and seal."

Reality of Assent

Mutual assent by parties is essential to every contract; that is, each must have agreed with the other under her own free will. If a party has become a party to a contract against her free will, the contract is voidable at her election. A party's will may be overcome by deception (innocent misrepresentation or fraud), by fear (duress), by trust and confidence (undue influence), or by mistake (mutual mistake). In order to avoid the contract *(rescission),* the injured party must return any consideration she received under the contract. She, in turn, is entitled to the return of any consideration *(restitution)* she gave to the other party.

Fraud is the intentional misrepresentation or concealment (intentional nondisclosure) of a material fact upon which another contracting party justifiably relied (i.e., was deceived) to her detriment. For example, a seller of a house who painted over its basement walls to cover water marks left by flooding is guilty of fraud. As another example, a seller of a house was guilty of fraud when she intentionally failed to disclose to the buyer that the septic system backed up in wet weather.

Innocent misrepresentation is identical to fraud except that misrepresentation is not made intentionally.

Duress is any wrongful action or threat of action made by one contracting party against the other party to the contract or to her family under such circumstances as to force the latter out of fear to enter into the contract against her free will.

Undue influence occurs when one party places all of her trust and confidence in another so that the dominant party's will is in effect imposed upon that of the dominated party. For example: Juanita, the oldest child of Madera, lived with and cared for Madera for twenty-five years. During that time Madera relied totally on Juanita's judgment in transacting financial and business transactions on Madera's behalf. Three years before Madera died, she sold 900 acres of prime farm land located in the heart of Iowa to Juanita for $1,000. The sale to Juanita is voidable by the executor of Madera's estate on the basis of undue influence.

The law creates a presumption of undue influence as a matter of law whenever the parties to a real estate contract are in a fiduciary relationship with each other. To successfully overcome this presumption the dominant party in the relationship must prove that the contract is fair to the dominated party. Fairness can be established by evidence of one of the following:

1. That the agreed-upon price to be paid for the property is equal to or in excess of its actual market value
2. That the "dominated" party was represented by an attorney during the entire transaction
3. That the "dominated" party possessed knowledge in regard to the nature of the transaction that was superior to that of the "dominant" party

4. That the "dominated" party had full knowledge of all the details related to the transaction and either had the competency to understand or actually did fully understand their implications and consequences, but yet proceeded to enter into the contract

5. That the "dominated" party sought out, received, and acted upon the advice of a third party or parties before and during the completion of the contract

Some examples of fiduciary relationships are:

Dominant	Dominated
Real estate broker	Client
Attorney	Client
Accountant	Client
Guardian	Ward
Conservator	Ward
Doctor	Patient
Trustee	Beneficiary of the trust

Mutual mistake occurs when both parties contract under a mistaken belief that certain material facts regarding the contract are true, such as the terms of the contract; the identity of the parties; and the existence, nature, quantity, or identity of the subject matter. The mistake must be mutual. If only one party is mistaken, the contract is valid and enforceable against her.

For example: Tara, pursuant to a written contract dated October 3, 1989, sold her exclusive winter ski lodge located in Colorado to Dobler. Prior to delivery of a deed, Dobler discovered that the lodge had been destroyed by fire in September of 1989. Neither Tara nor Dobler knew that the lodge had been destroyed when they entered into the contract of sale in October. The contract is voidable for mutual mistake as to the existence of the subject matter of the contract.

Legally Competent Parties

Certain parties by operation of law do not have the legal capacity to enter into binding contracts. Parties lacking *legal capacity* include infants (minors), mentally ill persons, and drunkards. Contracts entered into by parties lacking legal capacity are voidable; that is, they are valid until disaffirmed. Only the party who lacks legal capacity has the right to disaffirm the contract. To *disaffirm,* a party having a legal incapacity need only tender return of any consideration she has received or its value and indicate that she no longer desires to be bound. Upon doing so, the disaffirming party is entitled to have any consideration previously transferred to the other party to the contract returned. After a party acquires legal capacity, she may become bound to her previously voidable contract by inaction or action on her part that indicates a willingness to be bound. When this occurs, she is said to have *ratified* the contract and thereby caused it to be enforceable against her.

Infants (Minors)

To have legal capacity, a party must be of legal age. In almost all states a person is an *infant* (minor) and does not become of legal age until she reaches age eighteen. The legal age does range as high as twenty-one in a few states. All infants' contracts are voidable even though the subject matter of the contract is a necessity to the infant. The infant has the right of disaffirmance prior to attaining her majority and within a reasonable time thereafter. The extent of the reasonable time depends on the circumstances. As an example, X, age seventeen, purchased a hardware store from Y for $50,000. Three days after X attained age eighteen, she decided to quit the hardware business and tendered back a deed to the hardware store to Y. Y refused to accept the deed or to pay back the $50,000. The contract is voidable by X. X may disaffirm the contract within a reasonable time after she attains age eighteen. Three days would be a reasonable time. X is entitled to the return of $50,000, and Y must accept the deed. As a general rule, the infant's right of disaffirmance is not destroyed by fraudulent misrepresentation of her age; however, such action may subject her to damages for fraud (i.e., in tort).

Mentally Ill Persons

If a contract is entered into by a party after she was declared insane or mentally *incompetent* by a court, the contract is void from its inception. Adjudication (court declaration) of insanity or mental incompetency removes all capacity to contract from a mentally incompetent person and usually transfers it to a legal representative named a *guardian* or *conservator*. As a general rule, where there has been no adjudication of insanity or mental incompetency, the test is whether or not a party's mental condition was such that she did not understand the nature and consequences of the transaction. If the contract is made by the incompetent prior to her court adjudication of insanity, the contract is merely voidable.

Drunkards

A party who is intoxicated to a degree that she did not understand the nature and consequences of the transaction can void a contract within a reasonable time after she becomes sober and acquires knowledge of the contract.

Corporations

A *corporation* is a legal entity created by and owing its continued existence to the law of the state of its incorporation. Its power to enter into valid contracts is governed by the law of the state of its incorporation and the express and implied powers granted to it in its articles of incorporation. Most corporations, through their agents, have the power to enter into contracts for the purchase, sale, mortgage, and lease of real estate.

A Legal Objective and Subject Matter

A contract is void from its inception if its objective or its subject matter is *illegal*. Neither party can enforce the contract by court action or recover any consideration given in completion of an illegal contract. Ignorance of the law is *not* a valid defense by any party. A contract will be *illegal* if it is in violation of the common law, is prohibited by statute, or is contrary to public policy.

Violation of Common Law

The *common law* is a body of legal rules and principles developed by the courts. A contract in violation of the common law is illegal and void. As an example, X sells her furniture store and business to Y. In the sales contract, X agrees not to compete with Y in the furniture business in the entire state of Illinois for a period of 100 years. This agreement not to compete is illegal and void because it imposes an unreasonable restraint of trade; therefore, it is in violation of the common law. A reasonable restraint of trade, on the other hand, is valid.

Prohibited by Statute

Legislatures, in exercising a government's inherent police power, regulate the making of contracts. One instance might be a state statute that renders invalid any oral listing agreement with a real estate broker. Another example is a state statute that voids any *exculpatory clause* in a lease, that is, any provision exonerating a landlord from liability for injuries caused to the tenant by the landlord's *own* negligence.

Contrary to Public Policy

The public policy of a state is reflected in its constitution, statutes, and judicial decisions. The public policy of one state may differ from that of another. A court will decide each case dealing with an alleged violation of public policy on its own facts. The following circumstances are generally held to be against public policy: (a) an agreement to pay a member of a zoning board a specified amount in return for her favorable vote on a zoning matter or (b) an agreement with a trustee of a land trust which, if carried out, would cause the trustee to breach her fiduciary duty to her beneficiary.

In some instances, an agreement is illegal in part only. In such cases, the court will enforce the legal part if it can be separated from the illegal part.

In Writing

All states have a statute that requires certain contracts to be in writing. This law is commonly referred to as a *Statute of Frauds*. A contract that is not in writing, as required by the Statute of Frauds, is not enforceable by the courts. However, if both of the parties have performed their obligations, the courts usually hold the oral agreement to be enforceable. For *a writing* to be sufficient, it may take the form of a formal contract or consist of a series of letters, a check, telegrams, receipts, or any combination thereof. It is only necessary that all of the writings incorporate each other by reference so the court recognizes them as the intended contract.

Most Statutes of Frauds also provide that the only parties bound to the contract are those who sign. Therefore, if one party signs, she is bound. If both sign, both parties are bound. If neither party signs, the contract is totally unenforceable. The *signature* may appear anywhere on any of the writings representing the contract.

In addition to the requirements previously mentioned, a writing to satisfy a Statute of Frauds must contain a sufficiently detailed description of the subject matter, identification of the parties and subject matter, the price, and a statement of the other essential terms of the contract.

An understanding of the following provisions of a typical Statute of Frauds is important to any study of real estate and real estate transactions. (See also Figure 4–4.)

Contract to Answer for the Debt or Default of Another Person (Guaranty or Suretyship)

A contractual promise to pay the debt owed by another person must be in writing to be enforceable. This statute applies only to *collateral* (secondary) promises. It does not apply to *original* (primary) promises. For example, a father tells a landowner that, if the latter will transfer (i.e., a gift, not a sale) title to his land to the

Statute of Frauds
(requirement of written contract)

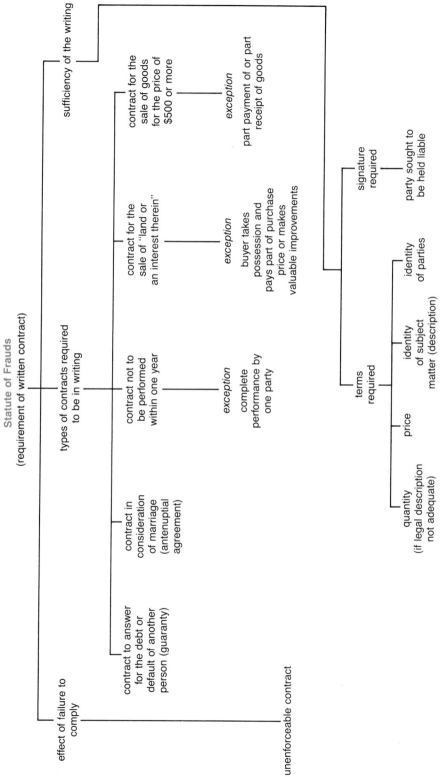

Figure 4–4   Statute of Frauds

son, he, the father will pay for it. The father's promise is original (primary) and need not be in writing under this particular Statute of Frauds. *Note:* The father's promise could be required to be in writing under a Statute of Frauds, subsequently discussed in this chapter, that applies to "contracts for the sale of an interest in real estate." As a contrasting example, X owns a ranch that is encumbered by a $250,000 mortgage debt. X sold the ranch to B under a contract of sale wherein B agreed to make a down payment of $200,000 and assumed and agreed to pay X's mortgage debt. B's promise to pay X's mortgage debt is collateral (secondary) and is not enforceable unless in writing.

Contract in Consideration of Marriage (Antenuptial Agreement)

A contract in consideration of marriage must be in writing to be enforceable. It occurs whenever an engagement (contract) to marry contains any promise that is additional to the mutual promises to marry; for example, the parties to an engagement agree to a property settlement (a division of real and personal property) should they legally separate after marriage.

Contracts Not to Be Performed Within One Year

Any contract that, by its terms, cannot be fully performed within one year of its date is unenforceable unless in writing. As an example, X and Y entered into an oral lease in which X agreed to lease a certain parcel of real estate to Y for a period of two years. The contract is unenforceable at its inception. *Exception:* Where one party to the contract has totally performed her promise, the entire contract is enforceable even though it is oral. For example, L and T entered into an eighteen-month oral lease. L insisted on and received the total amount of rent in advance. The oral lease is binding.

Contracts for the Sale of an Interest in Real Estate

Any contract that affects any private ownership rights in real estate must be in writing. For example, contracts to sell real property (real estate), a mortgage, a grant of a right to remove minerals or gravel, and grants or reservations of easements must be in writing. *Exception:* If a buyer under an oral contract to sell real estate takes possession and makes either valuable improvements *or* a payment (partial or total) of the purchase price, the contract is binding.

The distinction between real estate and personal property is important for the purposes of the Statute of Frauds. This distinction is a part of the law of property (discussed in Chapter 3).

Contracts for the Sale of Personal Property for the Price of $500 or More

Many buyers of real estate also simultaneously negotiate for the purchase of personal property found on the premises. The purchase price of the personal property frequently exceeds $500. In order to satisfy the provisions of the Statute of Frauds, the parties must either list the items of personal property in a written real estate contract or execute a separate written contract, commonly referred to as a *bill of sale. Exception:* If a buyer pays for or receives possession of some or all of the agreed-upon items of personal property, the contract is binding as to the items paid for or received even though the contract was oral.

Where the purchase price of the personal property is below $500, an oral contract is binding on the parties. Because of the difficulty of proving oral contracts, it would be advisable to list all items of personal property in a written real estate contract, regardless of the agreed-upon price.

REMEDIES UPON A BREACH OF CONTRACT

Contracting parties are allowed by law to state a sum to be received by one party as damages in case of breach by the other. This type of provision is called a *liquidated damages* clause. It is valid and enforceable as the sole remedy of the injured party, if the sum agreed upon was reasonably related to the probable damages that the parties forecast as resulting from a future breach. As an example, X enters into a contract for the sale of an apartment building to Y. X and Y agree that if possession of the apartment house is not delivered to Y on July 1, 1989, X is to pay Y $2,000 each month until the possession is delivered. The monthly rental revenue from the apartment house has been $1,800 each month for the last two years. This is a valid and enforceable liquidated damages clause. If the damages agreed upon in the contract are excessive, the liquidated damages provision will be void. If either an existing liquidated damages clause is void or if the parties neglected to include any liquidated damages provision and a breach occurs, the injured party has the right to assert the common law remedies explained in the following section and summarized in Table 4–1 against the party in default.

Remedies of the Buyer

If the seller defaults, the buyer can choose a remedy from among the following:

1. *Specific performance.* Under the remedy of *specific performance,* the buyer can obtain a decree by a court ordering the seller to perform the agreement. An example would be a court order requiring a defaulting seller of real estate to deliver a deed to the buyer conveying title to the property as agreed upon.
2. *Sue for damages.* The buyer can seek a judgment by a court ordering the seller to pay *damages* suffered by the buyer as a result of the seller's default. For example, X contracted to sell a factory building to Y. Upon X's default, Y purchased a substantially equivalent factory building from Z. However, six weeks elapsed before she was able to locate and purchase Z's building, and Y was required to pay $4,000 more to Z than the purchase price under her previous contract with X. Y is entitled to actual

	Remedies	Buyer	Seller
1.	Sue for damages (actual monetary loss)	X	X
2.	Specific performance	X	X*
3.	Rescission	X	X
4.	Restitution of earnest money	X	
5.	Retention of earnest money		X
6.	Liquidated damages if agreed upon in the contract of sale	X	X

*In most states.

Table 4–1   Remedies upon breach of real estate sales contract

damages, consisting of $4,000 plus a reasonable rental value of the factory building for the period of time that elapsed between X's default and Y's purchase of the factory building from Z.

3. *Rescission of the contract and restitution.* Upon a seller's default, the buyer is entitled to notify the seller that she considers the contract terminated *(rescission)* and can recover (obtain *restitution* of) any consideration (earnest money or down payments) previously paid to the seller.

Remedies of the Seller

Upon the buyer's breach of contract, the seller can choose a remedy from among the following:

1. *Sue for damages.* The seller is entitled to file a lawsuit and recover from the buyer the actual monetary loss *(damages)* suffered as a result of the buyer's breach.
2. *Rescission of the contract.* The seller has the right to notify the buyer that the contract is terminated. As a condition precedent to an effective *rescission,* the seller must return all payments (earnest money or down payments) previously received from the buyer.
3. *Specific performance.* As a general rule, *specific performance* is available to a seller of real estate. However, a few states do not allow this remedy.
4. *Retention of earnest money as damages.* Unless otherwise agreed in the contract, the seller has the right to rescind the contract and *retain the earnest money* as damages. *Earnest money* is a cash deposit paid by a prospective buyer as evidence of her good faith intention to perform her contractual obligation. If the amount is not unreasonably large (usually 10 percent or less), the courts will allow the seller to retain the earnest money as damages in case of the buyer's breach. Technically, a down payment is not intended to be earnest money; therefore, unless provided for in the contract, a seller does not have the right to retain a down payment as damages as a result of the buyer's breach.

REAL ESTATE CONTRACTS

No specific form of contract is necessary to bind parties to a real estate transaction. As previously discussed, the contractual agreement may be in the form of a letter, check, receipt, telegram, memorandum, or a combination of such writings. It is only necessary that the writing or group of writings contain all the essential elements of a contract and be signed by the parties. Persons engaged in all aspects of real estate transactions must be familiar with the numerous types of contracts to carry out their legal and ethical responsibilities successfully.

In actual practice today, most real estate transactions are begun and completed by use of local standard printed forms. Only in the more complicated transactions is there a tendency for the parties to require a contract whose provisions are tailor-made to their needs by an attorney. Printed forms used in the real estate business are not standardized throughout the United States or even in counties within a state. However, there is an increasing use of standardized forms prepared by state real estate boards. Where standardized forms have not been adopted, the forms in use differ in name, language, and scope of their coverage of subject matter. Therefore, it is important to the real estate broker and salesperson to be aware of the real estate form contracts commonly used in their market area and to understand the legal implications of the provisions in each. The provisions of a form contract entered into by the parties will determine their rights and obligations even though the parties may have misunderstood them when they signed. When choosing the appropriate form contract and aiding in its completion, the broker must be careful to see that the contractual provisions will legally fulfill the desires of the parties involved and protect their individual interests.

The contracts most commonly used in the real estate business are these:

1. Listing agreement
2. Deposit receipt and offer to purchase
3. Contract for the sale of real estate
4. Installment land contract
5. Option to buy or sell
6. Contract for the exchange of real estate
7. Lease

It is impossible to list and describe the multitude of form contracts currently used throughout the United States. The following discussion will explain the nature of the transaction involved (regardless of the form used) and describe the most common provisions found in representative real estate contracts.

The Listing Agreement

A *listing agreement* is a contract of employment whereby a broker is appointed as a special agent with limited authority to act for his principal in exchange for a commission. It is important that the agreement set forth the authority granted to the broker and the conditions upon which the principal is willing to dispose of her property. If the broker exceeds her authority or does not find a buyer ready, willing, and able to comply with the principal's conditions, the principal need not bargain with the buyer, and she is not obligated to pay a commission to the broker.

The formation and enforceability of a listing agreement is governed by general common law pertaining to contracts and by specific state statutes. Under the common law, the agreement need not be in writing. However, at least seventeen state statutes now require a written agreement for the broker to be entitled to his commission. Other states require a written agreement only for exclusive agency listing agreements.

The typical completed listing agreement form will usually contain the following information:

1. Names of broker and seller
2. Listing price
3. Agreed-upon amount of commission and time of payment
4. Description of the property involved
5. Seller's terms and conditions
6. Duration of the listing
7. Authority of the broker
8. Personal property to be included as part of the transaction
9. Type of listing (e.g., open listing, exclusive agency listing, or exclusive right to sell)

Many state laws or real estate commission regulations require inclusion as well as exclusion of certain provisions in listing agreements. It is the responsibility of the broker to ensure that the listing agreement she uses, whether it be in a form contract or otherwise, is binding and enforceable between herself and her principal and that it complies in every way with the laws in the state in which she is licensed and does business.

Mandatory Provisions

The following statements are often required in listing agreements: (a) It is illegal for either the principal or the broker to discriminate on the basis of race, color, religion, sex, or physical disability. (b) No amendment or alteration of the listing agreement shall be valid unless in writing and signed by the parties. (c) If the listing is exclusive, a statement of the exact duration of the contract must be included.

Prohibited Provisions

In addition to requiring minimum provisions, some state statutes also prohibit the inclusion of certain clauses, such as (a) a clause automatically extending the listing period, (b) a clause providing for a net listing agreement, or (c) a clause prohibiting recordation of the contract.

A more in-depth discussion of listing contracts and practices is found in Chapter 14.

Deposit Receipts and Offers to Purchase

During the process of negotiating a real estate contract, the original offer may have been made by either the seller or the buyer. Many *oral* offers and counteroffers may take place between the parties prior to a written finalization of their agreement. If oral negotiations are concluded with a definite offer and an unconditional acceptance, an oral contract is formed. However, as previously discussed in this chapter, oral contracts for the sale of an interest in real estate are not enforceable, under the provisions of the Statute of Frauds, by either the seller or the buyer. Consequently, it is essential that the parties state their agreement in some form of writing.

In some real estate market areas, a printed form designated a "Deposit Receipt" or an "Offer to Purchase" is used by brokers to set out the terms and conditions of the real estate sales contract. Although titled a *Deposit Receipt* or an *Offer to Purchase,* these forms contain all of the essential elements of a contract. These forms may be signed and initiated by either the seller or the buyer. The most common procedure is for the broker to have the buyer sign the form and forward it to the seller for signature.

Regardless of which party initiates negotiation, a completed and signed deposit receipt or offer to purchase constitutes a legal offer to enter a contract pursuant to its terms and conditions. Upon its acceptance, a contract is formed. An acceptance may be made orally or in writing, either by a separate, signed correspondence or by a signature on the deposit receipt or offer to purchase. Some type of written and signed acceptance is essential to bind the offeree under the Statute of Frauds, which provides that, for both parties to be bound, both parties must have signed the required writing. If one party (offeror) signs, she will be bound to the contract upon oral acceptance by the other party (offeree). The nonsigning party is not bound. She may choose to either become bound by signing the form or reject the contract as being unenforceable against her. For example, when a deposit (earnest money) is paid to the broker and the deposit receipt is signed by the prospective purchaser (offeror), the seller (offeree) is not bound until she signs the form itself or some other writing that indicates her acceptance.

Therefore, under the Statute of Frauds, the signatures of both parties are not necessary to enforce a printed form agreement that contains the necessary elements of a contract. A seller can enforce a written contract signed only by the buyer, and a buyer can enforce a written contract signed only by the seller.

The broker must be certain that the form contract contains only those terms and conditions of sale his principal had authorized in the listing agreement. Failure to do so will legally justify a refusal to accept the offer as well as a refusal to pay the broker's commission. However, if the seller accepts and signs the form contract containing materially different terms and conditions than she previously authorized, she is obligated to pay the broker the agreed-upon commission.

A deposit receipt usually contains a receipt for the required deposit, a description of the property involved, the terms and conditions of the sale, and a statement of the exact amount of the commission to be paid the broker. It may or may not require the formalization of a more detailed contract in the future. The offer to purchase differs from the deposit receipt in that it generally does not contain a receipt for "earnest money" or any statement of the amount of broker's commission.

Many buyers fail to realize that, under contract law and the Statute of Frauds, their signature on the deposit receipt or offer to purchase may bind them to its terms without a signature of the seller. Others believe that the receipt is a preliminary agreement prior to the completion of a subsequent detailed contract. In an attempt to reduce misunderstanding by the buyer who signs deposit receipts, at least one state, Illinois, prohibits the use of a form designated as *offer to purchase* when it is intended to be a *binding contract*. Illinois requires that all other forms used by brokers that are also intended to be binding must clearly so state in the heading of the form in enlarged bold type.

The Contract for the Sale of Real Estate

A contract for the sale of real estate does not convey legal title to the property. Only a deed properly executed and delivered to the buyer will convey legal title. However, after execution of the sales contract and prior to delivery of the deed, the buyer has an interest in the real estate known as **equitable title.** Having equitable title, the buyer may effectively record the contract. She also acquires an insurable interest in the property. The buyer and the seller are legally co-owners of the real estate until absolute title is transferred to the buyer by delivery and acceptance of a deed from the seller.

This contract is one of the most important and frequently used instruments in the real estate business. As we have said, a real estate contract may be legally sufficient in that it meets the minimum requirements of the law, yet it may be totally inadequate to protect the interests and fulfill the expectations and desires of both the seller and buyer. It is therefore important to use an adequate contract form. (See Figure 4–5.)

DEPOSIT RECEIPT & PURCHASE AND SALE AGREEMENT

DATE _____

I. Receipt is hereby acknowledged by _____ hereinafter called AGENT, of the sum

of $_____ from _____

_____ hereinafter called BUYER,

A. (which term may be singular or plural and shall include the heirs, successors, personal representatives and assigns of the BUYER) as a part of the purchase price on account

of offer to purchase the property of _____ hereinafter called SELLER (which term may be singular or plural and shall include the heirs, successors, personal representatives and assigns of the SELLER) said property being in _____

_____County,_____, and described as follows:

B. _____

_____

Also known as: _____

II. The SELLER hereby agrees to sell said property to the BUYER and the BUYER hereby agrees to purchase said property from the SELLER upon the following terms and conditions (if completed or marked):

III. 1. The total PURCHASE PRICE to be paid by the BUYER is payable as follows:

   (a) Earnest money deposit, receipt of which is herein acknowledged $_____

   (b) Additional payment $_____

   (c) Additional payment due at closing (not including costs of BUYER) $_____

   (d) Proceeds of new note and mortgage to be executed by BUYER to

      any lender other than the SELLER $_____

   (e) Existing mortgage balance encumbering the property to be

      assumed by the BUYER $_____

   (f) Balance due to the SELLER to be evidenced by a negotiable promissory note of the BUYER, secured by a valid purchase money mortgage, in a form acceptable to SELLER, on said property executed and delivered by the BUYER to the SELLER dated the date of closing,

     bearing interest at the rate of _____

     per annum and payable $_____ per_____ $_____

Privilege of prepayment ☐ does apply ☐ does not apply.

TOTAL PURCHASE PRICE: $_____

IV. 2. It is understood that the said property will be conveyed by WARRANTY Deed (Unless otherwise required) subject to current taxes, existing zoning ordinances, covenants, restrictions, and easements of record.

V. 3. The BUYER will pay for: ( ) Recording fees; ( ) Stamps on note; ( ) Intangible Tax on mortgage; ( ) Credit Report; ( ) _____ Attorney's fee; ( ) Mortgage transfer charge; ( ) Mortgagee's initial service fee; ( ) Photos; ( ) Appraisal fee; ( ) Mortgage insurance premium and review fee; ( ) Opinion of title;

Figure 4–5 Contract for the sale of real estate

Source: Reprinted with permission from *Real Estate,* by Kau, James B., and Sirmans, C. F., © 1985 by McGraw-Hill Book Company, N.Y., N.Y.

( ) _____ Title binder; ( ) prepaid insurance; taxes and
interest. ( ) _____
_____. Any incurred expense on behalf of BUYER will be
deducted from binder deposit in the event loan and or sale is not closed through no
fault of the SELLER.

4. The SELLER will pay for: ( ) Stamps and surtax on deed; ( ) Survey; ( ) _____
Attorney's fee; ( ) Appraisal fee; ( ) Real Estate sales commission; ( ) Abstract of title;
( ) Opinion of title; ( ) Mortgage discount; ( ) Satisfaction of Mortgage and recording
fee; ( ) Termite inspection; ( ) Repairs or replacements required by FHA or VA not to
exceed $_____ ( ).

5. PRORATIONS: All taxes for the current year, rentals, monthly mortgage insurance premiums, hazard insurance premiums and interest on existing mortgages (if any) shall be
prorated as of the date of closing. If part of the purchase price is to be evidenced by
the assumption of a mortgage requiring deposit of funds in escrow for payment of
taxes, insurance or other charges, the BUYER agrees to reimburse the SELLER for said
escrow funds assigned to BUYER at closing, with all mortgage payments to be current
at the time of closing.

6. TITLE EVIDENCE: WITHIN _____ days ( ) After date of acceptance ( )
After date of approval of mortgage loan, the SELLER will furnish and deliver to the
BUYER, AGENT or closing ATTORNEY: ( ) Title insurance binder for a fee policy in the
amount of the purchase price; ( )Title insurance binder for mortgage policy in the
amount of _____; ( ) A continuation abstract of title from the last title insuring policy or institutional mortgage.

VI. 7. SURVEY: Within _____ days ( ) after date of acceptance ( ) after date of
approval of mortgage loan, the SELLER will furnish and deliver showing all improvements
now existing thereon ( ) An accurate survey of said property certified within 3 months
of the date of closing; ( ) A copy of a previously made survey of sold property showing
all improvements now existing thereon; ( ) No survey is required.

8. TITLE EXAMINATION AND TIME FOR CLOSING. If said title evidence and survey as specified above show that the SELLER is vested with a good and insurable title to said property, subject to the usual exceptions contained in title insurance binders (such as exceptions for survey, current taxes, zoning ordinances, covenants, restrictions and
easements of record), the transaction shall be closed and the SELLER and BUYER shall
perform the agreements made herein on or before ( ) _____, ( ) _____
days after mortgage loan approval ( ) _____ days after date of acceptance.
The foregoing closing dates shall be extended to allow compliance with the Real Estate
Settlement Procedure Act. If title evidence and survey reveal any defects which are not
acceptable to the BUYER or Mortgagee, the BUYER or Mortgagee shall within 15 days
notify the SELLER of such title defects and the SELLER agrees to use reasonable diligence
to cure such defects and shall have 90 days to do so, in which event this transaction
shall be closed within ten days after delivery to the BUYER of evidence that such defects
have been cured. If the SELLER is unable to convey to the BUYER a good and insurable
title to said property, the BUYER shall have the right to demand and receive from the
AGENT all sums deposited hereunder, at the same time returning to the SELLER all the
evidence and surveys received from the SELLER and the BUYER's copy of the Agreement
where upon all rights and liabilities of the parties hereunder shall cease and determine;
or the BUYER shall have the right to accept such title as the SELLER may be able to convey, and to close this transaction upon the other terms as stated herein.

VII. 9. DEFAULT BY BUYER: If the said BUYER fails to perform the covenants herein contained
within the time specified, SELLER shall have the election of all remedies available under

Figure 4–5   (continued)

the law to include, but not limited to (a) require specific performance on the part of BUYER; (b) bring suit against BUYER for damages resulting from the breach; (c) after deducting any funds expended for Buyer or Seller's processing costs, the Owner shall retain as liquidated damages one-half of the remainder of the binder deposit. The remaining one-half of net deposit shall be paid to the Agent as compensation not to exceed the total amount of his commission.

10. DEFAULT BY SELLER: If the SELLER fails to perform any of the covenants of this Agreement, the aforesaid money paid by the BUYER at the option of the BUYER shall be returned to the BUYER on demand; the BUYER may bring suit against Seller for damages resulting from the breach, and the BUYER shall have the right of specific performance.

11. ATTORNEY'S FEES AND COSTS: In connection with any litigation arising out of the Agreement, the prevailing party shall be entitled to recover all costs incurred, including reasonable attorney's fees.

VIII. 12. LOSS OR DAMAGE: The risk of loss or damage to premises by fire, or otherwise, is assumed by SELLER until closing of this transaction.

13. THE SELLER agrees to deliver the property in its PRESENT AS IS CONDITION, excepting normal wear and tear. BUYER agrees that they have inspected the property in its present condition except as herein otherwise specified.

14. POSSESSION of the property shall be delivered to the BUYER _____

_____

IX. 15. ( ) FINANCING. It is agreed that the BUYER will require a mortgage loan in order to finance this transaction. The responsibility for arranging such a loan assumed by ( ) SELLER or ( ) BUYER; and in the event that such mortgage loan is not approved or attainable within _____ days of the date of acceptance of this Agreement, the SELLER shall have the right to terminate this AGREEMENT and thereupon the AGENT will return to the BUYER all sums deposited hereunder, less any incurred mortgage processing costs, and the BUYER will return to the SELLER all the title evidence and surveys received from the SELLER and BUYER'S copy of this Agreement. BUYER shall make application for financing within 5 days of the date of acceptance of this Agreement and furnish any and all credit, employment, financial and other information required by the Lender. The BUYER will reapply within 5 days at an alternate Lender in the event the original loan application is declined.

16. ( ) It is expressly agreed that, notwithstanding any other provisions of the Agreement, the BUYER shall not be obligated to complete the purchase of the property described herein or to incur any penalty by forfeiture of earnest money deposit or otherwise unless the SELLER has delivered to the BUYER a written statement issued by the Federal Housing Commissioner setting forth the appraised value of the property (excluding closing cost) of not less than $_____ which statement the SELLER hereby agrees to deliver to the BUYER promptly after such appraised value statement is made available to the SELLER. The BUYER shall, however, have the privilege and option of proceeding with the consummation of this Agreement without regard to the amount on the appraised valuation.

17. ( ) It is expressly agreed that, notwithstanding any other provisions of this Agreement, the BUYER shall not incur any penalty by forfeiture of earnest money or otherwise be obligated to complete the purchase of the property described herein, if the Agreement purchase price or cost exceeds the reasonable value of the property established by the Veterans Administration. The BUYER shall however have the privilege and option of proceeding with the consummation of this Agreement without regard to the amount of reasonable value established by the VA.

X. 18. ( ) TERMITE INSPECTION. The SELLER agrees to furnish, without expense to the

Figure 4–5   (continued)

BUYER, a termite inspection report showing all buildings on the premises to be visibly free and clear from infestation or damage by termites or other wood-destroying insects. This inspection report is to be furnished by a licensed firm. If a report shows such infestation or damage, the SELLER shall have the right to remedy the same within a reasonable time, and if the SELLER elects not to remedy same, the BUYER shall have the right to complete the transaction or to terminate this Agreement and receive a refund of all sums theretofore deposited with the AGENT.

19. ( ) ZONING. Unless the property is properly zoned for _____ use at the time of closing, the BUYER shall have the right to terminate this Agreement and receive a refund of all sums theretofore deposited with the AGENT.

XI. 20. ( ) PERSONAL PROPERTY TO BE INCLUDED IN THE PURCHASE PRICE. All fixed equipment, including drapery hardware, plants and shrubbery if now installed on said property. Additional personal property _____

_____

XII. 21. ( ) The offer of the BUYER shall terminate if the SELLER has not indicated his acceptance of this Agreement by signing and delivering same to the AGENT before 11:00 p.m. on _____

22. ( ) ADDITIONAL PROVISIONS: _____

_____

23. There are no agreements, promises or understandings between these parties except as specifically set forth herein. No alterations or changes shall be made to the Agreement except in writing and signed or initialed by the parties herein.

24. REAL ESTATE SALES FEE. The SELLER agrees to pay the listing AGENT a commission of _____% of the total purchase price accepted by him no later than at the closing of this transaction. Listing AGENT, _____, agrees to pay cooperating agent _____% of the sale price on closing.

25. This legal and binding Agreement shall not be recorded and if not understood parties hereto should seek competent legal advice.

26. SELLER and BUYER give AGENT authorization to advise surrounding neighbors who will be the new owner of the property.

27. TIME is of the essence in this Agreement except that time required for compliance with the Real Estate Settlement Procedures Act shall in no way invalidate this Agreement.

XIII. SIGNED, SEALED AND WITNESSED on the date and in the year herein stated.

_____	Date of Offer	BUYER

_____	Date of Offer	BUYER

2 witnesses as to the BUYER

_____	Date of Acceptance	SELLER

2 witnesses as to the SELLER | Date of Acceptance | SELLER

AGENT by the signature below acknowledges receipt of $_____ ( ) cash ( ) check which is the amount mentioned in the first paragraph of this Agreement. It will be held in escrow pending disbursement according to terms hereof.

_____

BY: _____

Figure 4–5   (continued)

The Parties

Every real estate sales contract must *name the seller and buyer* in order to be enforceable. The seller must agree to sell and the buyer to buy; otherwise the remedy of specific performance would not be available in case of default by either party.

Seller.   The seller must have clear legal title or be authorized to convey the property on behalf of the holder of title. A careful buyer will require up-to-date *evidence of title* or authority to convey title. To ensure title in the seller or her authority to convey title, the following matters must be considered by the buyer:

1. If title is held by a trustee, executor, administrator, conservator, or guardian, the buyer (or her representative) should examine the trust agreement under which the trustee acts or the court order granting power to convey to the executor, administrator, conservator, or guardian.
2. If title is in a corporation, the buyer must be certain that the corporate officers who sign the contract have the power to do so under the corporate charter and bylaws.
3. If title is held by co-owners, all must be named as sellers and each must sign the contract.
4. If title is held in severalty by a married person, the spouse of that person should sign the contract to release and extinguish any homestead or inchoate dower rights or rights in community property.
5. Where the contract is to be signed by an agent, the agent's authority to do so must be evidenced by a written power of attorney signed by the title holder and the spouse, if any.
6. If title is in a partnership, the partnership agreement should clearly indicate that the person who signs the contract has full authority to act.
7. If the title is held by an infant, a legal guardian must be appointed and authorized by a court to convey title in the infant's behalf.

Buyer.   The seller's primary concern for proper identification of the person who signs the contract as buyer is that she have legal capacity to do so as well as the financial ability to pay the purchase price. If there are two or more buyers, the contract should indicate the type of ownership by which they wish to acquire title (e.g., tenancy in common, joint tenancy, etc.).

Quality of Title

The contract should identify the *quality of title* to be conveyed to the buyer. Almost all real estate sales contracts are intended to convey fee simple title. Many form contracts do not expressly provide that fee simple is to be conveyed. However, most courts hold that a conveyance of a fee simple is intended when there is no indication otherwise. To avoid legal difficulties, the parties should specifically provide in the contract that the seller agrees to convey fee simple to the real estate.

Legal Description

A contract must contain a description of the property that is sufficient to provide a reasonably certain identification of the property. Whenever possible, a *legal description* of the property should be used; it should be the same as that appearing on the abstract of title, the seller's title policy, or the Torrens Certificate. A Torrens Certificate is written evidence that a court issued an order finding title to be in the named owner. If the property cannot be identified from the provisions in the contract itself, the courts hold the contract to be void. It is legally hazardous and not at all good practice to use only the street address to describe the property. The various types of legal descriptions were fully explained in Chapter 2.

In sales of residences and commercial properties, disputes may arise as to whether a certain item of property is or is not included in a sale. A contract for the sale of real estate does not include items of personal property unless the items are specifically listed. Whenever a sale includes items such as wall-to-wall carpeting, window air conditioners, drapes, or stoves that might legally be personal property, the interests of the parties should be protected in one of two ways: first, by providing a contract provision that lists the items in question and states that it is the intention of the parties that these items are to be considered as part of the transaction; second, by having a bill of sale convey title to such items. Many form contracts provide a space for the parties to list any personal property that is to be included as part of the sale.

Price

The purchase price and the method and time of its payment must be stated in such detail that there can be no ambiguity. No price terms should be left to be established by future negotiation or the contract is incomplete and unenforceable. The *purchase price* may be payable in cash or property. Where a cash payment is required, it is customary for the contract to require a partial payment at the time the contract is signed, with the balance to be paid upon delivery of the deed at closing. Where the property is to be sold encumbered by an existing mortgage, the contract should specify when and how much cash is to be paid and whether the buyer shall take "subject to" or "assume and agree to pay" the outstanding mortgage. In other situations, the contract may require that the seller receive a "purchase money mortgage" as part of the purchase price. In such a case, it is important that the contract specify in detail the terms and conditions of the mortgage. Mortgages are discussed in detail in Chapters 7 and 8.

Form of Deed

The contract should specify the *type of deed* to be delivered to the buyer. The usual deeds provided for in contracts are general warranty, special warranty, grant, bargain and sale, and quitclaim. Where the conveyance is to be by a trustee or executor, the type of deed to be given is usually provided for in the applicable state statutes. Most trustee or executor deeds take the form of a special warranty deed or a quitclaim deed.

If the contract is silent as to the type of deed to be given the buyer, most states allow the seller to give a deed without covenants, such as a quitclaim deed. Deeds are discussed in detail in the next chapter.

Title Exceptions

This provision of the contract sets forth the seller's intention to convey title subject to specified encumbrances and restrictions commonly referred to as *title exceptions.* A provision for specific exceptions implies an agreement that the title will be free from all others. Unless the contract provides otherwise, the seller must convey *marketable title* and the buyer is obligated to accept nothing less. A title is not marketable unless it is free from all liens, encumbrances, and restrictions not excepted in the contract. The exceptions commonly provided for in form contracts are as follows:

1. *Existing leases of a specified duration.* A lease is a conveyance of an estate in land and creates an encumbrance upon it. A buyer should investigate the rights of lessees by examining the lease prior to signing the contract.

2. *Special assessments.* Special assessments are imposed by a political unit, such as a city, for local improvements (e.g., streets, sidewalks, and drainage improvements).

3. *General taxes.* Real estate taxes become a lien during the year in which they are levied; however, they may not be due until the following year. Because the buyer must pay these taxes to release the lien, it is customary to provide that she receive a pro rata credit on the purchase price.

4. *Private restrictions on the use or enjoyment of the premises.* The use of land may be restricted by private restrictions created by a previous deed or subdivision plat. Contract forms usually provide that the seller will convey in fee simple and clear of encumbrances. Unless the contract is expressly made subject to existing private restrictions, the buyer may reject the title if it is subject to restrictions as to its use and enjoyment.

5. *Zoning and building codes or ordinances.* Although commonly found in form contracts, this exception is unnecessary and ineffective because zoning and building codes do not affect title. They merely regulate the use of the property. The buyer is held to have knowledge of the existence of these laws. Before signing the contract, a prudent buyer should examine all pertinent zoning, building, and fire and health regulations to determine whether these laws would prohibit her intended use of the property and whether the seller's current use of the property is in violation of these laws. This may be particularly important because of recent changes in land use controls and the enactment of new land conservation laws.

6. *Existing indebtedness.* For example, "Said real estate is subject to the following encumbrance: Mortgage to Savings and Loan Association in the amount of $50,000 which will be assumed by Buyer, if so provided herein, but if not so provided then it may be satisfied out of purchase price and released when deed is delivered." A seller's title is not considered marketable if encumbered by a mortgage. If the mortgage is not excepted, the buyer is not obligated to accept title. The contract clause quoted above is for the seller's benefit, because it allows the seller to use the proceeds from the sale to discharge an existing mortgage. It obligates the buyer to accept a deed upon release of the mortgage.

7. *Easements.* Unless excepted, easements of record render the title unmarketable.

8. *Encroachments.* Encroachments are improvements on land that extend over and upon neighboring land or on adjoining streets or alleys or improvements on neighboring land that extend over and upon the land to be sold. Encroachments render title unmarketable unless excepted in the contract. Where there may be any question as to the existence of encroachments, the buyer should insist that the contract require that the seller provide a survey.

An encroachment is a form of adverse possession of another person's real estate. If the encroachment has existed for the statutory period (i.e., commonly ten to twenty years), the adverse possessor may have acquired title to the land subject to

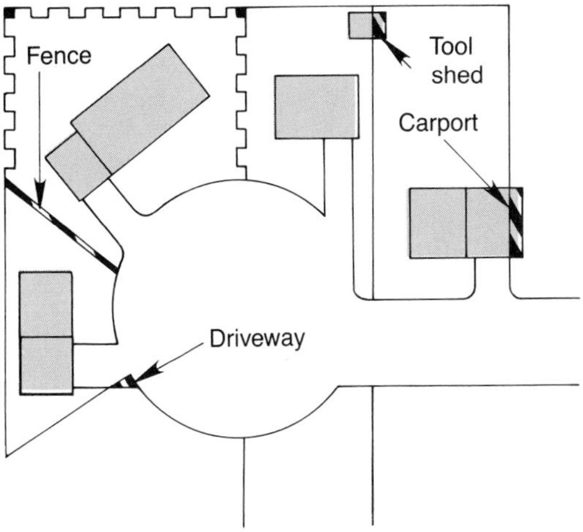

Figure 4–6   Typical
encroachments

CONTRACT LAW
AND REAL
ESTATE
CONTRACTS

the encroachment by adverse possession. See Figure 4–6 for illustrations of various types of encroachments.

Earnest Money Requirement

It is customary for form contracts to require the buyer to pay a cash deposit to the broker, her principal, or in escrow. This down payment or deposit is commonly known as **earnest money.** The contract usually provides that, if the buyer performs, the earnest money applies to the purchase price. To provide for the case of a buyer's default, the following provision is included in form contracts: "Then at the option of the seller, the earnest money shall be forfeited as liquidated damages and the contract shall be null and void." Courts have consistently upheld these provisions as long as the amount to be retained by the seller upon the buyer's default was not so large as to constitute a penalty.

Provision for Prorating

Form contracts generally provide for adjusting or **prorating** one or more of the following items as of the date of possession or delivery of deed. Where the parties desire a different date, such as in the case where the transaction is to be closed in escrow, the contract should specify such date. The mathematical calculations involved in prorating are covered in detail in Chapter 17.

General real estate taxes.   The contract usually provides for prorating based on the most recently ascertainable taxes, which usually consist of the latest amount paid.

Rents.   Unless otherwise agreed in the sales contract, the title holder on the date rent is due is entitled to the rent. The contract should, therefore, provide for prorating rent as of the closing date if the seller has received a prepayment.

Insurance premiums.   If the buyer is going to receive an assignment of the seller's fire insurance policy, the prepaid premium should be prorated.

Sewer and water and other utility charges.   These charges should be handled by instructing the municipality to read the meter at the date of closing and thereafter bill the buyer for water subsequently used. If utility charges have been prepaid according to some sort of "easy payment plan" or "level payment plan," they should be prorated.

Miscellaneous

The contract should specify all items to be adjusted or prorated, including

1. Fuel or supplies on hand; for example, LP (liquid propane) gas, firewood, coal, and fuel oil
2. Interest on mortgages to be taken subject to or assumed

Furnishing Evidence of Title

Unless agreed upon in the sales contract, the seller is not obligated to furnish the buyer evidence that her title is good. Without such a provision, the buyer would be legally obligated to make her own title search at her own expense. Form contracts usually provide that the seller furnish one of the following forms of evidence of title:

1. *Abstract of title.* An **abstract of title** is a chronological history of publicly recorded instruments, documents, and legal proceedings that have affected title to the property, commencing with government ownership of the real estate and brought up to the current date. Deeds, mortgages, other instruments or documents affecting title, and legal proceedings are all included in the abstract. For the most part, abstracts are prepared by lawyers and abstract companies. Each abstract includes an abstractor's certificate that discloses what records the abstractor *did* and *did not* examine and the last date covered by the search of the records. The buyer's attorney should examine the abstract and prepare an opinion as to the status of title.

2. *Title insurance policy.* A **title insurance policy** is a contract of indemnity. The title insurance company agrees to indemnify the owner (buyer) and/or her mortgagee against loss incurred by reason of those defects in the title not expressly excepted in the policy. The insurance company also agrees to defend, at its own expense, any lawsuit filed against the insured based on a defect in title. Only the buyer or other named insured (e.g., the buyer's mortgagee) is covered by a title insurance policy. Unless named as an insured in the title insurance policy, the seller is not covered. The seller is liable to the buyer for damages for breach of any title warranties expressed in or implied from the deed if title defects are subsequently discovered. Should the buyer suffer a loss because of a covered defect in title, the policy usually obligates the insurance company to pay the insured the actual financial loss plus any expenses, court costs, and attorney fees expended by the insured to protect or defend title. After such payment, the insurance company is authorized by the terms of its policy (i.e., a *subrogation clause*) to sue the seller for the seller's breach of any existing express or implied title warranties and collect from the seller any amounts it paid to its insured. (Title insurance is discussed in detail in Chapter 12.)

3. *Torrens Certificate.* A few cities and counties use the **Torrens system** of registration of title to land. Under this system, title is initially registered by written application to the county court in the county wherein it is located. A court hearing establishes ownership in the applicant, and the court issues an order for the registration of the real estate in the name of the owner. The title is registered with the Registrar of Titles. No lien or judgment is valid unless it is entered on the original title certif-

icate by the Registrar. Once registered, a certificate of title is appropriate evidence of title.

4. *Attorney's certificate of title.* When an **attorney's certificate of title** is required, no formal abstract of title is prepared. The attorney conducts her own search of the public records. Based on what is revealed by the examination, she will issue the written opinion *(certificate of title)* of the current status of the title.

At least eleven states have enacted "marketable title" statutes that void most adverse rights, interests, or claims to land that have been in existence for more than a specified period of years (e.g., forty years). These statutes typically exempt from their coverage the following adverse rights, interests, or claims:

1. Easements or other rights or interests that are discoverable by an inspection of the land
2. Title by adverse possession
3. Rights, interests, or claims of the U. S. government
4. Rights, interests, or claims of which the buyer has actual notice

Unless such rights, interests, or claims are recorded or rerecorded during the statutory period, they do not legally exist. A seller who has an uninterrupted chain of clear title of record in a parcel of land during the statutory period is held to possess a marketable title.

Fire Clause

Under common law, the **risk of loss** from fire or other casualty to the premises falls upon the purchaser during the pendency of the sale regardless of which party is in possession of the premises. Some courts have stated that the risk of loss remains on the seller until a deed is delivered to the buyer. Some states have resolved the conflict by enacting statutes *(Uniform Vendor and Purchaser Risk Act)* that provide that the seller retains the risk of loss until legal title is transferred to the buyer or the buyer is given possession of the premises.

A buyer may protect himself by including the following clause in the contract:

> If the premises are totally or substantially destroyed by fire or other casualty before this transaction is completed, the buyer may, at his option, accept the insurance proceeds or other settlement and complete the transaction or declare this contract void, and the amount of earnest money paid by the buyer is to be refunded. Seller at her own expense shall maintain insurance on the premises against fire with extended coverage for their full insurable value until this transaction is completed.

Provision for Escrow

The parties to a sales contract may choose to provide that the transaction be closed in escrow. An escrow arrangement protects the buyer against the death or incapacity of the seller and assures the seller that the money is available to close the transaction. Escrow arrangements are discussed in detail subsequently in this chapter and in Chapter 17.

Provision for Possession

The parties may agree to any **possession date;** however, without a contract provision to the contrary, the right of possession passes to the buyer at the time she receives the deed from the seller.

Time of the Essence Clause

Where the contract does not provide that *time is of the essence,* courts usually allow the buyer or seller a reasonable time after the agreed-upon closing date to comply with the terms of the sales contract. If the contract provides that time is of the essence, failure of the buyer or seller to close on the agreed-upon date places her immediately in default.

Installment Land Contract

The installment land contract is known by various names throughout the United States, such as "contract for deed," "land contract," or "installment contract." It is most correctly called an *installment land contract,* and the real estate is commonly referred to as being *sold under contract.* These real estate contracts are generally used when the buyer is unable to pay the entire purchase price herself or cannot obtain sufficient mortgage financing. For example, lenders often will not take a mortgage on unimproved land (i.e., land without a building). Another use is to spread taxable income from the sale of real estate over several years.

Under an installment land contract, the seller retains legal title as security for the payment of agreed-upon installments made up of principal and interest. The buyer becomes the "beneficial owner" immediately upon signing the contract and making a nominal down payment. However, the buyer is not entitled to delivery of deed until the full purchase price has been paid and all of her other obligations under the contract have been fully performed.

Unless the contract provides the contrary, the buyer is not entitled to possession until the entire purchase price has been paid and the deed is delivered to the buyer. However, it is common practice for the contract to give the buyer the right to immediate possession. Once the buyer rightfully does take possession, she has absolute and exclusive control over the property. There is, however, one qualification to the buyer's complete control. She may not commit *waste.* If the buyer commits any act toward the land that substantially impairs the security value of the real estate, the seller may get a court order restraining the buyer from such acts. Examples are a buyer who refuses to pay real estate taxes, allows buildings on the land to deteriorate, or materially changes the use of the property.

The interests of the seller and buyer are freely assignable during their lifetimes and pass by inheritance upon their deaths. The buyer is entitled to all profits from the land and must meet only the installment obligations to the seller.

To protect her interest against subsequent purchasers or mortgages taken out by the seller, the buyer must record the installment land contract.

A common installment land contract form contains certain provisions discussed in the following sections.

Description of Premises

The parties mutually agree to sell and buy property designated by its legal description.

Price and Terms

This clause in an installment land contract sets forth the total purchase price. It indicates the required down payment together with the amount of principal and accrued interest to be paid in installments. The time and place for payment of installments is stated in detail.

Possession of the Premises

The seller agrees to give exclusive possession of the property to the buyer on or before a specified date for the entire life of the contract, subject only to the buyer's default in any terms of the contract.

Escrow

An escrow agent is named and appointed for the seller and the buyer. This provision requires that the original signed copy of the installment land contract be deposited with the escrow agent. The seller is required to turn over to the escrow agent an executed general warranty deed to the buyer, together with either an abstract of title, a title insurance policy, or a Torrens certificate. Under the escrow agreement, which can be incorporated into the contract, the escrow agent binds herself not to deliver the seller's deed to the buyer until the buyer pays all installments of principal and interest and other charges provided for under the contract. Escrow arrangements are discussed even more fully subsequently in this chapter and in Chapter 17.

Right to Prepayment

This provision usually grants the buyer the right to prepay installments of principal and apply the prepayments against future installments.

Grace Period

The buyer is granted a period of time, usually thirty to sixty days after default, to make overdue payments. During the grace period, the seller is unable to declare a forfeiture. Also provided is an acceleration clause that authorizes the seller to declare the entire purchase price due and payable upon the buyer's failure to pay any one installment of principal and interest as required in the contract.

Right to Assign and to Mortgage

Here the seller retains the first option to repurchase the property from the buyer when the buyer wishes to sell or assign (transfer) her interest during the life of the contract. The provision usually requires that the buyer also secure written consent from the seller prior to mortgaging her interest.

Taxes and Assessments

This clause usually provides that the seller and buyer pay a pro rata share of their property taxes levied during the year the buyer takes possession. Prorating is done as of the date the buyer is given the right of possession. All subsequent taxes and assessments are required to be paid by the buyer.

Insurance

The buyer agrees to pay the seller the unearned portion of prepaid insurance currently in force on improvements on the premises and assigned to the buyer. The buyer also agrees to maintain insurance, from date of possession, on all improvements in a sufficient amount to cover the full insurable value of the improvements, payable to both the seller and buyer as their legal interests may appear.

Oil, Gas, and Mineral Rights

Unless oil, gas, or minerals are currently being removed from the premises, neither the seller nor the buyer alone has the right to remove oil, gas, or mineral deposits or lease rights to third parties. This provision should be included if the property is located in areas of oil and gas development. The parties should specify their respective mineral rights.

Default and Forfeiture

This provision requires the buyer to *forfeit* to the seller all payments made prior to her *default* on the terms of the contract. In most states, the seller is entitled to the payments as *liquidated damages* and is granted the right of immediate reentry and possession of the premises. In some states, such as California, statutory and common law restrictions are imposed to prevent a forfeiture of monies by a defaulting buyer. A few states allow the buyer a grace period after default when she can reinstate the contract by payment of monies in default.

When a buyer records the installment land contract and subsequently defaults, there is a cloud on the seller's title even though she has exercised her right of reentry and taken possession from the buyer. To clear her title, a seller may attempt to obtain a quitclaim deed from the defaulting buyer, file a strict foreclosure suit against the buyer, or file a bill to quiet title.

Options to Buy or Lease Real Estate

An *option* is a contract containing a continuing offer that grants the optionee the legal right to buy or lease real estate owned by the optionor at a stated, fixed price during a specified period of time. Because it is a contract, it cannot be revoked by the optionor. The optionee is not usually obligated to purchase the property or lease the premises; however, she can become bound if she expressly or impliedly accepts the offer within the time allowed in the option. To be enforceable under the Statute of Frauds, the option must be in writing. As an example, X, in exchange for $500, promises Y that if Y wants to purchase within thirty days of the current date, X will sell an identified apartment house to Y for a price of $150,000. The option may or may not provide that the consideration paid for the option be applied to the purchase price after acceptance of the option.

Some common types of options are listed below:

1. *Fixed price option.* The optionor is legally bound to sell or lease real estate to the optionee at a stated price (rent) or prices (rents) during the option period.
2. *Price step-up option.* This is usually a long-term option by whose terms the offered price (rent) of the real estate increases at stated levels during the entire option period.
3. *Conditional option.* The optionee's acceptance of the option offer is made conditional upon changes in zoning, obtaining licenses or building permits, securing options on adjacent land, or other events. If the conditional event does not occur, the optionee is not legally obligated to purchase or lease.
4. *Price-credit option.* In this option, the consideration paid to obtain the option is credited against the agreed-upon purchase price or rent if the option is exercised by the optionee.
5. *Renewable option.* This option is automatically renewable by the optionee at the end of the initial option period with a stepped-up option price.

An option contract can be negotiated by the parties to include any combination of the terms discussed above.

Contracts for the Exchange of Real Estate

Contracts for the exchange of real estate are essentially the same as contracts for the sale of real estate already discussed. The only important difference is that, in an exchange contract, both parties transfer title to real estate to each other, whereas in the sales contract the seller is required to transfer title to real estate in exchange for actual cash received or a promise to pay cash in the future. Where the market values of the exchanged properties are not equal, the contract will provide for a cash adjustment ("boot").

In other respects, exchange contracts are governed by the same common law and statutory rules and contain essentially the same provisions as sales contracts.

Leases

A lease is a contract whereby the owner (lessor) of real estate binds herself to give exclusive possession and control of all or a part of the premises to another person (lessee) in exchange for consideration (rent). Leases are discussed in detail in Chapter 6.

ASSIGNMENTS OF REAL ESTATE CONTRACTS

As a general rule, unless otherwise stated in the contract or prohibited by common law or statute, real estate contracts such as options, leases, and contracts for the sale or lease of real estate are freely assignable. An *assignment* is a legal transfer of rights a party possesses under a contract with another. For example, X enters into a contract for sale of real estate to Y. Y, finding herself unable to raise the purchase price, discovers Z, who agrees to pay Y $300 for Y's rights to purchase the property from X. A valid assignment was made, and X is legally bound to carry out the terms of the contract as if Z had been the original party.

ESCROW ARRANGEMENTS

Many real estate transactions are closed "in escrow." An *escrow arrangement* (Figure 4–7) consists of an oral or written contract under which a deed or other instrument, property, money, or any combination of these items is deposited with a third party (*escrow agent, escrowee,* or *escrow trustee*) to be held and delivered upon the performance of one or more specified conditions. The contract that specifies the conditions to be performed by the parties to the escrow is called the *escrow agreement* or *escrow instructions*.

A valid real estate closing in escrow is dependent upon the existence of an enforceable written contract for the sale of real estate. The contract for the sale of real estate may be found in a separate writing or in the escrow agreement. Once a valid escrow has been executed, the required instruments, property, or money have been delivered to the escrow agent, and all conditions in the contract for the sale of real estate and the escrow agreement are performed, the escrow is irrevocable.

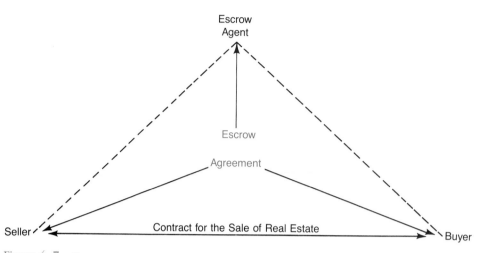

Figure 4-7   Escrow arrangement

Doctrine of Relation Back

Usually there is a length of time between the date the seller and buyer execute the contract of sale and the closing date (i.e., the date title is conveyed by deed and the purchase price paid). During this period of time, the seller or buyer may die or otherwise become legally incompetent. Without the *doctrine of relation back,* the decedent's estate would have to be probated or a conservator appointed as a result of the incompetency, thus causing expense and delay in closing the transaction. If, before the death or incompetency of the seller or buyer, a properly executed deed is deposited in escrow (under a valid contract of sale and escrow agreement) and is later delivered by the escrow agent in compliance with the escrow conditions, its delivery (transfer of title) *relates back* to (is effective on) the date that the deed was deposited with the escrow agent.

SUMMARY

Contracts are used extensively in the real estate business to assure transfer of title free of adverse interests. Several kinds of contracts are widely used for real estate transactions. These are the listing agreement, deposit receipt and offer to purchase, contract for sale of real estate, options, contract for the exchange of real estate, leases, and installment land contracts.

A legally enforceable contract must contain the following elements: an agreement (offer and acceptance), consideration, reality of assent, legally competent parties, and a legal objective and subject matter. It must also be in writing as required by state statutes.

The parties to a contract are allowed by law to agree upon the remedies available in case of a breach (e.g., liquidated damages and forfeiture by the seller). In the absence of an agreement to the contrary, the law grants several remedies to the parties. Upon the buyer's breach, the seller may sue for damages, rescind the contract, or sue in equity for specific performance. If the seller defaults, the buyer may sue in equity for specific performance, sue for damages, or rescind the contract and obtain restitution. Generally, real estate contracts are freely assignable to third parties by either gift or sale.

The most common form contracts are the listing agreement, deposit receipt, offer to purchase, contract for the sale of real estate, installment land contract, option, contract for the exchange of real estate, and lease. It is important to be aware of the legal implications of the provisions found in the form contracts being used in a market area.

Many real estate transactions are closed in escrow. An escrow is the deposit of a deed or other instrument, property, or money with a third person to be delivered by that person to the parties upon the performance of one or more agreed-upon conditions.

TERMS AND CONCEPTS

You can check your understanding of these terms against the glossary or by review in this chapter.

Abstract of title
Acceptance
Actual communication
Assignment
Attorney's certificate of
  title
Bilateral contract
Common law
Communicate
Complete and definite
  terms
Conditional option
Conservator
Constructive
  communication
Contractual intent
Corporation
Counteroffer
Damages
Default
Deposit receipt
Disaffirm
Doctrine of relation back
Duress
Earnest money
Equitable title
Escrow arrangement
Evidence of title
Exculpatory clause
Express contract
Fixed price option

Forfeiture
Fraud
Guardian
Illegal
Implied in fact contract
Incompetent
Infant
Innocent
  misrepresentation
Installment land contract
Lapse
Legal capacity
Legal description
Legally sufficient
  consideration
Liquidated damages
Listing agreement
Marketable title
Mutual mistake
Name the seller and
  buyer
Offer
Offeree
Offeror
Offer to purchase
Operation of law
Option
Possession date
Price-credit option
Price step-up option

Prorate
Purchase price
Quality of title
Ratify
Rejection
Renewable option
Rescission
Restitution
Retain the earnest
  money
Revoke
Risk of loss
Signature
Specific performance
Statute of Frauds
Time is of the essence
Title exceptions
Title insurance policy
Torrens system
Type of deed
Undue influence
Unenforceable contract
Uniform Vendor and
  Purchaser Risk Act
Unilateral contract
Valid
Voidable contract
Void contract
Waste
Writing

4-1. On June 1, B wrote S, "I'll buy your farm in McLean County for $150,000." S waited two weeks and then wrote B, "I accept your offer of June 1 to buy my farm." B received S's letter the next day and immediately wrote S, "Your acceptance is too late; I have already purchased a farm." S sues B for breach of contract. B defends on the following grounds: (a) no contract existed, and (b) even if a contract existed, the Statute of Frauds was not complied with. Are any of B's defenses valid? Explain.

4-2. B sent S an offer to buy S's farm for $50,000. S wired B, "Will you pay $69,500?" B wired back, "No." Thereupon S mailed an acceptance at the $50,000 price. Is there a contract? Explain.

4-3. B, in writing, offered to buy a tract of land for $75,000 from S and expressed a willingness to pay S $200 should S agree to allow B to purchase the land during the period of time between July 15 and August 31, 1989. S accepted B's offer and received payment of $200. On August 5, 1989, S tendered to B $200 and renounced any liability. On August 30, 1989, B advised S in writing that she wanted to buy S's land. S refused to sell. Was any contract formed? Explain.

4-4. S and B entered into a written contract for the sale of land for $200,000. During negotiations, S induced B to sign the contract by telling him that he had paid $225,000 for the land ten years ago, but that the land was currently worth $205,000. B later discovered the land to have a value of $150,000. B sued for rescission. What was the result? Explain.

4-5. On January 1, 1989, S sold and delivered to B a properly executed deed to a parcel of land. B paid a purchase price of $35,000. It was later discovered by both S and B that the land had a market value of $75,000 at the time of the sale to B. S sued to void the sale and deed on the grounds that she did not receive adequate consideration. Is she correct? Explain.

4-6. S had been declared incompetent by a court, and X had been appointed her conservator. Subsequently, S sold land and delivered an executed deed to B for $100,000 cash. B did not know of S's incompetency. X learned of the transaction between S and B and sued to declare the deed a nullity. What was the result? Explain

4-7. S owned a retail store in the city of Oz. Oz has a population of 50,000. There are other retail stores handling the same merchandise as is sold in S's store located in Oz. S sold his store to B and agreed not to open a competing retail store in Oz for at least two years. Two months later S opened a competing store approximately six blocks away. B sued S and requested a court order restraining S from conducting a retail business in the city of Oz. S defended on the basis that the contract was illegal. What was the result? Explain.

4-8. On September 5, 1989, S orally contracted to sell B ten acres of timberland for $50,000, deed to be delivered and purchase price paid on October 4, 1989. On October 4, 1989, B tendered the purchase price to S. S informed B that she did not wish to go ahead with the deal and refused B's money. B sued for specific performance. The court held in favor of S. Why? Explain.

4-9. On March 1, 1990, S and B entered into a written contract for the sale of a twenty-unit apartment house. The contract called for S to deliver possession and deed to B on April 1, 1990. The contract did not contain a "fire clause." On March 15, 1990, the apartment house was totally destroyed by fire. On April 1, 1990, S tendered possession and deed and demanded the purchase price from B. B refused to pay. S sued for the purchase price. What was the result? Explain. How could B have avoided the problem presented here?

4-10. Evans decided to purchase a 10-acre tract of land from Expando, Incorporated, the developer. The customary form contract of sale was prepared and signed by Evans and an authorized agent of Expando. The contract was silent in respect to marketable title and the type of deed to be delivered to the buyer. At the closing, Expando, Incorporated offered to Evans a quitclaim deed without covenants (warranties) of title and revealed that there was an existing mortgage on the land in the amount of $500,000.

(a) What effect does the omission of mentioned items have upon the validity of the contract?

(b) Assume that Evans refused to accept the quitclaim deed and pay the purchase price. Is her refusal legally justified?

(c) If her refusal is legally justified, what are her legal remedies against Expando, Incorporated?

4-11. S and B entered into a written contract for the sale of real estate that provided the deed to be delivered by S and the purchase price paid by B on May 1, 1989. The contract provided that "time is of the essence." S failed to deliver the deed on May 1, 1989, but was ready and willing to do so on the next day. B refused the deed and informed S he no longer considered the contract binding. S sued B for the purchase price. What was the result? Explain.

4-12. Tom Larson entered into a contract to sell a 4,000-acre farm to his son Scott for a sales price of $16,000,000. Tom Larson executed a deed to the farm naming Scott as grantee and delivered it to the Bank of Tarlock as escrow agent. Scott also deposited the purchase price with the Bank of Tarlock. Before the bank could deliver the deed to Scott, Tom was afflicted by a rare disease and died, leaving a will disposing of all his property to his wife, Lorraine, and his sons, Jeff, Eric, and Steve. In probate, Lorraine, Scott, Jeff, Eric, and Steve each claim to be owners of the 4,000-acre farm. Whose claim is correct? Explain.

4-13. O'Brien entered into a contract for the sale of Redacre (a 2,000-acre ranch) to Woodside for a price of $2,500,000. O'Brien agreed to deliver a deed to Woodside in exchange for the agreed-upon price on a closing date set for thirty days after the date of the contract. Three weeks after the date of the contract, Woodside realized that he would be unable to raise enough cash to meet his contractual obligations. He sought out Levy who had always "had his eye on Redacre" and successfully negotiated the sale of "his contract" with O'Brien to Levy for $300,000. On the closing date, Levy demanded a deed to Redacre conveying fee simple absolute title. Explain why each of the following statements is correct or incorrect as it relates to the facts stated above.
   (a) Levy is not legally entitled to receive a deed from O'Brien.
   (b) The contract for the sale of Redacre must satisfy all of the requirements of the Statute of Frauds in order to be enforceable.
   (c) If O'Brien wrongfully refuses to deliver a deed to Levy, Levy's only legal remedy is to sue O'Brien and recover damages for breach of contract.

4-14. Kozek purchased a 1,000-acre farm from Lebow under an installment land contract. The contract obligated Kozek to pay $6,000 each month for twenty years, at which time the $550,000 purchase price would be paid in full. The contract also provided that, upon Kozek's failure to pay any one monthly installment, Lebow could cancel the contract, repossess the farm and retain all payments previously made by Kozek as liquidated damages. Kozek operated the farm at a loss for five years and decided to sell out to Jacco. Kozek demanded that Lebow execute a deed to the farm and deliver it to him. Lebow refused. Several days later Kozek died leaving a will disposing all of his property to his wife, Carmen. Carmen, not being interested in farming, immediately sold her interest in the farm to Jacco. In the contract of sale, Jacco assumed and agreed to pay the outstanding balance owed on the installment land contract.
   (a) Was Kozek entitled to a deed from Lebow? Explain.
   (b) Assume that Kozek had defaulted on the contract. Could Lebow have retained Kozek's payments as liquidated damages for breach of contract? Explain.
   (c) If Carmen had chosen to do so, could she have enforced the installment land contract against Lebow? Explain.
   (d) Can Jacco enforce the installment land contract against Lebow?
   (e) Assume that Jacco took possession of the farm, made monthly payments of $6,000 to Lebow for six years and then defaulted. Is Jacco personally liable to Lebow for the balance of the purchase price? Explain.

4-15. On March 3, 1989, Simon sold and delivered to Lydia a properly executed deed to a parcel of land. In order to induce Lydia to purchase the land, Simon intentionally misrepresented to Lydia that the land was suitable for farming. To "clinch the deal," Simon falsely stated that the land yielded an average of 150 bushels of corn per acre over the previous five years. Upon taking possession, Lydia discovered that the land was not suitable for farming. Shortly thereafter Lydia discovered a huge deposit of sand and gravel 10 feet below the surface. Lydia was offered $1,000,000 by Raul for the rights to the deposit. Simon, after learning of the discovery, sued to rescind the sale to Lydia on the basis of fraud and to reclaim title to the land. Lydia asserted two defenses: (a) no fraud was perpetrated, and (b) even if fraud was perpetrated, Simon was not entitled to rescission. Are any of Lydia's defenses valid? Explain.

SUPPLEMENTARY READINGS

Dasso, Jerome, and Ring, Alfred A. *Real Estate Principles and Practices,* 11th ed. Englewood Cliffs, N.J.: Prentice-Hall, 1989. Chapters 10 and 11.

Jennings, Marianne M. *Real Estate Law,* 2nd ed. Boston: PWS-Kent, 1989. Chapters 11 and 13.

Kratovil, Robert, and Werner, Raymond J. *Real Estate Law.* 9th ed. Englewood Cliffs, N.J.: Prentice-Hall, 1988. Chapters 10–13.

Seidel, George. *Real Estate Law,* 2nd ed. St. Paul: West, 1989. Chapters 7 and 10.

Smith, Len Y., and Roberson, Gale G. *Business Law,* 7th ed. St. Paul: West, 1988. Chapters 7–16.

CHAPTER 5
Title Transfer, Deeds, and Recordation

As we know, land has several special physical characteristics—most importantly, immobility—that distinguish it from other kinds of property. Because of its immobility, the estates and rights in land and the methods required to transfer these estates and rights are prescribed by the laws of the state in which the land is located. As discussed in Chapter 3, title to land is in reality both the quantity and quality of rights a person possesses in a specific parcel of land. A person's title may be in fee simple or consist of some other interest in land. Unless otherwise stated, *title,* as used in this chapter, is defined as any ownership interest in land regardless of its quantity, quality, or duration.

Private title to land in the United States was originally acquired in two ways, by either a grant from the federal government or a grant from a foreign government. Thereafter, a recorded history of title to a given parcel of land may reveal a series of voluntary and involuntary transfers, involving private individuals as well as political and quasi-public units. This history of title is called a *chain of title.* The chain of title, when compiled in a written form together with a statement of all liens or liabilities to which the title may be subject, is referred to as an *abstract of title.*

INVOLUNTARY TRANSFER OF TITLE TO REAL ESTATE

There are several ways title to real estate can be transferred without the consent of its owner.

Condemnation

Condemnation is a legal proceeding whereby title to land, in exchange for just compensation, is taken by a governmental unit, permanently or temporarily, partially or totally, for a public purpose. The taking is pursuant to the government's power of eminent domain.

Adverse Possession

A private individual who has no interest in a parcel of land may acquire title to it by *adversely possessing* it for a statutory period of time. The required time of possession varies from state to state, with maximum durations ranging upward to twenty years. Some state laws provide shorter periods of possession when the possession is under *color of title* (possessor named as grantee in a void or otherwise ineffective deed) and/or accompanied with payment of real estate taxes assessed on the land.

For possession to result in ownership, it must be hostile (without permission) to the owner's title, actual, open, exclusive, notorious, and continuous during the statutory period.

Continuous adverse possession by different persons will result in title being acquired by the person in possession at the end of the statutory period. This process of obtaining the benefit of another's adverse possession is called *tacking*.

Even though a person has satisfied all the requirements to vest title in himself by adverse possession, the title of record will still be in the previous owner who recorded his deed. To obtain record title in himself, an adverse possessor must file a *bill to quiet title* with a court where the land is located. Upon finding title to be in the adverse possessor, the court will enter a judgment to that effect. The judgment is then recorded, showing title of record to be in the adverse possessor.

Foreclosure Sale

A *foreclosure* sale is an involuntary sale of a debtor's title to land pursuant to either an agreement between a debtor and creditor or by a decree of a court. The proceeds of the forced sale are used to satisfy the debtor's unpaid obligation. Foreclosure sales may arise out of the following circumstances.

1. A landowner defaults in payment of assessments or real estate taxes.
2. A mortgagor defaults in payment of his real estate mortgage debt.
3. A landowner fails to discharge a perfected mechanic's lien on his land.
4. A debtor fails to discharge a judgment lien attached to his land.

Partition Sale

A *partition* sale is a court-ordered sale for purposes of severing undivided interests in land such as joint tenancies and tenancies in common. Any co-owner may, without the consent of other owners, petition a court for an order of partition sale. Where the land cannot be physically divided without materially impairing the value of the land, the court will order the land sold and the proceeds divided according to the respective joint owners' undivided interests in the land.

Accretion

Accretion is an act by which one owner of land acquires title to a portion of land owned by another through the gradual and imperceptible deposit of quantities of sand or soil by natural causes, such as water or wind. Accretion of land may be the result of two processes, alluvion and dereliction. *Alluvion* is the process by which sand or soil is washed up on land by water or blown upon the land by wind to form firm ground. *Dereliction* occurs when a sea or stream shrinks and remains below its original water mark. *Erosion* is the sudden or gradual wearing away of land by the action of water, wind, or ice.

Escheat

Escheat is the legal process where title to land reverts to a county or state upon the death of a landowner who dies without a valid will and without leaving any heirs.

Community Property

If property qualifies as community property, title to one-half is automatically vested in each spouse. It is unimportant in whose name legal record title is held. Title to one-half of the real estate in a community property state vests in each spouse regardless of the intent. In that sense, transfer of title is involuntary.

VOLUNTARY TRANSFER OF TITLE TO REAL ESTATE

Where the owner of property initiates the transfer of title of his own accord, the transfer is considered voluntary.

Public Grant or Patent

A private person may obtain title to public lands either by a statutory *grant* or by *patent* from a state or federal government. A *patent* is a document that transfers title to land from a government to a private individual. A person may automatically receive title to public lands without a patent if legislation is passed granting title to him or to a class of persons to which he belongs *(grant)*.

Will (Testate Succession)

Title to real estate may be acquired by will. A *will* is a written instrument executed by an owner of property that disposes of title to his property, to take effect at the time of his death *(testate succession)*. The person executing a will is known as a *testator*. Upon his death he is said to have died *testate*. A gift of real estate by will is called a *devise,* and the person to receive the gift is known as the *devisee.*

Each state has enacted laws providing for the kinds of interests in property that may be disposed of by will. Any estate that an owner may transfer during his lifetime may usually be disposed of by will.

For a will to be valid, a testator must have *testamentary capacity;* that is, he must be a minimum age specified by law and have sufficient mental capacity at the time the will is executed. Most states have established age eighteen as the minimum age necessary to execute a will. Even though a testator may have been of legal age at the time he executed his will, the will may be voidable on the basis that he lacked sufficient mental capacity. A testator lacks mental capacity when he executes a will while "insane" or if he is induced to do so by undue influence, duress, fraud, or mistake.

In addition to the requirement of testamentary capacity, a will must usually be in writing and be executed with certain formalities. Oral wills are permitted only in a few states. As a general rule, the following requirements must be met in order to have a validly executed will.

1. *Writing.* The writing can be in any form (e.g., typewritten, handwritten, or printed).
2. *Signature.* Any mark that is intended to be the signature of the testator is valid. The signature may be located anywhere in the will. However, the most common and safest location of the signature is at the bottom of each page and at the end of the will.
3. *Publication.* The testator is required to declare to witnesses that the instrument is his last will and testament before or at the time of affixing his signature. He need not reveal the contents of the will.
4. *Attestation.* Formal wills are required to be witnessed and signed by two or more persons. The **attestation** clause says that the will was signed by the testator, that he declared it to be his last will and testament, and that the witnesses at the request of the testator and in his presence and in the presence of each other signed their names as attesting witnesses. In some states, a holographic will is an exception to the requirement that a will be attested by witnesses. A **holographic will** is one written entirely by the testator in his own handwriting and not witnessed or attested.

Specific provisions in a will or an entire will may be modified or revoked by a subsequent will or codicil of the testator, by a testator's deliberate and intentional destruction of the will, or by operation of law caused by certain changes in the testator's family relationships (marriage, divorce, birth of a child). A **codicil** is an instrument, executed with the formalities required of a will, that modifies or revokes an existing will.

Where a will has been revoked by the testator or is declared void by a court, the title to all property owned at the time of a person's death will pass according to intestate laws of descent and distribution.

Descent (Intestate Succession)

If a landowner dies without leaving a will, or if his will fails to dispose of all of his property, he is said to have died totally or partially **intestate.** By not choosing to execute a will, he has in a sense voluntarily allowed state law to designate those persons who are to receive title to his land upon his death.

The title to land is transferred to the heirs according to the statute of descent and distribution in the state in which the land is located. These statutes not only prescribe the persons to inherit the property, but also designate the proportionate share each is to receive.

The purpose of these statutes is to provide for an orderly transfer of title and also to carry out the probable intentions of an intestate decedent. Under these statutes, heirs who are blood relatives are most favored. The order of priority of inheritance and the amount inherited are usually determined by the closeness of an heir's relationship to the decedent. The following statements for descent and distribution of intestate property are typical of several state laws.

1. If there is a surviving spouse and also a descendant, spouse takes one-third of all property, surviving children share equally in two-thirds, and any descendants of deceased children share equally in the share that their parent would have taken if living (i.e., *per stirpes*).
2. If there is no surviving spouse but one or more surviving descendants, children share equally in the entire estate and any descendants of deceased children share equally in the share that their parent would have taken, if living (i.e., *per stirpes*).
3. If there is a surviving spouse but no surviving descendants, the surviving spouse takes the entire estate.
4. If there is no surviving spouse or surviving descendants, but a brother, sister, parent, or descendant of a deceased brother or sister is living, then parents, brothers, and sisters share equally in all the property (allowing a sole surviving parent a double share). Descendants of a deceased brother or sister share equally the portion their deceased parent would have taken, if living (i.e., *per stirpes*).
5. The order of distribution continues through the surviving maternal and paternal grandparents and their descendants; if none survive, then to the maternal and paternal great-grandparents and their descendants; and if none survive, then to collateral (uncles, aunts, and cousins) heirs.
6. Finally, if no spouse survives or known relative of the decedent is living, the real estate escheats to the county or state in which it is located.

Administration of Decedent's Estate

Whether a person dies testate or intestate, his estate must usually be submitted to a court for administration. If the decedent died testate, his will must be filed with the court and be probated to pass record title to the devisees. The court will appoint an ***executor*** who becomes the personal representative of the estate. The personal representative appointed by a court to administer an intestate estate is named an ***administrator.*** The personal representative's duties are to collect, preserve, and distribute all of the decedent's property; to pay all debts and taxes owed by the decedent and the estate; and to make final distribution of the decedent's property according to the will if the decedent died testate and, if not, according to law. The personal representative must file a final report with the court. Upon court approval of the report, he is legally discharged from his duties and the estate is ordered closed.

Transfer of Title by Sale

One of the most valuable rights of ownership is the right to sell. This right is legally protected, and any agreement or restriction depriving a landowner of the right to sell his land is null and void. The right to sell is limited only by the power of each state to regulate the methods and formal requirements for transfer of ownership to land within its jurisdiction.

Transfer of Title by Gift

Title to real estate may be transferred without an exchange of value. It is a landowner's right to give away his land if he wants; however, he may not do so with the intent to defraud his existing or subsequent creditors. Creditors may have a deed set aside if it was executed and delivered by the grantor to a grantee without receipt of adequate value in exchange. This is true even though the deed recites that value was received. On the other hand, a deed properly executed and delivered in exchange for a reasonable value will not ordinarily be set aside by the courts on the basis that it is in fraud of creditors. Even though a conveyance is not in fraud of creditors, it may be set aside if it violates a provision of the Federal Bankruptcy Reform Act of 1978 as amended by the Bankruptcy Amendments Act of 1984. For example, a conveyance is in violation of the act where it gives preference to one of the grantor's creditors as against another, if the conveyance was made within ninety days of the date a petition in bankruptcy was filed by or against the insolvent grantor.

The most common method of transferring title to real estate by *gift* is by an unconditional delivery of a deed to the intended grantee by the owner during his lifetime. The grantee may be a private person, a charitable organization, a religious institution, or a governmental entity. Where the grantee of a gift deed is a governmental entity, the transfer of title is said to be by *dedication.* Dedication may also occur by a subdivider's designation in a subdivision plat for certain streets and other areas to be for public use. The designated public areas become owned by the government unit upon its acceptance of the subdivision plat.

Conveyance by Deed

A *deed* is a written instrument properly executed and delivered by an owner of real estate to convey title to another person. For a deed to be operative, it must transfer a present legal interest. The person who executes the deed is called the *grantor,* and the recipient is the *grantee.*

The essential difference between a deed and a will is that the deed passes a present legal interest in the real estate, while a will does not become operative until the death of the testator. An instrument that attempts to transfer title at the death of its owner is void unless it is executed with the formalities required of a will. By their legal nature, deeds take effect upon delivery and are irrevocable, while wills are always revocable during the testator's lifetime and take effect only upon his death.

Unlike a contract, consideration is not necessary for a deed to be effective when it is properly executed and delivered to the intended grantee. A deed is further distinguished from a contract in that a contract for the sale of real estate transfers no legal title but binds the seller to execute and deliver a deed transferring legal title to real estate to the buyer. Where a deed contains covenants and is delivered in exchange for valuable consideration, however, the courts consider the covenants to be binding promises and award legal relief for their breach.

Requirements for a Valid Conveyance by Deed

There are a number of requirements that must be met before a conveyance by deed is valid. These requirements are described here, although all of them may not be required in each state.

A writing.   Statutes in most states require a conveyance of a freehold estate to be *in writing.* The document must be signed by the grantor or his duly authorized agent.

Names and addresses of parties. Every deed must have a ***grantor*** and a ***grantee.*** If a grantor or grantee or both are not named in the deed, it is void. Even though not generally required by state law, the addresses of the grantor and grantee should be given for identification. When the real estate is owned jointly, the deed should name all co-owners as grantors.

If the real estate is located in a state that provides for curtesy, dower, or homestead rights, the grantor's spouse must also be named as a grantor in order to release these rights. This is true even if the real estate is not jointly owned by the spouses.

Where property is to be conveyed jointly to two or more persons, each grantee must be named and the type of joint ownership identified. For example, "Maria Cisneros and Juan Cisneros, as joint tenants, with right of survivorship, not as tenants in common."

A grantor who acquired title to real estate prior to marriage must be identified in the deed by her maiden name and her married name. It is also important to set forth the marital status of the grantor in the deed to facilitate title search and help prevent ambiguities in the chain of title.

Signature of grantor. A deed must be ***signed by the grantor*** or his duly authorized agent. When a grantor is unable to write, his mark, properly witnessed, is a valid signature. A grantor who himself is unable to be physically present to sign a deed may appoint another person, called his ***attorney in fact,*** to sign in his behalf. The appointment of an attorney in fact must be contained in a written instrument, signed by the landowner and delivered to the appointed agent. This instrument is commonly referred to as a ***power of attorney.*** It includes authority to accomplish all acts necessary to sell and convey the landowner's real estate.

Where the grantor is to be a corporation, the deed must be signed by a duly authorized officer of the corporation. A corporate officer's authority to execute a deed and transfer title to corporate real estate must be granted by formal action by the board of directors. In some instances, formal action of the shareholders may be required in addition to formal action by the board of directors. As a general rule, the corporate seal must also be affixed to the deed.

Without the signature of the grantor or his duly authorized agent, the deed is void and conveys no title. A signature of the intended grantee is not required for a valid deed.

Legal capacity of grantor. A grantor must have ***legal capacity*** to convey title by deed. Legal capacity is established by state laws. State laws generally classify deeds as being void or voidable depending on the type and degree of incapacity of the grantor. A deed will be declared void whenever it has been executed by a person who has been judged incompetent by a court. In such cases, the ***incompetent*** is totally without legal capacity. His court-appointed guardian or conservator is the only person legally able to act in his behalf. Incompetency may be based upon mental illness, habitual drunkenness, drug addiction, or an inability to conduct business for any physical or mental reason.

A person who has not been adjudicated an incompetent may nevertheless not have sufficient legal capacity in certain circumstances. In such cases, he or his legal representative can void the deed within a reasonable time after he obtains legal capacity. A deed will be held to be voidable when it is executed by a minor, by any person who is under duress or undue influence, or by someone who is insane.

Description of the land.   The Statute of Frauds requires that the property being conveyed by a deed be **sufficiently described** so that it is clearly identifiable and distinguished from other parcels of land. A description in a deed is adequate if the land intended to be conveyed can be identified by reference to some other writing such as a plat, another deed, a contract, a map, or a survey. However, for the extrinsic writing to be incorporated by reference, it must be specifically referred to in the deed as containing the description of the land.

Granting clause.   The **granting clause** identifies as well as transfers title to the grantee. Where there is no clear indication in a deed that a lesser estate was intended to be transferred, the law assumes that the grantor intended to convey a fee simple. For example, a deed to "John Jones" as grantee is sufficient to convey a fee simple absolute.

To be effective as a deed, the writing must contain **words of conveyance.** In warranty deeds, the phrases "convey and warrant" or "grant, bargain, and sell" are commonly used as words of conveyance. In quitclaim deeds, the phrases are usually "convey and quitclaim," "remise, release, and quitclaim," or "quitclaim all interest." Words of conveyance indicate the grantor's intention to make a present conveyance. They also determine the grantor's warranties and obligations to the grantee should the grantor's title prove nonexistent or defective. Not all words of conveyance create warranties or impose obligations upon the grantor. Later in this chapter we will discuss types of deeds and warranties.

Delivery and acceptance.   A properly executed deed does not transfer title to real estate until it is delivered during the lifetime of the grantor. **Delivery** is the intent of the grantor that the deed shall presently transfer title to the grantee. The intent of the grantor can be shown by his words or conduct. The best evidence of delivery is the physical transfer of the deed from the grantor to the grantee or his agent without any reservation of right of control over the deed or any conditions attached.

An effective delivery may result even though there is no actual physical transfer of the deed to the grantee prior to the death or legal incapacity of the grantor. For delivery to occur this way, the words and conduct of the grantor must clearly show that he intended that the deed immediately convey title to the grantee. Consider the following examples: (a) The grantor, at the grantee's request, sends the deed to the grantee's agent, an attorney. Before the grantee receives the deed from his attorney, the grantor dies. (b) The grantor executes a deed and mails it to the grantee, but before the grantee receives the deed, the grantor dies. (c) A grantor transfers a deed to an escrow agent to be delivered upon the payment of the purchase price, but before the purchase price is paid and the escrow agent releases the deed to the grantee, the grantor dies. In each of these cases, the court held that an effective delivery had taken place.

A deed, even though physically transferred to the grantee, will not be held to have been delivered unless the grantor really intended to divest himself of possession of the deed and the title it represents. Such intention is not present where a grantor is under fraud, duress, undue influence, or mistake. Any deed obtained under any of these circumstances may be set aside by a court. As a general rule, a grantee must accept the deed from the grantor for a valid delivery to take place. *Acceptance of a deed* means that the grantee intended to obtain ownership of the real estate. His intention may be indicated expressly by his oral or written words or impliedly by his acts or other conduct.

Common Provisions Found in Deeds

Due to variations in state laws governing the transfer of title to real estate, deeds may vary in form and content. Nevertheless, almost all deeds have similar basic provisions. In addition to the previously discussed provisions required in a valid deed, the following provisions are usually included in deeds utilized throughout the United States.

Seal. In most states, a seal is not essential to the validity of a deed. In states where a *seal* is required, it is sufficient for the deed to contain a phrase stating that it is sealed or to use the written or printed word "Seal" or the phrase "Witness my hand and seal." The importance of the seal in those states where it is required is that it raises a presumption that consideration was given in exchange for the deed. To rebut the presumption, actual proof must be presented that no consideration was in fact paid in exchange for the deed.

Attestation. The act of witnessing a grantor's signature on a deed at his request and subscribing it as a witness is an *attestation.* In most states, attestation is not required for the validity of a deed, unless the signature on the deed is by mark. Even though not required, attestation is important for proof of a grantor's signature after his death or if he becomes otherwise unable to verify his own signature.

Acknowledgment. An *acknowledgment* is a formal declaration in a deed, by the grantor and before an authorized official, that the instrument was executed freely and voluntarily. The acknowledgment can be made before a notary public, a military officer, a judge, or a justice of the peace. An acknowledgment is usually unnecessary for the validity of the deed. However, in most states a deed cannot be recorded unless it is acknowledged. The inability to record a deed is serious. An unrecorded deed is not legally protected against innocent "purchasers" who acquire a lien or an interest in the real estate subsequent to the delivery of the unrecorded deed.

As a practical matter, all deeds should be acknowledged. Where a grantor is not available to testify in court, the acknowledgment itself may be introduced as evidence of the genuineness of the grantor's signature and of the instrument itself.

Recitation of consideration. Although not necessary for the validity of a deed, consideration is usually stated as having been received by the grantor. The consideration recited can be *nominal*; that is, the amount stated bears no relationship to the value of the real estate. An example would be, "$20.00 and other good and valuable consideration." Some state statutes require trustee and court-ordered deeds to recite the actual consideration received.

Exceptions or reservations. Following the description of the land, the deed may provide any *exceptions* or *reservations* to the grantor in the granting clause. An example of an exception would be a deed conveying "the West one-half of the Southwest Quarter of Section 25, . . . excepting therefrom one acre in the Southwest Quarter of said Southwest Quarter." An illustration of a reservation would be a deed conveying "Lots 36, 37, 38, and 39 of Pleasant Hills Subdivision in Section 1, . . . reserving, however, to the grantor, her heirs, and assigns forever, the minerals upon and underneath said land."

Habendum. The *habendum* establishes the quantity of the estate conveyed to the grantee. It usually begins with the words, "To have and hold the premises. . . ." Where there is a conflict between the granting clause and the *habendum,* the courts consistently hold that the estate described in the granting clause takes precedence over that described in the *habendum.* It is important that both clauses have an identical description of the estate conveyed to the grantee.

Any limitation, encumbrance, or restriction on the estate to be conveyed should be stated in the *habendum.* If not stated, the grantor is assumed to be making a conveyance that is free and clear of all such limitations, encumbrances, or restrictions.

Any intended limitation of the estate conveyed by the reservation of a life estate or by declaration of trust should be clearly set forth in the *habendum.*

When the grantee has agreed to take subject to or to assume and agree to pay an existing mortgage, the intent of the grantor and the grantee should be made clear. This is usually accomplished by the use of the words "subject to" or "the grantee hereby assumes and agrees to pay," followed by a detailed description and identification of the mortgage.

A subdivider often wants to control the future use of unimproved lots in a subdivision. His purpose is to create restrictions that can be enforced by and against the landowners in the restricted subdivision. These restrictions are called *restrictive covenants.* Restrictive covenants are listed in the *habendum* or in a separate instrument called a "declaration of restrictions" incorporated by reference in the deed.

Covenants of title. *Covenants* (warranties) *of title* may be expressly stated in a deed or implied from words of conveyance used by a grantor. The following are five important covenants (warranties) that may be expressed or implied in a deed:

1. *Covenant of seizin.* A promise by the grantor that he possesses title and has the right to convey it.
2. *Covenant of quiet enjoyment.* A promise by the grantor that the grantee shall not be disturbed in his possession of the property by the grantor or others having a better title to the property.
3. *Covenant against encumbrances.* A promise by the grantor that there are no existing encumbrances on the property.
4. *Covenant of further assurance.* A promise by the grantor that he will execute or obtain any additional document necessary to perfect title in the grantee.
5. *Covenant of warranty forever.* A promise by a grantor that he will forever warrant title to the property.

In many states, the five covenants (warranties) of title are implied by law when the grantor uses such words as "convey and warrant" or "warrant generally." Words of conveyance such as "grant, bargain, and sell," "convey and quitclaim" or "quitclaim all interest" do not imply covenants of title as a matter of law. For covenants to be made in a quitclaim deed, they must be expressly stated.

Covenants do not guarantee a marketable title or even any title to the grantee. However, a breach of covenant entitles a grantee to recover his actual damages against the grantor. The first three covenants bind the grantor only to the immediate grantee, while the last two may be enforced by subsequent grantees of the property in question.

Nontitle covenants or warranties. Unless expressly stated in the deed, a grantor is generally held not to have made any *nontitle covenants* or warranties. A grantee is said to take the property at his own risk. However, when a builder or real estate developer sells and delivers a deed to a newly constructed home to a grantee, many courts have modified the common law. They have established a common law warranty of *fitness for occupancy or use*. If the home purchased from the builder or developer is not reasonably fit for occupancy or use, the buyer can recover damages or rescind the sale. This warranty is not implied in a sale of a home by a homeowner other than a builder or developer.

Waiver of dower, curtesy, and homestead. In some states, the signature of a grantor's spouse on the deed is not enough to release dower, curtesy, and homestead rights. These states require that the deed contain a clause specifically releasing and relinquishing these rights.

Date. A date is not essential to the validity of a deed.

Common Types of Deeds

Quitclaim deed. A *quitclaim deed* contains no covenants or warranties, express or implied. It merely purports to transfer any title presently possessed by the grantor. A quitclaim deed usually contains words of coveyance such as "remise, release, and quitclaim," "convey and quitclaim," or "quitclaims all interest." The quitclaim deed is commonly used to remove a cloud on title or by a grantor who is not certain that he actually had title or that it is free from encumbrances and other adverse interests.

General warranty deed. A warranty deed contains the covenants (warranties) of seizin, quiet enjoyment, encumbrance, further assurance, and warranty forever. A *general warranty deed* usually contains words of conveyance such as "convey and warrant" or "warrant generally." The covenants of general warranty apply not only to defects coming into existence while the grantor possessed title but also to those that occurred before. If a grantor does not have any title to the real estate at the time he delivers the deed to the grantee but subsequently acquires title, the grantee is said to have good title. The grantor is stopped, by virtue of his covenants (warranties), from stating that he did not have title at the time he executed and delivered the warranty deed to the grantee. The grantee is held to possess title by virtue of the *doctrine of after acquired title*. This doctrine does not apply to conveyances by quitclaim deed.

Special warranty deed. A *special warranty deed* contains the same covenants (warranties), express or implied, as the general warranty deed, except that the gran-

111

tor covenants only against claims or defects of title arising during the time he possessed title. A special warranty deed usually contains words of conveyance such as "warrant specially." In some states, the use of the word "grant" alone will create a special warranty deed. The *doctrine of after acquired title* also applies to special warranty deeds. The special warranty deed is commonly used by grantors who have acquired title at a foreclosure sale or by guardians, trustees, executors, administrators.

Grant, bargain, and sale deed.   Most states provide that a ***grant, bargain, and sale deed*** usually carries with it two or three covenants (warranties). These covenants pertain only to claims asserted by, through, or under the grantor. The covenants commonly implied by law are these:

1. That the grantor has not divested himself of any interest in the property prior to delivery of the deed
2. That the title is free from any encumbrances brought about or allowed by the grantor
3. That the grantee shall not be disturbed in his possession (quiet enjoyment) of the property by the grantor or others having better title to the property

Specialty Deeds

Deeds used for special situations are called ***specialty deeds.*** Specialty deeds usually take the form of either a special warranty deed or a quitclaim deed. They derive their names either from the fiduciary status held by the grantor or from the special purpose they fulfill. Specialty deeds are generally used in circumstances where a grantor wishes to pass whatever title he may possess but does not wish to acquire the burden of all or any of the covenants (warranties) of title. Examples of specialty deeds are deed of trust, tax deed, executor's deed, guardian's deed, and deed in foreclosure.

RECORDING OF DEEDS AND OTHER INSTRUMENTS

All states have statutes allowing ***recordation*** (recording) of certain instruments that affect title to real estate. Although these laws vary from state to state, their provisions are substantially similar. The effect of a properly recorded instrument is to give *constructive notice* (public notice) to any person who subsequently acquires an interest in the real estate that a prior adverse interest exists. The process of recordation establishes priorities between adverse legal interests. As a general rule, the ***recording statutes*** provide that the first party to record his interest has first priority in law, if, at the time of recordation, he was without actual notice of an unrecorded adverse interest.

The purpose of recordation is twofold: first, it provides a means of protecting existing estates or other legal interests in real estate; and second, it protects the interests of subsequent purchasers against secret, unrecorded interests. The owner of an existing interest is assured protection only if he properly records his interest. A subsequent purchaser is assured of a superior interest in the real estate when he relies on the public record and acts in good faith, without *actual notice* of any unrecorded adverse interest.

As a general rule, any writing that affects title to real estate may be recorded. Most state laws allow the following instruments to be recorded: deeds, contracts for the sale of real estate, installment land contracts, leases, mortgages, deeds in trust, powers of attorney, releases of mortgages, assignments of mortgages, options, and *profits à prendre*. Deeds in a foreign language are recorded *only if* accompanied by a written English translation.

Each state law establishes the place where instruments must be recorded. As a general rule, a public office in the county in which the real estate is located is the designated office for recordation. The public officer who is required by statute to maintain these public records may be a county clerk, recorder, or registrar.

Recording Systems

Deeds and other instruments that have been recorded must be indexed by the county clerk, recorder, or registrar. Most states authorize two types of indexing systems, the *grantor-grantee index system* and the *tract index system.*

Grantor-Grantee Index

In the **grantor-grantee index** system, separate index books are maintained for "grantors" and "grantees." As each deed or other instrument is recorded, it is indexed by year and in alphabetical order both under the name of the "grantor" in the grantor's index and under the name of the "grantee" in the grantee's index. The *grantor's index* includes not only the names of grantors in deeds but also the names of lessors, mortgagors, trustors in deeds of trust (trust deeds), and other transferors of any legal interest in real estate. The *grantee's index* includes all grantees named in deeds, lessees, mortgagees, and others who received legal interests in real estate. Each index contains the following information: type of instrument; name of grantor and grantee; date of the instrument; description and index book; page and date of recordation.

Tract Index

A few states maintain a tract system of recordation. It differs from the grantor-grantee index system in that the **tract index system** is compiled according to parcels of land rather than by names of parties to a deed or other instrument. In each county, the recorder maintains a map that contains all parcels of land within a tract and their assigned reference (identification) numbers. The tract index contains a separate page for each parcel of land that identifies each parcel by its reference number and description. Each index page contains a list of all recorded deeds or other instruments affecting title to the identified parcel. To research the title to a parcel of land, the researcher need only locate the parcel on the recorder's map, obtain its reference number, and use the reference number to find the appropriate page in the tract index.

Requirements for Recordation

In order to be recorded, an estate or other interest in real estate must be evidenced by a writing. In most states, a deed or mortgage is not effectively recorded unless it is executed properly and contains an acknowledgment. A few states require an attestation in addition to the acknowledgment. An improperly executed deed, mortgage, or other instrument is not operative to give constructive notice to subsequent purchasers.

In at least one state, Illinois, no deed will be accepted for recordation by any recorder of deeds or registrar of titles unless revenue stamps, evidencing the payment of the state transfer of title tax, have been purchased from the appropriate public official and affixed to the deed. In addition, a written transfer declaration, signed by at least one buyer and one seller or their attorneys, must accompany the deed. The declaration must recite the full consideration paid for the property together with other details pertaining to the transaction. The effect of recording the declaration is to make public the actual purchase price of all real estate.

Chain of Title

Properly dated and recorded instruments reveal a continuous chain of title dating from an original grant from the government or from a foreign government up to present date. The *chain of title,* when compiled in a written chronological form together with a statement of all liens, court judgments, or other liabilities to which title may be subject, is referred to as an *abstract of title.*

Bona Fide Purchaser

A *bona fide purchaser* is a party who has paid value for an estate or other legal interest in real estate without actual or constructive notice of an already existing estate or legal interest in the same parcel. A purchaser has *actual notice* when he has knowledge of a prior unrecorded estate or other legal interest. He has *constructive notice* of recorded estates or legal interests. In addition, the law accords constructive notice of any adverse legal interests of the parties in possession of the real estate. This is true even though the subsequent purchaser does not inspect the premises and investigate the possible rights of those in possession. For example, A owns a home. He leases the basement to students from the local university. The leases are unrecorded. B purchases A's home. B does not inspect the home and is unaware of the leases. B is held to have constructive notice of the existing leases.

Effect of Unrecorded Instruments

An unrecorded instrument is valid between the parties to it; however, a subsequent bona fide purchaser acquiring an interest in the property will take priority over a prior unrecorded interest. For example, A deeds land to B; however, B does not take possession and also fails to record his deed. A deeds the same parcel of land to C, who pays value in good faith without actual notice of B's interest. C records her deed. One day later B records his deed. In this case, C is the exclusive owner of the parcel of land.

Not all existing liens need to be recorded to have priority over even a bona fide purchaser for value. These liens are statutory in nature and are either direct liens on specific parcels of real estate, such as real estate taxes, special assessments, and mechanic's liens, or general liens on all real estate owned by the debtor in the state. Examples of the latter liens are inheritance-tax, judgment, and franchise-tax liens.

The Torrens System of Title Registration

A few states have laws enabling cities and counties to adopt the *Torrens system* of land title registration voluntarily. Even where a county or city has established the

Torrens system, registration of titles is not compulsory upon the landowner. Consequently, in any given city or county under the system, a landowner need not register his title. The title would then remain under the system prescribed by state recording statutes. Once title to property has been registered, the property cannot be removed from the Torrens system except by court order.

Registration Procedure

The purpose of the registration procedure is to confirm and establish registered title in a present owner of real estate together with any outstanding adverse legal interests and encumbrances. Once title is registered, irrevocable ownership is established in the registrant, subject only to any adverse legal interests, liens, or encumbrances established by the court in the registration proceedings. Although the procedures for registering title vary, the following series of required steps appears to be common to all Torrens systems.

1. The owner of real estate files a written application to register title in a court in the county in which the real estate is located. The application is required to list all information regarding the owner's title, including any existing adverse legal interests, liens, or encumbrances. Registration is usually limited to fee simple estates.
2. The court refers the application to a title examiner whose duty is to conduct an extensive title search and submit to the court a report on the status of the title as revealed by the records.
3. The court sends actual notice of the title proceeding to all parties who appear to have an adverse legal interest in the owner's title. Constructive notice (notice by publication in a newspaper) is given to all other parties who may have a legal interest in the property.
4. The court holds a hearing and orders the recording officer to register the title in the owner in fee simple or otherwise, together with any adverse legal interests, liens, or encumbrances, and to issue a ***Certificate of Title*** to that effect.
5. The Registrar of Titles prepares an original and a duplicate copy of the Certificate of Title. The original is recorded in the registration book, and the duplicate is delivered to the owner.

After the title is registered, any adverse legal interest, lien (other than tax liens), or encumbrance acquired against the registered property is not valid unless it is filed with the Registrar of Titles and entered upon the original title certificate. Priority among registered interests, liens, or encumbrances is on a first-to-register, first-in-priority basis. The originals of all documents evidencing an adverse interest, lien, or encumbrance are usually retained by the Registrar of Titles until discharged or released.

Certain defects in title, such as tax liens and rights of a party in possession under a lease, may not be covered by a Torrens certificate. For protection, the buyer should require a tax search and make an inspection of the land.

Transfer of Ownership

Under the Torrens system, title to real estate does not pass upon the delivery of a deed to the grantee. The transfer of title occurs at the time a new certificate is registered and issued in the name of the grantee.

Where title to registered real estate passes by will, intestate succession, or judicial sale, the Registrar of Titles will make the appropriate change pursuant to court order.

Duty to Defend Title and Reimbursement for Loss

An owner of registered title is required to defend his title at his own expense if it is challenged. The Registrar of Titles is not required to defend the owner of registered title. Should the owner's title be defective due to an error made by the Registrar of Titles, the owner is entitled to recover actual losses by filing proof of his claim with the county. State laws require that an indemnity fund, made up of a portion of registration fees, be established to indemnify owners for their losses.

SUMMARY

Because of the immobility of land, the estates and rights in land, together with the methods required to transfer these estates and rights, are prescribed by law in each state. Private title to land in the United States originates in grants from either the federal government or a foreign country. Each subsequent transfer of title to a specific parcel of land is revealed in a recorded history of a series of voluntary and involuntary conveyances.

Title to real estate may be involuntarily divested from its owner by condemnation, adverse possession, foreclosure sale, partition sale, accretion, escheat, and community property.

An owner may accomplish a voluntary transfer of title to his land by will (testate succession), public grant or patent, descent (intestate succession), sale, or gift.

The most common legal device used to transfer title to real estate is the deed. For valid conveyance to be made by deed, the following legal requirements must be met: (a) a writing, (b) signature of the grantor, (c) sufficient description of the land, (d) legal capacity of the grantor, (e) identification of the grantor and grantee with reasonable certainty, (f) words of conveyance, and (g) delivery by the grantor and acceptance by the grantee.

In some states, the following additional requirements are necessary for the validity of a deed: (a) a seal, (b) attestation, and (c) an acknowledgment.

Due to variations in state laws governing the transfer of title to real estate, deeds vary in form and content. However, almost all deeds contain similar basic provisions, such as the names and addresses of the parties; a recitation of consideration; words of conveyance; a granting clause; a description of the real estate; exceptions and reservations; *habendum;* covenants of title; waiver of dower, curtesy, and homestead; date; signature; seal; attestation; and acknowledgment.

General warranty; special warranty; quit-claim; and grant, bargain, and sale deeds are the most common types. In addition, there are numerous specialty deeds that are designed and used to accomplish a specific purpose.

For a grantee or other person to protect his estate or legal interest in real estate against parties who may subsequently acquire rights in the same property, he must properly record the instrument, which serves as constructive notice to all persons who may subsequently deal with the property. Failure to record may result in an owner's complete loss of his legal interest or, at the very best, a subordination of his legal interest to that of a third party. All states have statutes allowing recordation of certain instruments that affect title to real estate. Recordation is made with the public officer who is in charge of the public records in the county where the real estate is located. For an instrument to be recorded effectively, it must be properly executed and (in some states) attested or acknowledged. The most common system of recordation is the grantor-grantee index. A few states use a tract index system for recordation.

Some states have passed laws providing for the Torrens system of title registration. Under this system, an owner of real estate may voluntarily initiate legal proceedings to confirm and establish registered title in his name. After a judicial hearing is held, title is registered in the owner with the county Registrar of Titles. Thereafter, transfer of title does not pass upon the delivery of a deed to the grantee, but rather it occurs at the time a new certificate is registered and issued in the name of the grantee. Registration of title passed by will, intestate succession, or judicial sale is accomplished pursuant to court order.

TERMS AND CONCEPTS

You can check your understanding of these terms against the glossary or by review in this chapter.

Abstract of title	Doctrine of after	Patent
Acceptance of a deed	acquired title	*Per stirpes*
Accretion	Escheat	Power of attorney
Acknowledgment	Exception	Quitclaim deed
Actual notice	Executor	Recordation
Administrator	Foreclosure	Recording statute
Adverse possession	General warranty deed	Reservation
Attestation	Gift	Restrictive covenants
Attorney in fact	Grant	Seal
Bill to quiet title	Grant, bargain, and sale	Signed by the grantor
Bona fide purchaser	deed	Specialty deed
Certificate of Title	Grantee	Special warranty deed
Chain of title	Granting clause	Sufficient description
Codicil	Grantor	Tacking
Color of title	Grantor-grantee index	Testamentary capacity
Condemnation	*Habendum*	Testate succession
Constructive notice	Holographic will	Torrens system
Covenants of title	Incompetent	Tract index system
Dedication	Intestate succession	Will
Deed	Legal capacity	Words of conveyance
Delivery	Nontitle covenants	Writing
Devise	Partition	

PROBLEMS

5-1. The city of Philadelphia passed an urban redevelopment law providing for the creation of a Redevelopment Authority. The purpose of the law was to clear, reconstruct, and rehabilitate blighted areas within the city. The Authority was given the power to acquire property by purchase or eminent domain and to sell or lease the property acquired to private developers. A lawsuit was filed, alleging that the law was invalid because it authorized the taking of property for private use. What was the result?

5-2. A, B, and C own a thousand acres of land in joint tenancy. B and C farm the land and share income from their operations with A. A became dissatisfied with merely receiving income from the farm and filed a lawsuit asking the court to sell the farm and divide the proceeds equally between A, B, and C. What was the result?

5-3. What effect, if any, do each of the following facts have upon the validity of a will?
   (a) The signature of the testator is only on the first page of a will consisting of three pages.
   (b) The instrument was handwritten by the testator.
   (c) The instrument contained the signature of one attesting witness.
   (d) The instrument did not purport to give away all of the testator's property.
   (e) The will was not delivered to the sole designated beneficiary before the testator died.
   (f) The testator, at the time he signed the will, thought that he was signing a contract for the purchase of cattle.
   (g) The testator, at the time he signed the will, was mentally ill.

5-4. T wanted to make a gift of a farm to each of her three sons. She properly executed three deeds conveying a parcel of farmland to each son. The deeds contained a proper attestation and acknowledgment. T placed the deeds in her safety deposit box and informed her sons of what she had done. She died, leaving a will disposing of all her property to her daughter. The sons and the daughter each claim title to the farms. Who has title to the land? Explain.

5-5. G sold land to B and delivered to B a general warranty deed. B later discovered that G never had title to the land. Nevertheless, he filed a lawsuit to quiet title on the basis that the warranties of title in the deed "guaranteed" title to him. During the lawsuit, X appeared and proved that she owned title to the land at the time G delivered his deed to B. Who presently has title to the land? Explain.

5-6. G, while insolvent, delivered a properly executed, attested, and acknowledged deed to E, the named grantee. The deed recited that it was given to E in exchange "for $20 and other good and valuable consideration." In a lawsuit to set aside the deed, G testified that she never intended to receive nor did she receive any consideration from E.
   (a) Will the deed be set aside? Explain.
   (b) Could X and Y, who were G's creditors at the time G delivered the deed to E, set aside the deed? Explain.

5-7. X subdivided his land into thirty-six residential lots. He recorded the subdivision plat together with a declaration of restrictions. One of the restrictions prohibited the construction of any "building" on any lot "other than one detached single-family dwelling." All deeds subsequently delivered were made subject to the restrictions. Y purchased a lot and constructed a large ranch-style home. Some years later he erected a 12-foot by 12-foot structure used as a playhouse by his children. Y's neighbor Z, who disliked Y intensely, filed a lawsuit asking the court to order the removal of the playhouse. What was the result? Explain.

5-8. S sold a parcel of land to B, delivering to B a general warranty deed. B did not take possession of the land or record her deed. S subsequently sold the same parcel of land to X, delivering to X a general warranty deed. X recorded his deed. X did not have knowledge of S's deed to B.
   (a) As between S and B, is B's unrecorded deed valid? Explain.
   (b) As between B and X, who owns title to the land? Explain.

5-9. Carson properly executed a quitclaim deed conveying his land, Redacre, to Dennis in exchange for a price of $150,000. Carson delivered the deed to Dennis, who promptly had it recorded. Several weeks later, Carson, being desperate for money, sold Redacre to Scott for $100,000. Carson properly executed and delivered a deed to Scott that contained the following words of conveyance, "convey and warrant generally." Scott also recorded his deed. Both Dennis and Scott claimed ownership of Redacre. Dennis filed a bill to quiet title against Carson and Scott. This lawsuit resulted in a judgment in favor of Dennis. A short time later Scott sued Carson for damages.
   (a) What was the legal rationale for the court to declare Dennis to be the owner of Redacre?
   (b) Will Scott be successful in his lawsuit against Carson? Explain.

5-10. List and explain the five types of covenants (warranties) made by a grantor who executes and delivers a general warranty deed to the grantee.

5-11. G executed and delivered a deed to B. The deed was not acknowledged. Is the deed valid? Explain. Will B have difficulty recording her deed? Explain.

5-12. Newly, the owner of Rancho Gordo, died intestate leaving Saul and Herb his sons and only heirs. A year later Saul conveyed "fee simple absolute" in Rancho Gordo to Maria by quitclaim deed. After Maria recorded her deed, Saul executed and delivered a general warranty deed conveying "fee simple absolute" in Rancho Gordo to Michelle. Six months later Herb died intestate leaving Saul as his only heir. What is the legal interest of Saul, Maria, and Michelle, if any, in Rancho Gordo? Explain.

5-13. Aldo owned a 5-acre tract of land with a house thereon in which he resided. Through fraud, Aldo was induced to convey the land to Cohen. The deed from Aldo to Cohen was properly recorded. Subsequently, Cohen sold and conveyed the land to Ezra by general warranty deed in exchange for $250,000. Aldo, upon learning of the fraud, sued Cohen and Ezra to have the deeds canceled and title of record vested in him. Ezra defended on the grounds that he was a bona fide purchaser for value. What was the result? Explain.

5-14. Garbarino and Bassi owned adjoining lots. Garbarino's lot was located to the west of the lot owned by Bassi. Bassi had purchased his lot from Kazcowiz in 1989. In 1960, Kazcowiz had constructed on the west side of her lot a garage and a driveway. The driveway and garage had been used by both Kazcowiz and Bassi. In 1990, after a bitter boundary dispute, Bassi had his lot surveyed. The survey revealed that the garage and the driveway encroached on Garbarino's lot 5 feet and that the encroachment extended the entire length of the line. Bassi immediately sued Garbarino, claiming title by adverse possession to the encroached-upon land. What was the result? Explain.

5-15. Beth properly executed a deed conveying Pleasant View to Rodwell but did not deliver it. Without Beth's knowledge, Rodwell took possession of the deed and recorded it. Rodwell subsequently sold Pleasant View to Spiro and executed and delivered a deed to him. Spiro recorded his deed from Rodwell. Both Beth and Spiro now claim ownership of Pleasant View. Who will prevail? Explain.

SUPPLEMENTARY READINGS

Burby, William E. *Real Estate,* 3rd ed. St. Paul, Minn.: West, 1965.

Dasso, Jerome, and Ring, Alfred A. *Real Estate Principles and Practices,* 11th ed. Englewood Cliffs, N. J.: Prentice-Hall, 1989, Chapters 11 and 12.

Jennings, Marianne M. *Real Estate Law,* 2nd ed. Boston: PWS-Kent, 1989. Chapters 9 and 14.

Kratovil, Robert, and Werner, Raymond J. *Real Estate Law,* 9th ed. Englewood Cliffs, N.J.: Prentice-Hall, 1988. Chapters 7, 9, and 15.

Seidel, George. *Real Estate Law,* 2nd ed. St. Paul: West, 1989. Chapter 8.

CHAPTER 6
Leases

The possessory rights to real estate may be temporarily transferred from one individual (the landlord) to another (the tenant) by a formal, written lease or by oral agreement. In either situation, a landlord-tenant relationship arises; however, there are important differences between the landlord-tenant relationship created by a formal, written lease and that created by periodic tenancy without a lease. In the first instance, the rights and duties of the parties to the lease are spelled out in the contract and are governed by rules of law. In the second instance, where no written lease exists, the duties and responsibilities of each party are implied by law. Although an oral lease for a year or less is valid, it is considered good business practice to put all leases in writing. Such practice usually minimizes disputes.

LEASES

A lease is both a *contract* and a *conveyance* of an interest in real estate. The contract element specifies the rights and duties of the parties to the lease. The lease also conveys the landlord's right to occupy the land to the tenant for the term of the lease. The parties to a lease are called the **lessor** or **landlord,** and the **lessee,** or **tenant.** The lessor's interest is called the **leased fee estate,** which consists of the right to receive the contract rent stipulated in the lease plus the *reversion* or the return of the property at the expiration of the lease. The lessee's interest is known as the **leasehold estate,** which consists of the use and occupancy of the property.

Upon occasion, the lessee may sublet the premises to a third party. In this instance, the original lessee is known as the **sublessor,** and the new tenant is known as the **sublessee.** The sublessor's interest is commonly referred to as the **sandwich leasehold** since the original lessee is sandwiched between the original owner (lessor) and the sublessee. Of course, further subletting is possible, thereby creating many tiers of subtenants and many possible leasehold estates.

LEASEHOLD ESTATES

There are four types of leasehold estates: (a) *estate for years;* (b) *estate from year to year;* (c) *estate at will;* (d) *estate by sufferance.* Each has different stipulations as to the rights of the lessee, period of time it covers, and manner in which it terminates.

Estate for Years (Estate for a Stated Term)

The term **estate for years** is misleading because the period of time (or term) of the lease may be any fixed period, whether two months, six months, one year, or two years. Thus, the more descriptive term, **estate for a stated term,** is often used. The estate for years (estate for a stated term) has a fixed beginning and a fixed end. The estate may be terminated by agreement of the parties at any time, by the expiration date stipulated in the lease without the need for prior notice by either party, or by merger of the leasehold and leased fee interests. An estate for a stated term is not terminated by the death of the landlord or tenant.

Estate from Year to Year (Estate from Period to Period)

An **estate from period to period** may be from week to week, month to month, year to year, or for several years. Such an estate is automatically renewed for succeeding periods unless proper notice of termination is given by the landlord or tenant. It differs from an estate for a stated term in that it does not have a definite termination date. The length of time for which the estate is renewed is dictated by the period for which the rent is paid.

An estate from period to period is generally created in one of two ways. First, the landlord and tenant may contract to rent by the month or by the year, without specifying the number of months or years the lease is to run. The rental arrangement then continues indefinitely for successive periods of time until one of the parties gives proper notice.

The estate from period to period may also be created through the actions of a holdover tenant and the landlord. When a tenant continues to occupy the leased premises after the expiration of the lease, he is called a **holdover tenant.** If the tenant continues to pay rent that is accepted by the landlord, and in the absence of an agreement to the contrary, an estate from period to period is created. (The landlord may, at her option, either hold over the tenant by accepting the rent, or have the tenant evicted). The successive period of the new estate cannot exceed one year. For example, if the original lease term was for six months, the newly established estate from period to period is six months. If the original lease term was five years, the newly established estate from period to period is limited to one year. Before an estate from period to period can be terminated, the landlord or tenant must give proper notice. Although the amount of notice varies from state to state, a notice of one week is generally required to terminate an estate from week to week; one month's notice is generally required to terminate an estate from month to month. The notice required to terminate an estate from year to year ranges from three to six months. In most states, notice must be in writing and delivered to the tenant or landlord or to a resident in the landlord's or tenant's residence (if above a certain age), or delivered by certified or registered mail with return receipt, or delivered by posting on the premises. This type of lease may be oral or written, depending on the term of the lease and the Statute of Frauds in the various states.

Estate at Will

An *estate at will* is an estate of indefinite duration that can be terminated at the "will" of either the landlord or tenant. It may arise by implication or by express agreement. Although common law rule does not require advance notice of termination by either party, statutory laws and judicial decisions in most states now require notice. An estate at will terminates upon the death of either the landlord or tenant.

Estate at Sufferance

An *estate at sufferance* occurs when a tenant comes into possession of the property lawfully and then, after her rights have expired, continues to hold possession of the property without the consent of the owner. Under common law, she is not entitled to any notice. Many states, however, have statutory provisions that require the landlord to give the same notice as that required under an estate at will. In at least one state, Illinois, recovery of double the annual rate of rent is allowed if the tenant fails to vacate after a proper written demand by the landlord. The nature of the estate at sufferance makes it the lowest estate in law.

LEASE REQUIREMENTS

Leases may be written, oral, or implied, depending on the term of the lease and various state statutes. The Statute of Frauds requires any lease with a term in excess of one year to be in writing. Some states, however, consider oral leases longer than one year to be valid. No particular form or wording is necessary to create a valid lease. If the intent to convey possession of property from one party to another for a specific period of time is clearly expressed in the lease and the lease meets all other requirements, a valid lease exists. A valid lease is a contract and must meet the requirements of a contract as specified in Chapter 4. These requirements include the following:

1. *A mutual agreement* (offer and acceptance)
2. *Consideration*
3. *Reality of assent*
4. *Legally competent parties*
5. *Legal objective*
6. *Description of the premises.* The leased property should be described with certainty to assure a "meeting of the minds." A street address should not be used exclusively because it does not specify what land or common property is included. The legal description of the property, combined with a statement of the lessee's right to light and air, use of hallways, staircases, elevators, sidewalks, drives, alleys, and so forth, should be used, especially if the property has several tenants.
7. *Terms of the lease.* The term of the lease should specifically indicate a date of beginning, a date of ending, and the duration of the lease. Some states have statutory laws that limit the term of the lease. In the absence of such laws, leases may be of any duration.
8. *Signatures.* The lease must be signed by the landlord because the courts construe the lease as a conveyance of real estate. The tenant need not sign the lease. Taking possession and paying rent constitutes acceptance of the lease by the tenant. As a practical matter, however, it is good business to get signatures from both the landlord and the tenant.

Joint and Several Liability

When two or more tenants sign the same lease, they are generally held to be *jointly and severally liable* for the rent. In other words, if three tenants share a building, all three tenants sign on the same lease, and two of the tenants fail to pay their share of the rent, the landlord can hold the third tenant liable for all the rent. The tenants would be able to avoid joint and several liability by signing separate leases that stipulate their separate obligations.

RIGHTS AND RESPONSIBILITIES OF PARTIES

In the absence of express provisions regarding the rights and responsibilities of the parties to the lease arising from the landlord-tenant relationship, those rights and responsibilities are implied and created by operation of the law. The nature of the implied rights and responsibilities of the landlord and tenant dictated by the operation of the law varies from state to state because of varying state statutes and court decisions.

The Uniform Residential Landlord and Tenant Act (URLTA) has been proposed by the National Conference of Commissioners on Uniform State Laws and has been submitted to all states for consideration and adoption. The purpose of URLTA is (a) to "simplify, clarify, modernize and revise the law governing the rental of dwelling units and the rights and obligations of landlords and tenants; and (b) to encourage landlords and tenants to maintain and improve the quality of housing." To date, over two dozen states have adopted modified versions of URLTA.

When the landlord and tenant expressly state *covenants* (promises) in a lease, they can bypass the operation of rules of law that would otherwise govern their relationship. A *covenant* is a promise to do something or refrain from doing something in regard to the leased property. Express covenants sometimes stipulate the remedy for the breach of a particular covenant. In the absence of an expressed remedy, the usual remedy is to sue for damages.

Some of the common covenants and conditions in a lease (whether implied or expressed) are described in the following sections.

Possession

The landlord implicitly convenants to give possession of the leased property to the tenant at the agreed-upon time. The tenant's right to use and occupy the premises gives her complete control of the property for the term of the lease. In the absence of lease provisions to the contrary, the tenant may refuse to allow the landlord to enter the leased property for almost any reason.

The landlord does have the right to enter premises that have been abandoned by the tenant in order to care for the property. In this situation, however, the landlord should exercise care so that her reentering the property is not misconstrued as an acceptance, without protest, of the tenant's surrendering of the property, thereby terminating the lease without tenant liability.

Once the current tenant gives notice to the landlord of her intention not to renew the lease, the landlord also has the right to enter the premises at reasonable times to show the rental property to prospective tenants. Most leases expressly provide that the landlord has the right to reenter the property, but they usually state the reasons for which she may enter. It would not be reasonable to let the landlord enter at will.

Use of the Property

In the absence of lease provisions to the contrary, the tenant has the implied right to use the property for any legal purpose. If she uses it for an illegal purpose, the landlord has grounds for eviction. In practice, leases may express that the property can be used only for certain purposes or may specifically prohibit other uses. The tenant may negotiate a provision in the lease that prevents the landlord from leasing other parts of the same building to a competitor. Such provisions are valid. When a tenant leases an entire building, she has the implied right to erect and maintain signs on the exterior of the building, so long as zoning codes do not prohibit them. As always, lease provisions to the contrary will overrule the implied right.

Rent

Most leases specify that the rent is to be paid in advance. In the absence of such a provision, in most states, the rent is due at the end of the term. When a tenant *assigns* her leasehold interest to a third party *(assignee),* the assignee becomes liable for the rent. This, however, does not release the original tenant from liability. If the assignee defaults on the rent, the landlord can bring action against the original tenant as well as the assignee. A *sublessee,* on the other hand, is usually not liable to the landlord for rent unless she specifically assumes such liability. Subleasing versus assigning the leasehold interest is more fully explained later in the chapter.

The amount of rent is usually stipulated in the lease. On long-term leases, *escalator clauses* are commonly inserted to allow for automatic rent increases to protect against inflation. In the unusual situation where the rent is not specified in the lease, the landlord is entitled to a reasonable rental value based on current market rent.

Repairs and Maintenance

By common law, the tenant has an implied duty to make the repairs that are necessary to prevent *waste* of the building and return it to the landlord at the expiration of the lease in the same condition she found it, normal wear and tear excepted. Until recently, the rule of *caveat emptor* (let the buyer beware) prevailed in the relationship of landlord and tenant, and the landlord was under no obligation to repair the leased premises. Today, however, many states have statutory laws requiring the landlord to keep any building leased for dwelling purposes in condition fit for habitation. Some states have granted the tenant of a dwelling unit the right to deduct minor repair bills from the rent to maintain habitability. The limitations of the right are many and they vary from state to state. The tenant may vacate the premises, if they become uninhabitable, on the grounds of *constructive eviction.* In multiple-tenant properties, the landlord has an implied duty to repair and maintain common areas such as hallways, elevators, stairways, entrances, and sidewalks. The lease should spell out the respective duties and responsibilities of the landlord and tenant to make repairs. If such provisions are stated, they should be worded very carefully. Generally, a lease provision to make repairs does not carry with it the duty to make any structural changes. If the tenant agrees to make repairs, she is generally obligated to keep the premises in reasonable repair. If the landlord agrees to make specific repairs, she has the implied assent to enter the building for such repairs. However, she is not obligated to make repairs not specified.

Improvements

Unless otherwise specified in the lease, neither the landlord nor the tenant has a duty to make improvements. Due to the tenant's implied duty to return the property in the same condition she found it, she is precluded from making any alterations or improvements unless the lease specifically allows it or the landlord agrees. Most long-term leases have provisions for making alterations and improvements to keep the building from becoming functionally obsolete. All improvements (fixtures) become the landlord's property unless otherwise specified. Occasionally, provisions may be made to allow the tenant to remove some improvements prior to the expiration of the lease. Certain items that are installed to aid the tenant in her trade are considered *trade fixtures* and, being classified as personal property, are removable before expiration of the lease.

Where the lease provides the tenant with the right to make improvements, the landlord should insure that she is protected from a mechanic's lien should the tenant fail to pay the subcontractors who did the work. The lease may stipulate that the tenant be required to obtain lien waivers from those performing the work, or the landlord may be given the right to pay off any mechanic's lien and add it to the amount of rent payable by the tenant.

Waste

As mentioned earlier, the tenant has an implied obligation not to commit waste. *Waste* is the neglect, alteration, destruction, or misuse of property committed by the party lawfully in possession to the detriment of the estate or interest of another party. Waste is generally classified as either voluntary or permissive. *Voluntary waste* is caused by any unreasonable or improper use of the leased property resulting in damage. *Permissive waste* is caused by an omission or failure to act to protect or preserve the leased property. A tenant who commits waste is liable to the landlord for damages.

Taxes, Assessments, and Insurance

Unless there are lease provisions to the contrary, the tenant is under no implied obligation to pay real estate taxes, special assessments, or insurance on the leased property. On long-term commercial leases, however, the lease may stipulate that the tenant is to pay such expenses. This type of lease is sometimes referred to as a *net lease.* If the tenant is to pay for the insurance, the lease should stipulate the amount of insurance to be carried and who is to receive the insurance award in case of a loss.

Security Deposits

Unless the lease states otherwise, the tenant is under no obligation to pay a security deposit to the landlord. Most leases, however, do provide for a security deposit. Where a security deposit is used, the courts usually allow the landlord to retain all or a part of it if the tenant breaches the lease. The amount retained by the landlord is usually determined by the amount of actual damages. Several states have passed legislation requiring the landlord to keep the security deposits in a separate escrow account or to pay interest to the tenant on the security deposit.

Exculpatory Clauses

Many standard leases contain *exculpatory clauses* that attempt to absolve the landlord from any liability to the tenant arising from negligence on the part of the landlord. The validity of such clauses is questionable under the common law. Several states have passed legislation outlawing them.

Option to Renew

There are several variations of an *option to renew* clause. Many standard lease forms contain automatic renewal clauses that bind the tenant to a new lease term equal to the original term if she does not provide sufficient notice in writing to the landlord stating her intent not to renew. In this instance, the careless tenant may find herself bound to an unwanted renewed lease.

To avoid this situation, some states require the landlord to notify the tenant of the automatic renewal clause prior to the date the lease is to terminate. Other states require that the automatic renewal clause stand out from the other lease provisions to prevent such an important clause from going unnoticed by the tenant.

Other common option to renew clauses provide that the tenant, at her option, is entitled to renew the lease at any time prior to the expiration of the lease.

Option to Purchase

An *option to purchase* is a unilateral contract in which the optionor agrees to keep an offer open and irrevocable for a stated period of time in return for the optionee's payment of money. In a lease containing an option to purchase, the rent provisions are considered sufficient consideration to support the option. In many instances, the terms of the option may provide that a percentage of the lease payments can be applied to the purchase price.

An *option to purchase* clause in the lease does not preclude the lessor from selling the property to someone other than the optionee. In such a case, however, the property is sold "subject to" the option. If the optionee decides to exercise her option, the new owner must sell it to her at the option price. Generally, when a lease with an option to purchase is assigned, the option to purchase is also transferred. The optionee may, however, assign the lease to one party and the option to purchase to a second party unless specific provisions in the lease prohibit it.

The option to purchase terminates upon termination of the lease. Death of the optionor or optionee does not affect an option.

Right of First Refusal

The *right of first refusal* clause provides the lessee with a prior right to purchase the leased property in the event the lessor decides to sell. It differs from the standard option to purchase in that the optionee in the option to purchase can compel the optionor to sell her property, whereas the holder of a first right of refusal cannot. Also, the holder of the first right of refusal has the right to match any offer that the lessor is willing to accept, whereas the optionee in any option to purchase must pay the agreed-upon option price if she decides to exercise her option.

Subordination Clause

A *subordination clause* is sometimes included in a lease to enable the lessor to place a first mortgage on the property after a lease has been executed. Without the subordination clause, leases signed before the mortgage have priority over the mortgage. The subordination clause acts to subordinate the senior position of the lease to the later recorded mortgage.

TYPES OF LEASES

Leases are contracts entered into for the mutual benefit of all parties. The varying needs of landlords and tenants require flexibility in the lease document. Leases are generally classified as long-term or short-term. This classification is rather arbitrary and has no legal significance, except that statutory provisions generally require leases with terms exceeding one year to be in writing. Leases are further subdivided according to how the amount of rental payment is derived. The most common types of leases are described on the following pages.

Fixed Rental Lease

A *fixed rental lease,* sometimes called a *flat lease,* stipulates a fixed rental that is to be paid over the duration of the lease. Fixed rental leases may be further classified as either gross leases or net leases.

Gross Lease

A *gross lease* requires that the landlord pay the taxes, insurance, and all other expenses out of the fixed rental amount received from the tenant.

Net Lease

The *net lease* requires that the tenant pay a net fixed rental to the landlord in addition to some or all of the fixed and operating expenses of the leased property. The net lease enables the landlord to receive a net rental return from the property over the years and assures that the amount will not diminish with increasing operating expenses.

Index Lease

Even with net leases, however, the corrosive effect of inflation diminishes the purchasing power of the landlord's fixed return. Consequently, an *escalation clause* may be inserted in the lease to guard against inflation. This is called an *index lease.* The escalation clause provides for an annual increase in rental payment based on a defined rule, formula, or index. One index commonly used is the **Consumer Price Index.**

Reappraisal Lease

In lieu of an escalation clause tied to an index, the lease may provide that the rental rate escalates in the same proportion as the market value of the property increases. Such a provision generally stipulates that the property be reappraised at certain intervals and the rental rate adjusted accordingly. The reappraisal lease is subject to attack, however, because of the uncertain nature of market value estimates. As a result, reappraisal leases are seldom used.

Percentage Lease

Percentage leases are very common in the retail trade business. The rental amount generally includes a base or minimum monthly rental plus a percentage of the gross sales over and above a specified amount. The tenant will usually demand that a maximum rental be stipulated in the lease.

Although the percentage rental is sometimes based on net income or gross profits rather than gross sales, such practice is generally not recommended because of the inability of the landlord (and sometimes the tenant) to determine either net income or gross profits. Since the landlord's rental is extremely dependent on the tenant's business operation, the landlord should enter into such leases only after careful analysis of the tenant's credit and past performance. Lease provisions should clearly define what is included in gross sales, when and what type of report the tenant is to submit to the landlord, and whether or not the landlord has the right to inspect or audit the tenant's books.

Agricultural Lease

Agricultural leases are as many and varied as residential or commercial leases. They may be long-term or short-term. Some may give the tenant full managerial responsibility, while others provide for considerable landlord supervision. Some leases are filled with elaborate covenants and conditions, while others include only the minimum requirements. Some common agricultural leases are discussed in the next sections.

Cash Rental Lease

The *cash rental lease* stipulates that the farm tenant is to pay the landlord a fixed amount per acre for the right to farm the land. The rent may vary from $2 or $3 per acre to over $200, depending on the region of the United States and the productivity of the land. The tenant buys his equipment, seed, fertilizer, and pays all other expenses associated with the farming operation. The landlord pays the real estate taxes only. All profits (and losses) from the farming operation accrue to the tenant. Cash rental leases are very common for pasture and grazing land.

Crop/Livestock Share Lease

Crop or *livestock share leases* are the most common agricultural leases in the United States. The lease stipulates the exact sharing of crops, livestock, and expenses between the landlord and tenant. In this type of lease, the landlord shares the risk involved in production and usually receives from 25 to 50 percent of the crops or livestock produced.

Share-Cash Lease

Occasionally, cash-rent provisions are spelled out for a part of the farming operation, with crop-share provisions applied to the balance. This arrangement is called a *share-cash lease*.

Sale-Leaseback

The *sale-leaseback* is a financing device that involves just what the name implies: An owner of real estate sells her property and simultaneously agrees to lease it back from the buyer, usually on a long-term, net lease basis. The parties to the lease are called the *seller-lessee* and the *buyer-lessor*.

Buy-Build-Sale-Leaseback

In some instances, a firm may purchase a site in a location of its preference, build a structure to suit its needs, and then search for an investor who is willing to buy the property and simultaneously lease it back to the seller, usually for a long period of time. In such cases, the firm gets the location and building it wants, and the subsequent sale-leaseback frees up fixed capital the firm had tied up in real estate and enables it to use all its funds in the day-to-day operation of the business.

Sale-Leaseback-Buyback

Occasionally, the sale-leaseback includes an option, called *sale-leaseback-buyback,* for the seller-lessee to repurchase the property at the end of the lease term. This financing device, in effect, allows the seller-lessee to obtain 100 percent financing on his building. Such leases must be carefully drawn to avoid Internal Revenue Service scrutiny. If the buyback price stated in the lease is a nominal value rather than fair market value at the time of sale, the Internal Revenue Service will probably rule that it was not a lease at all, but rather a long-term mortgage, and any tax benefits enjoyed during the lease term will be disallowed.

Advantages to Seller-Lessee

In summary, the major advantages of a sale-leaseback to the seller-lessee are these:

1. The sale frees up fixed capital that can be used more effectively as working capital or business expansion capital for an ongoing business.
2. The sale frees the seller-lessee of management problems associated with real estate ownership.
3. The seller-lessee retains use of the property.
4. The seller-lessee can deduct the total lease payments as a business expense from his income when calculating his income tax liability.
5. It enables the seller-lessee to obtain maximum financing without experiencing the many restrictive covenants that would be associated with bonds or other long-term financing devices.

Advantages to Buyer-Lessor

The buyer-lessor is usually a life insurance company, a pension fund, a church organization, or occasionally, an individual investor seeking a long-term relatively secure investment. The major advantages of a sale-leaseback to the buyer-lessor are these:

1. The rate of return on long-term leases is generally higher than that offered on first mortgages and other long-term investments of similar risk.
2. The buyer-lessor can commit large amounts of investment funds for a long period of time, thereby avoiding the recurring problem of reinvesting in shorter-term investments.
3. The buyer-lessor has more control over the real estate she owns than she would have if she merely held the first mortgage.
4. The buyer-lessor may take advantage of financial leverage by mortgaging her property.
5. The buyer-lessor can depreciate the building portion of her investment and deduct it when calculating her taxable income, thereby reducing tax liability.
6. The buyer-lessor benefits from any equity growth through property appreciation.

Ground Lease

A *ground lease* is an agreement for the rental of an unimproved parcel of real estate for a number of years in exchange for rental payments. The agreement usually provides for a building to be erected on the premises by the tenant. Lease terms of fifty to ninety-nine years are common. At the expiration of the lease, the building becomes the property of the landlord, unless otherwise provided. Since the building may have considerable value at the expiration of the lease, provisions are usually found in the lease that require the landlord to pay all or a part of the current, appraised value of the building. The ground rent paid by the lessee is sometimes expressed as a percentage of the value of the land. In order for the landlord to get a fair return on the appreciating value of his land, the lease usually provides for the land to be reappraised annually and the rents adjusted accordingly. In addition to the ground rent, the lessee usually pays the real estate taxes on the land as well.

TRANSFER OF INTEREST

Landlord's Interest

The landlord may freely sell, assign, or mortgage her *fee interest* in real estate. If she sells her interest, the grantee takes title *subject to* the lease and becomes liable for all the covenants in the lease. Such transfer, however, does not relieve the original landlord of her liability for the covenants unless the lease specifically releases her. Cancellation clauses are sometimes inserted in a lease to allow the landlord to cancel the lease upon proper notice if the property is sold. Possession of the property by a lessee is *constructive notice* to a potential purchaser that a lease exists. The purchaser, therefore, should determine the exact nature of the lease before proceeding with the purchase.

Finally, the landlord may mortgage her interest in the leased fee. If the landlord defaults on the mortgage, the tenant's interest may or may not be affected, depending on whether the mortgage was recorded prior to the lease or after the lease. If the lease was executed prior to the mortgage, the mortgagee must honor the lease unless a provision in the lease makes it *subject to* all the mortgages on the land. If the lease is made subsequent to the mortgage, the mortgagee can, upon foreclosure, terminate the rights of the tenant. To avoid eviction, the tenant may enter into a new lease arrangement with the mortgagee.

Tenant's Interest

The *leasehold interest* (tenant's interest) in real estate is considered personal property and may be freely assigned, sublet, or mortgaged unless provisions to the contrary are specified in the lease.

Assignment

When a tenant (assignor) assigns a lease, she transfers the entire remaining term of the lease to the assignee. In an *assignment* of the leasehold interest, the assignee becomes liable to the original landlord for rent. This, however, does not relieve the assignor from liability. The landlord may sue either the original tenant (assignor), or the assignee, or both for breach of the lease. If the original tenant is sued by the landlord for rent payments, the tenant has cause of action against the assignee.

Sublet

When a tenant transfers only part of the remaining term of the lease or only a part of the leased premises to the sublessee, she is subleasing. In a *sublease,* the sublessee is liable to the sublessor (original lessee) only, and not to the original landlord. The original tenant remains liable to the landlord unless she is expressly relieved of such liability by the landlord.

Mortgage

The value of the leasehold interest is the present value of the difference between the rent stipulated in the lease (contract rent) and the economic (market) rent. In some cases, the leasehold interest may be quite valuable.

When the tenant decides to mortgage her leasehold interest, she is confronted with *leasehold mortgage* payments in addition to lease payments. The double payments of the tenant greatly increase the risk of default and, upon foreclosure, the mortgagee is faced with the necessity of taking over the lease. As a result, leasehold mortgages are generally available only to tenants with excellent credit ratings. Many states have statutory laws to regulate which leasehold interests may be mortgaged. In Arizona, for example, for a life insurance company to place a leasehold mortgage, the unexpired term of the lease must be at least twenty-one years.

Many leases provide that the lease cannot be assigned, sublet, or mortgaged without the written consent of the landlord. Such provisions are valid. However, it is generally held to be against public policy for the landlord to unreasonably withhold consent.

Leases Subordinate to Mortgages

A lease on a property is *subject to* any existing mortgage or other lien on the property at the time the lease was made. In other words, the rights of the mortgagee or other senior lien claimant are superior to the rights of the tenant if the mortgage or other lien was recorded prior to the lease. Conversely, a mortgage recorded after the lease was made is subordinate to the lease. Upon signing of the lease, the tenant usually takes possession.

In addition, the tenant may also record the lease. Either possession or recording gives notice to others of the rights of the tenant. It is important to the tenant who plans on spending a considerable sum of money on improvements to inquire about existing mortgages or she runs the risk of having her lease terminated at foreclosure and losing her investment. It is also important for the lending institution to determine if there are any existing leases that would survive the mortgage. Although leases that are superior to a mortgage and thus survive a foreclosure may be an advantage to the mortgagee when she goes to sell the building, the lease terms may be very advantageous to the tenant, thereby having a negative impact on the leased fee value held as collateral by the mortgagee.

Leases often contain subordination clauses, which provide that the lease shall be subordinate to the mortgage up to a certain dollar amount. This allows the lessor or landlord to increase existing mortgages up to the agreed-upon amount.

REMEDIES OF THE LANDLORD

There are several remedies open to the landlord if the tenant defaults in the lease agreement.

Distress for Rent Due

Common law provides the landlord with the right of *distress for rent due,* which is to seize any property owned by the tenant for rent due. The property is usually seized without notice and is held by the landlord until the rent is paid or until a court order allows the landlord to sell it. Many leases specifically provide for the landlord's rights to distress. Many state statutes, however, have abolished or modified this questionable procedure because of constant misuse and abuse on the part of landlords.

Confession of Judgment

The *confession of judgment* lease provision allows the landlord's attorney to appear in court without the tenant's knowledge or consent and plead guilty on the tenant's behalf to any breach of the lease so charged by the landlord. Although such a provision is of questionable efficacy, it is still legal in several states. In states where it is not legal, the landlord can be protected by inserting a provision in the lease whereby she may deliver a written notice to the tenant, citing the nature of the contract breach. The clause further provides the tenant a reasonable period of time to correct the breach in order to prevent termination of the lease.

Sue for Rent Due

The landlord may sue on the lease to collect rent as stipulated in the agreement. Such rights are available to the landlord whether or not specified in the lease.

Actual Eviction by Law

Eviction is a legal process used to remove a tenant from the premises for breach of the lease. The landlord can have the tenant evicted if the tenant breaches the lease contract in any material way. She may then reenter the property and take possession. Generally, once the tenant is evicted, she has no further liability to pay rent unless the lease contained a survival clause. The *survival clause* provides that the tenant's liability survives the eviction.

TERMINATION OF LEASES

Leases may be terminated in a variety of ways. The most common methods are by (a) notice, (b) expiration of term, (c) breach of condition, (d) surrender and acceptance, (e) destruction of property, (f) condemnation, (g) merger, (h) constructive eviction, (i) actual eviction, and (j) foreclosure.

Notice

With estates from period to period, estates at will, and estates by sufferance, the lease may be terminated upon giving proper notice. If the period is from year to year, common law requires a notice of six months. Many states have shortened the notice requirement by statute. If the period is less than a year, the notice is usually equal to the period of the lease.

Expiration of Term

Estates for years (estates for a stated term) are terminated on the last day of the term without need of notification.

Breach of Condition

The lease usually gives the landlord the right to terminate the lease and to take possession of the leased property upon default of the tenant. Some states have statutes outlining the landlord's right to reenter upon default. In either case, the tenant should ensure that the landlord is required to give notice of default and allow the tenant a reasonable time to cure it.

Surrender and Acceptance

Surrender and acceptance involves the surrender of the unexpired portion of the lease by the tenant and the voluntary acceptance of the lease by the landlord. Upon surrender and acceptance, the landlord reacquires possession and relieves the tenant of future liability for rent. The Statute of Frauds in many states requires the surrender and acceptance to be in writing.

Surrender and acceptance should not be confused with *abandonment*. If a tenant abandons leased property, she does so without permission from the landlord and thereby remains liable for rent. The lease usually provides that the landlord may, upon the abandonment, reenter the property to protect it without having the courts construe it as a voluntary acceptance. In this way, the landlord may continue to hold the tenant liable for rent.

Destruction of Property

By common law, when agriculture was the predominant industry, the tenant was held liable for the rent even after the destruction of the improvements. It was felt that the tenant derived the majority of utility by farming the ground, not by using the buildings. Today, however, the majority of tenants are concerned primarily with the use value of the buildings. As a result, many states have passed statutes that relieve the tenant from the liability of paying rent if the improvements have been substantially damaged and that terminate the lease if the property has been destroyed. Many lease forms have similar provisions.

Condemnation

Unless otherwise specified in the lease, when all of the leased property is taken by condemnation, the lease is terminated and the tenant is reimbursed for the unexpired portion of the leasehold interest. As stated previously, the value of the leasehold interest is the present value of the difference between the rent stipulated in the lease *(contract rent)* and the *economic rent (market rent)* at the time the property was condemned. The tenant's claim to the award is superior to that of the landlord. The proceeds in a condemnation suit must first go to the tenant to satisfy her claim before the landlord acquires her share. Consequently, most landlords insert a *condemnation clause* in the lease, which provides that the lease will be terminated upon condemnation, with all the proceeds going to the landlord.

Merger

When the tenant's interest in real estate (leasehold interest) is merged with the landlord's interest (leased fee interest), the lease is terminated. A *merger* occurs when the tenant purchases or inherits the leased premises from the landlord. The leased fee interest merges with the leasehold interest to form fee simple ownership, and all property rights are vested in the new owner of the fee.

Eviction

An *eviction* is the dispossession or deprivation of the tenant from all or part of the leased premises at the instigation of the landlord. Evictions may be classified as actual eviction by law, constructive eviction, or partial eviction.

Actual eviction by law is a statutory right of the landlord if the tenant breaches the lease provisions. It involves a judicial proceeding to dispossess (evict) a tenant legally. If the judgment is in favor of the landlord and the tenant is dispossessed, the lease is terminated. Most state statutes list which conditions in the lease are grounds for legal eviction if breached.

Constructive eviction occurs when the leased premises become uninhabitable or untenantable for the use specified in the lease as a result of acts or omissions of the landlord that force the tenant to remove herself. Failure of the landlord to make repairs or to provide heat and electricity or other provisions agreed to in the lease may result in constructive eviction. Most states recognize constructive eviction as a basis for termination of the lease. The landlord can protect herself by inserting a provision in the lease calling for the tenant to provide written notice of any landlord failure. The clause would further provide the landlord time to remedy the situation before the tenant can terminate the lease through constructive eviction.

Partial eviction may be constructive or actual. *Partial constructive eviction* occurs when the landlord, due to her acts or omissions, makes a part of the leased premises untenantable. The tenant may move out of the entire leased premises and is no longer liable for rent. *Partial actual eviction,* on the other hand, occurs when the landlord actually evicts the tenant from only a part of the leased premises. In this situation, the tenant can continue to occupy the remainder of the premises without paying rent. Such a situation may arise when the landlord, whose business occupies a portion of the building, decides to expand and, in doing so, unlawfully evicts a tenant from an area previously occupied.

Foreclosure

As mentioned earlier, the landlord has the right to mortgage her leased fee interest. If the mortgage is foreclosed, however, and the mortgage is senior to the lease, the lease rights of the tenant are automatically cut off. This situation is not always attractive to the mortgagee since she becomes the owner of a newly unleased property with no income stream. Consequently, the mortgagor may insert a *nondisturbance clause* in the mortgage, which provides that, in case of foreclosure, the tenant's right will not be disturbed. If, on the other hand, the *lease antedates the mortgage,* the tenant's rights are not cut off by foreclosure. The mortgagee merely becomes the new landlord of the tenant, and both parties must adhere to the lease provisions.

Death of Parties

In an estate at will, the death of either the landlord or the tenant will terminate the lease.

The legal relationship between landlord and tenant was derived from the common law or custom established during the late fifteenth century and refined by centuries of judicial interpretation to satisfy the needs of an agrarian, feudal society. Land law was the first area of law to become established because the majority of wealth and, consequently, litigation stemmed from land and its ownership. It seems that those subjects of law that were settled earliest have become the most difficult to change.

The scales on the balance of justice have been tipped in favor of the landlord for centuries, because of his superior bargaining position. Now, however, consumer protection organizations have focused in on the inequitable landlord-tenant relationship and have encouraged tenants to organize and fight against the archaic one-sided law. Many state legislatures have responded to the demands of tenant unions by passing legislation to protect the tenant. As mentioned earlier, the Uniform Residential Landlord and Tenant Act (URLTA) has been adopted or is being considered in many states. In addition, the courts are handing down decisions in favor of the tenant by declaring certain provisions in the lease to be against public policy. The following list includes some of the recent laws or decisions affecting residential rental property in various parts of the country.

1. Distress has been outlawed in some states.
2. Exculpatory clauses releasing the landlord from all liability arising from her negligence have been found void in many cases.
3. Some statutes allow the tenant to make necessary repairs and deduct the cost from rent.
4. Some city ordinances require the landlord to deposit money in an escrow account to be released for repair work.
5. Evictions are legal only by court order in some states.
6. Some states require the landlord to pay interest on any security deposit she holds.
7. Certain contracts of adhesion where the landlord, with her superior bargaining position, dictates lease provisions on a "take it or leave it basis" have been held to be unconscionable and void.
8. Many states require the landlord to install smoke detectors in apartment units.
9. In some states, the landlord must install security devices at her expense, upon the request of the tenant..
10. Some states require the landlord to disclose to the tenants the name and address of the owner of the leased premises.
11. Some states provide that a tenant who has been dispossessed shall have the right to repossess the property after paying all rent in arrears. Generally, the lease must have five or more years remaining. To overcome this inconvenience, most landlords who draw up a lease will insert a clause in the lease expressly stating that the tenant agrees to waive her right of redemption.
12. Some states have passed legislation to protect tenants from unjust eviction. In these states, tenants can be evicted only for those reasons stated in the statutes. Although the permissible causes for eviction vary, they do tend to protect the tenant from certain unjust evictions.

The landlord-tenant laws affecting residential rental property vary considerably throughout the United States. Readers are encouraged to become familiar with the laws specific to their own state. Commercial leases continue to be enforced on the basis of the various clauses and covenants found in the lease, with few if any state statutes to the contrary.

SUMMARY

One of the many rights inherent in the total bundle of rights associated with ownership is the owner's right to occupy and use the premises. If the fee owner does not use the property herself, she may temporarily transfer the possession and use rights to a tenant by means of a lease, thereby providing the tenant with a leasehold estate or interest in the property for the duration of the lease. Various types of leasehold estates may be created, depending on the nature of the lease and the various state statutes. The four types of leasehold estates are (1) estate for years (estate for a stated term), (2) estate from year to year (estate from period to period), (3) estate at will, and (4) estate at sufferance. The lease must meet the requirements of a contract to be valid. The parties to a lease are called the landlord (lessor) and the tenant (lessee). The lease, whether oral or written, creates a landlord-tenant relationship between the lessor and lessee. The rights and responsibilities of the landlord and tenant are spelled out in the various clauses and covenants of the lease. In the absence of lease phrasing to the contrary, the relationship is determined by common law and state statute. Leases may be classified by (1) the length of the lease (long-term or short-term), (2) the type of property (residential, commercial, agricultural, industrial), or (3) how the amount of rent is derived (fixed-rental lease, reappraisal lease, percentage lease). The landlord's interest (leased fee) may be freely sold, assigned, or mortgaged. The tenant's interest (leasehold) may be assigned, sublet, or mortgaged unless phrasing in the lease prohibits it. The landlord has several remedies available if the tenant defaults in the lease agreement. They include distress for rent due, confession of judgment, suit for rent due, and eviction. Recent state statutes have provided the tenant with numerous remedies in case the landlord breaches the lease. Historically, common law has put the landlord in a superior bargaining position. Recently, however, the scales of justice have been tipping in the direction of the tenant, especially on residential leases.

TERMS AND CONCEPTS

You can check your understanding of these terms against the glossary or by review in this chapter.

Assign
Condemnation clause
Confession of judgment
Consumer Price Index
Covenants
Distress for rent due
Escalation clause
Estate for a stated term
Eviction
Exculpatory clause
Fee interest
Fixed rental lease

Ground lease
Holdover tenant
Jointly and severally
 liable
Lease antedating the
 mortgage
Leasehold interest
Leasehold mortgage
Lessee
Lessor
Market rent
Merger

Option to renew
Partial eviction
Permissive waste
Sale-leaseback
Sandwich leasehold
Sublessee
Sublessor
Subordination clause
Surrender and
 acceptance
Voluntary waste
Waste

What are the differences or relationships, if any, between the following?

Assignment and Sublease	Gross lease and Net lease	Right of first refusal and Option to purchase
Constructive eviction and Actual eviction	Leasehold estate and Leased fee estate	Sale-leaseback and Sale-leaseback-buyback
Contract rent and Economic rent	Nondisturbance clause and Survival clause	Sublessee and Assignee
Estate at sufferance and Estate at will	Partial constructive eviction and Partial actual eviction	Surrender and acceptance and Abandonment
Estate for years and Estate from period to period	Percentage lease and Index lease	

PROBLEMS

6-1. What is the main difference between a reappraisal lease and an index lease? Which of the two is most commonly used? Why?

6-2. How is an estate from year to year created? How is it terminated?

6-3. Comment on some of the remedies of the landlord that you feel are unfair to the tenant.

6-4. What is a nondisturbance clause in a lease? Whom does it protect?

6-5. What are the main advantages of a sale-leaseback to the seller-lessee?

6-6. What are the legal requirements for a valid lease?

6-7. Assume you own a building in a retail area and have a prospective tenant who is starting up an ice cream parlor. Her initial investment in equipment is high and her cash position is poor. What provisions in the lease would you suggest to entice the prospect into renting your building and allow you to make a satisfactory return on your investment?

6-8. Assume that, as lessee, you sign a lease on a building on January 1, 1989. In March of 1989 the lessor mortgages the leased premises. The lessor then defaults and the mortgagee forecloses. What are your rights, if any?

6-9. Give some examples to illustrate the difference between voluntary waste and permissive waste.

6-10. Under what circumstances will a court enforce an agreement that a security deposit shall serve as liquidated damages for a tenant's breach of a lease provision?

6-11. Give two examples of situations where a tenant might have the right to repair and deduct the repair costs by state statute or court decision.

6-12. Give two examples of landlords' liability with respect to common areas in leased premises.

6-13. What are the tenant rights when the landlord sells the property? What if the landlord dies?

6-14. Distinguish between a sublease and an assignment of a lease.

6-15. What are some of the risks of a landlord retaking possession of a leased premise without first resorting to legal action?

SUPPLEMENTARY READINGS

Anderson, Ronald A. *Business Law: Principles and Cases,* 7th ed. Cincinnati: South-Western, 1979.

Barlowe, Raleigh. *Land Resource Economics,* 4th ed. Englewood Cliffs, N.J.: Prentice-Hall, 1986. Chapter 14.

Bellavance, Russell C. *Real Estate Law.* St. Paul: West, 1978. Chapter 9.

Bergfield, Phillip B. *Real Estate Law.* New York: McGraw-Hill, 1979. Chapters 23 and 24.

Dasso, Jerome, and Ring, Alfred A. *Real Estate Principles and Practices,* 11th ed. Englewood Cliffs, N.J.: Prentice-Hall, 1989. Chapter 24.

Downs, James C. *Principles of Real Estate Management,* 12th ed. Chicago: Institute of Real Estate Management, 1980.

French, William B., and Lusk, Harold F. *Law of the Real Estate Business,* 5th ed. Homewood, Ill.: Irwin, 1984. Chapter 17.

Hoagland, Henry E., and Stone, Leo D. *Real Estate Finance.* Homewood, Ill.: Irwin, 1973. Chapters 9 and 10.

Institute of Real Estate Management. *Forms for Office Building Management and Operations Manual Guidelines.* Chicago, 1986.

Institute of Real Estate Management. *Marketing and Leasing of Office Space,* rev. ed. Chicago, 1986.

Kratovil, Robert, and Werner, Raymond J. *Real Estate Law,* 8th ed. Englewood Cliffs, N.J.: Prentice-Hall, 1983. Chapter 37.

Real Estate Education Company and Grubb & Ellis. *Successful Sales and Leasing of Office Space.* Chicago, 1980.

Real Estate Education Company and Grubb & Ellis. *Successful Sales and Leasing of Retail Property.* Chicago, 1980.

Roberts, Duane. *Marketing and Leasing of Office Space.* Chicago: Institute of Real Estate Management of the NATIONAL ASSOCIATION OF REALTORS®, 1979.

Shewkel, William M. *Modern Real Estate Management.* New York: McGraw-Hill, 1980.

Tosh, Dennis S., and Ordway, Nicholas. *Real Estate Principles for License Preparation.* Reston, Va.: Reston Publishing, 1979. Chapter 13.

Unger, Maurice A., and Karvel, George R. *Real Estate Principles and Practices,* 8th ed. Englewood Cliffs, N.J.: Prentice-Hall, 1987. Chapter 24.

Walters, William. *The Practice of Real Estate Management for the Experienced Property Manager.* Chicago: Institute of Real Estate Management, 1979.

CHAPTER 7
The Mortgage Market: Institutions and Agencies

The vast majority of all real estate purchases are financed through the use of credit. Most buyers provide a down payment and rely on debt financing to furnish the balance. The primary source of debt financing in real estate is the mortgage. A *mortgage* pledges a specific parcel of real estate as security for a debt. The mortgage creates a lien, which may be enforced by sale of the property to satisfy the debt. The borrower is called the *mortgagor* and the lender is the *mortgagee.* The mortgage is accompanied by a note, or promise to pay, which is usually a separate document. When the debt is repaid, the mortgage is extinguished.

A market exists for mortgages, just as a market exists for other products or services. The term *marketing* has been defined in many ways. In its broader sense, *marketing* is "human activity directed at satisfying needs and wants through an exchange process."[1] Although in its traditional use marketing relates to business activities, the broader definition is applicable to all organizations performing marketing-related activities. A *market* can then be defined as an aggregate of people or organizations involved in marketing. The *mortgage market* might therefore consist of people and organizations involved in marketing activities related to mortgages. The purpose of

---

[1]Philip Kotler, *Marketing Management,* 4th ed. Englewood Cliffs, N.J.: Prentice-Hall, 1980, p. 19.

a market is to satisfy human needs and wants. It also must involve something of value and be concerned with an exchange process.

Persons and organizations dealing in mortgages speak of the primary mortgage market and the secondary mortgage market. Marketing involves exchanges or transactions and also buyers and sellers in a competitive environment. In the ***primary mortgage market,*** for example, consumers are seeking favorable terms for a mortgage loan needed to purchase a home. Banks and others offer mortgage loans at terms intended to be competitive in the marketplace and yet profitable for the lender. Institutions that loan directly to the consumer are called ***primary lenders;*** they operate in the primary market.

Primary lenders promote their offerings just as any business would promote its products, and they design mortgages to appeal to particular consumer groups. A wide variety of mortgages has been particularly evident in the past decade because of a tight mortgage market and a shortage of borrowers able to handle traditional types of mortgages due to high interest rates. Distribution and communication programs bring borrowers and lenders together and provide feedback to ascertain the success or failure of the marketing operations. Three measures of the effectiveness of a lender's mortgage marketing effort are the volume of mortgage loans, lender's profits, and the rate of foreclosures.

A bank or other primary lending institution has only a certain amount of money available for lending. In the ***secondary mortgage market,*** private investors or government agencies are willing to purchase mortgages from primary lenders. Through such sales the primary lender obtains additional funds for loans to other consumers. This chapter will deal with the mortgage market in general, including the concepts and complexities of the primary and secondary markets.

MORTGAGES AND THE FINANCIAL MARKET

All types of debt instruments are bought and sold in the ***financial market,*** which is made up of two components, the money market and the capital market. The ***money market*** involves transactions and instruments of short duration, normally one year or less. Longer-term transactions involving debt instruments for more than one year (along with stocks) make up the ***capital market.*** Corporate, government, consumer, and mortgage debts are major components of the financial market. Corporate and consumer debts are split about evenly between the money market and the capital market, whereas the mortgage market utilizes long-term instruments almost exclusively and thus is part of the capital market.

All debt instruments having real property as security are considered to be in the mortgage market. The primary lender originates mortgages and either holds them or sells them to a secondary lender. In either case, the primary lender usually continues to service the loan by collecting the monthly payments from the borrower and forwarding payments to the secondary holder, less a servicing fee.

When we think of marketing and markets we usually think of markets for products. We can, however, think of money as a product in the financial market. There is a supply of and a demand for money. When the demand for money exceeds the supply, the price—the interest rate charged for borrowing the money—tends to increase. When the supply exceeds the demand, interest rates decline. Owing to the complexity of the financial markets, the price of money is not easy for the consumer to comprehend. This lack of awareness stems also from the fact that the consumer is not continually involved in financial market activities on a day-to-day basis. Interest rates on some instruments may fluctuate widely and/or frequently, whereas the mortgage interest rates fixed by lenders may change much more slowly. Many operations of the federal government affect the "price" of money.

Individuals, businesses, and government participate in the financial markets. Each of these participants receives income and budgets expenditures. Typically, individuals receive more income than they spend, with the difference going into savings or investments. Individual savings tend to provide sources of loans for others, since businesses and governments tend to need more money than they receive. The dollar amount of a real estate purchase, however, often makes it necessary for an individual to borrow to buy a home. Mortgage borrowers thus compete with other borrowers for the available supply of funds. Overall, however, individuals are net savers and their savings provide a source of funds for lending.

DEMAND FOR FUNDS IN THE MORTGAGE MARKET

Demand for real estate mortgages comes from individual households, land subdividers and developers, home builders, businesses, and investors. Individuals desire funds to build, buy, or remodel homes or to borrow against presently owned property to finance children's education. This demand is affected by economic conditions, living styles, marriage rates, employment, and number of families that are moving. Individuals, businesses, and investors usually want long-term credit, whereas developers and builders require relatively short-term credit. Investors also seek mortgages on residential apartments, office buildings, and shopping centers. Businesses demand mortgage credit for the purchase of stores, warehouses, hotels, and restaurants, together with the associated trade fixtures.

FLOW OF FUNDS

The financial markets provide a means whereby funds flow from individuals and other net savers to persons needing to borrow money, including those borrowing against real estate. The position of the mortgage market within the overall financial market makes it necessary to comprehend the flow of funds within the financial market as a whole. In other words, we need to understand how money gets from the individual savers to the borrowers. In most cases, there are no direct dealings between the savers and borrowers. Individuals place money in financial institutions, such as banks, who in turn make loans to borrowers. Pension funds and insurance companies also receive money from individuals; this money can, in turn, be lent to earn interest. In general, many individuals deposit small amounts that are accumulated by the intermediary, such as a bank, for use in making loans in larger amounts. The intermediary develops the systems and procedures to formally handle both the deposits and the loans and to lessen the risks. Private individuals who wish to borrow money go directly to the intermediary or financial institution. The process of gathering in funds as deposits and then lending out the funds to borrowers is called *intermediation*. These interactions are shown in Figure 7–1.

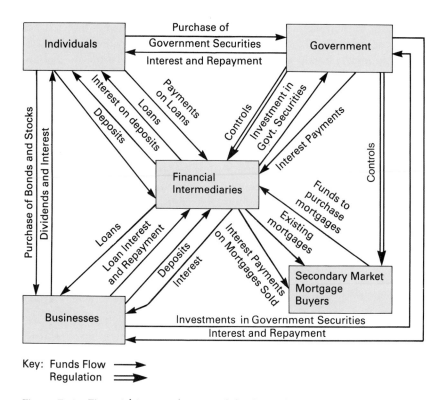

Key: Funds Flow ———➤
     Regulation ══➤

Figure 7–1 Financial intermediaries and the flow of funds

PRIMARY MORTGAGE MARKET

The *primary mortgage market* is comprised of borrowers who deal with banks and other institutional lenders or with others who originate mortgage loans. By definition, an *institutional lender* is a lender that meets two criteria: the institution accumulates deposits from individuals or businesses (such as savings accounts), pools the funds, and reinvests the funds in real estate mortgages or other loans or securities; and the institution conforms to state and/or federal regulations applicable to its charter.

Primary Mortgage Market Activities

The primary mortgage market deals with relationships between mortgage loan borrowers and lenders originating the loans. Some of the important activities primary lenders are involved with are included in the following discussion. The definitions often overlap; they are also not universally agreed upon.

Originating mortgage loans include the institutional lender's marketing activities to attract borrowers, contacts with potential borrowers, and the taking and processing of applications. Some primary lenders charge an *origination fee,* which is charged as a percentage of the face amount for loans completed. The term *origination* is sometimes used to include all activities related to bringing a loan into the lender's portfolio. The term may include only the solicitation to obtain mortgage loans and the taking of the loan application.

Loan processing includes the gathering and verification of information to enable the lender to either approve or disapprove the loan application. Loan approval is based on borrower credentials and property worth. It includes verification of creditworthiness and employment of the potential borrower. The processing of a loan is governed by state and federal regulations related to equal credit opportunity, fair credit reporting, kickbacks, truth-in-lending, and an elapsed time for the borrower to reconsider the agreement after signing. The person negotiating a loan for the lender is called the *loan correspondent,* who in some cases may later also service the loan. The papers, documents, and forms regarding a potential borrower and the property involved are referred to as a *loan submission.* When a loan has been accepted, the lender issues a *commitment letter* to the borrower, which permits the borrower to proceed with a purchase contract.

Underwriting, as used in primary lending, is the evaluation or analysis of the risks involved with a loan and the setting of an appropriate rate of return. In some cases it will be the determination as to whether a particular borrower and parcel of real estate meet a lender's minimum requirements. In other cases, a mortgage broker who originates a loan matches a potential mortgagor to the appropriate lender. The ratio of monthly payment to borrower income is often used as one criterion in the evaluation. Government agencies often specify minimum ratios.

Loan warehousing is the borrowing of funds by a mortgage broker on a short-term basis as necessary to fund the mortgage before it is sold to an investor or in the secondary market. Warehousing may involve the grouping of mortgages into a package, where the whole package is sold to the investor.

Closing of a loan is the settlement of a real estate transaction whereby the buyer takes the title; the seller gets his money; and the mortgage, note, and other documents are completed and signed.

Loan servicing is the collection of monthly payments, payment of taxes and insurance where appropriate, provision of annual interest expense and other data to the borrower, transmission of monies to secondary market lenders if appropriate, and the handling of foreclosures. A primary lender who sells a mortgage in the secondary market usually continues to service the loan for a fee paid by the secondary lender.

Deposit Insurance

The Federal Deposit Insurance Corporation (FDIC) was established in 1935 to insure bank deposits. The objective was to help stabilize the banking system following the financial collapse of the banking system in the early 1930s. The Federal Savings and Loan Insurance Corporation (FSLIC) was established later to insure deposits in savings and loan associations. Deposits are now insured up to $100,000 per account. National or state banks and savings and loans pay premiums based on a percentage of deposits and are subject to auditing and regulation.

SOURCES OF MORTGAGE MONEY IN THE PRIMARY MORTGAGE MARKET

Persons wanting mortgages have a variety of sources to which they can apply. The major sources of mortgage money are savings and loan associations, mutual savings banks, commercial banks, life insurance companies, mortgage companies, and pen-

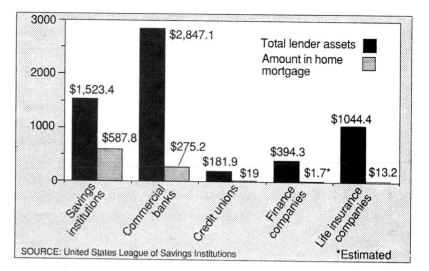

Figure 7–2 Lender assets and amount (in billions) in home mortgages for year-end 1987

sion funds, as well as individual lenders. Each of these organizations plays an important part as a source of mortgage money. Figure 7–2 shows that in 1987 savings institutions supplied more home mortgage money than all other lenders combined.

Savings and Loan Associations

Savings and loan associations (S&Ls) are private institutions that operate under state and federal regulations. There are over 5,000 state and federally chartered associations with combined assets of over $650 billion.

The purpose of organizing S&Ls is to encourage savings for home ownership. S&Ls are the second largest financial intermediary in the country. An *intermediary* accepts deposits from savers and uses the deposits to provide loans to borrowers. State and federal laws prescribe the standards for chartering new institutions, determine their operating procedures and constraints, and control the kinds of loans and investments that can be made.

Until the early 1960s, all savings accounts in S&Ls were of the passbook variety, and every account holder received the same rate of return, regardless of the size of the deposit or the length of time the deposit was held. The *certificate of deposit (CD)* was then introduced; it allowed thrift institutions to pay higher interest rates on larger savings accounts if the depositor agreed to leave the money invested for longer periods of time. By 1975, well over half the total deposits in thrift institutions were in certificates. In order to attract even more savings into the savings and loan industry, the *money market certificate (MMC)* was introduced. The yield on this certificate is tied to the twenty-six–week Federal Treasury Bill rate. The popularity of the CD and the MMC as alternatives to the lower-yielding passbook account is evidenced by the significant shift of savings into these higher-yielding instruments and out of passbook accounts.

In 1960, 100 percent of all savings accounts in all S&Ls were in passbook accounts. By 1975, only 43 percent of the savings accounts in S&Ls were passbook, while 57 percent were in higher-yielding CDs. By mid-1981, only 20 percent of all savings accounts were passbook, 40 percent were higher-yielding MMCs, and 40 percent were in various CDs.

Much of the money flowing into CDs and MMCs in the late 1970s and early 1980s came from funds within the S&L industry that were previously held in low-yielding passbook accounts. As a result, the overall cost of funds to the S&L business increased significantly from 6.32 percent in 1975 to an all-time high of 10.8 percent by mid-1981.

By 1978, the amount of new savings put into S&Ls had begun to slow down. Investors were looking elsewhere to place their funds into even more lucrative investments.

The S&L industry had been caught in a trap created by their thirty-year investment strategy of borrowing money on a short-term basis and lending money on a long-term basis at fixed rates. In earlier years, when interest rates were relatively stable and the cost of borrowing funds (passbook savings) was regulated, the S&L industry was dealing in known costs and its investment strategy worked fairly well. By 1981, with rapidly escalating interest rates, the S&L industry's overall *cost of funds* exceeded its overall *portfolio yield* by over 1 percent. In the early 1980s, S&Ls were failing at the fastest rate since the depression. In 1980, the *Federal Savings and Loan Insurance Corporation (FSLIC)* helped thirty troubled S&Ls work out mergers to prevent default. The FSLIC spent over $7 billion in 1981 to absorb the assets of failing institutions. The *Federal Home Loan Bank Board (FHLBB)* estimated that more than 75 percent of the associations operated in the red in 1981. Voluntary mergers of troubled S&Ls also increased.

Figure 7–3 shows the net annual savings flow of funds for S&Ls over a seven-year period. As can be seen, the first quarter of 1981 shows a $786 million outflow from S&Ls. Most outflow is attributable to investors moving their funds into high-yielding money-market mutual funds.

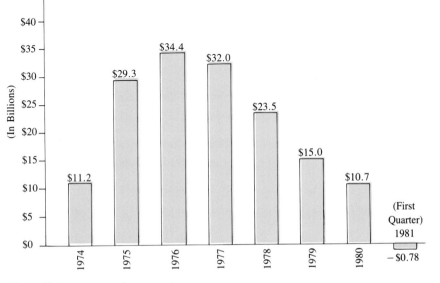

Figure 7–3   Net annual savings flow

Source: U. S. League of Savings Institutions

Changed Functions of Savings and Loan Associations

The *Depository Institutions Deregulation and Monetary Control Act of 1980* changed the role and functions of the S&Ls. Previously they had been specialized lending institutions and were, to a large extent, limited to making loans on improved real estate. Business and consumer loans were outside their scope, and the majority of their funds were invested in residential mortgages. Approximately one-half of all outstanding one- to four-family residence loans are with S&Ls. Although S&Ls are capable of making FHA and VA loans, most of their portfolio is made up of conventional loans. Typical S&L loans include:

- Construction loans on single-family homes, duplexes, fourplexes, condominiums, and cooperatives
- Permanent loans on the above-mentioned properties
- Short- and long-term loans on multifamily projects
- Short- and long-term loans on commercial and industrial properties
- Mobile home loans
- Loans on vacation homes

Prior to 1980, federally chartered S&Ls had to comply with a number of constraints that were removed by the Depository Institutions Deregulation and Monetary Control Act of 1980. In essence, the act allowed savings and loan associations to perform services similar to banks. The act

1. Allowed single-family and multifamily home loans up to a 90 percent loan-to-value ratio without dollar limitations on the amount of the loan
2. Removed geographical limitations on these loans
3. Permitted second mortgages up to the limitations of a 90 percent loan-to-value for all loans on a property
4. Permitted S&Ls to offer checking accounts, including interest-bearing checking accounts called *NOW (negotiated order of withdrawal) accounts*
5. Allowed the issuance of credit cards
6. Allowed investment in commercial paper and corporate debt securities, and the making of secured or unsecured personal loans up to a limit of 20 percent of the association's assets
7. Allowed consumer and commercial real estate loans up to 20 percent of assets
8. Allowed business and agricultural loans
9. Permitted an association to act as a trustee

The act also phased out Regulation Q, which allowed S&Ls to offer higher interest rates on deposits than banks. Over a period of six years, ceilings on savings account interest rates were abolished for all institutions. A further provision of the act allowed S&Ls the same access as banks to the Federal Reserve discount window. It also authorized the FSLIC to increase insurance on individual accounts up to $100,000.

The Garn-St. Germain Act of 1982 further restructured the thrift institutions and granted broader privileges to depository institutions as follows:

1. Federal thrift institutions may make business loans up to 10 percent of assets, consumer loans to 30 percent of assets, and leasing equipment loans up to 10 percent of assets.
2. Savings institutions are allowed to accept business and individual checking accounts.

3. Federal savings banks are allowed to hold up to 4 percent of assets in nonresidential mortgages.
4. HIFI (high-interest federal insurance) deposits with no interest rate ceilings are permitted.
5. Savings institutions are allowed some freedom in changing their names.
6. Interest rate differentials between thrifts and banks are discontinued.

In general, thrifts and banks become more alike.

Further S&L Problems in the 1980s

In response to thrifts' contention that they need to expand into other areas, such as loans for commercial real estate ventures, Congress passed laws allowing broader S&L operations.

In 1983, with falling interest rates and a booming Texas oil economy, thrifts poured billions of dollars (from government insured deposits) into real estate ventures. The precipitous fall of the Texas economy in 1984 resulted in declining property values and many loan defaults. In some cases, homeowners purposely defaulted on their own mortgage, walked away from the debt, and then bought a foreclosed property at a lower price and lower interest rate. These and other factors resulted in hundreds of insolvent thrifts nationwide. Only then did the Federal Home Loan Bank Board begin to inhibit lenient lending and accounting practices. In the face of increasing insolvencies, Congress allowed FSLIC to borrow more funds to close insolvent S&Ls. The Financing Corporation (FICO) was established in 1987 to help bail out the FSLIC. By 1989, the agency was consolidating insolvent institutions and attempting to sell them to investors. Bank and thrift failures over the past fifty years are shown in Figure 7–4. Federal government efforts continue to stabilize the S&L industry and to reduce future *default risks* (the possibility that a lender will not be

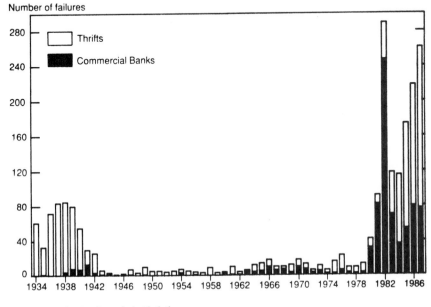

Figure 7–4 Bank and thrift failures

Source: Economic Report of the President, 1989

able to obtain repayment of the loan). The *Financial Institutions Reform, Recovery, and Enforcement Act of 1989* established the **Resolution Trust Corporation** to sell off sour loans and repossessed real estate. The law authorizes borrowing to shut down or merge more S&Ls and to buy up certificates of deposit issued by shaky thrifts to attract capital. The bill also increases the tangible capital requirements for S&Ls and provides for tougher criminal penalties for fraud. The Federal Home Loan Bank Board was dismantled and the **Savings Association Insurance Funds (SAIF)** were created to provide insurance for S&L deposits.

Mutual Savings Banks

Mutual savings banks started over 150 years ago in the industrialized northeastern part of the United States. Their purpose was to encourage savings by low- and moderate-income persons, especially factory workers. As the name implies, mutual savings banks are mutually owned; that is, there are no stockholders. The majority of their capital is in the form of demand deposits. Each mutual savings bank receives its charter from the state where it is located; therefore, regulations under which mutual savings banks operate vary considerably.

Today all mutual savings banks are located in eighteen states in the northeastern United States and in Puerto Rico. Approximately three-fourths of the total assets of all mutual savings banks are in Massachusetts and New York. Traditionally, savings banks operated under a less stringent lending policy than did S&Ls. Before 1950, lending policies restricted mutual savings banks to conventional mortgages within a geographical radius similar to that of S&Ls. As a result, mutual savings banks tended to invest more heavily in FHA and VA loans because, unlike conventional mortgage loans, these loans were not subject to the normal lending radius limitations and restrictions. Approximately 40 percent of the assets of savings banks are in FHA or VA loans and, of all single-family FHA and VA loans made, over half are originated by mutual savings banks. Nonetheless, with the geographic concentration of savings banks in the Northeast, the area often had an oversupply of funds. In 1950, laws were passed allowing out-of-state lending, thereby enabling lenders to move money from capital surplus areas to capital deficit areas across the country.

Today mutual savings bank loans comprise approximately 10 percent of all real estate mortgage loans, most of which are residential in nature. The loan-to-value ratio on conventional loans ranges from 60 to 90 percent. Some states have limitations on the maximum amount that can be borrowed on any one loan. Other limitations regarding mortgage terms and other factors vary from state to state.

Commercial Banks

Commercial banks are the largest of all lenders, in terms of both number of institutions and dollar value of outstanding loans. These include single-family, multifamily, and commercial mortgages. Their deposits are about four times greater than those of mutual savings banks, and they hold about 20 percent of the dollar volume of all real estate mortgages today. Commercial banks can be either state or federally chartered. State chartered banks are regulated by a state bank board and generally are given greater leeway on their lending practices than federally chartered banks. The latter are regulated by the Comptroller of Currency and Federal Reserve Board.

The deposits received by commercial banks are classified as either time or demand deposits. *Demand deposits* are withdrawable "on demand" and consequently cannot be used for long-term mortgages. ***Time deposits*** are expected to remain in the bank for a longer period of time, which may be from thirty days to thirty months. Since banks can expect to retain these deposits for set periods of time, they may be loaned to finance real estate. Since up to half of a bank's deposits are normally in demand deposits, commercial banks rarely have over 10 percent of their total deposits in mortgages. The remainder of the funds are in shorter-term business or consumer loans, and adequate reserves in marketable government obligations are retained.

Many commercial banks concentrate their lending efforts on short-term loans for construction. Generally, a mortgage banker originates or places a permanent loan with an institutional investor. In the interim, a construction loan is needed to finance the completion of the building project. Most commercial banks are willing to provide this interim financing if a firm commitment for the permanent loan has been obtained. This type of commitment is commonly referred to as an ***advance*** or ***forward commitment***. In other situations, a ***standby commitment*** may be used. The mortgage banker has obtained a commitment from a commercial bank to buy the mortgage at a substantial discount if the mortgage cannot be sold on more favorable terms to any other investor by the end of the commitment period. In other words, a commercial bank is "standing by " to purchase the permanent loan if necessary.

In some areas, commercial banks have developed strong mortgage departments and have become the dominant source of mortgage loans. In other parts of the country, the commercial banks usually purchase their mortgages from mortgage bankers rather than originating their own loans, thereby eliminating the need for a large, in-house mortgage department.

Lending Guidelines

In general, national banks were required to adhere to a number of loan guidelines prior to 1980. However, the Depository Institutions Deregulation and Monetary Control Act tends to homogenize all financial institutions; that is, it eliminates the essential differences in services between banks and savings and loan institutions. The act eliminated the interest rate limitations paid on passbook accounts and eliminated the ¼ point interest differential that S&Ls could pay on passbook accounts relative to banks.

The act also provided that commercial banks could lend up to a 90 percent loan-to-value ratio on first and second mortgages. It also provided that the Federal Reserve system would begin to charge both members and nonmembers for check clearing and other services. Furthermore, state usury limits on mortgage loans were preempted. Provisions of the act were discussed previously where they affected operations of S&Ls. As with prior deregulation in transportation and other areas, the small consumer is expected to benefit. In the long run some financial institutions will make out well, whereas others will be seriously hurt.

Life Insurance Companies

All life insurance companies are chartered under state laws and are regulated by the charter state as well as by other states in which they operate. Life insurance companies may be mutually owned by policyholders or may be stock companies privately owned by stockholders. The life insurance industry has assets in excess of $340 billion.

Their broad investment powers, coupled with their huge, relatively stable money resources, make life insurance companies a principal source of financing for commercial and multifamily mortgage financing. About 20 percent of the mortgages they hold are VA-guaranteed or FHA-insured. They are the most important source of financing for large, commercial real estate ventures.

The flow of premiums to life insurance companies on their policies is not subject to the same fluctuations as money held by most lenders. Consequently, life insurance companies have a more consistent availability of funds to be loaned for long terms. Approximately 40 percent of the life insurance industry's assets are invested in either real estate mortgages or in outright ownership of real estate.

The trend is for most life insurance companies to deal through mortgage companies and bankers when placing a mortgage loan rather than to operate their own lending offices. *Mortgage brokers* also package loan proposals for presentation to life insurance companies. Some small life insurance companies originate loans out of their home offices. The usual loan-to-value ratio for conventional loans placed by life insurance companies on residential property varies from 66⅔ to 80 percent.

Pension Funds

The first private pension fund was established by the American Express Agency in 1875. In the early 1900s, railroads and public utilities were developing their pension funds. In 1935, the civil service retirement system and the Old Age and Survivors Insurance Plan under the Social Security program were organized. Over the years, labor unions have bargained for and obtained employee pension fund programs in a wide variety of industries. Today pension funds have assets in excess of $1 trillion, and much of this is invested in mortgages.

Mortgage Bankers

Mortgage bankers (sometimes called *mortgage companies*) are primarily correspondent bankers for other lenders. They originate and service real estate loans for a fee, but usually do not hold them in their own portfolio. There are approximately 1,000 mortgage bankers today and they originate almost 20 percent of all new loans. As their name implies, they deal almost exclusively in mortgage loans. In addition to originating, selling, and servicing new loans, they often provide or arrange for interim financing on construction loans.

The correspondent nature of mortgage banking arose from the needs of life insurance companies. Most life insurance companies do not have their own mortgage loan department and do not originate their own mortgage loans; therefore, they purchase packages of mortgages from mortgage bankers. Today mortgage bankers originate, sell, and service both conventional and FHA-VA mortgage loans to life insurance companies, pension funds, and endowment funds, as well as to quasi-governmental agencies such as the *Federal National Mortgage Association (FNMA)* and the *Government National Mortgage Association (GNMA)*.

Other Sources of Mortgages

Savings and loan associations, commercial banks, mutual savings banks, and life insurance companies provide the bulk of funds for real estate mortgages. Pension funds, endowed institutions, direct governmental lending, real estate mortgage trusts

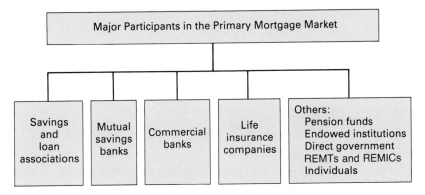

Figure 7–5   The primary mortgage market

(REMTs), real estate mortgage investment conduits (REMICs), and individuals are other sources that borrowers may use. REMTs and REMICs buy real estate mortgages whereas REITs (Chapter 3) purchase real property. These are summarized in Figure 7–5.

SECONDARY MORTGAGE MARKET

The secondary mortgage market consists of investors, lenders, or government agencies who buy and sell mortgages originated by primary lenders. It is essentially a market for the resale of existing loans originated in the primary mortgage market. The primary lender usually retains the function of servicing the loan for a fee and passes the amount collected on to the new owner of the mortgage.

The secondary mortgage market is usually thought of in connection with three agencies—FNMA, GNMA, and FHLMC—which are discussed in detail later. There are, however, some other parties who are active in the secondary market. The secondary market lender can either purchase a whole loan or purchase a *participation,* or part interest, in a loan. The latter case usually applies to larger projects where one lender cannot or will not carry the total loan. Figure 7–6 illustrates basic transactions in the mortgage market process.

In local market areas, the demand for mortgage money may not exactly equal the supply of funds available. If the supply and demand were always equal, there would be no need for the secondary market. In some areas the supply of funds is in excess,

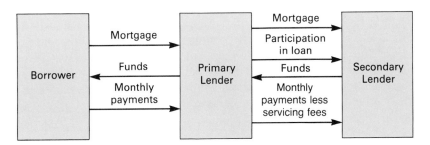

Figure 7–6   Basic transactions in the mortgage market

perhaps due to local recessionary conditions. In other areas where the population and construction are growing at rates faster than the U.S. average, there will be a shortage of funds to meet the higher demand for mortgages. The secondary market compensates for these differences.

Secondary Mortgage Market Activities

When funds become less available for mortgages in the private sector, the secondary credit agencies try to support the market through the purchase of existing mortgages from primary lenders. When the inflows into savings accounts are strong, monies tend to provide sufficient funds for mortgage lending. When inflows to savings accounts decrease, insufficient funds are available for mortgage lending. In cases where there is an actual outflow of funds from savings institutions *(disintermediation)*, it is even more necessary for support from the secondary market. Through the purchase of existing mortgages from banks and savings and loan associations by the secondary agencies, additional funds for new mortgages become available.

Continuing changes in the mortgage market reflect changing needs and fluctuations in the economy. The substantial growth of the secondary market has been one of the most pronounced changes. The emergence of and creation of a futures market in mortgage-backed securities are two major developments.

Selling Mortgages in the Secondary Mortgage Market

Why or under what conditions would a primary lender tend to sell mortgages it has originated? First, if the primary lender has insufficient funds to meet the need or demand for local mortgage loans, existing loans can be sold in the secondary market to obtain additional funds. A lender may also desire to enhance its image in the community by bringing in funds to loan in periods of tight money, perhaps in response to the needs of local builders and real estate brokers who depend on mortgage money availability for their livelihood.

Second, a primary lender can often handle bigger projects, such as a large building or a subdivision, by obtaining loan participation from other institutions. In some cases, commitments from FNMA or others may supply the additional funds. Sometimes larger commitments are needed for low- to moderate-income housing, where the projects are large.

Third, primary lenders who are members of FHLB (Federal Home Loan Bank) or FSLIC (Federal Savings and Loan Insurance Corporation) are required to diversify their funds so ratios of loan dollars to total assets and percentage limits on certain types of loans are maintained. By selling existing loans in the secondary markets, the primary lender can keep within the required limits.

As a fourth reason, sale of mortgages in the secondary market can result in increased profits. The primary lender usually continues to service the sold mortgages for a fee and can then earn new fees and service charges on loans originated with the new money. In some cases, an institution's loan portfolio can be expanded or diversified more easily through secondary market purchases. An investor can select mortgages to obtain the security and diversification wanted.

Finally, a primary lender usually originates loans only in the local area. By selling local loans, the lender can use the funds to purchase loans from other areas and thus geographically diversify its holdings.

A mortgage sold by a primary lender in the secondary market is usually sold at a discount or an amount less than the face value. The originator, however, usually retains the servicing of the loan for a fee ranging from one-quarter to one-half of 1 percent of the balance of the mortgage. A mortgage with a $50,000 balance, for example, would provide a yearly fee of $250, at a rate of one-half of 1 percent. The primary lender would then be free to place a new loan from the proceeds of the sale in the secondary market. A rule adopted by FNMA in 1989 requires that the primary lender selling a mortgage to a secondary lender must notify the mortgage holder of the name, address, and toll-free number of the new mortgage holder. The new mortgage holder must also send a confirmation of the acquisition. This rule came about because in the past mortgagors have been confused about where to send payments.

Why Primary Lenders Buy Mortgages in the Secondary Mortgage Market

Although government-related organizations are the main buyers in the secondary market, mortgages also can be purchased by institutions, such as banks, which are mainly primary lenders.

Certain conditions are conducive to the purchase of mortgages by a particular bank. Local rates may be very low, either due to lack of demand or because of local usury laws. Institutions in areas where rates are lower than the national average can purchase mortgages from higher-interest-rate areas and thus secure an improved rate of return on their money. The lending institutions may also want to diversify their holdings by including loans from different geographical areas. Or an institution may encounter excess liquidity related to increased local deposits or decreased local demand for loans. Institutions, normally primary lenders, can purchase mortgages in the secondary market and thereby obtain income from their excess funds.

Secondary Mortgage Market Transactions

When mortgages are bought and sold, the market price of the loan depends on the current market interest rates. The *market interest rate* for mortgages is the interest rate at which new mortgage loans are being made at that time. Time value of money calculations are also necessary to evaluate the present value of the loan.

The interest rate on a loan is called the *contract interest rate* and is negotiated between lender and borrower at the time the loan is originated. When the market interest rate is higher than the interest rate on an existing mortgage loan, the loan will sell at a *discount,* for less than the loan balance. The term *discounting* means to buy or sell, or offer to buy or sell, at a price below the loan balance. Conversely, if the market interest rate is lower than the interest rate on an existing loan, the loan will sell on the secondary market at a *premium.* A loan selling at a premium will sell for more than the loan balance.

A mortgage discount or premium can be expressed in terms of dollars, percentage, or points. Assume that a loan with a balance of $100,000 is sold for $95,000. The dollar discount would be $5,000, and

$$\text{Percent discount} = \frac{\text{Dollar discount}}{\text{Current loan balance}} \times 100\%$$

$$= \frac{\$5,000 \times 100\%}{\$100,000} = 5\%$$

155

This discount can also be expressed as 5 points, since a percent discount equals 1 point. Quotations or calculations are often made using basis points. A **basis point** is one-hundredth of a point. For example, a loan selling at 150 basis points off face value would be at 1.5 percent discount. If the loan with a face value of $100,000 were to sell at $104,000, we would say it is selling for a premium of $4,000, or a premium of 4 percent.

If a primary lender sells a mortgage in the secondary market, how does that action affect the original borrower? Essentially, there is no effect. The mortgage contract specifies the interest rate and payment procedures, which are not changed by the sale. Each party will continue to abide by the terms. Usually the originator, or primary lender, will continue to service the loan so payments will still be made as before.

Participation in the Secondary Mortgage Market by Commercial Banks

A number of additional considerations influence a commercial bank's decision to participate in the secondary mortgage market as a seller or buyer. A bank desires to continue servicing its customers or to acquire new customers to increase its total volume of business. The bank can acquire the money to continue to service these customers with all types of loans by selling mortgages in the secondary market when it is short of funds. Banks also must adhere to regulations governing the percentages of their assets that can be loaned and the ratios between various types of loans. By buying and selling loans in the secondary market, the ratios can be maintained without cutting off any particular types of loans to customers. Thus, the bank can maintain its function as a full-service bank at all times.

Banks earn origination fees on new mortgages and service fees by servicing mortgages sold to others in the secondary market. Careful management of these activities earns greater profits for the bank. Banks also provide services in-house or are dependent upon others such as appraisers, title companies, and attorneys. It is important to the bank to keep its performers of these functions busy. In addition, some special government programs make funds available to banks qualified to be regular participants in the secondary market. Without the bank's regular participation, the special program funds would not be available to customers.

Mortgage-Backed Securities

A **mortgage-backed security (MBS)** is a certificate issued by a holder of mortgages, usually in the secondary market. Mortgage-backed securities can be divided into two categories of pass-through securities: the investor holding the security receives principal and interest payments on a monthly basis, or the investor receives interest on a quarterly or annual basis with the principal due at maturity of the bond. Funds are paid to the primary lender and passed through the secondary lender to the investor. Some secondary holders guarantee the payments. In other cases, mortgages in the pool backing the security are insured by a private mortgage insurer.

A mortgage-backed security is different from a real estate bond because it is backed by a pool of mortgages instead of one or more mortgages. Furthermore, an MBS issued by a federally sponsored credit agency such as the Government National Mortgage Association is guaranteed by the government. Thus, the payments received by the holders of the securities do not depend on specific mortgages.

A high proportion of mortgage-backed securities are guaranteed by the government. The collateral can be either FHA, VA, or conventional mortgages, which are issued by banks or savings and loan associations.

A mortgage-backed security allows an investor to put funds into real estate without direct purchase of the property or a mortgage. It provides a fixed-income investment that pays more than a treasury bill, but still has a government guarantee. Brokerage houses offer unit investment trusts whereby an investor can participate with a $1,000 minimum. Units can then be sold or purchased on the open market. This permits the investor to obtain a higher yield without the greater risk and high administrative costs of directly originating and servicing mortgages. The yields, however, are not as high as the mortgages themselves. Those investors with current mortgage holdings can also diversify by acquiring mortgage-backed securities.

ROLE OF THE GOVERNMENT IN THE SECONDARY MORTGAGE MARKET

There is a need for a national mortgage market and a smooth flow of mortgage funds across the various submarkets. The government has supported the secondary mortgage market through several agencies to accomplish this need.

Federal National Mortgage Association (FNMA, "Fannie Mae")

Since its organization in 1938, the Federal National Mortgage Association (FNMA) has been the largest single holder of residential mortgages. It was organized primarily to establish a market for FHA-insured mortgages. An FHA-insured mortgage program had been in effect since 1934; however, the primary lenders were encountering difficulties in selling their holdings to secondary investors. This meant that the originators were short of funds to make additional mortgage loans.

In 1938 an administrative directive established the National Mortgage Association of Washington as a wholly owned subsidiary of the *Reconstruction Finance Corporation (RFC)*. This was soon changed to the FNMA and was referred to as *Fannie Mae.* It was authorized to purchase FHA-insured mortgages from all qualified sellers and also to grant direct loans for construction of rental housing. In 1948 FNMA was also authorized to purchase VA-guaranteed loans under the provisions of the Servicemen's Readjustment Act of 1944.

In 1954, FNMA was rechartered by Congress and allowed to sell mortgages as well as buy them. After being reorganized into a corporate structure, common stock was issued to dealers participating in FNMA programs and preferred stock sold to the U.S. Treasury. Under the new charter FNMA did not make direct loans. Purchases in the secondary market were discounted rather than being at par value as before, and the primary lenders continued to service the mortgages for a 0.5 percent fee. Under the new charter, the FNMA was also authorized to

1. Establish secondary mortgage market functions for FHA and VA loans
2. Establish or improve distribution of funds for real estate financing
3. Manage and liquidate mortgages acquired by FNMA prior to 1954
4. Establish *special assistance functions (SAFs)* to supervise housing loans created under public assistance programs

157

FNMA was authorized to establish its own standards for acceptability of the mortgages it would purchase. In some cases mortgages were higher than the FHA or VA minimum standards. Under the charter of 1954, FNMA was considered to be a quasi-government organization with the objective of operating at a profit.

FNMA was changed into a private corporation by the Housing and Urban Development Act of 1968. The existing stock held by the government was redeemed and common stock sold to the public. FNMA common stock is currently traded on the New York Stock Exchange. FNMA was intended as a profit-making enterprise and was subject to federal income taxes. It is, however, still subject to some governmental supervision by the Secretary of HUD and the Secretary of the Treasury when issuing securities. The Emergency Housing Act of 1970 allowed FNMA to purchase conventional mortgages. Figure 7–7 shows the composition of its mortgage portfolio, where intermediate-term mortgages are those not exceeding twenty years.

FNMA Organization and Procedures

A fifteen-member Board of Directors runs the Federal National Mortgage Association. Three members are elected by the stockholders. FNMA is set up in a manner similar to that of a private corporation and has a chief executive officer, president, and other officers. In addition, an FNMA Advisory Council has members from banks and other leaders in housing, home financing, and related organizations. The purpose of the Advisory Council is to bring new points of view from outside sources related to FNMA policies and procedures. FNMA publishes financial statements, again as any other corporation. FNMA raises money through the sale of bonds and mortgage-backed securities.

A procedure called the Free Market System Auction is used by FNMA to buy mortgages. Banks, savings and loan associations, insurance companies, or mortgage bankers send in bids offering to sell mortgages. The auctions are usually held bi-weekly on Mondays; FNMA then reviews the bids and decides how much it will commit at that time.

A seller may also submit a noncompetitive bid and be assured of getting a commitment at the average yield that FNMA accepts at that day's auction. In either of the above procedures, the primary lender must agree to continue servicing the mortgages.

Government National Mortgage Association (GNMA, "Ginnie Mae")

With the splitting of the Federal National Mortgage Association into two entities in 1968, Fannie Mae was allowed to concentrate on its primary function of maintaining an active secondary market for mortgages and was relieved of its two secondary responsibilities by the newly formed Government National Mortgage Association (GNMA) within the Department of Housing and Urban Development.

GNMA has three major activities. First, the *mortgage-backed securities (MBS)* program increases the available mortgage credit for federally underwritten mortgages. Second, the *special assistance functions (SAFs)* provide previously unavailable financing for low-income families and counteract declines in housing construction. The third activity is the responsibility for administration and liquidation of federally owned mortgages taken over from FNMA. The power to purchase conventional and government-backed mortgages on an emergency basis lapsed on October

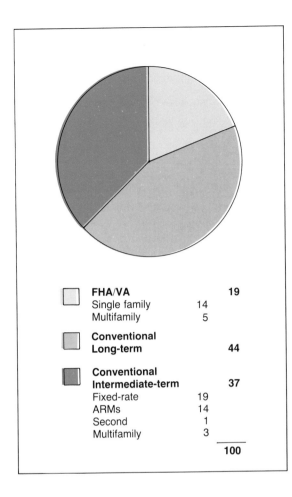

Figure 7–7   FNMA portfolio
composition as of Dec. 31, 1987,
in percent

Source: FNMA 1987 Annual Report

THE MORTGAGE
MARKET:
INSTITUTIONS
AND AGENCIES

FHA/VA		**19**
Single family	14	
Multifamily	5	
Conventional Long-term		**44**
Conventional Intermediate-term		**37**
Fixed-rate	19	
ARMs	14	
Second	1	
Multifamily	3	
		100

1, 1981. In any fiscal year, GNMA attempts to match its mortgage sales and purchases to minimize impact on the federal budget.

Under the mortgage-backed securities program, FHA-approved lenders (mainly mortgage bankers) issue mortgage-backed pass-through securities sometimes called *Ginnie Maes*. GNMA provides a guarantee to the purchaser of the security that timely payments of the scheduled monthly interest and principal will be received as well as the principal recovered. If the homeowners fail to make timely payments on their mortgages, the issuers—primary lenders—of the securities must advance the due amounts to the security holders. The GNMA guarantee is backed by the U.S. government so its securities are as safe and liquid as Treasury securities. The original issuer is responsible to service the mortgage.

Since its inception in 1970, the MBS program has been credited with helping to increase and stabilize the overall supply of mortgage credit. It also reduces credit cost by making funds that normally are restricted to the securities and bond markets flow into residential mortgages. Previously the primary mortgage market has been geographically limited, with local lenders satisfying the needs of local borrowers. The MBS program brought the resources of the national securities market to the secondary mortgage market. The result has been to increase the flow of funds from the securities market to the residential mortgage market and also to cause flow of funds from capital-surplus regions of the United States to capital-short areas.

From 1954 to 1968 FNMA handled *special assistance programs*. Congress cited two purposes when the SAF programs were originally started.

1. To provide financing of selected mortgages from programs designated to provide housing for segments of the national population unable to obtain adequate housing under regular programs
2. To provide financing for mortgages as a means of slowing or stopping a decline in home building activities

In 1968 the SAF programs were transferred to GNMA, and are often referred to as *Tandem programs* because originally they were joint GNMA-FNMA programs. Through the Tandem programs, GNMA assures builders and developers that permanent financing will be available for an approved project. GNMA provides a commitment to purchase FHA-insured, multifamily mortgages that meet the eligibility criteria at below-market interest rate. With this commitment, a builder or developer is better able to secure interim construction financing because the permanent financing is assured. GNMA will sometimes pay an above-market price, which is more than a private investor would be willing to pay. This results in a lower cost of the residential financing, making it possible for developers to build these projects.

A three-member Mortgage Distribution Board approves all sales of mortgage securities by GNMA. One objective is to match the volume of sales with the volume of purchases to minimize the effect of any GNMA program on the federal budget. Most sales are handled through bimonthly auctions.

The Federal Home Loan Bank (FHLB) System

The *Federal Home Loan Bank (FHLB)* system was created by Congress in the midst of the financial crisis of 1932. The *FHLB system* is similar to the Federal Reserve system. It is composed of a federal home loan bank board, twelve regional banks, and member institutions. All federally chartered savings and loan associations are required by law to belong to the system. Qualified state chartered savings and loan associations, mutual savings banks, and life insurance companies may join voluntarily and be insured by FSLIC. The primary purpose of the FHLB is to provide its member institutions with a line of credit to meet the changing demands for mortgage money in their local areas and to supplement the lending resources of institutions in capital-deficit areas by helping to shift funds from capital-surplus areas.

Lastly, and most important, the system ties the mortgage-lending institutions to the capital markets through the efforts of its subsidiary, the Federal Home Loan Mortgage Corporation ("Freddie Mac"). The FHLB system regulates and oversees its members. It does not originate loans to home buyers, but rather acts as a conduit to provide loanable funds to member institutions.

Federal Home Loan Mortgage Corporation ("Freddie Mac")

The *Federal Home Loan Mortgage Corporation (FHLMC)* was established in 1970 to create a secondary mortgage market for conventional mortgages. FHLMC is called *Freddie Mac* and is a private corporation owned by the Federal Home Loan Bank system. It buys, sells, and pools conventional mortgages and sells bonds or other instruments to investors with the mortgages as security.

Freddie Mac attempts to sell most of its assets in the form of pass-through securities. Investors purchase these directly from Freddie Mac or through brokers. Investors can also purchase whole loans, participation certificates, or bonds backed by mortgages. The advantages to investors are an increased effective yield at a minimized risk along with a regular flow of funds without the administrative burden of holding real estate loans directly. This provides additional funds so Freddie Mac can purchase additional mortgages. The Freddie Mac Collateralized Mortgage Obligation (CMO) was introduced in 1983 to offer additional investment incentives, under which interest payments are deferred and added to principal.

FHLMC provides liquidity and capital for the mortgage market by purchasing mortgages from the original lender, such as savings and loan institutions. Competitive auctions are held in which lenders submit telephone offers for review by FHLMC. If accepted, loan packages are delivered to a regional office to ascertain that the credit information on the borrower and the appraised property meet FHLMC guidelines. For acceptable loans, the funds are transferred to the original lender in exchange for the mortgages. In some cases lenders prefer to take *participation certificates (PCs)* in exchange for the mortgages. The original lender continues to service the loans by collecting the monthly payments and remitting them along with monthly reports to FHLMC.

The Freddie Mac *guaranteed mortgage certificate (GMC)* is more of a bond-type instrument and was first issued in 1975. It was originally intended for pension funds and other investors who are restricted to instruments that pay semiannual interest, return the principal at maturity, and are fully backed by FHLMC. GMCs are issued in amounts of $100,000, $500,000, and $1,000,000. The GMC gives the institutional investor many of the attributes of corporate bonds and fewer of the administrative problems of mortgages.

FHLMC Operations

Several other aspects of FHLMC activities are important to an understanding of Freddie Mac. Some of these are described as follows:

1. FHLMC will purchase interest in conventional multifamily mortgages in the same way as they purchase single-family interests.
2. In 1981, FHLMC introduced a program to create a secondary market for adjustable rate mortgages (ARMs). Uniform documents for ARMs were developed.
3. In 1981, FHLMC started the first nationwide secondary market for home improvement loans.
4. By purchasing mortgages in deficit areas, FHLMC recycles funds to that area.
5. In mid-1982, Freddie Mac started to deal in *growing-equity mortgages (GEMs)*.

The 1989 S&L bailout bill made changes in FHLMC to make it more like FNMA.

OTHER GOVERNMENT PROGRAMS

The Farm Credit System (FCS), established in 1917, is comprised of Farm Credit Banks (which lend directly to farmers) and Banks for Cooperatives (which lend to farmer-owned cooperatives). Considerable publicity has accompanied the plight of the farmers in the 1980s. A farmer who mortgaged property when prices were high was confronted with values dropping below the mortgage balance by the mid-1980s, a period of unfavorable prices for farm products. In 1988 Congress established the Financial Assistance Corporation (FAC) to help bail out the FCS.

Federal Land Banks make first mortgages to farmers and ranchers through local Federal Land Bank Associations. Loans can also be made on first mortgages or single-family homes in rural areas. These *rural areas* are defined to include towns or villages with populations not exceeding 2,500. The Federal Land Bank Association can make loans to buy, build, remodel, improve, repair, or refinance a house. Properties are carefully evaluated as security, and loans cannot exceed 85 percent of the appraised value of the real estate.

The *Farmers Home Administration (FmHA)* was created in 1946 by the Farmers Home Administration Act. The act provided the Farmers Home Administration with the authority to insure or make loans to farmers unable to obtain loans, such as for housing, elsewhere. In 1961 authority was granted to provide loans for water, sewer, and waste disposal. The Federal Housing Act of 1961 made rural nonfarm residents eligible for FmHA housing loans. In 1962 the services were expanded to include loans to finance low-rent apartment projects for senior citizens living in rural areas. The definition of *rural areas* has gradually changed so that by 1974 it included towns with a population up to 20,000. The FmHA was also authorized to make loans on mobile homes and condominiums. FmHA has thus become a primary housing agency for nonmetropolitan areas.

SUMMARY

The varying risks involved in financing different types of real estate in localized markets across the United States have hampered the development of a national mortgage market. However, the federal government has been instrumental in creating new and better means of mortgage financing and making mortgage funds more available to purchasers through governmentally guaranteed, insured, or subsidized programs. Two of the most important of these are the FHA and the VA programs.

In addition, the Federal National Mortgage Association (FNMA), Government National Mortgage Association (GNMA), and the Federal Home Loan Mortgage Corporation (FHLMC) operate in the secondary mortgage market to ensure a smooth flow of funds back into the primary market so that lenders have sufficient loanable funds to finance the housing demand.

The purchaser of real estate is able to obtain a mortgage loan from any one of several institutions across the country. The primary sources are savings and loan associations, mutual savings banks, commercial banks, and life insurance companies.

TERMS AND CONCEPTS

You can check your understanding of these terms against the glossary or by review in this chapter.

Basis point
Capital market
Certificate of deposit (CD)
Closing
Commercial bank
Commitment
Contract interest rate
Cost of funds
Default risk
Demand deposit
Depository Institutions Deregulation and Monetary Control Act of 1980
Discount
Discounting
Disintermediation
Farmers Home Administration (FmHA)
Federal Home Loan Bank Board (FHLBB)
Federal Home Loan Mortgage Corporation (FHLMC)
Federal Land Bank
Federal National Mortgage Association (FNMA)

Federal Savings and Loan Insurance Corporation (FSLIC)
FHLB system
Financial market
Forward commitment
Government National Mortgage Association (GNMA)
Growing-equity mortgage
Guaranteed mortgage certificate
Institutional lender
Intermediary
Intermediation
Loan correspondent
Loan processing
Loan servicing
Loan submission
Loan warehousing
Market interest rate
Money market
Money market certificate
Mortgage
Mortgage-backed security (MBS)
Mortgage banker
Mortgage broker
Mortgage company

Mortgagee
Mortgagor
Mutual savings bank
NOW accounts
Origination
Origination fee
Participation
Participation certificate
Portfolio yield
Premium
Primary lenders
Primary mortgage market
Reconstruction Finance Corporation
Resolution Trust Corporation
Savings and loan association
Savings Association Insurance Funds
Secondary mortgage market
Special assistance function
Standby commitment
Tandem program
Time deposit
Underwriting

What are the differences or relationships, if any, between the following?

Fannie Mae, Ginnie Mae, and Freddie Mac
Intermediation and Disintermediation
Money market and Capital market

Portfolio yield and Cost of funds
Primary mortgage market and Secondary mortgage market

S&Ls and Mutual savings banks
Time deposits and Demand deposits

PROBLEMS

7-1. Explain, in general, how the secondary mortgage market functions.

7-2. What is the relationship between the primary and secondary mortgage markets?

7-3. How can the Federal Reserve influence the availability and cost of credit?

7-4. Why do you think the government allowed FNMA and FHLMC to become private corporations?

7-5. Complete or check the appropriate spaces in Figure 7–8 to indicate the functions of each of the agencies listed.

7-6. What are the provisions of the Depository Institutions Deregulation and Monetary Control Act of 1980? Discuss its impact on (a) banks and (b) savings and loan associations.

7-7. As a board member of an S&L, what would be some of your responsibilities?

7-8. Discuss the impact of the Garn-St. Germain Act on thrift institutions.

	Full Name and Nickname	Insure Deposits	Make Direct Loans	Operate in Secondary Markets	Insure and Guarantee Loans	Special Assistance Functions	Market Stimulation	Sell Mortgage Securities
GNMA								
FHLMC								
FNMA								
FHA								
VA								
FHLB								
FDIC								
FSLIC								
FmHA								
FLB								

Figure 7–8

SUPPLEMENTARY READINGS

Bellavance, Russell C. *Real Estate Law*. St. Paul: West, 1979. Chapter 8.

Britton, James A., and Kerwood, Lewis O. *Financing Income Producing Real Estate, A Theory and Casebook*. New York: McGraw-Hill, 1977.

Brueggman, William B., and Stone, Leo D. *Real Estate Finance,* 8th ed. Homewood, Ill.: Irwin, 1989.

Cummings, Jack. *Complete Guide to Real Estate Financing,* Englewood Cliffs, N.J.: Prentice-Hall, 1978.

Epley, Donald R., and Miller, James A. *Basic Real Estate Finance and Investments,* 3rd ed. New York: Wiley, 1988.

Findley, A. Chapman. *Real Estate Portfolio Analysis*. Lexington, Mass.: Lexington Books, 1983.

FNMA Annual Report. Washington, D.C. (yearly).

Freddie Mac Annual Report. Washington, D.C. (yearly).

GNMA Annual Report. Washington, D.C. (yearly).

Institute of Financial Education. *Mortgage Lending Principles and Practices,* 3rd ed. Chicago, 1978.

Johnson, Ross H., and Henderson, Thomas P. *Real Estate Finance*. Columbus, OH: Merrill, 1985.

Maisel, Sherman J., and Roulac, Stephen E. *Real Estate Investment and Finance*. New York: McGraw-Hill, 1976.

Santi, Albert. *Questions and Answers for FHA, VA, and Conventional Loans*. Memphis, TN: Mortgage Techniques, 1987.

Shenkel, William M. *Real Estate Finance*. Dallas: Business Publications, 1988.

Sirmans, C. F. *Real Estate Finance,* 2nd ed. New York: McGraw-Hill, 1989.

Sirota, David. *Essentials of Real Estate Finance,* 4th ed. Chicago: Real Estate Education Company, 1986.

Warner, Arthur. *Real Estate Finance*. Reston, Va.: Reston, 1985.

Weidemer, John P. *Real Estate Finance,* 5th ed. Reston, Va.: Reston, 1987.

CHAPTER 8
Instruments of Finance

The primary source of debt financing in real estate is the mortgage. Generally, a mortgage involves two instruments, the mortgage and a note; however, a bond is used in some states rather than a note. This chapter describes the numerous mortgages that are available today, along with a detailed explanation of the various clauses and covenants found in the typical mortgage.

In several states, the ***deed of trust*** (or ***trust deed***) is used frequently instead of the mortgage. The deed of trust serves the same purpose as the mortgage; however, the deed of trust involves three parties instead of two, as illustrated in Figure 8–1. The borrower (trustor) executes the deed of trust, which conveys the property to a third party (the trustee). The title that the borrower conveys to the trustee is referred to as a *naked* or *bare title,* and *true title* rests with the borrower. The title held by the trustee is limited to what is required to carry out the terms of the trust. Referring to Figure 8–1, we see that when a note has been repaid in full under a mortgage, the lender cancels the note and provides the borrower with a mortgage release. The borrower would then record the release to give "public notice" that the mortgage has been paid and no longer encumbers the title to the property. With a deed of trust, the lender sends the trustee the deed of trust, the note, and a request for reconveyance. At this point, the trustee cancels the note and

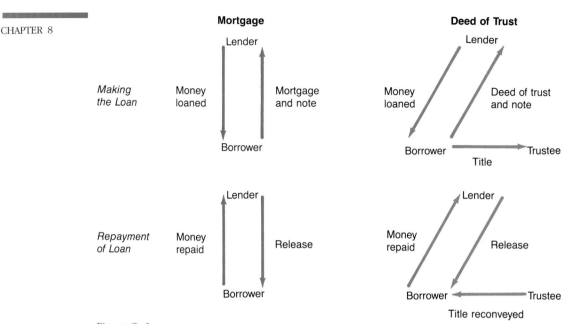

Figure 8–1   Mortgage compared to a deed of trust

provides the borrower with a reconveyance deed, which reconveys title back to the borrower. Again, the borrower records the reconveyance deed to provide "public notice" to the world that she now has unencumbered title to the property.

If the borrower defaults under a deed of trust, the lender delivers the deed of trust to the trustee and requests her to sell the property and pay off the delinquent note. The trustee is empowered to sell the property without a foreclosure proceeding because of the ***power of sale*** clause in the deed of trust.

The primary advantage of deeds of trust is that the lender can take possession immediately of properties in default. This prevents the defaulting borrower from damaging the property or fleeing with the rents. Since the trustee holds title and is empowered to sell the delinquent property, the foreclosure process is quicker and less expensive than with mortgages. Lastly, once the sale has occurred, most states do not provide for a statutory right of redemption to the borrower, which would allow her to redeem the property after foreclosure upon payment of all arrears. This precludes additional delays in the foreclosure process.

The remainder of this chapter discusses mortgage requirements, classifications of mortgages including many new creative financing methods, and remedies available to the lender upon default. The reader should note, however, that the material is pertinent to both mortgages and deeds of trust.

MORTGAGES

The ***mortgage*** is a contract between the ***mortgagor*** (borrower) and the ***mortgagee*** (lender) that pledges a specific parcel of property as security for a debt. The mortgage contract is not fully standardized but rather can be adapted to fit the needs of a variety of lender and borrower situations. The mortgage contract refers to the note (or bond) and the debt. It also lists the rights of the mortgagee and the responsibilities of the mortgagor arising from the debt. Both a debt and a pledge of property must be present for a mortgage to exist. The mortgage follows the debt and exists for the life of the debt. If the debt is paid or becomes unenforceable, the mortgage is *defeated* and the borrower obtains a title unencumbered by the mortgage.

The Note

The *note* is a contract that gives evidence of the debt. The person who mortgages property incurs a personal liability to repay the debt. Essentially, a general lien against all the debtor's property exists until the note is paid off. As a result, upon the default of the debtor, the creditor may obtain a deficiency judgment against other assets of the debtor if the foreclosure sale does not bring sufficient proceeds to cover the debt. Occasionally, however, the debtor and creditor may agree that the specific property pledged in the mortgage is the sole security for the debt, in which case deficiency judgments could not be obtained. Some states do not allow deficiency judgments.

The Pledged Property

In general, any interest in real estate that can be sold or assigned can also be mortgaged. Personal property also may be mortgaged by means of a *chattel mortgage*. A relatively new concept in real estate financing is the use of a *package mortgage,* which combines a loan on real estate with a loan on personal property such as furniture and appliances. Whatever the type of mortgage used, the pledged property should be adequately identified by a legal description, if real estate, or by serial number if personal property.

History of the Mortgage

Real estate has been used as security for loans for centuries. The concept of mortgages originated in England around the fourteenth century. The earliest mortgage was actually a deed of the property to the lender with a provision for return of the property to the borrower upon payment of the debt. If the borrower defaulted on the debt, the pledged security was lost to the lender without need of a foreclosure sale. In addition, the borrower still remained liable for the debt. Although by law the lender was entitled to take possession of the property at the time the mortgage was signed, he usually allowed the borrower to keep possession. This early interpretation of mortgage law fostered many abuses among lenders. It was common for lenders actually to encourage default, thereby obtaining absolute ownership of the mortgaged property. Many borrowers who felt that they were unjustly deprived of their property petitioned the king for relief. In cases of extreme hardship, the king would give the borrowers a chance to redeem their property upon payment of the delinquent obligation. Thus, the *equity of redemption* was born around 1625.

With the equity of redemption operating in favor of the borrower, the lender found himself in an untenable position. There was no time limit within which the borrower had to exercise his right of redemption. The lender was forced to reconvey the property to the borrower whenever he paid the delinquent debt. This obvious inequity was eventually eliminated when the courts began allowing the lender to bring suit against the borrower to cut off or foreclose his equity of redemption after a stated period of time, usually from six months to two years. This action is known as *strict foreclosure* and is still used today to some extent. The more common practice today is *foreclosure by sale.* The pledged property is sold at public auction, and the proceeds are used to pay off the debt. Any sale proceeds in excess of the debt are turned over to the borrower. The foreclosure by sale also acts to foreclose or cut off the equity of redemption. Some states have passed a *statutory right of redemption,* which allows the borrower to redeem her property within a period of time after the foreclosure sale. The time within which an individual is able to exercise her statutory right of redemption varies from state to state, but it is usually one to two years.

Three Theories of Mortgages

As the mortgage law evolved in England over the years, different schools of thought developed and have given rise to three different mortgage theories in the United States today.

Title Theory

States that recognize and practice the *title theory* of mortgage law require that title and possession of the mortgaged property transfer to the lender upon execution of the mortgage. In title theory states, a *defeasance clause* is included in the mortgage contract. This double-edged provision allows the borrower to defeat the mortgage and reacquire possession and ownership upon the full payment of the debt. On the other hand, if the borrower defaults, her rights are automatically terminated and the defeasance clause allows the lender to retain title to the property. In some states the title theory has been modified to allow the borrower to remain in possession of the mortgaged property as long as she abides by the terms of the mortgage contract. Fifteen states along the East Coast use the title theory.

Lien Theory

States that recognize and practice the *lien theory* of mortgage law hold that the mortgage, when executed, merely creates a lien in favor of the lender, and the borrower retains both possession and title. Again, the equity of redemption allows the delinquent borrower the right to redeem the property at any time prior to foreclosure by paying off the debt. The borrower also has the opportunity to redeem her property after foreclosure in those states having a statutory right of redemption. Lien theory is practiced in thirty-two states.

Intermediate Theory

Four states have adopted a mortgage theory that combines the title theory and lien theory. This *intermediate theory* holds that when the mortgage is originated it is a lien on the property. If the mortgagor defaults, title passes to the mortgagee, who then forecloses on the property. This theory is used in four states.

MINIMUM REQUIREMENTS OF A MORTGAGE OR DEED OF TRUST

Many organizations have encouraged the adoption of a standardized mortgage document, and at the present time, the Federal National Mortgage Association (FNMA), in conjunction with the Federal Home Loan Mortgage Corporation (FHLMC), has developed the most widely used instrument. Appendix K illustrates the FNMA/ FHLMC Uniform Mortgage instrument. Every mortgage contract must meet certain minimum requirements in order to be valid. The requirements for a valid mortgage contract are these:

1. The mortgage contract must be in writing.
2. Parties to the mortgage contract must be competent and must have the capacity to enter into a contract.
3. A mortgaging or granting clause must be included in the contract. This clause *pledges* or *grants* the property as security for the debt depending upon whether the state subscribes to lien theory or title theory.
4. A legal description of the pledged property must be included. Also, if any personal property is covered by the mortgage, it must be identified.
5. A description of the debt and the terms of the debt should be stated with sufficient accuracy to prevent the parties from substituting other debts in its place. In practice, the note is usually made a part of the mortgage by referring to it in the mortgage. The *note* is generally not recorded, because the mortgagor is reluctant to tell the world about her debts. The *mortgage,* on the other hand, should be recorded to protect the mortgagee's priority. A mortgage must be acknowledged before it can be recorded; however, an unrecorded mortgage is valid between the mortgagor and the mortgagee.
6. The specific promises or covenants agreed to by the mortgagor must be included. These are the *dos* and *don'ts* the mortgagor agrees to in exchange for the loan.
7. The mortgage must be executed (signed) by the mortgagor and the mortgagor's spouse (if married) to waive dower and homestead rights. These rights have been modified or eliminated in some states.

COMMON MORTGAGE COVENANTS AND CLAUSES

There is no single, standardized mortgage contract today. The provisions in each mortgage and/or note will differ somewhat because of the varying needs of the borrowers, the varying degrees of security offered by the pledged properties, changing conditions in the mortgage market, localized lending policies, and state laws. However, certain clauses are common to most residential mortgages and to deeds of trust. They are as follows:

1. *Covenant* or *promise to pay indebtedness.*
2. *Covenant to pay taxes and insurance.* The mortgagor agrees to pay the taxes and insurance on the mortgaged property. The mortgagee is very concerned that the mortgagor pay the taxes because unpaid taxes become a first lien on the property. The insurance clause insures the pledged property against loss by fire, wind, and rain. The mortgagee is usually provided with the right to pay any unpaid taxes, assessments, or insurance premiums and add such payments to the amount owed on the mortgage. Many lenders ensure that taxes and insurance are paid by providing the mortgagor with a budget mortgage, whereby the monthly payment includes not only principal and interest but also taxes and insurance.
3. *Covenant against removal.* This clause prohibits the mortgagor from removing or demolishing any of the buildings or fixtures from the pledged property because such removal could cause a loss in property value.

4. *Estoppel certificate* or *certificate of no defense.* This clause obligates the mortgagor to furnish the mortgagee, upon request, a written statement acknowledging the current loan balance and whether or not any defenses exist against the debt. The rule of estoppel means that the mortgagor cannot later assert that the balance due was different from that stated on the certificate.

The mortgagee uses the **estoppel certificate** if and when she decides to sell the mortgage. Since neither the mortgage contract nor the note specifies the exact loan balance at a given time, the certificate is given to the mortgage purchaser to assure her of the existing balance of the loan and to certify that the mortgagor has no defenses against the claim.

A number of other clauses are found in mortgages. The acceleration clause, interest escalation clause, and prepayment clauses are in most mortgages. These and other special clauses are described in the following sections.

Acceleration Clause

The mortgage contract and the associated note often stipulate that any default in payments or in any of the other agreed-upon covenants will cause the remaining loan balance to become immediately due and payable. This provision is called the **acceleration clause.** In the absence of this provision, the mortgagee's only recourse in case of default is to sue on the note or to foreclose. In either of these actions, the mortgagee can collect only the amount presently due rather than the entire debt. This would create the need for a series of actions rather than a single, final action.

Foreclosure proceedings are expensive and cumbersome and generally create bad public relations. As a result, most lenders provide a grace period before they exercise the acceleration option. They are willing to accept late payments or restructure the terms of the loan to facilitate payment. These practices, however, do not constitute a waiver of the mortgagee's right to accelerate the debt if she deems it necessary.

Interest Escalation Clause

The rate of interest to be paid on the debt is stated in the note and sometimes, although not necessarily so, in the mortgage. Two types of **interest escalation clauses** are common. The first generally provides that the rate of interest on the mortgage loan will automatically escalate to the highest legal rate upon default. The second provides that the rate of interest charged on the debt will vary according to some standard index. Heretofore this clause has been more common in commercial or business loans, but it is now becoming extremely popular in residential mortgages during this period of fluctuating interest rates.

Prepayment Clause

The **prepayment clause** allows the mortgagor to prepay the debt before it becomes due. Without this provision, the lender is not required to accept advance payments. The prepayment clause may allow full or partial prepayment and may, at the discretion of the lender, include a penalty for prepayment. Some lenders place provisions in contracts allowing up to 20 percent of the unpaid balance to be paid in any one year. Many lenders use a clause requiring a prepayment penalty only if the mortgagor is refinancing with another lender.

The mortgagor exercises her prepayment option when she sells the property and pays off the loan before its maturity. It also allows the mortgagor to refinance during periods of falling interest rates. Occasionally, the prepayment penalty on commercial loans is too severe to make refinancing a feasible alternative.

Covenant to Pay Attorney's Fees

This provision stipulates that, if it becomes necessary for the mortgagee to hire legal counsel to collect the debt or to foreclose the mortgage, the legal fees will be paid by the mortgagor.

Receiver Clause

The *receiver clause* is common in mortgages on income-producing property. It provides that, in case of default, a court-appointed receiver steps in and collects the rents and pays the necessary bills between the commencement of foreclosure action and the actual sale. Such a provision prevents the mortgagor from "milking" the property during the interim period and ensures that proper maintenance will be performed to protect the property value.

Owner's Rent Clause

The *owner's rent clause* provides that, in case of default, the mortgagor agrees to pay rent to a court-appointed receiver during the interim between the commencement of foreclosure action and the actual sale. This provision is a necessary supplement to the *receiver clause* when the mortgagor occupies the pledged premises, because the receiver is entitled to enforce only those contracts that the owner had. The owner obviously did not have a contract with herself. As a result, the owner's rent clause becomes necessary if the rent is to be collected from the owner herself.

Subordination Clause

Generally, the priority of mortgages as to lien rights is determined by the date of recording of each lien. The mortgage that is recorded first establishes the earliest lien right. In case of foreclosure, the holder of the earliest lien is paid from the sales proceeds first. Junior lien right holders are then paid off in ascending order. The established order of priority can be altered through the use of a subordination clause. Simply stated, the *subordination clause* provides that the holder of a prior lien right agrees to subordinate her priority to a subsequent lienholder. The question arises as to why anyone would subordinate her priority on a voluntary basis. The following example illustrates the use of a subordination clause.

The seller of a vacant parcel of land may take back a "purchase money mortgage" from the buyer as part of the selling price. In such a case, the seller becomes the mortgagee rather than a financial institution. When she records the purchase money mortgage (PM mortgage), the priority of her lien right is established. If the buyer plans to obtain a construction loan later in order to build on the vacant land, she must ensure that the purchase money mortgage contains a subordination clause under which the seller subordinates her prior lien to that of the lending institution furnishing the construction loan. This is necessary because lending institutions are not allowed to make construction loans on anything other than first mortgages. By agreeing to a subordination clause, a land developer may facilitate the sale of her land and may be able to command a somewhat higher selling price. Also, even though the seller has taken a junior lienholder position, the construction of the improvement on the mortgaged land increases the value of the pledged property and thereby provides additional security to the original seller in case of foreclosure.

Default in Prior Mortgage Clause

This *default clause* is commonly used in junior mortgages to protect the junior mortgage lender. It provides that, in the event the mortgagor defaults on the first mortgage, the junior mortgage holder may pay the delinquent amount and add it to the balance of the second mortgage loan. This right is exercised by the junior mortgage lender upon default of a prior mortgage when the real estate market is temporarily depressed, and the possibility exists that the proceeds from a foreclosure sale would not be sufficient to cover the junior lienholder.

Alienation Clause (Due on Sale)

Many mortgages contain an *alienation clause* that gives the lender the right to call the entire balance due if the property is sold, thereby preventing borrowers from passing on their low-interest mortgages to new home buyers via loan assumptions. This provision is also referred to as the *due-on-sale clause.* The original purpose of the due-on-sale clause was to protect the lender's security interest in the property from the *risks* of property depreciation or mortgage default that might result if the property were sold and the loan assumed by a person who either failed to maintain the property or was unable to make the required mortgage payments. In recent years, however, savings and loans across the country have attempted to enforce the due-on-sale clause in order to reduce the large number of low-yielding, fixed-rate mortgages found on their books. These low-yielding mortgages are then replaced with new, higher-yielding mortgages, many of which are of the adjustable-rate variety.

CLASSIFICATION OF MORTGAGES BY REPAYMENT METHOD

The varying needs of borrowers and lenders give rise to many variations in the way in which mortgages are repaid. The note and mortgage will define the repayment method to be used on the basis of the needs of the lender and the borrower. Some currently used repayment methods are described in the following sections. First, amortization and types of amortized loans are discussed; then various flexible-rate mortgages are covered.

Term Loan (or Straight Loan)

The *straight* or *term mortgage* loan provides for repayment of the principal amount of the loan at maturity. No provision is made to reduce the principal during the term of the loan. The borrower pays interest only at stated intervals, usually monthly, quarterly, semiannually, or annually. At the end of the loan term, the principal amount of the loan must be paid off along with the unpaid interest. The term of the loan usually varies from one to five years.

Term mortgages were very common on residential loans before the depression;

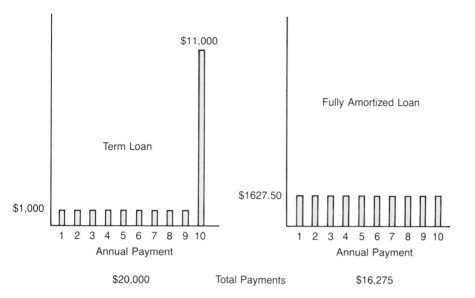

$11,000

Term Loan

$1,000

1 2 3 4 5 6 7 8 9 10
Annual Payment

Fully Amortized Loan

$1627.50

1 2 3 4 5 6 7 8 9 10
Annual Payment

$20,000   Total Payments $16,275

Figure 8–2   Term loan vs. amortized loan ($10,000 at 10 percent interest, annual payments)

however, the financial crisis of the 1930s precipitated large numbers of foreclosures because of the inability of borrowers to pay the lump sum upon maturity. For this reason, this type of loan has become less common.

Figure 8–2 compares a term loan to a fully amortized loan of $10,000 at 10 percent interest with a term of ten years with annual payments. As can be seen, the term loan requires annual payment of $1,000 for ten years for interest alone. In addition, at the end of the ten-year term, the entire principal (loan amount) of $10,000 is due. The borrower pays a total of $20,000 over the ten years. With the amortized loan, the borrower makes annual payments of $1,627.50 for ten years, or a total of $16,275.

As mentioned, the term loans of the 1930s contributed to high foreclosure rates because of the borrowers' inability to pay the large, lump-sum payment at the end of the loan term. From this sad experience, we learned that most people can budget somewhat larger payments throughout the terms of the loan in order to eliminate the burden of the large, lump-sum payment at the end of a term loan.

Fully Amortized Mortgages

The *fully amortized mortgage* provides for gradual repayment of the total principal amount over the term of the loan. The borrower makes periodic payments, usually monthly, quarterly, semiannually, or annually, which include both principal and interest. At maturity, the outstanding loan balance has been reduced to zero. The term of fully amortized residential mortgages generally varies from fifteen to thirty-five years. Table 8–1 shows the repayment schedule on a $10,000 fully amortized, ten-year loan at 10 percent interest with annual payments. The first annual payment was derived from Table E–2 in Appendix E. Refer to Table E–2, read across the table to find 10 percent, then read down to find ten years. You'll find the figure $162.75.

Table 8–1 Repayment of a
$10,000, ten-year, fully amortized
loan at 10 percent interest with
annual payments

Year	Loan balance (beginning of year)	Annual principal and interest payment		Loan balance (end of year)
		Interest	Principal reduction	
1	$10,000.00 × 10% =	$1,000.00	$ 627.50	$9,372.50
2	9,372.50 × 10% =	937.25	690.25	8,682.25
3	8,682.25 × 10% =	868.23	759.27	7,922.98
4	7,922.98 × 10% =	792.30	835.20	7,087.78
5	7,087.78 × 10% =	707.78	919.72	6,168.06
6	6,168.06 × 10% =	616.81	1,010.69	5,157.37
7	5,157.37 × 10% =	515.74	1,111.76	4,045.61
8	4,045.61 × 10% =	404.56	1,222.94	2,822.67
9	2,822.67 × 10% =	282.27	1,345.23	1,477.44
10	1,477.44 × 10% =	147.74	1,479.76	-0-

This is the annual payment per $1,000 at 10 percent for ten years. Since we are dealing with a $10,000 loan, multiply the $162.75 by ten to get the annual payment for a $10,000 loan ($162.75 × 10 = $1,627.50). This payment is sometimes referred to as the *P&I payment* (principal and interest payment) or the *debt service*. As mentioned, the debt service payment of $1,627.50 remains constant through the life of the loan. The allocation of the debt service between principal and interest is what changes. As can be seen, as the loan balance is reduced, the interest paid is reduced, leaving more of the fixed monthly service payment ($1,627.50) to go toward reducing the principal (loan) balance. By the end of the tenth year, the loan balance has been reduced to zero. There is a slight error due to rounding.

Table 8–2 shows part of an amortization schedule on a $77,500, thirty-year fully amortized loan with an interest rate of 9½ percent. The principal and interest payment on the loan is $651.66. In the first month, this $651.66 payment consists of $38.12 in *principal,* and the remainder ($613.54) is *interest* payment on the loan. At the end of the month, the original loan balance of $77,500 has been reduced by the principal payment of $38.12 to $77,461.88. The *interest portion* of the payment in the second month of the loan is calculated as follows:

$$\text{Principal Balance} \times \text{Interest Rate} = \frac{\text{Annual Interest Expense}}{12 \text{ months}}$$

$$\$77,461.88 \times .095 = \frac{\$7,358.87}{12} = \$613.24$$

As the years go by, the remaining loan balance continues to decrease, thereby causing less and less of the total monthly payment to go toward interest expense and more and more toward principal reduction. Referring to monthly payment number 360 of the amortization chart, we see that all but $5.15 of the monthly payment was for principal reduction.

Partially Amortized Mortgages

The *partially amortized mortgage* provides for gradual repayment of a part of the principal over the term of the loan. The borrower makes periodic payments that include both principal and interest, so that, at maturity, only part of the principal is paid off. The balance of the principal (the *balloon payment*) is due at maturity. The periodic payments on the partially amortized mortgage are less than those of a fully amortized mortgage of the same amount with the same terms. These reduced payments toward the principal will necessarily leave a loan balance at maturity, however. Newly formed businesses with large start-up costs and cash flow problems are likely candidates for partially amortized mortgages. The lender logically assumes that the cash-flow crisis experienced by the new firm is short-term and that within a few years, when the loan has matured, the then more experienced firm will be in a position to either pay off or refinance the balance.

FIXED-RATE MORTGAGES (FRM)

A *fixed-rate mortgage (FRM)* is any loan having an interest rate that remains unchanged over the life of the mortgage. The FRM was initially developed by the Federal Housing Administration after the depression as a financing device that would better meet the needs of the homebuyer than the straight or term mortgages that had been used in the past. The typical term of fixed-rate mortgages varies from fifteen to forty years. The most popular fixed-rate mortgage is the fully amortized loan. This and other versions of the fixed-rate mortgage are discussed below.

Renegotiable-Rate Mortgages (RRM)

The *renegotiable-rate mortgage (RRM)* is essentially a series of short-term loans of three to five years secured by a fixed-rate mortgage that amortizes the loan payments over a twenty-five- to thirty-five-year period but with a *call* provision requiring the note to be paid off or renegotiated within the three- to five-year period. This type of mortgage was very popular in Canada; hence, it is frequently referred to in this country as a *Canadian rollover loan.* When the loan was renewed at the three- to five-year intervals, the interest rate was renegotiated to whatever the prevailing market rate was at the time, and the principal and interest payment was adjusted to reflect the new rate.

When the RRMs were first introduced in 1980, the Federal Home Loan Bank Board issued limitations stating that the rate adjustment could not exceed a ½ percentage point a year nor more than 5 percentage points over the life of the loan.

In 1981, the Federal Home Loan Bank Board and the Comptroller of the Currency cancelled the RRM in favor of the more liberal adjustable-rate mortgage loans.

Growing-Equity Mortgages (GEM)

The *growing-equity mortgage (GEM)* has provisions that appeal to many homeowners. With the GEM mortgage, loans of 80, 90, or 95 percent loan-to-value are common, with fixed interest rates and loan terms of twenty-five to thirty years. Although the interest rate is fixed, the monthly payment increases by a predetermined

Table 8–2   Amortization
schedule

Mortgage Amount: $77,500.00			
Interest Rate: .0950000			
P&I Constant: $651.66			
First Payment: $651.66			

Payment number	Interest payment	Principal payment	Principal balance
1	613.54	38.12	77,461.88
2	613.24	38.42	77,423.46
3	612.94	38.72	77,384.74
4	612.63	39.03	77,345.71
5	612.32	39.34	77,306.37
6	612.01	39.65	77,266.72
7	611.69	39.97	77,226.75
8	611.38	40.28	77,186.47
9	611.06	40.60	77,145.87
10	610.74	40.92	77,104.95
11	610.41	41.25	77,063.70
12	610.09	41.57	77,022.13
13	609.76	41.90	76,980.23
14	609.43	42.23	76,938.00
15	609.09	42.57	76,895.43
16	608.76	42.90	76,852.53
17	608.42	43.24	76,809.29
18	608.07	43.59	76,765.70
19	607.73	43.93	76,721.77
20	607.38	44.28	76,677.49
21	607.03	44.63	76,632.86
22	606.68	44.98	76,587.88
23	606.32	45.34	76,542.54

3–4 percent per year. This increase in the amount of the monthly payment is used to reduce the mortgage balance, thereby accelerating the payoff on the mortgage.

For example, the monthly principal and interest payment on a standard thirty-year, fixed-rate, $70,000 mortgage with an interest rate of 15 percent would be $885.11. With a GEM mortgage, the first monthly payment would also be $885.11, but it would increase by 3.75 percent to $918.30 the second year, $952.74 the third year, and so on. By the twelfth year, the payment would go up to $1,327, but the loan would be completely paid off at the end of that year. With the GEM mortgage, the amount of interest paid over the life of the loan (twelve years) is only $97,810.36, whereas with the traditional thirty-year fixed-rate mortgage, the interest paid in the

Table 8–2 (continued)

INSTRUMENTS OF
FINANCE

Payment number	Interest payment	Principal payment	Principal balance
24	605.96	45.70	76,496.84
25	605.60	46.06	76,450.78
26	605.24	46.42	76,404.36
27	604.87	46.79	76,357.57
28	604.50	47.16	76,310.41
29	604.12	47.54	76,262.87
30	603.75	47.91	76,214.96
31	603.37	48.29	76,166.67
32	602.99	48.67	76,118.00
33	602.60	49.06	76,068.94
34	602.21	49.45	76,019.49
35	601.82	49.84	75,969.65
36	601.43	50.23	75,919.42
348	63.52	588.14	7,435.83
349	58.87	592.79	6,843.04
350	54.17	597.49	6,245.55
351	49.44	602.22	5,643.33
352	44.68	606.98	5,036.35
353	39.87	611.79	4,424.56
354	35.03	616.63	3,807.93
355	30.15	621.51	3,186.42
356	25.23	626.43	2,559.99
357	20.27	631.39	1,928.60
358	15.27	636.39	1,292.21
359	10.23	641.43	650.78
360	5.15	646.51	4.27
361	.03	4.27	

first twelve years and eight months of the thirty-year mortgage is $129,994.64, and there is still a mortgage balance of 65,458.03! See Tables 8–3 and 8–4. The specific advantages of GEM are as follows:

1. The homeowner will own the home free and clear in less than fifteen years.
2. The total interest paid is much less.
3. Lending institutions can sell the mortgages to Freddie Mac (the Federal Home Loan Mortgage Corporation) in the secondary mortgage market.
4. Loans can be up to 80 percent of home value, or up to 95 percent of home value if private mortgage insurance is obtained.

Table 8–3 Schedule of payments and amortization for a $70,000 growing equity mortgage*

Year	Monthly payment	Annual interest	Annual principal	Percent of principal repaid to date	Remaining balance
1	$ 885.11	$10,491.30	$ 130.02	0.2	$69,869.98
2	918.30	10,441.84	577.76	1.0	69,292.22
3	952.74	10,319.32	1,113.56	2.6	68,178.66
4	988.47	10,109.58	1,752.06	5.1	66,426.60
5	1,025.54	9,796.04	2,510.44	8.7	63,916.16
6	1,064.00	9,359.38	3,408.62	13.6	60,507.54
7	1,103.90	8,777.10	4,469.70	19.9	56,037.84
8	1,145.30	8,022.95	5,720.65	28.1	50,317.19
9	1,188.25	7,066.39	7,192.61	38.4	43,124.58
10	1,232.81	5,871.82	8,921.90	51.1	34,202.69
11	1,279.04	4,397.78	10,950.70	66.8	23,251.98
12	1,327.00	2,596.17	13,327.83	85.8	9,924.15
12 + 1 mo.	1,327.00	124.05	1,202.95	87.5	8,721.20
12 + 2	1,327.00	109.02	1,217.98	89.3	7,503.22
12 + 3	1,327.00	93.79	1,233.21	91.0	6,270.01
12 + 4	1,327.00	78.38	1,248.62	92.8	5,021.39
12 + 5	1,327.00	62.77	1,264.23	94.6	3,757.16
12 + 6	1,327.00	46.96	1,280.04	96.5	2,477.12
12 + 7	1,327.00	30.96	1,296.04	98.3	1,181.08
12 + 8	1,195.84	14.76	1,181.08	100.0	-0-
		$97,810.36	$70,000.00		

TOTAL PAYMENTS $167,810.36

*Initial payment based on 15 percent interest rate and thirty-year amortization with 3.75 percent per year increase in payments applied to principal

In addition to being attractive to potential borrowers, this instrument should find broad appeal among institutional investors and pension funds because of the relatively secure nature of the investment and the shorter period of time over which their capital is tied up.

The main disadvantage of the GEM mortgage is that the monthly payment increases may outstrip the borrower's salary increases, thereby increasing the possibility of default.

Rapid-Payment Mortgages (RPM)

The advantages of the previously described GEM mortgage are obvious. The borrower can save thousands of dollars in interest expense over the life of a loan and pay off the entire loan balance in less than half the time of the conventional, thirty-year fixed-rate loan. However, the ever-increasing payments on a GEM loan may

Table 8–4   Schedule of payments and amortization over the first twelve years and eight
months for a $70,000 conventional loan at 15 percent amortized over thirty years

Year	Monthly payment	Annual interest	Annual principal	Percent of principal repaid to date	Remaining balance
1	$885.11	$ 10,491.30	$ 130.03	0.2	$69,869.97
2	885.11	10,470.40	150.91	0.4	69,719.06
3	885.11	10,446.13	175.18	0.7	69,543.88
4	885.11	10,417.97	203.34	0.3	69,340.54
5	885.11	10,385.29	236.02	1.3	69,104.52
6	885.11	10,347.34	273.97	1.7	68,830.55
7	885.11	10,303.30	318.01	2.1	68,512.54
8	885.11	10,252.18	369.13	2.7	68,143.41
9	885.11	10,192.84	428.47	3.3	67,714.94
10	885.11	10,123.96	497.35	4.0	67,217.59
11	885.11	10,044.01	577.30	4.8	66,640.29
12	885.11	9,951.20	670.11	5.8	65,970.18
12 + 8 mo.	885.11	6,568.72	512.15	6.5	65,458.03
		$129,994.64	$4,541.96		

TOTAL PAYMENTS $134,536.96

constitute a real risk to the borrower. The ***rapid-payment mortgage (RPM)*** is another means of obtaining the benefits of the GEM mortgage without incurring the
primary disadvantage of increasing monthly payments. Essentially, the RPM is nothing more than the standard, fixed-rate mortgage with its term shortened from the
traditional twenty-five or thirty years to ten or fifteen years. It would seem that short-
ening the term of the loan would greatly increase the fixed monthly principal and
interest payment. Such is not the case. For example, on a $50,000, thirty-year, 12.5
percent, fixed-rate mortgage, the monthly principal and interest payment is $533.63.
The principal and interest payment on a $50,000, fifteen-year mortgage at 12.5 per-
cent is $616.26—a difference of only $82.63 per month (see Table 8–5).

As an incentive to the borrower, many lenders will offer a reduced interest rate
of from .5 to 1 percent below the thirty-year rates on the RPM mortgage since the
loan will be repaid in half the time of the traditional, thirty-year mortgage. Considering this, the monthly payment differential between the RPM fifteen-year loan and
the traditional thirty-year mortgage is even less, and the mortgage is paid off in half
the time. The monthly principal and interest differential on a $50,000, thirty-year
loan at 12.5 percent, as compared to a $50,000, fifteen-year loan at 11 percent, is
only $34.67 (see Table 8–5).

Biweekly Mortgages (Yuppie Mortgages)

The ***biweekly mortgage*** is another variation of the thirty-year, fixed-rate mortgage.
It was developed in Canada and was introduced in the United States in 1985. Basi-

Table 8–5 Amount of principal paid off at the end of each year on a thirty-year, fixed-rate mortgage vs. two fifteen-year, fixed-rate rapid payment mortgage (RPM) loans for $50,000

Term		30 Years	15 Years	15 Years
Interest rate		12.5%	12.5%	11%
Principal and interest		$533.63	$616.26	$568.30
Year	1	$ 163	$ 1,213	$ 1,388
	2	347	2,587	2,937
	3	555	4,142	4,665
	4	792	5,904	6,593
	5	1,036	7,899	8,744
	6	1,362	10,518	11,144
	7	1,705	12,716	13,822
	8	2,094	15,613	16,810
	9	2,533	18,893	20,143
	10	3,032	22,608	23,863
	11	3,596	26,815	28,379
	12	4,235	31,579	32,642
	13	4,598	36,973	37,807
	14	5,777	43,082	43,571
	15	6,705	50,000	50,000
	20	13,545		
	25	26,283		
	30	50,000		

cally, the difference between this and the traditional thirty-year, fixed-rate mortgage is that the borrower makes a payment every two weeks instead of every month. The biweekly payments reduce the principal balance faster, resulting in a greatly shortened loan term. For example, with the traditional thirty-year, fixed-rate mortgage on a $100,000 loan at 12.5 percent, the monthly payments would be $1,067.26, and the loan, of course, would be paid off in thirty years. During the term of the loan, the borrower would have paid interest totaling $284,203.97. With the biweekly loan, the biweekly payment would be $533.63, the loan would be paid off in eighteen and one-half years, and the borrower would have paid a total of $157,241.84 in interest— a savings of $126,962.14. It is interesting to note that the loan balance on the traditional thirty-year fixed-rate mortgage with monthly payments after eighteen and one-half years would be $78,190.15. Since the lenders have their money loaned out for a shorter period of time, they may offer the biweekly mortgage at an interest rate of ½–1 percent less than the traditional thirty-year mortgage. The biweekly mortgage appears to be gaining popularity.

Graduated-Payment Mortgages (GPM)

The *graduated-payment mortgage (GPM)* provides for reduced monthly payments during the early years of the loan. The payments will graduate by a predetermined amount every year for an agreed-upon amount of time, usually up to ten years. The payments then remain fixed for the balance of the mortgage term. This type of mortgage allows the buyer to purchase more home than she could otherwise afford because of the lower monthly payments initially. The primary disadvantages are negative amortization and increasing monthly payments in the early years of the loan.

Negative Amortization

Whenever the monthly payment on a loan is insufficient to cover all the interest charges, the deferred (unpaid) interest charges are added to the loan balance. In this instance, the loan balance actually increases rather than decreases. This phenomenon is known as *negative amortization.* The term *negative amortization* has a negative connotation. Consequently, lenders sometimes refer to it as deferred or capitalized interest. Whatever term is used, negative amortization is not always bad. In the event the borrower lives in an area where the value of housing is growing at a faster rate than the outstanding loan balance is increasing yearly, it would pay for the borrower to buy the house now, using a GPM mortgage.

VARIABLE-RATE MORTGAGES (VRM)

The first flexible-rate mortgage to be authorized by the Federal Home Loan Bank Board (FHLBB) was the variable-rate mortgage, which was authorized nationally by the FHLBB in 1979. As the name implies, the *variable-rate mortgage (VRM)* was a contract wherein the interest rate charged varied or fluctuated over the life of the loan. The rate charged was generally tied to the prevailing interest rates in the bond and money markets. This mortgage contract was designed to alleviate the problems of lending institutions during periods of inflation when they were holding low-yielding fixed-rate mortgages (FRM) but had to pay increasing rates of interest for money, thereby reducing the spread and ending up with lower profits. The variable-rate mortgage avoided the problem of committing mortgage funds for long periods of time at fixed rates of interest, and it ensured an acceptable spread between the cost of funds and the mortgage rates charged by the lender.

The governing rules issued by the FHLBB concerning VRMs included many of the safeguards suggested by consumer advocates. The interest rate adjustment was limited to a ½ percentage point per year, with a maximum increase not to exceed 2½ percentage points over the life of the loan. The regulations further required that fixed-rate mortgages also be available and that the lenders furnish the borrower with a comparison of the terms of both mortgages. The loan-to-value ratios and loan terms were similar to those of the more traditional, fixed-rate mortgage. The FHLBB governing rules on this type of mortgage subsequently were superseded by the more flexible guidelines of the newer adjustable-rate mortgage loans (ARM), which eliminated most consumer safeguards. The VRM was cancelled. Some state-chartered savings and loans still offer the VRM.

ADJUSTABLE-RATE MORTGAGES (ARM)

In 1980, the Comptroller of the Currency adopted regulations allowing the *adjustable-rate mortgage (ARM).* In 1981, the Federal Home Loan Bank Board did likewise, although for the first couple of years they called it the *adjustable mortgage loan (AML).* In 1983, the FHLBB stopped using the name AML and adopted ARM. Today, there is the trend to standardize the ARM instrument. This movement is led by FNMA and FHLMC.

At present, there are many different types of ARMs. However, all ARMs have four common features, each of which is negotiable between the lender and borrower. They are

1. *Initial Interest Rate.* This is the beginning interest rate on the ARM. It is usually somewhat lower than the market rate for fixed-rate mortgages. It will remain the same until the first adjustment period mentioned in the mortgage. At that time, it may be adjusted upward or downward.

2. *Adjustment Period.* This is the interval of time between changes in interest rate and/or monthly payment. Typically, the adjustment periods are one, three, or five years; however, other adjustment periods can be negotiated. As a borrower, if you anticipate interest rates are moving upward, it is in your best interest to negotiate for a long adjustment period. Conversely, if you anticipate lower interest rates in the future, a short adjustment period would be more favorable.

3. *Index.* Any economic index that can be readily verified by the borrower and is beyond the control of the lender may be used. Some of the more common indexes are

Federal Home Loan Bank Board (FHLBB) series of closed loans
Monthly average interest rate on loans closed by S&Ls
Six-month Treasury Bill rates
One-, three-, and five-year U.S. Treasury issues

Figure 8–3 shows the movement of some of these indexes over time. Most indexes are readily accessible via the *Wall Street Journal* or other financial publications. When the index is coupled with the margin, the result can be used to calculate the revised interest rate for the mortgage at the time of adjustment.

4. *Margin.* This is the spread or **margin** that the lender adds to the index to establish the interest rate on the loan. The amount of the margin will vary depending on the adjustment interval and initial interest rate. The borrower would negotiate for as small a "spread" or margin as possible.

In addition to the four basic features of all ARMs, several *optional features* are offered.

Interest Rate Caps, or Limits

The interest rate cap will limit the amount the interest rate on the mortgage can increase or decrease at the time of each adjustment or over the life of the mortgage. Typical caps are 2 percent limits per adjustment period and 5 percent limits over the life of the mortgage. With this protection, even if the index rate plus the margin indicates a new rate in excess of the cap, the increase is limited by the cap and the lender foregoes the lost interest forever unless there is a **carryover provision** in the mortgage. With a carryover provision, the lender is allowed to carry over to the next adjustment period any increase (or decrease) not allowed by the cap.

While the borrower's cost for this protection varies from lender to lender, it appears that, generally, a 1 percent annual cap costs about .5 percent more interest

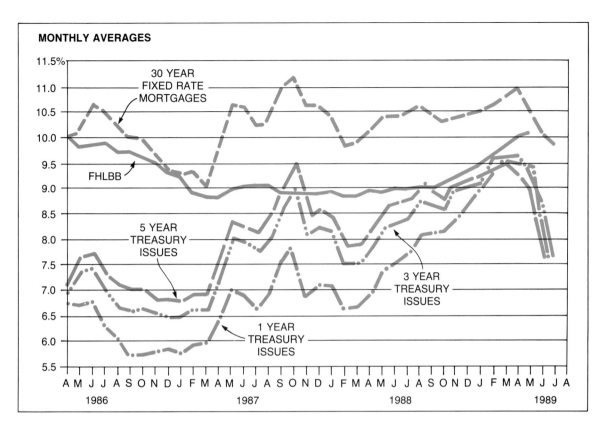

This chart is designed to show the trends of some of the more common indexes used to set rates on adjustable mortgages. Borrowers facing adjustments can use the numbers at the top to compute what their new rate is likely to be, assuming no caps or other special limitations. To do that, add the lender's margin to the applicable index. Data on 30-year fixed-rate loans are included for reference.

Figure 8–3   Some common indexes for adjustable-rate mortgages

Source: Federal National Mortgage Association: Federal Home Loan Mortgage Corp: U.S. Treasury

on the mortgage than a loan without the cap. Figure 8–4 illustrates a mortgage with an annual interest rate cap.

Monthly Payment Cap, or Limit

Another borrower or consumer protection feature that may be offered is a cap, or limit, on the amount by which the monthly mortgage payment will increase at adjustment time. The cap offered most often is 7.5 percent yearly. In other words, if the borrower's initial monthly payment was $500, any increase or decrease would be limited to 7.5 percent or $37.50 on the first adjustment period. The borrower should be cautioned, however, that by limiting the monthly payment, she may not be paying enough to cover the interest that would be charged during periods of rising interest rates. In such cases, *negative amortization* will result as the lender is allowed to add the unpaid interest to the outstanding loan balance.

Example 8–1 illustrates an ARM loan that has the features of coinciding interest rate and payment changes.

Figure 8–4 **Example of an ARM with annual interest rate cap**

Source: Mortgage Bankers Association. Used by permission.

Loan Amount	$50,000
Loan Term	30 years
Initial Interest Rate	12%
Adjustment Interval	Annually
Index	One-year Treasury security yield
Margin	1.5%
Interest Rate Cap	Yes, 2% annually
Monthly Payment (not including taxes, insurance, and mortgage insurance premiums, if any) for the first year	$514.31

Assume that, at the end of the first year, the index rate is 13%. Add the index rate (13%) and the margin (1.5%) to get the new interest rate (14.5%). Because, during one year, you have paid $181.44 on your loan principal, your new rate will be figured on a balance of $49,818.56 and on a term of 29 years because your loan is one year old.

But, because you have a 2% annual interest rate cap, your interest rate can only go from 12% (the initial rate) to 14%, even though the new index rate (13%) plus the margin (1.5%) calls for a 14.5% rate.

At 14%, your new monthly payment is now	$591.66
Your monthly payment on principal and interest has increased	$77.35
If you had not had the 2% annual cap on your interest rate, your new payment would have been based on the 14.5% rate called for by the new index (13%) plus the margin (1.5%), and would have been	$611.33
With a cap, you saved	$19.67

And you have no negative amortization.

Remember, without a cap on the amount the interest rate can go up over the life of the loan, your interest rate could increase two percentage points each year.

Example 8–1   ARM Mortgage

The type of ARM profiled in this example provides for coinciding interest rate and payment changes, and therefore negative amortization will not occur (see Table 8–6).

Table 8–6 The adjustable-rate mortgage (ARM)

Month	Index value	Index change	Interest rate	Payment	Loan balance
1st Month of Loan:					
Feb. 1990	15.53		13.5%	$572.71	$50,000.00
1st Payment Month					
March 1990	15.53		13.5	572.71	49,989.79
April 1990	15.53		13.5	572.71	49,979.47
May 1990	15.53		13.5	572.71	49,969.03
June 1990	15.53		13.5	572.71	49,958.47
July 1990	15.53		13.5	572.71	49,947.79
August 1990	15.53		13.5	572.71	49,936.99
September 1990	15.53		13.5	572.71	49,926.07
October 1990	15.53		13.5	572.71	49,915.03
November 1990	15.53		13.5	572.71	49,903.86
December 1990	15.53		13.5	572.71	49,892.57
January 1991	15.53		13.5	572.71	49,881.15
February 1991	15.53		13.5	572.71	49,869.60
March 1991	13.44	− 2.09	11.5	495.86	49,851.66
April 1991	13.44		11.5	495.86	49,833.54
May 1991	13.44		11.5	495.86	49,815.25
June 1991	13.44		11.5	495.86	49,796.79
July 1991	13.44		11.5	495.86	49,778.15
August 1991	13.44		11.5	495.86	49,759.33
September 1991	13.44		11.5	495.86	49,740.33
October 1991	13.44		11.5	495.86	49,721.15
November 1991	13.44		11.5	495.86	49,701.78
December 1991	13.44		11.5	495.86	49,682.23
January 1992	13.44		11.5	495.86	49,662.49
February 1992	13.44		11.5	495.86	49,642.56
March 1992	14.37	+ 0.93	12.375	528.77	49,625.73
April 1992	14.37		12.375	528.77	49,608.73
May 1992	14.37		12.375	528.77	49,591.55

Loan Amount: $50,000   Term: 30 years
Contract interest rate: 13.5%   Initial payment: $572.71
Initial index value: 15.53% (Set at closing)
First rate adjustment: − 2% (assume new index value of 13.44)
Second rate adjustment: + 0.875 (Assume new index value of 14.37)
Date of first payment adjustment: February 1, 1991 (based on first rate adjustment)
First adjusted payment due: March 1, 1991
Payment adjustment notice sent: January 15, 1991

For this loan there is an annual rate and payment adjustment. The maximum interest rate change at one time is 2 percent. All rate changes will result in a corresponding payment change, subject to the limitations stated above. At payment adjustment, the payment change will be sufficient to reestablish the amortization schedule.

The Index is FHLBB National Average Mortgage contract rate for major lenders on the purchase of previously occupied homes. Assuming a closing date of February 1, 1990, the first payment will be due March 1, 1990.

Introductory Rates

This is an initial rate for the ARM that is lower than the prevailing market rate. The rate may be from 1 to 5 points below market rates. The extremely low introductory rates are sometimes used by lenders to entice borrowers into opting for an ARM. These are sometimes called *teaser rates*. These rates will jump considerably at the first adjustment period and may cause "payment shock" if the borrower is not fully informed. The interest rate for the first adjustment period is generally not based on the introductory rate plus the margin, but rather on the market rate at the time of the adjustment or on the "normal" initial interest rate plus the margin. The difference can be shocking.

Convertibility

Another consumer protection feature offered by some lenders is the ability to convert the ARM loan into a fixed-rate loan, usually within a specified period of time. Some lenders will charge a fee; others provide the feature at no cost to the borrower. If the borrower is certain that interest rates will be going up and staying up, it may be in her best interest to convert.

Assumability

This feature enables the borrower to allow a new homebuyer to assume her ARM mortgage, usually at the same rate, if the new buyer meets the lender's minimum underwriting requirements. In the past, on fixed-rate loans with low interest rates, such a feature was a real advantage. Today, however, the interest rate on an ARM is generally much closer to the prevailing market rate and therefore is not much of an advantage to the new homebuyer. Nonetheless, if the lender offers this feature without charge, the borrower should accept it.

Disclosure Statements

Initial Disclosure Statement

Every ARM that is originated by a lender must include a detailed disclosure statement to the borrower specifically outlining all of the features of the loan. Among other things, this initial disclosure statement must include the following:

1. General information regarding the ARM
2. Information that the rate may change
3. Information identifying the index used and where it is published
4. Frequency of adjustment

5. Information on any possible negative amortization
6. Method used to implement the rate change
7. Prepayment provisions
8. Chart showing a ten-year history of index used
9. Worst-case example

In addition, the lender must provide the borrower with a copy of the "Consumer Handbook on Adjustable Rate Mortgages" published by the Federal Reserve and the Federal Home Loan Bank Board. The booklet explains the ARM terminology and provides examples of how an ARM works. The disclosure information must be provided to the borrower at the time a loan application is given to her or whenever she pays a nonrefundable fee, whichever comes first. If a loan application is taken by phone or by a third party such as a realtor, the lender has three days following the receipt of the application to provide the disclosure information.

FNMA ARM Limitations

The Federal National Mortgage Association (FNMA) is the largest purchaser of mortgages in the secondary mortgage market. As of 1985, FNMA had over $80 billion invested in mortgages. In order to reduce the risk of investing in mortgages, FNMA has issued guidelines, or limitations, on which mortgage loans they will purchase in the secondary market. Since most primary lending institutions are interested in packaging and selling their mortgages in the secondary market to maintain their liquidity, they generally heed these limitations. The guidelines can change over time. The reader is encouraged to contact the regional office of the Federal National Mortgage Association to obtain the current limitations. If the lenders want to sell an ARM mortgage to FNMA, they must adhere to the limitations. Figures 8–5 and 8–6 are helpful guides or checklists to assist the consumer shopping for an ARM loan.

By law, every important feature of the ARM is negotiable, except for the maximum term of the loan, which is forty years. Features most commonly negotiated include a limit or cap on the amount the rate can change in a year or over the life of the loan. Another negotiable item includes the method of adjusting for the interest rate change. The various methods include adjusting the monthly principal and interest payment, adjusting the loan term, and/or adjusting the loan balance. The smorgasbord of indexes to choose from will most likely create confusion and anxiety among consumers initially. Eventually, however, the number of indexes offered will probably boil down to two or three of those most popularly requested.

Graduated Payment–Adjustable Rate Mortgages (GP-ARM)

Another form of ARM is sometimes referred to as a *graduated payment–adjustable rate mortgage (GP-ARM)*. The advantage of the GP-ARM is that the borrower has lower payments initially and is therefore able to purchase more house than she could otherwise afford. As with any graduated payment mortgage, however, negative amortization occurs because the reduced monthly payments at the outset of the mortgage are insufficient to cover the interest costs and the lender is allowed to add the unpaid interest charges to the outstanding loan balance. In essence, the lender is merely postponing the payment of some of the early years' interest charges. In addition, even though the monthly payments increase by a predetermined amount in the early years, the interest rate is tied to an index that may go up or down. If

1. Initial Interest Rate	How long is it compared with the market rate, and how soon can it change? Has the rate been bought down?
2. Adjustment Period	Is it one, three, or five years? Is it another period?
3. Index	To what index will the ARM interest rate be tied? Is it a relatively stable rate, or does it fluctuate more than others?
4. Margin	What margin will be added to the index at each adjustment period?
5. Interest Rate Caps	How much can the rate change? How often? Will the cap apply to the first adjustment, or begin with a subsequent adjustment? Does the cap apply to a "teaser" rate or a buydown rate?
6. Monthly Payment Cap	Does the ARM have a payment cap? How much is it? When does it apply?
7. Graduated Payments	How much can your payments go up annually? Does it result in negative amortization? Is the initial interest rate fixed for the period of graduating payments?
8. Negative Amortization	Does the ARM allow negative amortization? How much negative amortization is allowed?
9. "Introductory" Rate	How much lower is the "introductory" rate than the "going" rate? When will it adjust? Is there a limit on how much the interest rate can go up at the time of adjustment?
10. Assumability	Can the ARM be transferred to another borrower? Is there a fee?
11. Convertibility	Can the ARM be converted to a fixed-rate mortgage without additional fees? Will the interest rate be higher or lower than the interest rate on the ARM?
12. Prepayment Privilege	Can the mortgage be paid off before the full term of the loan? Is a fee charged?
13. Points	How many points is the lender charging? Can the seller as well as the buyer pay them?

Figure 8–5   Things to consider when shopping for an ARM

Source: Mortgage Bankers Association. Used by permission.

the index plus the margin is higher than the initial rate, additional negative amortization results.

Elastic Mortgages

The *elastic mortgage,* a crossbreed of a fixed-rate and an adjustable-rate mortgage, was developed in 1985. It offers the predictable, fixed monthly payment found in the conventional fixed-rate mortgage and the advantages of an adjustable-rate mortgage should interest rates decline. In addition, no negative amortization will ever be experienced, and the borrower can pay off the loan early with no prepayment pen-

ARM Checklist	Lender 1	Lender 2	Lender 3	Lender 4	Lender 5	Lender 6
1. Initial Interest Rate						
2. Adjustment Interval						
3. Index						
4. Margin						
5. Interest Rate Caps						
6. Monthly Payment Cap						
7. Graduated Payments						
8. Negative Amortization						
9. "Introductory" Rate						
10. Assumability						
11. Convertibility						
12. Prepayment Privilege						
13. Points (Including origination fee)						

Figure 8–6   ARM checklist

Source: Mortgage Bankers Association. Used by permission.

alty. The mortgage begins as a fifteen-year loan with a total of 180 payments. The interest rate on the mortgage is tied to an index. If the interest rate index declines, the term of the elastic mortgage shrinks; that is, the total number of monthly payments needed to pay off the loan is reduced. If interest rates increase, the term of the loan on the elastic mortgage increases. In other words, the fifteen-year loan is reamortized every year to reflect the changes in interest rates. As with most ARMs, the mortgage offers a 4 percent lifetime cap on the interest rate, and the initial interest rate is 1 to 2 percent lower than the traditional, thirty-year fixed-rate loans. As with all fifteen-year loans, the monthly payment is higher than on a traditional thirty-year loan and may be prohibitive to some borrowers; however, the loan is paid off in approximately half the time.

Shared Appreciation Mortgages (SAM)

The *shared-appreciation,* or *equity-participation,* loan has been used by commercial lenders for several years. However, the **shared-appreciation mortgage (SAM)** concept is relatively new to the residential mortgage market. With a SAM, the lender offers the borrower a fixed-rate mortgage at below market rates in exchange for a share of the profits either (a) upon resale, or (b) after a stipulated period of time, usually five to ten years. Under the terms of the mortgage, the lender usually guarantees to refinance the property with a long-term mortgage after the predesignated five- to ten-year period, thereby enabling the buyer to pay the lender her share of the property appreciation even if she decides not to sell.

The advantage of a SAM to the lender is the ability to share in any property appreciation. Today, however, most S&Ls cannot justify adding to their burgeoning portfolio of below-market, fixed-rate mortgages in hopes of being compensated by property appreciation. As of this writing, property values in many areas of the country have not appreciated for up to two years. Some areas have experienced 10 to 15 percent losses in property value. No one knows these facts better than the lending institutions. Other troublesome questions regarding the SAM are

1. Who determines how much the property has appreciated if the homeowner does not desire to sell after the agreed-upon five- or ten-year period of time?
2. How will a home improvement made by the buyer be handled?
3. Does the lending institution share equally in any property loss that might occur?
4. If the property is sold rather than refinanced after ten years, who pays any realtor fee and other selling expenses?
5. How will the appreciation payment made to the lender be treated by the IRS? Is it a deductible interest expense? Who pays what amount of capital gains tax? Is the appreciation payment to the lender interest income or long-term capital gain?

Example 8–2 illustrates one of the problems associated with a SAM mortgage.

The shared appreciation mortgage has not been widely accepted across the country by either lenders or borrowers. It appears that the SAM instrument was hastily drafted without giving due consideration to the many questions that have emerged concerning its mechanics. In 1989, the Federal Housing Administration (FHA) abolished their SAM mortgage.

Example 8–2   A SAM Payoff

Assume a buyer purchases a $75,000 home with a $60,000, thirty-year, below-market, fixed-rate SAM mortgage at 9 percent interest in exchange for giving up one-third of the property appreciation to the lender. The buyer is required to pay the lender her share of the appreciation either in ten years or when the property sells, whichever occurs first. Assume further that the property appreciates 10 percent per year or doubles in value over the ten years. At the end of ten years, the buyer owes the lender one-third of the $75,000 appreciation, or $25,000. In addition, the buyer still has a mortgage balance on the loan of $53,658. The total debt ($25,000 + $53,658) of $78,658 exceeds the original purchase price of the house and quite likely the buyer would be forced to refinance the entire $78,658 (possibly at a much higher rate) in order to pay off the lender.

Reverse Annuity Mortgages (RAM)

In many instances, older people on fixed incomes require additional money to cover the rising costs of living. Rather than sell their home to raise the additional money needed to cover their expenses, they may enter into a *reverse annuity mortgage (RAM)* contract to satisfy their income needs. Once they sign the RAM, the monthly payments they were making stop and a reverse procedure begins. The elderly couple begin to receive monthly annuity payments from the lending institution. Essentially, the couple are borrowing the equity that they have built up in the house over their lifetime. They are charged the going rate of interest for the loan. The loan is paid off whenever the property is ultimately sold or upon the death of the mortgagor.

One variation of the RAM provides that the lending institution will loan up to 80 percent of the equity in one lump sum. The mortgagor will then purchase a single-premium life annuity insurance contract with the proceeds. Again, the RAM is paid off when the property is sold or upon the death of the mortgagor. In Texas, the state homestead law prevents the homeowner from using a RAM mortgage on her principal residence.

Budget Mortgages

When a property is financed with a high loan-to-value mortgage, the lending institution may require that, in addition to monthly principal and interest payments, the borrower also pay monthly installments on the real estate taxes and insurance for the pledged property. This *budget mortgage* assures the mortgagee that these expenses will be paid when due and allows the mortgagor to budget the expenses over twelve months rather than incur one lump sum payment.

OTHER MORTGAGE CLASSIFICATIONS

Previously, we classified mortgages by repayment method. Mortgages can also be grouped according to what is included in the mortgage or by other special provisions. Some of the often-used types of mortgages are discussed in the following sections.

Package Mortgages

The *package mortgage* is a recent concept in which the mortgage loan covers not only the real property itself, but also the fixtures and equipment that are customarily sold with the property. Types of items that may be covered include dishwashers, dryers, garbage disposals, air conditioners, refrigerators, and stoves. Package mortgages provide several advantages to the borrower, who:

1. Need obtain only one loan instead of several
2. Deals with only one lender and makes only one payment
3. Spreads the cost of the equipment over a much longer period of time
4. Pays a much lower rate of interest than would be allowed on an installment plan

The combined effects of a lower interest rate and a much longer loan term result in a much lower monthly payment, thereby making the purchase more affordable for most consumers.

Blanket Mortgages

A *blanket mortgage* covers or blankets several pieces of real estate as security for a loan. Such mortgages are common in financing a new subdivision. As the individual lots are sold to various customers, the subdivider/mortgagor must free the lots from the mortgage to convey title. This is accomplished by the insertion of a *partial release clause* in the mortgage. It stipulates that, upon payment of a certain release price, each lot will be individually released from the mortgage. Since, as a rule, the best lots in a subdivision are sold first, the release price for individual lots will usually be considerably higher than the average mortgage value of the individual lots, thereby assuring adequate security for the remaining loan balance.

As an example, assume a blanket mortgage covers ten lots as security for a $200,000 loan. The average mortgage value of the individual lots is $20,000 ($200,000 ÷ 10). However, the individual release price for each lot may be as high as $25,000 to compensate for the earlier sale of the best lots.

Open-End Mortgages

A borrower may require additional funds to repair and/or improve her mortgaged property in the years following the original mortgage loan. An *open-end mortgage* allows the borrower to obtain such funds under the original terms of the mortgage or under other terms stipulated in the mortgage. The total loan normally cannot exceed the original loan amount. Such advances are available at very little extra cost and may be repaid over the term of the loan. As a result, open-end mortgages provide more favorable terms than the standard home improvement loan, which has a much higher interest rate and must be repaid in a few short years.

Questions of priority arise when intervening liens are created between the time of the original mortgage and the subsequent reopening of the mortgage for the additional loan. Most states subscribe to the theory that the priority of the additional debt depends upon whether or not such advances were obligatory. If the lender was obligated to make such additional advances to the borrower as a result of a written or verbal commitment, the priority of the additional advance coincides with the priority of the original mortgage. On the other hand, if the lender was not obligated to make the additional advance of funds (i.e., if it was a discretionary loan), the intervening lien has priority over the additional advance of funds.

Purchase Money (PM) Mortgages

A *purchase money mortgage* is given by the purchaser of real estate to the seller as partial payment of the purchase price. The seller is generally willing to take back a PM mortgage to facilitate a sale during periods of "tight" money or when she sells on an installment contract in order to spread her gain over several years. The purchase money mortgage may be a junior or senior lien.

Wrap-Around Mortgages

A *wrap-around mortgage (WAM)* is actually a second mortgage that engulfs or wraps around an existing first mortgage. Only those first mortgage loans without a due-on-sale clause can be wrapped. A wrap-around mortgage is used primarily to obtain additional funds when it is impossible or impractical to refinance the existing loan. The wrap-around loan is based on the property's current market value. The funds advanced to the borrower represent the difference between the principal amount of the wrap-around loan and the current loan balance on the first mortgage loan. The borrower and the original lender or first mortgagee have no future dealings. The borrower makes her payments to the wrap-around lender who, in turn, funnels a portion of the payment to the first mortgagee to cover the debt service on the first mortgage (see Examples 8–3 and 8–4).

Until the Federal Home Loan Bank Board's regulation changed in 1981, federally chartered S&Ls could not make second mortgage loans on property. Today, the federally chartered S&Ls can use the wrap second mortgage to assist buyers and sellers in financing a transaction. In essence, the use of a wrap-around second mortgage can reduce the down-payment requirement of a buyer who is attempting to "assume" a low-interest-rate loan.

Construction Loans (Interim Financing)

Construction loans are used to provide the funds necessary to pay for material and labor during the construction process. These are called *interim loans.* Since high

---

Example 8–3   Wrap-Around Second Mortgage

An investor purchased an apartment building ten years ago for $125,000 with 80 percent financing at 8 percent interest for twenty-five years, fully amortized. Today, her property is worth $200,000, and she would like to obtain some extra funds by refinancing, but her first mortgage has a heavy prepayment penalty. She decides to use a wrap-around second mortgage, with these results:

Ten years earlier

Original purchase price	$125,000
Original first mortgage loan (80% of $125,000)	$100,000, 25-year, 8 percent interest rate with annual principal and interest payments of $9,368.

Ten years later

Current market value	$200,000
Wrap-around second mortgage	$160,000, 25-year, 15 percent interest rate with annual principal and interest payments of $24,752.
Funds advanced to borrower (wrap-around second mortgage loan less first mortgage loan balance: $160,000 − $80,000)	$80,000

The borrower receives an additional $80,000 in funds. She pays $24,752 in principal and interest on the $160,000 second mortgage (wrap-around) to the wrap-around lender who, in turn, funnels $9,368 to the original lender for debt-service payments on the original $100,000 loan. The balance of the payment is retained by the wrap-around lender and is used to reduce the $80,000 loan she advanced. The "wrap" lender realizes an "effective" yield on the $80,000 of 19 percent!

Example 8–4 Wrap-Around Mortgage by a Seller

The wrap-around mortgage can also be used by a seller to sell a property that has an existing low-interest-rate-mortgage with no due-on-sale clause. For example, let's assume a seller has a first mortgage loan of $55,000 at an interest rate of 9 percent, and yearly payments of $4,950. She wishes to sell her property for $80,000 and is willing to take back a second wrap-around mortgage of $65,000 with a $15,000 down payment from the buyer. The wrap-around mortgage is to be at 13 percent interest for a term of thirty years. Figure 8–7 depicts the wrap-around.

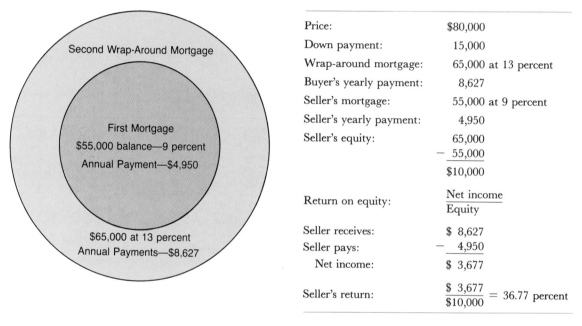

Price:	$80,000
Down payment:	15,000
Wrap-around mortgage:	65,000 at 13 percent
Buyer's yearly payment:	8,627
Seller's mortgage:	55,000 at 9 percent
Seller's yearly payment:	4,950
Seller's equity:	65,000
	− 55,000
	$10,000

Return on equity: $\dfrac{\text{Net income}}{\text{Equity}}$

Seller receives:	$ 8,627
Seller pays:	− 4,950
Net income:	$ 3,677

Seller's return: $\dfrac{\$ 3,677}{\$10,000} = 36.77$ percent

Figure 8–7 Wrap-around mortgage

Figure 8–8 Calculating the wrap-around yield

The seller can sell her property and at the same time generate an attractive yield on her remaining investment in the property by financing the sale. The yield is calculated in Figure 8–8.

risks are involved in completing a building on time and within the projected budget, the interest rate charged on such loans is higher than on conventional financing. In most instances, before a lending institution will commit to a construction loan, it will require a "standby" or "takeout" commitment from a permanent lender, whereby that institution agrees to provide the permanent financing upon completion of the project. The "takeout" commitment assures the construction lender that the construction loan will be paid off once the building project is completed. Although the construction loan may finance the entire cost of construction, most lending institutions place the funds in an escrow account from which the funds are released at various stages of construction.

Senior Mortgages

The order of priority of mortgages or deeds of trust is generally determined by the date they are recorded. A *senior mortgage* is a first mortgage that was recorded prior to any junior mortgage. A *junior mortgage* may be a second, third, or fourth mortgage, depending on how many mortgages were recorded ahead of it. Priority of a mortgage determines the degree of risk exposure to the lender. Senior mortgages create the least risk and result in lower interest rates charged to the borrower than that charged on junior mortgages. In the event of default and foreclosure of a mortgage, the proceeds from the foreclosure sale are distributed to the various mortgagees in order of their priority.

Junior or secondary financing is used when: (a) the buyer lacks sufficient funds to pay the difference between the first mortgage loan and the purchase price of the property; or (b) the buyer wants to maximize her financial leverage; or (c) the owner wants to "free up" some equity in her property.

FHA, VA, AND CONVENTIONAL MORTGAGES

There are three types of mortgages, classified as to whether or not a government agency insures or guarantees the loan.

FHA Insured Mortgages

The Federal Housing Act of 1934 created the Federal Housing Administration (FHA), whose primary objective was to stimulate the depressed housing industry by providing more and better means of financing mortgage loans. The FHA has been a leader in adopting loan reforms. Some of their accomplishments are as follows:

1. They were the first to introduce the fully amortized mortgage. As mentioned, prior to the depression, straight or term loans were used almost exclusively.
2. They were the first to offer mortgages with loan-to-value ratios of 80 percent. Formerly, the typical loan-to-value was 50 to 60 percent.
3. FHA was the first organization to develop minimum property standards.
4. FHA was the first to eliminate prepayment penalties for paying a mortgage off early. Some conventional lenders still impose prepayment penalties, but they are becoming a thing of the past in residential lending.
5. They were the first to allow loans to be assumed at the original interest rate.
6. FHA was the first to introduce the graduated-payment mortgage (GPM), thereby allowing prospective homeowners a chance to buy more house than they could otherwise afford.

The FHA is essentially an insuring agency. It generally does not make loans itself, but rather insures approved FHA lenders against loss on mortgages placed by them. Both the property and the borrower must meet certain standards and requirements to qualify for an *FHA insured mortgage* loan. An approved FHA appraiser must appraise the property before a loan is made.

FHA 203(b) Loans
Section 203(b) loans (loans on one- to four-family housing) enable the borrower to obtain up to 97 percent of the acquisition cost. The acquisition cost is the selling

Table 8–7   Maximum FHA 203(b) loans on housing in Dallas, Texas

1-Family	$101,250
2-Family	$114,000
3-Family	$138,000
4-Family	$160,500

price plus the estimated closing costs. A table of estimated closing costs for FHA loans is found in Appendix G.

The maximum loan amount for one-to-four-family residences under the 203(b) program varies by area of the country. The current maximum loan amounts for the area of Dallas, Texas are shown in Table 8–7.

Investors   These borrowers are able to obtain loans of 75 percent of the acquisition cost on one- to four-family properties up to the maximum loan amounts stated in Table 8–7.

Negotiated interest rate.   For years the Secretary of Housing and Urban Development set the interest rate on all FHA mortgages. Today, the interest rate is freely negotiated between the borrower and the lender on all FHA loans except for the FHA 232 and 235 programs.

FHA underwriting guidelines.   Contrary to popular belief, the FHA 203(b) program is available to anyone who meets the underwriting guidelines. There are no income limits beyond which a person is prevented from using the program. In 1986, President Reagan suggested that no family making in excess of $40,000 be allowed to use the FHA 203(b) program, but as of this writing, no such limitation exists.

FHA Underwriting Ratios

The FHA formerly used ratios that were based on a borrower's net effective (before tax) income rather than gross income to qualify a prospective borrower for a loan. In addition, they considered maintenance expense and estimated utility costs as part of the house payment. The revised underwriting ratios implemented in the spring of 1989 are as follows:

		Not to Exceed
1)	House Payment-to-Gross Income Ratio	29%
2)	Long-Term Debt-to-Gross Income Ratio	41%

These ratios are similar to the guidelines used by conventional lenders in that they are based on gross income. The *first ratio* is sometimes referred to as the income ratio, and it represents the allowable percentage of a borrower's gross income that can be used to cover the house payment. The house payment must include a provision for principal, interest, real estate taxes, and hazard insurance. The *second ratio* is sometimes called the debt ratio, and it represents the allowable percentage of a borrower's gross income that can be used to cover long-term debt. Long-term debt includes the house payment plus any other debt with twelve or more months remaining. Generally speaking, both of these guidelines must be met in order to obtain loan approval.

One-Time Mortgage Insurance Premium (MIP)

The borrower pays a premium for FHA insurance, which protects the lender from loss in case the borrower defaults on the mortgage. Up until 1983, the FHA insurance premium was collected monthly along with the principal and interest payment on the mortgage. Today, the FHA charges a *one-time mortgage insurance premium (MIP)* for most of their loans. The borrower has two options with regard to payment of the MIP. She may either pay the entire premium in cash at the closing or finance 100 percent of the premium. The premium rates vary depending on the length of the loan and whether the premium is financed or paid for in cash. See Table 8–8. The loan amount is multiplied by the appropriate premium factor to determine the one-time premium. The borrower is entitled to a refund of the unearned MIP upon early cancellation of the loan.

Other FHA Programs

FHA 222 (military-in-service). Military personnel on active duty for at least two years are eligible to obtain an FHA loan with a reduced down payment (no down payment on the first $25,000, 95 percent financing of the price that exceeds $25,000). The maximum loan amounts are the same as those under FHA 203(b). In addition, the government pays the mortgage insurance premium.

FHA 245 (graduated payment). The FHA 245 programs are all graduated-payment mortgages designed to reduce the buyer's monthly payments in the early years of the mortgage, thereby allowing her to qualify for a larger mortgage than under the standard FHA 203(b) program. There are presently five FHA graduated-payment plans:

1. Plan 1, wherein payments increase 2.5 percent per year for five years, then level out.
2. Plan 2, wherein payments increase 5 percent per year for five years, then level out.
3. Plan 3, wherein payments increase 7.5 percent per year for five years, then level out (this is the most popular plan).
4. Plan 4, wherein payments increase 2 percent per year for ten years, then level out.
5. Plan 5, wherein payments increase 3 percent per year for ten years, then level out.

Table 8–8 FHA mortgage insurance premium factors

Portion of MIP financed	Term of the loan			
	Less than 18	18–22	23–25	over 25
100%	.02400	.0300	.03600	.03800
0%	.02344	.02913	.03475	.03661

Note: Multiply the appropriate factor from the table above by the loan amount to obtain the one-time premium.

The GPM loans are available on single-family, owner-occupied homes only. Each of the plans has the same beneficial features of any other FHA mortgage. The primary disadvantages to the graduated payment plans are the increasing mortgage payments, the fact that higher discount points must be paid by the seller because of the limited appeal of this type of mortgage in the secondary market, and finally, the increase rather than decrease of the mortgage balance over the graduated period. This phenomenon of negative amortization is caused by the reduced monthly payments in the early years, which are insufficient to cover the interest alone. Hence, the interest accrues and is added to the mortgage balance.

FHA adjustable-rate mortgage. In 1984, the Federal Housing Administration announced a new FHA-insured adjustable-rate mortgage. The interest rate is indexed to the weekly average yield on one-year treasury securities. The interest rate is adjusted annually and cannot change more than 1 percent per year or more than 5 percent over the life of the loan. No negative amortization is allowed. The loans are available to owner-occupants of one- to four-family homes and single-family condominiums and for rehabilitation loans under the FHA 203(k) program.

FHA 235 program. The FHA 235 program is a government-subsidized mortgage to assist low-income families in purchasing a home. The applicant cannot exceed a certain income level to qualify. The mortgaged property must be either new or rehabilitated. If the applicant qualifies, the government will subsidize the monthly mortgage payment down to 4 percent interest. Until recently, the subsidy was an outright grant or gift to the borrower. Today, however, there is a *recapture provision* in the mortgage, which requires the borrower to pay back to FHA the lesser of

1. the total amount of the mortgage assistance payments; or
2. 50 percent of the net appreciation of the mortgaged property upon resale.

FHA growing-equity mortgage (GEM). The GEM mortgage provides for a fixed-rate thirty-year mortgage with an annual increase in the monthly payments after the first year. The *entire* increase in the monthly payment is applied to the principal, thereby paying off the loan in twelve to eighteen years, depending on the exact terms of the mortgage. Today FHA offers two GEM programs. The first plan provides for a 2 percent payment increase per year for ten years. The second plan calls for a 3 percent payment increase per year for ten years. In the eleventh year of both plans the payments level off.

Price-Level Adjusted Mortgage (PLAM)

FHA is about to unveil a revolutionary instrument called the ***price-level adjusted mortgage.*** The PLAM is a long-term, fully amortized mortgage in which the monthly payments are structured to be constant in purchasing power for the term of the loan. The initial payment is based on a long-term, fixed-rate loan at the prevailing real rate of interest, generally between 3 to 5 percent. Thereafter, the *monthly payment* and the *outstanding loan balance* are adjusted to reflect changes in the price level. The payments and the loan balance will be adjusted monthly based on the change in the seasonally adjusted Consumer Price Index, All Urban Consumers (CPI-U).

For example, a $100,000, thirty-year PLAM mortgage with a beginning real interest rate of 4 percent would have a monthly payment of $477.42 in the first month. The real rate of interest realized on mortgage loans since the war years has been at about 4 percent. If inflation increases at the rate of 6 percent per year for the term of the loan, the last monthly payment would have been adjusted up to $2,740. Although this looks like a shocking payment change, the $2,740 represents the same purchasing power as the $477.42 did thirty years prior. If the borrower's income just keeps pace with inflation, the monthly payment, in real dollars, will be no more than when the loan began.

The PLAM mortgage will allow home buyers to qualify for a larger initial loan because the payments are significantly lower at the beginning of the term. In the first fifteen years of the PLAM mortgage, negative amortization will most likely occur since the principal reduction on the mortgage will be less than the inflation adjustment.

FHA Assumptions

For all FHA loans originating after December 1, 1987, assumptions are not permitted without first notifying the lender. In addition, unless the original borrower obtains a written release of liability from the lender, she remains liable for a period of five years after the transfer.

The rule for notification varies, depending on whether the original owner is an owner-occupant or an investor. If the original owner was an *owner-occupant,* any person assuming the loan within *one year* of the original mortgage *must qualify* using FHA underwriting guidelines. If the original owner was an *investor,* any person assuming the loan within two years of the original mortgage must qualify using FHA underwriting guidelines.

After this one- or two-year period, loans are freely assumable without qualifying, and both parties are jointly and severally liable for the debt for five years. After the five-year period, full liability rests with the party assuming the loan. In effect, this eliminates the *simple assumption* for FHA loans originating after December 1, 1987. The rules for assumptions of loans originating after February 5, 1988, include:

- If an investor assumes a high-ratio loan-to-value (L-T-V) originated by an owner-occupant, the mortgage must be paid down to 75 percent loan-to-value if the seller is to be released from liability.
- If an investor assumes an 85 percent L-T-V for a secondary residence, the mortgage must be paid down to 75 percent if the seller is to be released from liability.
- If an owner-occupant assumes a high L-T-V mortgage for a secondary residence, the mortgage must be paid down to 85 percent L-T-V if the seller is to be released from liability.

The sales contract should indicate whether the original appraised value or a current appraisal is to be used to determine the loan-to-value ratio. If the contract calls for a current appraisal, the lender should use the higher of the two appraisals when calculating the loan to value.

Finally, a borrower is generally eligible for only one owner-occupied, high loan-to-value loan at any one time. If a borrower intends to keep for rent an FHA insured property and purchase another one using FHA financing, either the new one or the previously acquired property must be paid down to 75 percent loan-to-value.

Advantages of FHA Financing

- Low down payment—as mentioned, financing up to 97 percent of the acquisition cost is possible on owner-occupied residences.
- Lower initial monthly payments are possible with an FHA GPM.
- Loans originating prior to December 1, 1987, are fully assumable—no due-on-sale clause. In 1987 FHA began including a limited due-on-sale clause.
- No prepayment penalty—FHA requires that no prepayment penalty exist in an FHA mortgage.

Disadvantages of FHA Financing

- FHA loans generally take longer to process and approve than do conventional loans. Recently, however, many local lenders have been approved by FHA as "direct endorsers" and can approve loans without first submitting them to FHA. This "direct endorsement" program has helped expedite FHA loan approval.
- Some sellers are concerned that FHA appraisals and inspections may hinder the sale. In the past, FHA had their own appraisers and the turnaround time was slow. Today, FHA uses independent fee appraisers and the turnaround time has been curtailed. In addition, the quality of the appraisals has increased.
- Maximum loan amounts may be too low for some market areas. However, they are under constant review by FHA.
- FHA discount points are charged. Until a few years ago, the discount points had to be paid by the seller. The buyer was not allowed to pay the discount points. Today, however, the discount points that are charged may be paid by either the buyer or the seller. Example 8–5 demonstrates the use of discount points.

VA Guaranteed Loans

The Servicemen's Readjustment Act of 1944 (the GI Bill) was passed to provide benefits for World War II veterans. It has since been amended to include veterans of Korea and Vietnam. Veterans who served 180 days or more active duty after January, 1955, are eligible. Vietnam veterans need to have served only ninety days active duty. Section 503 enables the veteran to obtain a partially guaranteed, first-mortgage real estate loan on a one- to four-family, owner-occupied property. Both the borrower and the property must meet certain requirements. To qualify for VA financing, the veteran applies for a "Certificate of Eligibility." If the property is approved, a "Certificate of Reasonable Value" is issued. The Veterans' Administration guarantees lenders against loss in the event that the veteran defaults and the foreclosure sale does not bring sufficient money to cover the mortgage debt.

The following veterans are eligible:

1. A veteran who served at any time during the period *September 16, 1940, to July 25, 1947; June 27, 1950, to January 31, 1955; or August 5, 1964, to May 7, 1975,* and was discharged under conditions other than dishonorable after at least ninety days' active service (or less than ninety days in case of service connected disability).
2. Veterans whose active duty service occurred during the period after *July 25, 1947, and prior to June 27, 1950; after January 31, 1955, and before August 5, 1964; or after May 7, 1975, and prior to September 8, 1980,* and who served for a period of 181 days or more and were discharged or released under conditions

Example 8–5   Computing FHA Discount Points

FHA mortgage rates are made competitive with conventional mortgage rates through a process known as *discounting* that uses **discount points.** To discount means, of course, to take away. Generally, 1 point of the mortgage principal is discounted for each one-eighth of 1 percent difference between the FHA interest rate and the conventional interest rate. For example, in a $50,000 thirty-year mortgage, if the FHA rate stood at 15 percent and the conventional rate was 15.5 percent, the one half of one percent difference is equivalent to $\frac{4}{8}$; thus, the face amount of the mortgage would be discounted 4 points, as shown below:

<table>
<tr><td align="center">FHA</td><td align="center">Conventional</td></tr>
<tr><td colspan="2" align="center">15%—½% difference—15.5%</td></tr>
<tr><td colspan="2" align="center">equals</td></tr>
<tr><td colspan="2" align="center">⅛ or 4 points</td></tr>
<tr><td>Face amount of note</td><td>$50,000</td></tr>
<tr><td>Discounted by 4%</td><td>− 2,000</td></tr>
<tr><td>Lender's cash advance</td><td>$48,000</td></tr>
<tr><td>Points (4) paid</td><td>+ 2,000</td></tr>
<tr><td>Total</td><td>$50,000</td></tr>
</table>

The investor who lends $48,000 for a $50,000, 15 percent mortgage will receive $7,500 interest (15 percent) the first year plus a $2,000 (4 percent) discount. In other words, if the mortgage were paid off in the first year, the loan would yield 19 percent. However, if the loan ran the full thirty years, the lender's yield would be 15 percent interest plus one-thirtieth of 4 percent per year—since the total discount must be divided by the life of the loan. Historically, lenders have found that the average life of a single-family mortgage is eight years; consequently, most lenders compute 1 percent of discount as equal to one-eighth of 1 percent interest. In the above example, the effective FHA yield would be 15 percent per annum interest plus ⅛ or one-half of 1 percent interest, or an effective yield of 15.5 percent on the loan.

other than dishonorable or who served for a lesser period and were discharged or released for a service-connected disability.

3. Veterans whose active duty service began *after September 7, 1980, and who completed at least twenty-four months* of their original enlistment and were discharged or released under conditions other than dishonorable or who served at least 181 days and were discharged for hardship or disability reasons, or who served for less than 181 days and were discharged for service-connected disability.

4. Certain United States citizens who served in the armed forces of a government allied with the United States in World War II.

5. Unmarried surviving spouses of the above-described eligible persons who died as the result of service or service-connected injuries.

6. Service personnel whose service began prior to September 8, 1980, and who have served at least 181 days in active duty status, or whose service began after September 7, 1980, and who have served at least twenty-four months of the original

enlistment, even though not discharged, while their service continues without a break.

7. The spouse of any member of the armed forces serving on active duty who is listed as missing in action, or is a prisoner of war and has been so listed for a total of more than ninety days.

There is *no time limit* within which the veteran must use his **entitlement.** If the veteran pays off a VA loan and sells the property or it is assumed by a veteran who substitutes entitlement, the original *veteran's full* entitlement is *restored* and may be *reused.* In addition, any increases in entitlement that are passed by Congress are available to the veteran. If the veteran has *sufficient partial entitlement, he may obtain a second VA loan* to purchase another residence.

Generally speaking, the money for a VA loan is provided by an approved lender, who determines the maximum loan amount. The VA, however, sets the maximum allowable interest rate on the loan and appraises the property before committing to the loan guarantee. No down payment is required on a VA loan, and terms of thirty years are available. In some areas of the country where VA lenders are not available, the VA will make a direct loan.

Entitlement. The amount of the entitlement available to the veteran establishes the maximum loan amount he can receive with no down payment. The Veteran's Administration does not set the maximum loan amount, only the maximum guarantee or entitlement. The lending industry has set the maximum loan amount with no money down at four times the veteran's remaining entitlement, thereby resulting in a 75 percent "at-risk" factor for the lending institution. In other words, if a veteran still has his full entitlement, he can usually get a loan of up to $144,000 with no down payment ($36,000 × 4 = $144,000), 25 percent of which is guaranteed by the VA.

Partial entitlement. Even though a veteran has purchased a home using his VA entitlement, he may be able to acquire a second home using a second VA loan even though the first home has not been sold. In order to determine whether or not a second home can be purchased, the following must be determined:

1. The date the first home was purchased
2. The VA entitlement on the date of purchase of the first home
3. The entitlement that was used for the first purchase, calculated by applying the dates and figures from Table 8–9. Determine the remaining or residual entitlement that is left, if any.
4. The amount the guaranty has increased since the date of purchase to the present. Add this figure to the residual entitlement remaining, if any.

For example, let's assume a veteran purchased his first home in August of 1968 for $30,000. In looking at Table 8–9, we see that the maximum entitlement was the lesser of 60 percent of the selling price of $30,000 ($30,000 × .60 = $18,000) or $12,500. We can see that the veteran has no residual entitlement remaining from the original $12,500. However, there have been several increases in entitlement since 1968 (see Table 8–9) amounting to a total of $23,500 ($36,000 − $12,500). The veteran has acquired an additional $23,500 of entitlement and can now borrow up to $94,000 on a second home with no down payment, assuming he qualifies other-

Table 8–9   VA entitlement

Entitlement	Date
Original amount—$2,000	Before 1945
50% of the loan or $4,000, whichever is less	December 28, 1945
60% of the loan or $7,500, whichever is less	July 12, 1950
60% of the loan or $12,500, whichever is less	May 7, 1968
60% of the loan or $17,500, whichever is less	December 31, 1974
60% of the loan or $25,000, whichever is less	October 1, 1978
60% of the loan or $27,500, whichever is less	October 1, 1980
Feb. 1, 1988	*For loans of $45,000 or less:* 50% of loan or $36,000, whichever is less
	For loans above $45,000: 40% of the loan or $36,000, whichever is less, but never less than $22,500
	Therefore, for loans from $45,001 to $56,250, the minimum guaranty will exceed 40 percent.
	Manufactured home loans: The guaranty is 40 percent of the loan or $20,000, whichever is less.

wise. Remember, the lending institution will loan up to four times the remaining entitlement with no money down ($23,500 × 4 = $94,000 loan). Again, if the veteran wanted to borrow more than $94,000, he would be required to pay 25 percent of the excess over $94,000 as a down payment. The veteran's loan may be used to purchase a new home, to refinance an existing mortgage, to finance the remodeling of an existing home, or to purchase a condominium. The loan term is up to thirty years and no down payment is required.

Discount points.   As mentioned, lenders who place FHA or VA loans usually charge borrower's points. A point represents 1 percent of the loan amount. Discount points are used to increase the effective yield on a mortgage.

Discount points on FHA loans are negotiable between the buyer and seller. VA discount points *must* be paid by the seller.

Guarantee or funding fee.   The Veterans Administration charges the veteran borrower a fee for issuing a loan guarantee. It is referred to as a VA funding or guarantee fee. The fee is currently 1 percent of the loan amount.

VA underwriting guidelines.   The Veterans Administration uses the amount of money remaining after all appropriate expenses are deducted from the family's total gross income as an underwriting guideline. This residual amount is called the *balance available for family support*. The amount necessary to qualify for a loan varies by family size and by region. These figures may be obtained from the VA office in your area. The amount necessary to qualify for a VA loan in Houston, Texas, is

Veteran	$350
Veteran and spouse	$500
Each additional dependent	$ 90

Debt ratio. In addition to meeting the above residual income requirement, the veteran's long-term debt-to-gross income cannot exceed 41 percent. The Veteran's Administration defines long-term debt as any obligation with six or more months remaining.

Assumption of VA Loans

For all VA loans originating before March 1, 1988, there are three different types of assumptions.

1. *Simple assumption.* With a simple assumption, the original borrower is not released of liability to pay the loan and the original veteran's entitlement is not restored. Consequently, the new borrower need not be a veteran or approved by the Veterans Administration.
2. *Assumption with release of liability.* With this type of assumption, the original borrower is given a release of liability from the debt. However, the original veteran's entitlement is not restored. The new borrower need not be a veteran but the loan application must be approved by the VA.
3. *Assumption with release of liability and restoration of original veteran's entitlement.* When the new borrower is a veteran with sufficient remaining entitlement, and who is willing to use his entitlement, the original borrower will be given a release of liability and his *entitlement is restored.* Again, the VA must approve the loan application of the new veteran.

For all VA loans originating after March 1, 1988, the selling veteran must notify his lender before the property is sold so that the lender can qualify the buyer using VA underwriting guidelines. If the buyer qualifies, the loan is current, and the buyer agrees to assume the obligation, the selling veteran can be released from liability. If the selling veteran does not notify the lender before the property is sold, or if the buyer does not qualify, the lender can call the loan due and payable immediately. The first page of the mortgage must, in large, bold letters, indicate the following:

THIS LOAN IS NOT ASSUMABLE WITHOUT THE APPROVAL OF THE VETERANS ADMINISTRATION OR ITS AGENT.

A *processing fee* of up to $500 may be charged. In addition, a *transfer fee* of one-half of 1 percent of the remaining loan balance is charged.

Other VA Loans

The VA offers graduated payment mortgages (GPM), buy-down mortgages, growing equity mortgages (GEMs), and second mortgage loans in addition to the traditional thirty-year, fixed-rate mortgage.

Conventional Underwriting Guidelines

Although each of the various conventional lenders is free to determine its own underwriting guidelines for **conventional mortgages,** most have adopted those developed by the Federal National Mortgage Association and the Federal Home Loan Mortgage Corporation. As you learned in Chapter 7, these are the two biggest agencies operating in the secondary mortgage market. If any lender wants to sell packages of mortgages to these two agencies, they must comply with their underwriting guidelines. The current FNMA/FHLMC underwriting guidelines are as follows:

House Payment-to-Income Ratio.   Beginning in 1989, the maximum amount a borrower may spend on monthly payments for housing is 28 percent of her total gross monthly income, regardless of the loan-to-value or type of mortgage. The monthly house payment includes principal, interest, taxes, hazard insurance, private mortgage insurance (PMI), and association dues, if applicable.

Long-Term Debt-to-Income Ratio.   The maximum amount a borrower may spend on long-term debt is 33 percent of her total gross monthly income on 95 percent loans. On 90 percent loans and below, the ratio is 36 percent. According to FNMA, long-term debt must include all installment debt with ten months or more remaining and must include the monthly house payment as explained above.

Loans of 90 percent and 95 percent are available to owner-occupants. If the borrower is an investor who does not plan to occupy the property herself, 70 percent loans are available. Currently, the borrower may own up to four properties that are mortgaged, including her primary residence. This limitation is based on the borrower's total ownership, not just the number of loans sold to FNMA.

FNMA Loan-to-Value Limits on Refinancing

When all of the refinance proceeds are being used for purposes related to the property (e.g. home improvement, refinancing the mortgage), the maximum loan-to-value for the new loan is 90 percent for owner-occupied and 80 percent for investor-owned properties.

When any portion of the refinance proceeds are used for purposes unrelated to the subject property, the maximum loan-to-value for the new loan is 80 percent.

Equity takeout refinancing on properties that are not owner occupied is not allowed by FNMA.

FNMA Limitations on Buy-downs

Buy-down mortgages are used to allow a buyer to qualify for a larger mortgage than the borrower would otherwise obtain with a conventional mortgage. The lender collects a one-time, lump sum payment at the inception of the loan to buy the interest rate down below the prevailing market rate. The borrower is then qualified on the basis of the reduced (bought down) interest rate.

When a mortgage loan involves an interest rate buy-down, a downward adjustment in the selling price is necessary whenever the seller's cost of the buy-down or any other concession *exceeds:*

1. 6 percent of the lesser of the sales price or appraised value if the loan-to-value is greater than 90 percent.
2. 10 percent of the lesser of the sales price or appraised value if loan-to-value is 90 percent or less.

The sales price should be adjusted downward by the amount of the excess when calculating the loan amount.

Borrower Qualification on Buy-down Mortgages

If the property being financed is owner occupied and the loan is a fixed-rate mortgage, the borrower is qualified at the buy-down rate.

If the property being financed is owner occupied and the loan is an adjustable-rate mortgage with a loan-to-value of 80 percent or less, the borrower is qualified at the buy-down rate.

The Federal National Mortgage Association (FNMA) has announced that they will not purchase buy-down mortgages on investment properties.

FNMA/FHLMC Loan Limits

Effective January 1, 1986, FNMA/FHLMC announced an increase in the loan limits on mortgages they buy from lenders. The new limits are shown in Table 8–10.

OTHER FINANCING DEVICES

Installment Land Contract

The *installment land contract* (or, as described in Chapter 4, *contract for deed*) is a common method of financing the purchase of real estate when money is tight. The buyer and seller enter into a contract that provides that the buyer is to furnish a down payment to the seller and pay the balance of the selling price to the seller on an installment basis over a period of years. The buyer takes possession at the signing of the contract and pays the taxes and insurance on the property. The seller contractually agrees to deliver the deed to the buyer upon final payment of the selling price. Meanwhile, the deed is usually held in escrow. In case of default, the contract seller generally retains the down payment and all other payments as liquidated damages. Installment land contract sales generally command a higher selling price than ordinary sales because of the generally lower down payment requirement and the minimal closing costs.

Participation Agreements

Participation agreements in a mortgage, sometimes called *kickers,* enable the lending institution to participate in the earnings or equity growth of the property that it is financing. The use of kickers or sweeteners is prevalent during periods of tight money to induce the reluctant lender into making the loan.

Assuming Versus Taking Title Subject to Existing Financing

Another method of financing real estate is to take over the existing financing on the property being sold. Such a strategy may be very advantageous in periods of tight money or when the interest rate on the seller's property is considerably lower than prevailing rates and the buyer is able to take over the existing mortgage balance at the lower rate. The buyer may either **assume and agree to pay** the existing mortgage debt, or she may purchase **subject to** the existing mortgage. Under either alternative, the buyer must make the mortgage payments and abide by all other pro-

Table 8–10   FNMA/FHLMC loan limits

	Maximum Loan
Single-Family	$187,600
2-Family	$239,950
3-Family	$290,000
4-Family	$360,450

visions stipulated in the mortgage or she may lose the property through foreclosure.

When the buyer purchases *subject to* an existing mortgage, she is not personally liable to pay the debt. The worst that can happen to her upon default and foreclosure is that she will lose her property and any equity she had in it. If the foreclosure sale does not bring sufficient proceeds to cover the debt, the lender has recourse against only the original mortgage holder and may sue her for a deficiency judgment.

On the other hand, if the purchaser *assumes* the existing mortgage, she assumes personal liability and becomes coguarantor on the debt. In the event of default and foreclosure, the lender has recourse against both the buyer and the original mortgagor (the seller) for any deficiency. The buyer is primarily liable; but if she does not have sufficient assets to pay the deficiency judgment, the lender will sue the seller. The seller, in turn, will take legal action against the buyer to collect on the deficient monies owed.

Upon occasion, when the financial standing of the buyer is strong or the pledged property itself is sufficient protection, the lending institution will give the seller under an assumed mortgage a *release of liability.* However, institutions are not usually inclined to do so.

Sale-and-Leasebacks

The *sale-and-leaseback* is a financing device whereby an investor either purchases or builds a building, sells it, and simultaneously leases it back for a long-term period. Many different variations of a sale-leaseback exist; they were covered in depth in Chapter 6.

Municipal Bonds (Tax Exempt)

Recently, cities have raised single-family mortgage money by selling tax-exempt *municipal bonds.* The bond proceeds are loaned through local savings and loans who earn a fee for processing the loan and collecting the monthly payments. The municipalities determine who qualifies for the bond money. Most cities reserve the money for low- and moderate-income families. Since the interest on such bonds is not taxable to the purchaser of the bonds, the mortgage money can be offered at rates of anywhere from 1.5 to 3 percent below the going rate on conventional mortgage loans. The concept is not without its critics. Some complain that pouring low-interest mortgage money on the housing market will only increase the inflation of home prices. Others are concerned that the large influx of bond offerings will hinder the sale of municipal bonds for the more traditional public building programs. Savings and loan associations that do not participate in the program complain that those who do so engage in unfair competition. The Internal Revenue Service, which could lose millions of tax dollars, complained sufficiently to cause President Reagan to call for legislation limiting the use of such bonds.

The *Omnibus Reconciliation Act of 1980* placed the following federal limitations on the use of tax-exempt bonds to finance home ownership:

1. In any state, dollar volume per year cannot exceed $200 million or 9 percent of that state's average mortgage activity within the last three years, whichever is smaller.

2. The funds must be used to originate a new mortgage; they cannot be used to replace an existing mortgage.

3. The mortgagor must not have been a homeowner within the three years prior to application, except for those seeking rehabilitation loans or loans in "targeted" areas.

4. The home financed must be the borrower's primary residence.

5. Mortgage loans can be used to finance one- to four-family units; however, in the case of multiunit structures, one of the units must be owner occupied.

6. The value of the home purchased with a municipal mortgage bond may not exceed 90 percent of the median value of homes in the Standard Metropolitan Statistical Area or 110 percent of the median value in a "targeted" area.

7. Whenever a purchaser assumes a mortgage financed by the tax-exempt loan money, she also must meet the three-year requirement, the primary-residence requirement, and the purchase-price restrictions.

8. "Targeted" areas are defined as census areas wherein 70 percent of the family incomes amount to only 80 percent or less of the state's median income. Other "targeted" areas may be designated by the individual states in economically distressed areas.

As can be seen, these limitations are numerous and complex. Many states have decided not to fight the bureaucratic red tape involved in the issuance of such bonds. Consequently, the number of issues across the country has diminished. The 1986 Tax Reform Act further restricts the use of bond issues to finance real estate.

Mortgage Credit Certificate (MCC)

In most participating states, the first-time home buyer can receive a tax credit of 20 percent of the yearly interest paid on a mortgage to purchase a single-family primary residence. In other states, the tax credit may vary from 10 to 15 percent. The credit cannot exceed the taxpayer's tax liability for the year. Any unused credit may be carried forward. There are maximum income and property cost limitations that apply to the program, and they vary from state to state. The tax credit is available each year as long as the taxpayer continues to reside at the property.

For example, assume a primary residence is purchased using a $60,000 mortgage at 10 percent interest over thirty years. The purchaser would pay $6,000 in interest expense the first year. The 20 percent tax credit, $1,200, reduces the purchaser's tax liability by that amount. This program may be used in conjunction with either FHA, VA, or conventional loans. The participating lenders determine the specific terms of the loan.

Refinancing

Refinancing occurs when an investor obtains a new loan to pay off an old one. Properties are generally refinanced for one of the following reasons:

1. To take advantage of falling interest rates or longer mortgage terms, thereby reducing debt service payments and increasing the cash flow to the equity investor.

2. To generate more investment capital for the investor by borrowing against the increased equity created primarily through property appreciation. This creates "tax free" cash that may be reinvested in other properties, thereby increasing

Example 8–6   Refinancing to "Free up" Owner's Equity

Assume a property was purchased ten years ago for $125,000. The investor purchased it with an 80 percent, twenty-five-year, 9 percent interest, fully amortized mortgage. The property has been appreciating 5 percent per year since the purchase. By refinancing, the investor can generate $68,000 tax free cash as follows:

Ten years earlier

Purchase price	$125,000	$100,000 first mortgage
5% appreciation per year or 50% over the ten-year period		Loan balance being reduced annually through amortization of the loan
		$82,000 loan balance in ten years

Ten years later

Market value, now	$187,500
	× .80
New first mortgage	$150,000
Pay-off balance of old mortgage	− 82,000
"Tax-free" cash generated for owner's use	$ 68,000

The interest rate on the new $150,000 first mortgage is at the prevailing rate at the time the refinancing took place, thereby necessitating an adjustment of the principal and interest payment. Also, most lenders charge a 2- or 3-point refinancing fee which is figured on the amount of the new loan.

---

investment holdings. This refinancing process is known as *pyramiding*. Example 8–6 illustrates how refinancing can free up the owner's equity in an investment.

3. To pay off the seller in a contract-for-deed sale containing a refinancing clause that requires the contract buyer to pay off the contract in a stipulated period of time.
4. To generate cash to meet any other financial obligations.

The reader is reminded that FNMA has set refinancing limitations on any loans they purchase.

ALTERNATIVE FINANCING METHODS

Buy-down Mortgages

As discussed earlier, a **buy-down mortgage** is an instrument that decreases the interest rate on a mortgage by means of making a lump-sum, advance payment of cash, which thereby reduces the monthly mortgage payments during the buy-down period and enables more prospective buyers to qualify for the loan. The buy-down period of time is usually from one to five years; funds for the buy-down payment can be provided by any source. Many builders arrange for buy-down mortgages and make the "buy-down" payment in order to provide below-market financing for their prospective purchasers. Individual home sellers and friends or relatives of purchasers are now assisting with buy-down payments as a creative way to enable the purchaser to buy a property in spite of the prevailing high interest rates.

The Federal National Mortgage Association (FNMA), the nation's largest purchaser of mortgages in the secondary mortgage market, has agreed to purchase certain buy-down mortgages. For a list of the current limitations on mortgage buy-downs, contact the nearest FNMA office. Example 8–7 illustrates an FHA graduated buy-down.

Until recently, customers for a buy-down mortgage were qualified on the basis of their ability to handle the first year's principal, interest, taxes, and insurance payments. This underwriting practice enabled more people to qualify for a buy-down mortgage than the standard mortgage. Conventional, FHA, and VA lenders all have a different policy regarding borrower qualifications on a buy-down mortgage. The Federal National Mortgage Association (FNMA) allows conventional lenders to qualify borrowers at the buy-down rate on owner-occupied properties financed with either fixed-rate mortgages or ARMs with a loan-to-value of 80 percent or less. FHA lenders will allow borrowers to be qualified on the buy-down rate not to exceed 2 percent below the market rate. The Veteran's Administration qualifies borrowers at the note rate or market rate, not the buy-down rate. Each of these lenders has changed their policy on this matter several times in the last two years. The reader is encouraged to contact local lenders for any up-to-the-minute changes.

Direct Purchase Loans

One of the frequently used methods of financing in periods of rising interest rates has been the use of *first purchase-money mortgages.* For instance, when a seller is attempting to sell her "free-and-clear" home (i.e., a home without a mortgage encumbrance), she may agree to offer a below-market first purchase-money (PM) mortgage to entice a prospective purchaser. The terms of the PM mortgage are similar to those of a conventional mortgage, except they usually contain a "call provision" that requires the buyer to refinance and pay off the seller in a stated period of time, usually two to five years. In the meantime, the buyer makes the monthly principal and interest payments to the seller. The problem with this type of financing is that the seller is locked into an investment that can't readily be converted to cash in an emergency. Also, the buyer is faced with a "balloon" payment and the prospects of refinancing at what could be even higher rates in the future.

These problems have been alleviated somewhat by the introduction of ***direct purchase loans*** by the Federal National Mortgage Association (FNMA). The FNMA has announced their willingness to purchase both first and second purchase-money mortgages that have been negotiated between the buyer and the seller if they meet certain guidelines. This direct purchase program will make it considerably easier for sellers who offer buyers purchase-money mortgages to convert such loans into cash by selling the mortgages to FNMA. The mortgage must comply with the following guidelines to be acceptable for purchase by FNMA.

1. The mortgage must originate with the help of a mortgage banker, savings and loan association, or a bank that normally works with the FNMA.

Example 8–7   Graduated 3-2-1 Buy-Down

Sales price:	$62,000	Down payment:	$13,150.00	
Mortgage amount:	$48,850	Buy-down period:	3-year	
Mortgage term:	30 years	Buy-down type:	Graduated 3-2-1	
Current rate:	15.5			

Months	Interest rate	P&I payment	Monthly buy-down payment	Annual buy-down payment
1–12	12.5	$521.36	$115.90 × 12 =	$1390.80
13–24	13.5	559.53	77.73 × 12 =	932.76
25–36	14.5	598.20	39.06 × 12 =	468.72
37–360	15.5	637.26	—	—
			Total buy-down cost	$2792.28

The first year's monthly buy-down payment is calculated by subtracting the monthly P&I payment at 12.5 percent ($521.36) from the monthly P&I payment at 15.5 percent ($637.26), resulting in a buy-down cost of $115.90 per month for year one.

	Conventionals loan qualification	
	Buy-down mortgage	Standard mortgage
Monthly P&I payment (first year)	$521.36	$637.26
Monthly mortgage insurance	20.34	20.34
Monthly homeowners insurance	18	18
Monthly RE taxes	60	60
Total monthly	$619.70	$735.60
Annual PITI* payment	$7436.40 ÷ .28 =	$8827.20 ÷ .28 =
Income needed to qualify	$26,558.57	$31,525.71

*Principal + Interest + Taxes + Insurance

2. The lender assisting in the mortgage origination must comply with sound underwriting procedures regarding the property appraisal and the borrower's creditworthiness.
3. The mortgage must provide regular twenty- to thirty-year level monthly payments with no balloon.
4. The mortgage and note used must be the standard FNMA instruments.

The local bank or S&L that the seller uses to assist in originating the mortgage will perform all the standard functions of a normal loan transaction except supply the money. In exchange for their help, the lending institution will receive a service fee of three-eighths of 1 percent of the loan balance from FNMA. When the seller is ready to sell the mortgage, she contacts the lending institution servicing the loan, which will get a commitment from FNMA to buy the loan at a certain price. The price offered will depend on the relationship between the rate stated in the mortgage and current rates. Meanwhile, the buyer will continue to make payments to the lender servicing the loan without the worry of making a balloon payment in the near future. The willingness of FNMA to convert approved first and second purchase-money mortgages held by sellers into cash provides a valuable financing device which should alleviate at least some of the seller's concerns about "taking back" a note in order to assist the buyer in the home purchase.

Ground Lease

Some developers sell the buyer the house but lease her the ground. This arrangement can often reduce the down payment and the monthly mortgage payments. The ground lease usually contains an option-to-purchase provision.

Lease-Option

A *lease-option contract* provides the lessee-optionee with the use of property for a prescribed period along with the option to purchase the property within a certain period of time. The contract includes the price of the property and the term of the option. At some time during the term of the option, the lessee decides whether or not she wants to exercise the option. If she does, the provisions in the lease usually allow some of the rent payment to go toward the purchase price. Unless specific provisions in the lease prohibit it, the lessee may sell or assign her option rights. If and when an option is assigned to a third party, the assignee may then exercise her option and acquire title to the property. If the lease itself is assigned, the option rights are assigned with it unless specific provisions prohibit that. Finally, the lessee may assign the lease to one party and the option rights to another party, unless specifically prohibited.

Lease-Purchase

The *lease-purchase instrument* enables a buyer to lease the property for a stated period of time, usually one to two years, after which she purchases it at a prearranged price. The lease period gives the lessee time to save the required down payment and/or to allow interest rates to decline before the purchase. It differs from a lease-option in that the lessee-optionee is not obligated to exercise her option-to-purchase, whereas the lessee in a lease-purchase agreement has legally obligated herself to purchase.

Shared Equity

Some builders with an unsold inventory of homes are offering prospective buyers the opportunity to buy one-half ownership in a home, while the builder retains ownership of the other one-half. The buyer generally supplies one-half the required down payment and the builder supplies the other half. The buyer is charged an agreed-upon rent for the right to occupy the home, and the two partners share equally in the remainder of the mortgage payment and other expenses. This arrangement appears attractive to the prospective purchaser who could not otherwise afford a full down payment or a higher monthly payment. However, the shared equity has some of the same problems the SAM mortgage faces.

Financing the Down Payment

The majority of this chapter has concentrated on methods of financing home purchases. Most of these methods require a small down payment. With today's inflation, more and more potential home buyers are having difficulty saving the required down payment for a home purchase. Figure 8–9 enumerates several sources to consider in obtaining the necessary funds for the down payment.

Proposed Housing Legislation

The National Affordable Housing Act of 1989 proposed that individuals who have not owned a home within the last three years be allowed to use their retirement accounts for a down payment on the purchase of a primary residence. Massachusetts Governor Michael Dukakis and some senators have suggested similar legislation.

Figure 8–9 Sources of down payment

- Obtain a loan from a friend or relative.
- Obtain a loan from your credit union.
- Obtain a salary advance.
- Borrow on the cash surrender value of your life insurance.
- Refinance other property.
- Obtain an unsecured loan from your bank.
- Sell your silver or gold jewelry.
- Refinance your car.
- Obtain a second mortgage loan from the seller or a third party.
- Ask for cash as your wedding gift with an explanation.
- Pledge any securities.
- Income tax refunds.
- Purchase on "contract" with no money down.
- Sell your antiques.
- Lease-option and save, save, save during option period.
- Use sweat equity.
- Sell any company stock you hold.
- Pledge the company stock as collateral for a loan.
- Acquire a VA Mortgage—100% financing.
- Acquire an FHA mortgage—low down payment requirement.
- Assume an FHA or VA loan with small down payment requirement.
- Negotiate an "assumption" on a foreclosed property held by a lending institution requiring little or no down payment.

Since home ownership has declined in the last few years and first-time homeowners are having increasing difficulty in saving for a down payment, some version of this legislation is likely to pass.

REMEDIES OF THE LENDER UPON DEFAULT

The purpose of the mortgage is to provide security for the lender in case of default by the mortgagor. Because of this security, the lender is more willing to lend the money. If default does occur, there are several remedies available to the mortgagee to recover the money due.

Strict Foreclosure

Under *strict foreclosure* or foreclosure by writ of entry, the lender petitions the court and asks that the mortgagor's equity of redemption be cut off or foreclosed. The court then establishes a period of time within which the mortgagor must pay the debt or forfeit all interest in the property forever to the lender. There is no judicial foreclosure sale. If the value of the property exceeds the amount of the debt, the lender has profited. If the value of the property is less than the debt, the borrower may still be held liable for the deficiency. Very few states permit strict foreclosure today. Its two main advantages are that it eliminates both the expensive and time-consuming judicial sale and the statutory redemption period.

Judicial Foreclosure

Judicial foreclosure is the most commonly accepted remedy in most states today. Although the procedures vary from state to state, the action involves a court proceeding to foreclose or cut off the mortgagor's equity of redemption and to sell the pledged property at a public auction to pay off the debt. If the sale proceeds are not sufficient to cover the debt, the lender may sue for a deficiency judgment; however, deficiency judgments have been eliminated in several states. If the proceeds from the foreclosure sale are in excess of the senior lienholder's claims, the excess is distributed according to the property rights of junior lienholders or the mortgagor. If there is no excess, the junior lienholders may seek a judgment for full payment of their claims. In those states not having a statutory right of redemption, the successful bidder at the foreclosure sale receives a chancellor's or sheriff's deed. Some states provide the mortgagor one last chance to redeem her property after foreclosure for a set period of time. This statutory period of redemption varies from state to state and may be as long as two years. In these states, the successful bidder is given a *certificate of sale* and receives the deed after the statutory period of redemption has expired.

Steps in a Foreclosure

The following procedures are included in a *foreclosure:*

1. The title is searched or an abstract is prepared to identify all parties who have an interest in the property to be foreclosed. The search may reveal junior lienholders who will be summoned to the foreclosure proceedings so that they may protect whatever interest in the property they have.

2. Summons and complaint are served on the mortgagor and any junior lienholders revealed in the title search.
3. If the mortgagor has a defense against the foreclosure, she files an answer to the complaint, resulting in a trial by jury.
4. If the mortgagor does not answer the complaint, foreclosure proceeds to a conclusion, and a judgment decree is obtained by the mortgagee on the amount to be collected. This decree is filed with the court, and a court order directs the property to be sold at a public auction.
5. Notice of the foreclosure sale is given to all known defendants and published in a local newspaper.
6. Bids are made on the property. The mortgagee can, and usually does, bid on the property up to the amount of the mortgage to protect her interest in it. The successful bidder receives a certificate of sale in those states having *statutory rights of redemption*. A deed would be given to the successful bidder in those states not having a statutory right of redemption.
7. If surplus money remains after the first mortgage is paid off, junior mortgagees who have filed a **surplus money action** will be paid off in order of their priority. If the sale proceeds are not sufficient to pay off the first mortgage, the mortgagee may file for a **deficiency judgment** on the note unless the mortgaged property alone is security for the debt (nonrecourse loan). (Some states do not allow deficiency judgments.)
8. After all periods of redemption expire, the successful bidder receives a deed.

Foreclosure by Exercise of Power of Sale (Foreclosure by Advertisement)

In several states, nonjudicial foreclosure by exercise of power of sale (foreclosure by advertisement) is permitted. This type of foreclosure requires that the mortgage contain a *power of sale* clause, which stipulates that the mortgagee may advertise, sell, and disperse the proceeds of the pledged property without the need of judicial action. Although this method of foreclosure is speedier and less expensive than judicial foreclosure, in many states the mortgagee relinquishes her right to deficiency judgments and the mortgagor relinquishes her redemption rights. Since foreclosure by exercise of power of sale is not confirmed by a judicial proceeding, it is subject to attack. However, the mortgagee can request a judicial foreclosure rather than foreclosure by exercise of power of sale if she prefers to do so.

Foreclosure by Management

Lenders may stipulate in the mortgage agreement that, upon default by the borrower, the lender can take over the property and manage it until the delinquent amounts have been paid. This places the mortgagee in a position of property manager.

Foreclosure by Entry

Foreclosure by entry is allowed in Massachusetts, Rhode Island, Maine, and New Hampshire. There the mortgagee may peaceably enter the property (unopposed by the mortgagor) in the presence of witnesses. She can then place the property for sale. If the mortgaged property has a market value that is higher than the debt, the mortgagor is entitled to the difference. She is also given a statutory right of redemption that varies from one to three years.

Foreclosure by Voluntary Deed

The mortgagor may voluntarily quitclaim deed her interest in the mortgaged property to the lending institution to avoid the embarrassment of a foreclosure. If the *voluntary deed* procedure is followed, the mortgagor may later claim that she was pressured into signing the quitclaim deed and seek to have it invalidated. Junior liens are not satisfied or eliminated by a voluntary deed, which leaves it as a less satisfactory method.

SUMMARY

The mortgage instruments of today evolved from concepts developed in early England. Most states recognize and practice either the title theory or the lien theory of mortgage law. A small number of states recognize a form of mortgage law that combines some of the characteristics of each of the other two theories. These states are known as intermediary states.

Each mortgage (deed of trust) contains covenants and clauses that are common to all. These covenants and clauses outline the duties and responsibilities of the mortgagor with respect to caring for the mortgaged property and the method of repaying the debt. In addition, other clauses outline the remedies available to the lender in case the borrower defaults or breaches any of the covenants in the mortgage.

In recent years, the number of different types of mortgage instruments has increased dramatically. Skyrocketing interest rates from 1979 to 1982 forced the S&L industry to reevaluate their investment policy of borrowing short-term and lending on a long-term, fixed-rate basis. The number of flexible rate and graduated payment mortgages is mushrooming. The adjustable-rate mortgage (ARM), elastic mortgage, and rapid-payment mortgage (RPM) are all relatively new mortgage instruments designed to aid the troubled S&L industry and still provide some type of financing for the potential home purchaser. Home purchasers often use some form of "creative" or alternative financing methods. The most commonly used forms of creative financing include contract-for-deed sales, mortgage buy-downs, land-leases, and purchase money mortgages.

High unemployment, decreasing property values, poor underwriting and appraisal practice, and a sluggish economy have all led to record high mortgage defaults and subsequent foreclosures. Judicial foreclosure is the most commonly accepted remedy in most states. Foreclosure by exercise of power of sale, by entry, by management, and by voluntary deed are other, less common remedies.

You can check your understanding of these terms against the glossary in Appendix A or by review in this chapter.

Adjustable-rate mortgage (ARM)
Alienation clause
Balloon payment
Budget mortgage
Buy-down mortgage
Call
Carryover provision
Certificate of sale
Conventional mortgage
Deed of trust
Default clause
Deficiency judgment
Direct purchase loans
Discount points
Due-on-sale clause
Elastic mortgage
Entitlement
Estoppel certificate
FHA insured mortgage
FHLB board
Fixed-rate mortgage
Foreclosure
Foreclosure by sale
Fully amortized mortgage
Graduated-payment adjustable-rate mortgage (GP-ARM)

Graduated-payment mortgage (GPM)
Growing-equity mortgage (GEM)
Installment land contract
Interest escalation clause
Interim loan
Intermediate theory
Junior mortgage
Lease-option contract
Lease-purchase instrument
Margin or spread
Mortgage
Mortgage credit certificate (MCC)
Mortgagee
Mortgage insurance premium (MIP)
Mortgagor
Municipal bonds
Negative amortization
Note
Omnibus Reconciliation Act of 1980
Open-end mortgage
Owner's rent clause
Partial release clause

Partially amortized mortgage
Power of sale
Prepayment clause
Price-level adjusted mortgage (PLAM)
Receiver clause
Refinancing
Renegotiable rate mortgage (RRM)
Reverse annuity mortgage (RAM)
Sale-and-leaseback
Senior mortgage
Shared appreciation mortgage (SAM)
Straight (term) mortgage
Subordination clause
Surplus money action
Trust deed or deed of trust
VA guaranteed loan
Variable-rate mortgage (VRM)
Voluntary deed
Wrap-around mortgage (WAM)

What are the differences or relationships, if any, between the following?

Acceleration clause and Interest escalation clause
"Assuming" and Taking title "subject to"
Equity of redemption and Statutory right of redemption
FNMA and GNMA
Fully amortized mortgage and Partially amortized mortgage
GEM and RPM

GPM and GP-ARM mortgage
Installment land contract and Contract for deed
Lease-purchase instrument and Lease-option contract
Lien theory and Title theory
Package mortgage and Blanket mortgage
Renegotiable rate mortgage and

Canadian rollover mortgage
RPM and Biweekly mortgage
SAM and GEM mortgage
Senior mortgage and Junior mortgage
Strict foreclosure and Judicial foreclosure
Wrap-around mortgage and Purchase money mortgage

PROBLEMS

8-1. Why is an owner's rent clause inserted in a mortgage contract? How does it differ from a receiver clause?

8-2. When is a wrap-around mortgage used?

8-3. Differentiate between an FHA insured and a VA guaranteed loan.

8-4. Assume that landowner A is selling her farm to developer B on contract for deed. Why might the developer insist on a subordination clause in the sales contract? What might the landowner request if she agrees to subordinate?

8-5. What are the alternatives available to the mortgagee in case of default of the mortgagor?

8-6. If you had a chance to *assume* a VA mortgage or take it *subject to,* which would be the better deal? Answer the same question for a conventional mortgage.

8-7. Differentiate between title theory and lien theory of mortgage law.

8-8. What is the effect of a due-on-sale clause in a mortgage contract?

8-9. What kind of title is held by the trustee in a deed of trust?

8-10. What are the advantages and disadvantages of a SAM mortgage?

8-11. What are the primary advantages to a deed of trust over a mortgage?

8-12. Explain the mortgage *buy-down* concept.

8-13. Explain FNMA's *direct purchase* program.

8-14. Using Table E–1 in Appendix E, calculate the monthly principal and interest payment on a $74,000 loan at 12 percent, thirty years.

8-15. Referring to the above question, what would be the total cost of a three-year, three-two-one buy-down?

8-16. What is the balance on the above loan after five years? after ten years? after 20 years? (Use Table F–9, Appendix F.)

8-17. How does a growing-equity mortgage (GEM) differ from a rapid-payment mortgage (RPM)?

8-18. Describe the features of the elastic mortgage.

8-19. What are the four common features of all ARM loans? What are some of the optional features found in most ARM programs?

8-20. Discuss the FNMA underwriting ratios used by most conventional lenders.

SUPPLEMENTARY READINGS

Beaton, William R. *Real Estate Finance,* 2nd ed. Englewood Cliffs, N.J.: Prentice-Hall, 1982.

Boykin, James H. *Financing Real Estate.* Lexington, Mass.: D.C. Heath & Co., 1979.

Case, Frederick E., and Clopp, John M. *Real Estate Financing.* New York: Wiley, 1978.

Dennis, Marshall. *Fundamentals of Mortgage Lending.* Reston, Va.: Reston Publishing, 1978.

Hoagland, Henry E. *Real Estate Finance,* 6th ed. Homewood, Ill.: Irwin, 1977.

Johnson, Ross, and Henderson, Thomas. *Real Estate Finance.* Columbus, Oh.: Merrill, 1985.

Kratovil, Robert, and Werner, Raymond J. *Real Estate Law,* 8th ed. Englewood Cliffs, N.J.: Prentice-Hall, 1983. Chapters 20 and 21.

Melicher, Ronald, and Unger, Maurice A. *Real Estate Finance,* 3rd ed. Cincinnati, Ohio, South-Western Publishing Co., 1989.

Sirota, David. *Essentials of Real Estate Finance,* 4th ed. Chicago, Ill.: Real Estate Education, 1986.

Wiedemer, John P. *Real Estate Finance,* 5th ed. Reston, Va.: Reston Publishing, 1987.

CHAPTER 9
Taxes and Liens

The rights and interests of people who own real estate have been discussed. These rights, however, are subject to the rights and needs of others, including the public and the government. Taxes and liens are two means of exercising these external rights.

Funds obtained from real estate taxes are used to support public schools, street improvements, parks, police and fire protection, and other governmental operations. The power to tax is vested in the legislative branch of the government and is limited by the Constitution. The taxes are levied on real property by cities, counties, or other local governing agencies. The amount of taxes and the method of levy and assessment vary considerably from state to state and from town to town within a state; however, the procedures involved are usually very similar.

An understanding of taxes and the taxing system is important when handling real estate transactions for two reasons. First, the taxes on property entail such a substantial amount of money that they act as a constraining influence on buyers in purchase decisions. A real property tax is a charge or burden that must be paid each year; thus, it affects the value of the property. Second, at the closing of a real estate transaction, the taxes are prorated such that the seller and buyer pay their correct portions. This *proration,* or allocation, affects the amount of money needed by the buyer at the closing.

Two basic types of taxes are related to real property. The first is the *general tax,* which is based on the value of the property. The second type consists of *special assessments.* A special assessment is a levy to cover costs of improvements, such as sidewalks or street lights, which primarily benefit certain properties.

General Taxes

General taxes are levied by local governing agencies such as cities, towns, counties, and school districts. Taxes levied on real estate provide a substantial portion of the funds required for the general operations of local government, including schools, fire and police protection, parks, and salaries. These taxes, being based on the value of the property, are called *ad valorem* (from the Latin, *at value*) taxes. General taxes are levied on the basis of the ability to pay concept, since owners of more expensive property pay higher taxes than owners of lower-priced property.

The taxation process consists of several steps. These steps occur in sequence as follows:

1. Determination and appropriation of the amounts of money needed to operate the government
2. Assessment of property and allocation of the levy to each property
3. Collection of the taxes

Budget and Levies

Budgeting is the first step in the taxing process. At the beginning of the budgetary period, which is usually every year, the legislative body determines how much money is needed by each segment of the local government, such as the schools or street maintenance. These needs are then compared to an estimate of the money available from taxes. If the projected funds available do not meet the expected expenses, either the expenditures must be reduced or the sources of money must be expanded. This budgeting step is then followed by an *appropriation,* which is a formal enactment or law defining exactly how all of the money is to be spent and indicating the sources of the funds, including the real property tax. Following the appropriation, the legislative body of the town, county, or other taxing unit votes to decide the method used to impose this tax on persons or property. This process is called *tax levy.* Frequently, the maximum amount or rate of tax that taxing bodies can levy on real estate is limited by law or local referendum.

Assessed Value

Each parcel of real property in a locality is assigned an assessed value in order to determine the amount of taxes to be paid by the property owner. The property value is estimated by a tax assessor employed by the city, county, or other governing organization. The total property value is generally estimated separately for the land and building and then combined on the tax bill. The methods and procedures for appraisal will be covered in Chapter 19. However, the value for tax assessment purposes is sometimes quite different from the market value or expected selling price. Frequently, state laws or local rules establish the assessed value as a certain percentage of market value.

These percentages vary from 25 to 100 percent. Farm property is an exception, for farms are often assessed at market value even though other property is assessed at a lower percentage. The town, county, or tax district making the tax levy maintains a tax list (usually called an *assessment roll*) that defines each piece of property under its jurisdiction, together with its latest assessed value.

When estimating property value, the assessor considers factors such as recent selling prices of similar property, estimated cost of reproducing the structure, location, depreciation, and income from the property. The typical assessor is experienced in the profession and uses systematic procedures to arrive at property values. The assessor tries to assess all property in a locality at a fixed percentage of its market value, so that the tax will be equitable. Constitutional provisions require that property taxation be uniform in a locality to ensure that owners of similarly valued property pay the same amount of taxes; however, this uniformity is not always easy to achieve because of the many variables affecting value.

Since there is considerable room for difference of opinion as to the value of a specified parcel of property, property owners who do not agree with their assessed value or who feel that an error was made can *appeal* their assessment to the established local review agency. This agency may be called the *board of review, board of organization, town tribunal,* or *board of appeal,* depending on the taxing unit. Property owners who still do not agree with the rulings of those agencies can appeal further to the courts.

Tax Calculations

The general tax is based upon the assessed value and the tax rate. Assume that a house has an estimated market value of $60,000 and that the local policy is to assess property at 60 percent of market value. The assessed value can be calculated as follows:

$$\text{Assessed value} = 0.60 \times \$60{,}000 = \$36{,}000$$

The tax rate is determined by dividing the amount of money needed by the city (assume $4 million) by the assessed value of all property (assume $200 million). In this case, the city would need to collect two cents for each dollar of assessed valuation or, in other words, $2.00 per $100 of assessed valuation.

$$\text{Tax rate} = \frac{\$4,000,000}{\$200,000,000} = .020$$

Tax rates are usually expressed as dollars per $100 of assessed value, or mills per dollar. Assume that the tax rate was $2.00 per $100 of assessed value, which is the same as $.020 per dollar or 20 mills per dollar. The tax in our example would be figured in this way:

$$\text{Tax} = .020 \times \$36,000 = \$720$$

or, by the other method of calculation:

$$\text{Tax} = 2.00 \times \frac{\$36,000}{100} = \$720$$

The tax of $720 would then be billed to the taxpayer.

Tax Collection

States and localities differ in billing methods and the date when a tax is due. In most cases, the taxpayer is allowed to pay the taxes in installments. For example, half of the year's taxes could be due in May and the remaining half in September. Often a city, county, school district, or other unit will set its own tax rate. In order to avoid duplication in the tax-bill mailings, however, it is standard practice for the county to collect the total taxes on a combined bill.

Enforcement

Taxes and special assessments must be valid and enforceable, however. This means the tax must be for a legal purpose, must be levied properly, and must be applied uniformly to the affected properties. General taxes, if not paid, become a tax lien against the property. Tax liens take priority over any other existing liens (as discussed later in this chapter), and the property can be sold—within the constraints of the law—to satisfy the lien.

If a property is sold at a tax sale, the original owner of the real estate, who lost the property due to nonpayment of taxes, has a right in some states to redeem the property within a specific period of time, defined by individual state statute. This is known as the ***statutory right of redemption.*** If an owner should redeem his property by later payment of the tax, he will be required to pay an additional interest penalty—often as much as 2 percent per month, depending upon state law.

Equalization

Sometimes taxes are levied by the state government on the basis of property values. To avoid duplication of the assessing functions, the state will base the taxes upon the assessments made by local assessors under local rules. To assure that all property owners in the state pay a fair and uniform share of the state tax, an ***equalization factor*** is established by the state. For example, property in a county that assesses property at 60 percent of market value would be adjusted relative to other counties in the same state that assess their property at 50 percent of market value. To illustrate, assume there are similar houses in each of two counties, with a market value of $40,000 each. The assessed value in the first country would be 0.60 × $40,000, or $24,000. In the second county, the assessed value would be 0.50 × $40,000, or

$20,000. If the state equalization factor were based on 50 percent of market value, the assessed value in the first county would be equalized by multiplying the assessed value of $24,000 by ⅚, resulting in $20,000, the same as the assessed value in the other county. The objective is to levy a state tax on assessed values already on the books (so that a separate state assessment is not needed), but to adjust the tax so that all state residents pay a tax in the same proportion to market value.

These equalization factors are established by a body, usually called the state *board of equalization*. Some states have passed laws that require all real property to be assessed at 100 percent of market value. In such a case, equalization is not needed.

Exemptions

Most states have laws that exempt certain types of property from real estate taxes, provided the property is used for tax-exempt purposes. Typical properties not taxed are hospitals, educational institutions, and real estate owned by religious organizations. Also, governments or their agencies do not tax themselves or each other. So property owned by the state or federal government and properties used for parks, schools, or recreation are tax exempt. It is important that taxing bodies use great care to determine the tax-exempt status of a given property because, when any property is exempt from taxes, other properties must bear a higher tax burden.

Many states have a provision whereby the property taxes of senior citizens are reduced. Usually, a formula that is based on income and ability to pay is specified by state law to reduce the tax. This provision has been adopted because older persons often purchased their homes in the 1930s or 1940s. They are now retired and have lower incomes. It is not uncommon for a house to have appreciated from $5,000 to $40,000 since the 1930s. This would bring about a proportional increase in taxes. The objective of the special law is to prevent loss of property by these senior citizens due to their inability to pay the property tax. Some states also have special veterans' exemptions.

Local governments sometimes grant tax *exemptions* or reductions in tax in order to attract new industries. The rationale is that the economic advantage provided by the new industry outweighs the tax loss.

Variations in Property Taxes

Property taxes vary considerably throughout the United States. Tax rates are usually lower in small towns, but they also vary widely from city to city. Property taxes on a $60,000 house may be less than $200 in one place and up to $3,000 in other locations. This wide variation can result from different types of property in the community, level of services offered, government efficiency, and other sources of revenue available. Some cities in the Southwest obtain income from oil wells on city property. Northern cities may have considerable expenses for snow removal. Some towns collect separate trash collection fees and add sewer fees to water bills. In other cities, higher taxes result from such things as larger welfare payments, subsidized public transportation, more parks, libraries, or other services. In California, Proposition 13 to severely limit property taxes was approved by voters. Similar referendums have passed in other states. All of these factors affect property taxes.

Large amounts of exempt property also cause rates to be higher; however, the federal government will reimburse local governments in areas where federal installations exist. Areas with high-priced homes usually generate more taxes than they consume in services. Many local areas benefit from more taxes than they consume in services; many also benefit from federal government revenue sharing. Higher wage rates in some large cities result in higher tax rates. Last, but not least, some cities are managed more efficiently than others, either due to the layout of the city or because of better management.

Variations may also exist within a city, even though it is the objective to have equal taxes for properties of equal value. Sometimes properties sold are automatically reassessed on the basis of the sale price, whereas other properties may not be reassessed until the regular periodic schedule. All of these factors affect the amount of taxes in a locality. One state, Pennsylvania, gives cities the choice of a land tax as an alternative to the property tax. Under the land tax concept, land is taxed heavily and there is no tax on buildings and other improvements. The concept was promoted by nineteenth-century American economist Henry George and is intended to promote the development of land. Some cities in Pennsylvania use a modified land tax.

Special Assessments

Certain municipal improvements benefit the community as a whole, whereas other improvements mainly benefit the owners of specific parcels of real estate or residents of limited areas. Installation of sidewalks in a residential area would typically fall into the second category. *Special assessments* are taxes levied upon specific parcels of real estate where owners will primarily be benefited by a proposed improvement. Where the primary purpose of an improvement is to benefit the public in general, such as widening a street to facilitate through traffic, the improvement is normally not financed by special assessments, even though incidental benefits may also accrue to the properties in the immediate neighborhood.

Originating an Assessment

Procedures for originating and implementing a special assessment will vary from state to state; however, certain steps are usually involved. The idea for improvement may originate in either of two ways. First, the legislative authority in the locality, such as the city council, may originate the proposed improvement. The second method is for the property owners who want the improvement to petition for it. In either case, notices would be given to property owners affected, and hearings would be held to hear their views and to ascertain the pros and cons of the proposal. Following the hearings, the authorized legislative authority (such as the city council) may pass an ordinance approving the action and setting forth the costs and the properties to receive the special assessment.

Assessment Roll Spread

A method is needed to allocate the total improvement cost among the benefited property owners fairly and equitably. The amount of assessment allocated to each parcel of real estate is determined by either (a) front footage or (b) estimated benefit from the improvement. Thus, each piece of property will not necessarily be assessed the same amount. This allocation is often called the *assessment roll spread.* Following any hearing, if the assessment is approved, it becomes a lien on the properties involved and bills are issued to property owners for payment. Property owners usually have the option to pay the full amount at one time or to pay yearly install-ments with interest on the unpaid balance. Special assessments are enforced by the same means as general property taxes.

LIENS

A *lien* is a claim by a creditor, taxing body, or court *(lienor)* against a property owner *(lienee)* whereby the property is security for payment of a debt. It is a legal right that permits a creditor to have the debt satisfied out of the property of the debtor. The lien may entitle the creditor to have the property of the debtor sold to satisfy the debt, whether or not the debtor agrees. The enforcement of the lien is normally carried out through a court action. Liens can be categorized in different ways. The first category groups liens as either equitable liens or statutory liens. An *equitable lien* is sometimes called a *voluntary lien* and is placed with the consent of the owner. For example, consider this case: an owner requests a mortgage and signs the note to obtain the loan. In the process, the mortgagee acquires a lien on the property. *Statutory liens* are different and exist where the law allows a creditor to file a lien without owner concurrence; for this reason, these liens are also called *involuntary* liens.

Liens are also classified as either specific liens or general liens. A *specific lien* is placed against a specific parcel of real estate. These include mechanic's liens, mort-gages, tax liens, and other liens against a single parcel of property. A *general lien,* in contrast, affects all real and personal property of a debtor and might result from state or federal inheritance taxes, judgments, or debts of a deceased person.

Each state has its own law or statutory provision covering requirements for liens. An understanding of liens is important in the real estate business because a lien affects the value or marketability of a parcel of property. When a piece of property is forceably sold to satisfy one or more creditors, liens are paid off in the sequence in which they are recorded, except in the case of tax liens, which have priority. The buyer in a real estate transaction must make sure as part of the title examination that the property being purchased is not encumbered by liens. If there were liens on the property, the liens would remain as a liability for whoever owns the property. The lienholder could foreclose and force sale of the property to satisfy the lien. Therefore, liens must be paid off or otherwise settled prior to or during the closing of the transaction.

A pending lawsuit relating directly to the land can be recorded as a *lis pendens.* The purchaser of a property would then take the title subject to the rights of parties as finally determined by the judgment or decree.

Types of Specific Liens

Specific liens are against one parcel of real estate and do not affect other property of the debtor. There are several different types of specific liens, including mechanic's liens, mortgage liens, vendor's liens, vendee's liens, and attachments.

Mechanic's Liens

Mechanics are persons such as carpenters or electricians who provide the labor or services used in the construction or improvement of real property. Material sup-pliers provide the lumber or other supplies used in the construction. Laws in all states give these mechanics (whether they be contractors, subcontractors, or laborers) and material suppliers some security that they will be compensated for their work and material by granting them the right to place a ***mechanic's lien*** against the property on which the labor or materials were used. Some states include services of surveyors, truckers, and architects. This right is derived from the theory that the value of the property has been enhanced, and therefore the parties contributing to the increased value should have a right of security for the work or materials furnished. The mechanic's lien is a specific lien because only the property on which the work was performed and improved in value is subject to the lien.

The fact that work was carried out is not always sufficient to allow a lien to exist. In some states, the lien claimant must show proof of being hired by the property owner. In other states, it is sufficient if the lien claimant can show that the property owner had knowledge of the work, even though the work was ordered by someone else. Laws governing these latter cases are known as ***consent statutes.*** The owner is said to give implied consent because he had knowledge of the work and did not object to it. Thus, the agreement to perform the work can be *express* or *implied,* but need not be in writing.

A mechanic's lien is usually established when the claimant files a notice of the claim under oath with the county clerk. Some states require that a copy of the notice also be mailed to the owner of the property against which the lien is being filed. The lien must contain a description of the property, the name of the owner, the name and address of the lien claimant, the name of the person who originally ordered the work, and dates when work was ordered, started, and completed. These dates are very important since some states allow liens to take precedence on the basis of the date when the work was ordered, whereas others use the date on which the work was started. The contract price, amount paid to date, and balance due must also be given on the notice of claim. The balance due then becomes the amount of the lien.

Since property owners are sometimes subjected to false claims, there are also statutory provisions to protect them. Frequently, the owner will hire a ***contractor,*** and the contractor in turn may hire one or more ***subcontractors.*** When a contractor has completed his work, the property owner has the right to hold back a portion of the amount due until the contractor has furnished an affidavit or proof that all subcontractors and material suppliers have been paid. This procedure is important, since in many states subcontractors, as well as the general contractor, have the right to file a lien against the property on which they performed their work.

The law in these states imposes upon the property owner the obligation to assure that subcontractors as well as the contractor are paid. What happens when an owner pays the contractor, but the contractor fails to pay the workers or the material supplier? Sometimes a contractor may run short of cash and use the money for other projects he is working on. The fact that the contractor had been paid by the owner does not remove the right of a subcontractor to file a lien. This means that the property owner must be careful to require the contractor to have signed releases from all workers and suppliers before the owner pays the contractor. An alternative is to assure that the contractor is bonded. Other states require subcontractors to give the property owner advance notice of amounts due to them so that the owner can know how much to withhold.

Sometimes a tenant will order work on the property he rents. An owner is not, however, liable for payment for work ordered by a tenant without the owner's knowledge and consent. If a person holding less than a fee simple estate authorizes work to be done, only his interest can be attached.

Mechanics and material suppliers are allowed a set period of time in which to record a lien; therefore, a lien might exist but not appear on the record in the recorder's office. The lien must, however, be filed while the work is still in progress or within a period established by law (typically three months) after completion of the work to maintain its priority. When filed, it is effective retroactively in priority to the date the work was completed or the supplies were furnished. In cases where a mechanic fails to file within the set period and pretends to perform additional work, the courts have not allowed this pretense to preserve the priority beyond the allowed period.

A lien does not continue for an indefinite period of time, nor does it automatically assure the lien claimant of his money. The lien expires in a time set by state law, usually one or two years, unless the lien claimant takes action to enforce the lien. Enforcement consists of taking action to foreclose the lien by initiating a court action resulting in a sale of the property and paying off the lien from the sale proceeds. Since there is often a considerable amount of time from the filing of a lawsuit until the judgment is rendered, a creditor can give notice of his claim against a parcel of real estate by recording the notice in the county where the real estate is located as a *lis pendens*. Its filing prevents the expiration of the lien and takes priority among liens at the time the notice is recorded. The right to a mechanic's lien is coupled with the right of the mechanic or material supplier to take legal action against the persons who ordered the work on the basis of contractual liability.

Discharge of a mechanic's lien.   There are several ways to remove or make ineffective a mechanic's lien:

1. The property owner can pay the amount of the claimed debt to the lien claimant. A **certificate of execution** or **satisfaction of lien** would then be signed by the lien claimant, acknowledged, and filed with the county clerk's office.
2. A lien expires after a set period of time unless an action has been taken by the lien claimant to enforce it. A court order can then be obtained to remove the lien from the record.
3. The owner can deposit money into court or post a bond equal to the amount of the lien. The property is then freed and the lien claimant has recourse to the bond or money deposited.
4. The property owner may disagree with the lien and have the lien claimant served with notice to commence action to foreclose within a period of thirty days. The objective is to bring the claim into court for trial. If the lien claimant should fail to prosecute or should lose the court action, the lien is discharged by order of the court.

Mortgage Lien

A mortgage is executed by the property owner to borrow money, using the property as security. The property owner signs a mortgage note that becomes a lien against the property. (Mortgages were discussed fully in Chapter 7). When the mortgage is paid off, the lien is discharged. If the mortgage payments are not paid when due, the mortgagee can foreclose on the property. A mortgage lien is a voluntary lien, since the owner requests the mortgage and agrees to the lien upon execution of the mortgage instrument. It is also a specific lien, since the lien is against only the specific parcel(s) of real estate. Most mortgage institutions will accept only a first mortgage; thus there will be no other liens with higher priority. Any second or further mortgages would have a lower priority, just as would any liens filed at a later time. A mortgage lien can be transferred by the mortgagee to another party by assignment of the mortgage and mortgage note.

Tax Lien

If taxes or special assessments are not paid, they become a specific lien against the property on which they were levied. Property tax liens take priority over other liens, even though other liens may have been recorded earlier. The property can be sold to enforce the tax lien. Mortgage institutions, in order to preclude the possibility of having tax liens take priority over their mortgage liens, often require that the mortgagor pay amounts each month in addition to interest and payment on principal. The lending institution will then accumulate these monies and pay the tax when due. These monies are called *impounds;* some institutions pay interest on these impounds, whereas others do not.

Environmental Lien

The federal Superfund statute (or CERCLA) imposes strict cleanup liability on the owner or operator of property where hazardous substances exist. Thus, a purchaser of contaminated property may become liable for the cleanup of pollution from a prior owner's business.

Some state laws provide for similar cleanup liens. Other states have statutes dealing with such concerns as restoration of mines and wells and regulation of service stations, often containing provisions for liens. Sometimes statutes provide for "superliens," liens for reimbursement of cleanup expenses that have priority over existing liens, except taxes.

Vendor's Lien

A *vendor's lien* or (*seller's lien*) arises when a seller conveys real estate and receives a mortgage from the purchaser for the balance of the purchase price. The seller receives a *purchase money mortgage* that becomes a lien on the property for the balance due. The lien can be enforced by foreclosure if the buyer does not make payments in accordance with the contract agreement.

Vendee's Lien

A *vendee's lien* (or *buyer's lien*) arises when a contract is drawn up for a real estate transaction, the buyer gives the seller a deposit, and then the seller defaults. Since the seller defaults and refuses to go through with the transaction, the buyer then has a lien against the property. This lien would be for monies paid as deposits under contract plus any other money expended by the buyer as part of examining the title for the property. This type of lien can also be enforced by foreclosure, as can any other lien.

Attachments

Suppose that one person A is suing another person B for monetary damages. Under certain circumstances, the plaintiff A is allowed by statute to file a lien, or *attachment,* against real property of the defendant B, pending the outcome of the court action. The objective of the plaintiff's action is to assure that, when the court action is completed and a judgment is rendered, there will be property of the defendant available to pay the amount awarded by the court. The plaintiff must file a bond to pay any costs and damages that the defendant may suffer if the defendant wins the suit. This condition tends to protect against malicious, nuisance, and other unjusitified suits.

Bail Bond Lien

A bail bond is used to release a person from jail where he is being held on a criminal charge. Real property can be used as bail in lieu of cash, and a bail bond lien is then filed against the property to secure the bond. When the person is released, the bail bond lien is discharged by a certificate obtained from the state's attorney or a court.

Conditional Bills of Sale

Certain articles of personal property, such as stoves, furnaces, air conditioners, elevators, or other items, can be installed in real estate as a property improvement. The articles can be purchased under an agreement called a **conditional bill of sale.** The title does not pass until the goods have been paid for completely. The seller can file the conditional sales agreement in the county recorder's office in the same way that any real estate document is recorded. It then takes priority in the same manner as a lien.

Types of General Liens

General liens normally affect all of the debtor's property, both real and personal. General liens can come about from judgments, decedent's debts, state inheritance taxes, federal estate taxes, corporation franchise taxes, and conditional bills of sale. Each of these can constitute a claim or lien against real property.

Judgments

A *judgment* is a court order that may result in an award of money to the plaintiff. A judgment for an award of money becomes a lien against real and personal property of the debtor. The court order is accompanied by a **writ of execution** that may direct the sheriff to seize and sell the debtor's property in sufficient amount to pay the judgment and any expenses involved in the sale. The judgment can take priority over other liens on the basis of the date the judgment was entered in court, the date the writ of execution was issued, or the date the judgment was filed. The priority depends on the individual state law. A judgment lien is attached to all real property held by the debtor and under the jurisdiction of the court. It remains in effect for a period of time governed by state statute, usually ten years.

When any judgment is paid or otherwise satisfied, the debtor should obtain a formal receipt from the lien claimant or court to be recorded so that there is no later question that the judgment has been satisfied and no longer exists as an encumbrance on the property.

Decedent's Debts

Upon someone's death, title to his real property passes to his devisees by will or to his heirs by law if there is no will. The property is subject to liens existing at the time of the debtor's death. In addition, debts of the deceased person can become liens against the property. In the process of settling the estate, the debts are paid first out of personal property in the estate; but if debts still remain, the real property can be sold to pay the debts. Until these debts are paid, they are a lien against the decedent's real property. A buyer of property from an estate should obtain proof that all debts of the decedent have been paid; if not, the property can be taken to satisfy the debt.

Federal Estate Tax

Transfer of the net estate of a decedent is subject to a federal estate tax. The tax is progressive, so that larger estates are taxed at a higher percentage. A resident of the United States is allowed a certain exemption. A general lien can be filed by the federal government for this tax that attaches to all property in the estate.

State Inheritance Tax

In most states, a tax is levied against an inheritance. By statute, the state acquires a lien upon the real property of the estate, and a clear title cannot be given until the tax is paid. Persons purchasing property from an estate should make sure that any inheritance taxes have been paid or that the title has been cleared.

Corporation Franchise Tax

Corporations are assessed a franchise tax in accordance with the state law. The tax is based upon either capital stock or income and becomes a lien on the property of the corporation until paid.

Priority of Liens

As mentioned, liens usually take priority in the order in which they are filed or recorded. If there is a foreclosure on the property and it is sold for less than the value of all liens and mortgages, the liens of highest priority would be paid first and other lien holders would be paid in the order of their priority. A holder of a lien may willfully make it subservient to another lien. For example, the holder of a lien on a parcel of land in a development may agree to make his lien subordinate to a construction mortgage for a house.

Taxes and special assessments, if not paid, become the highest priority liens without regard to dates. Mortgage institutions usually require the homeowner to deposit monthly installments on the tax *(impounds)* to assure that the tax is paid when due, so that no tax lien takes priority over the mortgage lien.

SUMMARY

Real property taxes are an important means of obtaining funds for schools, street construction and repair, and other functions of local government. Taxes fall into the two primary groupings of general taxes and special assessments. General taxes are levied throughout the community on the basis of estimated property values as related to the funds needed by the local government. Special assessments are levied on properties that benefit from special work being done, and the amount is based on the cost apportioned according to the benefit each property owner receives from the improvement.

A lien is a claim against a property owner causing the property to become security for payment of a debt. Of the many types of liens, two primary groups are the most important. Statutory (involuntary) liens are allowed by law, whereas equitable (voluntary) liens are those in which the property owner requests or agrees to the lien. An example of an equitable lien is a mortgage. Liens can also be classified as specific or general. Specific liens attach to one parcel of property, whereas general liens attach to all of a person's property. With some exceptions, liens take priority by date of recordation, so that any foreclosure and sale of a property will result in higher priority liens being paid first. This could mean that some lienholders may not be paid.

TERMS AND CONCEPTS

You can check your understanding of these terms against the glossary or by review in this chapter.

Ad valorem	Equalization factor	Purchase money
Appropriation	Exemption	mortgage
Assessment roll spread	Impound	Satisfaction of lien
Attachment	Judgment	Statutory right of
Certificate of execution	*Lis pendens*	redemption
Conditional bill of sale	Mechanic's lien	Tax levy
Consent statutes	Proration	Writ of execution

What are the differences or relationship, if any, between the following?

Contractor and	General taxes and	Vendor's lien and
Subcontractor	Special assessments	Vendee's lien
Equitable liens and	Specific liens and	
Statutory liens	General liens	

PROBLEMS

9-1. The objective in a community is to have the assessment be 40 percent of market value. If the assessment is $24,000, what would you expect the house to sell for in the open market?

9-2. The assessed value on property A is $21,000. The general tax rate is $1.85 per $100 of assessed value. What is the tax?

9-3. The tax rate in Jarvis township is 24 mills per dollar of assessed value. The assessed value of house B is $19,400. What is the yearly tax?

9-4. The general tax on property C is $684 per year. The lending institution wants the mortgagor to make monthly deposits with them. How much should be paid each month in addition to interest and payment on principal to have sufficient funds to pay taxes when due?

9-5. What is the order of priority among a number of liens on the same property?

9-6. If you were building a house or having a substantial improvement made, what precautions could you take against mechanic's liens?

9-7. Describe what a mechanic must do to enforce a mechanic's lien.

9-8. List the types of government services that a property owner helps finance by paying property taxes.

9-9. If a property is foreclosed and the proceeds are more than sufficient to pay a tax lien or mechanic's lien, what happens to the surplus? What if the proceeds are not sufficient?

9-10. If a property owner disagrees with a property tax assessment, describe the steps that can be taken to contest the assessment.

9-11. Outline the steps a local taxing body would take in arriving at a tax rate.

9-12. A city has a budget of $740,000 to be paid out of property taxes. Total taxable property in the city has a market value of $100,000,000, and the assessment ratio is 40 percent. Determine the total assessed value of property and the tax rate needed to support the budget.

9-13. Mr. D'Angelo owns a house and lot with a 188 ft. frontage. His property has a market value of $97,000, with a city assessment ratio of 55 percent. His yearly tax bill was $1,997.00. Calculate the millage rate (mills per dollar) in the city. Also determine his bill if the city were to assess owners $45 per front foot for paving the street.

9-14. D'Angelo is considering buying another property with a market value of $76,550. The current assessment rate is 70 percent, and the tax rate is 31 mills. What is the property tax?

9-15. Mr. Jones signed an agreement to sell his house to Mr. and Mrs. Axon. Prior to closing, the Axons' attorney found a mechanic's lien on the property. What options are available to the buyer and seller?

9-16. All counties but one in a state assess property at 50 percent of market value. County K assesses at 65 percent of market. Property A in County K is assessed at $13,000. If a state tax were imposed based on assessed property values, to what value should property A be revalued, based on an equalization factor?

9-17. Proposition 13 was passed by voter referendum in California. Voters elsewhere have approved similar provisions, which limit tax rates on real estate. Discuss some implications of these actions.

━━━━━━━━ SUPPLEMENTARY READINGS

Beeman, William J. *The Property Tax and the Spatial Pattern of Growth Within Urban Areas.* Washington, D.C.: Urban Land Institute, 1969.

Case, Karl E. *Property Taxation: The Need for Reform.* Cambridge, Mass.: Ballinger, 1978.

Faber, Stuart J. *Real Estate Liens, Encumbrances, and Secured Transactions,* 2nd ed. Los Angeles: Lega Books, 1979.

French, William B., and Lusk, Harold F. *Law of the Real Estate Business,* 5th ed. Homewood, Ill.: Irwin, 1984. Chapter 20.

Gold, David G. *Property Tax Relief.* Lexington, Mass.: Lexington Books, 1979.

Guerin, Sanford M. *Taxation of Real Estate Dispositions.* New York: McGraw-Hill, 1982.

King, Alvin T. *Property Taxes, Amenities and Residential Land Values.* Cambridge, Mass.: Ballinger, 1973.

Kratovil, Robert, and Werner, Raymond J. *Real Estate Law,* 8th ed. Englewood Cliffs, N.J.: Prentice-Hall, 1983. Chapter 39.

Peterson, George E. *Property Taxes, Housing, and the Cities.* Lexington, Mass.: Lexington Books, 1973.

Rawson, Mary. *Property Taxation and Urban Development: Effects of the Property Tax on City Growth and Change.* Washington, D.C.: Urban Land Institute, 1961.

Ring, Alfred A., and Dasso, Jerome. *Real Estate Principles and Practices,* 11th ed. Englewood Cliffs, N.J.: Prentice-Hall, 1989. Chapter 25.

CHAPTER 10
Land Use Planning and Zoning

Land can be used for farming, industry, commerce, residential living, or recreation. A particular parcel of land could be used for any one or more of these possible uses. The use that gives the land the greatest value is called the highest and best use. Experience has shown that land usually holds it value better when its use is controlled and it is surrounded by land used for similar purposes. As an urban area expands, it becomes important to plan the use of land rather than to let it be developed in an unplanned manner.

Land use planning can originate from either public or private sources. Public agencies plan for the orderly and logical development of a community. The objective of private planning is to maximize the efficiency and utility of a parcel of land.

To be effective, land use plans must provide a means to assure that the objectives are achieved. A variety of legal measures are available, both public and private, to restrict uses and assure conformance to the plan. Public planning can be enforced by zoning. Private plans can be implemented by restrictions or covenants placed in deeds, plats, or related documents.

Most public land use planning takes place in urban areas or land surrounding the urban area. Substantial changes in urban areas are brought about by economic, social, and political forces. The resulting expansion of urban areas is often rapid and accompanied by the creation of blight areas and slum areas as well as problems in transportation, water pollution, and sewage. Many cities or urban areas have commissions to deal with urban expansion and its related problems. These commissions have been established in order to bring about orderly, planned change. Their primary approach is to establish a ***master plan*** for the urban area. The master plan attempts to balance the residential, industrial, commercial, and recreational areas. It is then necessary to enforce the plan through restrictions on land use that are implemented by (a) zoning regulations and building codes (as discussed in this chapter) and (b) requirements for starting subdivisions of residential or industrial construction (as discussed in Chapter 18).

URBAN PLANNING

The transition from horse-and-buggy to heavy automobile and truck traffic has caused the cities to undergo substantial changes. In the past, many cities expanded without controls or plans. In fact, in the 1920s, cities frequently developed in a manner that blocked further orderly growth. Areas were developed without provision for utilities, transportation, or parking (although the future needs for off-street parking could not have been foreseen at that time). Since 1950, however, most urban areas have set up commissions to establish a plan and enforce it. In some cases, the commissions have been established as advisory, making subsequent enforcement difficult if not impossible.

In the 1950s and 1960s, urban planning progressed to the stage of a profession in itself. Today, some universities offer undergraduate and graduate degrees in urban planning to prepare people to assume responsible positions in city government. City planning has become as much an art as a science, involving ecological considerations, human relations, and economic knowledge, in addition to the ability to solve the technical problems of urban areas.

Although there was a trend of heavy population movement to urban areas in the years from 1940 to 1960, there has also been a concurrent trend for urban areas to decentralize. The growth of the total urban area is often accompanied by the establishment of suburban communities. Some of these communities resist being formally incorporated into the nearby city because of the higher tax burden imposed.

In a sense, urban planning results from competition between urban areas as well as from pressures from within the area. New industries locate in urban areas where there are social advantages and pleasant living, as well as in areas having lower costs and other economic advantages. Carefully planned industrial parks attract industries, whether they be companies just starting or older companies moving from a site that is too small or from an area that has become blighted.

Levels of Planning

Urban area planning takes place at the federal, regional, state, and local levels. Federal planning may deal with overall national needs, whereas a regional plan may deal with a problem in a particular area. As examples of regional planning, urban areas around the Great Lakes work together on water conservation problems, communities around New York City work together on transportation and traffic, and communities around Los Angeles cooperate on smog control.

Cities and urban areas derive their planning powers from state laws. State laws authorize municipalities to incorporate under a charter from the state and to operate within these delegated powers. State legislatures have also given these municipalities the right to establish planning commissions under legislation referred to as *enabling acts.*

A local area will then establish a planning commission to set objectives and to set up the means for control. This planning body may be either elective or appointed. It may be either advisory or have executive responsibility, although experience has shown that a planning commission, in order to be effective, needs the authority to enforce its decisions.

The development and implementation of the master plan require funds. Initial funds can be secured from bond issues because the plan usually results in building projects that increase taxable values. Thus, bond issues for master plans provide for a return through future taxes of amounts substantially higher than the original costs of the master plan.

Planning Procedure

The planning commission will usually begin by reviewing the present community layout. Meeting with local civic and business organizations is an important step in learning their needs and gaining support for plans as they are formulated. The commission will normally require a staff to carry out much of the work, usually under the guidance of a director. An initial step is to make a land survey or prepare a map showing all the physical aspects of the area, including streets, land elevation, existing buildings, utilities available, and other important factors.

Along with the physical layout, the urban area economics must be extensively analyzed. Many questions must be answered. What is the past and future economic character of the area? What types of industry are prevalent and what other industries might be attracted to the area? Is industry in the area sufficiently diversified to avoid economic downturns or situations where certain industries become depressed or obsolete?

The primary technique for analyzing community income and economic prospects is *economic base analysis.* This process is carried out by determining planned increases in employment for the various types of industry in the area. Part of the analysis will include a study of the effects of industrial employment upon service employment in the area. Sources of service employment are barber shops, restaurants, retail stores, and other businesses where the customers are primarily local. Other measures of economic activity should also be measured and projected. These factors would include the number of households, commercial structures, bank deposits, and motor vehicles. The past and present population should be studied along with future projections. This study should include racial makeup, occupations, employment, and any apparent long-term trends. Another factor to consider is the *dependency ratio,* which compares the dependent part of the population to the productive segment as follows:

$$\text{Dependency ratio} = \frac{\text{population under age 20 or over age 65}}{\text{population age 20 to 65}}$$

The result of this initial effort is the master plan for the area. It designates areas for residential, commercial, recreational, and industrial use. It may also break areas down into lower classifications, such as the type of residences permitted. The planners will then determine what public facilities are needed to support the master plan. These facilities include utilities, transportation, schools, and recreational areas.

Those responsible for planning also have to consider how the master plan will influence the tax structure, so that an excessive burden is not placed on some individuals or organizations. Excessive tax burdens could force companies or individuals to avoid or move out of the urban center or community to a more favorable tax area.

The plan should also include requirements and procedures for developers of subdivisions to submit plans for approval. Those responsible for reviewing the plans will see whether the proposed development conforms to the master plan and whether it provides adequate utilities, open area, parking facilities, or school areas needed to support the master plan objectives. These would include water supply, sewage disposal, and utility needs. Subdivision plans must be approved before any work can start. The procedures of submitting a plan and having it approved apply to industrial site developments as well as to commercial and residential area developments. See Chapter 18 for the procedures involved.

Planned Unit Development (PUD)

Residential developments of ten acres or more that incorporate areas for public, commercial, or industrial use are often defined as *planned unit developments (PUDs)*. The original plan will set aside areas for single-family residences, apartments, retail store areas, parking, schools, parks, golf courses, and sometimes industrial use.

The objective of the PUD is to provide for commercial, recreational, and educational facilities located convenient to the housing. The plan may provide for a variety of residential uses such as single-family dwellings, apartments, townhouses, or condominiums. Typically, each type of area would have a specified limit of the allowable density (persons per acre). For example, the planned community of Columbia, Maryland, specified average residential area limits of 3.8 persons per acre. See Figure 10–1, which illustrates the Wilde Lake development in Columbia.

A PUD requires extensive planning and a large initial investment. It is frequently necessary to work out arrangements with local governments to obtain approval for different concepts in zoning and taxing. The PUD would then replace the existing land use provisions. Usually, a considerable number of years would be needed to complete the planned unit development.

Traffic Design

Quite often urban plans will suggest street layouts such that certain streets carry through traffic whereas other streets are curved or laid out so as to be free from heavy traffic. Buffer zones are often prescribed to separate industrial areas from residential areas. Many downtown areas or residential areas have traffic routed around them. The important criterion is to make sure that people and material can be moved readily throughout the area. Public transportation must also be considered as part of the total traffic design.

Much of the rest of urban planning revolves around the traffic plan. It is better to establish streets, beltways, and freeways that meet the overall urban requirements

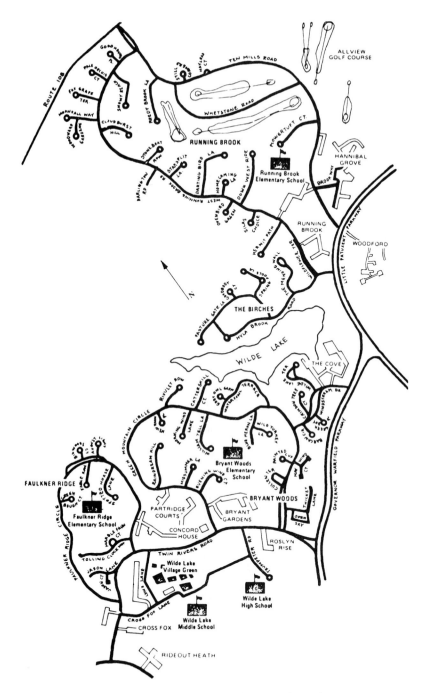

Figure 10–1   Wilde Lake community of Columbia, where elementary schools help to define the neighborhoods

Source: National Association of Home Builders. *Land Development Manual*. Washington, D.C. 1974, p. 59.

than to improve existing transportation to meet needs as congestion develops. It is also important to separate the through traffic from the local traffic. In large urban areas, the through traffic includes vehicles going from one part of the urban area to another.

Urban Renewal

As part of the overall urban master plan, certain areas are often selected for complete renovation or renewal. Areas of severe deterioration, frequently located near city centers, are good candidates for renewal. The most drastic procedure is to level all structures in an area and completely rebuild. This step can be initiated and financed either by public bonds, federal assistance, or private financing. In other areas where deterioration is less severe, some properties are renovated, often to retain aesthetic advantages, whereas other buildings are demolished and rebuilt. Areas near downtown Philadelphia, St. Louis, and Baltimore offer good examples of some areas that were completely demolished and rebuilt, while areas in other cities have been largely renovated.

Federal, state, and local authorities also provide public housing in areas to be rehabilitated or provide subsidies for such projects. Some of these projects have been successful; others have not. Those projects that allow the occupants to own or eventually own their homes tend to be more successful in maintaining a desirable environment than those that rent or lease units.

Enterprise Zones

Enterprise zoning is a recent approach to urban renewal of depressed areas. The concept originated in Great Britain. A new business starting in the designated area is given tax breaks and may be freed from certain government regulations. The objective is to attract new business firms and help revive the area.

A number of provisions might apply to a designated enterprise zone:

1. Rent control may not apply.
2. Property taxes are reduced.
3. Government-owned land would be auctioned off.
4. Laws would not be changed for a set number of years.

Factors affecting health and safety, such as building codes, are not relaxed. The enterprise zone status would be guaranteed for a specified number of years.

Land Reutilization Authorities

Several cities have established a *land reutilization authority* (LRA) to acquire and manage tax delinquent and foreclosed land. Parcels can be set aside until larger tracts are accumulated for possible reuse. The parcels are then marketed for development.

Ground Leases

Considering that the cost of land is 20 to 25 percent of the cost of a development project, ground leasing becomes one of the major incentives (along with a tax abatement) that a local government can offer to developers. Vacant or underutilized land owned by educational or religious organizations, railroads, or pension funds can be leased to developers. This provides profits for the lessee and savings in initial investment for the developer.

Transfer Development Rights

The process of land use planning and zoning tends to be unfair to landowners who are prevented from developing their land. At the same time, those owners whose property is authorized for development often obtain windfall gains. Since some land is needed for the more valuable uses and other land must be reserved for open areas, the property owners involved have been placed in a position of conflict. Fairer solutions have been sought.

Transfer development rights (TDR) is a new concept in the direction of alleviating this conflict. Under the TDR concept, all land in a community carries transfer development rights. These rights are considered much like one of the bundle of rights going with land ownership. The owner whose land has been designated as open space can sell her TDR to another landowner. This other landowner can then develop the land with a greater *land use intensity* (LUI). Figure 10–2 shows (a) how a developer can develop a quarter acre parcel with regular rights, (b) how it could be developed if she owned TDR from an additional quarter acre, and (c) how it could be developed if she owned TDR for an additional three-quarters of an acre. Under this concept, TDRs could be sold on the open market.

The TDR concept can also be used to save historical sites. Developer D owns a landmark building that she plans to demolish to build an apartment. D also owns other land nearby. The city can transfer the development rights of the landmark site so that D can build a more extensive building on the other land than would normally be permitted. A similar approach can be taken to preserve farmland or open land. Farmland can be preserved by the farmer selling the development rights. The taxable value (and taxes) of the land without development rights would then be much less than land on the edge of a city that could be developed.

Local and state governments sometimes find it desirable to limit growth in order to curtail congestion, to preserve aesthetic factors, or to avoid overloading existing

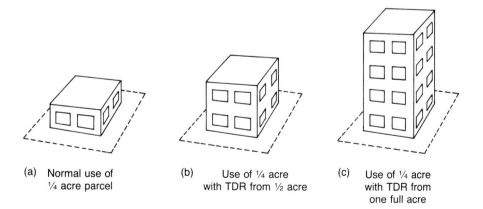

(a) Normal use of ¼ acre parcel

(b) Use of ¼ acre with TDR from ½ acre

(c) Use of ¼ acre with TDR from one full acre

Figure 10–2   Implementation of transfer development rights (TDR)

utilities. These objectives may all be accomplished through the use of transfer development rights.

Building Codes

Building codes define basic requirements to regulate construction, in order to protect the safety, health, and general welfare of the users of the building. There are standard codes that become law when adopted by the city, town, or county. Codes govern such features as electric wiring, plumbing, and building materials.

In the past, most codes specified permissible materials or construction methods. Recently, *performance standards* have come into frequent use. They may specify strength, durability, or other performance characteristics rather than stating specific materials or designs. This provides greater flexibility for use of new materials or designs as they are developed and eliminates the need to continually revise the building codes.

Approvals

Prior to starting new construction or significant modifications to an existing structure, plans must be submitted to the local authority and a building permit must be obtained. As the construction progresses, it is checked by inspectors employed by the city or county. Upon satisfactory completion, a certificate of occupancy is issued.

Building Moratoriums

Sometimes a community decides it needs more time to study growth problems. It has the right to withhold building permits and approval of new subdivisions and to delay permits to connect with municipal sewer or water supplies. A temporary suppression is called a *building moratorium,* or sometimes, a *zoning freeze.* In shoreline developments, this moratorium may be imposed while an environmental impact study is being made.

Density Controls

Overcrowding in certain areas can be a severe urban problem. Better planning for a balance in the community can be achieved through zoning regulations to limit population growth. Some ordinances designed to achieve this, however, have been declared invalid by the courts. Examples of ordinances declared invalid were those that (a) restricted apartment buildings to a certain number of units; (b) prohibited multifamily unit constructions; (c) specified minimum lot sizes; (d) specified minimum floor areas; or (e) specified minimum cubic feet in the building. Courts have held these to be invalid in certain cases where the primary result was to restrict an area to more affluent families, to exclude newcomers to the area in order to avoid burdens on public utilities, or to discriminate against the poor or certain racial groups.

Housing Codes

Codes affecting use and occupation of residential property are called *housing codes.* These codes also vary from locality to locality. A local code may include requirements for number of occupants per unit, window area per room, or lighting needed for stairways.

Implementing the plan for an urban area depends heavily upon the power to zone. *Zoning* is a means for regulating and controlling land and its use even though property is privately owned.

The right to regulate land usage derives from the ***police power of government***. Usually, municipalities acquire the rights to establish and enforce zoning requirements from state laws.

Although there have been court challenges to zoning on the grounds that it interferes with a person's rights guaranteed by the constitution, courts have upheld the rights of municipalities to exercise and enforce zoning powers. The basis has been that the rights of the majority cannot be infringed by rights of particular individuals.

Some zoning ordinances have been challenged in the courts as discriminatory on the basis that requirements for minimum lot size and for single-family dwellings discriminate against lower income persons. In some cases, the courts have struck down those ordinances as having been created to exclude certain people rather than to protect the general public or to plan the urban area.

Purpose of Zoning

The first real zoning ordinance was passed by New York City in 1916. The objective was to control land use to keep undesirable activities out of residential areas, hold down population densities, and provide for more homogeneous use of land. More recent laws have cited additional reasons, such as promoting health and morals; reducing traffic congestion; providing safety from fire, panic, vandalism, and crime; and providing adequate air and light. To accomplish this, zoning must be consistent with an overall urban master plan.

The following exemplify typical types of ***protective zoning***:

1. Limits on height or width of construction
2. Maximum or minimum setback from street or minimum distance of structure from property lines
3. Type of materials or procedures used in construction, wiring, or plumbing
4. Restrictions on display of signs or billboards
5. Limitation on type of business allowed or usage of property
6. Limit on number of occupants per apartment
7. Limit on number of families per residence
8. Specific way to position garages or other structures on the lot
9. Minimum lot sizes

Zoning is often used as a planning tool to encourage land usage for its highest and best use. This is called ***directive zoning***. Zoning ordinances must be integrated into overall urban planning. However, experience has shown that highly restrictive zoning tends to cause the area to remain underdeveloped.

Bulk zoning is used where the primary purpose of the requirement is to control density and avoid overcrowding. Restrictions on setbacks, side or court areas, building height and size, and percentage of open area are examples of bulk zoning. Figure 10–3 shows a method by which the allowable height of a structure varies with the area or distance from the lot line. *FAR* (floor area ratio) is the index of building bulk and height used to assess the intensity of land use. It is the total floor area in the building divided by the lot area:

$$\frac{\text{Total floor area}}{\text{Lot area}} = \text{Floor area ratio (FAR)}$$

Some ordinances also specify a required amount of off-street parking area, or they may require off-street loading areas for trucks to unload in shopping areas. Some zoning ordinances go beyond these limits. Certain cities, such as Williamsburg, Virginia, require that new buildings conform to a certain type of architecture. This is known as *aesthetic zoning* and sometimes applies to shopping or other areas. *Incentive zoning* specifies that the street floors of office buildings be used for retail establishments. This has been used effectively to provide retail areas where investors are primarily interested in constructing office space.

When authorities are studying an area for original zoning or changes in zoning, *hold zoning* or *interim zoning* can be applied. This prevents developers from initiating usage of the land in a way that would negate the study results.

Zoning Categories

Zoning regulations generally restrict the use of land to one of several overall classifications: residential, commercial, industrial, agricultural, and recreational. These are called *land use districts.* A district limited to single-family residential units is typically designated R–1. Other designations might be R–2, R–3, B–1 (business), C–1 (commercial), and so forth. The objective is to provide a degree of use that is homogeneous within an area and to avoid mixtures among the categories.

Restrictions to *residential use* are the best known to most people. These restrictions prevent commercial or industrial buildings in an area, or they restrict signs. Usually the residential restriction would allow only a particular type of use. The highest classification (R–1, for example) would be for single-family residences. Sometimes, a higher classification would also specify minimum lot sizes for each

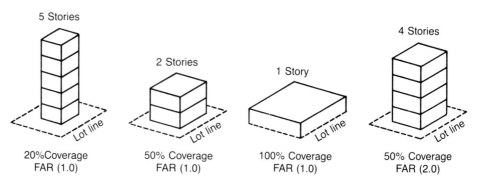

Figure 10–3   Configurations illustrating FAR (floor area ratio)

Source: National Association of Home Builders. *Land Development Manual.* Washington, D.C. 1974, p. 12.

home. The next category (R–2) typically permits structures designed for from two to four families, or it permits row houses—a series of houses having common walls. The third level or category of residential use (R–3) allows apartments, schools, and churches. Normally, zoning is *cumulative* such that R–3 would permit all uses from R–1 and R–2.

Commercial zoning is also subdivided. The highest group (i.e., C–1) would include shops, restaurants, or office buildings. Usages considered less desirable, such as service stations or garages, would have a lower classification (i.e., C–2).

Industrial zoning is the third category, which may also be broken down further into groupings such as light, medium, and heavy manufacturing. The classification of industries by group would also take into consideration noise, smoke, and other factors that particular industries might introduce into the area. Some communities use *performance zoning* rather than listing prohibited industries. Standards are established for noise, air pollution, fire, and explosives. Industries are then permitted in the area as long as the standards are met.

Agricultural zoning permits farming, dairying, and raising of animals or poultry. It often excludes commercial or industrial uses.

Recreational zoning includes parks and similar uses.

Spot zoning sets aside certain areas for purposes different from the general area requirements. Spot zoning has been ruled illegal in almost every city in the United States.

Some urban areas have also restricted the construction of residences or apartments in industrial or commercial areas. These regulations protect industrial users against possible future lawsuits. Without these restrictions, the owner of the residential properties could claim that the industrial use adversely affects her health or welfare because of noise, odors, or traffic. At that point, the fact that the industries were there first could lose its impact, and a company could be forced to move or to install expensive abatement equipment. Sometimes, C–1 or R properties are not permitted in C–2 areas; this is called *noncumulative zoning.* If specific purposes are prohibited (e.g., drive-in theaters or mobile home parks), the zoning is called *exclusionary zoning.*

A new concept, inclusionary zoning, was first used in California in 1979. *Inclusionary zoning* laws require that new housing developments contain a certain percentage of low- or moderate-income properties.

Enforcement

All zoning laws, housing codes, and building codes contain provisions that allow the local authorities to enforce the regulations. Without these provisions, the regulations would be meaningless. Before initiating new construction or making a change in existing construction, the property owner must obtain a permit. At that time, she must submit evidence to show that the contemplated project complies with zoning requirements. If a private party initiates construction or takes action to change existing construction without having approval, any citizen or official can ask for an *abatement* or court order to halt the action.

If any unauthorized change is made without approval, a court order can be requested to require the building to be restored to its original status. In a situation where a building is occupied by more than the allowable number of persons or families, a court order can be obtained to end the violation. In addition to these methods of enforcement, the municipality can levy fines either in place of or in addition to the other remedies. Frequently, a fine will be levied on a time basis, such as a fine of $20.00 per day until the violation is remedied. This counteracts intentional stalling.

A written permit must be obtained from the local authorities before starting new construction or remodeling. It must be displayed at the scene of construction. As construction proceeds, an inspector will check the work to make sure it complies with building codes. Before the new or remodeled structure can be used, a notice of completion must be filed and a certificate of occupancy obtained. This certificate can be applied for when the building permit is requested; however, the certificate must be signed by the authorized inspector prior to actual occupancy of the building. If this certificate is not approved, use of the building or release of mortgage funds may be held up. It is important to understand these procedures and requirements, since a delay in occupancy may result in substantial financial loss to the owner and builder.

Changes in Zoning

Action to change zoning can be initiated by a property owner, either to tighten restrictions or to make a restriction more lax. For example, a property developer may request a zoning status change from farm area to single-family residential to protect her investment and assure potential home buyers that future construction or use will not cause the area to deteriorate and reduce property values. On the other hand, an owner of property in a deteriorating neighborhood or changing area may request rezoning to commercial or apartment usage to increase the value and possible uses of the property.

The first step in requesting a zoning change is to submit a petition to the local board or body having zoning authority. Usually, this petition must be published in a local newspaper by either the petitioner or the authorities. A sign describing the pending action must also be displayed at the property for a specified period of time. The notifications should specify a time and place for a public hearing on the proposed change. This public hearing provides a place for all interested parties to be present and heard before any decision is made. The decision of the board is not always final, however, since any person who feels that she has been aggrieved may appeal to higher authority or eventually to the courts. If other remedies are prescribed, such as appeal to other boards or officials, these appeals must be carried out before an appeal is made to the courts. Judicial relief from burdensome zoning must usually be based on constitutional grounds. Courts usually have upheld zoning ordinances; however, the courts in many cases have granted relief from arbitrary, unreasonable, or discriminatory zoning provisions.

Nonconforming Use

Whenever any zoning regulation is enacted, existing structures or uses that do not comply with the new requirements must be protected. Provisions allow this ***nonconforming use*** since it would not be fair to a property owner to have retroactive zoning requirements. If there already was a service station in an area designated residential, the service station could continue to operate. This condition may prevail only as long as the use is continuous. If, however, the facility was not used as a service station for a set period of time designated by law (such as three years), then the service station could not be reactivated. If the service station was destroyed by a fire, the regulation would not usually allow it to be rebuilt on the same site. Usually a zoning ordinance will also prohibit any enlarging or modification of the structure intended to continue it in a nonconforming use.

Some ordinances contain **amortization** provisions to establish the time by which nonconforming uses must be phased out. The theory is that the purpose of the zoning change cannot be fully realized as long as nonconforming uses exist. Courts have held this to be a reasonable exercise of police power.

Relief by Administrative Action

Instead of going through the zoning change procedure, a property owner may seek relief from strict compliance with a zoning ordinance or building codes through zoning authorities. Generally, authorities can grant either variances or conditional use permits. These actions are allowed to permit sufficient flexibility to meet hardship cases, situations where the relief would not disrupt the general zoning scheme, or special needs.

Conditional Use Permit

A **conditional use permit** allows a special use if deemed desirable for public convenience. A service station may be built in an area zoned for industrial use where the service to people in the area is necessary.

Variance

A nonconforming use involves a use that existed prior to the enactment of the ordinance. A **variance,** on the other hand, permits doing something that an existing zoning ordinance forbids. Variances or exceptions are granted where the ordinance brings about a harsh or unique hardship for an individual. As an example, a lot may be of such size or shape that it would be unreasonable to build a structure that conforms to the setback requirements. In another instance, a lot may be too narrow to allow construction conforming to side area restrictions. A variance may then be allowed to permit a structure that violates the side area requirement. In any decision to grant a variance, though, the approving body must still consider the broad intent of the zoning ordinance, and not permit just any usage.

The procedure for obtaining a variance is similar to that for requesting a change in zoning. The zoning board will hear petitions for changes in zoning or variances from the zoning requirements. The board must, however, act within any area master plan in its decisions. The burden of proof lies with the person making the petition. Usually the board will make an on-site inspection of the property involved to establish the validity of the request. A variance will usually be turned down if it is felt that the primary intent is to increase the value of the property to the owner. Petitions to obtain a variance that extends a present nonconforming use will usually be rejected.

Recent Developments

Recently the Supreme Court has ruled that municipalities may be required to pay landowners when new government regulations prohibit full use of private property.

Rulings do not, however, affect regulations preserving historic landmarks or coastal areas.

The term *downzoning* is used where a new regulation or change in zoning severely restricts use of privately owned property, resulting in loss of value. In a particular case, land zoned residential was rezoned to "agriculture only," and the court ruled that compensation was owed to the property owner.

In another case, the Supreme Court overturned a lower court ruling that allowed the public to walk along the beach between a private home and the Pacific Ocean. The ruling reaffirmed the property owner's rights to the beach.

SUMMARY

Land use planning is a necessary prerequisite to achieving balanced city or suburban growth. Although the primary responsibility for land use planning rests with the municipal government, it can receive substantial assistance from state and federal agencies. While orderly growth takes financial backing, the funds generated often more than compensate for the initial costs.

Zoning is a key factor in implementing and enforcing any land use plan. One objective of zoning is to allocate areas for residential, commercial, industrial, and recreational use so that the well-being of the public as a whole is enhanced. Building codes and other restrictions are aimed at safeguarding the health, welfare, and safety of the area population. Means are available to change zoning or to obtain exceptions where hardship has resulted.

TERMS AND CONCEPTS

You can check your understanding of these terms against the glossary or by review in this chapter.

Abatement	Enterprise zoning	Planned unit
Amortization	FAR	development (PUD)
Building moratorium	Inclusionary zoning	Police power of
Bulk zoning	Land use district	government
Conditional use permit	Land use intensity	Transfer development
Downzoning	Master plan	rights (TDR)
Economic base analysis	Performance standards	Zoning freeze
Enabling acts		

What are the differences or relationships, if any, between the following?

Aesthetic zoning and Incentive zoning	Hold zoning and Interim zoning	Planning and Zoning
Building codes and Housing codes	Nonconforming use and Variance	Residential, Commercial, Industrial, Agricultural, and Recreational
Cumulative and Noncumulative zoning	Performance zoning and Exclusionary zoning	zoning
Directive zoning and Protective zoning		Variance and Spot zoning

10-1. List the steps necessary to secure a change in zoning.

10-2. Make a rough sketch of your community and label land allocations.

10-3. Identify streets in your community that are designed to carry through traffic.

10-4. List the elements of a good land use master plan.

10-5. Look for examples of two of the following in your community:
(a) Nonconforming use
(b) Variance
(c) Spot zoning
(d) Conditional use permit

10-6. Discuss how a planned unit development (PUD) is different from a normal development in zoning requirements, degree of planning, and amount of investment needed.

10-7. An acre of land is allowed development rights sufficient for six townhouses. If transfer development rights are allowed, from how much land must the developer obtain rights in order to construct fifteen townhouses on the acre plot?

10-8. Smith owned a lot in an R–1 zone and desired to build a duplex, so he applied for a variance. Comment on his approach.

10-9. If you wanted to construct a garage closer to the lot line than allowed by zoning or the building code, what technique would you use?

10-10. In what cases do you feel a court of law might set aside zoning restrictions?

10-11. How is interim zoning of benefit to the community planning board?

10-12. Why might a community want to limit growth? What are some means of accomplishing this?

10-13. Discuss the advantages and disadvantages of using enterprise zones.

SUPPLEMENTARY READINGS ▬▬▬

Berman, Daniel S. *Urban Renewal.* Englewood Cliffs, N.J.: Prentice-Hall, 1969.

Beuscher, Jacob H.; Wright, Robert W.; and Gilelman, Morton. *Land Use—Urban Planning.* St. Paul, Minn.: West, 1976.

Clawson, Marion, ed. *Modernizing Urban Land Policy.* Baltimore: Johns Hopkins University Press, 1973.

Correale, William H. *A Building Code Primer.* New York: McGraw-Hill, 1979.

Crawford, Clair. *Strategy on Tactics in Municipal Zoning.* Englewood Cliffs, N.J.: Prentice-Hall, 1969.

Crawford, Clair. *Handbook of Zoning and Land Use Ordinances—With Forms.* Englewood Cliffs, N.J.: Prentice-Hall, 1974.

David, Philip. *Urban Land Development.* Homewood, Ill.: Irwin, 1970.

Gold, Seymour M. *Urban Recreation Planning.* Philadelphia: Lea & Febiger, 1973.

Goodman, William L., and Freund, Eric C. *Principle and Practice of Urban Planning.* Washington, D.C.: International City Managers Association, 1979.

Grieson, Ronald E. *Urban Economy and Housing.* Lexington, Mass.: Lexington Books, 1982.

Hagman, Donald G. *Urban Planning and Land Development Control Laws,* 2nd ed. St. Paul, Minn.: West, 1986.

Harrison, Bennett. *Urban Economic Development.* Washington, D.C.: Urban Institute, 1974.

Heilbrun, James. *Urban Economics and Public Policy,* 3rd ed. New York: St. Martin's Press, 1987.

Hinds, D. S. *Winning at Zoning.* New York: McGraw-Hill, 1979.

Krueckeberg, Donald A., and Silvers, Arthur L. *Urban Planning Analysis,* 2nd ed. New York: Wiley, 1988.

National Association of Home Builders. *Land Development Manual.* Washington, D.C.: 1981.

Sayalyn, Lynne B. *Zoning and Housing Costs.* New Brunswick, N.J.: Center for Urban Policy Research, Rutgers University, 1973.

Siedel, George J., III. *Real Estate Law.* St. Paul, Minn.: West, 1979. Chapter 13.

Smith, Halbert C.; Tschappat, Carl J.; and Racster, Ronald. *Real Estate and Urban Development,* 3rd ed. Homewood, Ill.: Irwin, 1981, Chapter 14.

Witheford, David K. *Zoning, Parking, and Traffic.* Saugatuck, Conn.: Eno Foundation for Transportation, 1972.

CHAPTER 11
Home Ownership

The trend in home ownership in the United States is changing. Economic conditions have made it more difficult for the average American to own a home. The composition of the American housing market is also changing. These changes, along with their impact on the homebuilder, the savings and loan industry, and the consumer himself, are discussed in this chapter.

TRENDS IN HOME OWNERSHIP

In 1890, approximately half the families in the United States owned their own homes. The United States was primarily rural then, and each family worked together as a productive unit using its home as a place of work as well as a residence. Later the industrial revolution pulled much of the population away from the farm and into urban areas to take advantage of employment opportunities. Urbanization of the young work force led to a decrease in home ownership and a corresponding increase in renters. By 1920, home ownership had dropped to 46 percent. In the early 1920s the downward trend reversed, and home ownership increased to about 48 percent. Then the crash of the stock market in 1929 signalled the beginning of the Depression, which resulted in thousands of mortgage foreclosures. Home ownership decreased every year for the next ten years. By 1940, only 44 percent of families in the United States owned their own homes. The Depression spawned dozens of federal statutes designed to cure the ills of our economy. The Federal Housing Act of 1934, which created the Federal Housing Agency, was one of the more successful programs. The FHA introduced long-term amortized loans with high loan-to-value ratios. It provided insured loans to many qualified borrowers who would otherwise have been unable to finance a home purchase. The Federal National Mortgage Association ("Fannie Mae") created a secondary market for mortgages to encourage the flow of mortgage funds from areas of cash surplus to cash deficit areas. The federal government's commitment to better housing and more favorable mortgage financing provided the impetus for an unprecedented increase in home ownership between 1940 and 1960, when the percentage jumped from 44 percent to 62 percent. Between 1960 and 1970, home ownership increased at a very slow pace. The slow increase was attributable to rising land and construction costs, the tight money market, and a dramatic shift in the composition of our population. This population shift resulted in quite a large number of very old and very young heads of households who typically rent rather than buy.

THE CHANGING REAL ESTATE MARKET

The postwar baby-boomers are maturing into a large segment of the home-buying market. *Baby-boomers* are those born during the postwar years of 1946 to 1960. It is projected that by the first quarter of the twenty-first century they will represent the largest portion of the adult population. According to the U.S. Census Bureau, the largest age group in the year 2000 will be those ranging in age from 45 to 64.

The Shrinking Middle Class

Until recently in the United States, we took for granted that our standard of living would steadily improve generation after generation. However, in the 1970s, individual incomes began losing the battle with inflation. Recently, the Economic Policy Institute, a Washington, D.C. think tank, conducted research on income growth and concluded the following:

- The bottom two-fifths of the population saw no real growth in income between 1979 and 1986.
- The middle fifth showed only marginal increase.

- The second highest fifth shared proportionally with overall income growth.
- Only the top fifth gained proportionally during this decade.

The average husband's salary fell 4 percent from 1979 to 1986, after adjusting for inflation. The only way the standard of living could be maintained or increased was to add a second income to the family. By 1988, nearly 60 percent of women worked outside the home, a 20 percent increase from the year 1965. The Census Bureau reports that since 1976, married households with both spouses employed and with children (so-called *"DIWKS"*, double income with kids) have increased by 61 percent. Two-thirds of the college-educated women with children under the age of one are working outside the home. Married households with double income and no kids (*"DINKS"*, double income no kids) have increased 31 percent. Because the only way many families could stay in the middle class was to add a second income, single parents with children have problems maintaining their standard of living.

Most economists use the following ranges to describe low-, middle-, and upper-class incomes:

Low	under $20,000
Middle	$20,000 to $50,000
Upper	over $50,000

The Brookings Institution found that the number of families in the upper class rose 38 percent between 1973 and 1986, the middle class shrank, and the lower class remained about the same size. Today, one-third of all children are living in a lower class family and one in six children are living in poverty. Although women's pay has been increasing over the years, they still earn only 68 percent of the income of their male counterparts. The segment of our population suffering most in the struggle to maintain their standard of living has been those without a college education. The Brookings Institute study found that men between ages twenty-five to thirty-four with only a high school diploma experienced a 16 percent decrease in inflation-adjusted income between 1973 and 1986. Although these figures should underscore the importance of education, many areas of our country are experiencing 40 and 50 percent high school drop-out rates.

By 1987, the number of Americans living in poverty was increasing. According to the U.S. Census Bureau, 32.5 million people, or 13.5 percent of our population, lived in poverty. Poverty by ethnic background was as follows:

	Number	*% of ethnic group*
White	21.4 million	10.5
Hispanic	5.4 million	28.2
Black	9.7 million	33.0

In 1987, poverty-level income for a family of four was $11,611.

Home Ownership Declines in the 1980s

In 1980, the home ownership rate peaked at 65.8 percent. By 1988, home ownership had declined to about 64 percent. The decline is much more significant among the younger households. In 1981, 63 percent of the households headed by people under age 30 owned their homes. By 1988, this figure had dropped to 52 percent. According to Frank Levy of the School of Public Affairs at the University of Maryland, a 30-

year-old homeowner in the 1950s could satisfy his monthly mortgage payment using only 14 percent of his gross monthly pay. In 1973, it took 21 percent and in 1984, 44 percent. In the late 1980s it had declined somewhat. However, these figures point up a family's need for two incomes in order to service the mortgage payment.

By 1988, more than half the baby-boom households were homeowners. This large number of baby-boom homeowners will tend to keep the housing market strong for the next decade as they "trade up" to bigger, more expensive homes. However, the person looking to buy his first home is faced with rising interest rates, rising housing costs, and a shrinking standard of living, which makes it extremely difficult to save for the down payment. A 1988 poll for the National Housing Institute showed that two-thirds of those polled under age thirty-five who do not own a home consider it an important goal.

The reasons first-time home buyers under the age of forty give for buying a home are summarized in figure 11–1. The largest single reason given was the tax and investment advantages offered by home ownership. Figure 11–2 summarizes the reasons prospective first-time home buyers are still renting.

Household Characteristics of the Buyer

Household Composition

Approximately 73 percent of home buyers in 1988 were married couples. Ten percent of the home buyers were single males and 10 percent were single females. The remaining 7 percent of home buyers were made up of unmarried couples, friends, or siblings (See Figure 11–3).

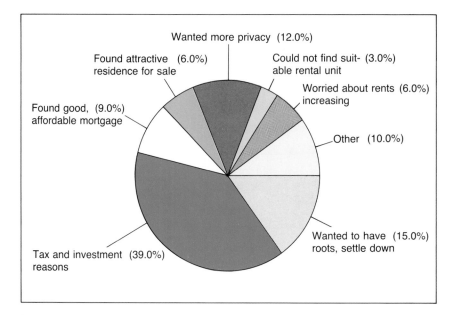

Figure 11–1　The home purchase decision

Source: 1986 NAR homeownership survey.

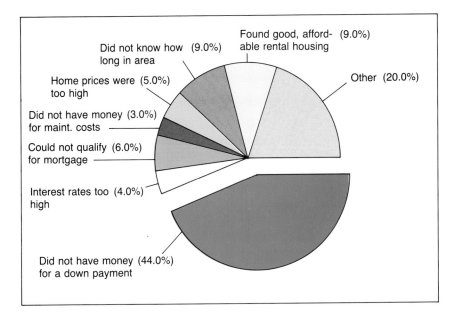
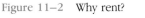

Figure 11–2   Why rent?

Source: 1986 NAR homeownership survey.

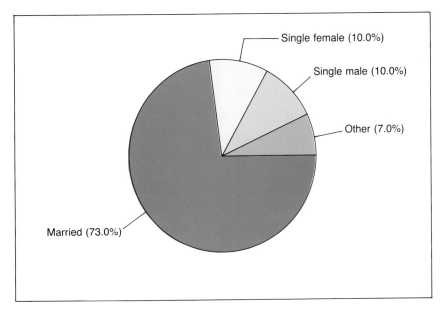

Figure 11–3   Characteristics of the buyer—household composition

Source: NATIONAL ASSOCIATION OF REALTORS®, 1988.

Income

Thirty-two percent of the buyers had family incomes over $60,000, 60 percent earned between $25,000 and $60,000 annually, while only 8 percent had incomes of less than $25,000. The average buyer's family income was $49,300 (See figure 11–4).

Age

Only 3 percent of the home buyers were under twenty-five years of age. Thirty-nine percent of the home buyers were in the twenty-five-to-thirty-four age group. Another 39 percent were in the thirty-five-to-forty-four age group. The forty-five-to-sixty-five age group comprised 17 percent of all home buyers. The over-sixty-five age group accounted for the remaining 2 percent. The average age home buyer was 39 (See figure 11–5).

Consumers' Housing Preferences

According to a NATIONAL ASSOCIATION OF REALTORS® survey conducted in the fall of 1988, consumers' housing preferences were as follows:

Property Type

Single-family detached	85%
Townhouse or rowhouse	6%
Condominium	4%
Duplex or triplex	5%

New Versus Existing

New home	17%
Existing home	83%
Average living area	1,800 square feet
Average lot size	29,300 square feet

Bedrooms

5 or more	8%
4	25%
3	53%
2	13%
1	1%

Air Conditioning

No air conditioning	35%
Air conditioning	65%

Basement

No basement	50%
Basement, unfinished	31%
Basement, finished	19%

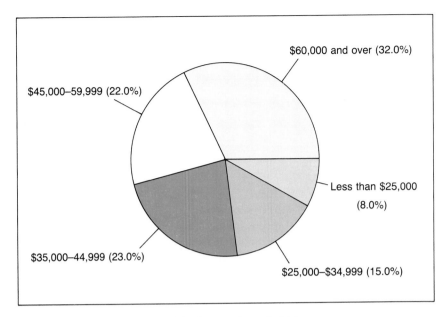

$60,000 and over (32.0%)

$45,000–59,999 (22.0%)

Less than $25,000
(8.0%)

$35,000–44,999 (23.0%)

$25,000–$34,999 (15.0%)

Figure 11–4   Characteristics of the buyer—household income
Source: NATIONAL ASSOCIATION OF REALTORS®, 1988.

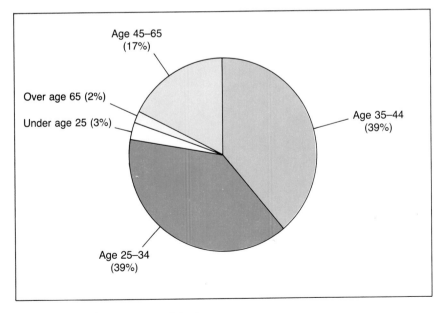

Age 45–65
(17%)

Over age 65 (2%)

Under age 25 (3%)

Age 35–44
(39%)

Age 25–34
(39%)

Figure 11–5   Characteristics of the buyer—age
Source: NATIONAL ASSOCIATION OF REALTORS®, 1988.

Existing Single-Family Home Sales

Existing single-family home sales increased to a seasonably adjusted annual rate of 3,710,000 units in 1988, 10 percent higher than 1987. Much of this activity is attributed to the strong repeat home buyer market (see Figure 11–6).

New Single-Family Home Sales

New home sales for 1988 show a 7 percent increase over the previous year. The seasonally adjusted annual rate for new home sales is 671,000 units (see Figure 11–7).

Housing Affordability Index

The NATIONAL ASSOCIATION OF REALTORS® uses an index to measure housing affordability. In November of 1988, the *Housing Affordability Index* dropped slightly to 112.9. An index of 112.9 means that a family earning the median income of $31,996 has 112.9 percent of the income necessary to qualify for an 80 percent loan-to-value conventional loan on the median existing home price of $87,900 at prevailing interest rates. This assumes the buyer has a 20 percent down payment. See Figure 11–8.

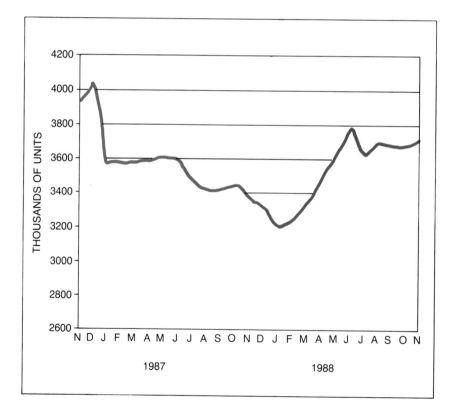

Figure 11–6   Existing single-family home sales (seasonally adjusted)

Source: NATIONAL ASSOCIATION OF REALTORS®

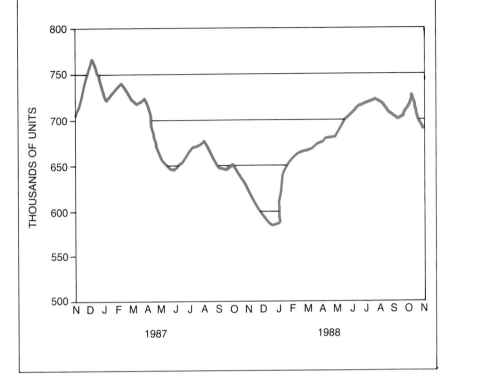

Figure 11–7   New single-family home sales (seasonally adjusted)

Source: NATIONAL ASSOCIATION OF REALTORS®; Bureau of the Census

Existing Single-Family Home Sale Prices

Figure 11–9 shows the percentage of existing single-family homes that were sold in various price ranges throughout the United States and also by region in November 1988. For the U.S. market, 33.1 percent of the homes sold at a price of $120,000 or more. The Northeast region of the United States shows 63.3 percent of the homes sold for $120,000 or more. The Midwest region reports the smallest percent of homes sold over $120,000.

New Home Sales Prices

Figure 11–10 on page 260 shows the distribution of new home sales prices for the United States in 1988. As can be seen, 43 percent of the homes sold for $120,000 and over, 28 percent sold in the $80,000 to $119,999 range, 20 percent sold for $60,000 to $79,999 and 9 percent sold for less than $60,000.

ADVANTAGES OF HOME OWNERSHIP

The advantages of home ownership are many and complex, and their importance varies with each homeowner. The many advantages can be broadly classified into

Figure 11–8   Housing affordability index

Source: NATIONAL ASSOCIATION OF REALTORS®

two areas: (a) social or psychological and (b) economic. Legislation has also been favorable toward homeowners.

Social or Psychological Advantages

The socio-psychological advantages may be further subdivided into four areas.

Security

Home ownership provides the family with a sense of security and belongingness that is not available to the renter. The homeowner is not under the constant threat of increasing rents or eviction. He is able to remodel or repair his home as he pleases and when he pleases, without having to obtain the consent of a recalcitrant landlord. The homeowner thereby acquires a certain "peace of mind."

Civic Responsibility

Through ownership, the individual becomes keenly aware of real estate taxes, special assessments, zoning restrictions, and other police powers that are unfamiliar to most renters. The homeowner can determine where his tax dollars go and whether they are being utilized efficiently and effectively. Special assessments are levied against him to finance certain improvements that accrue to specific properties. The homeowner again has an opportunity to determine the need for such improvements

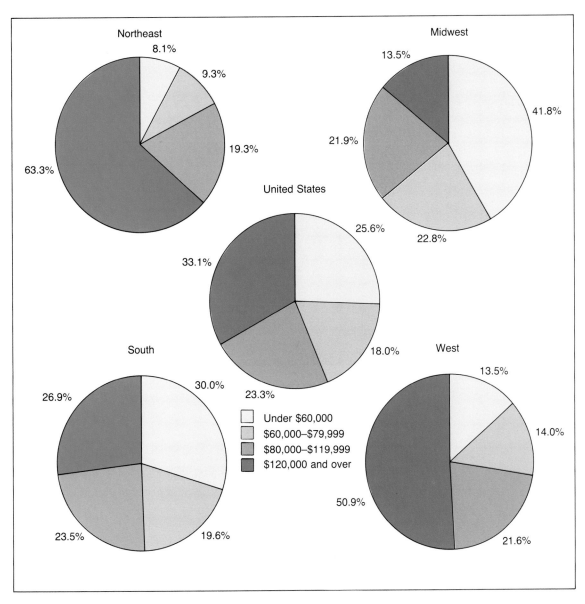

Figure 11–9 Existing single-family home sales by price class
Source: NATIONAL ASSOCIATION OF REALTORS®, 1988.

and may voice his opinion at a public hearing. Also, the homeowner is faced with zoning restrictions that are implemented by local municipalities to control land use and growth. The objectives of zoning ordinances are honorable, but political favoritism can sometimes make them a farce. The homeowner becomes sensitive to any zoning changes that may adversely affect his property value. He soon learns that 50 to 70 percent of the real estate tax dollar goes toward financing local schools and roads. As a result, he is interested in efficiently run public schools and road construction programs and acts to guard against mismanagement or misappropriation

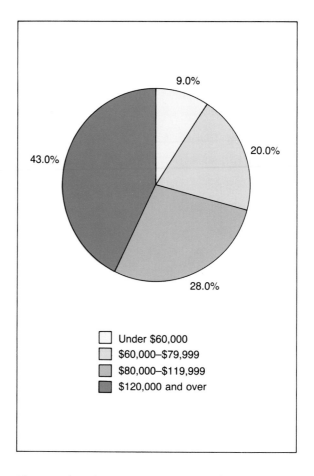

Figure 11–10 New houses sold by sales price class

Source: U.S. Department of Commerce, Bureau of the Census, 1988.

9.0%

20.0%

43.0%

28.0%

☐ Under $60,000
☐ $60,000–$79,999
☐ $80,000–$119,999
■ $120,000 and over

of the tax dollar. These political, economic, and social implications of home ownership provide the basis of an understanding of local government and help develop a sense of civic responsibility.

Pride

Most homeowners are exceptionally proud of their homes, and this pride is manifested in the care given their investment. A neighborhood with a high percentage of owner-occupied homes will typically be better cared for than a neighborhood that has a substantial portion of rental units. The typical renter, having no vested interest in the property, usually does not exercise the same care in maintaining the property as an owner does.

Enhanced Self-Image

Although certain segments of our society claim to dismiss materialism as a reflection of success, most people still perceive a strong relationship. Also, a home enables many people to extend their personality and express themselves creatively and tangibly through interior decorating, landscaping, and architecture.

Economic Advantages

Several real economic advantages accrue from home ownership.

Investment

Nearly all home purchases are financed by mortgage loans. The loans are amortized so that a portion of each monthly payment goes toward principal and a portion toward interest. The principal portion of the payment reduces the loan balance and produces a corresponding increase in the owner's equity, provided property values remain constant. If property values increase, the total increase accrues to the equity owner even though he has only a small down payment invested in the property. The monthly loan payment therefore acts as a "forced savings" for the home buyer.

Hedge Against Inflation

In an inflationary economy, wise investors place their money in investments that keep pace with or exceed the rate of inflation. Otherwise, the investor's purchasing power diminishes. Real estate is one of the few investments that has historically kept pace with or exceeded the general rate of inflation, and thus is considered a *hedge against inflation.*

Credit

Merchants and financial institutions are particularly interested in an individual's home ownership status when extending credit. Home ownership implies stability, responsibility, and civic pride, all of which are personal traits that tend to reduce the risk to the creditor and increase the possibility of credit being extended to the homeowner.

Favorable Legislation

Homestead Act

The *Homestead Act* of 1862 was enacted to provide free land to settlers in the West. Many states today recognize *homestead* property rights. Such rights vary from state to state, but they generally exempt a homestead from forced sale or foreclosure. Also, a homestead cannot be mortgaged or sold during the lifetime of the husband or wife without the consent of both parties. Upon the death of a spouse, the remaining spouse and/or children can continue to live on the homestead until the children reach majority age, without regard to the provisions in the deceased spouse's will or creditor's claims. If the living spouse remarries, homestead rights for both the spouse and the children are usually relinquished.

In 1989, the states of Iowa and Minnesota announced a homestead program whereby a family could homestead a tract or land (40 acres) in selected or targeted areas of the two states for five years and the property would be deeded over to them.

Example 11–1   Actual Costs of Buying a Home Today

To highlight the total after-tax costs of purchasing a home today, let us examine in detail the purchase of an existing home priced at $67,900 financed with an 80 percent loan-to-value, 12 percent interest, 30-year, fixed-rate conventional mortgage. Let's assume the home buyer is in the 28 percent tax bracket. Examine figures in the two accompanying forms for a complete breakdown of the "before-" and "after-tax" costs to purchase.

COST TO PURCHASE ESTIMATE

Name ___ Mr. and Mrs. Homebuyer ___

Proposed Property ___ 123 Neat Street, Anytown, U.S.A. ___

Proposed Purchase Price ___ $67,900 ___
(80%, 30-year fixed-rate loan at 12% interest.
Loan amount $54,320)

Loan Fee ___ $ 1,629.60 (3% of loan amount) ___

Appraisal ___ 200.00 estimate ___

Record Deed ___ 5.00 estimate ___

Record Mortgage ___ 5.00 estimate ___

Mortgage Policy ___ 55.00 estimate ___

Homeowners Insurance ___ 300.00 estimate ___

First Month's Interest ___ 543.20 (54,320 × .12 ÷ 12) ___

Attorney Fees ___ 200.00 estimate ___

Other ___

Total ___ 2,937.80 ___

Cash Downpayment ___ 13,580 (20% of purchase price) ___

Total Cash Needed ___ $16,517.80 ___

OTHER INFORMATION

PAYMENTS: Principal & Interest ___ $558.95 (See Tables in Appendix) ___

Insurance ___ 25.00 (300 ÷ 12) ___

Taxes ___ 113.00 (based on 33% assessed value; ___

Other ___ tax rate of $6/100 ___
of assessed valuation)

Total Monthly Payment $696.95

AFTER TAX ANALYSIS OF HOME OWNERSHIP COSTS
(For Taxpayer Using Itemized Deductions)

Prepared for: __Mr. and Mrs. Homebuyer__

1. Sale Price of Home: $ __67,900__

2. Cash Required: $ __16,362.80__

   Down Payment   __13,580__

   Closing Costs   __2,782.80__

3. Loan: $ __54,320__ , __30__ years at __12__ % interest

4. Monthly Payments, Principal and Interest: $ __558.95__

5. Monthly Deposit for Taxes, Approximately: $ __113.00__

6. Monthly Deposit for Insurance, Approximately: $ __25.00__

7. TOTAL MONTHLY PAYMENT: $ __696.95__

8. EXPENSE ITEMS FOR INCOME TAX PURPOSES:

9. First Month's Interest: $ __543.20__

10. Monthly tax deposit: $ __113.00__

11. TOTAL DEDUCTIONS: $ __656.20__

12. In 15% tax bracket, deduct cash saving per month $ _____

13. In 28% tax bracket, deduct cash saving per month $ __183.74__

14. In 30% tax bracket, deduct cash saving per month $ _____

15. In 20% tax bracket, deduct cash saving per month $ _____
   (To calculate, multiply tax bracket by "TOTAL
   DEDUCTIONS," Line 11)

14. Total Monthly Payment (Line 7): $ __696.95__

15. Subtract Applicable Deduction (Line 12, 13, 14, or 15): $ __−183.74__

16. ACTUAL MONTHLY PAYMENT: $ __513.21__

17. Subtract EQUITY which is being gained monthly: $ __− 15.75__
    (Line 4 minus Line 9)

18. ACTUAL MONTHLY COST (After Taxes): $ __497.46__

Note:

  ● Interest decreases by a small amount each month: equity increases by the same amount.

  ● The actual after-tax cost will be lower if property increases in value and higher if the property decreases in value. Historically, home values have equaled or exceeded the general rate of inflation.

Homestead Tax Exemption

Some states provide the taxpayer relief by exempting the first $500 to $5,000 of assessed property value on a principal residence from taxation.

TAX BENEFITS OF HOME OWNERSHIP

Home ownership also provides many tax benefits, which are discussed on the following pages.

Interest Deductions on First and Second Homes

As of 1989, the taxpayer may take advantage of two types of interest rate deductions on his principal or second residence, namely, *acquisition indebtedness* and *home-equity debt.*

Acquisition Indebtedness

The law allows the taxpayer to fully deduct the interest on debt incurred to acquire, construct, or substantially improve any principal or second residence valued up to $1 million ($500,000 if married filing separately). For example, if a taxpayer purchases a principal residence using an $800,000 mortgage to finance it and then uses a $400,000 mortgage to finance a second home, he would exceed the maximum annual acquisition indebtedness by $200,000.

The acquisition indebtedness also includes any indebtedness secured by the residence as a result of refinancing, but only to the extent that the *new indebtedness* does not exceed the limit of the *refinanced indebtedness.* Acquisition indebtedness is reduced as payments are made and cannot be increased by refinancing *unless the additional proceeds are used to make improvements to the residence.*

For example, if a taxpayer purchases a residence for $300,000 using a $270,000 mortgage, the entire $270,000 is acquisition indebtedness. If he pays it down $70,000 over the years and obtains a second mortgage in the amount of $70,000 to buy an airplane, only the remaining $200,000 balance of the original loan is *acquisition indebtedness.* If the taxpayer had used the $70,000 to finance home improvements, then the additional $70,000 borrowed would also be acquisition indebtedness.

The Internal Revenue Service has ruled that if a buyer purchases a home for cash and obtains financing within ninety days, that financing will qualify for the deduction.

Home-Equity Debt

The taxpayer may borrow an additional home equity loan of $100,000 per year ($50,000 if married filing separately) secured by his principal or second residence, as long as the combined indebtedness does not exceed a 100 percent loan-to-value mortgage. As contrasted with acquisition indebtedness, there are *no restrictions* on the use of debt proceeds for the home equity loans. This provision will most likely be used to convert personal, high-interest rate loans, which by 1991 will no longer be deductible, to a home-equity loan, which will most likely be at a lower interest rate and is 100 percent deductible. Sorry Texas, but your homestead law prevents you from pulling cash out of your primary residence so let's hope you have a second home to take advantage of this provision. A motor home or a boat with living facilities qualifies as a second home, and the interest on the loan to purchase it is fully deductible.

In summary, under the new tax laws that went into effect on January 1, 1988, you may deduct interest on up to a $1 million loan used to acquire, build, or improve either your principal residence or a second home. In addition, you may deduct the interest on a home-equity loan of up to $100,000 whose proceeds may be used for any purpose (except in Texas).

Deductibility of Interest on Consumer Loans

Because consumer debt is no longer deductible at all as of 1991, many homeowners are replacing such debt with a home equity loan, where the interest charged is still deductible.

The deductibility of interest on consumer or personal loans is being phased out completely over a five-year period as follows:

1987	65% deductible
1988	40%
1989	20%
1990	10%
1991	0%

Real Estate Taxes

Real estate taxes on the home are also tax deductible. The combined deductions of interest expense and real estate taxes can add up to several thousand dollars in the early years of the loan.

Depreciation

Although a single-family, owner-occupied home cannot be depreciated for tax purposes, if the home is a duplex and the extra unit is rented out, the rental unit can be depreciated. Depreciation is a tax deductible, noncash flow expense. Chapter 21 provides a detailed explanation of various available depreciation techniques.

Favorable Tax Treatment

The taxable gain, if any, on the sale of a personal residence is computed by determining the **amount realized on the sale,** the **adjusted sales price,** the *adjusted basis of the property sold,* and the *cost of the new residence,* if one is purchased.

The *amount realized* on the sale is calculated by subtracting the expenses of the sale from the selling price. The selling price includes the total amount of money and fair market value of property received plus the amount of all notes, mortgages, and other liabilities that are a part of the consideration for the sale. The selling price does not include the amount received for the sale of any personal property items like furniture. The *selling expenses* that are subtracted include such items as commissions, advertising, legal fees, and title services.

The **realized gain** on the sale is the difference between the *amount realized* on the sale and the **adjusted basis** of the residence sold. The *adjusted basis* of the residence is the original cost plus any capital improvements and minus any depreciation taken, reimbursed casualty losses, or deferred gain from a previous sale.

Example 11–2 Computing a Deferred Gain

House purchased	1986	$100,000
Sold	1988	150,000
Realized gain		$ 50,000
New house purchased	1991	$150,000
Less: Adjusted selling price of old residence		−150,000
No recognized gain		0

Adjusted basis of new residence:	
Cost new	$150,000
Less: Deferred gain	−50,000
	$100,000

Examples of capital improvements that are part of the property's basis are room additions, installation of central air conditioning, furnaces, driveways, and professional landscaping. For a residence limited to personal use, there would be no depreciation.

When a sale of a taxpayer's principal residence is followed within a period of twenty-four months by the purchase of a new residence, or if a new residence was purchased within twenty-four months prior to the sale of the old residence, any gain is recognized *(recognized gain)* and taxed only so far as the *adjusted sales price* of

Example 11–3 Computing Recognized and Realized Gain

Assume the same facts as in Example 11–2 except that the new home purchased was less than the selling price of the old residence. Some of the $50,000 gain will be *recognized* and *taxed* as follows:

New home purchased	$140,000
Adjusted selling price of old residence	150,000
Recognized gain	$ 10,000
Adjusted basis of new residence:	
Cost new	$140,000
Less: Deferred gain ($50,000 − $10,000)	−40,000
	$100,000

Any realized gain that is deferred on the old residence reduces the adjusted basis of the new residence.

If the new home is sold in 1988 for $280,000, the amount of capital gain finally realized is calculated as follows:

Amount realized on sale	$280,000
Less: Adjusted basis of residence	−100,000
Realized gain	$180,000

the old residence exceeds the cost of the new one. The remainder is **deferred gain.** There is not a limit on the holding period of the old residence to take advantage of the gain deferral.

To reiterate, the total *cost of the new residence,* including purchase price, attorney fees, and so forth, *must equal or exceed* the *adjusted sales price* of the old residence for *all* of the gain to be deferred.

The *realized gain* will be *recognized* by the amount that the *adjusted sales price* of the old residence exceeds the cost of the new residence.

The *adjusted sales price* is calculated by subtracting *fixing-up expenses* from the *amount realized* on the sale of the old residence. In order for *fixing-up expenses* to be deducted, they must be for work performed during a ninety-day period ending with the date contracted to sell the house, and they must be paid for within thirty days after the date the house is sold and not be considered capital expenditures or improvements. Painting, yard manicuring, and minor repairs are examples of typical fixing-up expenditures. Example 11–4 illustrates the computations described above.

Since a personal residence is classified as a capital asset in the internal revenue code, the $1,100 recognized gain in Example 11–4 would be classified as a capital gain. On a personal residence sale, capital gains are taxable, while capital losses would be nondeductible. The $1,100 gain would be added to the taxpayer's other income and taxed at ordinary income tax rates applicable to the taxpayer.

Rollover of the Gain on Personal Residence Sales

As previously described, a taxpayer can **rollover** all or a portion of the *realized gain* on the sale of a personal residence into a newly acquired residence if the cost of a replacement residence equaled or exceeded the *adjusted sales price* of the sold residence and the replacement residence was purchased either twenty-four months before or twenty-four months after the sale of the old residence. The deferred gain simply reduced the basis of the new residence. Prior to the Revenue Act of 1978, if more than one residence was purchased within twenty-four months of the sale of the old residence, only the last residence purchased qualified for the deferment of the gain. Any gain on intervening sales would be recognized for tax purposes.

Effective for sales of principal residences after July 26, 1978, the Revenue Act of 1978 provides for the deferment of more than one gain within twenty-four months of the sale of the initial residence when (1) the sale of the residence is in connection with the commencement of work by the taxpayer as an employee or as a self-employed individual at a new principal place of employment and (2) the distance between the taxpayer's new principal place of employment and his former residence is 35 miles greater than the distance from his former primary place of employment to his former residence. To qualify, the individual must be a full-time employee in the general location of his new place of employment for at least thirty-nine weeks of the twelve-month period immediately following his arrival in the general location.

Once-in-a-Lifetime $125,000 Exclusion
on the Sale of a Personal Residence

Effective for sales after July 26, 1978, the Revenue Act of 1978 has provided a one-time election (the **over-55 exemption**) to exclude up to $125,000 ($62,500 for married taxpayers filing separately) of the gain realized on the sale of a homeowner's principal residence. To qualify for the exclusion, a homeowner or the homeowner's spouse (if the property is held jointly) must be at least fifty-five years of age before the sale and must have owned and used the residence as their principal residence

Example 11–4   Calculating Adjusted Sales Price

In May of 1987 a residence was sold for $35,000 after the sellers incurred fixing-up expenses of $600. Commissions and other expenses of sale amounted to $2,800. The original purchase price of the home was $25,500. Capital improvements over the years totaled $4,000. In November of 1990, a new residence was purchased for $30,500.

Calculation:

May, 1987		
	Selling price	$35,000
	Less: Selling expenses	− 2,800
	Amount realized	$32,200
	Less: Basis of old home ($25,500 + $4,000)	− 29,500
	Realized gain	$2,700
	Amount realized	$32,200
	Less: Fixing-up expenses	− 600
	Adjusted sales price	$31,600
	Less: Cost of new residence	− 30,500
	Recognized (taxable) gain	$1,100
Nov. 1990	Cost of new residence	$30,500
	Less: Deferred gain on old residence	− 1,600
	Adjusted basis of new residence	28,900

Example 11–5   Deferred Gains

Al Smith, a real estate associate, lived and worked in Bloomington, Illinois. On January 15, 1990, Al moved to Chicago, 130 miles away, and sold his home in Bloomington (adjusted sales price $55,000). Al purchased a new home in Chicago on February 15, 1990, for $75,000. In March 1990, Al's employer transferred Al to Clearwater Beach, Florida. Al sold his home in Chicago on April 15, 1990 (adjusted sales price $76,000) and purchased a home in Clearwater Beach for $91,000 on May 15, 1990.

January 15, 1990	February 15, 1990	April 15, 1990	May 15, 1990
Sold home #1 in Bloomington	Purchased home #2 in Chicago	Sold home #2 due to job transfer	Purchased home #3 in Clearwater Beach

Prior to July 26, 1978, only the gain on the last home purchased twenty-four months after the sale of Al's Bloomington residence would qualify as the new residence for the deferment of gain rules. Therefore, the gain on the Chicago residence (residence #2) would be recognized (taxable) for tax purposes. Effective for sales after July 26, 1978, all gains are deferred, consequently reducing the basis of the Clearwater Beach residence.

for a total of at least three years during the last five-year period ending on the date of the sale of the residence. The three-year usage need not be consecutive.

Two points of caution! First, this election is available only *once in a lifetime* to a taxpayer. A married couple is considered as one taxpayer by the Internal Revenue Service. The election does not apply separately to each spouse. If spouses make an election during marriage and subsequently divorce, no further elections are available to either of them or to their spouses, should they remarry. If the excludable gain is less than $125,000, the remaining balance of the $125,000 exclusion is lost forever.

The Internal Revenue Code allows a taxpayer to elect the $125,000 gain exclusion and also to defer, rather than recognize any realized gain over $125,000 if a replacement residence is purchased within the twenty-four month replacement period described earlier.

Example 11–6 Once-in-a-Lifetime Exclusion

On November 2, 1989, a fifty-nine-year-old taxpayer sold his residence for $250,000. The home, which he purchased twenty years ago, had a basis of $100,000 at the time of the sale. His selling expenses were $13,000. If he elects to take the $125,000 exclusion, his taxable gain would be computed as follows:

Sales price		$250,000
Less: Selling expenses	$ 13,000	
Basis	100,000	
		−113,000
Realized gain		$137,000
Less: Exclusion		−125,000
Gain recognized for tax purposes		$ 12,000

Example 11–7 Deferment of Gain

If the taxpayer in Example 11–6 purchased another residence within twenty-four months of the sale of the first residence, he would have to compare the cost of the new home with his revised adjusted sales price as follows:

Sales price		$250,000
Less: Selling expenses	$ 13,000	
Exclusion	125,000	
		−138,000
Revised adjusted sales price		$112,000

If the taxpayer purchases another home costing at least $112,000 within twenty-four months, none of the $37,000 gain on the sale of the first residence would be recognized. It would be deferred, thereby reducing the basis of the new residence. If the new home costs between \$100,000 and \$112,000, the recognized gain would be calculated by subtracting the cost of the new home from \$137,000. If the new home costs \$100,000 or less, the entire \$37,000 gain would be recognized. The 1986 Tax Reform Act does not affect the once-in-a-lifetime exclusion.

Formulas for Calculating Adjusted Basis, Realized Gain, and Recognized (Taxable) Gain

Calculation #1:

Calculation of the "adjusted basis" of a residence:

\$ Purchase price

\+ Capital improvements (driveways, furnaces, etc.)

\- Depreciation

\- Casualty losses

\- Deferred gain on the sale of prior residence

\$ Adjusted basis

Calculation #2:

Calculation of the "realized gain":

\$ Amount realized on the sale (selling price less selling expenses)

\- Adjusted basis of old residence (See Calculation #1)

\$ Realized gain

Calculation #3:

Calculation of the "recognized gain":

\$ Adjusted selling price of old residence (amount realized less fixing-up expenses)

\- Cost of new residence

\$ Recognized gain (taxable)

DISADVANTAGES OF HOME OWNERSHIP

Although the list of ownership advantages is lengthy, the prospective home owner would be remiss if he did not consider the many disadvantages, any one of which may be important enough to dissuade a person from purchasing.

Down Payment Required

First, the down payment required may be sufficiently burdensome to keep many prospects from purchasing a home. If the family nest egg is used as a down payment for the purchase of a house, the family may be unable to meet other financial emergencies and may be forced to curtail other activities requiring money. If an individual already owns a home, the nonliquid nature of the real estate investment precludes the homeowner from rapidly converting ownership equity into emergency cash. He may be able to obtain a second mortgage loan, but this takes time and is expensive.

Property Taxes

Real estate taxes, which have increased in recent years create an additional burden. Even though the taxes are deductible from ordinary income, they nevertheless require a cash outflow from savings. On an annual basis, real estate taxes range from 1 to 3 percent of the property's value. Special assessments are occasionally levied against specific properties to improve streets, sidewalks, and sewage facilities. Such assessments, although payable over several years, can amount to several thousand dollars.

Maintenance

Wide fluctuations in repair and maintenance costs can be incurred, depending on the age of the building, the quality of the construction, and the extent to which the homeowner can do the maintenance himself. The prospective homeowner should allow for annual repair and maintenance expenses of from 1.5 to 2.5 percent of the value of the structure. If the prospective homeowner does much of the maintenance and repair work himself, he necessarily curtails his leisure activities. The maintenance, repair, and yard work necessary in owning a home may create an undesirable hardship.

Commuting

The suburban location of many single-family homes requires expensive and time-consuming commuting. It also decreases the opportunity to attend the cultural activities located in central business districts.

Illiquid Investment

Finally, the homeowner may be forced to sell at a time when the real estate market is in a slump. If so, he must be willing to either accept a low offer for the home or retain ownership until the market recovers. In the meantime, he may need to purchase another home in a new location. The traumatic experience of double house payments, even if for just a short time, may be enough to turn the most ardent homeowner into a lifelong tenant.

Expenses of Sale

When the homeowner does sell, he incurs the expense of the broker's sales commission and legal fees. These expenses range from 8 to 10 percent of the value of the property and can negate the paper profit on many homes that have been held for under three years. Obviously, then, a fundamental factor in the prospective homeowner's decision whether or not to buy is the length of time he expects to occupy the home. If it appears that the holding period will be less than three years, it may be economically unsound to buy.

RENT VERSUS BUY

The topic of rent versus buy is popular on radio, television, and in the press. The proponents of renting state their case or the columnist dutifully lists the advantages of renting, and the proponents of buying counter by advancing their theories. Occasionally, impressive looking rent-versus-buy analysis forms are used to quantify and compare the two alternatives. Who wins usually depends upon the vested interest of the designer of the forms. The apartment owner convincingly uses the forms to demonstrate that renting is definitely the best alternative. Conversely, the broker who sells homes is just as convincing in arriving at the opposite conclusion. Unfortunately, many people try to compare the high cost of owning a twelve-room house with the low cost of renting a six-room apartment. Obviously, comparing apples to oranges is seldom enlightening.

In addition, any attempt to quantify or measure the value of pride, independence, civic responsibility, and the other nonquantifiable advantages of home ownership or the nonquantifiable advantages of renting would be a gross oversimplification.

How, then, can one attach any credence to such oversimplified comparisons? A more realistic approach would require the individual to compare the satisfaction (or utility) gained from tenancy in relation to its cost against the satisfaction derived from home ownership against its cost. The satisfaction derived from renting or owning may be monetary or nonmonetary, just as the costs may be.

The satisfaction derived and costs incurred will vary from individual to individual. As a result, there will be a continuing demand for rentable units from those people who conduct their own analysis and determine for themselves that renting is more advantageous than buying. There will also be more and more demand for owner-occupied homes by those people who analyze their needs and conclude they will be best satisfied by purchasing a home. Family circumstances, family composition, changing cultural beliefs, income, age, and increasing mobility of the work force will strongly influence the relative merits of these two ways of life.

HOME OWNERSHIP CONSIDERATIONS

For families, the decision to purchase a home is the largest financial undertaking of a lifetime. The median selling price of a new home in the United States is now nearly $115,000.

It is not uncommon for the typical family to own and occupy four to five homes in a lifetime. Nonetheless, many pitfalls await the unwary purchaser. When shopping for a home, the purchaser may want to seek the help of a realtor. Realtors are professionally trained in all phases of real estate marketing, and they subscribe to a strict code of professional ethics.

CONDOMINIUM OWNERSHIP

The many advantages and disadvantages of home ownership described in this chapter also apply to the condominium, with some exceptions. *Condominium ownership* consists of an individual interest (just like a single-family dwelling) in an apartment, plus an undivided common interest in the common areas such as elevators, halls, lawn, parking area, heating plant, and so forth. The condominium owner can sell, mortgage, lease, or otherwise transfer the unit just as he would a regular residence. In addition to residential condominiums, professional buildings, office buildings, medical clinics, or recreational developments can use the condominium form of ownership.

Formation

State condominium laws provide that a developer or property owner must execute and record a master deed to the condominium. The deed must be accompanied by a declaration, bylaws, detailed layout *(condominium map)*, floor plans, and elevations of all sides. An *elevation* is a pictorial drawing as seen from one side of a building. Once filed, the condominium status of the property can be removed only with the consent of *all* owners. Provisions are made for transfer of the developer's rights to the owners association when all units have been sold. It is important that the common units be conveyed free of any liens or encumbrances.

Advantages

The condominium concept has a number of advantages, with the result that the increase in the number of units built and sold since 1970 has been phenomenal.

1. The cost of owning a condominium is generally lower than the cost of a single-family dwelling of similar size.
2. The owner can enjoy the use of common facilities, such as a swimming pool, for a fraction of the cost of owning a pool individually.
3. The owner does not need to do the actual work of maintaining the yard, the exterior of the building, or the heating and air conditioning systems, although he does share in these maintenance costs. He still maintains the interior of his own unit, however. In response to public acceptance of condominiums, many apartments are being converted to condominium ownership.

Disadvantages

The main cause of dissatisfaction among condominium owners derives from their lack of control of how things are to be done. Since the majority rules, the association may spend more money than some tenants desire, or there may be a difference of opinion as to how the association money should be spent. Frequently, the monthly payments for maintenance and operation turn out to be well above the original estimate. Inefficiency or excessive management fees can contribute to this. Friction can also arise between the developer and the tenants as to who has certain maintenance responsibilities during the period of time when some of the units are yet unsold. The transition period up until the time there is full control by the association can result in problems or litigation. Sometimes items thought to be commonly owned elements, such as the recreational facilities, are actually, by terms in the agreement, leased facilities, and the leasing cost continues over a longer period. In other cases, the recreational facilities described to the unit buyer turn out not to be part of the original purchase, but rather have to be added later at extra cost. In other cases, bankruptcy of the developer creates problems for the owners. In some condominiums, parking spaces may cost extra or be leased. Although many of these problems can be avoided by careful scrutiny of the purchase agreement, the possibility of friction among unit owners still exists. Other disadvantages often voiced are similar to the disadvantages of renting, such as lack of privacy, noise, and being too close to the neighbors.

Time-Sharing

Some condominiums in recreational areas are sold on a time-sharing basis. For example, the Massanutten Development Company in Virginia sold fee simple interest in units for two weeks out of each year. In other words, a person can own the unit for the first two weeks in June of every year. This interest can be sold or transferred just as any other property.

Condominium Conversion

Many apartment owners are converting their apartment buildings to condominiums. Often, the current renters in an apartment to be converted would prefer to rent rather than purchase a condominium and therefore oppose the conversion. In 1979, the city of Chicago implemented a moratorium on condominium conversions, thereby preventing existing apartment building owners from converting them to condominiums. Later, however, a federal judge struck down the moratorium.

COOPERATIVE OWNERSHIP

A cooperative is different from a condominium in many ways. In *cooperative ownership* a person purchases shares in a corporation that owns the entire building. In return for ownership of stock in the corporation, the owner receives a lease for occupancy of a unit. This legal interest is considered personal property. Each unit owner pays a share of the total expenses, but the corporation pays property taxes and maintenance and holds the mortgage. Usually, there are restrictions on a person's ability to assign the lease, and approval of the board of directors is usually needed to sell an interest in a cooperative. A typical sales contract for a co-op interest might read, "Fifteen shares of stock in Alton Apartments, Inc., entitling owners to proprietary use of Apartment #29 and parking area #29, along with use of all common elements." All decisions are made by a board of directors elected by the shareholders.

In the cooperative, if one tenant-owner fails to pay his share of the taxes or mortgage debt, the others may have to make up the difference or run the risk of foreclosure. Also, if a person leaves the cooperative, he receives only his original investment, and the property appreciation accrues to the remaining owners.

SUMMARY

Home ownership peaked in 1980 at 65.8 percent. Since then, home ownership has been on the decline. The decline in home ownership is related to other trends. The U.S. population is getting older. By the year 2000, the largest age group will be those ranging in age from forty-five to sixty-four. The middle class is shrinking. The decade of the 80s saw the average worker's salary decrease after adjusting for inflation. The standard of living was maintained by adding a second income to the household. By 1988, nearly 60 percent of women worked outside the home. Single parents with children thus lost ground to inflation in the 1980s, and the total number of those living in poverty increased. According to the Census Bureau, 13.5 percent of the American population overall and over 33 percent of the American black population live in poverty.

By 1988, home ownership had declined to about 64 percent. The decline was most significant among the households headed by individuals under age 30, dropping from 63 percent in 1981 to 52 percent in 1988. The single biggest barrier to home ownership for the young household is the lack of a down payment. Most households still look favorably upon home ownership. The primary reason given by first-time buyers was the tax and investment advantages of home ownership. Other advantages of home ownership include that it provides the homeowner security, pride, and civic responsibility. The disadvantages of home ownership include the need for a down payment, the costs of maintenance and real estate taxes, the expenses involved in the sale of the property, and the illiquid nature of the investment. These factors must be carefully considered by the heads of households when making their decision to rent or buy. In addition, the potential homeowner must evaluate the alternative forms of home ownership.

TERMS AND CONCEPTS

You can check your understanding of these terms against the glossary or by review in this chapter.

Acquisition indebtedness	"Dinks"	Housing Affordability
Adjusted basis	"Diwks"	Index
Adjusted sales price	Fixing-up expenses	Over-55 exemption
Baby-boomers	Home-equity debt	Recognized gain
Deferred gain	Homestead Act	Rollover of gain

What are the differences or relationships, if any, between the following?

Adjusted sales price and Amount realized on sale	Condominium ownership and Cooperative ownership	Recognized gain and Realized gain

PROBLEMS

11-1. Ted Taxpayer purchased a residence in 1988 for $45,000. He spent $5,000 on capital improvements and sold the property in 1991 for $80,000. He incurred selling expenses of $5,200. What is the amount of the realized gain?

11-2. Referring to problem 1, assume Mr. Taxpayer purchases a new home within six months after he sold his old residence. He paid $70,000 for his new home. How much of the gain is taxed? How much is deferred?

11-3. What is the rule governing fixing-up expenses? Are they used in calculating realized gain?

11-4. At age 57, Iris Incometax sells her home for $75,000 and retires to Florida. She paid $25,000 for the home seven years ago. Assuming that she is entitled to the over-55 exemption, how much of the gain is taxable? Assume she sold the house for $175,000. How much would be taxable.

11-5. Explain the "over age 55 exemption from long-term capital gain" on the sale of a principal residence.

11-6. Should and can the conversion of apartments to condominiums be restricted?

11-7. List the main advantages and disadvantages of condominium ownership.

11-8. Mr. and Mrs. Janski purchased their residence in 1987 for $75,000. They incurred $300 in legal fees in the purchase. During their three-year ownership, they made $10,800 in capital improvements. In 1990, they sold their home for $93,000 and incurred selling expenses of $6,148. In addition they incurred fixing-up expenses of $750. They bought a new home for

$92,000 that same year. Calculate both realized and recognized gain, if any.

11-9. How has the rate of home ownership changed since 1980? Where were the most significant changes?

11-10. What was the major barrier to home ownership for the young, potential homeowner?

11-11. Explain how the NATIONAL ASSOCIATION OF REALTORS'® Housing Affordability Index works.

11-12. What is the maximum *acquisition indebtedness* that a homeowner can deduct from his taxes as of 1988? What is the rule on the deductibility of a *home-equity* loan?

11-13. Discuss the phase-out of the deductibility of interest on consumer loans.

▬▬▬▬ SUPPLEMENTARY READINGS

Bloom, George F. *Real Estate,* 8th ed. New York: Wiley, 1982.

Galaty, Filmore W., et al. *Modern Real Estate Practice,* 10th ed. Chicago: Real Estate Education Co., 1986.

Harrison, Henry S., and Leonard, Margery B. *Home Buying.* Chicago: Realtors National Marketing Institute of the NATIONAL ASSOCIATION OF REALTORS®, 1980.

Harwood, Bruce. *Real Estate Principles,* 4th ed. Reston, Va.: Reston Publishing, 1986.

Pearson, Karl G. *Real Estate Principles and Practices.* Columbus, Oh.: Grid, 1978. Chapters 15–18.

Ratcliff, Richard U. *Real Estate Analysis.* New York: McGraw-Hill, 1961. Chapter 8.

Ring, Alfred A., and Dasso, Jerome, *Real Estate Principles and Practices,* 10th ed. Englewood Cliffs, N.J.: Prentice-Hall, 1985. Chapter 22.

Salins, Peter D. *The Ecology of Housing Destruction.* New York: New York University Press, 1980.

Shenkel, William M. *Modern Real Estate Principles,* 3rd ed. Dallas: Business Publications, 1984. Chapter 21.

Unger, Maurice A., and Karvel, George R. *Real Estate Principles and Practices,* 8th ed. Cincinnati: South-Western, 1987. Chapter 10.

Urban Land Institute. *Housing for a Maturing Population.* Washington, D.C., 1983.

Wendt, Paul F., and Cerf, Alan. *Real Estate Investment Analysis and Taxation.* New York: McGraw-Hill, 1979. Chapters 1 and 4.

CHAPTER 12
Real Property Insurance

Although insurance is a specialized professional field of its own, it relates to real estate, or real property, in a number of ways. Knowledge of real property insurance is important to the owner for her own protection, to the property manager so that she can properly manage the property, and to the real estate broker, who often is asked to advise clients as to their insurance needs.

Insurance is a contract arrangement between two parties whereby one party, called the *insurer,* agrees to indemnify the other party, called the *insured,* against losses the insured may incur. The insurance company is taking the risk that a particular event will not occur. The insurance contract, called the *insurance policy,* describes the risks covered. Usually, the policy is on a standard printed form and must conform to state requirements. In exchange for the coverage against loss, the insured pays a *premium* to the insurer. Premiums paid to the insurance company are used to pay expenses and dividends to stockholders and to build up reserves to pay losses due under the policies. Optional coverage to the basic insurance policy can be added by an *endorsement* or *rider.*

A property owner does not have to take out insurance, since all risks can be assumed by the owner. Actually, a homeowner does take certain risks, but the wise property owner will at least insure against those risks for which she could not stand the loss, such as complete or substantial destruction of the property. The homeowner can, of course, try to eliminate or reduce the risk. Some businesses or individuals become *self-insurers* by setting aside certain funds to cover risks. They feel that it is more economical to save the premium and take the risk; however, they must make sure that there are actually sufficient funds available to handle potential risks. Usually, a lending institution will require sufficient insurance to cover its interest if there is a mortgage on the property.

When a property owner takes out insurance, considerable confidence is placed in the insurance company. Often, homeowners have a significant part of their life savings invested in the home. They would undergo a substantial loss if the insurance company could not make good on the policy. States have responded to this problem by closely regulating insurance companies through requirements for incorporation or operation, as well as for audits and reporting.

Insurance companies are in a position of great responsibility and large potential risk. To avoid the possibility of incurring losses simultaneously on a substantial portion of their policies, companies try to diversify their risks. They diversify in two ways. First they seek policy holders over a wide geographical area. The other method is to handle a variety of different types of insurance, such as life, fire, and automobile insurance. Some insurance companies reinsure some of their policies with other insurance carriers.

Many large insurance companies have salespeople in many different cities and towns. Because of the need to cover widespread areas, some smaller companies use independent brokers to handle their policy sales. These independent brokers will usually handle policies for a number of different insurance companies.

Insurance provides many social and economic benefits. Many businesses could not operate without this protection. It provides a means whereby a major financial loss does not fall upon one or a few individuals, but rather many pay a small share of the total loss. A number of different types of insurance are related to real property. They are listed by perils as follows:

1. Loss due to fire, windstorm, or other natural elements
2. Loss due to breakdown of artificial elements, such as water pipes or sprinkler systems
3. Liability for injury of other persons due to the condition of the property, or damage to another person's property due to conditions on the insured property
4. Theft, vandalism, or other crime
5. Business interruption
6. Loss of property due to defects in the title or loss in value of the property due to defects or problems related to the title
7. Construction defects in a home
8. Mortgage insurance

The first five perils are handled through regular property insurance companies, but the last three coverages are by separate policies with companies specializing in those types of insurance.

TYPES OF PROPERTY INSURANCE COVERAGE

The following are covered through regular property insurance companies.

Insurance Against the Elements

Property damage can be caused by the elements of fire, air, water, and earth. This can result from windstorm, flood, and earthquake, although a basic real property insurance policy may cover only fire or fire and windstorm, excluding water and earthquake damage. In some locations, these additional coverages can be obtained by paying extra premiums and obtaining *endorsements* to the policy.

Until 1968, flood insurance was not offered by most insurance companies. It was felt that only those in high-risk areas would be interested, and that would cause the rates to be very high. A joint effort of the insurance industry and the federal government resulted in the National Flood Insurance Program. As an encouragement to purchase flood insurance, the federal government subsidizes rates and reinsures companies against catastrophic losses. At the same time, the federal government desires to discourage further construction in flood-prone sites. Therefore, before flood insurance can be sold in an area, the community must enact and enforce restrictions against further construction in locations subject to flooding.

Liability Insurance

Liability insurance protects the property owner against claims for injury to others or damage to the property of others. Legal principles hold a property owner liable for compensating payments where it can be shown that another person suffered loss or injury due to the property owner's negligence. These claims can arise due to a condition of the property or activities that take place on the property. A property owner is required to take ordinary care of the property and to use ordinary skill in managing it. When a third party is injured because of owner negligence, the property owner may be held liable. For instance, a fall on a sidewalk not cleared of ice could be a result of inadequate care. Sometimes a property owner's liability will depend on whether or not the third party had a valid right to be on the property. A trespasser will have less chance of recovery than would a repair person or friend who had a legitimate reason to be on the property. The owner of land is required to exercise a greater degree of care toward his invitee than toward a trespasser on his land.

Loss from Crime

Insurance can be purchased against losses from burglary, theft, or other criminal acts. Insurance policies may provide coverage primarily related to personal property within the real property. The loss could be perpetrated either by trespassers or by a person allowed on the premises. If a policy covers only burglary, the insurer will probably require some evidence of forceable entry, such as visible marks of tools or other means of entry. Sometimes it is difficult to tell whether an item such as a wristwatch was stolen or lost or just misplaced. Some companies use a "mysterious disappearance" clause which, for an extra premium, reimburses for a loss without evidence of burglary.

INSURANCE PRINCIPLES AND PRACTICES

Although land itself is considered to be indestructible, any structures on the land are subject to damage from fire, wind, other natural elements, or human causes. Insurance protects against loss from these risks.

Coverage

Usually, a person will pay a premium sufficient to cover damage to a certain percentage of the market value of the property. This is reasonable, since the land itself is indestructible. If a property owner does not carry sufficient insurance, the insured is a *coinsurer* and the insurance company would pay only a portion of the loss. Usually, insurance companies agree that insurance covering 80 percent of property value is sufficient to allow full reimbursement for any partial loss. Sometimes an individual may have sufficient resources to cover losses and will not purchase insurance. This person is a *self-insurer;* however, most people are not willing or able to assume the risk of a large loss.

If there is a mortgage on the property, the mortgagee or lender will require the property owner to carry sufficient insurance to cover the interest the mortgagee has in the property.

Indemnity

It is not intended that a person be able to profit from insurance; nor is insurance intended as a gambling or speculative proposition. The principle of **indemnity** states that the purpose of insurance is to reimburse the insured for any loss, and the objective is to restore her to the place she was before the loss occurred. To collect the insurance, the applicant must have an **insurable interest** in the property at the time of the loss. This means that, in the event of property destruction, the person would suffer a financial loss. As an example, X could not take out insurance on the property of a friend, Y, unless X was in a situation to suffer financial loss if damage occurred to Y's property.

Insurance Rates

The insured pays a premium for a certain amount of coverage. This relationship of premium to coverage is called a **rate.** If a person pays $120 a year for $40,000 fire insurance coverage, the yearly rate would be computed as follows:

$$\text{Rate} = \frac{\$120}{40,000} = .003$$

or $3.00 per $1,000 of coverage. The rate will depend on the amount of risk involved according to the type of construction, location of the property, or any other factor that affects the likelihood of the event insured against. It will also vary with the quality of and distance from fire protection. Typically, brick homes would have lower rates than frame homes; tile roofs would have a lower rate than wood shingle roofs. An area with a past history of tornadoes or a site near a forest fire area would have higher rates than locations where the threat was less likely. Rural properties distant from a water hydrant would have a higher rate than city properties. This type of rate system provides an incentive to construct safer structures and select better locations. In some cases, policies may allow special deductions for safety devices—fire extinguishers, special locks, alarm systems, or anything that tends to prevent or reduce the loss potential. Usually, the insurance company will set up standard rates for classes of property in order to avoid an involved analysis of each property to be insured.

Cancellation of Policy

The insured can cancel a policy and receive a rebate of unearned premium; however, this rebate will not usually be a proportional part of the total paid. Frequently, the insurance rates for a three-year period will be less than three times the one-year rate. If a person cancelled a three-year policy at the end of the first year, she would then be charged at the one-year rate or **short-rate,** so that the refund would be less than two-thirds of the total paid. This provision could apply even though the company allowed the insured to pay the three-year premium in installments. The insured should also remember to notify the company as soon as she desires a cancellation. If a person sold a home but failed to notify the insurance company, the insured might receive a rebate only from the date of notification rather than from the date of title transfer.

If the company cancels the policy, it must give advance notice as required by state law and refund a proportionate amount rather than the short rate. Concealment or misrepresentation of facts by the insured can void the policy. For example, the insured may fraudulently conceal from the company that rooms are rented out in order to obtain a lower rate, making the policy voidable. Policy coverage can also be denied if, in violation of a policy provision, a person allows a risk to increase, such as leaving the home vacant for sixty days without notifying the insurance company.

Deductible Amounts

The primary purpose of insurance is to protect a person against a risk she cannot afford. Where full coverage is provided against any amount of risk, the insurance company must handle a large number of small claims. Often, the paperwork for a small claim takes as much time as that for a large claim. To encourage policyholders to be self-insurers on small losses, insurers provide **deductible amount** clauses in policies. For a $50 deductible policy, the property owner would pay the first $50 of any loss. This option also tends to encourage policyholders to take greater care to prevent losses. Deductible policies cost considerably less than full coverage policies. Because property owners can absorb these smaller losses, and because some state laws permit only deductible policies, they are frequently used in real property insurance policies.

TYPES OF POLICIES

Fire Insurance

The basic protection against property loss has been the standard fire insurance policy. Most companies use a standard form. The policy indemnifies the property owner against losses incurred due to what courts term "unfriendly fires." If the insured person deliberately sets a fire, the insurance could not be collected.

The basic policy insures against direct loss from fire or lightning. In case of fire, the insured is reimbursed for the actual loss up to the face value of the policy and no more. This includes the costs to remove personal property from a home endangered by fire. Damage from smoke would also be included, but not from smoke resulting from a defective chimney or situation where the fire was not classified as "unfriendly." The policy also excludes damage from fire caused by war, rebellion, or civil disturbance; however, these coverages are available as an extended coverage endorsement.

The insured value is usually interpreted to be the maximum amount to reproduce the lost property. If there is a partial loss, the insurer will pay the amount required to reproduce the original property less depreciation. Usually when a loss occurs, the insured obtains estimates of repair or replacement. Sometimes it is necessary to call in an appraiser to establish the original property value and the value remaining after the loss. If the insured and the insurer cannot agree on the loss, an arbitrator may be selected. Once in a while, the dispute will go to the courts for settlement.

The policy will describe the property insured. It may or may not include structures such as garages, barns, or other outbuildings.

Extended Coverage

Endorsements can be added to a basic fire insurance policy to extend the coverage either to additional structures on the property or even off the property, or to additional perils such as windstorm, hail, riot, civil disturbance, falling trees, or bursting water pipes. Other policies also have *extended coverage* for theft, losses associated with personal property, and liability, either by separate endorsement or by use of a broad form that includes coverage of other risks, such as those perils just listed. Some mortgage companies will insist that the owner carry extended coverage as a condition to making a mortgage loan.

Homeowner's Policy

The *homeowner's policy* is a single package policy designed to give the property owner protection against a wide variety of risks. These include losses from fire, windstorm, and other natural elements plus other possible risks. The additional risks might include liability to third parties, theft, water damage, explosion, vandalism, riot and commotion, fall of aircraft, smoke, earthquake, and glass breakage. The homeowner is able to secure all of these coverages in one policy at a lower cost than by purchasing them under separate endorsements.

Homeowner policies provide various types of coverage and cover different uses. For example, HO-1 (Homeowner One), HO-2, and HO-5 are for owner-occupied dwellings. HO-4 is primarily for tenants and covers personal property only. HO-6 is for owners of condominium units.

Rent and Leasehold Insurance

An owner of an apartment or other income-producing property is subject to the same risks as the homeowner and other additional risks. If rental property is damaged, the owner can lose the rent from the property as well as incur expenses related to repairs or restoration. *Rent insurance* can be purchased to give the owner continued income in case of loss of rent due to fire or other covered provisions. *Rental insurance* provides reimbursement for potential—rather than actual—rent loss and would cover apartments vacant when the fire occurred.

In some instances, a tenant on a long-term lease may be paying considerably less than economic (market) rent. This situation creates a positive leasehold interest that may have considerable value to the tenant. Destruction of the leased property could wipe out the tenant's leasehold interest. She can protect herself against this loss by purchasing a *leasehold insurance* policy.

Business Property Insurance

The various types of businesses and differences in types of properties associated with each business necessitate a variety of insurance coverages. The risks due to fire, windstorm, and other elements are similar to residential risks. In addition, many businesses have considerable merchandise or inventories that also need to be insured. A business is also subject to loss of earnings if the damage causes the business to be interrupted or closed. This is often referred to as a *consequential loss* since it is not directly due to the peril insured against. Insurance for these risks can be obtained either by individual policies, as extensions to a basic policy, or in a package policy similar to a homeowner's policy. Public liability is also an important factor in a business, since the premises are frequented by customers. Businesses face possible lawsuits resulting from bodily injury or property damage through negligence or alleged negligence of the business owner. The insurance ordinarily covers not only the actual damages paid, but also the legal costs associated with the lawsuit.

Condominium Insurance

Insurance for a condominium should be in the name of the board of directors to cover the common areas, including public liability. If the overall policy covers destruction of units, the premium costs are shared by the unit owners. In some cases unit owners purchase coverage for their own property, both real and personal. Some states have laws specifying how condominium insurance is to be handled.

OTHER POLICY PROVISIONS

A person purchasing real property insurance should be aware of a variety of clauses that may appear in policies and restrict coverage. Homeowners are often not aware of the meaning of these provisions until a loss occurs and coverage is denied.

Pro Rata and Coinsurance

Since it is not the intent of insurance to provide a recovery greater than the actual loss, the policy will usually contain a pro rata liability clause. The following pro rata liability clause or one similar to it will appear in most policies.

> This insurer shall not be liable for a greater portion of any loss than the amount insured against bears to the total insurance carried on the property against the peril involved, whether collectible or not.

This *pro rata clause* prevents a property owner from collecting an amount greater than the actual loss through policies with different insurance companies. For example, assume an owner has $10,000 insurance with Company X and $30,000 with Company Y. Loss was determined to be $20,000. Each company would be liable in the same proportion as the insurance carried. Thus Company X would be liable for ¼ × $20,000, or $5,000, and Company Y would pay ¾ × $20,000, or $15,000, giving the insured the exact amount of the loss. The owner could not collect more than the actual loss.

A *coinsurance clause* is different; it can result in the insured being a partial self-insurer. In the past, property owners often reasoned that most losses are less than the entire value, and therefore they would carry insurance less than the total value. This was unfair to the insurance company and other insured owners who carry full coverage, since it would cause rates to increase. Today the typical homeowner's policy will provide that coverage to 80 percent of the property value is required in order to warrant the reimbursement of 100 percent of losses. Therefore, on a property valued at $80,000, the owner must carry 80 percent, or $64,000 insurance coverage to collect 100 percent of the losses.

If, for example, the above property owner carried only $48,000 insurance, the company would say that the homeowner carried the balance of $16,000 at her own risk. If there were a loss of $20,000, the insurance company would calculate its portion of liability in this way:

$$\text{Amount Recovered} = \frac{\text{Amount Carried}}{\text{Amount Required}} \times \text{Loss}$$

$$= 48/64 \times \$20,000$$

$$= \$15,000$$

The owner would have to make up the $5,000 balance on her own. Thus, a homeowner should carry insurance to 80 percent of the value and increase the insurance as the property value grows due to inflation or improvements. Otherwise, she may find herself in the position of being a coinsurer without intending to be.

Many companies provide policies with automatic increases in coverage based on an inflation index. The company then guarantees full coverage in case of a loss.

Diminution by Loss

When an insurance company pays a loss on a policy, the insurance remaining in force often becomes less than the original policy value. (Some homeowners' policies state different provisions.) If an insured had a $30,000 policy and then a $5,000 loss was paid, the remaining coverage would be only $25,000, even after the repair was made. This is called *diminution by loss* of the policy value. It is necessary to apply for a new policy in the original amount and pay an additional premium in order to reinstate the full coverage.

Subrogation

Assume that party A had fire insurance on her property. The property was damaged by a fire that was caused by the negligence of B. Party A can collect from her insurance company; however, the principle of *subrogation* provides that the insurance company can attempt to collect from B. In this process, the insurer can go to court as a representative of A, and a provision to this extent will usually appear in the policy.

Actual Cash Value

Many homes are old and have lost value due to deterioration. If an *actual cash value* clause appeared in the policy and the home were destroyed, the company would pay the reproduction cost, minus depreciation. This means that the homeowner would not be able to replace the home without adding some of her own money. If the words "replacement cost" were substituted in the policy for "actual cash value," the insurance company would not deduct for depreciation. Premiums are substantially higher when the policy provides for payment of loss at replacement cost.

Loss Payable Endorsement

A *loss payable endorsement* clause is always required by mortgage companies to protect their interest. If there is a loss, the proceeds check is made payable to the owner and mortgagee jointly.

Named on Policy Clause

Only the person whose name appears on a policy (or the heirs if the person named dies) can collect on the policy restricted by a *named on policy clause.* If the property is sold, the former owner no longer has an insurable interest in the property. The policy does not cover the new owner unless the insurance company accepts her as the insured. In another application, if two owners own a property on a fifty-fifty basis, but only one person's name appears on the policy, only half of the loss can be recovered.

CLAIM PROCEDURES AND ESTABLISHING AMOUNT OF LOSS

If a loss occurs, it will be necessary to determine the amount of reimbursement due. After suffering a loss, the policyholder will usually file a claim with the insurance company as an initial step. There are several approaches to determining loss. One way to establish the amount is to determine the property value just prior to the loss and then try to establish how much the value is reduced by the loss. Estimating the cost of replacement is another approach; however, other factors such as depreciation or obsolescence may have reduced the value such that a restoration would actually leave the owner with a property of greater value than originally. To avoid a profit by the property owner, the usual procedure is to determine the restoration cost and subtract for depreciation. Thus, the owner would pay part of the restoration cost. In cases when the value or loss cannot be so easily measured, such as in personal injury cases, the matter usually must be resolved by negotiation or court appeal.

CURRENT ISSUES IN PROPERTY INSURANCE

Insurance is sometimes difficult to obtain for real estate in blighted or high-risk areas. The term *redlining* refers to the alleged practice of discouraging the writing of insurance policies for properties in high-risk areas. Redlining received its name from the old underwriting practice of outlining in red ink on a map those areas deemed to be high-risk areas and advising agents not to write policies in these areas.

Redlining by lending institutions is in violation of Title VIII of the Federal Civil Rights Act and the Federal Home Loan Bank Board regulations. A recent federal district court decision held that insurance policies must be available in all neighborhoods; however, the insurance company can charge higher rates in neighborhoods that have higher loss ratios.

Lack of available insurance retards the rebuilding of blighted areas. Under a program operated by the insurance industry called FAIR, participating companies can purchase reinsurance against riot from the Federal Insurance Administration. The insurance offered, however, is still at rates higher than normal.

TITLE INSURANCE

When a piece of real property is purchased, it may be difficult to completely prove that the title is clear and that there will be no future claims on the title. Sometimes claims or other defects in the title unexpectedly show up later to cast a cloud on the title or otherwise reduce its value or make it difficult to sell. As an example, a woman may claim to be the wife of a deceased owner, whereas the records showed the deceased owner to be single. A *title insurance* policy protects against loss of value or marketability. The insured pays a one-time premium when purchasing a title policy. Title insurance companies almost always have an established staff to investigate records and examine titles before the company accepts the risk of insuring a particular piece of property.

There are two kinds of title insurance—owner's and lender's. An owner's title policy safeguards the property owner (and lender) for as long as it is owned by the insured or heirs or devisees. A lender's policy covers only the lender's mortgage balance; the amount of insurer's liability decreases as the loan is paid off, and the policy terminates when the mortgage loan has been completely paid.

Covered Risks

The following are risks that are usually covered by a title insurance policy:

1. Someone else owning an interest in the property
2. A document affecting the chain of title not being properly signed or acknowledged, or any defect in the recording of the title
3. Problems resulting from fraud, forgery, lack of legal competence, incapacity, or impersonation
4. Lack of a legal access to the land, or restrictive covenants seriously limiting use of the land
5. An undetected lien on the property prior to the policy date
6. Unrecorded and unknown easements, leases, contracts, or options resulting in an unmarketable title
7. Being forced to remove or substantially alter the structure because of encroachment, violations of zoning requirements, or restrictive covenants
8. Inability to build a single-family residence due to the reasons cited in item 7

Exclusions

A typical title policy does not guard against the following losses:

1. Condemnation (eminent domain) after policy date
2. Expenses resulting from the exercise of police powers or environmental protection
3. Any of the above-covered risks agreed to or known to owner but not to insurer, or any risks that do not result in an actual loss to the owner

4. Rights to streets, alleys, and so forth, outside the legal description of the insured property

Options of the Insurer

The insurer can satisfy a claim by the insured by selecting one or more of the following options:

1. Pay the claim
2. Pay the cost of a successful defense of the title or take other action to defend owner
3. Pay the face amount of the policy and any attorney's fees or other costs up to that time
4. Negotiate a settlement

Cost of Title Insurance

The cost of a title insurance policy is based upon the value of the property at the time of acquisition or the face amount on the policy. There will usually be a minimum cost of $50 to $75 even if the value is only $1,000. A typical rate structure scale graduates to $125 for $10,000, $200 for $30,000, and $300 for $60,000.

A *binder policy,* as sold in many states, is designed for buyers who plan to sell within a short time. By paying about 110 percent of the normal premium, the owner can get a refund of all except 10 percent if the property is sold in one or two years.

PRIVATE MORTGAGE INSURANCE (PMI)

Private mortgage insurance (PMI) is offered by private profit-oriented companies. The Mortgage Guaranty Insurance Company (MGIC) was formed in 1957 as the first to offer PMI; however, today there are over a dozen firms.

Banks and savings and loan associations that originate mortgages exceeding 80 (or sometimes 90) percent of the home's appraised value require PMI. The policy covers only the top 20 to 25 percent of the loan value and the borrower pays the premium. The objective is to protect lenders against foreclosure losses on these higher-risk loans. After several years, when the loan-to-value drops below 80 percent of the current market value of the property, PMI can usually be canceled.

MUTUAL MORTGAGE INSURANCE

FHA insures loans on real property made by approved lending institutions. Mutual mortgage insurance plans insure against homeowner defaults so that the lending institution does not incur significant losses on these loans.

LIFE INSURANCE WITH MORTGAGE

Most lenders offer an insurance policy whereby the borrower pays a premium for life insurance. The policy pays off the balance of the mortgage if the primary wage earner dies, or it is available for a higher premium to insure against the death of either wage earner. This policy can be canceled at any time by the insured.

INSURANCE AGAINST STRUCTURAL DEFECTS

New home buyers can purchase a warranty against structural defects under the Home Owners Warranty *(HOW)* Program. The Home Owners Warranty Corporation (a private company) offers policies that cover single-family homes as well as high-rise or low-rise condominiums. If a builder has been approved by the company, the buyer of a new home can purchase a policy. Before 1980 the cost was $2 per $1,000 of sale price, but by 1981 the cost had risen to the range of $2.60 to $3.15, depending on loss experience figures. During the first two years the builder agrees to repair all structural defects. If the builder fails to comply due to bankruptcy or other reason, HOW will cover the cost but with a $250 deductible. After the first two years, HOW warrants the next eight years of the ten-year policy with a deductible amount equal to 1 percent of the home purchase price. Homeowners with complaints are required to participate in a conciliation process to attempt to resolve any dispute before it goes to final arbitration.

Many builders provide uninsured one-year warranties against defects backed up only by their own integrity. Two states, New Jersey and Minnesota, have related laws. New Jersey law requires builders to register with the state and requires the builder to offer ten-year protection through either a state or private plan. Minnesota law requires builders to provide an express warranty to the buyer. In most states, courts will enforce an implied warranty of fitness upon builders.

The Federal Housing Administration (FHA) and Veterans Administration (VA) require one-year warranties for their loans on new homes; they insure the home against structural defects for four years.

SUMMARY

Insurance is a means of shifting and distributing the burden of loss so that one or a few individuals do not suffer a very large loss. The insured pays a premium to the insurance company, and the insurer in turn takes the risk of loss from fire, windstorm, theft, liability, or other perils defined in the policy. Coverage for title defects, structural defects, and mortgage insurance are handled with special policies.

There are a variety of perils that can be insured against, and the insured can select those she desires and then pay the rate for that coverage. She can also select deductible amounts and thereby assume a portion of the risk. Sometimes, the insured assumes this proportionate risk unintentionally by not maintaining adequate coverage. Those insured should be careful to maintain sufficient property insurance to keep up with the current value of their property.

TERMS AND CONCEPTS

You can check your understanding of these terms against the glossary or by review in this chapter.

Consequential loss   Indemnity   Redlining
Diminution by loss   Insurable interest   Self-insurer
Endorsement   Liability insurance   Short rate
Extended coverage   Premium   Subrogation
Homeowner's policy   Rate   Title insurance
HOW

What are the differences or relationship, if any, between the following?

Deductible amount and   Pro rata liability and   Rent insurance and
    Pro rata   Coinsurance   Rental insurance
Insured and Insurer   Rent insurance and
                              Leasehold insurance

PROBLEMS

12-1. The fire insurance policy on your home is to be renewed. It covers protection against fire and lightning. What additional coverage might you consider and when is each appropriate?

12-2. Your homeowner's policy has not been changed for four years and home values in the area have increased by 30 percent during that period. List and explain factors to evaluate so as to determine if the present coverage is sufficient.

12-3. A fire insurance policy contains an 80 percent coinsurance clause. The original cost of the property was $24,000; the present value is $32,000. The insurance carried at present is $22,000. If there is a fire loss of $8,000, what portion will the insurance company pay, assuming no reduction for depreciation?

12-4. Describe the effect of each of the following clauses in an insurance policy if a loss occurs.
   (a) Actual cash value
   (b) Replacement cost
   (c) Subrogation
   (d) Diminution by loss
   (e) Named on policy

12-5. Calculate the annual fire insurance premium for a $64,000 policy at a rate of $.365 per $100 of coverage.

12-6. The rate for a homeowner's policy is $.39 per $100. The insurance company will offer a two-year policy at 1.85 times the annual rate and a three-year policy at 2.7 times the annual rate. On a $50,000 house, determine the saving for a two-year policy or a three-year policy over a six-year period.

12-7. In problem 12-6, assume that Mr. Roth took out a three-year policy. If he canceled after one year, what would be his refund at the short rate?

12-8. A property owner had a fire loss of $20,000. He had carried a $30,000 policy with company A and a $40,000 policy with company B on a property valued at $35,000. What would the owner collect from each company?

12-9. Kurt and Karla Schmidt carried $40,000 insurance on a residence valued at $70,000. They suffer a loss of $15,000. The company would have paid the entire loss if they had carried 80 percent coverage. What can the owners recover on the loss?

12-10. Ms. Alton pays $4.20 per $1,000 on her homeowner's policy with a face value of $60,000. Her home was recently appraised at $84,000. If she wants to be insured 100 percent against losses, how much additional premium would she have to pay?

12-11. Suppose a policyholder's home is partially damaged by fire. What are some factors that will determine if the insurance company will pay the full amount of the loss?

12-12. Discuss how the construction materials in a home affect the amount of insurance needed or the cost of the policy.

12-13. Discuss the usefulness of title insurance in each of the following situations:
   (a) Betty and Bob Jones purchased a home from Mr. Sellars who had the deed in his name and claimed he was never married. Three years later Mr. Sellars died and a woman identified herself as Mrs. Sellars and claimed a dower right in the property.

The property was located in a state where the dower right was a one-third fee simple estate.

(b) Joan and Billy Smith paid $60,000 for a home that the seller claimed he had bought for $48,000 two years ago and then added $19,000 in improvements and repairs. Six months later an appraiser valued the home at $56,000. The Smiths presented a claim for $4,000 to the title company.

(c) Joe and Agnes Beyer purchased a home from a widow, the only known heir of her husband, who died without a will. Later a man claiming to be the son of the widow's husband by a prior marriage appears and claims a share in the property. The son had been living away and the widow claimed she did not know of his existence.

(d) At the time Al Jack deeded a lot to the Borths, Al showed evidence that he was of age. One year later Al appears with proof that he just became of legal age last week and was disaffirming the sale and wanted the property back. The Borths had started construction of a home.

(e) Eleven months after the purchase of a home, the buyers noticed cracks in the foundation due to settling of the soil. They needed to sell the home and move to a different city, but were unable to find a real estate broker to list the property and filed a claim with the title company.

SUPPLEMENTARY READINGS

Bickelhoupt, David L. *General Insurance,* 11th ed., Homewood, Ill.: Irwin, 1983. Chapters 4, 5, 8, 18, 19, and 21.

Greene, Mark R., and Trieschmann, James S. *Risk and Insurance,* 7th ed., Cincinnati: South-Western, 1988.

Huebner, S. S. *Property and Liability Insurance,* 3rd ed., Englewood Cliffs, N.J.: Prentice-Hall, 1982.

Long, J. D., and Gregg, D. W. *Property and Liability Insurance Handbook.* Homewood, Ill.: Irwin, 1965. Chapters 5–10, 19, 23–27, 31, 32, 41, and 49.

Mehr, Robert I., and Cammock, Emerson. *Principles of Insurance,* 8th ed., Homewood, Ill: Irwin, 1985. Chapters 13, 15, 16, 22, 29, and 32.

Nelson, David Robert. "Why Builders Should Know HOW." *Real Estate Review,* vol. 8, no. 1 (Spring 1978), pp. 46–53.

Vaughn, Emmett J., *Fundamentals of Risk and Insurance,* 4th ed., New York: Wiley, 1986.

CHAPTER 13
Brokerage

Real estate brokerage can include one or more of the following functions: listing, selling, buying, leasing, renting, exchanging, appraising, or managing real property. License laws usually define a real estate *broker* as a person or firm who, *for compensation,* engages in buying, selling, renting, leasing, or exchanging real estate *for others.* In all states it is unlawful to engage in real estate brokerage without a valid broker's license.

A real estate broker's primary asset is expertise or know-how. A broker does not sell a product, but rather provides a service. Consequently, success depends upon skill in bringing interested and willing parties together in order to complete transactions successfully. To be effective, brokers must have the necessary background, including knowledge of the law, the locality, property values, ownership, and sources of financing. They also need managerial and sales ability.

Proper representation of a seller and adequate service to a buyer require that brokers possess specialized knowledge and qualifications. They need to be aware of local property values. They must be able to correlate the needs of a buyer with the various available properties. They must be aware of building activities, the local real estate market, and the availability of financing. They must also know the state and local statutes and regulations and have enough knowledge of the law to handle the interests of the seller and buyer properly and to avoid jeopardy to all persons involved. A willingness to put in hard work and long hours and the ability to get along with people are also important attributes. Since real estate can be bought and sold without a broker's services, brokers must be able to convince a prospective client that it is worthwhile to pay the fee or commission, rather than to try to handle it alone. In all of its facets, brokerage requires extensive knowledge.

What a Broker Is Not

Some aspects of real estate should not or cannot be performed by the broker. Brokers must recognize those activities that are beyond their legal and practical limitations—those that require the services of an attorney, surveyor, or other professional. The continued success of a brokerage depends upon the ability to acquire clients, to integrate all facets of the business, and to complete transactions both quickly and to the satisfaction of the client's needs and interests.

Specializing Brokers

The brokerage business can be segmented into groupings based on either the type of property or the type of service. Residential brokers deal primarily with single-family units or those housing two to four families. Others might deal mainly with apartments. Commercial brokers work with income-producing properties. Industrial brokers handle transactions involving industrial properties.

Some brokers handle transactions other than sales, such as negotiating leases, securing mortgages, or handling exchanges of property. Exchanges of property often provide tax advantages to the parties involved. In selling real estate, the broker who is also willing to take property in trade on a sale can sometimes encourage transactions that otherwise might not be within the financial capability of a buyer. In most exchanges, both parties pay a commission based upon the value of their property sold or exchanged. These commission rates may differ from rates customarily charged in sales of property. As in regular sales transactions, the contract agreements must make each party aware that both are paying a commission to the broker. Failure to do so would result in a breach of the broker's duty to the client.

When brokers negotiate leases, they are usually paid a percentage of the rent to be collected.

Buyer Brokering

In the traditional relationship, the listing broker and selling broker are considered to be the agent and subagent of the seller, respectively. Although some consumers may think that the broker is a middleman, the broker's fee is paid by the seller and the agent or subagent is hired to act in the seller's best interest. In response to buyers' needs for representation, some brokers have set up their firm as a buyer's brokerage. A buyer's broker is employed by and represents only the buyer in the transaction. This relationship exists whether a fee is paid by the buyer or the commission paid by the seller is split, with the buyer's broker receiving a portion.

The following services are typical of those offered by a buyer's brokerage:

1. Searches to locate property meeting the buyer's needs
2. Tours of the community neighborhoods
3. Suggestions on making offers and assistance in negotiations
4. Counseling on financing

The FHA and most conventional lenders allow a buyer's agent fee to be included in the financing; the VA currently does not, however.

THE BROKER AS AGENT

Any person or entity who acts at the request and in behalf of another in dealing with third persons is an *agent,* and the person for whom the agent acts is known as the *principal.* The status of agent does not automatically carry with it the authority to enter into contracts in behalf of the principal. Either that authority must be expressly granted to the agent or the principal must in some way represent the agent to a *third party* as having authority.

By law, an *agent* is defined as one employed by and under the control of another (principal) to represent the principal in dealings with others. The *agency* creates a *fiduciary* relationship, meaning that each must place trust and confidence in the other, and each must also exercise a certain degree of fairness and good faith.

Types of Agents

Agents can be classified either by how the agency arises or by the extent of authorization. If the authorization has been delegated by the principal, the relationship is an *actual agency.* When a third person has relied upon the principal's express or implied representations that the agency existed, the agency is called an *ostensible agency.*

Classification as to extent of authorization creates either a universal agent, a general agent, or a special agent. A *universal agent* has the authorization to perform all lawful acts for the principal. A *general agent* has the authorization to transact all business in either a certain place or of a specific type, such as all real estate affairs. Finally, the *special agent* is authorized by the principal only to perform a certain action or to handle a particular affair. The most common type is the special agency, where the broker is authorized by a seller to find a buyer for a particular parcel of property.

Agency Relationship

A principal/agent relationship arises whenever a person or entity is given authority to negotiate for or to buy, sell, exchange, or lease real property or any interest therein. However, the typical real estate broker usually does not have the authority to contract with third persons in behalf of a principal.

Most brokers are usually hired to produce a specified result, that is, to obtain a buyer or lessee who is ready, willing, and able to comply with the principal's terms. Once the principal/agent relationship is established, it is subject to common law and applicable state statutes.

Salespersons

While conducting a brokerage business, the broker may hire sales representatives to perform some or all of the necessary activities. It is the salesperson who is usually in active personal contact with prospective buyers or lessees and negotiates the transaction according to the terms requested by the principal. The broker, however, remains responsible to the principal for the performance of their agreement.

Contract of Employment

In most states, the contract of employment (or listing agreement) between the principal and the broker must be in writing in order to be binding. In some states, however, verbal listing agreements are fully enforceable. A written agreement should always be executed to establish proof of employment and to leave no doubt as to the rights and duties of the parties. A written agreement typically contains the (a) property identification or address, (b) seller's name, (c) broker's name, (d) listing price, (e) commission, (f) duration of agreement, and (g) type of listing (as described in Chapter 14).

Any person who is legally competent to enter into a contract (see Chapter 3) can be legally bound to a listing agreement. A person who is able to contract is not only legally capable of appointing an agent but also of acting as an agent. The authority of a real estate broker to act as an agent for a buyer or a seller is based on the provisions of the applicable state licensing law and of the terms of the listing agreement. A broker's authority to act cannot be unlimited or unrestricted. Any action by the broker against public policy or in violation of state licensing laws may result in a fine or loss of license.

Duties

The broker has a number of responsibilities not only to the principal, but also to the third party involved in a transaction. If the seller were the principal, a potential buyer would be a third party and the broker would have certain responsibilities toward the buyer.

Representation

The broker is responsible to represent a property to the buyer properly. In dealing with the buyer, the broker violates his duty to the principal (seller) if he indicates that the seller will accept less than the listed price. All offers received by an agent must be submitted to the principal. If the broker is hired by a seller and makes a willful misrepresentation to the buyer, the broker can be held liable. For example, if the broker stated that a basement was dry and it turned out to have water problems, the buyer could hold the broker responsible. The buyer would also have recourse against the seller, since the broker was his agent; however, the seller can then sue the broker for fraudulent misrepresentation. This assumes, of course, that the seller did not misrepresent the situation to the broker in the first place. In any case, the broker would have only secondhand knowledge of the basement condition. The broker should, however, ask the seller significant questions about the condition of the property at the time the listing agreement is made. When a broker employs a salesperson to deal directly with the buyer, the broker is responsible for the salesperson's actions. A multiple-listing broker who himself does not have the listing is still an agent of the seller, since any commission would come from the seller.

Care and Skill

The broker is also required to exercise care and skill in carrying out his duties. For example, assume the broker drew up an offer and acceptance that was signed by both parties, and the buyer decided later not to go through with the contract. If it was judged that the buyer was not obligated because the document was poorly worded, the seller could hold the broker responsible for damages. It is the responsibility of the broker to understand his business and to know when it is necessary to obtain legal advice. The broker can also be held accountable for misconduct by secretly buying property from his principal, making secret profits, not disclosing material facts to the principal, or not accounting for deposits he holds.

Loyalty

The broker has the duty to be loyal to his principal. For instance, he cannot act for both parties in the transaction without the knowledge of both. Obviously the seller, who is looking for the highest price, and the buyer, who is looking for the lowest price, have conflicting interests. Even though the broker's task involves bringing buyers and sellers together, he is still responsible as an agent to his principal. The fact that he thought he was acting in the interest of both parties does not help. The situation might occur that a broker is hired by a buyer to find a certain type of property. He happens to have a listing on a similar piece of property. If a contract is made with only the broker and buyer knowing about the dual representation and the broker collects a commission from the seller, the seller may sue the broker. In addition, the buyer may refuse to pay a commission. The broker would be guilty of fraud and could lose either or both commissions as well as his license.

Conflict of Interest

The broker cannot have any other conflict of interest. For example, he cannot receive a fee from a lending institution for placing a mortgage, since he would not then be acting in the client's best interest to obtain the best available mortgage rate.

Keep Principal Informed

All significant information that comes to the attention of the broker must be disclosed to his principal. The broker must give his client notice of information or conditions, such as changes in the mortgage market, changes in zoning, or information on other offers. In a recent Iowa case, a seller had listed a tract of farmland with the broker. The broker found a purchaser who lacked the full down payment, and loaned the buyer the difference without telling the seller. Other problems later came up and the seller refused to pay the commission. The Iowa Supreme Court found that the broker had breached his duty by not making a full disclosure of the loan and therefore was not entitled to the commission.

Duty to Buyers

The broker has his primary responsibility to sellers from whom he holds listings, but he still has certain responsibilities to prospective buyers. Some courts have held that the broker has an agency duty to purchasers, especially where they lack knowledge of real estate transactions. The solution is to require the broker to make the buyer aware of the need for independent legal or other advice in handling the real estate transaction and of the agency relationships binding the broker to the seller. Over half the states now require that the agent disclose to the buyer that the agent represents the seller.

Agency—Further Ramifications

Usually an agent is authorized by the principal to perform certain acts on his behalf. The agent is bound within these constraints in any action taken. The principal need not accept acts performed outside of the agent's authority; however, the principal may ratify acts performed by the agent outside of those authorized. The principal then, in effect, has authorized the act. The principal can ratify by direct or express confirmation of the act or by implication. If the agent performs an unauthorized act in the presence of the principal and the third party, the principal implies ratification by not interfering or countermanding a statement. The third party has been led to believe that the agent was acting within the principal's authorization. The principal cannot in any case, however, ratify a portion of the act and not the whole act.

Negligence

A broker can be held responsible for any negligence in performing duties as an agent; the agent, however, cannot be held liable for an honest mistake. Suppose a broker has a letter from authorities stating that a residence is now in school district A, and tells this to the prospective buyer. If, in the meantime, the district has been changed back to B, an honest mistake has been made and the broker would not be held liable. If, on the other hand, the agent told a prospective buyer that a developer would pave the streets without having knowledge that it was certain, the broker could be held liable for misrepresentation and the broker is open to lawsuit by the parties to the transaction.

Although responsible for statements misrepresenting the property, the agent cannot be held responsible for exaggerations that are clearly not true. For example, the statement by a salesperson that "the owner is the best housekeeper in town" would not normally be construed by a prudent buyer to be factual.

Frequently, a broker is employed by a principal to negotiate, but is not to reveal the identity of the principal. In this case, the broker can either state that he is representing a principal who wants to be kept unknown or proceed as if he is buying on his own account. If conditions later place the seller in a position to sue, he can sue the broker in either of these situations. If a true principal is later revealed, the seller can also sue that principal if there is cause. If, however, the broker states that he is acting for an undisclosed principal, he can state in the contract agreement that he does not assume any liability under the agreement. This clause is binding if the third party agrees to the provision by signing the contract.

Broker's Liability to Parties

In the previous discussion it becomes apparent that a broker has responsibilities to both the seller and buyer, and courts have imposed liabilities on brokers for failure to disclose material facts to a buyer in regard to a transaction. In a 1984 California case, Easton v. Strasburger, a broker was sued for failure to inform a buyer that a house he purchased was built on fill land and was vulnerable to earth slides. A slide later damaged the home and the buyer sued and recovered from the broker. In another California case, the seller accepted an unsecured note as part of the sale transaction, and the buyer later defaulted. The seller successfully sued the broker for concealing the buyer's weak financial position. In a recent Illinois case, however, the court said that a real estate salesperson has no duty to identify and disclose latent defects that are not disclosed by the seller.

Although the listing broker is clearly the agent of the seller, a recent Federal Trade Commission study indicated that more than half of the buyers surveyed were of the opinion that the selling broker was looking after their interests. The broker handling the sale prepares the offer, may suggest terms, and responds to questions by the buyer. The broker's responsibilities to the buyer are primarily in the disclosure of property defects and making proper representation of the facts.

Duration of Agency

Listing agreements usually specify the broker's period of employment. This is required by law in some states. The broker earns his commission only if he procures, within the specified time period, a prospect who is ready, willing, and able to purchase. If, after the agreement expires, the seller advertises and a prospect appears and enters into a contract, no commission is due, even though the buyer may have previously negotiated with the broker. In other cases, the broker has been awarded the commission if the owner shows bad faith, or deliberately delays the negotiations, or if the negotiations had begun during the listing agreement period and were concluded beyond the listing expiration time. A listing agreement will usually contain a clause extending for 60, 90, or 120 days the right to a commission from a sale where the agent had negotiated with that buyer during the listing agreement period.

When no specific listing time period is agreed upon, the seller may, without liability, terminate the listing after a reasonable time. This is true even if the broker is in the process of negotiating, unless the negotiation is essentially complete. In this case, the broker's expenditure of money and time does not prevent revocation, since his taking of a listing is expected to result in his spending time and money. The definition of reasonable time will vary with the task, since it might be expected that a typical single-family residence would sell more quickly than a tract of land or a special-purpose building.

If the agreement provides for extraordinary expenditures by the broker, however, the seller might be responsible for damages if the seller terminates the listing agreement. As an example, a listing agreement that provides that the broker spend money to improve the property to make it more saleable could not be arbitrarily terminated by the seller. Provisions like this make the listing agreement more like a *bilateral contract,* or *agency coupled with an interest.* A listing agreement providing that the broker advertise at least twice a week in the local newspapers identifies a legal obligation of the broker. In these cases, revocation of the agreement by the seller has not been sustained by court decisions.

The agency, of course, terminates when the real estate has been sold. After a broker has performed by providing a buyer, the owner cannot terminate the agreement. With an open listing where more than one broker can sell, it is understood that the agreement with all brokers ends when any one broker or the owner himself locates a buyer. The owner is not responsible for notifying each broker, since the brokers recognize that the property might be sold and the agency terminated at any time. In good practice, however, the owner is expected to notify the brokers within a reasonable time if the property is sold, and a prudent owner will do this as promptly as possible. In the case where a broker finds a buyer but does not notify the owner, and the owner in the meantime signs a contract with another buyer, the first broker loses his commission. It is the duty of the broker to promptly notify the owner when he finds a buyer.

Deposits and Accountability

The broker, as an agent of the principal, is responsible for monies or property entrusted to the agency. In some ways, the broker is acting in the position of a trustee and can be held responsible under laws pertaining to trustees as well as those regulating brokers. The agent must not mix funds held for the client with agency funds. A broker normally maintains a special account for holding funds of clients. State laws make mixing *(commingling)* of clients' funds with the broker's own funds a basis for revocation of license.

Without authority in the listing agreement, the broker does not have the right to accept an **earnest money deposit** from the buyer on behalf of the seller. If the contract has not been signed and the broker embezzles a deposit, the buyer must bear the loss if it cannot be recovered. The broker is, however, liable to the seller if he refunds a buyer's deposit without the seller's consent.

It is important that the contract specify what happens to an earnest money deposit if there is a default. If no statement exists, the deposit holder must file an *interpleader* with a court to ascertain disposition.

Agency Termination

There are several ways for an agency to terminate:

1. An agency is terminated upon completion of the desired act. If a buyer is found who is ready, willing, and able to purchase the property, the agency is completed.
2. The agency terminates when the stated period ends. The principal *may* terminate an agency at any time; however, compensation may be due to the agent for services performed, such as for advertising or time spent on the property. If the broker has provided a buyer ready, willing, and able to buy, termination of the agency will not preclude the recovery of the commission. Nor can the principal terminate a contract without commission if the agent is in the process of negotiating with a third party. If an agency is wrongfully terminated by the principal before the act is completed, the agent could collect damages.
3. Death or insanity of either party terminates an agency.
4. An agency *may* be terminated by bankruptcy of the principal.
5. In the case of an agency to handle real estate, the agency will be terminated if the property is destroyed.
6. An agency is terminated if the agent's license is revoked or suspended.

More Than One Broker

There are some situations that involve more than one broker in a listing or transaction. Due to the frequency of cobrokering and the use of multiple listing services, it is important to examine the relationships between the persons involved.

More Than One Broker Employed by Seller

The seller can employ more than one broker by using an open listing (whereby the owner can also sell the property without paying a commission). The law is clear in this case that if one of the brokers, or the owner, sells the property, the sale terminates the agencies of the others by removing the subject property from the market. If more than one broker was involved with the same client, it may be difficult to resolve who was actually the ***procuring cause***. A generally accepted rule is that if a broker sets in motion a sequence of events without break in continuity and a sale results, he is entitled to a commission even though he may not have conducted all of the negotiations. The mere fact that a broker showed a property first does not assure that he becomes the procuring cause. If he abandons a prospect, another broker who later shows the property and completes the sale may be considered the procuring cause. If more than one contract is offered, the seller has the right to accept any one or none of them.

Cobrokering

The practice of cobrokerage is recognized as a valuable marketing procedure for seller, buyer, and brokers. Figure 13–1 shows the fiduciary relationships between the persons involved, whether they are part of a multiple listing service or not.

The ***cobrokers*** are subagents of the listing broker as well as agents of the principal. Thus cobrokers and their salespersons, as well as the salespersons of the listing broker, owe a fiduciary duty to both the seller and the listing broker. This, however, does not remove the listing broker's responsibility if there is a problem. A fiduciary relationship requires all involved to exercise good faith, professional skill, and diligence in accordance with the instructions of either principal. Failure to discharge a duty by any of these would result in a breach of the fiduciary relationship that could make the agent (or agents) liable. Generally, it is assumed that the agents will share the commission in the event that a subagent procures a sale.

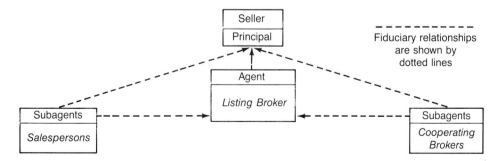

Figure 13–1   Fiduciary relationships in cobrokerage

COMMISSIONS

The broker is compensated for handling transactions, usually in the form of a **commission** or percentage of the price. The broker is entitled to the commission when he has obtained a buyer ready, willing, and able to purchase. Once this purchaser is found, even if the seller reconsiders and decides not to sell before the contract is signed, the commission is still due. Thus, the seller can decline a contract and not sell the house, but he still owes a commission to the broker. The seller has no responsibility to the buyer until the contract is signed. Even if the buyer, after the contract is signed, refuses to go through with the contract, the broker has still done his job and is owed the commission.

The commission rate paid by the seller is negotiable; however, some brokers have a policy of a set rate of, for example, 6 percent. Although the salesperson normally receives a proportion of the commission, some brokerages operate differently. For example, RE/MAX International in Washington, D.C. allows sales associates to retain 100 percent of the commission; however, each pays a monthly fee to be associated with the firm.

A listing agreement can usually be terminated by a seller upon proper notice to the broker, but only before the broker has spent time or money on the listing. The seller can also terminate the listing if the broker is not complying with the terms. If the listing is nonexclusive, it can be terminated by the seller at any time.

When Is Commission Due?

In discussing brokerage operations, it is important to define the terms **ready, willing, and able** in order to determine when commissions are due. *Able* means to have the necessary funds to make the payments required and to close the deal within the specified time. The buyer need not actually have the funds in hand, but should be able to borrow them or secure a mortgage. A *willing* buyer is one who is willing to enter into a valid contract to purchase the property. The broker has produced a *ready* buyer when the buyer is identified by name to the seller.

If the sale is not completed because of some fault of the seller, the broker is still entitled to a commission. This could occur if either the owner or spouse refuses to sign the contract or deed, if there are defects in the title, if the owner is guilty of fraud, if the buyer and seller agree to cancel the sale, or if the seller is unable or unwilling to give possession within a reasonable time.

Some agreements between the seller and broker include a clause to the effect that, if the deal is not completed, there is no commission. An equivalent provision may specify that the commission will be paid out of the sale price. In either case, the broker receives no commission if the buyer defaults or if the title cannot be cleared; however, courts have held that the arbitrary refusal by the seller to complete the contract does not mean that the commission is not due.

Procuring Cause

Other factors affect whether or not a commission is due. If the broker does not have the exclusive right to sell, the broker who has been the procuring cause in the sale is due a commission. When the owner and several brokers have been active in the selling process, the broker must prove that he was the procuring cause and that the commission is due. Where more than one broker was involved, the courts have held that the broker whose efforts predominated is entitled to the commission. If a broker finds and introduces a prospect to the owner, but the owner alone carries out the negotiations, courts have held the broker to be the procuring cause. To avoid these potential problems, brokers prefer a listing where they have the exclusive right to sell.

Sale by Owner

When an owner has hired a broker and then later, without knowing that the agent dealt with the buyer, sells the property to a buyer procured by the agent, the broker might be entitled to a commission. Courts have held that the seller might reasonably suspect that the buyer was procured by the agent and should check with the broker regarding each prospect. It could not be reasonably expected that a buyer, trying to get a good price, would reveal this fact. In some states, however, courts would not award a commission, holding that the broker should have advised the seller of each prospect encountered. The broker can provide protection to the agency by being careful in the listing agreement and in agency operations. The listing agreement should specify that the commission is due if the property is sold within a specified time to a person with whom the broker had negotiated. The broker might also advise the seller of each prospect with whom he negotiates.

Failure to Pay Commission Due

If the seller fails to pay the commission due, the broker's only remedy is to sue and obtain a judgment against the seller. The broker cannot block the sale of the property or file a lien against the property unless the listing contract provides this right. In order to enforce payment in litigation, the broker would need to (a) show that he was employed by the client, (b) show that he was the procuring cause of the sale, and (c) show that the buyer was ready, willing, and able, as defined above. In most cases, these factors are subject to various interpretations. If the listing agreement were silent as to the rate of commission, the agent would be allowed a reasonable rate. Some states require that the commission be specified in the listing agreement.

Restraint of Trade

Certain activities have been held to be a violation of antitrust laws. In Baltimore, Maryland, several real estate brokerage firms were convicted by jury of a conspiracy to raise commissions on residential properties from 6 to 7 percent. The U.S. Department of Justice has instituted suits where real estate boards were accused of fixing commission rates in the area. Tie-in arrangements have also been declared illegal. In real estate, a *tie-in* arrangement exists, for example, when a condition of the sale of a lot is that the purchaser will not resell the lot unless it is listed with a specific broker. Courts have held, however, that a broker has the right to cooperate with other brokers of his choosing and to make business decisions as to which brokers to work with.

Trades and Exchanges

Property trades or exchanges may be the result of financing difficulties, convenience to the property owners, or tax saving purposes. One broker may be acting for two or more principals and may receive a commission from each. Each principal must be informed as to the multiple commission and dual agency situation. The broker has the responsibility to deal with each principal impartially and honestly. Some brokers may specialize in exchanges and may belong to the International Traders Club.

ORGANIZATION OF BROKERAGE OPERATIONS

A real estate brokerage operation—like any other business—may be organized as an individual proprietorship, a partnership, or a corporation. The individual proprietorship is the most common, especially where the enterprise is small and can be readily managed by one person. In this case, the individual proprietor owns the business and directs its operation. He may operate the business under his own name, a trade name, or an alias. If operating under an alias, he must register the assumed name in the office of the local recorder and usually must have the state registration under the alias so that any person can readily determine his true identity. The objective is to prevent any broker from using an alias for fraudulent purposes.

Two or more persons can enter into a legal agreement to go into business jointly in the form of a partnership. State regulations and the partnership agreement define their responsibilities to each other and to the public. In most cases, a written agreement between the partners is required by law. It must be registered in the local recorder's office. A partnership can be either a general partnership or a special partnership. A *special partnership* is formed for a specific purpose, such as the sale of lots in a subdivision. In contrast, a partnership entered into for the purpose of carrying on a business, such as a real estate business, is called a *general partnership*. Real estate brokerage operations are often general partnerships. State laws require that all partners doing real estate business be licensed as brokers.

Incorporation is the third form of business organization. A corporation is an enterprise that has the status of an individual in many ways but is separate from the individuals operating the company. The owners of the business have a limited financial liability in its operation. A person can invest a sum in the business and be financially liable only for the amount invested. State laws regulate the organization and operation of corporations. Typically, the owners invest money in exchange for shares of stock in the business. The distribution of the shares of stock represents the degree of ownership by each.

Advantages and Disadvantages

Each form of organization has advantages and disadvantages. Some of these are outlined below.

Proprietorship

Advantages	*Disadvantages*
Ease of formation	Personal liability for business losses
Personal satisfaction in running business	Limited capital available
Ability of owner to do as he desires	
All profits to owner	

Partnership

Advantages	*Disadvantages*

Advantages
Greater capital available
More skills and experience
Not subject to corporation taxes

Disadvantages
Personal liability for financial losses
Disagreements (unanimity is usually required for major decisions)
Limited sources of new capital (loans, increase in number of partners, or new contribution of existing partners)

Corporation

Advantages
Limited liability of stockholders
Greater capital available (through sale of stock)
Life extends beyond death of any owners
Greater ease of business growth

Disadvantages
Close state or federal regulation
Double taxation (taxes on the corporation's earnings in addition to income taxes for individual stockholders)
Greater costs in initial organization

The Broker as a Manager

In addition to fulfilling duties as an agent, a broker has the responsibility of running a profitable business. These management responsibilities involve pursuing a number of activities to various degrees, depending on the size of the operation. The securing of listings is, of course, one of the important functions. The implementation of programs in advertising, publicity, and sales promotion are also important elements, just as they are in any business. Staffing and managing the sales force becomes a greater task as the size of the sales force grows. Finally, the broker has the responsibility of selecting the location for the office, defining the type of business or the type of clients to be served, financing the operation, and assuring that the operation continues on a profitable basis.

The Office and Its Location

The location of the brokerage office and its layout greatly influence the efficiency of the operation. In addition, the office projects the firm's image to the public. The office location should be convenient to the salespeople as well as close to many of the properties handled. The office should also be highly visible to the public to help attract both potential buyers and sellers.

FRANCHISED BROKERS

There has been a tremendous growth in *franchised* brokerage operations. These franchisors do not own the individual franchises directly, but rather they lease their trade names, service marks, operating procedures, reputations, and national referral services to the individual broker. In return for this, the *franchisee-broker* is expected to follow certain prescribed methods of operation, to pay a one-time fee for the franchise, and to pay a percentage of gross sales or net profits. The franchisor usually also offers national advertising and training for salespeople. Examples of franchises are Century-21, Coldwell-Banker, ERA, and Travelers Realty Network.

Many states have enacted special laws or regulations to alleviate some problems that have occurred with franchises. Some clients have expected that, if a problem occurs with the franchisee-broker, the client can hold the franchisor responsible. This is not the case. Also, in some instances, there are two or more franchisees of the same franchisor in one metropolitan area. A client who has dealt with one of them may remember the broker only by the *service mark* and have difficulty identifying the particular broker contacted. To prevent this confusion, it is usually required that, in advertising, the broker's name be at least as prominent as the franchisor's name or service mark. The public interest is served under this system of organization by the efficiency of a large-scale operation, licensee training, the national referral service, and the requirement of the Lanham Act that the owner of a service mark police those it licenses.

STAFFING THE OPERATION

In expanding his business, the broker will be involved in hiring two kinds of employees. One group consists of salespeople who perform the actual showing and selling of property. These persons may be full- or part-time employees. State license laws usually define a *real estate salesperson* as one employed by a licensed real estate broker to negotiate the sale, purchase, lease, or exchange of real estate for others and for compensation under the broker's direction and guidance. The salesperson, in his actions with the public, acts for the employing broker and not in his own capacity as an individual. Agreements are drawn up by a salesperson in the name of the broker and usually must be signed by the broker. Thus, the broker is responsible for the dealings of his sales force. Any litigation would be with the broker rather than with individual salespeople. Each representative is, however, bound by the same rules and regulations as the broker and must exercise good faith to all parties and faithfulness to the principal.

The second category of employees, the office personnel, run the office and handle the other business functions. Both groups support the broker in his operations; the broker is responsible for the actions of each salesperson and each employee.

Staffing the brokerage office with qualified and competent personnel involves techniques similar to staffing any business operation. Employees usually appreciate certain considerations from their employer, including fair wages, continuing employment in exchange for competent performance, fair working hours, pleasant working conditions, a feeling of contribution to the firm, respect, and the ability to improve earnings and status. The broker also wants employees who will contribute to the goals of growth, reputation, and profit. The broker can work toward achieving these objectives through guidelines such as to:

1. Provide a worthy firm image, as well as self-image.
2. Seek qualified job applicants through advertisements or placement offices.
3. Carefully screen applicants for both their physical and mental capabilities. It is better not to have the reputation of hiring frequently and letting people go who do not perform. Physical exams before employment are important. Job applications should be used to collect data on the applicants. The broker should check

the references and the validity of data supplied, particularly from any prior employers. State licensing requirements also help screen candidates for technical competence.

4. Carefully interview each applicant. Determine career objectives, reasons for entering the real estate business, previous employment and reasons for changing, family status, outside interests, education, and expected earnings.
5. After hiring, introduce the new employee to others in the office. Provide training and help during the early weeks of employment. Regular follow-up discussions with employees are important to their continuing satisfactory performance.
6. Define a specified trial period for new employees.
7. Give periodic performance appraisals to review performance, suggest improvements, and provide opportunity for increases in compensation. Keep abreast of what competitors are paying to stay competitive and to retain the best salespeople.

Employee Versus Independent Contractor

Whether a real estate salesperson is an employee or an independent contractor is significant. If the agents are legally *employees,* the broker would have to pay FICA taxes for them, withhold for income tax purposes, carry Workmen's Compensation Insurance, and incur liability for on-the-job accidents. In determining the form of relationship between a broker and the sales force, the Internal Revenue Service looks more at the details of the operation than at the terminology used by a particular broker. In either case, the broker can provide office space, telephone service, and secretarial services.

The Tax Equity and Fiscal Responsibility Act of 1982 sets forth three criteria for classification as an *independent contractor:*

1. The individual must be a licensed real estate agent.
2. Substantially all remuneration for services performed must be directly related to sales or output rather than number of hours worked.
3. A written contract with the broker must exist, defining the salesperson's status as an independent contractor.

Compensation

The most common method used to compensate real estate salespeople is by *commission.* The employment agreement between each sales representative and the broker should specify how commissions are shared between the broker and salesperson. If a broker held a listing and one of his salespeople made the sale, the salesperson could receive from 30 to 70 percent of the commission received, depending on the employment agreement. Brokers allow experienced salespeople or broker-salespeople a greater share since they are able to handle most aspects of a transaction on their own. An inexperienced salesperson would require more guidance and assistance in carrying out a transaction.

Often the salesperson is expected to furnish an automobile for business use and to pay the associated expenses such as gas and maintenance. The salesperson is entitled to take these expenses as deductions on his federal income tax return. To support the tax deduction, there should be a written agreement between the broker and salesperson. The salesperson should also keep records of mileage and expenses.

Some brokers have adopted a system whereby the salesperson gets 100 percent of the commission. In return, the salesperson pays "rent" to the broker for use of the office space, the broker's name, and other services.

TRENDS

Prior to the 1970s independent real estate brokerages were dominant. A brokerage may have had branch offices, but the branches were within the same geographical area. In the 1960s, some brokers began to cooperate with brokers in other cities. A broker who sold a client's home might contact another broker in the town where that client was moving. Networks of cooperating brokers developed, and the referring broker usually received a share of the commission if a sale resulted from the referral.

The use of franchises, such as Century 21, developed in the early 1970s. Other franchises are ERA Real Estate, Inc., Red Carpet Corp., and Realty World International, Inc. For a fee paid to the franchisor, a broker can use the franchise name and logo and can participate in training and other programs sponsored by the franchisor. The broker (franchisee) is required to conform to certain policies.

Example 13–1   Dividing a Typical Commission

In a typical case, the commission is paid by the seller upon selling the property and completing the transaction. If the selling price were $120,000, a typical 6 percent commission would be $7,200. It is common for the salesperson who procured the listing to receive from 10 to 25 percent of the total commission upon sale of the listed property. This is also a usual practice if the property is multiple-listed. The sharing of the commission between the listing broker and the selling broker is based on individual agreements or local practice. In the example, if the listing broker's share was 50 percent, the brokerage would receive 50 percent of $7,200, or $3,600. This compensates for time and effort spent on promotion and advertising of the property. It also includes the listing salesperson's share of 10 percent of $7,200, or $720. In the example, the selling broker would receive 50 percent, and that would give the selling broker $3,600. Suppose that the employment agreement between the salesperson making the sale and his broker provided 60 percent to the salesperson, then the selling salesperson would receive 0.6 × $3,600, or $2,160; the selling broker gets 0.4 × $3,600, or $1,440. The complete breakdown is as follows:

Listing salesperson	$ 720
Listing broker	2,880
Selling salesperson	2,160
Selling broker	1,440
Total	7,200

Again, the breakdown varies with local custom and agreements between particular brokers. The salesperson should fully understand his employment agreement so that there will be no misunderstanding when a sale is completed.

Acquisitions

Also, starting in 1969, some real estate brokers expanded their operations by acquiring other brokerages in different cities. For example, by 1981 Coldwell Banker & Co. of Los Angeles had acquired offices in over ten other cities, employing over 10,000 salespeople.

In the late 1970s a new trend developed. Certain companies not previously associated with real estate brokerage began to expand into the field. Merrill Lynch (previously only a stockbrokerage) established a separate division known as Merrill Lynch Realty Associates. By 1981 the division had acquired thirteen real estate firms in over twelve cities with more than 5,000 employees. In 1981 Sears Roebuck acquired Coldwell Banker, which became part of its Saraco Group. The objective was to provide a variety of real estate services under one division. Sears now offers financing, including VA and FHA loans, as well as mortgage insurance.

Errors and Omissions (E&O) Insurance

In recent years there has been a trend among professionals to increase the amount of liability insurance carried. This has included physicians, surgeons, dentists, lawyers, business executives, and now, real estate brokers. There has been a growing number of lawsuits by real estate buyers and sellers against brokers claiming malpractice. Insurance companies have responded by offering Errors and Omissions (E&O) Insurance to brokers.

SUMMARY

Real estate brokerage usually includes the function of bringing real estate buyers and sellers together. The functions of managing or leasing real property, renting, and handling property exchanges are also included. State laws regulate the operations of real estate brokers.

The success of the real estate broker depends upon his technical and managerial skills. His source of income primarily derives from commissions or fees for performing services for clients. There is an agency relationship between the broker and the client, who are the agent and principal, respectively, and the authority of the broker depends upon their mutual agreement. The broker must understand his responsibilities as an agent and act accordingly with respect to the principal, cobrokers, his salespeople, and third parties.

One of the important functions of a broker is to hold deposits belonging to others. Therefore, he is obligated to set up a special account separate from his own funds.

In addition to responsibilities as an agent, the broker has the responsibility of managing a business. This includes financing, marketing, organizing, staffing, and controlling the organization. It is important for the broker to understand the ramifications of the employee versus independent contractor concepts, since they affect dealings with the IRS.

Recently, there has been increased franchising of real estate brokerages by national franchisors. This has resulted in advantages to clients; however, the public has often been confused by the responsibilities and obligations of the franchisor. Consequently, special regulations have been issued by state real estate commissions that apply to franchised operations.

TERMS AND CONCEPTS

You can check your understanding of these terms against the glossary or by review in this chapter.

Agency	Earnest money deposit	Ready, willing, and able
Bilateral contract	Fiduciary	Service mark
Broker	Franchise	Special agent
Cobroker	General agent	Third party
Commingle	Principal	Tie-in
Commission	Procuring cause	Universal agent

What are the differences or relationship, if any, between the following?

Actual agency and Ostensible agency	Employee and Independent contractor	Listing agreement and Agency coupled with an interest
Agent and Agency		
Agent and Procuring cause	Franchisee and Broker	Universal agent and General agent

PROBLEMS

13-1. List the three methods of organizing a real estate brokerage office. State two advantages and two disadvantages of each method.

13-2. List some things that a broker can do to achieve better broker-salesperson relationships.

13-3. Broker A had an agreement with his salesperson E that the salesperson would receive 10 percent of the total commission for each listing obtained, plus 40 percent of all monies coming to the brokerage from property sold. The multiple-listing service of which brokers A, B, and C were members provided that the listing salespeople got 10 percent of the commission, the selling broker got 50 percent, and the listing broker got 40 percent. Salesperson E listed a house for $84,000 and later sold it to a client for $80,000. The commission was 6 percent. Determine the commissions earned by both Salesperson E and Broker A.

13-4. In 13-3, salesperson F, working for broker B, listed a house at $108,000. Salesperson E sold the property at the list price. Determine the allocation of commission.

13-5. In 13-3, E listed a property at $64,000. Salesperson F, working for broker B, presented A with a signed offer for $64,000 and a check for

$2,000 earnest money. B presented the offer to Kaiser, the owner of the house, who said he had changed his mind. Who is entitled to how much commission, if any?

13-6. What are the three types of agents? Give an example of a real estate broker acting as each type of agent.

13-7. What are some functions of a broker in marketing real estate for clients?

13-8. What are some of the responsibilities of a broker from a business/finance point of view?

13-9. If you were a broker, would you prefer to have your salespeople be *employees* or *independent contractors*? What are some ways to convince the IRS that your salespeople are what you say they are?

13-10. What actions are important to an agent in a fiduciary relationship?

13-11. List some provisions in a listing agreement that may cause it to be considered noncancellable by the principal.

13-12. How can a franchisee-broker advertisement cause possible confusion to a client?

13-13. What actions by a broker or group of brokers might be considered restraint of trade?

13-14. List some of the possible pitfalls threatening a homeowner selling his own home without using a broker's services.

13-15. What are some possible pitfalls in selecting a broker to list a home?

13-16. Jack Broker has stated his unwritten buy-out policy to his salespeople. He guarantees that if a home is listed with the firm and is not sold within sixty days, the firm will buy the home at 90 percent of the list price. Jack, however, must approve each home before the guarantee applies. Betty, one of his salespeople, writes the guarantee into a listing agreement as an inducement to get the listing. After sixty days the seller requests the firm to honor the guarantee. Jack points out that he had never approved the listing agreement. The seller files a complaint with the local real estate board. Give your opinion of the likely result.

13-17. In a Washington case a listing broker gave another broker incorrect information on a property boundary, which was passed on to a client, who purchased the property. The listing agreement stated the correct boundary. A buyer discovered the error after closing the transaction and filed suit against both brokers. Give your opinion.

13-18. In a recent Alabama case a husband and wife owned a home jointly. The husband listed the house with a broker who shortly found a buyer. The husband signed the contract to sell. Neither the listing nor the sale contract was signed by the wife, and she refused to sign the deed. Give your prediction on the outcome.

SUPPLEMENTARY READINGS

Case, Frederic E. *Real Estate Brokerage.* Englewood Cliffs, N.J.: Prentice-Hall, 1982. Chapters 3 and 4.

Cyr, John E., and Sobeck, Joan M. *Real Estate Brokerage.* Chicago: Real Estate Education Company, 1982.

French, William B., and Lusk, Harold F. *Law of the Real Estate Business.* Homewood, Ill.: Irwin, 1975. Chapter 11.

Levine, Arthur M. "Dual Agency Trap." *Real Estate Review,* Spring 1985, pp. 109–112.

Lindeman, Bruce. *Real Estate Brokerage Management.* Reston, Va.: Reston Publishing, 1981.

NATIONAL ASSOCIATION OF REALTORS®. *Handbook on Multiple Listing Policy.* Chicago, 1975.

Realtors National Marketing Institute. *Real Estate Office Management—People, Functions, Systems.* Chicago, 1975. Chapters 7–19.

Schneider, Jules, and Tune, Bill. *Who's My Boss?* Scottsdale, Ariz.: Gorsuch Scarisbrick Publishers, 1989.

Semenow, Robert W. *Selected Cases in Real Estate.* Englewood Cliffs, N.J.: Prentice-Hall, 1973, pp. 90–265.

Semenow, Robert W. *Questions and Answers in Real Estate.* Englewood Cliffs, N.J.: Prentice-Hall, 1978. Chapter 1.

Shenkel, William M. *Marketing Real Estate,* 2nd ed. Englewood Cliffs, N.J.: Prentice-Hall, 1985. Chapters 12–14.

Warkentin, James B. *Buyer Brokering,* 6th ed. Springfield, Va.: Charter Press, 1987.

CHAPTER 14
Marketing Real Estate

Marketing is the process of planning and executing the conception, pricing, promotion, and distribution of ideas, goods, and services to create exchanges that satisfy individual and organizational objectives.[1] The objective of this chapter is to describe marketing concepts as they apply to real estate, looking especially at the practices covered by real estate professionals.

The real estate broker deals both with sellers and prospective buyers of real estate. The broker's relationship with the seller involves obtaining properties to list. The dominant reasons that home sellers turn to real estate brokers rather than trying to sell their property on their own are because they need technical assistance and are hesitant to take risks. Many have difficulty making a decision as to the price to ask and want advice in preparing their homes for showing. The seller also needs assistance in obtaining mortgages for prospective buyers and in making contact with potential buyers.

Statistics indicate that home owners who try to sell for themselves are often not successful. They also show that sales completed by the owners themselves often are at a lower price than with an agent, possibly due to the seller's lack of bargaining or appraisal skills. Since a prospective buyer may hesitate to tell a homeowner her reasons for rejecting the property, the owner may not get the

---

[1]American Marketing Association (AMA) Board, *Marketing News,* March 1, 1985.

feedback that an agent could obtain. Sometimes these comments can be used effectively to improve the property for future showings. Minor paint damage, pets in the house, or other factors can often be easily corrected and may make a significant difference. The agent is trained to screen prospective buyers, whereas the homeowner selling on her own would be subject to visits of people who are just looking or possibly even persons evaluating the house for future burglary. Finally, when a buyer is found, the inexperienced seller may execute an invalid contract or a contract that does not protect against potential problems. Research indicates that about five out of six home buyers come into contact with a broker in the buying process.

LISTING AGREEMENTS

The broker can be either the agent of the seller or the agent of the buyer. When the broker is the seller's agent, the listing agreement, usually called the *listing,* serves as the contract between the seller and the broker. Listings are important since they form a reservoir of properties for future sales.

Sources of Listings

There are many ways a broker or salesperson can secure listings. The following are important sources:

1. Company reputation and previous client referrals
2. Sold signs (another home may now be needed by sellers)
3. Classified advertising (a nice ad attracts other sellers)
4. Calling on owners who have homes for sale
5. Expired listings of other firms
6. Building contractors
7. Referrals from out-of-town brokers
8. Company personnel departments (new employees)
9. Recently promoted employees (who may desire upgrading of their home)
10. Recent marriages, deaths, or births (a different home is needed)
11. Vacant rental properties
12. Door-to-door canvassing (some might decide to sell later)

Working with the Seller

As mentioned, the needs for technical assistance and for avoiding risks dominate sellers' reasons to use brokers to handle their property. Therefore, in the attempt to obtain a listing, the broker can concentrate on providing this assistance and on building confidence in her ability as a broker to bring about a sale. Salespeople can increase their chances of obtaining a signed listing agreement in the following ways:

1. Prepare a competitive market analysis showing prices of comparable properties sold recently.
2. Be aware of other properties for sale in the area and the degree of buyer interest.
3. Present to the seller a route to approach the property that would pass by other nice properties and avoid those with less eye appeal.
4. Check the county offices to determine plat or other information about the property.

5. Bring measuring equipment or other materials necessary to obtain data to complete a listing form.
6. Be able to describe arrangements with sources of mortgages for potential buyers.
7. Check out school districts.

The broker or salesperson can gain the seller's confidence by any of a number of approaches:

1. Present data showing a favorable selling record.
2. Make constructive suggestions for increasing the property's marketability.
3. Discuss the agent's methods for screening and qualifying buyers.
4. Show how contacts with brokers can increase the number of prospective buyers.
5. Describe resources of the agency, such as number of salespeople or advertising budget.
6. Present a schedule that outlines when advertising will start and other factors related to getting the project underway.
7. Explain benefits of a multiple-listing service, referral system, home protection plan, or other services.

Once a property owner selects a broker to list the property, the broker must establish the price and other terms and complete the necessary forms and documents.

Establishing Price

Establishing the price is often the broker's most difficult task. The owner naturally wants to secure the highest price, but may have an unrealistic opinion about the property's value. Some unscrupulous brokers inflate the value of a prospective lister's property to obtain the listing; the intent is often to induce the owner to reduce the price later when early sales efforts fail. This practice is not considered ethical, especially since the broker is the seller's agent. In doing this, the broker is not acting in the best interest of the principal. This practice not only delays the sale, but also causes the broker to spend extra money, time, and effort during the time when the property is listed at an unrealistic price. Prudent brokers will refuse to list property where the owner insists upon an unrealistically high price. These brokers, in turn, often develop a reputation for rapid turnover of properties, which works to their long-term benefit. Before accepting a listing, it is the duty of the broker to estimate the property value and prepare an estimate of the net proceeds to the seller from the sale.

A careful inspection of the property by the broker or salesperson is very important. It is necessary not only to help estimate the value but also to aid the broker to show the property favorably. In the inspection process, the broker can also make suggestions that may improve the salability of the property, improvements that may cost little or nothing (such as rearranging the furniture to make a room appear larger), or other changes where the increased sale value would considerably exceed the cost of improvement. Expensive changes or those that may delay sale of the property should not be recommended.

After the home is ready to place on the market, it is best to have the owner sign a disclosure statement listing any property defects. The objective is to protect the seller and agent against buyer claims after sale closing.

Listing Forms

Figure 14–1 shows part of a listing form for a residence. A photograph of the house and an accurately completed listing form provide the basic essential data to promote the property. In a multiple-listing system, the photos and listing forms are either published in a bound book or distributed on individual pages to all brokers and salespeople for insertion in a loose-leaf notebook.

Whether bound or loose, the listings are usually grouped in the following order: first residential property, then commercial, and finally lots and acreage. Within each grouping, properties are placed in price sequence. In larger cities, the listings may also be grouped by location. In some cases, there will be a separate section for suburban or farm properties. A map of the metropolitan area is always included in the booklet to assist agents in locating homes in a specific area. As a broker completes the listing form, she can also use it as a checklist for points to inspect and questions to ask of the property owner. Different listing forms are available to suit the particular needs of sellers and brokers. Figure 14–2 illustrates typical listing information for commercial, farm, lots, and acreage properties.

TYPES OF LISTINGS

There are three basic types of listings: the open listing, the exclusive agency, and the exclusive right to sell. These differ mainly in restrictions as to who can sell and when a commission is due. The net listing is an additional category, but it overlaps the three basic categories.

Area		Address		City		$
Listing No.		No. Rms.		Bedrooms		Baths
Owner		Ph.		Tenant		Ph.
Lot Size		Zoning	Taxes		Style	Age
Basement/Crawl/Slab			Garage		AC	Fireplace
Rooms	Size	Floor	Brms.	Size	Floor	Elementary
LR			1			Jr. High
DR			2			Private
Fam.			3			High School
Kit.			4			Possession
Lender				Special Assessments: $		
Mortgage Bal.		Int. Rate		Sewer	Heat	
Payment (Principal & Interest)				Water	Roof	
Reason For Selling				Water Heater		
				Windows	Septic Tank	
Remarks:						
Showing Instructions				Commission		
Listing Broker			Key			
This information is believed to be accurate but is not warranted			Phone		Sales Rep.	

Figure 14–1   Listing information for a residential property

Area		Address		Town			$	
Listing No.				Lot Size				
Owner			Phone			Zoning		
Construction			Roof		Gas	Taxes		Year
Age	Floors		Water		Heat	Electricity		Basement
Parking	AC		Sewer		Rest Roms	Possession		
Schools								
Terms:						Possession		
Gross Income		$						
Less Operating Expense		$						
Net Yield		$						
Present Lease:								
Remarks								
Showing instructions:					Key:			
Listing Broker					Phone			
Salesperson					Phone			
This information is believed to be accurate but is not warranted					Commission			

Figure 14–2 Listing information for a farm or commercial property

Open Listing

Unless specified otherwise, a listing agreement creates an open listing. Open listings are often handled informally without a written agreement; however, some states require that all listing agreements be written. An owner who declares, "I'm ready to pay a commission to anyone who finds a buyer for my house" would, in effect, be creating an open listing. With an *open listing,* either the property owner, the broker, or other hired brokers can sell the property; however, only the broker who is actually the *procuring cause* is entitled to a commission. If the property owner sells the property, no commission would be paid to the broker. A broker is the procuring cause, however, if she is the primary cause of the buyer and seller getting together and completing a transaction, even though the owner actually handles the sale.

There are several disadvantages to an open listing. One is the possibility of disagreement as to who was the procuring cause in a particular transaction. Disagreement can occur when more than one offer is made at about the same time. Brokers holding open listings will seldom do any advertising and will hesitate to exert much effort because of the uncertainty of receiving any commission. Open listings are used frequently, however, because an owner may not be willing to give up the right to sell the property herself in order to avoid paying a commission.

Exclusive Agency Listing

An *exclusive agency listing* bars the property owner from hiring more than one broker, but it still allows the owner to sell the property herself without paying a commission. If the property is sold through the owner's own efforts, the listing

315

agreement comes to an end. There is then no liability on the owner's part to pay a commission. The broker will usually prefer an exclusive agency listing over an open listing since it is more likely that her efforts will result in a commission. She may be willing to advertise the property, since other brokers cannot compete. The property owner, in turn, can expect a greater effort from a particular single broker than if other brokers were also involved.

A controversy can arise from the exclusive agency agreement, however, if the seller sells directly to a person who had also dealt with the broker. Usually, the listing agreement will specify a period of time when a commission is still due if a person who has dealt with the broker buys the property directly from the seller. In some localities a *coexclusive agency* can be used whereby either of two brokers or the owner can sell.

Exclusive Right to Sell

An ***exclusive right (or authorization) to sell*** provides that the broker will receive a commission if the property is sold within the time limit prescribed in the listing agreement, regardless of who sells it. The owner can still sell the property; however, a commission would be due to the broker. Usually, the exclusive right to sell names a time after the listing agreement ends wherein the broker is still entitled to a commission if the property is sold to a party who inspected the property during the listing agreement period. A broker preparing a listing contract should clearly state in the agreement that a commission will be due if the property owner sells the

Example 14–1 Computing a Fair Price in Lieu of a Net Listing

To illustrate the possible problems arising from this type of listing, suppose a property owner wants $120,000 for a property. The broker may advertise the property at $132,000. Assume that she showed the property to a customer, and the customer made an offer of $120,600. This would place the broker in an unfair position, especially if she had spent considerable funds in promotion of the property. The broker must present each offer to the property owner. If the offer of $120,600 was accepted by the owner, the broker would receive only $600 for her efforts. On the other hand, a broker may get an unsuspecting client to set a "net" amount far below market value and pocket an exorbitant fee.

To avoid this conflict of interest, a broker, if offered a net listing by the seller, normally should calculate a fair commission and offer to list the property at a list price calculated as follows:

$$
\begin{aligned}
&\text{Owner wants} && \$120,000 \\
&\text{Commission desired} && 6\% \text{ of price} \\
&\text{Price} = \$120,000 + .06 \times \text{Price} \\
&\text{Price} - .06 \text{ Price} = \$120,000 \\
&\text{Price} = \frac{\$120,000}{1 - .06} = \frac{\$120,000}{0.94} = \$127,660
\end{aligned}
$$

If sold at $127,660, the commission is $.06 \times \$127,660 = \$7660$, and the owner gets the balance of $120,000. Establishing a listing price this way reduces the possible conflict of interest or other problems that may arise.

property, since courts have held that the words "exclusive right to sell" might not be sufficiently clear to the average property seller. If both parties do not fully understand the agreement, the courts might hold that there was no meeting of the minds and that, therefore, the contract is not valid.

Net Listing

A *net listing* provides that the seller will receive a predetermined or net amount of money for the property. A net listing agreement may be any one of the three types already discussed. The broker is then considered free to set any selling price and retain all money received above the seller's specified amount. The theory is that the broker is able to receive a fee based on selling ability, and the seller is guaranteed a net amount. The net listing is illegal in some states. Its concept is basically questionable, both ethically and legally. See example 14.1.

MULTIPLE LISTING SERVICE

A *Multiple Listing Service* (MLS) consists of a formal arrangement between real estate brokers in an area where any member broker has the opportunity to sell listings held by other members. Listing agreements entered into between member brokers and property owners provide that the listing will be distributed to other member brokers. One advantage is that the seller receives greater coverage, since many brokers can show the property. The advantage to the potential buyer is that one agent can show all of the multiple-listed properties. The buyer need not spend time telling several agents about her needs and desires. The broker, too, will be more likely to find a suitable property for a particular customer. Multiple Listing Services recommend a listing contract period (usually about ninety days) for residential properties. The listing period for commercial, industrial, or agricultural properties usually ranges from 90 to 180 days. These periods allow the broker a reasonable time to advertise and sell the property.

Commissions Under MLS

The commission rate is a matter for negotiation between the seller and the broker at the time the listing agreement is made. Any indications of rate-fixing by local real estate boards are subject to the scrutiny of the Federal Trade Commission as violations of antitrust laws. In 1980 the Supreme Court ruled that brokers may be sued under federal antitrust laws if they conspire to fix the fees involved in the buying and selling of homes. Some firms have been found guilty under this decision. The real estate industry argued unsuccessfully that commissions tend to be uniform because of economic and marketing conditions.

Typical commission ranges are as follows:

1. Single-family residence—4 to 7 percent
2. Rural or farmland—6 to 10 percent
3. Commercial or apartments—3 to 5 percent

There is a growing tendency to use flat rates, however, such as $5,000 for a residential property of any price.

In the usual multiple-listing arrangement, the commission is divided between the listing broker and the selling broker in accordance with rules agreed upon by the member brokers. The salesperson obtaining the listing gets a portion of the broker's share. The salesperson's listing and selling commission may vary from area to area or in accordance with the agreement with the broker.

Procedures

Brokers and salespeople pay an initiation fee for joining the Multiple Listing Service in their locality. They also pay a monthly membership fee for which they receive copies of the listings or weekly books showing all multiple-listed properties for sale in the area. Multiple Listing Services formerly required that all multiple-listed properties be taken as an exclusive right-to-sell listing; however, the NATIONAL ASSOCIATION OF REALTORS® currently recommends that exclusive agency listings also be accepted.

Some boards allow the seller one or two "named exceptions" in the exclusive right-to-sell contract. If one of the exceptions buys the property during the term specified in the listing, the seller need not pay the listing broker the sales commission. Boards in some areas permit a broker to hold a listing agreement for a specified number of days before it is given to the multiple-listing service. During this period, the listing broker can attempt to sell the property. The prudent seller, however, may object to this lapse and specify in the agreement that the listing be provided to the multiple-listing service immediately.

MLS Policy

Multiple Listing Services subscribe to certain policies dealing with what the service does and does not do. Some of the important provisions are:

1. An MLS does not fix or recommend commission rates, nor does it suggest sharing arrangements.
2. An MLS has neither dealings with nor responsibilities to buyers or sellers.
3. There are no restrictions on cooperation with nonmembers or on sharing arrangements between members.
4. An MLS does not regulate advertising or the use of "For Sale" or "Sold" signs.
5. An MLS does not restrict political activities of members.
6. An MLS does not reject listings on the basis of price, quality of property, or rate of commission.
7. It is open to any REALTOR® who wants to join.
8. The preferred method of financial support is a monthly fee per member plus a fee per listing.
9. Net listings are not accepted, and all contingencies must be noted on the listing agreement.
10. Listed properties can be withdrawn at any time.
11. Negotiations are to be handled through the listing broker.
12. Statistical marketing data is compiled by MLS.
13. The MLS serves as a mechanism by which participants may extend a blanket offer of subagency to other participants.
14. An MLS participant has the right to accept any offer of subagency. Once a participant begins working on a listing, the offer of subagency is accepted, the fiduciary duty to the seller begins. An MLS member who represents the buyer

should disclose this fact to the seller (or seller's agent) and reject the subagency offer in writing. Failure to do this could result in an undisclosed *dual agency,* subjecting the broker to a possible lawsuit.

Local Market Data

The United States can be thought of as a set of markets or regions whose activities or production are summed up to create a Gross National Product (GNP). Although the GNP may continually grow from year to year, some local markets grow faster and others may actually decline. Real estate markets are local. The distance from one market to another may be as close as 50 to 100 miles. The following economic factors have a strong bearing on a local real estate market:

1. Percentage of persons unemployed
2. Sales
3. Total personal income
4. Industries moving into or out of area

Local sales data are often available to brokers through the local multiple-listing service that publishes weekly and quarterly summaries of sales data for the area. Table 14–1 shows a typical report. This type of information can be used by a real estate broker to

1. Compare quantity and dollar figures to earlier years
2. Show weekly trends
3. Compute the firm's share of the market

Table 14–1 Weekly data compiled by a typical Multiple Listing Service

Weekly Market Analysis	
Total number of active listings	621
$ Amount of all active listings	38,248,121.00
Total number of new listings	68
$ Amount of all new listings	3,959,831.00
Total number of sold listings	31
$ Amount of all sold listings	1,463,857.00
Total number of co-op sales	17
$ Amount of all co-op sales	684,200.00
Average listed prices:	
All active units	79,841.40
Expireds and withdrawns	70,160.24
All sold units	66,291.18
Actual sold price average	67,221.20
Average list-to-sale price difference	1,118.04
% of sale price to list price	96.42%
Average days on market (actives)	91 days
Average days on market (solds)	78 days

A broker can use the following ratios to judge her performance, as well as the local market performance:

1. Percent of homes in area for sale
2. Sales volume compared to prior years
3. Share of property sales
4. Share of listings

PROMOTION

Selling is aided by promotion, which includes activities such as advertising, public relations, holding open houses, and distributing brochures or publications. These activities help present the broker's products or professional abilities to prospective purchasers or sellers and to the public in general. Brokers who concentrate on residential properties will have different promotion strategies from brokers who emphasize commercial or farm real estate.

Promotion is an important part of the real estate broker's effort, just as marketing is part of any business effort. As such, it requires a strategy, a budget, planning, and controls, all as integral parts of the brokerage operation. Strategy considers what the broker has to sell and who the potential customers will be. It also considers the constraints of the resources available, such as number of salespeople and financial resources, as well as the resources of competitors. Thus, strategy involves factors external to the operation as well as internal aspects.

Sometimes promotion is used as a device to mislead by providing improper or insufficient information; however, research has shown that misleading promotion usually does the advertiser more harm than good. Promotion should be better utilized as a method of providing information to prospective buyers to help them make good purchases.

Advertising

Real estate advertising can be classified according to its objective or the medium used. Understanding each of these factors helps one select a good advertising strategy and implement it successfully.

Kinds of Advertising and Their Objectives

Advertising can be classified as specific advertising, name advertising, and institutional advertising. *Specific advertising* promotes individual parcels of real estate or particular related services. The objective is to sell or rent a specific property described in the ad or to secure customers for the broker's services. Specific advertising usually appears in newspapers, brochures, or flyers.

The second category is *name advertising.* The purpose of name advertising is to display the name of the firm before the public. This advertising aims to enhance the firm's reputation and image in the eyes of potential home buyers or sellers. Newspaper advertising can accomplish this goal, as can radio or television announcements, billboards, office signs, or activity news items in newspapers.

Institutional advertising has as its objective the creation of a favorable public opinion toward the real estate brokerage business. It is intended to influence public opinion so that potential sellers or buyers will select a broker rather than sell or buy on their own. Membership or other fees provide the funds to support much of today's institutional advertising.

Advertising Media

Newspapers are the most widely used medium for advertising by real estate brokers. They are used to implement specific, name, and institutional advertising. Classified advertising in newspapers is used primarily for specific advertising of property, but the ads also are designed for name advertising. Brokers group their specific listings into attractive arrangements not only to exhibit their available listings, but also to place their names attractively before the public. A seller in the process of selecting a broker often looks in the classified section of the local newspaper to choose a broker who uses attractive advertising. Thus, the specific ads also act as name advertising.

Since potential buyers are interested in up-to-the-minute information on available property, the daily newspaper serves the broker well. Sunday newspapers tend to carry a greater number of listings, since the local potential buyers often have more leisure time to carry out their search on Sundays. In addition, out-of-town buyers often look for real estate on weekends.

Other advertising media suitable for real estate brokers' ads are magazines, radio, television, outdoor signs, booklets, home shows, and other displays. Industrial properties, rural estates, farms, or unusual properties are often advertised in nationally distributed specialty or trade magazines that reach particular groups of readers. Whereas newspapers have a short life, magazines often lie around and are read over a period of months in libraries, waiting rooms, and so forth. Signs, booklets, and displays are primarily intended to bring the broker's name before the public.

Real estate advertising is often positioned to provide notice to people who visit specific places such as motels, restaurants, or personnel departments of local industries. Some brokers maintain connections with a referral network of brokers in other cities to get contacts with potential buyers before their families actually visit the community.

Billboards, bus signs, and signs on real estate offices are common ways to reach the public. The billboard in Figure 14–3 meets three important criteria: (a) the copy

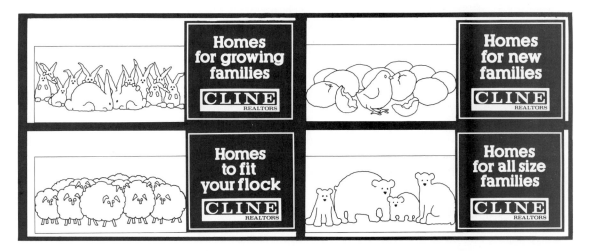

Figure 14–3   Example of billboard advertising

Source: Cline REALTORS®, Cincinnati, Ohio. Material is protected by international copyright. Billboard advertising is being marketed through Identity Campaigns, Inc., 565 East 4500 South, Suite A210, Salt Lake City, Utah 84107. Permission granted limits reprint use to textbook publication only.

is simple enough for drivers to read; (b) the elements catch the eye; and (c) the name of the company is large enough to be easily read.

"For Sale" and "Sold" signs on listed properties are one of the best means of providing name advertising. These signs provide name advertising for the broker, as well as specific advertising for the individual house.

Some communities have passed laws prohibiting "Sold" and/or "For Sale" signs on homes. The arguments for these laws have been based on the concepts of "detracting from appearance" and "preventing panic selling." A Baltimore city sign ban was challenged in court. In 1981 the United States Supreme Court let stand a lower court ruling that the city's sign ban was unconstitutional.

HOME BUYERS

Motivations

Studies show that lack of knowledge of real estate and perceived high risks in selling are the primary motivators for potential home buyers to select the services of real estate brokers. About 80 percent of home buyers come into contact with one or more real estate brokers during the search process, usually to help them with difficult decisions. The problems that buyers must resolve relate to determining the price that they can afford to pay, the right time to purchase, where to buy, and the means to obtain financing. The decisions are easier for people who have previously purchased a home than for first-time buyers, so that a higher percentage of first-time buyers rely on brokers. Buyers new to an area also have more need for technical information. In addition, they often have only a short time in which to look and decide, which forces them to place greater reliance upon a broker. (However, sometimes potential buyers suspect brokers of bias and therefore turn to friends or relatives or rely on their own intuition in the home-buying process.)

Brokers and salespeople should try to understand why people buy rather than rent homes. Several significant advantages of home ownership were discussed in greater detail in Chapter 11. The salesperson can use these to convince a potential buyer of the advantages of home ownership.

Sources of Buyers

Real estate brokers seek potential buyers from a number of sources. People moving to the area from other places, usually as a result of a change in job, provide an important source. Although advertising in local newspapers and listings in the yellow pages provide some contact with these people, many brokers count upon referrals through company personnel departments, banks, and others. Some brokers also have arrangements with brokers in other cities. People selling their homes in one city provide early contacts when they let their broker know of their plans to move to another particular city.

Qualifying Prospective Buyers

Prospective buyers for real estate can be grouped into three categories: (a) those who need a place to live; (b) those who prefer a place different from their present residence; and (c) those who are looking but not yet seriously interested. The constraints and motivations of buyers from each group will be different. A large portion of those in the first group are moving from another area. For them the home selection process is affected by time requirements, since the family does not want to be divided for a lengthy period. A frequent problem of these buyers is the inability to sell their currently owned property. These people need to find a satisfactory place to live within cost and time constraints.

The second group of potential buyers simply want to move to a different property, whether bigger, smaller, better located, or otherwise different. In this case, the prospective buyer can afford to inspect a number of alternative properties carefully over a period of time while searching for a bargain or a property that meets all desires. In this case, the broker or salesperson can expect to spend more time and effort to conclude a transaction.

The broker in either case should spend time to evaluate and qualify each prospective buyer carefully to serve the client better and to make the most efficient use of her own time. It does not serve the best interests of either the client, the seller, or the broker to show properties not within the buyer's price and need constraints. This does not, however, preclude the possibility that prospective buyers will change their constraints. This possibility should always be kept in mind. In almost all cases, one or more of their desires will have to be set aside as the available alternatives are considered. Frequently, buyers will learn early that their monetary limits were too low for the quality of home desired. Also, their specifications may change as they are further exposed to properties. The broker should determine each client's resources and the type of property that will meet the client's needs by asking questions. The following information is needed to evaluate a prospective client's needs and qualifications:

1. Name, address, and telephone number
2. Business address and telephone number
3. Desired price range for property
4. Address of present property owned and whether it is presently for sale or will need to be sold before buying another home
5. Money available for a down payment, family income, and desired monthly payment
6. Marital status and family size
7. Type of home desired (size, style, and location)
8. Reasons for moving
9. How long client has been looking
10. Why client came to this brokerage office
11. Whether client is working with other brokers
12. What homes have been looked at
13. Any special needs (i.e., basement, fireplace, garage, etc.)
14. If right home is found, any reason that might prevent them from purchasing immediately

Once this analysis of the buyer has been completed, the salesperson can make plans and formulate a strategy to serve the buyer's interest and also to plan the most efficient use of her own time.

THE SALESPERSON

Making a living as a real estate salesperson involves two primary tasks: (a) obtaining property to list and (b) securing buyers for property. Success depends upon many facets, such as understanding the motivations of sellers and buyers, knowing advertising and selling techniques, and having the ability to close a sale by bringing the parties into an agreement.

Attributes of Salespeople

Surveys have shown that people in the process of buying homes prefer certain characteristics displayed by salespeople, including the following:

1. Friendly, cooperative, and unpressuring manner
2. Willingness to help and give time to the customer
3. Sincerity, honesty, and straightforward approach
4. Ability to provide helpful information
5. Efficient planning, showing properties of interest, and following through on buyer's requests for more information

In contrast, certain practices used by some salespeople have been identified as the most negative:

1. Showing homes that did not fit needs
2. Misrepresentation or attempt to mislead
3. Using pressure techniques or being too aggressive
4. Not taking adequate time
5. Lack of knowledge about homes, locations, financing, or other pertinent information

Selling Ability

The art of "salesmanship" is sometimes considered to be dependent upon personality and persistence. In the real estate business, possibly more than in other sales occupations, the technical capabilities and approaches used by the broker and salesperson are usually more significant. A systematic sales approach will include an analysis and frequent reanalysis of the needs of the potential buyer, a systematic evaluation of the available properties listed, a careful plan to show the properties efficiently so that the buyer's time is not wasted, and a willingness to provide factual information that the buyer needs to make the proper decisions.

As the seller's agent, the broker must help the seller list the property at a realistic price, and he must also provide advice on preparing the property for showing. This coordinated approach, working with both the seller and buyer, and particularly considering one's responsibility to the seller, can result in successful selling and satisfied buyers and sellers. Satisfied buyers and sellers make future prospective clients themselves who also recommend other potential clients.

Product Knowledge

As in any marketing operation, the salesperson must be familiar with the product. In real estate marketing, this can be broken down into groups of knowledge as follows:

1. Knowledge of the profession, including laws and financing
2. Knowledge of the community and neighborhoods, including schools and shopping facilities

3. Knowledge of houses in general, including constructions, heating costs, taxes
4. Knowledge of the specific property being shown—reasons for selling and other information not on the listing agreement

Of further importance is an understanding of the buyer and her needs, financial abilities, and personal desires. Keeping aware of available properties is another requirement. Knowledge of location, lot size, age and construction of buildings on the market, and existing mortgage money availability are all necessary to respond to queries of the buyer as the property is shown.

Some salespeople have successfully used the *locational farm concept.* This means that the salesperson concentrates efforts in a specific geographic area within the local community.

Closing the Sale

When properties have been shown, it is important for the salesperson to be able to judge which properties the prospective buyer likes and to proceed to close the sale and obtain a signed agreement to purchase. (*Closing* may not always have the same meaning, since sometimes settlement and closing are used interchangeably for the meeting where the title is transferred.) The buyer can be encouraged to think of herself as the owner. This might involve thinking about the good and bad points about each property and handling questions or objections concerning each property. The closing is critical, since a salesperson's success and livelihood depends on actual sales completed. Successful salespeople are able to guide the prospective buyer to a decision, without pressing the prospect into uncomfortable situations or beyond desired constraints.

Evaluation of Salespersons

It is important to evaluate all salespersons, but especially the newer employees. The objectives of evaluation are (1) to determine if a salesperson should be retained, (2) to identify areas where additional training or supervision is needed, and (3) to determine those who can take on greater responsibilities and thus receive a larger portion of the commissions.

Daily activity reports from each salesperson, along with personal observation, are useful in accomplishing these objectives. The identification of a person's strengths and weaknesses provides a helpful guideline in making positive recommendations for improvement.

OTHER MARKETING CONCEPTS

Relocation Services

Many brokers have been successful by placing emphasis on relocation services. Two approaches are often used. Under the first approach, real estate brokers become associated with networks of other brokers. A broker in Columbus, for example, may list the home of a person moving to Baltimore, so she would identify a Baltimore broker and mention the prospective move to him. With the second approach, a broker may work closely with a company in assisting persons being transferred to other locations. A combination of the two approaches is often utilized.

Trade-in Plans

Some brokers utilize trade-in arrangements as part of their marketing strategy. The plan is directed at home sellers who need greater assurance that their existing home will be sold. Trade-in plans can take varied approaches, but the guaranteed trade-in is one of the more popular. Under this plan, the broker guarantees the sellers a set price, usually lower than the list price, less brokerage fees, if the home does not sell at the list price in a period such as ninety days. After the ninety days, if the house is not sold the broker takes title to the home at the set price. There are variations to this plan. In any case, it is necessary to define the terms very carefully when the listing agreement is made.

Sale by Auction

The sale of real estate is frequently handled by public auction. Notices of auctions are published as paid advertisements in local newspapers. A notice of an auction is considered to be an invitation to make an offer on the property. Bids can either be written or oral. By the terms of some auctions the owner need not accept the highest bid received at the auction and has the right to reject all offers. Most state licensing laws require an auctioneer's license, but not a real estate salesperson's or broker's license, to auction real property.

The terms of the auction are usually specified in the auction notice; however, to meet the Statute of Frauds requirement, the written contract is usually completed as soon as possible following the auction.

SUMMARY

The degree of success of a broker or salesperson depends primarily upon her ability to secure listings from sellers and then to consummate sales to prospective buyers. This ability depends heavily upon technical knowledge of real estate. It also depends upon understanding the motivations of sellers and buyers and being able to satisfy their needs and provide the services they expect.

The open listing, exclusive agency listing, and exclusive right to sell are the three basic types of listing contracts. Most real estate brokers, as well as Multiple Listing Services, prefer the exclusive right to sell, which provides that the broker earns a commission regardless of who sells the property, as long as a ready, willing, and able buyer is found within the period specified in the listing agreement.

The success of the broker also depends upon promotion. The real estate broker has several advertising media open to her, but the newspaper is the most heavily used. Well-designed advertising not only helps the broker to sell the advertised properties, but also attracts potential buyers and other sellers to the broker.

You can check your understanding of these terms against the glossary or by review in this chapter.

Locational farm concept   Net listing   Procuring cause

Multiple Listing Service   Open listing

What are the differences or relationships, if any, between the following?

Exclusive agency listing
   and Exclusive right to
   sell

Name advertising,
   Institutional advertising,
   and Specific advertising

PROBLEMS ▮▮▮▮

14-1. Joanne Cushing, a salesperson for C & R Realty, has talked with Bob Axel, who has been trying to sell his home on his own. It is a three-bedroom home, which Bob has priced at $86,000. Bob has asked Joanne to come over and discuss the possibility of having an open listing of the property with C & R Realty. Make a list of material and information that Joanne should bring to the meeting with Bob.

14-2. What type of listing should Joanne recommend? Make a list of information to present to Bob to justify this recommendation.

14-3. If Bob desires a net listing at $84,000, what listing price would you suggest to obtain a commission of 6 percent?

14-4. After listing Bob's property, Joanne receives a long-distance call from Julio Marcos who is coming to town on Saturday to look for a home. Prepare a list of questions to ask Mr. Marcos.

14-5. What are the different types of advertising and their objectives?

14-6. What are some quantitative measures of local market activity that the broker could compile from MLS data?

14-7. What are some quantitative measures that a broker could use to determine the performance of his business?

14-8. What are some quantitative measures that a salesperson could use to compare her performance with that of other salespersons?

14-9. Discuss whether a real estate salesperson is selling a product or a service.

14-10. Visit a broker's office or a model home. Make a list of the promotional devices used. Which do you think are most effective? Least effective? What other devices should have been used?

14-11. How might a real estate firm determine which of its advertising methods are most effective?

14-12. Cut out the classified ad section from a local newspaper and select what you judge to be the five most effective ads. What were your criteria for the selections?

14-13. Mr. Honer and his wife were moving to another city and placed an ad in the classified section of the newspaper. The ad stated, "For Sale by Owner." Make a list of the things the Honers should do at this point.

14-14. In the prior problem, several calls were received from interested parties, as well as six calls from real estate agents wanting to list the property. The Honers had felt that they were not making sufficient progress in selling the home and decided to talk with some of the agents. Make a list of things to be brought up at the meetings with brokers to help in making a selection of broker.

14-15. After talking with six brokers from the above problems, the Honers compiled the fact sheet shown in Table 14-2. Summarize the important facts useful in arriving at a conclusion.

14-16. Which broker would you select and why? Which would you not select and why?

Table 14–2

Broker	Type of Listing Suggested	List Price Suggested	Commission Rate	Length of Listing Suggested
A	Exclusive right to sell	$86,000	6%	60 days
B	Exclusive right to sell	84,400	6%	90 days
C	Open	79,900	6%	30 days
D	Exclusive agency	85,000	6%	60 days
E	Exclusive agency	83,500	6%	60 days
F	Exclusive right to sell	98,500	5%	120 days

SUPPLEMENTARY READINGS

Bloom, George F. *Real Estate,* 8th ed. New York: Wiley, 1982. Chapter 16.

Conover, Joseph A. *Thirty Days to Great New Success in Real Estate Sales.* Englewood Cliffs, N.J.: Executive Reports Corporation, 1973.

Day, Joe, II. "Farming: The Hydroponic Method." *Real Estate Today,* Jan. 1986, pp. 49–51.

Godi, Art, and Reyhons, Ken. *Creative Listing Handbook.* Chicago: REALTORS® National Marketing Institute, 1980.

Jones, Talova L. *Real Estate Success Habits.* Oklahoma City: TLC, 1984.

Litka, Michael P., and Shilliff, Karl A. *Contemporary Real Estate Incidents.* Columbus, Ohio: Grid, 1980.

McMichael, Stanley A. *How to Operate a Real Estate Business.* Englewood Cliffs, N.J.: Prentice-Hall, 1967.

McMichael, Stanley A. *The Real Estate Salesman's Handbook.* Chicago: NATIONAL ASSOCIATION OF REALTORS®, 1969.

NATIONAL ASSOCIATION OF REALTORS®. *Handbook on Multiple Listing Policy.* Chicago, 1975.

Shenkel, William M. *Marketing Real Estate,* 2nd ed. Englewood Cliffs, N.J.: Prentice-Hall, 1985. Chapters 1–22.

Wigginton, F. Peter. *The Complete Guide to Profitable Real Estate Listings.* Homewood, Ill.: Dow Jones-Irwin, 1977.

CHAPTER 15
Federal Regulations, State Licensing, and Ethics

Federal, state, and local laws, in addition to professional ethics, directly affect practices in the real estate profession. Particular areas where federal laws apply include low-income housing, urban renewal, insured or guaranteed mortgages, fair housing, and laws designed to protect the consumer. State laws, on the other hand, primarily control the licensing and practice of real estate brokers, salespersons, and others in related activities. Ethical considerations serve as a self-governing force among professionals in day-to-day real estate transactions.

State licensing requirements vary considerably from state to state. Many of the provisions, however, tend to be consistent. The NATIONAL ASSOCIATION OF REALTORS® has worked toward consistency in licensing regulations from state to state. The License Law Committee of NAR, in cooperation with the National Association of Real Estate License Law Officials (NARELLO), has published a suggested pattern for real estate license law.[1]

Federal regulations concerning real estate financing and mortgages were discussed in Chapter 7; legislation covering urban renewal, land use, and low-income housing was discussed in Chapter 10. Other aspects of federal and state law are discussed in other chapters as they relate to specific topics.

---

[1]NATIONAL ASSOCIATION OF REALTORS®. *Real Estate License Law—Suggested Pattern,* 4th ed. Chicago: 1975.

FEDERAL HOUSING

Since the formation of the Public Housing Administration in 1937, the federal government has become increasingly involved in providing housing within the financial means of more families. The original program was supplemented by the Housing Acts of 1949, 1954, and 1961. In 1965, another law provided a rent supplement program that subsidized payments to the landlord so that low-income families would pay no more than 25 percent of their income for rent. There have been several extensions of the law since then.

The first government endeavors in housing resulted in public housing projects owned by a local housing authority. Initial projects were concentrated in inner-city areas; however, later projects have spread to suburban areas. Although the local government authority has the primary responsibility for starting and administering the current projects, the Department of Housing and Urban Development (HUD) is available to provide technical assistance when requested. Projects are begun only after a local housing authority studies the community and the available housing. The study determines existing low-income family housing standards, extent of blighted areas, vacancies available, and overcrowding. Based on the findings, HUD may approve a proposed program and allocate certain units to a community. Assistance from HUD is available in the form of grants, annual subsidy contributions, loans, and government guarantees of bond issues. The grants and loan guarantees are used to initiate projects, whereas the annual federal contributions help maintain the availability of housing for the lowest income groups.

LAWS RELATED TO FAIR HOUSING

A basis for protection against discrimination was begun with the Civil Rights Act of 1866 and was supplemented 102 years later by the Fair Housing Act of 1968. These laws make it illegal to interfere with the rights of individuals and provide penalties for enforcement. It is illegal to coerce, interfere, intimidate, or threaten a person in the process of buying, selling, or renting real estate.

Civil Rights Act of 1866

Congress passed the *Civil Rights Act* of 1866 following the Civil War. This act provided that "all citizens of the United States shall have the same right, in every State and Territory, as is enjoyed by white citizens thereof to inherit, purchase, lease, sell, hold and convey real and personal property." The intent of the act was to prohibit discrimination based on race.

The law provides means to enforce the provisions. Where there is an instance of racial discrimination, the complainant can take the case to a federal court. A Supreme Court decision in 1883, however, effectively limited the act's application to federal housing. An executive order in 1962 required the elimination of discrimination on (a) real estate owned by the federal government (including real estate it leases to others), (b) property affected by federal grants or funds, or (c) government insured mortgages. Title VI of the Civil Rights Act of 1964 broadened the scope of antidiscrimination into any areas where the federal government provided assistance.

In a situation where a real estate broker or salesperson is found to have discriminated because of race, the court could force the sale or rental of the property or could award damages.

Fair Housing Act of 1968

The *Fair Housing Act* of 1968 expands the Civil Rights Act by making it illegal to discriminate on the basis of race, color, religion, or national origin in connection with the rental or sale of most housing as well as land designated for residential use. The act clearly covers both single-family housing and multifamily housing as follows:

1. Single-family housing
   (a) Houses not privately owned
   (b) Houses privately owned by an individual who owns three or more houses, or who, in any two-year period, sells more than one of which he was not the most recent occupant
   (c) Privately owned housing when a broker or other person involved in the business of selling or renting houses is used and/or when discriminatory advertising is used
2. Multifamily housing
   (a) Housing of five or more units
   (b) Housing of four or fewer units, if none of the units is occupied by the owner

The 1968 Fair Housing Act prohibits certain acts if based on race, color, religion, or national origin:

1. Refusal to sell or rent to, negotiate with, or deal with a person
2. Stating different terms or conditions for buying or renting to different people
3. Advertising housing as available only to certain persons
4. Making false statements concerning the availability of housing for sale or rent
5. Calling attention to the possibility that minority groups may move into an area in order to persuade an owner to sell or rent
6. Any practices by banks, savings and loan associations, insurance companies, or other commercial lenders that deny loans or specify different terms or conditions to different persons
7. Refusing to admit anyone into a brokers' organization, Multiple Listing Service, or other service

Where there is an apparent violation of the Fair Housing Law of 1968, the complainant can report it to Fair Housing, HUD, Washington, D.C. 20410, or to the nearest regional office. The complainant may write a personal letter or fill out a form provided by any post office or HUD office to report a complaint. When the complaint is received, HUD will send a copy to the person charged, who then can file a written answer. After an investigation, HUD may take a number of actions. HUD can (a) attempt informal conciliation to end any discriminatory practice; (b) inform the complainant of his right to court action; or (c) refer the complaint to the Attorney General or to an equivalent state or local agency. The individual may, as an alternative, seek remedy by local, state, or federal court action. A 1972 amendment to the law requires an Equal Housing Opportunity logo and poster.

Supreme Court Ruling on Balanced Neighborhoods, 1979

A racially mixed group of residents of Bellwood, Illinois, brought suit under the Fair Housing Act in 1979 to stop real estate agents from attempting to illegally tip the racial balance in a neighborhood. The suit charged two real estate agencies with steering black home buyers to the integrated Bellwood neighborhood while guiding whites into other predominantly white areas. The U.S. Supreme Court, in ruling against the real estate agents, stated that everyone in Bellwood could suffer economic losses if the area's stability were undermined.

Related Local Ordinances

In another later ruling, a federal judge declared two other Bellwood ordinances unconstitutional. One ordinance required a real estate agent to obtain a permit from the village before soliciting for listings. A second ordinance required all property owners and agents to give the village notice of the intent to sell or rent property. The judge ruled that the restrictions violated due process protections.

Housing and Urban-Rural Recovery Act of 1983

As part of the Housing and Urban-Rural Recovery Act of 1983, the Department of Housing and Urban Development (HUD) administers a program to encourage the production of market-rate residential housing. Developers can take advantage of a federal subsidy if the developer's project offers at least 20 percent of the units at below-market rentals to low-income occupants. A developer can receive a grant or low-interest loan of up to 50 percent of eligible project costs. The law also provided for an Urban Development Action Grant Program to encourage private development in distressed cities.

Fair Housing Amendments Act of 1988

The 1988 fair housing law bars discrimination against (1) families with children and (2) the handicapped. The conditions of prior fair housing laws are extended to these groups; however, there are a number of exemptions to the first category relative to property primarily for senior citizens.

State Antidiscrimination and Fair Housing Laws

Most of the states have adopted fair housing laws paralleling the federal laws. The provisions are very similar to those defined above for the federal laws. Some states have recently expanded the provisions to prohibit discrimination based on sex, marital status, age, physical handicap, or other factors. The provisions for each state are covered in booklets available from sources listed in Appendix C.

CONSUMER PROTECTION

A number of federal laws and regulations were designed to protect the consumer against unscrupulous persons involved in real estate. These laws have been promoted by both consumer interest groups and legitimate business interests.

Consumers may be involved with real estate transactions only a few times in their lives, and the amount of money they allocate toward a real estate transaction is usually substantial. Many of the provisions—the "fine print" in the documents—are difficult for the consumer to comprehend. Much legislation is designed to help the consumer in this respect.

Truth-in-Lending Law

The federal *Truth-in-Lending Law* is part of the Consumer Credit Protection Act of 1968. The Board of Governors of the Federal Reserve System was given responsibility to implement the law and subsequently issued *Regulation Z,* which went into effect on July 1, 1969. Its objective is to let consumers know exactly what they will be paying in credit charges for a transaction so that they can compare sources of credit for possible savings. The law does not regulate interest rates on loans, since legal limits on interest that can be charged for specific purposes are governed by state usury laws. The law and Regulation Z require that the interest rate be clearly specified and that it include any charges listed under other names that are legally defined as interest.

Compliance with Truth-in-Lending

The act requires that anyone who offers, extends, or arranges credit must make certain disclosures to the consumer. The most important disclosures are (a) the total finance charge; (b) the annual percentage rate (APR); (c) date finance charge begins; (d) number of payments; (e) due dates of payments; (f) prepayment penalties, and (g) total of all payments. However, the total of all payments need not be stated in cases involving a first mortgage or contract for deed on a dwelling. The *annual percentage rate* is the total annual cost of credit and must include not only the interest, but also the points and any other fees. The following fees must be included in the calculation: application fees, inspection fees, finders' fees, termite inspection costs, disclosure statement fees, closing fees, points, loan discount fees, prepaid interest, VA funding fees, or prepaid mortgage insurance premium (MIP) on FHA loans. The objective is to provide the borrower with the means to compare financing costs. Fines have been levied for noncompliance. In 1981 eleven builders agreed to pay Federal Trade Commission fines of up to $90,000 each for advertising simple interest rates rather than APR.

Truth-in-Lending and Advertising

When the Truth-in-Lending Law became effective on July 1, 1969, the advertising of real estate credit was placed under the jurisdiction of the Federal Trade Commission (FTC). The intent of this law is to make bait advertising of credit terms a federal offense. For example, if an advertisement offers homes at $1,000 down, the ad is in violation if the seller will not usually accept this amount as a full down payment. Or if an advertisement mentions credit terms, the annual percentage rate must be spelled out and stated as such in those words. The words "Buyer can assume 9% mortgage" would be improper in an advertisement if other charges will be made that fall into the definition of finance charges. Any rate of interest or finance charge must be expressed as an annual percentage rate (APR). The act provides both criminal and civil penalties for violations.

Consumer Credit Protection Act

The *Consumer Credit Protection Act* of 1968 and Regulation Z apply to consumer credit transactions where the security for the loan is real property used as the principal residence of the borrower. The act provides that the customer receive a notice of his right to rescind certain transactions up through the third business day following receipt of the disclosure and rescission notice. If the customer decides to rescind the transaction, he must notify the creditor in writing and is then not liable for any charge. The lender must return any deposits or property given as a down payment.

Equal Credit Opportunity Act of 1975

The *Equal Credit Opportunity Act* prohibits discrimination in obtaining credit because of race, color, national origin, religion, age, sex, or marital status. Prior to this time, these factors were often taken into account when a lender evaluated the loan application of a potential borrower. For example, single or divorced women often had difficulty in obtaining mortgage loans. Mortgage lenders must also observe Regulation B of the Federal Reserve Board, which outlines procedures to follow in determining the eligibility of mortgage loan applicants.

Real Estate Settlement Procedures Act (RESPA)

The Real Estate Settlement Procedures Act, administered by HUD, has the objective of providing potential home buyers who are arranging financing with information on the total costs involved. The lender must advise the buyer, seller, and any others involved of all charges to be levied. Each person who applies for a home mortgage loan must be furnished with a booklet entitled *Settlement Costs* published by HUD. The lender usually provides an estimate of total closing costs. The purposes are (a) to allow a buyer to shop around and compare costs and (b) to let the buyer know how much cash will be needed at settlement. RESPA applies to all first mortgage loans of one- to four-family residential properties where the lender is under federal regulations. The law also bans referral fees and bars sellers from requiring buyers to purchase title insurance from any particular company. The law does not apply to commercial property. Procedures in the law are discussed in greater detail in Chapter 16.

Magnuson-Moss Consumer Product Warranty Act

The Magnuson-Moss Consumer Product Warranty Act is designed to protect the consumer in the sale of goods where warranties are specified, including protection when builders offer such warranties in respect to home appliances. A warranty must be designated as "full" or "limited," and the rights of the buyer must be defined in case defects should occur. Warranties must also be written in simple, easily understood language. A builder who offers a warranty that does not meet the requirements of the act could be subject to a $10,000 per day fine. The act does not, however, require that warranties be given.

A builder seeking to offer a warranty, then, has three alternatives: (a) warrant the structure and consumer products (e.g., the water heater); (b) assign manufacturer's warranties to the buyer and make no warranties on his own part; (c) specifically list the items or parts of the structure that are warranted. The Home Owners Warranty (HOW) program discussed in Chapter 12 meets the provisions of the Magnuson-Moss Act.

Many states have additional laws of their own designed to protect real estate purchasers. In New Jersey, for example, a state law passed in 1979 requires builders to offer an insured warranty.

Disclosure of Insulation

Beginning in September 1981, an FTC regulation required that brokers include insulation information on all listings of new homes. This should include the "R" values for exterior walls and the ceiling. The regulation further requires that the insulation values also be stated in the sales contracts by the seller.

Interstate Land Sales Full Disclosure Act (ILSFDA or ILSA)

During the early 1960s, it came to the attention of the U.S. Senate Special Committee on Aging that elderly persons were being persuaded to purchase retirement or other property that often turned out to be useless or undesirable. Sometimes land that was represented as a vacation retreat or retirement property turned out to be a swamp or desert. The *Interstate Land Sales Full Disclosure Act,* passed by Congress in 1968, has been successful in limiting fraudulent schemes or other activities involving misrepresentation, sight unseen selling, and overdevelopment of available water resources.

Jurisdiction of ILSFDA

ILSFDA provides that anyone selling or leasing fifty or more (or potentially fifty or more) lots of unimproved land as part of a common plan in interstate commerce must comply with provisions of the act. HUD has taken the position that a condominium of fifty or more units may fall within the act's jurisdiction. The law does not apply to situations where all lots are 5 acres or more, to cemetery land, to certain commercial or industrial developments, or to cases where 100 percent of the sales are intrastate.

Statement of Record and Property Report

The developer under the ILSFDA must file a *statement of record* with HUD containing information on the nature of the development, including title condition, encumbrances, location of roads, improvements, utilities, schools, recreational areas, and other services available to the property owner. It must also include copies of the legal instruments used in selling, such as contracts, deeds, bills of sale, and so forth. A second document, called a *property report,* is also required. It has less detail than the statement of record. A copy of the property report must be given to purchasers prior to purchase of any property. Its purpose is to make purchasers aware of planned improvements, possible problems such as wet property in low areas, planned utilities and their cost, availability of roads and their condition and maintenance, and many other items that potential purchasers should know about. Although the forms are filed with HUD, HUD does not approve the project or endorse the development in any way. The main purpose of these two documents is to make the information available. The buyer of a property in a subdivision under ILSFDA has three working days to rescind the purchase. Each purchaser receives a notice similar to that in Figure 15–1.

Figure 15–1   Notice of right of rescission

NOTICE OF RIGHT OF RESCISSION

Notice To Customer As Required By Federal Law:

You have entered into a transaction on _____
(Date)
which may result in a lien, mortgage, or other security interest on your home. You have a legal right under federal law to cancel this transaction, if you desire to do so, without any penalty or obligation within three business days from the above date or any later date on which all material disclosures required under the Truth in Lending Act have been given to you. If you so cancel the transaction, any lien, mortgage, or other security interest on your home arising from this transaction is automatically void. You are also entitled to receive a refund of any downpayment or other consideration if you cancel. If you decide to cancel this transaction, you may do so by notifying the following:

_____
Name of Creditor

at _____
Address of Creditor's Place of Business
by mail or telegram sent not later than midnight of

_____
Date
You may also use any other form of written notice identifying this transaction if the notice is delivered to the above address not later than the specified time. This notice may be used for that purpose by dating and signing below.
I hereby cancel this transaction.

_____   _____
Date   (Customer's Signature)

State Regulations

Some states also have regulations that apply to intrastate land sales, whereas some supplement the federal ILSFDA. Arkansas and Pennsylvania, for example, require that any developer proposing sale within the state of land located outside the state shall submit particulars to the state Real Estate Commission for approval.

Many states have laws related to the purchase or lease of subdivided land within the state. New York, for example, requires the filing of an *offering statement* with the Department of State. In one of its provisions, the statement prohibits the conveyance of land if it is encumbered by a mortgage or lien that might affect clear title.

ENVIRONMENTAL CONTROLS

A broad interpretation of the word *environment* would include physical, social, cultural, and aesthetic factors. As related to real estate, environmental concerns can be limited to actions that will affect land, air, water, minerals, and objects of aesthetic or historic significance.

We shall briefly define the government environmental legislation that affects real estate transactions. Prior to the 1960s, the laws of police power, trespass, and nuisance served to protect owners' enjoyment of their property and the health of the public in general. Due to population growth, new industries, and increased awareness of problems, the government has enacted legislation intended to protect the environment.

National Environmental Policy Act (NEPA), 1969

The stated purposes of NEPA are (a) to declare a national policy to encourage harmony between humans and their environment; (b) to promote efforts to reduce damage to the environment; (c) to increase understanding of the environment; and (d) to establish a Council on Environmental Quality. The act refers to federal actions, but the agency guidelines extend to private activities. Proposed actions affecting real estate include an *environmental impact statement* (EIS) that considers the impact of proposed major projects on the quality of the environment, including indirect as well as direct effects. Although the act does not prescribe sanctions for failure to comply, complaining parties have generally sought injunctions that have frequently been granted. The Environmental Protection Agency (EPA) was established by executive order in 1970 to establish and enforce standards. Many of the states have followed up with similar legislation.

Air Pollution Controls

The Air Quality Act of 1967, as amended in 1970, requires the Environmental Protection Agency to establish air quality standards to protect the public health and welfare. The individual states are given primary responsibility for control within their boundaries. Air pollution is related to land use since the location and design of industrial buildings and transportation facilities have an influence on the climate and air in the cities.

Water Quality

Although owners of riparian land have always had the right to take actions in cases where watercourses were polluted, the problem has become too general to be resolved by individual lawsuits. Two types of water pollution exist. *Chemical pollution* results from the release of toxic chemicals into rivers and lakes (e.g., the damage caused by the release of Kepone into the James River). The discharge of sewage or other wastes results in *biological pollution.* The objectives of the Federal Water Pollution Control Act, as amended in 1972, are to restore and maintain the chemical, physical, and biological integrity of the nation's waters. The legislation deals with (a) elimination of the discharge of pollutants into navigable waters by 1985; (b) protection of fish and wildlife; (c) prohibition of the discharge of toxic pollutants; (d) financial assistance for publicly owned waste treatment works; and (e) encouragement of research and development.

The Safe Drinking Water Act of 1974 has as its purpose the assurance of minimum standards for water supply systems. The EPA was entrusted with formulating the regulations and administrating the program.

Coastal Zones

In 1972, Congress passed the Marine Protection, Research and Sanctuaries Act (sometimes called the Federal Ocean Dumping Act), which regulates the discharge and dumping of waste into the offshore areas of the ocean. In the same year, the Coastal Zone Management Act was passed to encourage states to preserve, protect, develop, and restore coastal areas. This act has greatly influenced real estate activities, since coastal waters are defined to include the Great Lakes area and their connecting waters, harbors, bays, marshes, and other areas that have a measurable quantity of seawater. The federal government provides grants to share in the administration costs of programs. It also requires permits for new developments or other projects, in addition to environmental impact statements.

Noise Control

The Noise Control Act of 1972 impacts upon real estate values and uses including, but not limited to, aircraft noise. Although noise control responsibility rests primarily with the states, federal legislation extends to vehicles that move about in interstate commerce. Noise from aircraft can substantially affect land values near airports.

Solid Waste

The Resource and Recovery Act of 1976 replaced the federal Solid Waste Disposal Act. The term *solid waste* might be more appropriately referred to as *discarded materials*. Dumps for discarded materials can pose a threat to health and the environment as well as to property values. The new act deals with recoverable materials, hazardous wastes, waste as a potential source of energy, and guidelines for waste disposal.

Land Ownership by Aliens

In the years before 1979, citizens and corporations in other countries acquired real estate in the United States at a record rate. Many U.S. citizens are concerned that rich agricultural land is being bought up and converted to other uses, thereby threatening future food sources.

Legislation on alien ownership of land dates back to the last century when laws were enacted to prevent foreign investors from acquiring large tracts for tenant farming. Currently, seven states (Connecticut, Indiana, Kentucky, Mississippi, Nebraska, New Hampshire, and Oklahoma) prohibit land ownership by nonresident aliens. About half the states have some restrictions on alien ownership.

On the federal level, there is no restriction on land purchased by aliens; however, the Agricultural Foreign Investment Act of 1978 requires foreign citizens and corporations to disclose their U.S. farm and timberland holdings to the Secretary of Agriculture. Federal restrictions also exist that limit how alien land can be used.

STATE LICENSING

All states and the District of Columbia have laws regulating the licensing of real estate brokers and salespeople. The primary purpose of these laws is to protect the public against incompetency or dishonesty in real estate transactions. The laws are also intended to enhance standards by which brokers and salespeople perform their functions and to protect licensed brokers and salespeople from improper or unfair competition. These laws control the issuance of licenses to practice, as well as their suspension or revocation when violated. In most states, the law establishes a state board or real estate commission that has the responsibility to implement the laws and the right to issue and enforce regulations. The commission has the power to issue, suspend, or revoke licenses of real estate brokers or salespersons. The commission can also turn over evidence of violations to the state's attorney general for prosecution or request a court to issue an injunction. In some states, other people involved in real estate, such as appraisers (states of Oregon and Nebraska) or escrow agents (state of Washington), require licenses.

The Financial Institutions Reform, Recovery, and Enforcement Act of 1989 set requirements for anyone completing a real estate appraisal used to justify a loan insured by certain federal agencies. This was done because many S & L defaults were attributed to overvalued appraisals.

The Right to License

The legal basis for a state's right to license derives from the police power of the state. The exercise of this control is especially important in real estate because the average person transacts real estate business very infrequently. In addition, the amount of money involved is relatively large, usually including much of a person's total life savings or potential future earnings.

Courts have upheld the constitutionality of real estate licensing laws when tested as violating the Fourteenth Amendment. The tests charged that the laws deprive a person of a means of making a livelihood in selling real estate. The courts have responded that the restrictive requirements are not unreasonable in that the real estate business requires skill, competence, and trust to protect the interest of the public. In some states, however, courts have struck down requirements that applicants be U.S. citizens or residents of the state for one year. This licensing authority is not unusual. States also regulate the practice of law, medicine, nursing, teaching, pharmacy, and other areas where a degree of competency is required.

Educational Requirements

Real estate professionals recognize that experience alone is not adequate to meet competition and provide the proper service to clients. Activities carried out by real estate professionals depend heavily upon an academic base. The increased need for educational depth and background in these and other subjects has been recognized by both professional associations and state legislative bodies. State statutes include educational prerequisites for taking licensing examinations. Professional associations also have educational or classroom prerequisites for professional designations. Concurrently, there has been an increasing trend for universities and community colleges to either expand the number of real estate courses offered or provide degrees or majors in real estate. More than sixteen states require further periodic continuing education courses for licensed salespersons.

Examinations

Many states contract with testing agencies to administer real estate licensing examinations. These include (1) the Uniform Real Estate Licensing Examination administered by the Educational Testing Service (ETS) of Princeton, New Jersey, (2) American College Test services (ACT), (3) the multistate examination, or (4) the Real Estate Assessment for Licensure (REAL) program administered by the ASI Processing Center in Philadelphia. Those successful in passing the test then apply to the real estate commission in their state for a license.

Typical Licensing Regulations

Although the regulations for obtaining and maintaining a license vary from state to state, similarities do exist:

1. *License.* A broker or salesperson must be licensed before participating in a real estate transaction for a fee.
2. *Education.* Frequently, a high school diploma and/or a specified number of hours of classroom study are required for either a salesperson or a broker. In some states (e.g., Oregon), continuing periodic courses are required. In Indiana, a B.S. degree is required for a broker's license.
3. *Experience.* Experience in real estate prior to application for a broker's license is needed in some states.
4. *Examination.* Sales candidates and broker candidates take different examinations.
5. *Fees.* Fees are required for both the original license and periodic renewals. Fees are used to administer and enforce the law and to provide education.
6. *Reputation.* Applicants must submit evidence of good reputation and competency. Written references from real estate professionals or others are usually needed.
7. *Sponsor.* State laws often require that a salesperson be sponsored by a licensed broker for whom he will work after obtaining the license.
8. *Reciprocity.* Most states have reciprocal agreements allowing credit for experience or a license from another state.
9. *Minimum age.* The minimum age is usually eighteen for a salesperson and twenty-one for a broker.
10. *Recovery fund.* Some states require licensees to furnish a surety bond or contribute to a **recovery fund.** Persons who sustain losses due to negligence or fraud by a licensee and cannot make recovery from the licensee may obtain reimbursement from the fund.
11. *Individual licenses.* Licenses are issued to individuals and not to associations or corporations.
12. *Display.* Display of the license in the broker's place of business is required. Pocket cards are also carried by each licensed sales representative and broker.
13. *Employment severance.* Salespersons' licenses are usually returned to the state when employment with a particular broker ends.
14. *Administration.* The license law is handled by an appointed body, different in name from state to state (see Appendix C), but made up of paid officials and employees.
15. *Suspension.* Fraudulent activities or violations of state regulations or laws can result in suspension of licenses.
16. *Exemptions.* It is common practice to exempt certain persons from the need to have a license as follows:
    (a) A public officer in duties related to real estate
    (b) Attorneys at law acting in their capacity related to real estate
    (c) Court-appointed administrators or executors
    (d) Any person selling or buying real estate for himself or through a power of attorney
17. *Brokerage.* Operations must be physically separated from other types of business.

18. *Advertising.* Advertising must include the broker's registered name.
19. *Prizes.* Many states have barred the use of prizes and lotteries to induce business; however, in 1985 the Illinois Supreme Court overturned the restriction and litigation is pending in other states.
20. *Fair housing.* Regulations exist to support fair housing laws.

Typical Violations

Although a person should be familiar with the laws and regulations in his individual state, a number of violations are clearly defined as part of many state laws. These include the following:

1. Placing a "For Sale" or "For Rent" sign on a property without consent of the owner
2. Failure of a broker to keep a client's funds (i.e., deposit on a purchase) separate from the broker's business account
3. Untruthful or misleading advertising
4. Misrepresentation, whether intentional or innocent
5. Acting for more than one party in a transaction without both parties' knowledge
6. Accepting compensation or other items of value from anyone other than an employing broker for real estate–related activity
7. Payment of fees, gifts, or other consideration by a broker to other than the broker's employees or other licensed brokers
8. Conviction of a felony
9. Using blind ads, that is, ads without the registered broker's name
10. Performing services ordinarily performed only by licensed attorneys at law
11. Failure to give a client a copy of the listing agreement

ETHICS

Most professional businesspeople—whether lawyers, bankers, or engineers—although competitive with each other in their day-to-day dealings, work together to implement the ethical and professional aspects of their professions. In a specific city or town, real estate brokers compete to list property and to make sales. At the same time, these brokers work together to maintain ethical standards in their dealings with the public, their clients, and fellow brokers. In most states, statutes also govern certain ethical considerations. These standards are more important in real estate brokerage than they are in some other businesses where the clients and the public are more familiar with the service performed or the product provided. As we know, over a lifetime, a person may only use a broker's service once or twice and, therefore, may not comprehend all of the numerous and involved details. The typical real estate transaction may include appraisal, financing, and other elements with which most clients are unfamiliar. Furthermore, the transaction is important because of the large amount of money involved. The sale or purchase of a home may affect the life savings of a family.

Ethics means different things to different people and the rules are not as rigid as those described in the chapters on real estate law. Often, ethics deals with subjective factors, but that fact does not reduce the importance of ethics in the real estate business. Most communities have a large number of independent brokers, each of whom has considerable freedom of action in carrying out business. The ethical or unethical practices of a few brokers or salespeople can reflect on the profession as a whole within a certain community. These examples illustrate some practices that might occur.

> *Example 1:* Ms. Adams, a broker, knew that two other brokers had offered to list the Bayes' home at $55,000. Ms. Adams told the owners that she would list it at $65,000, and she did not mention that this was much higher than a recent sale price for a similar home. Is this ethical?

> *Example 2:* Mr. Broker held an exclusive listing on the Karls' home, and Mr. and Mrs. Prospect had just given him an offer at the listed price. Mr. Broker knew that Mr. Karl had become very ill two days before and that the Karls would probably not be able to afford the new home they were planning to build. Mr. Broker knew, however, that by law the Karls would be bound to sell and he would earn a commission. Should he take the offer?

In some cases, a broker will be faced with decisions of ethics versus immediate returns. As with any business, however, the ethical way may preserve the good company image and do the business the most good in the long run.

How can we judge what is ethical and what is not? Professional associations establish sets of guidelines. State laws and/or regulations define certain actions that are not permitted. If a situation arises that is not defined by either of these, a broker or salesperson might ask, "What if the public knew I did this?"

ETHICS IN PRACTICE

State laws, professional association codes, and tradition have resulted in a substantial number of practices that are generally considered ethical and others that are considered unethical. Most persons engaged in the real estate business try to be completely ethical in all aspects of their work. There are always a few, however, who may not act scrupulously. In some cases, the novice may act unethically without realizing the implications. It is with these thoughts in mind that we explore ethics in practice.

Much of the remainder of this chapter will center around illustrative examples. Because state statutes and regulations differ, some actions cited as unethical may also be unlawful in some states. Even in these cases, however, there are always borderline cases requiring interpretation.

Ethics in Listing a Client's Property

In the example cited earlier, a broker offered to list a property at $65,000 even though she knew that comparable properties had sold closer to the $55,000 price suggested by other brokers. Her reasoning may have been that, once she got the listing, she could later recommend a drop in the listed price.

It is the responsibility of a real estate broker to advise a prospective client of the fair market value of a property. He should suggest that a property appraiser be consulted if the appraisal is beyond his own capabilities. It is unethical to list a property either too high or too low without advising the owner of the reasonable market value. To do this would violate the broker's duty as an agent of the seller. It is clearly unethical to suggest a high list price to a client as a strategy to obtain a listing.

Consider Brooks Realty. They have acquired a reputation of fast turnover of the properties they list. Ms. Ames, in hearing of this reputation, offered to list her house with Brooks at $69,500. Mr. Brooks, on examination of the property, stated he could take the listing only if the price were $66,000. He cited recent comparable sales. In this case, Mr. Brooks had built his reputation on selling his clients' property within a reasonable time, and he felt that his reputation was more important than just another listing. He might also have considered that the time he spent showing a home priced too high could be better spent elsewhere.

Some brokers think in terms of never turning down any listing, on the basis that they might somehow sell the property. This is clearly unethical. If a broker lacks the expertise needed to handle a certain type of industrial property, for example, the listing should not be accepted. If a broker becomes ill and cannot serve his principal in a diligent manner, the listing should be given up. If a property is in an area of the city distant from the broker's office where he cannot properly handle it, he should refuse to list it.

A broker who is a member of a multiple-listing service should distribute the listing information to other brokers immediately. It is unethical to delay distribution and try to sell it himself.

As another example illustrating ethics, a broker should not take listings that compete with his own operations. If the broker owns lots for sale, he could not usually be expected to adequately serve a seller of similar lots.

A listing whereby the broker will buy the property at a lower price if it is not sold in sixty days also presents ethical conflicts. If the purchase and resale prospects look good, the broker might not give the principal diligent service while acting as his agent.

Relationships with Buyers

Although the broker has primary responsibilities as agent of the seller, the broker also has duties and obligations to the buyer. The stated primary purpose of licensing real estate brokers and salespersons is to protect the public. One way to do this is to educate licensees so that they are aware of the legal and professional aspects of the job of broker or salesperson. Many buyers have never owned or purchased a home and depend upon the licensee for guidance.

In some cases, the broker will be the agent of the buyer. If a prospect came to town and asked of a broker, "Can you find me a home with about 5 to 10 acres?" the broker would then act for the buyer in this search. If it turned out that the broker could match up one of his listed properties with the buyer's needs, the broker would be obligated to inform both parties if he expects to collect a commission from each.

Buyer Qualification

The process whereby the broker obtains information about the buyer's needs, family size, income, available down payment, and so on, is called *buyer qualification.* Both ethically and from the standpoint of efficient use of everyone's time, the broker should restrict showings to properties that the buyer can reasonably be expected to purchase. Also it would not be ethical to lead the buyer into a contract where the monthly payments would be beyond his abilities.

Legal Matters

Although a real estate broker or salesperson needs knowledge of laws as they apply to real estate, he must take care not to engage in activities considered to be the practice of law. One of these borderline areas is the drawing up of a contract. As a general practice, attorneys and real estate professionals have agreed that the broker can fill in printed contract forms for the parties to sign. If the contract is more complicated, it should be drawn up by an attorney.

It is unethical for a real estate broker to give legal advice or to engage in activities considered to be the practice of law. Instead, he should recommend that a buyer or seller obtain legal counsel for legal matters. If asked by a client to perform a legal task, the broker should refuse and suggest that the client consult an attorney. Even if a form contract is used, the broker or salesperson should suggest that the client is free to consult an attorney before signing. If the client asks the broker to recommend an attorney, the broker should suggest three or more alternative names of attorneys.

In some localities, the tax assessor reviews current real estate transaction documents for use in updating the assessments. The broker should not be a party to showing misleading figures on legal documents. If a house sold for $50,000, it is improper to show $40,000 on the deed to mislead the tax assessor. It would be proper to state a nominal value such as "$5.00 and other consideration," however. Anyone should know this is not the real sale price and would not be misled.

Frequently, a buyer might need a larger mortgage so that he will have more funds to make improvements on a house he desires to purchase. It would be unethical for the salesperson to suggest actions to mislead the lending institution or others, such as using extra tax stamps on the deed to make it appear that a higher purchase price was paid.

Ethics in Selling

When a broker tries to close a particular sale, it is sometimes tempting to use statements or actions that are misleading, untrue, or otherwise unethical. A statement to the buyer that the owners will probably take less because "they have to be moved by June 1," "the husband is very ill," or "they are getting divorced" is unethical unless the seller has authorized use of the information. Lack of diligence by the broker in representing his principal or in making factually unsupported statements about the property are not ethical. For this reason, a broker should never accept a listing that he does not intend to pursue diligently.

Courts, in deciding cases involving misrepresentation, take into account the seller's ability to comprehend or evaluate facts about the property. The broker or salesperson (and perhaps the seller) often has or should have superior knowledge about such factors as the community, zoning, soil conditions or problems, and services available. A broker who purchases a parcel of property from a client, when only the broker knows the land is going to be rezoned as commercial, would be acting unethically. A salesperson who knows the land is not suitable for a septic system would be acting improperly to show the land to a prospective builder.

Buyers will frequently ask questions about the condition of the property. Questions about the condition of an appliance, for example, usually cannot be answered by the salesperson without further checking. Any statements made without consulting the owner would be improper. Representing that a home is well insulated should usually be based on expert knowledge. Stating that "The view from the property is beautiful" would, however, fall into the acceptable category of *"puffing."* The salesperson must be able to determine the line between puffing (mere opinion) and misrepresentation of fact.

Responsibilities to the General Public

A broker or salesperson has responsibilities to third parties. Consider a buyer who wants to purchase a lot on the edge of a residential area and have it rezoned as a liquor store. Should the broker lend assistance in obtaining the zoning change? The broker could expect to place himself in the position of opposing the residents who would resist the change. If he were successful, he could earn a commission, but he could also tarnish his public image. From a purely ethical point of view, is he doing the right thing? If he lived in the area, he would probably not like the change.

Real estate brokers have considerable influence over the formation and character of a community. They can promote premature speculative subdivision development or conversion of open areas to use. They can also lend opposition or support to tax increases to provide schools or parks or to set aside historical sites.

Sometimes a broker publicizes the sale of a property to a minority family in the hopes that it will induce others in the neighborhood to list and sell with him; this is called **blockbusting,** a practice that is both unethical and illegal in all states. The broker can go even further and try to purchase adjacent property at distressed prices. A broker has ethical duties to others beyond those with whom he deals directly.

ETHICS IN ADVERTISING

We sometimes hear of cases of blatant misrepresentation in advertising. If there is a likelihood or intention that an ad may deceive the intended reader, it probably falls into the unethical category. The following are some examples of advertising that might be likely to deceive the intended reader:

1. Stating "Sale by Owner" and listing the licensee's telephone number (illegal by many state laws)
2. Using the word *institute* or some word implying nonprofit in the agency name
3. Advertising an attractive home when there is really no intent to sell in order to draw prospective buyers to look at less attractive homes, sometimes called the *bait and switch* tactic
4. Allowing an ad to run after the property has been sold
5. Advertising a low price that does not mention incomplete construction (e.g., appliances, furnace) or that calls them "extras" in small print
6. Using altered photographs, such as adding trees, grass, or a lake where none exists, or touching up the photos to add a sidewalk or paved street
7. Including a garage, porch, or patio in the advertised square foot area
8. Using the phrases "sacrifice price" or "below market value" without ascertaining the true appraised price

9. For investment property, showing income based on unrealistic expenses or permanently full occupancy
10. Stating "four bedrooms" when one of those rooms is 6 × 7 feet, or "two baths," when one lacks a shower or tub

It is also unethical (and sometimes illegal) for a broker to advertise a property before obtaining a clear intent to sell from the owner.

Relations with Other Real Estate Professionals

A broker should conduct his business so as to be fair to his fellow brokers. Legitimate disagreements between brokers should be settled by the local board whenever possible. Brokers should also be fair to other brokers in referrals or other instances where there is a dual contribution. Advertisements derogatory to other brokers or implying better deals or commission rates would be improper. The following are some examples of unethical actions:

1. Rejecting an offer submitted by another broker without submitting the offer to the principal or owner
2. Leaving a sign on a property after the expiration of a listing or alongside the sign of the new exclusive listing broker
3. Soliciting a listing from a home owner listed with another broker or asking when an exclusive listing will expire
4. Criticizing other brokers on the basis of untrue or unproven information
5. Delaying a sale due to a dispute with another broker
6. Collaborating with another broker to set commission rates
7. Starting litigation against another broker before attempting to negotiate the dispute

Local chapters of professional associations provide a means whereby real estate licensees can resolve differences.

MISREPRESENTATION

The term *misrepresentation* relates to false statements. A victim of misrepresentation can recover in a court of law; however, certain elements must be proved:

1. That a representation regarding a material fact was made as a statement of fact, which was untrue and known to be untrue by the party making it, or else recklessly or innocently made
2. That it was made for the purpose of inducing the other party to act upon it
3. That the other party did, in fact, rely on the representation
4. That the other party was damaged by reliance upon the statement

A recent case—Ford v. Cournale 36 C.A. 3d 172 (Ca. 1977)—was an action for misrepresentation against a real estate broker and his sales representative. In this case, the court found that the broker had misrepresented facts about the income of an apartment house by assuring the purchaser that the apartment house would give a net income of between $700 and $900 per month. Neither the broker nor the salesperson made any check on the expenses in connection with the operation of the apartment house. The salesperson admitted that the statement was based on 100 percent occupancy and that he knew the vacancy figures were not and could not be totally accurate. The broker also admitted that he did not expect the purchaser to conduct an independent investigation or check any other information, and he was aware that she was depending on his representations. The court allowed the plaintiff a judgment against the broker.

There are other possible serious consequences of misrepresentation:

1. The buyer may be able to cancel the contract for sale of the property.
2. The buyer may be able to collect damages.
3. The principal, if damaged, may collect damages or refuse to pay a commission.
4. The broker or salesperson may lose his license.

No longer entirely valid is the old law of *caveat emptor* (let the buyer beware) which held that, if the buyer failed to discover defects, that was his bad luck. Courts are getting away from this concept. We will now discuss the different types of misrepresentation.

Intentional Misrepresentation—Fraud

A seller (or salesperson) states that a basement is dry even though he knows that water comes in when it rains. In this case, the person making the statement knows that it is false; hence, this is called *intentional misrepresentation*. Reckless or careless statements are usually taken by courts to be intentional misrepresentation also, if they are not true.

Negligent, Without Due Diligence

A broker may be careless or negligent in his statements and, as a result, someone is damaged; for example, a broker advertises a three-family apartment with potential income of $480 per month. After the sale, the buyer learns that the neighborhood was zoned for a limit of two families per building. In this case, the broker should have determined the limitation.

Innocent Misrepresentation

A salesperson may make a statement, believing it to be true. As an example of *innocent misrepresentation,* the seller might indicate to the salesperson that the basement is dry, and the salesperson repeats it to the buyer, who relies on it. In this case, if it were later shown to be false, the buyer could probably either sue the seller for damages or cancel the contract. The broker may still be due a commission.

In a recent Kansas case, an agent repeated a seller's statement (not knowing it to be false). The court held the seller liable but not the agent.

Nondisclosure—Concealment

Is mere silence a misrepresentation? In our previous example, assume that the salesperson knew that water came into the basement during heavy rains; however, the buyer never asked anything, and the salesperson remained silent about the matter. Courts have held that it is the responsibility of the principal or agent to disclose *latent defects,* that is, those not observable by reasonable inspection of the property. The salesperson's silence can be considered misrepresentation through *nondisclosure* (fraud). As another example, a broker's silence on a known pending change in zoning or a flaw in the title could also be considered misrepresentation by conceal-ment. If the salesperson had not known about the leaky basement or the broker had not known about the pending change in zoning, the misrepresentation would have been innocent. Suppose that, in the leaky basement example, the seller had recently repainted the basement walls so that evidence of water would not be noticed. A court decision, Batey v. Stone 192 SE2d 528 (Ga. 1972), held this to be fraud, even though no statement was made; thus, intentional misrepresentation (or fraud) can take place by acts as well as words.

In a recent Alabama case, a seller knew his septic tank was faulty but did not reveal this to the broker or buyer. After purchase, the buyer filed suit against the seller and the broker for failure to disclose the defect. The court ruled in favor of the buyer, saying that it was a broker's responsibility to learn about deficiencies and to inform prospective buyers of such defects.

In Texas and North Carolina cases, the seller was aware of the fact that the house was constructed on disturbed soil which had settled or was likely to settle. The court ruled in favor of the purchaser, saying that the seller and/or agent are under a duty to disclose defects or potential problems to prospective buyers.

Recent Ruling

In a recent ruling, an FTC administrative law judge found that a company with head-quarters in New York used deceptive practices and high-pressure tactics to sell thou-sands of undeveloped, isolated, barren lots in New Mexico, Florida, and Missouri as investment properties. The judge ordered the company to stop its unfair practices. In addition, the judge ordered the company to take the following remedial mea-sures.

1. The company must provide the following warning to potential buyers at least two days prior to any sales contract:

   THE SELLER ADVISES YOU THAT IT IS NOT SELLING THE LOTS IN THIS SUBDIVISION AS A FINANCIAL INVESTMENT. THEREFORE, DO NOT COUNT ON YOUR LOT RISING IN VALUE OR YOUR BEING ABLE TO RESELL IT. THE FUTURE VALUE OF LAND IS VERY UNCERTAIN.

2. A ten-day "cooling off" period was ordered during which a customer may cancel a sales contract and company personnel are barred from contacting the customer.

3. Consumers who buy land "site unseen" were given the right to inspect the land six months after the sale and cancel the sale within three days after their on-site inspection.

4. The company was ordered to give written notice to all persons who purchased land from them prior to the date the FTC complaint was issued, advising them of their current rights.

The judge found deceptive practices in the company's repeated claims that the lots were "bargain buys" and would make a "good investment" for the future, when in fact the company's constantly rising prices were three to five times the appraised market value of the lots. The evidence revealed that purchasers usually signed pur-chase contracts at free dinner parties. At these parties, the judge said that prospective purchasers were wined and dined and company salesmen used an "organized of-fense" to work customers up to a high pitch of emotion and then quickly sign them up before this emotional state died away.

Not a Case of Misrepresentation

In a 1978 North Carolina case, an appellate court held that a home buyer, who had unrestricted opportunity to inspect the premises, was not entitled to recover damages from the seller or broker on the basis of their innocent misrepresentation of the square footage of the house. In this case the seller listed and the broker advertised the house as having 1,700 heated square feet. The buyer was shown the inside and the outside of the house by the broker. At the time of the showing, the broker reiterated that the house contained 1,700 heated square feet of living space. The buyer signed a contract to purchase that did not state the square footage of the house. Subsequently, the buyer discovered that the house contained approximately 1,400 square feet.

The court held that the buyer could not recover for misrepresentation because he had access to the correct amount of square footage and should have discovered the mistake. Other courts, however, have upheld buyer's claims in similar situations. Thus the broker has a duty to ascertain the area because of his greater expertise.

Some Suggestions

What can brokers or salespeople do to protect themselves against these possible situations? The following are some positive actions they may take:

1. Ask the seller outright about the roof, basement, septic system, and other potentially problematic aspects of the property. Make a list of facts detailing everything.
2. Guard against making statements regarding unknowns such as the condition of the furnace, presence of termites, or property value. If the buyer asks about them, an expert can be called in.
3. Any stated defects to be taken "as is," such as a damaged swimming pool, should be stated in the contract agreement.
4. The contract should state that the appliances, the furnace, and so on, are to be in good working order on the date of closing.
5. Where work is still being done on a house, the down payment should be held in a trust account until the work is completed.

Thus, we see that misrepresentation is not always within the control of brokers or salespeople; however, they can take certain actions to protect themselves, as well as the buyers and sellers. As of January 1, 1988, all sellers in California must give buyers a written statement (also signed by the agent) listing all known defects in the house.

PROFESSIONAL ASSOCIATIONS

Real estate brokers have organized both nationally and locally to promote high professional standards. The goals and objectives of professional real estate associations are to:

1. Promote high standards
2. Protect the public
3. Exchange ideas and information
4. Support legislation in the interest of the public and of real estate professionals
5. Cooperate in the growth of urban and rural areas with respect to real estate

Other types of real estate specialists can belong to independent professional groups in their special area, or they can join institutes that are part of the NATIONAL ASSOCIATION OF REALTORS®.

SUMMARY

Federal legislation in the areas of civil rights, fair housing, consumer protection, and environmental protection affects the activities of all persons engaged in the real estate business. All people involved in any area of real estate should fully understand these laws and how they affect their occupations. State legislation follows, implements, or supplements the federal regulations, but provisions differ from state to state.

All states have statutes requiring the licensing of real estate brokers and salespeople. Some states also license others in the real estate business. The laws provide a state commission to implement the law and define penalties for violations.

Ethics is an important consideration in all aspects of real estate transactions. Ethical standards appear in codes of professional organizations or state laws and regulations; however, all aspects of ethics are not specifically defined. Therefore, brokers and salespeople should have an understanding of a wide variety of actions that could have unfavorable consequences or tarnish their public image.

TERMS AND CONCEPTS

You can check your understanding of these terms against the glossary or by review of this chapter.

Annual percentage rate	Equal Credit	Latent defects
Biological pollution	Opportunity Act	Misrepresentation
Blockbusting	Fair Housing Act	Nondisclosure
Buyer qualification	Innocent	Property report
Caveat emptor	misrepresentation	Recovery fund
Chemical pollution	Intentional	Regulation Z
Civil Rights Act	misrepresentation	Statement of record
Consumer Credit	Interstate Land Sales Full	Truth-in-Lending Law
Protection Act	Disclosure Act	
Environment		
Environmental impact		
statement		

PROBLEMS

15-1. List several legislative acts that are designed to protect the consumer, and state the intended purpose of each law.

15-2. What arguments can be made for and against consumer protection laws?

15-3. What types of situations are covered by environmental protection laws?

15-4. What factors do you think might be covered in an environmental impact statement?

15-5. List six examples of actions with respect to real estate that would require an environmental impact statement.

15-6. Why do you think that commercial real estate transactions are exempt from RESPA?

15-7. What does *disclosure* mean? List three laws and what they require to be disclosed.

15-8. Why do some federal laws encourage states to establish laws rather than impose federal requirements? Give two examples of laws that do this.

15-9. *Redlining* is defined as a practice whereby lenders refuse to lend money for purchase of homes in certain neighborhoods. Give arguments for and against this practice.

15-10. Give an example of a type of improper activity that may have induced RESPA, Truth-in-Lending, and the Interstate Land Sales Full Disclosure Act.

15-11. What actions can a state Real Estate Commission take to enforce the state law? Can the commission impose fines or imprisonment for violations?

15-12. Can a person recover from a state recovery fund for each of the following? Must other steps be taken first in each case?
   (a) The contract price was $5,000 higher than appraised value.
   (b) A broker represented a septic system as being in good order when it was defective.
   (c) A real estate salesperson stated that a client must purchase title insurance from company A. The client later discovered that she paid $200 more than another company charges.

15-13. If a person sells real estate for others but charges no fee or commission, does he need a license? Discuss.

15-14. List some persons from whom a real estate salesperson cannot receive compensation or gifts of value.

15-15. How does the Bellwood ruling by the U.S. Supreme Court affect real estate brokers?

15-16. In a recent Maine case a buyer purchased an unimproved lot. He relied on the seller's statement that the lot had been approved for septic tank installation, without making further inquiry to verify the statement. After purchase, the buyer learned the lot was not approved for septic system installation. What is the court's decision and why?

After reading each of the following cases, review the text and give your opinion as to whether or not a legal or an ethical violation took place:

15-17. Broker A, as the agent of Seller B, sold a house to Buyer C, filling in a standard contract of purchase drafted by legal counsel. At the time Broker A presented the contract for Buyer C's signature, she explained that the contract was a standard form generally used in the area. She suggested that the buyer have his own attorney review it. Buyer C said he would read it over carefully, and if there was any lack of clarity in it he would consult an attorney about it. He later returned with a signed contract, saying it was clear and satisfactory to him.

At the closing, Buyer C said he misunderstood the date of possession of the property.

15-18. Broker A was approached by Client B to appraise a house for rental purposes. Client B explained he had recently inherited the property, recognized that it had been neglected, and wanted the appraisal in order to have some definite idea of the property's value before discussing it with negotiators for the local urban renewal agency.

Several months later, Client B complained to the broker, specifying that he had been overcharged for the appraisal. Broker A explained that the appraisal fee he had agreed upon with Client B was one-tenth of 1 percent of the valuation shown in his appraisal report.

15-19. As she had done in the past, Broker A mailed to her fellow brokers descriptions of properties listed with her. Her objective was to invite the cooperation of the other brokers. As indicated in her mailing, some of the properties described were listed exclusively with Broker A, and some were listed on an open or nonexclusive basis. Broker B received a copy of Broker A's mailing, became interested in one property described, noted that it was not exclusively listed with Broker A, contacted the owner directly, and obtained his own nonexclusive listing of the property. When this action came to the attention of Broker A, she filed a complaint with the Board of Realtors charging Broker B with unethical conduct.

15-20. Broker A used a classified advertisement including a description of a property with the words, "Call Ms. J, 429–8406."

15-21. Property Manager A, acting as management agent for Owner B, offered a house for rent to a tenant, stating to the prospect that the house was in good condition. Shortly after, the tenant entered into a lease and moved into the house. He later filed a complaint against the property manager charging misrepresentation because he found a clogged sewer line and a defective oven.

15-22. Broker J usually sent out letters to each of the neighbors after he sold a house and the buyers moved in. The letter suggested that the residents should stop by and visit the new neighbor. What do you think of this practice?

15-23. Seller K, in accepting an offer from Buyer B through Broker X, insisted that the contract contain a clause stating that the house is purchased "as is." What should the broker do? What should he say to the clients?

15-24. List some statements that could be considered "puffing."

15-25. List some defects in a home where nondisclosure could be considered as misrepresentation. What do these defects have in common?

15-26. The Beyers moved into a home they had just purchased through Broker B. One week later it rained hard and about an inch of water came into the basement. The possibility of this defect was never mentioned during the negotiations. The broker claimed that he knew nothing about the problem before the Beyers mentioned it. What can the Beyers do?

15-27. Mr. James, a broker, has the policy that the seller should always set the purchase price of the property. James has never suggested to a seller that the price was too low or too high, nor has he ever turned down a listing. What are the business, ethical, and legal considerations of his policy?

15-28. Mr. and Mrs. Seller advertised their own home and located the buyers. Due to lack of knowledge on how to handle the sale contract, they went to Jack Broker for assistance. Jack said he could help only if he wrote up a listing agreement, which he would do for 3 percent instead of the usual 6 percent. Comment on this situation.

SUPPLEMENTARY READINGS

Bergfield, Philip B. *Real Estate Law.* New York: McGraw-Hill, 1979. Chapter 21.

Ellis, John T., and Beck, John A. *Guide to the ASI Real Estate License Examination.* Englewood Cliffs, N.J.: Prentice-Hall, 1984.

French, William B.; Martin, Stephen J.; and Battle III, Thomas. *Guide to Real Estate Licensing Examinations,* 5th ed. New York: John Wiley & Sons, 1988.

Galaty, Fillmore W.; Allaway, Wellington J.; and Kyle, Robert C. *Modern Real Estate Practice,* 11th ed. Chicago: Real Estate Education Corporation, 1988. Chapter 21.

Harwood, Bruce. *Real Estate Principles,* 4th ed. Reston, Va.: Reston, 1986. Chapter 18.

Henderson, Thomas P.; Johnson, Ross H.; Kruse, Dennis; and Ficek, Edmund F. *Real Estate Examinations Guide.* Columbus, Ohio: Charles E. Merrill, 1977. Chapter 12 and Appendixes.

Henszey, Benjamin N., and Friedman, Ronald M. *Real Estate Law,* 2nd ed. New York: Wiley, 1984.

NATIONAL ASSOCIATION OF REALTORS®. *Interpretation of the Code of Ethics.* Chicago: 1978.

Pivar, William H. *Real Estate Ethics.* Chicago: Real Estate Education Company, 1979.

Reilly, John W. *The Language of Real Estate,* 3rd ed. Chicago: Real Estate Education Company, 1989.

Reilly, John W., and Vitousek, Paige B. *Questions and Answers to Help You Pass the Real Estate Exam,* 2nd ed. Chicago: Real Estate Education Co., 1984.

Rose, Daniel. "Landmarks Preservation and the Law." *Real Estate Issues,* Summer 1979.

Semenow, Robert W. *Questions and Answers on Real Estate.* Englewood Cliffs, N.J.: Prentice-Hall, 1978. Chapter 9.

Shenkel, William M. *Modern Real Estate Principles,* 3rd ed. Dallas: Business Publications, 1984. Chapters 3, 4, 16, and 22.

Smith, Halbert C.; Tschappat, Carl J.; and Racster, Ronald L. *Real Estate and Urban Development,* 3rd ed. Homewood, Ill.: Irwin, 1981. Chapters 15, 17, and 18.

State laws governing licensing of brokers and salespeople can be obtained from the office of the real estate commissioner (or equivalent) in each state. (See Appendix C for the addresses of state agencies.)

Tosh, Dennis, and Ordway, Nicholas. *Real Estate Principles for License Preparation.* Reston, Va.: Reston, 1985.

CHAPTER 16
The Transaction— from Offer to Closing

Prior chapters have dealt with a great many facets of real estate. The present chapter will integrate this material as it applies to a residential property transaction from offer to closing (settlement). Chapter 17 will then cover the completion of the transaction with the closing.

The 1986 Tax Reform Act requires that those responsible for real estate closings after January 1, 1987, must report the terms of the sale to the IRS.

OVERVIEW OF TRANSACTION

Once a client has decided to purchase a parcel of real estate, the broker or sales-person plays a key part in bringing about a valid agreement between the two parties. The agent should also assure to the greatest extent possible that the necessary steps take place to prepare for the closing and final conveyance of the property from seller to buyer. The broker has an ethical responsibility to assist both the seller and the buyer, who may lack knowledge or experience in the steps that must take place prior to the closing. The salesperson and broker are also fulfilling their own inter-ests, since in most cases the seller, as principal, plans to pay the broker from the proceeds of the sale. This chapter will detail the events from the time the buyer decides to make an offer on a parcel of real estate up through the point where all the contingencies are settled and questions of title validity are resolved.

As discussed in Chapter 4, the transfer of title to real estate from one party to another is usually initiated by a written contractual agreement. The primary reason is to protect the interests of both parties. When an item of personal property is purchased, such as an automobile or refrigerator, the item purchased is quickly turned over to the buyer. Real estate is different because, at the time of agreement to buy, the purchaser has no assurance that the title is without defects or even that the seller is in fact the sole or true owner. A contract is necessary to bind the purchaser and seller while the necessary investigations and steps are carried out to bring about a valid conveyance of the property from the seller to the buyer.

The lay person may consider the documents and procedures cumbersome; how-ever, shortcuts can lead to problems. The omission of provisions or failure to use precise terminology can lead to disagreements or misunderstandings, and possibly even lawsuits.

The flow chart in Figure 16–1 shows the steps involved in a typical residential transaction from the offer until the closing (or settlement). The chart also shows who usually has the primary responsibility for each step.

THE OFFER AND ACCEPTANCE

Prior to the sale, the property had been listed with a real estate broker at an agreed-upon list price. The listing agreement between the broker and seller provides that a commission will be paid to the broker when she has produced a buyer who is ready, willing, and able to purchase the property. Several steps are necessary to bring about this contractual agreement between the buyer and seller. Assume a broker or one of her salespeople locates a prospective purchaser who has inspected a house and wants to make an offer. If the prospective purchaser is very anxious to buy the property and believes that the price is firm (i.e., the seller will not reduce the price), she may offer to pay the list price. The purchaser might also offer to pay the list price if the property is newly listed or she otherwise feels that someone else may stop her from getting the property by coming in with another offer at the list price. The salesperson/broker first prepares the offer. The salesperson/broker se-cures the purchaser's signature and presents the written offer along with the buyer's deposit check, or *earnest money,* as it is usually called, to the seller for acceptance. If there are no contingencies or exceptions to the seller's listing conditions and no other offers have been previously accepted, then the broker has provided a ready, willing, and able buyer and has earned the commission.

Seller's Attorney	Seller	Real Estate Agent	Buyer	Buyer's Attorney	Financial Institution
			Inspect property		
			Make offer		
		Prepare offer			
			Sign offer and make earnest money deposit		
May review offer				May review offer	
	Accept, reject, or make counteroffer	Earnest money deposit in escrow account			
			Accept, reject, or make counteroffer		
If a two-step contract, prepare formal contract		Signed agreement *			
	Clear contingencies	Assist buyer and seller in each step as needed	Seek financing		Appraisal and credit check — Commitment letter and estimate of closing costs

**

From this point, the escrow agent and/or attorneys or their delegates prepare deed, obtain survey, handle title search or title insurance and prepare other legal documents. (Also see Figures 17–1 and 17–2).

Note: If there is to be an escrow closing, the materials can be turned over to the escrow agent at * or at**

Figure 16–1 Flow chart of steps involved in a typical transaction to purchase residential real estate

In some states, it is customary to use a *deposit receipt* when the broker is accepting earnest money from a prospective buyer where the intent is to meet all terms of the listing. When the broker plans to use a deposit receipt, it becomes more important that the listing agreement define all terms carefully. The well-designed deposit receipt will contain the provisions of a lawful binding agreement as discussed in Chapter 4.

Listing Is Not an Offer to Sell

If a broker presented an offer from a buyer at the full listing price without contingencies, does the seller have to sell? The answer is NO! For both an *offer* and an *acceptance* are required to have a binding contract. If a listing could be construed to be an offer to sell, then acceptance at full price would be the contract. If the listing is not an offer, then the buyer is merely making an offer to purchase.

Courts have held that the listing agreement is only a private contract between the broker and the property owner and does not concern the buyer. It is an agency agreement that binds a seller to pay a commission if the broker finds a buyer. If the buyer's offer meets all the terms specified in the listing agreement, the seller may owe a commission. However, the buyer cannot force the consummation of the sale unless the buyer's offer is accepted by the seller or her duly authorized agent (i.e., attorney in fact under a written power of attorney from the seller).

Inspection of the Property

In any transaction, the buyer or her representative should inspect the property for any noticeable *defects* or problems. A prudent buyer will also question the seller about defects not readily observable *(latent defects)* such as roof leaks or basement seepage, which could only be noticed in wet weather. The seller and the broker have a legal responsibility to disclose any known latent defects to the buyer, and the lack of disclosure or falsification is possible cause for rescinding the contract later or for recovery of damages from either the seller or the broker. The principle of *caveat emptor* (let the buyer beware) does, however, apply to defects that can be observed by a reasonable inspection. Sale contracts usually contain a clause that the buyer has inspected the property and finds it acceptable. Some home sellers disclose any known defects and then sell the home "as is" to avoid liability for problems that may arise after the sale.

Negotiation and Contingencies

The case where the prospective buyer offers at full list price and in accord with all of the seller's conditions is not common. In most instances, the buyer makes an offer to purchase either at an amount below the listed price or with certain contingencies, exceptions, or provisions. Some common differences between the listing and offer are as follows:

1. Offer at a price lower than the list price
2. Offer contingent upon buyer being able to obtain a mortgage at a specified interest rate and repayment term
3. Offer contingent upon occupancy by the buyer at a date different from that in the listing agreement

4. Offer contingent upon including certain additional items with the sale, such as carpeting, TV antenna, draperies, or appliances
5. Offer contingent upon the seller giving the buyer a ***purchase-money mortgage***— essentially a loan made by the seller to the prospective buyer when the buyer may not have a sufficient down payment and asks the seller to accept a mortgage on the property as part of the price
6. Offer contingent upon evidence of freedom from termites
7. Offer contingent upon sale of other property presently owned by the buyer

All of these contingencies except the last one can usually be resolved or negotiated within a few days. The last contingency depends upon an event that is highly uncertain and, therefore, would usually be unacceptable to the seller. Acceptance of condition number 7 might tie up the property for an indefinite period of time. Sometimes a seller can accept this provision with the condition that if the seller receives another offer, the first offeror has five days after notification to sign the contract without the contingency.

After the broker or the salesperson has prepared the offer, including the contingencies desired by the potential buyer, the offer is presented to the seller with an earnest money deposit. The judicious buyer will specify in the offer the time limit within which the seller must accept the offer. If the offer is not accepted by the specified date, the buyer can then proceed to make another offer without the risk of being under contract to purchase two properties. The buyer can, however, revoke the offer at any time *prior* to acceptance.

If the seller accepts the buyer's offer, she will sign it. If the offer is made up correctly, as discussed in Chapter 4 on contract law, a binding agreement exists. Frequently, however, the seller may agree to some of the proposed conditions in the written offer but not to others. She may make a ***counteroffer,*** whereby she agrees to some of the conditions and proposes a compromise on the price. Typical compromise conditions might include:

1. A change in price
2. A requirement that the buyer apply for a mortgage within three days and obtain a commitment within two weeks, or some other specified number of days, assuring the seller that the property will not be off the market for a long period in case the buyer has difficulty obtaining a mortgage commitment from a financial institution

If a counteroffer is to be made, the salesperson/broker will make the changes in the offer form and have the seller initial them and sign the form; then the counteroffer is presented to the prospective buyer. Legally, this means the seller has rejected the original offer. The seller cannot later change her mind and accept it and require the buyer to abide by the original offer. Upon being advised of the counteroffer, the buyer can now either accept it or reject it or make a further counteroffer. This process continues until either an agreement is reached or one party discontinues the process.

Postoccupancy Agreement

Sometimes a seller will desire to occupy the sold property for a period of time after the closing. Normally it is preferable for occupancy to be given on the date of closing; however, there may be special circumstances. If this extended occupancy is to be allowed, the best procedure is to enter into a ***postoccupancy agreement*** rather than a lease, since the lease could inadvertently give the seller additional rights under applicable landlord and tenant laws. The postoccupancy agreement is essentially a license to stay in the property for a fixed short period. The buyer should receive a security deposit to be held in escrow until the buyer makes final inspection of the property. Sometimes a provision is made for the rent to increase significantly if the specified occupancy termination date is exceeded.

A BINDING AGREEMENT

In the selling process, the real estate broker needs to bring about a binding agreement between the seller and buyer such that any differences between them are resolved. A more formal contract can be drawn up later by legal counsel, who may add other suggested provisions. In some cases, the buyer and seller might go directly to legal counsel to have the contract drawn up without going through the offer and acceptance process. In other cases, the buyer and seller can draw up a valid contract themselves without the aid of a broker or a lawyer; however, legal advice is recommended to make sure a binding agreement is formed (Chapter 4). If the initial document drawn up is the final contract, it is called a ***one-step transaction.***

Some offer and acceptance forms provide that a more formal contract will be drawn up within two to ten days *(two-step transaction);* however, the buyer and seller should always assume that the form being signed is a valid contract.

Forms

Printed offer and acceptance forms for transfer of real estate can be purchased in most stationery stores. State or local Boards of REALTORS® have their own recommended forms. However, there is actually no set required form or format. A typical offer to purchase agreement form is shown in Figure 16–2. In our discussions in this chapter, other clauses will be discussed in addition to those shown in that figure.

Provisions in the Agreement

It is sometimes said that the usual offer and acceptance is not a binding agreement; however, its validity as a contract depends on its provisions. It is not necessary to have a lawyer prepare a contract to make it binding. Both parties should assume that they are entering an enforceable agreement. In Chapter 4 we saw that a binding contract has the following elements:

1. Competent parties to the contract—seller and purchaser
2. Offer and acceptance—a meeting of the minds
3. Consideration—each party must obligate herself
4. Adequate property description
5. In writing and for a legal purpose

In the case of married persons, it is frequently said that it takes two to sell and one to buy. Either of the married partners can become obligated to purchase; however, both parties must agree to sell property that is owned jointly.

OFFER TO PURCHASE AGREEMENT

This AGREEMENT made as of _____, 19_____,

among _____ (herein called "Purchaser"),

and _____ (herein called "Seller"),

and _____ (herein called "Broker"),
provides that Purchaser agrees to buy through Broker as agent for Seller, and Seller agrees to sell the following described real estate, and all improvements
thereon, located in the jurisdiction of _____,
(all herein called "the property"): _____

_____, and more commonly known as _____

_____(street address).

    1. The purchase price of the property is _____

Dollars ($_____), and such purchase price shall be paid as follows:
_____

    2. Purchaser has made a deposit of _____ Dollars ($_____)
with Broker, receipt of which is hereby acknowledged, and such deposit shall be held by Broker in escrow until the date of settlement and then applied
to the purchase price, or returned to Purchaser if the title to the property is not marketable.

    3. Seller agrees to convey the property to Purchaser by Deed with the usual covenants of title and free and clear from all monetary encumbrances,
tenancies, liens (for taxes or otherwise), except as may be otherwise provided above, but subject to applicable restrictive covenants of record. Seller further
agrees to deliver possession of the property to Purchaser on the date of settlement and to pay the expense of preparing the deed of conveyance.

    4. Settlement shall be made at _____ on or before
_____, 19_____, or as soon thereafter as title can be examined and necessary documents prepared, with allowance of
a reasonable time for Seller to correct any defects reported by the title examiner.

    5. All taxes, interest, rent, and impound escrow deposits, if any, shall be prorated as of the date of settlement.

    6. All risk of loss or damage to the property by fire, windstorm, casualty, or other cause is assumed by Seller until the date of settlement.

    7. Purchaser and Seller agree that Broker was the sole procuring cause of this Contract of Purchase, and Seller agrees to pay Broker for services
rendered a cash fee of _____ per cent of the purchase price. If either Purchaser or Seller defaults under such Contract, such defaulting party shall
be liable for the cash fee of Broker and any expenses incurred by the non-defaulting party in connection with this transaction.

Subject to: _____

_____

_____

_____

    8. Purchaser represents that an inspection satisfactory to Purchaser has been made of the property, and Purchaser agrees to accept the property in
its present condition except as may be otherwise provided in the description of the property above.

    9. This Contract of Purchase constitutes the entire agreement among the parties and may not be modified or changed except by written instrument
executed by all of the parties, including Broker.

    10. This Contract of Purchase shall be construed, interpreted, and applied according to the law of the jurisdiction of _____ and shall
be binding upon and shall inure to the benefit of the heirs, personal representatives, successors, and assigns of the parties.

All parties to this agreement acknowledge receipt of a certified copy.

WITNESS the following signatures:

_____   _____
Seller   Purchaser

_____   _____
Seller   Purchaser

_____
Broker

Deposit Rec'd $ _____

Personal Check   Cash

Cashier's Check   Company Check

Sales Agent:

Figure 16–2   A sample offer to purchase agreement form

The sales agreement should also contain the following facts:

1. Date agreement is prepared.
2. Names and addresses of purchaser and seller.
3. Name of broker (not necessary for a binding agreement between purchaser and seller).
4. Location of property.
5. Description of property (usually the legal description; it must be sufficient to assure there is a meeting of minds concerning the property involved). The street address is usually included.
6. The price to be paid for the property, defining the earnest money deposit made at the time of the acceptance of the offer and exactly how and when the balance of the purchase price is to be paid. Any elements left to later negotiation may make the contract unenforceable. Provisions may include the following:
   (a) Additional deposit to be paid upon signing a formal contract, usually bringing the total deposit up to about 10 percent of the purchase price (if a two-step agreement).
   (b) Assumption of the seller's existing mortgage by the buyer.
   (c) Seller to take a purchase-money mortgage from the buyer.
   (d) Balance due at closing. It will often specify payment in cash or certified check, since ownership of the property will be transferred at the closing and the seller will not want to risk being involved with a bad check.
7. Type of deed to be furnished. The buyer should normally require a warranty deed (or a deed with English covenants). This is the most desirable deed from the buyer's viewpoint. In some states the *grant deed,* backed up by title insurance, is common. In a *warranty deed,* the seller assumes full responsibility for a valid title without limit of time and, at any time in the future, the buyer has recourse for damages against the seller if the title is defective.
8. Place and date of settlement (closing).
9. Provision for proration of taxes, interest (if an assumption), and rent or expenses if an income property.
10. Responsibility if damage occurs to property before settlement. The fairest provision is to have seller responsible as long as she has possession of the property.
11. Statement establishing broker's fee may be given.
12. Contingencies (discussed in next section):
    (a) Provision for termite inspection.
    (b) Ability of buyer to obtain an adequate mortgage at a specified percentage of purchase price and specified interest rate.
    (c) Provisions related to tenants, easements, or other factors.
13. Statement that purchaser has inspected property and finds it acceptable (does not waive latent or hidden defects).
14. Signature of purchaser and seller (broker's signature is optional).

CLEARING CONTINGENCIES

Conditions in the agreement stating actions that must take place before the agreement becomes binding are called *contingencies.* The buyer may insert a clause that the contract is contingent "upon her obtaining an 80 percent mortgage at no greater than 14 percent interest for 30 years." The buyer should specify that a certificate will be provided showing no termite infestation or structural damage, or that if termites are found, the seller will pay for treatment. If the buyer plans a commercial venture, for example, she may insert a clause that the sale is contingent on getting the zoning changed. As another example, the buyer may specify that the sale is contingent on being able to obtain the seller's existing liquor license. In the case of a building lot, the contingency may specify favorable soil tests for drainage or the ability to support footings for an eight-story building.

If a conditional clause is put in the contract by the buyer for her own benefit, she may later waive it and still have a valid contract. If the buyer inserts a condition that requires her own action, such as securing a mortgage, but she makes no effort to secure the mortgage, the clause is no longer in effect. The buyer is still bound to the remaining terms of the contract. The seller should protect herself against unreasonable delay to fulfill a condition by specifying a time allowed for the buyer to apply for a mortgage. The seller takes the risk that, if the buyer changes her mind on the purchase, she may make only a token effort to obtain the mortgage. The contingency should also specify the terms of the mortgage required, or the buyer may judge the terms unacceptable. If no terms were specified, a court will determine whether or not the terms obtained by the buyer are reasonable. If found to be reasonable, the court will enforce the contract.

It is in the broker's interest to see that these conditions are cleared as soon as possible. For instance, she could order the termite inspection, with concurrence of the seller. She could use her contacts to find a mortgage lender, help the buyer apply for the mortgage, and then follow up with the financial institution to obtain a response. A letter of commitment furnished by the financial lending institution to make a mortgage loan at the specified rate will satisfy this condition, but the lending institution will want an appraisal and credit report first. If for any reason the buyer will not be able to obtain a mortgage, prompt determination of that fact will permit the seller to place the property back on the market. Sometimes a *back-up offer* is written if another client is also interested in the property. If done, the second offer should be an unconditional offer to become binding if the first offer fails or to become inoperative if all contingencies in the first offer are fulfilled.

ESCROW

When the agreement is completed and the contingencies are cleared, the buyer and seller will need to decide if they will have a *regular closing (settlement)* with a meeting or if they will want an *escrow closing*. This chapter will discuss the advantages and disadvantages of the escrow closing, and Chapter 17 will explain the closing steps by means of flow charts.

If the buyer and seller agree on an *escrow closing,* they will jointly select a third person, called an *escrow agent, escrow holder, escrowee,* or *escrow officer,* to carry out the remaining steps to complete the real estate transaction. The escrow procedure is used widely on the West Coast. It is used in other areas when one or more of the parties cannot be present at the closing or for other reasons. The escrow agent is the agent of both the buyer and the seller. The buyer gives sufficient funds to the escrow agent to complete the transaction, along with precise written instructions. The seller gives the escrow agent the deed and other documents, along with instructions. The instructions are usually contained in an *escrow agreement* between the buyer, seller, and escrow agent. After all instructions have been complied with, the escrow agent will convey the property.

The escrow agent can be a bank, a title insurance company, or an independent escrow company. One dictionary defines *escrow* as "a deed, bond, or other written engagement, given to a third person, and delivered to the grantee when specified conditions have been fulfilled." The escrow agent is a trustee who holds the money and documents but usually does not perform the functions of an attorney. In California, escrow agents are licensed, bonded corporations. They are permitted to prepare legal forms for buyer and seller signature that in other parts of the United States only attorneys at law can prepare. In some cases, the escrow agreement gives the escrow agent the responsibility to clear all contingencies.

Why Escrows Are Used

The use of escrow in real property transactions dates back to England in the fifteenth century. Some advantages of the escrow method of closing follow.

Conditional and Irrevocable Agreement

When the documents are turned over to the escrow agent, the money from the buyer is turned over also. This deposit is **conditional** and **irrevocable** in that the buyer will get the money back if all the conditions of the contract agreement (such as clear title) cannot be met; however, the buyer cannot revoke the agreement if all conditions are met. This is also true without an escrow closing; however, the nonescrow closing may require court action to reach a settlement of differences. Therefore, we can say that the escrow closing is less likely to "fall through."

Death of Seller

In an escrow closing, the title to the property actually passes to the buyer when the materials are turned over to the escrow agent. When the escrow is not used, death of the seller before the closing often raises complications in executing the deed, sometimes resulting in a judicial proceeding. If the deed was properly executed by the grantor, the principle of **relation back** would cause title to be passed at the time the deed was delivered to the escrow agent.

Several Parties

Sometimes real estate transactions involve several parties, especially if a tract is being split up or if property exchanges are involved. A formal meeting for all parties at a regular closing may become burdensome, so an escrow closing is used.

Broker Tasks

In a regular closing, the listing broker may have responsibility for preparing some of the closing papers. She also is accountable for the earnest money deposit until the time of closing. With an escrow closing, the broker is relieved of this responsibility. Also, the death of the broker could not interfere with an escrow closing.

SEEKING A LOAN

A borrower who takes sufficient time to shop around and learn the types of mortgages, interest rates, and other terms available from various lenders can often achieve a significant savings. In any locality, it is common to find differences in mortgage terms available from alternative lenders. For a $50,000 loan, a one-quarter of 1 percent reduction in interest rate means about a $10 reduction in each monthly payment. The many new types of mortgages provide certain advantages and risks. The borrower who has a few days available to select a lender can often take advantage of these possibilities. A borrower who is in the locality only for a weekend while hunting for a property may have to rely on the real estate agent's knowledge of available mortgage terms.

After evaluating alternative sources of financing, the borrower can apply to one or more lenders for a loan. The application form is prepared, and the lending institution evaluates the borrower and the property. The lender may have limited funds and thus will be selecting prospective borrowers on the basis of the risks involved with the borrower or the property. In other cases, where funds are readily available, the lender will be making loans as long as the borrower and the property meet the standards set by the lender.

The loan officer can apply certain rules of thumb to determine if the application process should continue; for example:

1. Does the client have a stable job?
2. Will monthly payments for mortgage, taxes, and insurance exceed 25 to 30 percent of client's gross monthly income?
3. Do other existing monthly payments on long-term obligations plus (2) above exceed 45 percent of gross monthly income?
4. Is the real estate acceptable?
5. Does the borrower have sufficient liquid assets for down payment, closing, and moving expenses?
6. What is the borrower's reason for moving?

When the loan officer can answer the above questions favorably, she can proceed to obtain a loan application from the borrower.

Certain risks enter into the decision to accept or reject specific mortgage applications. Some of these relate to the borrower, while other risks relate to the specific property used as security for the mortgage.

As a precaution against risks related to the borrower, the lender interviews the prospective borrower, runs a credit check, and verifies information on employment and borrower's available assets.

As a precaution against risks related to the real estate itself, the lender has the property inspected and appraised, has the title checked or insured, investigates required property insurance, and evaluates potential zoning or neighborhood changes.

To be approved, a borrower must have the available cash for the down payment, closing costs, and moving expenses. The borrower's income must also be sufficient to handle the periodic mortgage payments, property taxes, and insurance. The borrower's other long-term obligations and living style need to be considered as part of a total evaluation. Most lending institutions send a Request for Verification of Employment to the borrower's employer for verification of income and evaluation of the probability of continued employment. They also send a Request for Verification of Deposit to the borrower's bank, mutual funds, and other accounts.

A *property appraisal* protects both the lender and the borrower, and is, therefore, a key step in the lender's decision-making process. The amount of the loan is based on the appraised value or price paid for the real estate, whichever is less.

Most lenders employ a professional to perform the appraisal, at the borrower's expense. Appraisal methods and procedures are discussed in Chapter 19.

A *commitment* by the lending institution to the borrower is a key step in the lending process. It commits the lender to provide a loan to the particular buyer on a specific property at a certain interest rate and for a set number of years. The commitment also designates a time limit (such as thirty, sixty, or ninety days) beyond which the lender may not honor the commitment. Prior to giving the commitment, the lender will have evaluated the property and checked the creditworthiness of the borrower. The lender also considers the market conditions, such as interest rates and inflation risks. Since checking the title takes more time and involves legal costs, the lender usually issues a commitment without a title search, but reserves the right to deny the loan if the title is not clear or title insurance is not obtainable.

The loan commitment is an important step because it permits the contract for purchase of the real estate to become binding. The sale agreement normally contains a clause making the contract contingent upon the buyer's ability to secure a mortgage for a given amount at a certain rate and term. When a loan commitment satisfies this contingency, the seller then has a binding agreement, and the real estate agent has earned a commission.

STEPS OR POSSIBLE OBSTACLES TO COMPLETION OF THE TRANSACTION

The parties to the transaction and the broker should understand the types of problems that can be encountered and their consequences. Two categories of obstacles could prevent the completion of the transaction. The first type is the failure of one party, either intentionally or unintentionally, to carry out her obligations. The second includes defects in title or the inability of the seller or buyer to conform to a contingency clause in the contract. This second category prevents the fulfillment of the agreement and would usually make the contract null and void, unless both parties were willing to change the contract and accept the conditions. Some other steps are also necessary prior to closing the transaction.

Failure to Perform

Either the buyer or the seller might fail to carry out one or more of the provisions stated in the contractual agreement. This failure to perform usually does not affect the right of the broker to her commission; however, it will interfere with the completion or closing of the contract and thus delay the availability of the commission or result in litigation. If one party fails to perform in accordance with the contractual agreement, there are various remedies available to the other party. (These are discussed in Chapter 4 and reviewed here.) They are similar whether it be the buyer or seller who reneges; however, it is not as easy for the seller to enforce some remedies as it is for the buyer.

Sometimes the seller changes her mind or is unwilling to go through with the agreement. She may receive a better offer or decide not to sell. In this case, the buyer may agree that the contract be rescinded and ask for return of the earnest money together with any costs that may have been incurred. A second alternative would be to sue for breach of contract, with the intent of securing damages for the breach of agreement. The third alternative is to sue for specific performance. A court can force either party to carry out the contract agreement and complete the transaction. This forced compliance to the contract is called *specific performance.*

A buyer may also have a change of mind. For example, if she had intended to move to the town to take a new job and the job offer was canceled, she would not buy the house. If the buyer refused to carry out the contractual obligation to purchase the property, the seller may sue for damages, sue for specific performance, or declare the contract void and keep the earnest money or deposit. If the buyer who refuses to carry out the contract was from out of state or did not own real estate, the cost of enforcing the contract may not be worth the effort. Forfeiture of the earnest money is often the most practical course of action. In this case, the broker may settle for part of the earnest money in lieu of a full commission, especially if the broker regains the listing and the chance to sell the property again.

In either of these cases, the party who refuses to comply with the contract should be advised of the potential results of failure to perform. In the case of the buyer with the canceled job offer, the broker could suggest that the buyer confirm the obligation to buy and then have the broker resell the property.

Marketability of Title

A *marketable title* is a title free from all liens and encumbrances. Conversely, an unmarketable title either has a serious defect or is encumbered. Normally, the encumbrances are to be removed by settlement or suit. Before settlement and transfer of title, the purchaser or mortgage lending institution should require an examination of the title to see if there are any defects or encumbrances. Four types of title examination procedures are used to determine the marketability of the title: (a) abstract and opinion; (b) attorney direct search and opinion; (c) title insurance; and (d) the Torrens System.

Abstract and Opinion

When an abstract is used, an abstractor searches the records and prepares an *abstract* (chain of title) showing all recorded legal instruments affecting the property. The abstractor certifies that the abstract is complete and turns it over to the purchaser's attorney who renders an opinion on the marketability of the title.

Attorney Direct Search and Opinion

The attorney makes a direct examination of the records in the recorder's office, compiles a *brief of title,* and renders an opinion as to the marketability of the title. The purchaser and the lending institution rely on the opinion of the attorney. If the attorney has made a mistake and the title later turns out to be defective, the purchaser can sue the lawyer for damages. A lawyer will usually carry insurance against this risk.

Title Insurance

Title insurance companies are authorized to do business in the various states in which they operate. They issue policies insuring the title to property on the basis of the abstract or the company's own records. As in any title examination, the records must be updated to the closing date of the transaction. If a subsequent defect in title becomes evident, the insurance company must pay the costs or losses of the insured owner. (See Chapter 12.)

Survey

The buyer should find out if a recent survey of the property exists. If not, a survey should be performed. The *survey* will identify the exact boundaries of the property and determine if all structures are completely within property boundaries. It will establish whether the improvements are in complete compliance with municipal ordinances, such as being set back a minimum distance from the lot line of any structures. It also will show if any structures on the property encroach upon property belonging to someone else. A garage extending onto the neighboring property is an example of an *encroachment.* Encroachments onto the property would also be identified.

Surveys are performed by licensed land surveyors. They are an essential step prior to any contemplated purchase of real estate, new property construction, modification to existing structures, or fence construction. The survey assures that the structure would comply with all existing setback requirements. It would also establish if a fence is within the property line. The survey is especially important if any new construction is part of the purchased property. The drawing showing the results of the survey should then be turned over for examination as part of the title search. Since many mortgage institutions require a survey by a licensed surveyor, the buyer should coordinate with the mortgage company to avoid duplication of effort and cost.

Destruction of the Property

What happens if structures on the property are destroyed by fire or windstorm after the contract agreement? The common-law rule is that the property has been sold upon signing of the contract, and the buyer is obligated to go through with the purchase transaction. Another view states that the seller has agreed to provide the property in the condition existing at the time of agreement and, therefore, further risk is the *seller's.* Laws or court decisions in California, Connecticut, Illinois, Kentucky, Maine, Massachusetts, Michigan, New Hampshire, New York, Oregon, Rhode Island, South Carolina, South Dakota, and Wisconsin have put the risk on the seller who, having possession, is in the best position to protect the property. In all states, the risk is placed on the seller where loss is due to seller negligence or where a delay in closing is the fault of the seller or a good marketable title could not be furnished. In the absence of any specific provision in the contract, a court may set an equitable settlement.

The party in possession is in the better position to prevent fire damage. Thus, possession is an important factor in determining liability. Some states have adopted the Uniform Vendor and Purchaser Risk Act, which provides that, in the absence of specific provisions in the contract, the party in possession is liable for destruction of the property between the time of contract signing and the closing.

A well-written contract will specify exactly what is to happen if the property is damaged or destroyed so that litigation will not be necessary. A commonly used clause provides that, in case the property is damaged, the buyer will accept the insurance and the remainder of the damaged property as settlement. With this clause, the purchaser needs to make sure that the insurance coverage is adequate not only to restore or replace the property, but also to compensate for the lack of ability to use the property as a place to live or source of income while being rebuilt. If the contract does not contain a specific provision to cover damage or destruction of the property, it is best for both parties to assume that they would have the responsibility and protect their respective interests by seeing that there is adequate insurance.

Time Is of the Essence

If an agreement specifies that *time is of the essence,* it means that the parties have agreed that time is a critical factor and that failure to conform to dates specified will cause a breach of contract that can terminate the deal. If this clause is not in the contract, either party has a reasonable amount of time to perform after the date specified for closing. Since it is easy for delays to come about in the transaction, this clause should not be used unless dates are critical.

Death of One Party

A contract will normally state that the agreement is binding on heirs. If either the buyer or seller dies, the other can enforce the contract against the decedent's estate. If the sellers are joint tenants and one dies, the survivor then has legal title and is bound to complete the contract. If husband and wife have contracted to purchase real property and one dies, the survivor and the estate of the deceased would be liable to the seller if there were default on the contract.

Warranties or Representations by Seller

Sometimes the seller makes warranties or representations in the contract regarding such factors as zoning, condition of septic system, or nonreceipt of violation notices. The best procedure for the buyer is to state in the contract that the representation or warranty survives the closing. Another procedure is to place the warranty in the deed also. If either of these is not done or the representation is stated in the contract as a condition and the buyer goes ahead and closes without making sure the warranty is met, the buyer, by closing, will be held to have either agreed the condition was met or to have waived the warranty. This is called a *merger of the contract into the deed.*

Real Estate Settlement Procedures Act

The Real Estate Settlement Procedures Act *(RESPA)* was first enacted by Congress in 1974 and amended in 1975. The primary objective of the act was to assist home buyers in understanding the settlement process and the related costs. By requiring the lending institution to provide a "good faith" estimate of all of these costs for the home buyer, it was reasoned that home buyers could shop around and perhaps obtain better terms. The act requires the use of a standard form when a lending institution finances the sale of a one-family residence. A prospective buyer who applies to a lending institution is furnished with the booklet, *Settlement Costs and*

You—A HUD Guide for Home Buyers.[1] This booklet describes the many aspects of a settlement under the following categories:

1. *What happens and when.* This describes the sequence of events from the time a home is selected until the settlement. Chapters 16 and 17 of this book cover these same events.
2. *Shopping for services.* This portion deals with the role of the real estate broker, selecting an attorney, selecting a mortgage lender, and securing title services.
3. *Home buyers' rights.* This section describes the estimates the borrower is entitled to receive, including effective interest rates. It also describes certain unfair practices and the rights of the home buyer to file complaints to HUD.
4. *Home buyers' obligations.* This section describes the obligations of the home buyer to repay the loan and to maintain the property in a proper state of repair.

Part Two of the booklet provides an item-by-item discussion of possible settlement services home buyers may require and for which they may be charged. The booklet contains the Uniform Settlement Statement form along with worksheets for use in comparing costs.

Other Objectives of RESPA

In addition to providing assistance to home buyers, the act provides them with certain other safeguards. It prohibits the acceptance of fees or *kickbacks* for referrals where no service is performed. For example, a title insurance company could not pay a fee to an attorney for referral of business. RESPA also prohibits a seller of real property from requiring that the buyer purchase title insurance from a particular company. Escrow deposits or *impounds* are payments collected along with the mortgage payments that are placed in a special account to pay property taxes or insurance when due. Some lenders do not pay interest to the borrower on these deposits. RESPA prohibits the lending institution from collecting amounts greater than those needed to make the tax and insurance payments.

Itemized Disclosure

The act provides that an itemized disclosure (settlement statement) be provided to both the buyer and the seller on a standard form. The following items or costs must be specified.

1. Contract sales price
2. Personal property
3. Settlement charges
4. Prorated adjustments paid by seller
5. Gross amount due from borrower
6. Deposit or earnest money
7. Principal amount of loan(s)
8. Existing loan(s) taken subject to
9. Prorations credited to borrower
10. Total amounts paid by or in behalf of borrower

---

[1]*Settlement Costs and You—A HUD Guide for Home Buyers.* Available from savings and loan institutions or others handling mortgages. Washington, D.C.: Department of Housing and Urban Development, 1976.

11. Cash required from borrower
12. Real estate brokers' sales compensation
13. Loan origination fees (expenses of lender to originate loan, usually a percentage of the loan)
14. Loan discount points (where a point is 1 percent of the loaned amount)
15. Appraisal fee
16. Charge for credit report
17. Lender's inspection fee
18. Mortgage insurance application fee (for FHA or VA loans)
19. Assumption/refinancing fee
20. Prepaid interest (from settlement date to first monthly payment)
21. Prepaid mortgage insurance premiums (required for FHA loans)
22. Prepaid hazard insurance premium (fire or homeowner's insurance policy)
23. Reserves deposited with lender (for lender to make future tax and insurance payments)
24. Settlement, closing, or escrow fee
25. Title charges
26. Notary fees
27. Attorney's fees
28. Title insurance
29. Government transfer taxes and charges
30. Survey
31. Inspections (presale inspections for buyer's benefit, including termite or pest inspections to be paid by seller)

A completed form is to be provided to seller and buyer at settlement date. If the exact charges are not yet known, the lender must provide a good faith estimate. The booklet also provides other information useful to the buyer.

USE OF COMPUTERS IN PREPARATION FOR CLOSING

Mortgage departments in banks and savings and loan associations are making increased use of computers in the closing preparation. The need for computer use has grown due to a large volume of closings, the increased number of government forms required, and the many calculations that must be performed.

As the steps are completed for a mortgage loan transaction, the information is placed into the computer. At any time, the status of the transaction can be checked to determine what uncompleted steps remain. When all the steps have been completed, the calculations are made by the computer, and the parties can proceed with the closing.

SUMMARY

A residential property transaction begins when a potential buyer decides to make an offer on a parcel of property. When an agreement is reached, a contract will result between the buyer and the seller. If the agreement includes any contingencies, each must be cleared before an enforceable binding agreement exists.

An agreement will specify either the date of closing when the parties will complete the transaction or, in the case of an escrow closing, the name of the escrow agent who will handle the transaction for the two parties.

A number of obstacles could interfere with the completion of the property transaction. These may occur either because one of the parties fails to perform her responsibilities or because of something not controllable by either party. The broker and the parties to the transaction should take steps to help assure that the transaction will be completed.

TERMS AND CONCEPTS

You can check your understanding of these terms against the glossary or by review in this chapter.

Abstract	Escrow agent	Purchase-money
Acceptance	Escrow agreement	mortgage
Caveat emptor	Marketable title	Relation back
Commitment	Merger of contract into	RESPA
Contingency	deed	Settlement
Counteroffer	Offer	Specific performance
Earnest money	Postoccupancy	Survey
Encroachment	agreement	Time is of the essence
Escrow	Property appraisal	

What are the differences or relationship, if any, between the following? Check your responses from the chapter text or from the glossary.

Conditional and	Escrow closing and	One-step transaction and
Irrevocable	Regular closing	Two-step transaction
Defects and Latent	Grant deed and	
defects	Warranty deed	

PROBLEMS

16-1. Seller A and buyer B sign a contract for sale of a house. Prior to closing, some defects in the title are discovered. What options does the buyer have? What options are open to the seller?

16-2. Seller A and buyer B have signed a contract for sale of a house. Prior to the closing, seller A tells buyer B and the broker that she will not go through with the sale and offers to return the earnest money to B. What options are open to the buyer? What options does the broker have? What do you recommend the broker say?

16-3. Broker X has just obtained the necessary signatures to complete the contract for sale of a house. Make a checklist of things he should do prior to closing.

16-4. Prepare a checklist for a broker to use when drawing up a binding agreement.

16-5. Seller A and buyer B have signed a contract for sale of a house; X was the listing and selling broker. B later advises the broker that the job offer he had was rescinded, and he will not be moving to town. What options are open to broker X?

16-6. A broker holds an exclusive right to sell a listing and brings a signed offer to the seller at the list price with no conditions. Is the seller obligated to sell? To pay the commission?

16-7. A clause in a contract states that the seller will replace the furnace. If this is not completed by the time of closing, what can the buyer do? What if the buyer wants to obtain possession, but the seller refuses to replace the furnace? Can you suggest a better wording for the contract clause?

16-8. A buyer submits an offer contingent upon obtaining a mortgage. Does the seller need to insert any clause to protect himself before signing?

16-9. You have signed a contract to purchase a property. When the survey is completed, it shows the garage roof overhangs one foot on the neighboring lot. What are your possible options?

16-10. If a contract to purchase real estate is both conditional and irrevocable whether there is an escrow closing or not, how does the escrow closing give greater protection to the seller?

16-11. A house under contract was two-thirds destroyed by fire prior to the closing. What would happen if the contract stated the property was held at risk of the seller? Of the buyer? What if there were no risk clause in the contract?

SUPPLEMENTARY READINGS

Bergfield, Philip B. *Real Estate Law.* New York: McGraw-Hill, 1979. Chapter 13.

Friedman, Milton R. *Contracts and Conveyances of Real Property,* 4th ed. New York: Practicing Law Institute, 1986.

Goldstein, Paul. *Real Estate Transactions,* 2nd ed. St. Paul: Foundation Press, 1985.

Gray, Charles D., and Steinberg, Joseph C. *Real Estate Contracts: From Preparation Through Closing.* Englewood Cliffs, N.J.: Prentice-Hall, 1970.

Harvey, David C. B. *Harvey Law of Real Property Title and Closing.* New York: Clark Boardman Company, 1972. 3 vols.

Mann, John. *Escrows—Their Use and Value.* Chicago: Chicago Title and Trust Company, 1975.

Plattner, Robert H. *Real Estate Principles.* San Diego: Harcourt Brace Jovanovich, 1984.

Reilly, John W. *The Language of Real Estate,* 3rd ed. Chicago: Real Estate Education Company, 1988.

Semenow, Robert W. *Questions and Answers on Real Estate.* Englewood Cliffs, N.J.: Prentice-Hall, 1979. Chapter 2.

U.S. Department of Housing and Urban Development. *Settlement Costs and You—A HUD Guide for Home Buyers.* Washington, D.C.: 1976.

CHAPTER 17
Closing and Conveyancing

The legal title to a parcel of real property passes from the seller to the buyer when the instrument of *conveyance* (deed) is delivered to the buyer. Completion of the transaction (closing or settlement) takes place at a meeting of the parties concerned except when an escrow closing has been selected.

Usually, a meeting is held during which all of the pertinent documents are available and the transaction is concluded. If the buyer is obtaining a mortgage, the buyer's loan will be closed at the same meeting, and the mortgage funds will be disbursed by the lender. Figure 17–1 illustrates the main elements of the transaction. At this meeting, the financial aspects will be settled, the deed will be signed and delivered, and the key or token of possession will be transferred from the seller to the buyer. Sometimes, however, the actual date of property possession may be later or earlier than the title transfer date. This meeting—called a *closing* or *settlement*—includes the buyer and seller, their attorneys, representatives of any lending institution involved, and the real estate broker. The alternative to the meeting is to appoint an escrow agent to handle the closing, as in Figure 17–2.

The contract of sale should specify that the closing take place by a certain date and at a specified place. The contract terms should provide enough time from con-

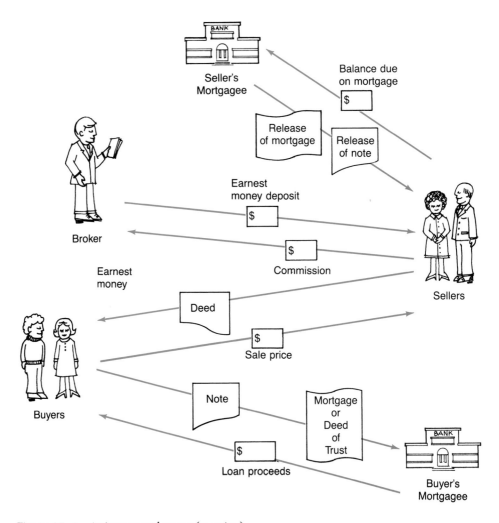

Figure 17–1   Actions at settlement (meeting)

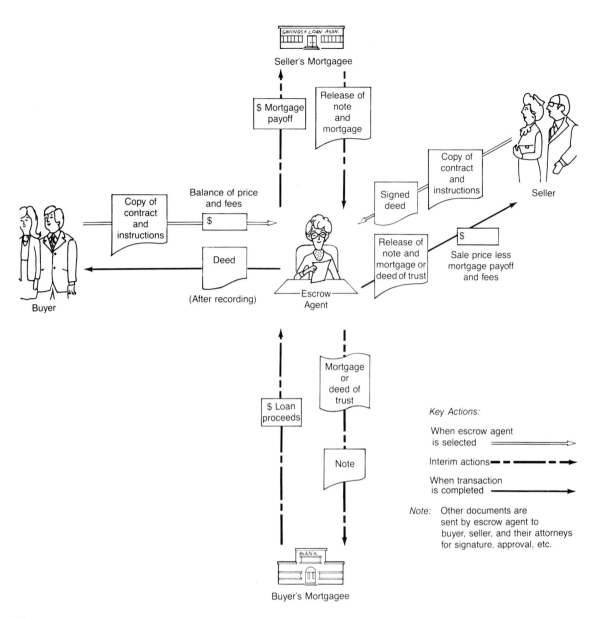

Figure 17–2   Actions for escrow closing

tract execution to the closing to permit completion of the title search, survey, inspections, removal of encumbrances, and any other matters that must be completed before the conveyance of the property. If the time of closing is not specified in the contract, the courts will usually require it to take place within a reasonable time. If it does not take place by the time specified in the contract, usually a monetary adjustment will be worked out to compensate for the delay. If the seller is unable to deliver on the required date, usually the buyer will receive a per diem payment. If the contract specifies that "time is of the essence," the conveyance must take place on the date specified.

ESCROW CLOSING

In some states, most residential real estate transactions are closed in *escrow.* In any state, however, it is sometimes not convenient for either the buyer or the seller to be present at the closing. This might happen if the seller were moving to a distant city before the date of closing. In this case (as discussed in more detail in Chapter 16), the buyer and the seller may select a third party to carry out the closing and complete the transaction. This procedure is called *closing in escrow,* and the person or institution who handles the transaction is called an *escrow agent.* The escrow agent serves both the buyer and the seller. In some states, such as California, escrow agents are licensed and bonded. In other cases the escrow agent can be an officer of a title company or a disinterested attorney trusted by both parties.

The seller delivers the deed to the escrow agent, and the buyer gives the necessary money to the escrow agent. The escrow agent is instructed to have the title examined. If the title is shown to be valid, the escrow agent pays the proceeds of the sale to the seller. In an escrow closing, the title officially is divested from the grantor when the deed is delivered to the escrow agent; however, the title does not pass to the grantee until all conditions are cleared and the deed is delivered to the grantee. The transaction is usually considered irrevocable after it is turned over to the escrow agent, a fact that is referred to as the *relation-back doctrine.* Even if the grantor or grantee dies, marries, or goes bankrupt in the interim period between delivery of the deed to the escrow agent and completion of the proceedings, the transaction is still carried through, as shown in Figure 17–2.

DOCUMENTS REQUIRED AT CLOSING

Certain documents are needed at the closing, whether regular or escrow, to verify that the contract requirements have been met and to provide the necessary information and documentation to complete the transaction. The following documents should be available at closing.

Deed

The deed should be properly executed and ready for delivery to the buyer. It must be the type specified in the contract (e.g., a warranty deed) and must comply with all provisions of the contract. It must (a) be in a form acceptable for recording, (b) show the marital status of grantor(s) and grantee(s), and (c) meet all specified elements for a valid deed, including words of conveyance, specified consideration, and property description.

Lien Discharges

The seller must provide a certificate showing discharge of each lien and mortgage, if there are any.

Insurance Policies

If insurance policies are to be transferred from seller to buyer, the seller must secure insurance company approval, have the policy assigned to the buyer, and bring these documents to the closing. If the buyer is obtaining a new policy, a copy must be available to assure the mortgagee that adequate protection exists.

Cashier's Check

It may be required that the balance due from the buyer be paid by a cashier's check, especially if the buyer uses an out-of-town bank.

Receipts

The seller should bring current receipts for taxes paid, assessment receipts, and receipts for sewage or water service payments.

Title Insurance

If the seller is required to supply title insurance or an abstract, these should be brought to the closing along with any attorney's opinions needed.

Affidavit of Title

The seller must furnish an *affidavit of title* covering the period between completion of the title search and the actual closing. The affidavit should be signed by the seller and state that, during this interim period, there have been no divorce proceedings, judgments, bankruptcy proceedings, or other events that have affected title. The affidavit also states that no repairs or improvements have been made or that any made have been paid for in full. This action protects the buyer against possible liens or claims that originated during this period. The affidavit may also state that fixtures or any personal belongings in the property are paid for, that there are no existing violations or defects in title, and that the seller is the sole current owner.

Certificate of Occupancy

If the property is newly constructed or improved, the seller is required to furnish a *certificate of occupancy,* signed by the proper government official, stating the property is fit for occupancy and that plumbing and electrical requirements and other building code requirements are met.

Survey

The seller must provide a *survey* if so specified in the contract. The survey is used to provide evidence of the existence or nonexistence of encroachments.

Leases

If the property is leased, the seller must assign and deliver the leases to the purchaser. The seller should also furnish an affidavit stating the amounts of rent collected to date and the exact amount of security deposits held by the seller. The security deposits are turned over to the buyer. The seller should send a letter to each tenant advising the tenant of the change in ownership, and copies of the letters should be brought to the closing.

Termite Certificates

Termite certificates should be supplied by the seller if required by the contract.

Fees and Commissions

The attorney's fees and broker's commission are usually paid at the settlement.

Employee Records

If the property (e.g., an apartment building) should involve paid employees, the seller should bring their employment records and data, along with copies of letters notifying each employee, the property manager, or any other involved persons of the change in ownership.

Bill of Sale

A bill of sale is prepared if any personal property is to be transferred by the seller to the buyer.

INSPECTION PRIOR TO CLOSING

Immediately prior to closing it is important for the buyer to make an inspection of the property being purchased. The agent should accompany the buyer. They should make sure that the fixtures included when the home was shown and any personal property (such as stove, refrigerator, or other items) listed as going with the house are still there. The inspection should confirm that appliances and furnace are in operating condition. This inspection should take place after the seller's furniture has been moved out and before closing.

CLOSING COSTS

The costs related to completion of the real estate transaction are called *closing costs* or *settlement costs*. These costs may be fees charged by attorneys, broker, or mortgage institutions; taxes; or the amount necessary to compensate the other party in the transaction. The contract should specify the costs to be paid by each party. Specific costs are usually borne by one party or another in accord with law or custom in the particular state, county, or municipality. Recently, a few lenders have begun offering mortgages that eliminate some or all closing costs if borrowers are willing to pay for the service in higher interest rates and monthly payments throughout the life of the loan. In the following discussion, the costs are assigned by the most frequent method, but variations often exist among localities.

Buyer's Costs

At closing, the buyer is required to pay for fees, services, or other costs stipulated in the contract agreement. If a mortgage is involved, the lending institution usually provides the buyer with a good faith estimate of closing costs. This permits a buyer to compare costs between lenders and also to make sure he has sufficient money ready. The following possible fees or costs would apply where applicable, depending on the contract and the lending institution agreement.

1. *Appraisal fee.* Usually required by the mortgage-lending institution for a new mortgage.
2. **Points charged by lender.** This can be a loan origination fee or a one-time charge by the lender to increase the effective interest yield.
3. *Survey cost.* If required by lending institution or desired by buyer, the survey cost will be due unless the buyer has paid for it separately.
4. *Assumption fee.* Frequently required by the lending institution if the buyer is assuming the seller's mortgage.
5. *Title insurance premium.* If required and not paid by seller.
6. *Recording fee.* Paid by buyer to record deed and any mortgages.
7. *Legal fee.* Paid by buyer for attorney to examine title and render opinion in an abstract. Sometimes the buyer will have his own attorney in addition to the institution's attorney.
8. *Attorney's fee.* Includes contract preparation or review and evaluation of the title.
9. *Interest.* If the lending institution charges mortgage interest a month in advance, the purchaser would owe the interest on a new mortgage from the closing date to the next scheduled payment date.
10. *Impounds.* In addition to the principal and interest payment, borrowers having VA or FHA loans or loans with PMI (private mortgage insurance) are required to make monthly payments to be held by the lender and used to pay taxes and insurance when due. These are called **impounds** and assure that money will be available to make the payment when due. The lending institution protects itself by paying the fire insurance premium and taxes when due, so that a tax lien will not assume precedence over the mortgage lien. Some institutions deduct the impounds as they are received each month from the loan balance, so that the homeowner gains the benefit of reduced interest.

Seller's Costs

The contract or custom in the community may require that certain costs be paid by the seller. The costs may include any of these:

1. *Legal fees.* Costs of title insurance, preparation of abstract, deed preparation, and fees charged by the seller's attorney.
2. *Pay-off of encumbrances.* Any mortgages not assumed as well as any liens or other encumbrances must be paid and discharged before or at closing. This may include penalties, if applicable, to pay off loans in advance of final due date or fees for required releases.
3. *Transfer taxes* (sometimes called *transaction taxes*). Taxes customarily based on selling price.
4. *FHA or VA fees.* These fees would be paid, if due, by seller.

PRORATION

On the day of closing, the seller's ownership terminates and the buyer's ownership begins. It is, therefore, customary to apportion or prorate costs, interest, taxes, and rental income between the buyer and the seller so that both pay their prorated share for the period each owns the property.

The contract between the buyer and the seller usually states that the interest, taxes, insurance, rent, expenses, and utilities are to be prorated where applicable. In some cases, the seller has paid the cost in advance, covering some amount of time after the seller's ownership ends. In that case, the buyer would be obliged to reimburse the seller for that payment. In other cases, the seller may not have paid an expense accrued before the closing and, in that case, the seller would be obliged to credit the buyer's account so that the buyer can pay the bill when it later becomes due. Often there is a considerable amount of money involved, so it is important to allocate it properly and fairly. This necessitates a method of establishing the number of days each owns the property so that a proportionate share can be calculated. In most states or localities, it is customary that the day of closing be assigned to the seller for both costs and income for the purposes of proration.

Proration Methods

There are different methods of making the *proration* calculations, depending upon the contractual provisions and the customary procedures in the local area. The computations in this text carry division and multiplication to three decimal places. The final proration figure is then rounded off to two decimal places.

The Uniform Method (Actual Days in Month)

The uniform method calculates the monthly amount the same way as the statutory month method, by dividing the yearly rate by 12. The daily amount is calculated by dividing the monthly amount by the actual number of days in the month. If the yearly taxes were $600 and the closing date were August 20, the calculations would be as follows:

$$\text{Monthly rate} = \frac{\$600}{12} = \$50$$

$$\text{Daily rate} = \frac{\$50}{31} = \$1.613$$

Taxes from January 1 to August 20 would be calculated as follows:

$$7 \text{ months} \times \$50 = \$350.00$$
$$20 \text{ days} \times 1.613 = \underline{\quad 32.26}$$
$$\text{Total} \quad \$382.26$$

Statutory Month Method (Year = 12 Months of 30 Days Each)

In this method, the yearly amount is divided by 12 to obtain the monthly amount. The monthly amount is then divided by 30 to determine the daily amount.

Actual Days in the Year Method

The actual days in the year method has traditionally been used on all commercial sales, apartment sales, and transactions where the dollar amount is large. Prorations are carried out by dividing the yearly amount by the actual days in the year (365 or

366) to obtain the daily rate. The actual days owned by the party are then calculated for the year. If the closing is August 20, and the yearly interest is $6,000, the calculation is as follows:

$$\text{Interest} = \frac{\$6,000}{365} = \$16.438 \text{ per day}$$

January	31 days
February	28
March	31
April	30
May	31
June	30
July	31
August	20

January 1 to August 20 = 232 days

The interest through August 20 is 232 days × $16.438 = $3,813.62. This method will be used in this text for all problems dealing with commercial, industrial, or apartment properties.

Interest Proration

In closing transactions where the seller's mortgage is to be assumed by the purchaser, it will normally be necessary to prorate or apportion the interest between the buyer and the seller. If there is more than one mortgage to be assumed, interest on each mortgage will be prorated. Consider an example where the closing date was April 12 and the seller of the home had made the mortgage payment on April 1, including payment of interest through April 30. The mortgage balance was $20,800 on April 1 and the interest is 8 percent per annum. The portion of interest due the seller is calculated as follows:

$$\text{One month's interest} = \frac{\$20,800 \times 0.08}{12}$$

$$= \frac{1664}{12} = \$138.667$$

$$\text{The daily interest} = \frac{138.667}{30}$$

$$= \$4.622$$

$$\text{Interest for 18 days} = 18 \times 4.622$$

$$= \$83.20$$

Figure 17–3 shows the schedule of interest with respect to ownership, including the eighteen days for which the buyer should reimburse the seller.

Tax Proration

All transactions involving real estate will require allocation of the taxes between the parties. The taxation laws of the particular state or other jurisdiction where the property is located determine whether the seller owes money to the buyer or vice versa.

Figure 17–3   Schedule of interest with respect to ownership

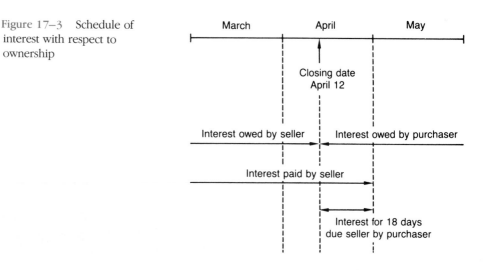

Some examples will illustrate how the taxes are prorated under various taxation laws.

Taxes Required to Be Paid in Current Year

Assume that the taxes of $800 for 1991 are due May 1, 1991. The closing date of the real estate transaction is set for April 10, 1991. The schedule in Figure 17–4 shows the relationship of due date to closing date. The seller must pay to the purchaser the taxes for the period the property was owned by the seller from January 1 to April 10 because the buyer would be billed for the whole year's taxes on May 1, 1991.

$$\text{Monthly rate} = \frac{\$800}{12} = \$66.667$$

$$\text{Daily rate} = \frac{\$66.667}{30} = \$\ 2.222$$

Amount due purchaser

$$3 \text{ months} \times \$66.667 = \$200.001$$
$$10 \text{ days} \times \$2.222 = \underline{\quad 22.220}$$
$$\text{Total} = \$222.221$$
$$\text{or (rounded) } \$222.22$$

Figure 17–4   Relationship of tax due date to closing date

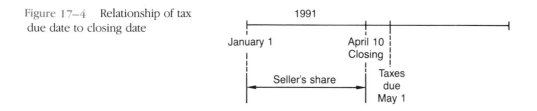

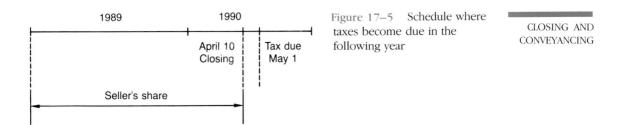

Figure 17–5 Schedule where taxes become due in the following year

As another example, assume the closing date were September 18, 1991, and taxes were due May 1, 1991. The seller would have paid all of the 1991 taxes and would be due an amount from the purchaser to cover the rest of the year after September 18 as follows:

Sept. 19–Sept. 30 (12 days)

$$12 \times \$2.222 = \$ 26.664$$

Oct.–Dec. (3 months)

$$3 \times \$66.667 = \underline{200.001}$$
$$\text{Total} = \$226.665$$
$$\text{or (rounded) } \$226.67$$

In this example, the lending institution may request the buyer to deposit additional money in an escrow account toward payment of the 1992 taxes due May 1, 1992. If the institution's policy is to deduct the impound from the mortgage balance until paid, the homeowner benefits with respect to the interest charged.

Taxes Paid in Following Year

Assume the taxes of $800 for 1990 are due on May 1, 1990. The closing date is April 10, 1990. Figure 17–5 shows the relationship between closing date and tax due date. In this situation, the buyer would be billed for the 1989 taxes on May 1, 1990, and the following year he would be billed for the 1990 taxes on May 1, 1991. The seller owned the property during all of 1989 and part of 1990, so the seller owes the buyer as follows:

1989 taxes		$=$	$ 800.000
3 months in 1990	$3 \times \$66.667$	$=$	200.001
10 days of April	$10 \times \$ 2.222$	$=$	22.220
	Total	$=$	$1022.221
	or (rounded) $1022.22		

The closing statement should then give the buyer credit for the full $1,022.22, and the same amount is debited to the seller.

Installment Payment of Taxes

Some states allow taxes to be paid in installments. Assume that one-half of the 1989 taxes are due on May 1, 1989, and the other half on September 1, 1989. The yearly taxes are $800 and the closing date is July 24, 1989. The May 1 payment was paid by the seller. The following shows the calculations to determine the credit due the buyer:

$$
\begin{array}{lcl}
\text{Taxes 1989} & = & \$800 \\
\text{Half-payment made by seller} & = & -\,400 \\
\text{Balance} & = & \$400 \\
\text{Taxes 1990 6 months} \times \$66.667 & = & \$400.002 \\
\qquad\qquad 24 \text{ days} \quad \times \$\ 2.222 & = & \underline{\quad 53.328} \\
& & \$853.330
\end{array}
$$

The buyer should receive $853.33 from the seller so he can pay the $400 for 1989 on September 1, 1990, and the 1990 taxes when due in 1991.

Insurance Proration

An insurance proration is necessary when the purchaser is taking over the insurance policy from the seller. Insurance policies are often written to provide coverage over a three- or five-year period. It is important to determine how much of the unexpired policy has been paid by the seller. Since insurance policies do not ordinarily run in calendar-year periods, the calculation is performed differently from the tax and interest prorations. Assume the seller has a three-year paid-up policy expiring July 21, 1993, for which the seller paid the $390 premium in full. The closing date for the property transaction is May 17, 1992. Calculations are made to determine the amount due to the seller from the buyer in order to compensate for the paid-up insurance coverage that the buyer is to receive from the seller. First determine the daily cost of the policy. (*Note:* Insurance prorations always use thirty days for a month.)

$$
\text{Yearly amount} = \frac{\$390}{3} = \$130
$$

$$
\text{Monthly amount} = \frac{\$130}{12} = \$10.833
$$

$$
\text{Daily amount} = \frac{\$10.833}{30} = \$0.361
$$

Subtract the closing date from the expiration date to determine the policy period remaining as follows:

	Year	Month	Day
Expiration date	1993	7	21
Closing date	1992	5	17
Unexpired period	1	2	4

To subtract, start with the day column, and proceed just as with any subtraction problem. The total value of the unexpired portion of the policy is then calculated as follows:

$$
\begin{array}{lcl}
1 \text{ year} \times \$130 & = & \$130.000 \\
2 \text{ months} \times \$10.833 & = & 21.666 \\
4 \text{ days} \times \$0.361 & = & \underline{\quad 1.444} \\
\text{Total due seller} & = & \$153.110
\end{array}
$$

In cases where the buyer wants to purchase his own insurance, it is not necessary to make any proration calculations. The seller would apply for a rebate from the insurance company for the unused portion of the policy, and the insurance would not be prorated.

To illustrate another situation, assume the same problem with the closing date now set at October 24, 1991. The calculations are as follows:

	Year	Month	Day
Expiration date	1993	7	21
Closing date	1991	10	24

In starting to perform subtraction, the 24 cannot be taken from the 21; therefore, it is necessary to borrow 30 days from the 7 in the month column to arrive at 51 in the day column. The subtraction in the day column can now take place.

	Year	Month	Day
Expiration date	1993	6	51
Closing date	1991	10	24
			27

Now the subtraction cannot take place in the month column; therefore, 12 months are borrowed from the 1993 in the year column to arrive at 18 months in the month column, as follows:

	Year	Month	Day
Expiration date	1992	18	51
Closing date	1991	10	24
Unexpired portion of policy	1	8	27

The amount due the seller is calculated as follows:

$$
\begin{aligned}
1 \text{ year} \times \$130 &= \$130.000 \\
8 \text{ months} \times \$10.833 &= 86.664 \\
27 \text{ days} \times \$0.361 &= 9.747 \\
\text{Total due seller} &= \$226.411 \\
(\text{rounded to } \$226.41)
\end{aligned}
$$

In this problem, if the seller had been paying on a yearly installment basis, he would have paid only through July 21, 1992. Thus the amount the buyer owes the seller would be $130 less than the $226.41, or $96.41. The $96.41 would then appear as a credit to the seller on the closing statement.

Rental Income and Wages

When the property involves rental income or wages for employees, an amount may be due to either the buyer or seller, depending on the specific situation. Assume a building has two apartments and each tenant pays $640 per month. The closing is May 12 and the seller has collected the rent for May in advance. It is necessary to calculate the amount due from the seller to the buyer. (Use actual days in the month for income and wages.)

$$\text{For one apartment, daily rent} = \frac{640}{31} = \$\ 20.65$$

$$\text{Days remaining} = 31 - 12 = 19$$

For one apartment: 19 days × $20.65	= $392.35
For two apartments	× 2
Due purchaser on both apartments	$784.70

As mentioned before, the day of closing is considered a day of income and expense for the seller. In addition to rents paid or due, we must consider any damage deposits given to the landlord by a tenant. Any deposits that were received from tenants and are being held by the seller will be turned over to the buyer or credited to him at the closing.

Apartments often have a janitorial service. The wages or salaries must be prorated so that the buyer and seller pay the wages for the period that each owns the property. Assume an apartment building had a janitor who was paid $500 per week for a seven-day workweek. He was paid last on May 9 for the week ending May 9. Closing is May 12, so the janitor is owed three days' pay.

$$\text{Daily rate} = \frac{\$500}{7} = \$\ 71.429$$

Days	× 3
Due purchaser	$214.287

(rounded to $214.29)

The $214.29 would be credited to the buyer on the closing statement.

Utilities

Usually, the power company or the gas company will read the meter at the property location on the day of closing and bill each party separately for his portion. Sometimes, however, especially in the case of water, the meter is not read, and it is necessary to prorate the charges. Consider a case where the water and sewage fee of $30 is paid quarterly in advance and the closing is May 6. On April 1 the seller paid in advance for water for the months of April, May, and June, and therefore the purchaser owes the seller for more than one month's use. It is prorated in the same manner as rental income.

THE SETTLEMENT STATEMENT

The *settlement* (closing) *statement* itemizes and allocates all costs and monies between the various parties to the transaction. Its purpose is to allocate these funds clearly and accurately. Calculating the figures in advance allows each party to arrange to have adequate funds available at the closing to complete the transaction. Although the preliminary copy of the closing statement may require minor adjustments later, it does serve as a basis for determining the approximate amount each party owes or will receive and also permits each party to check its accuracy before the settlement.

A typical settlement statement form is shown in Figure 17–6. Some forms have only two columns and may include a separate settlement portion for the broker to settle with the seller. Sometimes separate settlement statements are prepared for the buyer and seller.

The various entries are shown in Figure 17–6. The buyer's debit column is totaled first. The amount "Due from buyer to close" is entered in an amount that will cause the buyer's credit and debit column to have equal totals. The seller's credit column is then totaled. Then the amount "Due to seller to close" is entered so that the seller's debit and credit columns have equal totals.

Property Address _1821 MASON_   Broker _HENDERSON REALTY_
Seller _KEVIN AND KATHY BECK_   Date of contract _JUNE 2, 1991_
Buyer _ALFRED AND AMY CROSS_

SETTLEMENT DATE: JULY 15, 1991	BUYER'S STATEMENT		SELLER'S STATEMENT	
	DEBIT	CREDIT	DEBIT	CREDIT
1. PURCHASE PRICE	57,500.00			57,500.00
2. EARNEST MONEY DEPOSIT		5,750.00		
3. MORTGAGE BALANCE		42,000.00	42,000.00	
4. PURCHASE MONEY MORTGAGE		8,000.00	8,000.00	
5. MORTGAGE INTEREST		160.89	160.89	
6. INSURANCE	413.34			413.34
7. GENERAL TAXES		378.23	378.23	
8. TRANSFER TAX			15.50	
9. TITLE INSURANCE	92.00		92.00	
10. ASSUMPTION FEE	100.00			
11. AGENT'S COMMISSION			3450.00	
12. LEGAL FEES			310.00	
13. SURVEY	85.00			
14. TERMITE INSPECTION			30.00	
15. OIL	66.00			66.00
DUE FROM BUYER TO CLOSE		1967.22		
DUE TO SELLER TO CLOSE			3542.72	
TOTALS:	58256.34	58256.34	57979.34	57979.34

Figure 17–6   Settlement statement

Example 17–1   A Typical Residential Closing

Example 17–1 provides information on a sample real estate transaction. The closing statement shown in Figure 17–6 has been prepared from the information given.

Kevin and Kathy Beck of 1821 Mason Street in Foxboro have listed their house with Henderson Realty for $59,000. A 6 percent commission is to be paid on the actual sale price. The existing mortgage has a balance of $42,000 after the June 30, 1991, monthly payment was credited. No further payment was made. Monthly mortgage payments of $430 are due on the last day of each month and include the interest through and including that date. Interest on the mortgage balance is at 9.5 percent. On June 2, 1991, Alfred and Amy Cross signed a contract to purchase the house for $57,500. It was specified that they would assume the present mortgage. The Becks also agreed to take a purchase money mortgage of $8,000.

The buyers gave the broker a 10 percent earnest-money deposit, and the broker now holds this in his escrow account. The closing date is set for July 15, 1991. The agreement provided that the buyers and sellers would each pay half of the title insurance policy of $184. The real estate general tax for 1991 was $700 and was paid in full on June 1, 1991. The buyers have agreed to pay for the 120 gallons of oil in the tank at $0.55 per gallon. A four-year insurance policy on the house was paid in full by the Becks. It cost $800 and expires August 9, 1991. The buyers have agreed to take over this policy. The sellers will pay the transfer tax of $0.50 per $500 or fraction thereof. Prorations are based on the actual number of days in the month.

The buyers will pay an assumption fee of $100. The buyers are also to pay $85 for a survey. The sellers owe $30 for a termite inspection. The sellers' legal fees total $310.

Refer to Figure 17–6 as the settlement statement is completed.

Purchase Price

The purchase price of $57,500 is entered as a credit to the sellers and a debit to the buyers.

Earnest Money

The earnest money has already been paid by the buyers, and it appears as a credit of $5,750. It does not appear as a debit to the sellers unless they have already received the deposit from the broker.

Mortgage

Assumed mortgage: The $42,000 balance of the assumed mortgage is credited to the buyers since they assume this as a debt to be paid off in the future. It is entered as a debit to the sellers since this is deducted from their proceeds.

New mortgage: A new mortgage is always a credit to the buyers since they assume this obligation for future payment.

Purchase money mortgage: The $8,000 purchase money mortgage is credited to the buyers since they assume the obligation for future payment. It is also debited to the sellers since they do not receive it now.

Mortgage Interest

Assumed mortgage: Under an assumed mortgage the mortgage interest is prorated over the month of closing. The sellers pay up to and including the closing date, and the buyers pay for the rest of the month. If the sellers paid the month's interest in advance, the buyers will owe the sellers money. If the interest is paid at the end of the month, the sellers will owe the buyers money.

$$\text{Yearly interest} = \$42{,}000 \times \$0.095 = \$3990.00$$

$$\text{Monthly interest} = \frac{3990}{12} = \$332.50$$

$$\text{Daily interest (July)} = \frac{332.50}{31} = \$10.726$$

$$\text{Interest (July 1--15)} = 10.726 \times 15 \text{ days} = \$160.89$$

The $160.89 is credited to the buyers and debited to the sellers since it is not paid until the end of the month.

New mortgage: At the closing, the buyers and the mortgagee will select a day of the month for future loan payments. If it is different from the settlement date, the buyers may have to pay interest in advance from the settlement date to the next loan payment date. This would appear as a debit to the buyers.

Second mortgage: Any second or other mortgages are handled the same as the first mortgage.

Taxes

If the taxes were paid in advance, the sellers are due a credit for the period the property is owned by the buyers. These taxes are then shown as a credit to the sellers. If the taxes have not been paid for a period of time over which the sellers owned the property, they are debited this amount. It is also credited to the buyers. The buyers will then pay taxes when due.

In our case, the 1987 tax was paid by the sellers on June 1, 1991. Since the 1991 tax is not known, it is customary to use the tax from the prior year, which in this case is $700. The monthly and daily taxes are figured as follows:

$$\text{Monthly tax} = \frac{\$700}{12} = \$58.333$$

$$\text{Daily tax} = \frac{\$58.333}{31} = \$1.882 \text{ (for July)}$$

The sellers' share of the 1991 tax is from January 1 to July 15, or

$$6 \text{ months} \times \$58.333 = \$349.998$$
$$15 \text{ days} \times \$1.882 = \underline{28.230}$$
$$\$378.228$$
$$\text{(rounded to } \$378.23)$$

This amount is credited to the buyers since they will have to pay the total 1991 tax on June 1, 1992.

In Figure 17–6 the prorated taxes are debited to the sellers and credited to the buyers.

Special Assessments

These assessments are owed by the owner as of January 1 each year and do not appear on the settlement sheets unless specified in the contract.

Insurance

New policy: The premium for a new policy is debited to the purchasers.
Assumed policy: Where an insurance policy is paid for by the sellers and taken over by the buyers, the buyers must pay the sellers for the remaining value of the policy. In our example, the sellers had paid the insurance policy premium in advance and, therefore,

should be credited with the unused portion. The value of the policy from July 15, 1991, to the expiration date of August 9, 1993, is calculated as follows:

$$\text{Yearly cost} = \frac{\$800}{4} = \$200$$

$$\text{Monthly cost} = \frac{\$200}{12} = \$16.667$$

$$\text{Daily cost} = \frac{\$16.667}{30} = \$0.556$$

	Year	Month	Day
Expiration date	1993	8^7	9^{39}
Closing date	1991	7	15
	2	0	24

$$2 \text{ years} \times \$200 = \$400.00$$
$$0 \text{ months} \times \$16.667 = 0.00$$
$$24 \text{ days} \times \$0.556 = 13.34$$
$$\text{Unexpired value} = \$413.34$$

This amount is credited to the sellers and debited to the buyers.

Transfer Tax

The transfer tax is debited to the party responsible for paying it. The transfer tax on revenue stamps is computed at $0.50 per $500 or portion thereof. If there is no mortgage, the tax is based on the purchase price. Where there is a mortgage, the stamps are usually figured on the difference between the purchase price and the assumed mortgage, which in this case is

$$\$57,500 - \$42,000 = \$15,500$$

$$\text{Transfer tax} = \$0.50 \times \frac{15,500}{500} = \$15.50$$

This charge is debited to the seller.

Title Insurance

The cost of title insurance is debited to the party responsible. In our problem, the title insurance cost is shared so that half is debited to the buyers and half to the sellers.

Loan Origination Fee (Points)

This fee is usually paid by the buyers and is computed as a percentage of the amount borrowed. For FHA loans it is paid by the sellers. There are no points in our example.

Assumption Fee

Where the mortgage is assumed, the buyers usually pay an assumption fee. In our example, $100 is debited to the buyers.

Agent's Commission

The real estate broker's commission to be paid by the sellers is figured as 6 percent of the purchase price of $57,500.

$$\text{Commission} = .06 \times \$57,500 = \$3,450$$

Legal Fees

The fees of an attorney are debited to the responsible party. In our example, the sellers pay $310.

Appraisal Fee

An appraisal fee is often required by the lender and is usually paid for by the buyer.

Survey

Sometimes a survey is required by a lender and paid for by the buyer unless the contract specifies otherwise. In our problem, $85 is paid by the buyers for a survey.

Termite Inspection

The cost of inspection plus any treatment necessary is paid for by the seller. In our problem, $30 is paid by the sellers for a termite inspection.

Water Bill

Usually, utility meters are read on the date of closing. If they are not, the cost is prorated on the basis of the last paid bill.

Oil

It is normal practice to charge the buyer for oil left in the tank and credit this to the seller. In our example,

$$120 \text{ gal.} \times \$0.55 = \$66.00$$

Impounds (Escrows)

If the seller has accumulated money in an escrow account kept by the mortgagee to pay taxes and insurance, it is credited to the seller.

Chattels (Personal Property)

If the buyer arranges to purchase personal property from the seller, this is handled by a bill of sale. It is a debit to the buyer and a credit to the seller.

Rents

For leased property, it may be necessary to prorate rents. Rent collected in advance is debited to the seller and credited to the buyer. Overdue rent is credited to the seller and debited to the buyer.

Salaries

Any salaries of persons (e.g., janitors who care for rental apartments) must be prorated as of the day of the closing. If a salary is unpaid, the seller will be debited his share, and the buyer will receive a credit.

Penalties to Pay off Loan

The mortgagee may charge a penalty to pay off a loan balance. This penalty is debited to the seller.

Lien Satisfaction

Any outstanding liens may be handled at the closing by a debit to the seller unless the payment was made directly to the lienholder.

ACTIONS SUBSEQUENT TO CLOSING

After the closing is completed, the buyer or his attorney or agent should do the following:

1. Record deed obtained from the seller in recorder's office. The recorded deed then is retained by the new owner.
2. If the old mortgage was paid off, record the release of the mortgage, showing that the lending institution has no further legal interest in the property.
3. Have evidence of title brought down to closing date to show that no actions that could result in a lien or title defect took place between completion of title search and closing date.
4. Obtain home and liability insurance if not already purchased.
5. If persons are employed on the property, obtain workmen's compensation and employer's liability insurance. Arrange for janitorial and any other services. Notify tenants to pay rent to the buyer.

The seller should make sure that the water, gas, and electric bills are transferred to the buyer's name. If there is a purchase money mortgage, the seller should have it recorded.

The lending institution should assure that its mortgage or deed of trust is recorded for its protection as discussed in Chapter 9 on liens and their priority.

SUMMARY

The closing (or settlement) is the procedure or event by which the property ownership transfers from the seller to the buyer. This can be handled at a meeting where the buyer and seller are present, or it may be handled by an escrow agent who looks after the interests of both parties and completes the transaction if and when each party's obligations are complied with.

At the closing, the monetary aspects of the transaction are completed such that the seller is paid the amount due him at the time the title is transferred to the buyer.

Many of the items, such as mortgage interest, taxes, insurance, utilities, and income from rental property, may need to be apportioned so that each party pays or receives his proper share. This apportionment is called *proration*. All of these figures are calculated and entered in the closing (settlement) statement to show the amounts due to seller and to be paid by buyer. The amounts due to the broker, the attorneys, the county recorder, and others can be handled on the same form or separately. A wide variety of forms are used in different localities.

TERMS AND CONCEPTS

You can check your understanding of these terms against the glossary or by review in this chapter.

Affidavit of title	Escrow	Relation-back doctrine
Certificate of occupancy	Escrow agent	Settlement
Closing	Impounds	Settlement statement
Closing in escrow	Points	Survey
Conveyance	Proration	

PROBLEMS

Prepare closing statements for each of the following transactions. (Consider the date of closing to belong to the seller, unless designated otherwise by your instructor.) You may reproduce copies of Figure 17–7 to record the results.

17-1. John and Sally O'Brian listed their home at 2429 Reston Avenue with the Henderson Real Estate Company. The selling price was $84,500, and possession was to be given four weeks following the signing of the contract. The listing agreement stated that the broker was to receive a commission of 6 percent of the selling price. On March, 1, 1987, the balance on the mortgage was $53,700. The payments on the mortgage are $260 per month plus interest at the rate of 12 percent per annum on the unpaid balance. The O'Brians are willing to sell the property subject to the existing mortgage if the prospective purchasers can provide the necessary cash difference. They are not able to take a purchase money mortgage.

On March 18, 1987, Henderson Real Estate Company submitted a contract offer to the O'Brians from Peg and Bill Miller. Mr. and Mrs. Miller offered $82,000 if they could take title subject to the existing mortgage. The O'Brians signed the acceptance on March 29, 1987. Closing was set for April 15, 1987, at the office of the Henderson Real Estate Company. A check for

$8,000 was deposited with the broker as earnest money.

The sellers were to pay $320 for title service. They also owed the amount for revenue stamps at the rate of $0.50 per $500 or fraction thereof and $14 for recording. There were two paid-up insurance policies for $30,000 and $50,000. The $30,000 policy cost $300 for three years and expires August 15, 1988. The five-year policy for $50,000 expires March 1, 1989, and has a premium of $450. General taxes for 1986 are due on June 1, 1987, in the amount of $840.

The seller paid the mortgage payment due April 1, 1987, covering interest through March 31. The contract stated that taxes, insurance, and interest are to be prorated, and the buyer is to pay a $150 assumption fee.

(a) Prepare the settlement statement using the statutory month method.

(b) Prepare the closing statement using the uniform method.

17-2. Mr. Ray Galt is selling his house at 984 Dunes Drive to a Mr. and Mrs. Prince. The contract is dated July 17, 1992, and has been signed by the buyer and the seller. The purchase price is $67,500. An earnest money deposit was paid to the Johnson Real Estate Company in the amount of $6,750. Johnson was employed by Mr. Galt.

Purchaser is to take title subject to the exist-

Property Address _____   Broker _____

Seller _____   Date of contract _____

Buyer _____   _____

SETTLEMENT DATE:	BUYER'S STATEMENT		SELLER'S STATEMENT	
	DEBIT	CREDIT	DEBIT	CREDIT

Figure 17–7   Settlement statement worksheet

ing mortgage, which has an unpaid balance of $52,500. Payments are due quarterly on the last day of March, June, September, and December in the amount of $250 on the principal plus interest at 10 percent per annum on the amount of principal outstanding since the last quarterly payment. The last payment was made June 20, 1992.

Real estate taxes in the amount of $1,260 for 1991 were paid in full on June 1, 1992. The seller has a $60,000 fire insurance policy written for a three-year term that expires November 24,

1993, for which he paid a three-year premium of $570. The quarterly water bill in the amount of $96 was paid for the three months ending June 30, 1992. Closing is set for August 8, 1992.

The seller will pay the attorney $360 for the abstract. The seller owes the recording fees of $20 and the revenue stamps at $0.50 per $500 or fraction thereof. The commission on the sale was 6 percent. The buyer will pay 2 points for the assumption fee.

Prepare the settlement statement using the uniform method.

17-3. Bruce Allen and his wife Samantha are selling their four-apartment structure to Betsy Ball, an unmarried woman, of 2820 Vine Street, Archdale, Nebraska. The property is at 6820 Main Street, Archdale, Nebraska. The lot is approximately 50 by 165 ft. and is described as lot 9 in block 4 of Ipex subdivision in the SW quarter of Section 34, Township 2 North, Range 1 East of the Sixth Principal Meridian.

The binder was drawn up on March 24, 1988, and a formal contract was executed April 1, 1988. The sale price was $289,000, and the buyer deposited $28,000 as earnest money with the Ficek Realty Company. Ficek was employed as a broker by Allen. The title will be conveyed by warranty deed, and the sale will be closed on May 7, 1988. The purchaser is to assume the unpaid balance of the existing mortgage. The mortgage was originally for $220,000 and is payable at $400 per month plus 10 percent interest on the outstanding balance at each payment. Payments are due on the first day of each month and in-

clude interest for the previous month. The May 1, 1988, payment has been made; the mortgage balance is $198,400 on May 1, 1988. The buyer will pay an assumption fee of $800.

The 1986 real estate tax was $4,200 and was paid on June 1, 1987. The 1987 tax is not yet known. The fire insurance policy for $280,000 expires September 3, 1990. The three-year premium of $3,000 was paid in full. There are 1,000 gallons of oil in the tank priced at $1.31 per gallon.

The two-month water bill for the period ending May 15, 1988, of $180 is paid. The electric bill of $1,440 for the two-month period ending April 17, 1988, is paid. The following personal property is included in the sale price: lawn mower, storm doors and windows, TV antenna, and refrigerators and stoves in three apartments. Possession is to be given on the date of closing.

The three apartments are rented under leases expiring November 30, 1988. Monthly rent is $600, payable in advance on the first day of each month. The rent for May was paid May 1, 1988. Purchaser asked for and seller agreed to provide a survey (cost of $240) showing that the garage and building are within lot lines and that there are no encroachments.

The seller will owe $925 to the title company for the title examination and will pay $280 for tax stamps. The exclusive listing defined the commission as 4 percent of the gross selling price.

Prepare the closing statement using the actual days of the year method.

SUPPLEMENTARY READINGS

Bellavance, Russel C. *Real Estate Law.* St. Paul: West, 1978. Chapter 11.

Bergfield, Philip B. *Principles of Real Estate Law.* New York: McGraw-Hill, 1979. Chapter 13.

Cogswell, John E.; Lansford, Raymond W.; and Nystrom, Arthur N. *The Professional Guide to Real Estate Closing.* Independence: Arcola Real Estate, 1979.

Ellis, John T. *Guide to the ACT Real Estate License Examinations.* Englewood Cliffs, N.J.: Prentice-Hall, 1984.

Ellis, John T. *Guide to the ASI Real Estate License Examinations.* Englewood Cliffs, N.J.: Prentice-Hall, 1984.

Estes, Jack C., and Kokus, John, Jr. *Real Estate License Preparation Course for the Uniform Examinations.* New York: McGraw-Hill, 1976. Chapter 15.

French, William B.; Martin, Stephen J.; and Battle, Thomas E., III. *Guide to Real Estate Licensing Examinations,* 5th ed. Boston: Warren, Gorham, and Lamont, 1988. Chapter 17.

Galaty, Fillmore W.; Alloway, Wellington J.; and Kyle, Robert C. *Modern Real Estate Practice,* 11th ed. Chicago: Real Estate Education Corporation, 1988. Chapter 23.

Ring, Alfred A., and Dasso, Jerome. *Real Estate Principles and Practices,* 11th ed. Englewood Cliffs, N.J.: Prentice-Hall, 1989. Chapter 12.

Siedel, George J., III. *Real Estate Law.* St Paul: West, 1979. Chapter 10.

Tosh, Dennis S., and Ordway, Nicholas. *Real Estate Principles for License Preparation,* 2nd ed. Reston, Va.: Reston, 1985. Appendix B.

CHAPTER 18
Subdivision, Development, and Construction

The development of land and the construction of improvements is one of the most important single contributions to gross national product in the United States. Over three million persons are employed in the production of real estate improvements, and two million more are employed in manufacturing products going into homes and other new construction.

A large portion of this real estate production is the development of raw land into residential, industrial, or other usage. Cities and towns grow primarily through the process of developing unimproved parcels of land. When a tract of land is divided into smaller parts for development, the process is called *subdividing*. A *land developer* builds homes on the lots and sells them.

Subdivision and land development take time and involve a number of steps. The up-and-down cycles of the economy and the real estate business provide further risks to the *subdivider* or land developer. In view of these complexities, the care spent in planning a real estate project can determine its success or failure.

RESIDENTIAL SUBDIVISION AND DEVELOPMENT

The requirements and methods for developing raw land into residential or industrial subdivisions have changed considerably in the past thirty years. Residential development, in particular, has been subject to increasingly stringent standards and controls. These include federal and state regulations, as well as local standards.

Past Problems

In the recent past, many residential developments have been very successful, whereas others have been far less than successful. Some have not only been financial disasters for the developers, but they have also resulted in severe problems for the families who purchased sites or homes.

A few subdivision and land development projects have made developers wealthy at the expense of the people who invested in the real estate. Many of these problems can be traced to inadequate planning, inadequate financing, or a lack of concern by the developer for the long-term success of the property. Others were the result of unscrupulous developers, intent only upon their own interests, who "let the buyer beware." During the last thirty years, developers frequently were concerned only with a one-time development of a small parcel of land. Because of their inexperience, ineptness, or lack of concern, they proceeded without adequate planning. The developers, financial backers, and land purchasers, as well as the community, all lose out if a development is unsuccessful.

The resulting problems have led to the following changes in the process and the control of subdivision development.

1. There are now strict municipal regulations and controls over new subdivision developments. These include more stringent administration of zoning and building codes, as described in Chapter 10.
2. All states have stringent licensing requirements for those involved in real estate.
3. General urban area master plans have been prepared specifying use restrictions for urban land and land adjacent to the area.
4. Controls over existing utilities and their extension or the increase in demand for present capacity have been implemented.

Planning Steps

There are several steps in the planning and execution of a subdivision project. The following steps are typical.

1. Analyze the market to determine the desires and needs of potential customers in the area.
2. Identify alternative locations and select the best prospects for a successful development.
3. Draw a preliminary layout of the prospective areas. Investigate financing and the availability of utilities. Make a preliminary submission of a plat and plan to the municipal authorities.
4. Make a final decision on a location. Have a formal survey made and plat layout drawn including lots, streets, utilities, and land use restrictions.
5. Submit a formal plan to municipal authorities for approval.

6. Construct the necessary roads, provide grading and erosion control, and bring in utilities.
7. Sell sites to potential builders and begin construction of homes.
8. Complete roads, sidewalks, or other items under the responsibility of the developer. Provide for maintenance under developer's responsibility.

Market Evaluation

An evaluation of the market is comprised of a number of closely integrated investigations, analyses, and decisions. The objective is to end up with homes or home sites that customers will want within their price and location constraints.

Prior to purchase of land or initiation of any evaluation work, the developer should research overall market conditions. The general state of the economy is a first consideration. The local business picture is also important, as are local population trends. If a residential project is contemplated, the present availability of homes and apartment units should be analyzed. This availability is then compared to the findings of a market survey to determine who the potential buyers are and what they are looking for.

Information on potential buyers would include present living locations, work locations, earnings, family sizes, and other needs or desires. Next, the developer should investigate the competition. Which areas of need are the competitors aiming for? What can be done to provide better values than the competition has? One result will be a forecast of the number of homes needed on a year-by-year basis. From this evaluation, a line of residences can be chosen at prices, sizes, and styles that will have a good chance of selling.

The developer then must determine what land resources are available as well as the financial backing and the other resources needed and whether or not they are available. The human assets to accomplish the job are also significant. A marketing organization is needed to market the properties, whether it be the developer's own personnel or independent real estate brokers. Construction, site survey, planning, and legal services are also needed.

The search for a site will probably start with identifying a number of alternatives and a *locational analysis* considering accessibility to needs and conveniences. Sometimes a prospective developer will start with a property that she already owns; however, it is still wise to consider other alternatives. If the land under consideration does not have the attributes desired, it may be financially advantageous to abandon it and select a different site.

Planning Trade-Offs

The information from the market evaluation will help determine the attributes desired for the proposed subdivision. Municipality restrictions will, of course, have to be considered also. There is no standard list of attributes from which to make the final set of designs; however, the following choices should be carefully considered:

1. Privacy provided by large lots versus economy allowed by smaller lots
2. Privacy and appearance provided by trees and vegetation versus economy of more efficient construction on bare or cleared land
3. Privacy provided by distance from schools and commercial areas versus convenience in having schools and shopping areas close by

4. Narrow winding roads to discourage traffic versus wider streets with curbs and sidewalks to accommodate pedestrian and automobile traffic
5. Recreation areas versus economy of complete use of all land for home building
6. Features such as family rooms and two baths versus economy

Some developments are planned around a particular recreation site or facility such as a golf course, country club, waterfront area, lake, school, or shopping center. Other innovative developments might center around a stable and riding track, as in Figure 18–1, or a private-plane airstrip.

Once a general type of development has been determined, the developer should look for an equivalent development completed in the past few years. A drive through that area and a talk with some residents may reveal positive attributes of their development as well as problems. Also, the places from which the people moved would give an indication of the source of buyers. After the general objectives and constraints have been established, the developer can select the final location. In the Planned Unit Development (PUD), the developers obtain special zoning approval to integrate residential, commercial, and possibly certain industrial uses into a single unit.

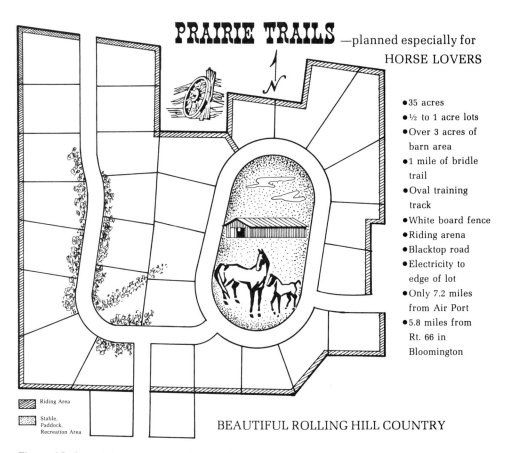

PRAIRIE TRAILS —planned especially for
HORSE LOVERS

- 35 acres
- ½ to 1 acre lots
- Over 3 acres of barn area
- 1 mile of bridle trail
- Oval training track
- White board fence
- Riding arena
- Blacktop road
- Electricity to edge of lot
- Only 7.2 miles from Air Port
- 5.8 miles from Rt. 66 in Bloomington

Riding Area

Stable, Paddock, Recreation Area

BEAUTIFUL ROLLING HILL COUNTRY

Figure 18–1   Subdivision centered around stable and riding track

Source: Hal Riss Real Estate, Normal, Illinois.

Steps Prior to Land Acquisition

At this stage in the planning process, one or more tracts are under consideration. The market evaluation has identified the important factors. The next step is to compare the alternative tracts of land, considering several factors.

Location

Is the tract in a location where natural growth or expansion of the urban area will proceed? Usually, the natural growth of an urban area will extend along important traffic routes that facilitate access. If a site is not in this natural expansion pattern, it could still be a satisfactory location; however, the costs of promotion will be greater and the rate of progress in selling the lots and homes and completing the project will be slower. Proximity to schools, shopping centers, and public transportation must also be considered.

Layout

Next, a rough layout is prepared of each area under consideration to determine how many lots could be expected. It would include proposed streets and a layout of the lots. An example of a layout is shown in Figure 18–2. Depending upon the terrain and other natural factors, a larger amount of acreage would not necessarily guarantee a greater number of lots. Some areas may not be usable because of the terrain.

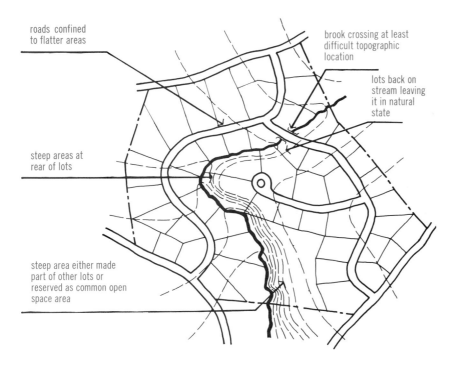

Figure 18–2 Tentative layouts of streets and lots

Source: State of New Hampshire, Office of State Planning. *Handbook of Subdivision Practice.* 1972.

Style

Along with the layout of each area, the style of homes or buildings proposed is considered, since it will have a significant impact upon the individual lot size. Of major importance in this decision is the style and price range of any existing properties in the area. The proximity and type of commercial and other properties must also be considered, since these factors affect marketability.

Topography and Geology

The nature of the soil on the site is important for several reasons. First, it must support structures and roadbeds. Erosion and drainage are important considerations. Factors such as rocky ground or high water level may preclude construction of basements. Filled land or underground mining operations can also affect the stability of the land. Another important factor is drainage. The ability to construct stable roadbeds and to have dry basements in the homes is important. The ability of the soil to drain or absorb water is also important where septic systems are planned.

Utilities

Electricity, gas, water, and sewage are important considerations. Septic systems can substitute for sewage systems, and wells substitute for city water. The developer should determine the nearest location of each of these utilities, the available capacity for expansion, and the cost of extending the lines or pipes to the desired site. The mere existence of these facilities does not mean that there is the necessary gas or water capacity, pressure, or sewage capacity. The size of the development will affect the amount that can be spent to bring in these utilities. The cost should be computed on a per lot basis. This method helps the developer understand how these costs will offset the sale price of the lots, since all costs must be recovered through lot sale. A large development will be able to support considerably more of these costs than would a small development.

Access

A large part of the early improvement costs will be in providing roads. These costs will have to be borne by the developer before receiving money from sale of lots. Road costs include displacement costs for soil, leveling, providing drainage and culverts or bridges, preparing a road base, paving, curbing, and sometimes providing sidewalks. Sometimes the street construction must be closely integrated with the utility extension, as shown in the two alternatives of Figure 18–3.

Local Zoning Restrictions

In considering any site, the local zoning regulations must be considered. If the property is not presently zoned for the lot size and type of construction contemplated, the procedures to change the zoning must be investigated. The developer sometimes wants to place tighter restrictions on the development than those set by the municipality. This will help assure consistency in construction, protection of property values, and protection of values of unsold or undeveloped property.

Access to Services

The developer should also consider access to fire protection, police protection, hospitals, schools, and churches. The tax rate of the municipality is also an important factor.

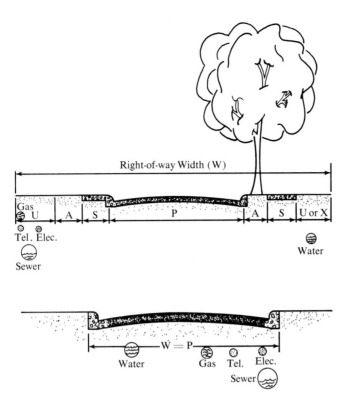

Figure 18–3 Two methods of integrating utilities with street construction

Source: National Association of Home Builders. *Land Development Manual.* Washington, D.C. 1974.

Government Reports

Depending on the type of subdivision or development, it may be necessary to file an environmental impact statement or, for land sales, a federal or state property report. (These reports and when they must be filed were described in Chapter 15.)

Financing

Most land developers require some type of financing. Prior to selecting a site, the available financing in that location must be investigated. This financing would include FHA, VA, and other federal program funds, as well as conventional mortgage loans. An investigation of available financing is appropriate whether or not the developer needs funds to purchase and develop the land. Even if she has those funds, she needs to establish financing commitments so that prospective property buyers will be able to finance their houses.

Often, the developer will purchase the land herself or form a syndicate to make the purchase. A *syndicate* is a group of persons who combine their financial resources to undertake a venture which, in this case, is the development of the real estate. The formation of a syndicate has certain tax advantages to the participants and permits accumulation of the large amounts of money needed to carry out a real estate development project.

If the developer has funds to purchase the land, she can then obtain a mortgage on it to finance further development and construction. Usually, however, a bank or other lender will require that the subdivision be surveyed and other tests performed before furnishing financing to make sure the land is fully usable for the proposed construction.

403

In the loan agreement, the developers can arrange terms so that individual sites can be released from the total mortgage and sold to buyers. The buyers can then arrange to build their own homes with individual loans. A typical release provision might allow the sale of a site free and clear to the buyer, with a portion of the money from each lot sold going to the lender to repay the loan gradually. In any case, the developer would probably develop a smaller portion of the total tract and later expand the development as the lots are sold. This procedure would then give her the additional funds from the lot sales to proceed with extended development of the whole tract.

The use of an option to purchase provides another alternative to the developer who is short of funds to purchase the entire tract that she desires to develop. If the developer is offered 150 acres, she may purchase 50 acres outright and obtain options to purchase additional tracts at some time in the future. This gives her the opportunity to develop the first tract and, if successful, she will then be able to go ahead and expand the project. If the original tract is not successful, she would not take up the option to purchase the remainder.

Subdivision Planning

Once the parcel of land to develop has been selected and purchased, the extensive and detailed steps of layout and planning of the subdivision must follow. In some cases, a developer may take an option on a tract of land pending completion of the more detailed surveys and layouts required. The option would provide greater assurance that all factors would work out satisfactorily before she actually made the land purchase.

The process of planning a subdivision requires a considerable initial outlay of money and time. However, careful planning can provide substantial monetary savings by allowing more efficient use of land as well as by identifying and avoiding potential problems. If unforeseen changes need to be made as a result of inadequate planning, the venture can become quite costly and the developer may go bankrupt. The plans prepared for the subdivision should describe the grading of roads, drainage, drainage dump, road paving, sidewalks, curbs, water mains, recreation areas, street signs, and municipal inspection fees. Some of the many preferred practices in the layout of a subdivision are shown in Figure 18–4. A *cluster layout,* for the same number of homes, can reduce street area and increase *open space* areas.

In addition to local constraints with which the developer must comply, if FHA financing is used there are standards for new subdivisions that must be met before FHA will approve loans. The development must contain the essential utilities, such as water, sewage, and electricity, and these must comply with local regulations. Minimum size lots are specified on the basis of home size to be built, and a uniform setback from the road is required. To secure FHA and VA loans, the roads must be of approved width and surfacing. The homes must meet approved structural and appearance constraints and must be consistent with other improved property in the area. Other features such as recreational areas and barriers from industrial or commercial establishments must be present, along with adequate access to shopping areas and schools.

Covenants and Restrictions

The developer of a subdivision will usually prepare *covenants* (or *restrictions*) that become binding upon the property owners in the subdivision. These requirements are in addition to zoning and other local municipal restrictions. They are made a part of the contracts to purchase lots. Each purchaser thereby agrees to these provisions when purchasing a lot. Either the developer or another property owner can take legal action to enforce any covenant or restriction. The purpose is to protect the interests of the residents and their property values. These covenants are particularly important if the subdivision is not under urban restrictions or is developed around a lake or other center of attraction where unauthorized persons may attempt to use the facilities. Some typical restrictions that appear in subdivision covenants are:

1. Restriction to use of lots for residential construction only
2. Approval of each home plan by the association or developer
3. Prohibition of outbuildings and fences in certain areas
4. Restrictions as to minimum house living area, minimum lot size, or setback of buildings
5. Restriction of type of exterior construction materials
6. Maintenance of lots in good order
7. Restriction on design of septic systems and disposal of trash
8. Restrictions on signs, animals, parking on roadways, or temporary structures
9. Easement rights
10. Rules for use of recreational facilities, lake, or other special areas
11. Membership in development association; power of association to levy fees and assessments; election of officers in association
12. Right of first refusal to other property owners or the developer if an owner wants to sell

In some cases courts have held that restrictions are in violation of Fair Housing laws. A restriction of lot sizes to a minimum of 40,000 square feet was struck down by a New Jersey superior court. The court decided that the purpose of the restriction was to reserve lots for affluent persons and to discourage use by lower-income persons and was therefore invalid. A restriction for a minimum floor area was held to be invalid in another court case. In other specific cases courts have given different opinions and found lot size restrictions to be enforceable. It is apparent from the decisions that large lot restrictions are not valid if the intent is to exclude certain economic or racial groups.

Plat Approval

Most states and municipal governments have laws regulating the subdividing of land. Many of these laws have been passed because of past incompetence or fraudulent practices used by subdividers. Most municipalities have planning commissions that are authorized to review and approve plats of all proposed new subdivisions. The *plat* must be prepared by a licensed land surveyor at the expense of the developer and submitted to the commission. Sometimes the submission must be made in two

Figure 18–4 Preferred practices in the layout of a subdivision

Source: State of New York, Office of Planning Services. *Control of Land Subdivision*. 1974.

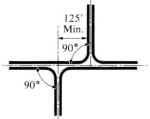

Undesirable offset street intersection

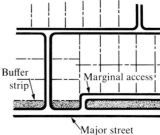

More desirable street intersection

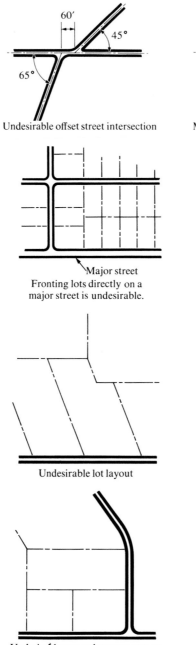

Major street
Fronting lots directly on a
major street is undesirable.

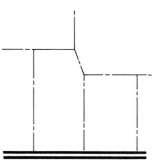

Buffer strip
Marginal access
Major street
Use of a buffer strip and marginal
access street is more desirable.

Undesirable lot layout

More desirable lot layout

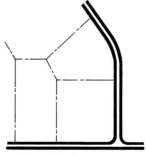

Undesirable corner lot arrangement

More desirable corner lot
arrangement

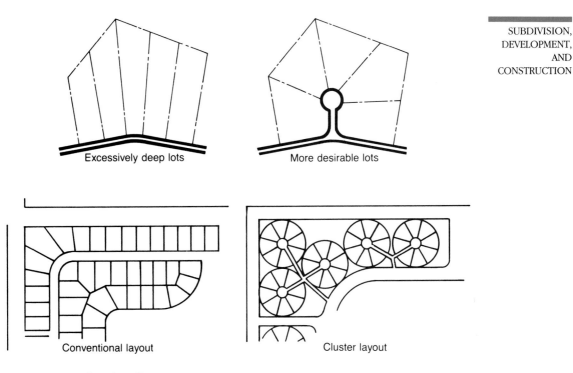

Excessively deep lots

More desirable lots

Conventional layout

Cluster layout

Figure 18–4   (continued)

or three steps. Figure 18–5 shows a preapplication sketch of a subdivision, with the planning board's comments added.

Depending on the local regulations, various requirements must usually be met by the developer. Some common requirements include the following:

1. Road cuts to specified width
2. Curbing
3. Sidewalks
4. Road paving, finishing, or oiling
5. Locations for wells and cesspools
6. National building codes
7. Lot size restrictions
8. Sufficient public areas (open space)

Normally, the developer must post a bond to assure that the actual construction is in accordance with the plat. The commissioner can then use the bond money to complete or reconstruct any work not in accordance with the approved plat. In some localities developers are required to pay *impact fees* to cover costs for expanding utilities, sewage facilities, and other items.

Figure 18–6 shows a final subdivision plat. Table 18–1 on page 410 shows a typical list of items that must be submitted with the plat. The table also shows a typical set of requirements that must be on the final plat. The final plat is then recorded. The act of recording becomes a public *dedication* of streets and designated open areas, such as a playground.

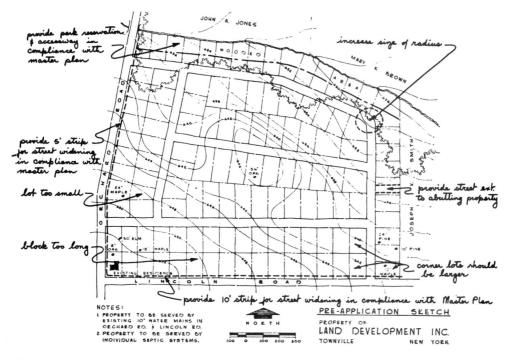

On the sketch (handwritten annotations):

provide park reservation & accessway in compliance with master plan

increase size of radius

provide 5' strip for street widening in compliance with master plan

lot too small

block too long

provide street ext. to abutting property

corner lots should be larger

provide 10' strip for street widening in compliance with Master Plan

JOHN A. JONES

WOODED

MARY K BROWN

AREA

SMITH

JOSEPH

EXISTING RESIDENCE

LINCOLN ROAD

NOTES:
1. PROPERTY TO BE SERVED BY EXISTING 10" WATER MAINS IN ORCHARD RD. & LINCOLN RD.
2. PROPERTY TO BE SERVED BY INDIVIDUAL SEPTIC SYSTEMS.

NORTH

100 0 100 200 300

PRE-APPLICATION SKETCH
PROPERTY OF
LAND DEVELOPMENT INC.
TOWNVILLE   NEW YORK

Figure 18–5   Preapplication sketch of a subdivision

Source: State of New York, Office of Planning Services. *Control of Land Subdivision.* 1974, p. 25.

COMMERCIAL AND INDUSTRIAL DEVELOPMENTS

Commercial property includes income-producing property such as shopping centers, office buildings, gasoline stations, retail establishments, parking lots, and hotels and motels. Industrial properties are used for the manufacture and warehousing of industrial and consumer products and include factories, utilities, warehouses, and mining or lumbering operations. The development of these types of properties requires steps and considerations similar in some ways to that of residential properties, but different in other ways.

Development for Retail Establishments

Retail facilities can vary from the *freestanding store* to the small *neighborhood centers,* shopping centers developed on a nonplanned basis called *suburban shopping districts,* the larger *community shopping center* anchored by a department store or variety store, or the *regional shopping center* anchored by two or three larger stores or branches of stores.

Many landowners have successfully developed retail shopping centers. However, a considerable amount of planning is required to assure the success of this type of endeavor. The designer of a shopping center will try to start with a **generative business** (e.g., a branch of a major department store) which, through advertising, will generate business of its own efforts. The developer can then attempt to obtain the many smaller **shared businesses** that can thrive due to the pulling power of the larger stores. The shopping center would also include **suscipient businesses** (e.g., restaurants), which attract people for purposes other than shopping. The general theory is that the clustering of stores increases the overall sales volume of each one.

The market evaluation would include an analysis of the demand in the area, determination of the future potential in the trade area, and an evaluation of current and contemplated competition. This would include a consumer survey in the area. The planning phase would include a preliminary layout, soil evaluation, utilities, road access, local restrictions, financing, and an investigation of applicable government regulations. These and the plat approval would follow to some extent the guidelines given for residential developments; however, the many differences that vary by locality and type of establishment are discussed in the supplementary readings at the end of this chapter.

Land Use for Office Space

Office buildings can be placed in two categories. Those designed and built for a specific company's use fall into the group of **custom construction.** Other office buildings are constructed on a speculative basis for rental. Between 1950 and today, the proportion of white-collar workers as a percentage of the total labor force expanded considerably. This factor, along with the growth of service industries during the same period, increased the demand for office space. One of the most significant

Figure 18–6   A subdivision plat

Source: State of New York, Office of Planning Services. *Control of Land Subdivision.* 1974, p. 28.

Table 18–1   Typical items to be submitted with a plat

Submission items		Required on final plat	
☐ Site survey map	☐ Sanitary sewerage computations	☐ Name of subdivision	☐ Open space (acreage noted)
☐ Site location map	☐ Fish and Game Department approval	☐ Name and address of owner	☐ Natural features
☐ Soils map	☐ Health and welfare: Division of Public Health approval	☐ North point	☐ Zoning district(s)
☐ Percolation test data		☐ Bar scale	☐ Future subdivisions
☐ Soils test data		☐ Date	☐ Topographic contour 5′ interval
☐ Watershed outline and drainage computations	☐ Public works and highway approval	☐ Area of site	
	☐ WSPCC approval for subdivision	☐ Parcel boundary	☐ Water mains and other utilities (final)
☐ Engineer's statement of suitability	☐ Water Resources Board approval	☐ Names and addresses of abutting owners	☐ Sanitary sewers (final)
☐ Statement of existing street work	☐ Fill and Dredge Special Board approval	☐ Subdivisions and buildings 100′ away	☐ Drainage system (final)
☐ Cost estimates		☐ Roads and drives 200′ away	☐ Name, address and seal of engineer
☐ Deed restrictions		☐ Buildings to remain	☐ Name, address and seal of surveyor
☐ Road profiles (final)	☐ Municipal water supply approval	☐ Existing and proposed street lines	
☐ Cross sections (final)	☐ Sewage disposal approval	☐ Existing and proposed street R.O.W. widths	☐ Bearings and distances
☐ Statement incorporating requirements of subdivision regulations	☐ Other municipal approval	☐ Street names	☐ Lot dimensions
	☐ Other state approval	☐ Lot lines	☐ Lot areas
		☐ Setback lines	☐ Lot numbering
☐ Statement of responsibility and liability		☐ Easements	☐ Stations
		☐ Watercourses	☐ Radii
			☐ Curve data
			☐ Pavement widths
			☐ Monument locations

Source: State of New Hampshire, Office of State Planning. *Handbook of Subdivision Practice*, 1972, p. 31.

trends over the past twenty-five years has been the shift of offices to the suburbs; however, the rehabilitation of downtown areas in large cities has also included new office construction.

Prior to acquiring land for office building construction on a speculative basis, a planner/developer should make a study of market demand. The developer needs initially to obtain one important figure, the current ratio of *net rented area* to *net rentable area* (in square feet) in the particular business community. A low ratio would indicate much unoccupied existing office space, and the contemplated project should probably be abandoned. If the ratio were high, the next phase of the study would be to forecast the needs in the area over the next five years. In this forecast, it is necessary to forecast new or increased business or government needs in the area and to convert the potential number of employees into office area needed. A figure of 275 to 300 square feet per employee is often used. Once the projected demand has been estimated, the developer will need to determine the types of uses contemplated. At that time, the type of building space to construct is selected, and the amount of potential space demand that the contemplated project could capture is estimated. Most other procedures in the planning and development for office space are similar to those for residential developments.

Industrial Sites

A company seeking a site for a plant has the choice of locating in an industrial park or on an individual site. Depending on the type of company, the following factors tend to be dominant in choosing a location:

1. Market-oriented companies tend to select locations near the consumers (users) of their products.
2. Labor-oriented companies tend to locate near sources of skilled labor to meet their needs.
3. Resource-oriented companies (such as steel) desire to locate near sources of raw materials. An aluminum company may choose to locate near sources of electric power.
4. A transportation-oriented firm would locate near the types of transport facilities that meet its needs.

Some industries tend to be independent of all these factors and thus have greater freedom in selecting sites for new plants; however, a developer of an industrial park should consider how these factors would affect potential tenants for the particular industrial park. The development and use of industrial parks has increased, largely due to their ability to provide superior facilities (such as utilities and transportation) and enforced land use controls. They also provide an attractive appearance, police protection, and pleasant and safe working conditions. Frequently, the industrial park will target its promotional campaign toward a certain category of industry. In any case, an industrial development will need to plan sites or construction to suit the needs of particular industries that decide to locate in the park.

THE BUILDING INDUSTRY

The building industry is one of the largest elements of the national economy. Many manufacturers depend upon it as a market for their products, and industries in general depend on it to expand capacity. A large segment of the total labor force is engaged in building construction. All of these facts together mean that the well-being of the construction industry has a heavy impact upon the national economic picture as a whole. The construction of individual residences makes up a large and important segment of the building industry. This enterprise will be dealt with here in greater detail than will other segments.

A house is a rather complex product, since it is comprised of a large variety of elements and materials. Often, single elements such as windows or doors are special either in size, design, or color; this can cause problems because all the necessary materials must be gathered and used in a certain sequence. Building materials are normally distributed by manufacturers either through wholesalers or directly to retail lumberyards. Builders then procure their materials through lumberyards, whole-sale plumbing supply houses, and many other sources. Many of these organizations do not sell directly to retail customers.

The bulky nature of most building products requires that those responsible for transporting and distributing them carefully control costs. Transportation, handling, and storage make up a considerable portion of the total costs of the delivered ma-terial. Some products such as plywood and gypsum board break easily or are dam-aged by weather. These factors further complicate their transportation and storage. Some manufacturers furnish preassembled or prefabricated units of various sizes. Moving the assembled or prefabricated units is possible, but it is more difficult because of their extreme bulk. This higher transportation cost and greater risk of breakage or damage is often, however, counterbalanced by the greater efficiency and cheaper labor that can be provided in the manufacturing facilities compared with site construction.

The Home Builders

Over past years, most homes have been built by the contractor on the building site. In recent years, however, more homes have been partially constructed at a manufac-turing plant and then transported to the building site, where the house is built from these prefabricated or partially assembled units.

Construction at the building site is carried out by specialists under the overall direction and responsibility of the builder or contractor. The electrical work, plumb-ing, plastering, brickwork, excavation, and pouring of concrete are often subcon-tracted out, as are a few other skill areas—depending frequently on the skills of the builder and labor force. Usually, the carpenters work directly for the builder on an hourly wage basis. All laborers who work on residential construction need some variety of skills and some knowledge of construction. Often, the same laborers who perform the rough carpentry will continue through the finished carpentry or wood-work, unless the contractor has a large operation and has several residences under way at the same time. The smaller operation still requires specialization, but workers with each type of skill, such as carpentry or masonry, will require a considerable amount of experience and background in order to adapt to the wide variety of types and stages of construction.

National Association of Home Builders (NAHB)

Persons in the business of building or rebuilding homes, apartments, or commercial or industrial structures can belong to the National Association of Home Builders *(NAHB)*. It has over 600 local affiliates and over 75,000 members. The association prepares and distributes literature dealing with building construction and land de-velopment. NAHB also conducts research related to new concepts in design, con-struction, and land use. In addition, NAHB provides a focal point for working with the federal government to improve housing and housing programs. It presents the views of the building industry to Congress and to the pertinent agencies and de-partments in the executive branch of the government.

Building Trades

The building trades are well organized in most cities. They tend to be organized along craft occupations, such as plumbers, carpenters, electricians, and bricklayers.

Thus, the building contractor must work with several organizations. These trade organizations have been quite successful in establishing relatively high wage scales for their workers. The higher wages compensate, to some extent, for the seasonal work and weather constraints that result in many days each year without work. The high labor rates have brought about greater competition from nonunionized personnel.

Where organized trades prevail, the labor unions control many of the hiring practices and training methods of apprentices and prescribe other restrictions as to how work is to be performed. Building trade organizations also tend to be slow in their acceptance of new methods and materials; this factor can impede the use of potential economies in building that might otherwise be adopted more quickly. All these factors support high wage rates in the building trades.

Manufactured Housing

The term *manufactured housing* refers to houses built away from the building site in one or more sections. Sections are often constructed in manufacturing plants where wages are lower than those for on-site construction. The sections are then combined into a complete house on the site. The end cost of the manufactured home is usually substantially lower than the cost of a home constructed completely at the site. Another advantage is a shorter time for construction. Thirty days are sometimes sufficient from order date to the time the customer can move in. By 1983, almost one-third of all new single-family homes sold in the United States were manufactured homes.[1] About half of these are in rental communities.

The Federal Housing and Community Act authorizes FHA loans for manufactured housing, including mobile homes. The 1974 Manufactured Housing Act empowers HUD to regulate the mobile home industry. Under a 1987 federal court ruling, homes with removable chassis must meet the same building codes applied to site-built homes. Many state legislatures have enacted laws prohibiting local restrictions that exclude manufactured homes just because they are manufactured off site. It is necessary only to meet the same zoning rules that govern regular housing. The most recent tendency is to treat manufactured houses and mobile homes as real property for tax purposes and other homeowner privileges.

Home Inspection

Home inspectors are often hired by home buyers to examine a home prior to purchase and point out existing or potential problems. Plumbing, electrical wiring, structure, roof, zoning, and other items are evaluated. This helps the buyer to choose between alternative homes and to understand problems related to the properties prior to making an offer to purchase. Sometimes the buyer can enter into a purchase contract contingent upon a satisfactory inspector's report. In other cases, a seller may seek an inspection report prior to placing a home on the market so that she and a potential buyer are both aware of any problems. If none are found, the report can give greater assurance to a buyer and help sell the home. Persons having a new home constructed also may request an inspection report prior to making the final payment to the contractor.

---

[1]Source: Rose, James L., and Duncan, Michael J. 1985. "Real Estate Developments." *Illinois Business Review,* June. Champaign: University of Illinois.

The American Society of Home Inspectors, Inc., is composed of members who meet certain qualifications. Also, some states are considering regulation of home inspections. The home inspection industry is seen as an outgrowth of consumerism and the problems that have sometimes occurred after buyers took possession of new homes.

Residential Construction

The construction of a new home can be closely integrated with the work of the developer, or it can involve only the owner of a single piece of property and the builder. Usually, the builder or a construction firm is involved in a particular project over a short period of time. However, the builder still faces a number of risks. Weather and labor strife always threaten delays and create uncertainties. During periods of inflation, costs of labor and materials can increase quickly, or there may even be shortages of materials. All of these factors lead to a relatively high rate of business failures in the building industry.

The construction of a typical residence can be separated into the following systematic steps:

1. Planning and estimating
2. Designing
3. Selecting a builder
4. Doing the construction work

Construction of an entire development differs somewhat from individual unit construction; however, the processes are quite similar in most ways.

Planning and Estimating

The first planning step is to select the building site or lot. The lot selection must be integrated closely with the design of the home. Usually, a subdivision or residential area is laid out to accommodate a certain size, price, or style of home, and this may be an initial constraint. Usually, there is also a price constraint to work with. The availability of mortgages and the percentage loan that can be obtained will also considerably influence the home size and price range.

The planning stage consists of the search for a number of alternative lots and some acceptable home designs and then the choice from among these alternatives.

Design of the Home

A person planning to build a home can either hire an architect to design an individual home or select from an architect's existing designs. Many companies provide a number of home designs for which the drawings and specifications can be purchased. In some cases, these specifications may have to be modified to comply with local restrictions or constraints or the person's individual preferences. However, minor modifications can usually be made easily. In either case, the architect prepares the basic drawings of a home, which include the floor plans as well as the front, side, and rear views. A typical floor plan is shown in Figure 18–7. The front elevation of that home is shown in Figure 18–8. The *floor plan* shows the exact room sizes and their interrelationships, whereas the *front elevation* shows the finished house as it would more normally appear to someone viewing it at ground level.

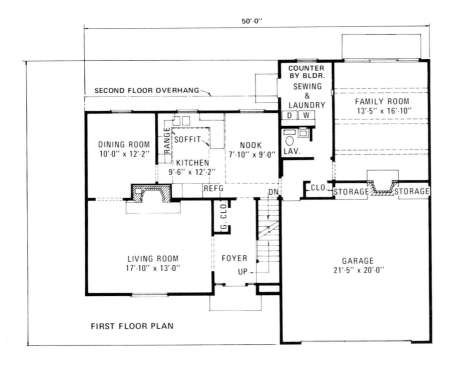

FIRST FLOOR PLAN

SECOND FLOOR PLAN

Figure 18–7 Typical single-family residence floor plans

Source: Used by permission Widerschein/Strandberg Corp., Toledo, Ohio.

Figure 18–8   Front elevation of
residence

In addition to the floor plan and external views, the architect prepares a specification and a bill of materials. The *specification* would describe requirements that might not be completely clear from the drawings. The type of framing, wood and nailing requirements, siding material, grade of concrete, and tests used to check the mixture are examples of items that might be in the specifications. Figure 18–9 shows some typical requirements.

The *bill of materials* would list the quantity of each item of material required to construct the house. If all of the items, such as studs, nails, and so on, are not specifically listed, the builder would have to determine this information by analysis of the drawings. Sometimes a bill of material is not furnished at all, and the prospective builder would need to figure quotations from the drawings to prepare a bid.

A survey then would show the layout of the house on the lot. An example is shown in Figure 18–10.

Selecting a Builder

Selecting a builder to perform the actual construction work usually involves obtaining competitive bids. The drawings of the house, the specifications, and the bill of materials provide the information as to what the builder is required to do. These documents would be sent to each prospective builder to bid on the project. In some instances, the developer or the property owner could select a builder based on past experience or by reputation, but the best practice is to seek competitive bids. In the competitive bidding process, each prospective builder quotes a price on the identical drawings and specifications, so that the lowest bid could probably be accepted. The prospective owner should also consider the builder's reputation for meeting quality and scheduling requirements, in addition to the competitive prices. The builder's ability to provide a bond or other evidence of financial stability is also important. Otherwise, there may be delays or problems if the builder cannot obtain sufficient funds to complete the project. Sometimes, however, a bidder may take exception to a requirement or suggest an alternative method of construction or type

SPECIFICATIONS FOR A HOME

The contractor shall provide all necessary labor and materials and perform all work of every nature whatsoever to be done in the erection of a residence for

Mr. and Mrs. John A. Halliburn

as owner, in accordance with these specifications and accompanying drawings. The location of the residence will be as follows:

421 Fourth Ave., Waynesboro, Va. 22980

General

The plans, elevations, sections, and detail drawings, together with these specifications, are to form the basis of the contract and are to be of equal force. The contractor shall comply with all health and building ordinances that are applicable.

Excavation and grading

The contractor shall do all necessary excavating and rough grading. The excavation shall be large enough to permit inspection of footings after the foundation has been completed. All excess dirt shall be hauled away by the contractor. Black surface loam shall be used in grading.

Concrete footings

Footings shall be of concrete having a minimum compressive strength of 2000#, 2500#, or 3000# per sq in at 28 days, whichever will be according to local code. Concrete shall be machine mixed with clean water to the proper consistency, and shall be placed immediately after mixing. Footings shall be thoroughly protected with hay or straw in freezing weather. All footings shall be set below the frost line and rest on firm soil, and shall be flat and level on the underside. Footings shall be of sizes shown on plan.

Basement walls and floor

Basement walls shall be constructed of 8 in concrete blocks of approved quality. Blocks shall be laid in a full bed of mortar, composed of one part of cement to three parts of sand. Mortar joints shall be filled thoroughly with cement mortar, neatly pointed on both sides. All walls shall have uniform bearing for framing, being straight, plumb, and level. Beam fill to be placed as shown on the plans. Basement walls shall be parged on exterior with ½ in cement mortar and waterproofed with 2 coats asphalt applied by brush. Basement floor shall be 4 in thick of concrete having minimum compressive strength of 2500# per sq in at 28 days and monolithically finished to a smooth hard surface and carefully pitched to drains.

Heating

Contractor shall and will provide all necessary labor and material and perform all heating work of every nature whatsoever to be done, including the installation of 135,000 BTU heating system of sufficient size to properly heat all parts of the house to 72°F at all times. If hot air system is to be used, it is to be installed according to the code of the National Society of Heating and Ventilating Engineers.

Figure 18–9 Typical requirements from a specification

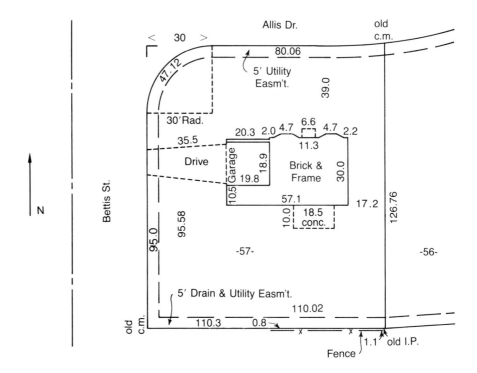

Figure 18–10   Survey—Layout of house on lot

of material. The property owner may accept the suggestion if it would improve the house or result in a lower cost. Since the total amount of money required to finance a home is substantial, most builders will require periodic payments as the work progresses. If so, the bids should clearly indicate the amounts and the point in construction when each is due.

Normally bids are requested for a *fixed price* for the entire building. The builder would estimate costs for material and labor and add on a profit. He would usually seek bids from subcontractors to install plumbing, electric wiring, concrete work, cabinets, or other portions that the builder does not plan to do himself. The builder would try to get fixed prices for these subcontracted tasks since he would want to make sure his subcontractors would not later raise their prices. The builder may also line up workers because, at times, good labor is difficult to find. Less competent laborers could cause delays and increased costs.

In order to avoid the risks related to a fixed price, some builders are willing to bid only on a *cost-plus-fixed-fee* basis. In this case, the property owner or developer would pay all the actual costs of labor and materials, and the builder would get a fixed fee. On a $40,000 house, the builder might get a typical fee of $4,000 above costs. This type of contract places more risk with the property owner and less risk with the builder. In this case, the builder would not need to estimate the job so carefully. It would also leave the property owner greater freedom in making changes as the work progressed. At the same time, the total cost may vary considerably from what was originally planned or expected. Another agreement may provide for a cost-plus-percentage-of-cost basis. If the agreed figure were 10 percent, and the costs came to $43,000, the builder would receive the $43,000 cost plus a $4,300 fee. Since it is somewhat unwise to give the builder an incentive to end up with greater costs, this type of contract is not widely used and is not recommended.

Once the builder has been selected, a contract is signed between the builder and the property owner. The contract would contain all of the provisions outlined above and would refer to the plans and specifications. Usually, it is wise to specify a schedule for completion.

Payments

The contract should specify that the builder provide a performance bond. The payments to the contractor would be scheduled (e.g., one-third when shell is completed, one-third when plastered, and one-third upon issuance of occupancy permit). Prior to each payment, the contractor should be required to provide an affidavit or receipts showing that materials and subcontractors have been paid, or else provide lien waivers if they have not been paid.

Construction Work

Once the contract has been negotiated and signed and a building permit has been issued by the designated public official, the builder can start construction. The nature of home construction requires that many tasks be performed in sequence. Some steps must be completed before others can start. The site preparation and completion of the foundation are necessary before the framing of the structure can begin. The next major steps are the framing, roof, and siding, since the protection provided by the roof and walls will permit much of the interior work to be carried out regardless of the weather. Figure 18–11 and Appendix B show residential construction details, including the *joists* supporting the floor, the *studs* forming the basis for the walls, and the *rafters* supporting the roof. Numerous other parts of a typical home are also identified.

The remaining steps still require careful planning and coordination by the builder so that the various specialists are scheduled to perform their tasks in the right sequence. For example, the heat ducts and electric wiring must be put in before the plaster. Then both the heating contractor and electrician must come back to finish the work that must be done after the plastering and interior painting. A delay at any stage can delay much of the other work. If a builder is constructing a number of homes, land clearance and digging can be initiated at one time for several houses. Then, as each step on one house is completed, the specialists can go on to the next house, so as to result in more efficient use of time, labor, and delivery of materials.

Inspection

The electrical, plumbing, and other work may need to be checked by the local inspector for conformance to building codes. The inspections often must take place before the work is covered up by later steps in the building sequence.

Energy Efficient Homes

The salesperson or broker can help the potential home buyer evaluate the home from an energy efficiency standpoint, just as it would be evaluated for construction details and other advantages or defects. The prudent home buyer looks at the energy

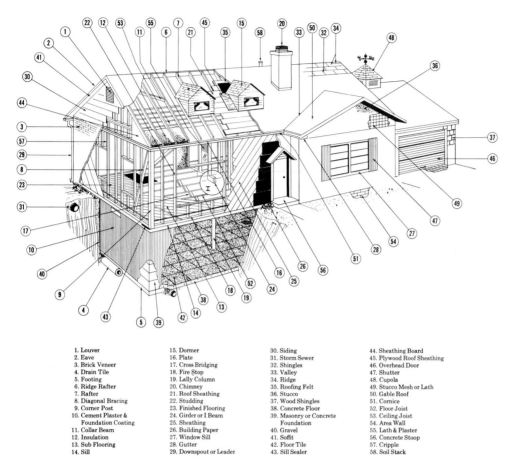

Figure 18–11 Residential construction details

Source: *Dodge Building Cost Calculator and Valuation Guide.* Copyright ©, 1980. McGraw-Hill Information Systems Company. 1221 Avenue of the Americas. New York, New York 10020.

1. Louver	15. Dormer	30. Siding	44. Sheathing Board
2. Eave	16. Plate	31. Storm Sewer	45. Plywood Roof Sheathing
3. Brick Veneer	17. Cross Bridging	32. Shingles	46. Overhead Door
4. Drain Tile	18. Fire Stop	33. Valley	47. Shutter
5. Footing	19. Lally Column	34. Ridge	48. Cupola
6. Ridge Rafter	20. Chimney	35. Roofing Felt	49. Stucco Mesh or Lath
7. Rafter	21. Roof Sheathing	36. Stucco	50. Gable Roof
8. Diagonal Bracing	22. Studding	37. Wood Shingles	51. Cornice
9. Corner Post	23. Finished Flooring	38. Concrete Floor	52. Floor Joist
10. Cement Plaster &	24. Girder or I Beam	39. Masonry or Concrete	53. Ceiling Joist
Foundation Coating	25. Sheathing	Foundation	54. Area Wall
11. Collar Beam	26. Building Paper	40. Gravel	55. Lath & Plaster
12. Insulation	27. Window Sill	41. Soffit	56. Concrete Stoop
13. Sub Flooring	28. Gutter	42. Floor Tile	57. Cripple
14. Sill	29. Downspout or Leader	43. Sill Sealer	58. Soil Stack

saving features of the home as closely as the heating bill, tax bill, and interior and exterior condition.

Most older dwellings need considerable work to make them energy efficient. As a general rule, homes can be compared in a specific area by their fuel costs; however, since the living habits of the homeowner can affect the heating cost significantly, several other items also need to be checked.

The following checklist will provide an idea as to how energy efficient an older home is (the numbering of the list refers to the numbers in Figure 18–12):

1. *Insulation* in ceiling, in walls, in attic floors, and in floors over garage and crawl space (refer to Figure 18–13 for R-values)
2. Vapor barrier wherever there is insulation
3. Perimeter insulation along and under edges of foundation
4. Double-glazed windows or storm sash
5. Storm doors
6. Insulation on air handling ducts or hot water pipes

Figure 18–12   An energy efficient home

Source: "Insulation for Thermal and Sound Control," p. 1, Owens-Corning Fiberglas Corporation. Reprinted with permission.

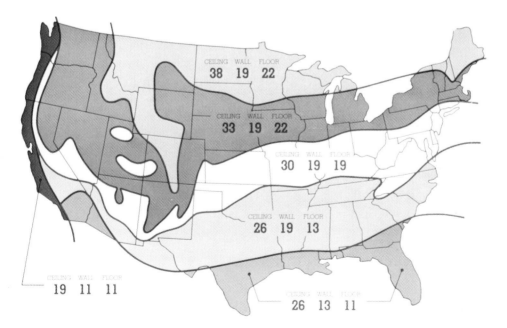

Figure 18–13   Recommended R-values for insulation

Source: *Guide to Constructing an Energy Efficient Home,* p. 17, Owens-Corning Fiberglas Corporation. Reprinted with permission.

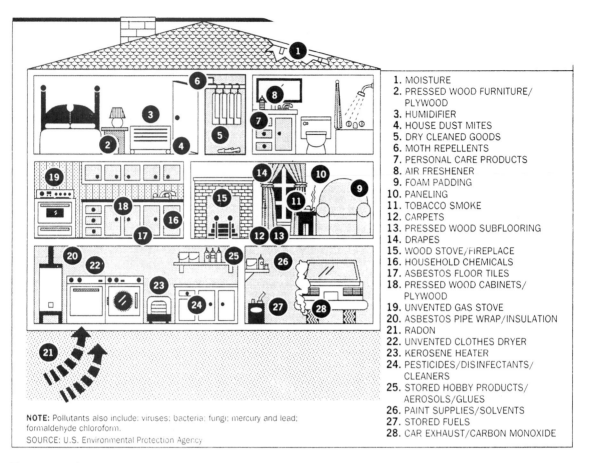

Figure 18–14 Potential air pollution hazards in a home

7. Weather-stripping on windows and doors
8. Caulking and sealing to prevent air infiltration
9. Ventilation to exhaust attic air and moisture
10. Proper size of heating and cooling equipment

An inspection by an insulation expert can be obtained if there is doubt as to the existing adequacy. Some utility companies offer free inspections to determine the energy efficiency of a home.

Inspection and Defects

In a recent nationwide survey of owners of new homes, many reported problems with their houses and difficulties in getting builders to correct them. More than thirty states now allow the owner of a defective new home to sue and recover damages from a builder on the basis of *implied warranty of habitability*—meaning the new home should be essentially free of major defects.

Home Pollution

The issue of indoor air quality was not recognized until the energy crisis of the 1970s prompted construction of airtight buildings that trap pollutants and encourage cost-conscious building managers to turn down ventilation. Many home buyers now insist on testing for radon as a contingency in contracts. Some potential hazards in a house are shown in Figure 18–14.

SUMMARY

Real estate construction represents a large and important segment of our national economy. The subdivision of land, its development, and the construction of homes make up a significant portion of this business. Other segments are the construction of commercial property, apartments, shopping centers, and industrial sites.

Experience has caused municipalities to place stringent restrictions on subdividers and developers. Whether the development is residential, commercial, or an industrial park, it requires extensive planning and a considerable financial outlay. Most subdividers and developers need to arrange for financing before they start any actual work. They should also carry out a market analysis and a variety of other investigations.

The construction of homes also requires experience and financial backing. The home builder faces risks due to uncertainties of weather, labor strife, and materials prices. Building a home requires planning and estimating, designing, and selecting a builder, as well as the actual construction work. The sequential nature of the construction makes it a complex task requiring considerable planning and careful supervision and control.

TERMS AND CONCEPTS

You can check your understanding of these terms against the glossary or by review in this chapter.

Bill of materials	Insulation	Shared business
Cluster layout	Joist	Specification
Covenant	Land developer	Stud
Custom construction	NAHB	Subdivider
Dedication	Open space	Subdividing
Floor plan	Plat	Suscipient business
Front elevation	Rafter	Syndicate
Generative business	Restriction	

What are the differences or relationships, if any, between the following?

Fixed price and Cost plus a fixed fee	Net rented area and Net rentable area	Subdivider and Land developer
Joists and Rafters		

PROBLEMS

18-1. List the important steps in planning a residential subdivision.

18-2. List some of the covenants that might appear in deeds for a residential subdivision.

18-3. Assume that you are considering the purchase of a lot in a residential development. Prepare a checklist of items to ask about or investigate.

18-4. Sketch a floor plan of your home or apartment.

18-5. Make a sketch of your lot and the position of the house on the lot.

18-6. Use the energy checklist provided in this chapter to check your home or apartment for energy efficiency.

18-7. Discuss reasons why a payment schedule is important when contracting to have a home built. Why is it important to obtain copies of receipts for materials and subcontract work before payments are made to the contractor?

18-8. Discuss reasons why a developer may impose further restrictions beyond the regular zoning restrictions in a new development.

18-9. Determine in square feet the heated living area for Figure 18–7.

18-10. In Figure 18–10, determine the lot size in square feet and acres.

18-11. In Figure 18–6, estimate the lot sizes for lots 41 and 23.

SUPPLEMENTARY READINGS

Ambrose, James. *Building Structures Primer*. New York: Wiley, 1981.

Burchell, Robert W., and Hughes, James W. *Planned Unit Development*. New Brunswick, N.J.: Rutgers University Center for Urban Policy, 1972.

Control of Land Subdivision. Albany, N.Y.: New York State Office of Planning Services, 1974.

David, Philip. *Urban Land Development*. Homewood, Ill.: Irwin, 1972. Chapter 15.

Derven, Ronald, and Nichols, Carol. *How to Cut Your Energy Bill*. Farmington, Mich.: Structures Publishing Company, 1976.

Farley, John H. *Dodge Building Cost Calculator and Valuation Guide*. New York: McGraw-Hill, 1974.

Handbook for Subdivision Practice. Washington, D.C.: National Association of Home Builders, 1975.

Handbook of Subdivision Practice. Office of State Planning, State of New Hampshire, 1972.

Herubin, Charles A. *Construction Site Planning and Development*. Englewood Cliffs, N.J.: Prentice-Hall, 1988.

Kinnard, William N.; Messner, Stephen D.; and Boyce, Byrl N. *Industrial Real Estate*. Washington, D.C.: Society of Industrial Realtors, 1979.

Kleeman, Leonard. *Real Estate Encyclopedia of Home Design, Construction, and Architecture*. Englewood Cliffs, N.J.: Prentice-Hall, 1981.

Land Development Manual. Washington, D.C.: National Association of Home Builders, 1981.

Land Use Controls. Urbana, Ill.: University of Illinois College of Agriculture Special Publication No. 7, 1963.

Lewis, Jack R. *Construction Specifications*. Englewood Cliffs, N.J.: Prentice-Hall, 1975.

Liebing, Ralph W. *Systematic Construction Inspection*. New York: Wiley, 1982.

McKeever, J. Ross. *The Community Builders Handbook*. Washington, D.C.: Urban Land Institute, 1968.

McMahan, John. *Property Development,* 2nd ed. New York: McGraw-Hill, 1988.

McNeill, Joseph G. *Principles of Home Inspection*. New York: Van Nostrand Reinhold, 1979.

Real Estate Atlas. Miami: Real Estate Data, Inc. (Updated annually for certain areas).

Residential Construction Costs. Los Angeles: Marshall and Swift Publication Company, 1982.

Smith, Halpert C.; Tschappat, Carl J.; and Racster, Ronald L. *Real Estate and Urban Development,* 3rd ed. Homewood, Ill.: Irwin, 1977. Chapter 12.

Smith, Wallace F. *Urban Development*. Berkeley: University of California Press, 1975.

Ventolo, William L. *Residential Construction*. Chicago: Real Estate Education Co., 1979.

CHAPTER 19
Appraisal and Value

An appraisal gives an unbiased estimate or opinion of value. Appraisals are performed to solve a problem or answer a question concerning value. The question or problem may be very simple, such as What is the market value of a particular house? In fact, the vast majority of appraisal assignments involve the estimation of market value. On the other hand, the question or problem involving value may be very complex, such as What is the value of the sublessee's leasehold interest on a thirty-year index lease that has twenty-three years remaining? The scope of the appraisal assignment will vary depending on the objective of the appraisal. This chapter will deal with some of the basic concepts.

TYPICAL APPRAISAL ASSIGNMENTS

Why are appraisals performed? Who uses appraisals? Some answers to these questions follow:

- *Investors* often seek an expert opinion on value before making decisions on buying, selling, or exchanging real estate.
- *Property owners* of multifamily, commercial, or industrial buildings may request an opinion as to the economic feasibility of a proposed remodeling or rehabilitation program.
- *Buyers and sellers* of single-family homes may request an opinion of value before they consummate a purchase or sale.
- *Subdividers* frequently request the help of an appraiser in determining the feasibility of a proposed subdivision.
- *Developers* may desire a "highest and best use" analysis of a particular site or building.
- *Insurance agents or adjustors* may request an appraiser to estimate the insurable value of a client's property.
- *Lawyers* frequently request professional opinions on value for purposes of estate planning, property settlements, condemnation, estate liquidation, lawsuits, or lease negotiations.
- *Lending institutions* who make loans on real estate seek the appraiser's opinion of the market value of real estate that is to be pledged as security for a loan.
- *Local and state governments* seek the appraiser's assistance in determining market value when they exercise their power of eminent domain to acquire private property for public use.

APPRAISAL AS A PROFESSION

Real estate appraising is the most specialized area within the real estate industry. The need for professional appraisal service has long been recognized by banks, savings and loan institutions, government agencies, investors, endowed institutions, and others who make important and frequent decisions based on estimates of property value. Some state legislatures have either passed or are considering legislation requiring licensing of real estate appraisers.

The recent crisis in mortgage lending, which has resulted in a record high number of foreclosures and bank failures, has created much alarm and finger-pointing within the real estate industry. In fact, several factors have contributed to the current crisis. Poor underwriting practices in qualifying borrowers, inflated property appraisals, atypical financing methods that unrealistically increase selling prices of properties, and a slowing of the rate of inflation have all combined to create the present turmoil in the industry. The industry needs to go back to less speculative lending, more dependable value estimates, and more responsible loan underwriting practices. These problems are now being addressed by the major appraisal organizations and leaders in the primary and secondary mortgage markets.

The varied and technical nature of real estate appraising and the important decisions that stem from appraisals underscore the need for very specialized training and adherence to a strict professional code of ethics by the appraiser. Appraisers must not accept an assignment they are not qualified to carry out, nor should they let their biases or emotions jeopardize accurate, objective findings of value. Two important professional appraisal organizations have contributed greatly in elevating appraisal to its current standing as a profession.

The American Institute of Real Estate Appraisers (AIREA) formed in 1932, an affiliate of the NATIONAL ASSOCIATION OF REALTORS ® (NAR), is a leader in appraisal education, publications, and professional standards of practice in the industry. Their members subscribe to a strict code of ethics and must meet stringent educational and experience requirements before they are awarded either the *MAI* (member, appraisal institute) or the *RM* (residential member) designation.

The Society of Real Estate Appraisers (*SREA*) is the other major professional appraisal group responsible for elevating the art of real estate appraisal to a professional status. The society is also heavily involved in appraisal education, research, and publications. Their members also face lengthy educational and experience requirements before they earn their designations. The society's designations include the **SRA** (senior residential appraiser), **SRPA** (senior real property appraiser), and the SREA (senior real estate analyst).

Other major appraisal organizations include the American Society of Appraisers, the American Society of Farm Managers and Rural Appraisers, the International Association of Assessing Officers, the International Right of Way Association, the National Association of Independent Fee Appraisers, and the National Society of Real Estate Appraisers. In recent years, many universities have increased their course offerings in real estate appraisal. Professionally designated appraisers and others highly trained and experienced in forming accurate, unbiased estimates of value will continue to be in great demand in the future.

Regulation of Appraisers

As of this writing, only twelve states[1] regulate appraisers under their licensing authority. In most states the individual is at liberty to "hang up his shingle" and begin his appraisal practice with no requirements whatsoever. At the federal level, various agencies impose regulations on appraisals and appraisers, but such efforts are inconsistent and inadequate. Within the appraisal industry itself, there are several professional associations that adhere to a strict code of ethics and provide quality educational programs to enhance professionalism. However, it is estimated that 75 percent of the appraisers in the country do not belong to any of these organizations.

The federal government has a significant interest in assuring that quality appraisals are being made. For instance, the Federal Savings and Loan Insurance Corporation (FSLIC) insures over $1 trillion in deposits held at savings and loans throughout the country. When these institutions fail, the federal government must pick up the tab. To date, hundreds of failed S&Ls have been closed down or merged, and many more are on the "troubled" list. It was estimated in 1989 that it would take $150 to $200 billion to bail out the failed savings and loan industry. Many of these failures were due, in part, to shoddy appraisal practices.

---

[1]*States currently requiring licenses include:* Texas, Illinois, Indiana, Florida, Michigan, Oregon, South Carolina, Pennsylvania, Rhode Island, Nebraska, Delaware, and Mississippi.

In addition to insuring S&L deposits throughout the country, the federal government insures or guarantees over $480 billion in mortgages through the FHA, VA, and Farmers Home Administration. In the late 1980s, these federal agencies were experiencing record high foreclosures, costing the government billions of dollars. All of these losses came at a time when the federal government was experiencing a record high national debt and recurring annual budget deficits in the hundreds of billions of dollars. The savings and loan crisis of the late 1980s focused attention on the relatively unregulated appraisal industry and stimulated congressional action.

Proposed Federal Regulation of Appraisers

The Real Estate Appraisal Reform Act of 1987 has as its purpose:

> To reorganize and consolidate in a new federal agency certain functions of the Federal Government relating to real estate appraisals and to authorize state appraiser certifying agencies, for the purpose of protecting the financial and public policy interests of the United States in certain real estate-related financial transactions.

In essence, the bill would allow the federal government to:

1. Set standards for appraisals
2. Set standards for appraiser qualifications
3. Provide that the states enforce the requirements

These standards would be established with strong input from an advisory committee consisting of users and regulators of appraisers and appraiser groups. The bill also includes a "sunset" provision that will automatically reduce the federal government's role once the standards have been set and the mechanism for state enforcement is in place. It is presumed this could be accomplished within a five-year period. At this writing, most of the reform measures discussed here were passed, and states are now required to certify or license appraisers as of a specified date.

TYPES OF VALUE

An *appraisal* has been defined as an estimate or opinion of value. Many different kinds of value exist. The specific type of value to be estimated depends on the intended use of the appraisal. Some of the common uses of appraisals and the respective types of values estimated for those appraisals are listed in Table 19–1. The

Table 19–1   Types of value determined by different appraisals

Use of appraisal	Type of value estimated
To determine listing price	Market value
To determine the price to pay for a given investment	Investment value
To determine insurance needs	Insurable value
To establish rental values	Market value
To establish value of collateral to allocate value between land and building for depreciation	Market value

three types of value most frequently estimated by the appraiser are market value, investment value, and insurable value.

Market Value

Most appraisal assignments involve the estimation of market value. *Market value* has no universal definition, but relates closely to the buying, selling, or exchanging of property. The various courts and jurisdictions around the country have fostered many different definitions, each definition having its own assumptions and limitations. Many definitions of market value are based on a decision by a California Supreme Court in an eminent domain case (Sacramento Railroad Company v. Heilbron). The court's definition was

> The highest price in terms of money which a property will bring in a competitive and open market under all conditions requisite to a fair sale, the buyer and seller each acting prudently, knowledgeably, and assuming the price is not affected by undue stimulus.

The ninth edition of *The Appraisal of Real Estate,* published by the American Institute of Real Estate Appraisers, defined market value as

> The most probable price as of a specified date in cash, terms equivalent to cash, or in other precisely revealed terms, for which the specified property rights should sell after reasonable exposure in a competitive market under all conditions requisite to fair sale, with the buyer and seller each acting prudently, knowledgeably, and for self-interest, and assuming that neither is under undue duress.

The assumptions and conditions presumed in the Institute's definition include

1. The property is exposed for a reasonable time on the open market. The determination of a "reasonable" period of time depends on the type of property involved and the existing market conditions. For instance, residential properties usually sell more quickly than commercial or industrial properties, and all properties tend to sell at a slower rate when mortgage rates are high.
2. Buyer and seller are well informed and act prudently.
3. Buyers and sellers are acting in their own best interests.
4. Payment is made in cash, its equivalent, or in other specific terms.
5. The specified financing, if any, may be the financing already in place or readily available financing.
6. The impact, if any, on market value of any atypical financing or other concessions shall be so indicated in the appraisal report.

Market value also represents "value in exchange" and could be envisioned as the expected selling price of a property. Many other definitions of market value have been advanced by courts, appraisal organizations, and scholars.

Since each definition of market value has its own assumptions and limitations, the value estimates may also differ. Consequently, it is imperative that each appraiser specifically define market value in his report.

Insurable Value

An appraiser may be asked to estimate the value of a building and its contents to determine the amount of insurance needed to fully indemnify or protect the insured in case of loss. Insurable value is generally based on the reproduction or replacement cost of the physical assets that are exposed to loss from some insurable hazard. Although the concept of *insurable value* is complex and beyond the scope of this book, it generally entails the following:

1. First, replacement value of the property is estimated.
2. Those portions of the property that are specifically exempt by the terms of the insurance contract are then subtracted. Examples are architectural fee, utility hookups, loan fee charges, and other construction costs that would not be incurred again in case of loss and reconstruction. These costs are deducted from the replacement value to arrive at *replacement cost, insurable.*
3. Depreciation for insurance purposes is subtracted next. Unlike depreciation as used in the general field of appraising (loss in value from any cause), *depreciation* for insurance purposes (loss in value from physical deterioration only) is subtracted from the replacement cost, insurable, to arrive at what appraisers call *insurable value, depreciated.* The insurance industry sometimes refers to insurable value, depreciated, as *actual cash value.* Appraisers feel this implies some relationship to market value, however, and since that is not the case, appraisers prefer to use the phrase *insurable value, depreciated.* Although there are different types of insurance policies, as discussed in Chapter 12, this is the usual insurable value.

Investment Value

Clients will often request an appraisal when considering the property as an investment. They could be considering the investment as a potential source of income or in speculation for future sale. *Investment value* can be considered as the present worth of the property's future income stream and property reversion to a specific investor.

The investment value to the individual is further influenced by the investor's ability to obtain financing, the amount and terms of available financing, the investor's other income, and how the acquisition of the property will affect the investor's tax bracket. Investment value represents "value in use" and is, therefore, a specific value to a particular or potential user. Considering this, a particular income-producing property may have a different investment value to each of several different potential investors. Investment value is used by clients making decisions whether or not to purchase a given property as an investment or by clients comparing alternative investment possibilities.

Plottage

Plottage is the incremental increase in value that results from the combination of two or more parcels of land to form one large parcel that has greater utility and hence a greater market value than the individual parcels. For example, assume existing zoning laws permit a four-unit apartment building on a 10,000 square foot lot. If an adjoining lot of the same size can be purchased, zoning laws will permit a ten-unit apartment building. If lots are selling for $5,000 per allowable unit, the parcels of land, when combined, will experience a $10,000 increase in value due to plottage.

Market value may be more than, equal to, or less than market price. *Market price* is the amount of money actually paid for a given property by a buyer who may or may not have been well informed and free of undue pressure. On the other hand, *market value* is the estimated price a property would sell for in the open market predicated upon knowledgeable behavior on the part of the buyer and seller and neither acting under undue pressure. The only way to determine whether or not a property actually sold for market value is to have it appraised. Market value may also be more than, equal to, or less than cost. *Cost* is the amount of money needed to bring a property into being. This includes the outlay for land, labor, capital, and management, including overhead and profit. A rational builder would not knowingly build a building on a site unless he expected market value to equal or exceed the cost of production. Unfortunately, the unknowledgeable buyer or builder who makes decisions without complete market knowledge may overbuild a site or overimprove a structure, thus incurring costs that cannot be recouped in the market place.

PREREQUISITES TO VALUE

Four basic elements are necessary for a property to have a market value. The degree to which each of these prerequisites is present determines the total value that can be assigned to the property.

Utility

Without utility or potential utility, there can be no market value. *Utility* is satisfaction derived from ownership of property, whether monetary return or psychological satisfaction. The utility of a property may increase or decrease overnight or may change gradually, depending on the forces at work in the marketplace. Although utility is essential before value can exist, utility alone does not create value. A common analogy clarifies this point. The air we breathe has considerable utility for all of us; however, there is no scarcity of air on the surface of the earth and, therefore, air has no market value. (Our society does incur certain indirect costs in order to provide *clean* air.)

Scarcity

Scarcity is a second prerequisite before market value can exist. Scarcity refers to the supply of an existing product relative to the demand for it. Since ordinary air is not scarce, it has no market value. Air to a deep-sea diver is scarce, however, and certainly does have *utility*. However, if all deep-sea divers were without funds, they would be prevented from purchasing the air. Without this *effective demand* or purchasing power, no market value would be created.

Effective Demand

Effective demand is an economic term meaning that there is a need or desire for an item backed up by purchasing power. Purchasing power is normally created by, or results from, a person's income, existing assets, and/or the extension of credit.

Since most real estate purchases rely extensively on borrowed funds, and as the cost of these funds rises, all else being equal, the effective demand for real estate will fall. Without purchasing power, no effective demand would exist.

Transferability

Even though an item has three of the four prerequisites to value, if that item has no *transferability,* market value cannot be created. The transferability of a property may be adversely affected by mechanic's liens, judgments, leases, mortgages, or other encumbrances or claims against the title to the property.

In summary, the interrelated prerequisites of utility, scarcity, effective demand, and transferability are all necessary to create market value. To the extent that all these prerequisites continue to exist, market value will be present. To the extent that these relationships change relative to one another, market value will change.

PRINCIPLES OF VALUE

Ten basic principles affect the value of real property.

Principle of Supply and Demand

As the supply of a particular type of property increases relative to demand, market value will decrease. As demand increases relative to supply, market value will increase. The interplay of supply and demand determine market value.

Principle of Change

The real estate market is dynamic and always changing. The forces of change affect specific properties, neighborhoods, cities, and nations. The wants and needs of buyers and sellers in the marketplace also change. Change affects supply and demand and, therefore, value.

Principle of Substitution

Properties that provide the same or similar utility are considered substitutes *(principle of substitution).* Among available substitutes, consumers will generally choose the one with the lowest price.

Principle of Conformity

The highest values are realized in properties that show a reasonable degree of sociological, economic, and architectural similarity. For instance, the introduction of heavy industrial establishments into a residential area resulting in heavy truck traffic, air pollution, and noise pollution will adversely affect residential property values. Reasonable conformity is not meant to imply monotonous uniformity.

Principle of Highest and Best Use

Property is most profitable if used in a way to which it is best adapted and for which the demand is greatest. The *highest and best use* is that legal and probable use which is expected to produce the highest net return. The highest and best use of a property may change over time.

Principle of Balance

Maximum value is created and maintained when the following four agents of production are in balance: (a) labor (wages); (b) capital; (c) management; (d) land (rents). When these agents are out of balance, value is adversely affected. For example, when an apartment building has been overimproved, the market rents are insufficient to provide a satisfactory return for the capital invested.

Principle of Contribution (Principle of Marginal Productivity)

The value of any one of the agents of production or any item of production is directly related to its contribution to the net income or present value of the property. The application of the *principle of contribution* is essential to any sound decision on remodeling or rehabilitating a building.

Principle of Increasing and Decreasing Returns

As mentioned earlier, real property value is affected by the contribution of the four agents of production, namely, labor, capital, management, and land (rents). Up to a point, incremental increases in capital invested (or any one of the other agents of production) will produce correspondingly greater increases in value *(principle of increasing returns)*. Once maximum value is developed, any additional incremental increase in capital will produce a less than corresponding increase in value *(principle of decreasing returns)*.

Principle of Competition

When a property generates a net income sufficient to satisfy the four agents of production, any excess is considered profit. In a competitive environment, uses of property that produce heavy profits attract competition. If this competition is excessive, it may result in a strongly competitive situation where few or none of the competitors make an adequate profit.

Principle of Anticipation

Value is created by the anticipated future benefits of ownership. Future benefits may be very different from those in the past. A realistic projection of future benefits is essential to an accurate appraisal of value.

FORCES INFLUENCING VALUE

Value is dynamic. It is not inherent in property, but rather is a dynamic characteristic that changes with the changing wants and needs of the market.

Four major forces are constantly at work nationally, regionally, locally, and within the specific property itself to influence value. These are (a) governmental/political, (b) economic, (c) social/psychological, and (d) physical forces.

Figure 19–1 summarizes the four major forces influencing value and gives some examples of each. The summary shows forces with which the appraiser is confronted

---

FORCES INFLUENCING VALUE

Governmental/Political Forces
Zoning regulations
Building codes
Taxes
Special assessments
Police and fire protection
Eminent domain
Rent controls

Economic Forces
Population growth
Wages, salaries, and savings
Availability and rates of mortgage money
Employment growth and sources
Labor availability and rates
New construction rates
Rental rates, vacancies, and existing supply of property
Price range of existing homes

Social/Psychological Forces
Demographic factors—Age, education, income, occupation, and number of
   children in family
Social factors—Social participation, mobility, life styles, class, or subcultures
Psychological factors—Self-concept, how risk is perceived, prestige

Physical Forces
Location of neighborhood, degree built up, and general appeal
Proximity to shopping, employment, recreation, schools, and churches
Quality of schools and churches
Street pattern, condition, sidewalks and curbs
Utilities available
Site size, shape, topography, subsoil, and landscaping
Improvement, age, size, condition, exterior
Interior, amenities, depreciation of buildings

Figure 19–1   The four forces influencing value

in collecting, organizing, and interpreting the necessary data to arrive at an estimate of value.

THE APPRAISAL PROCESS

To aid in planning and executing the appraisal assignment, the appraiser follows a systematic procedure called the appraisal process. This plan of action ensures efficient and effective use of the appraiser's time and resources. Figure 19–2 depicts the steps as described in the text.

Step 1—Define the Problem

The first step in the appraisal process consists of defining the problem:

1. *Identify the subject property by street address and legal description.*
2. *Identify the rights to be evaluated.* Although most appraisals estimate the value of

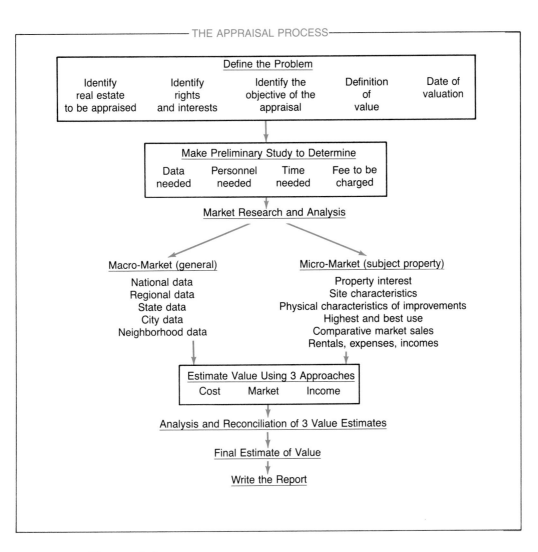

Define the Problem

| Identify real estate to be appraised | Identify rights and interests | Identify the objective of the appraisal | Definition of value | Date of valuation |

Make Preliminary Study to Determine

| Data needed | Personnel needed | Time needed | Fee to be charged |

Market Research and Analysis

Macro-Market (general)

National data
Regional data
State data
City data
Neighborhood data

Micro-Market (subject property)

Property interest
Site characteristics
Physical characteristics of improvements
Highest and best use
Comparative market sales
Rentals, expenses, incomes

Estimate Value Using 3 Approaches

| Cost | Market | Income |

Analysis and Reconciliation of 3 Value Estimates

Final Estimate of Value

Write the Report

Figure 19–2   The appraisal process

all the rights included in fee simple ownership, partial interests may also be considered and evaluated. For instance, appraisals may require evaluation of leasehold interests, leased fee interests, sublessee's interests, mineral rights, air rights, or other partial interests.

3. *Identify the objective of the appraisal.* Before taking on an appraisal assignment, the appraiser should clearly understand the client's objectives. Some appraisers and appraisal texts make a distinction between the *function* of an appraisal and its *purpose*. The **function of the appraisal** is concerned with the reason for the appraisal, that is, its use. The **purpose of the appraisal** is to estimate value. The function of the appraisal determines the specific type of value to be estimated, namely, market value, investment value, or insurable value. As mentioned earlier, most appraisal assignments involve the estimation of market value.

4. *State the date of the valuation.* It is essential that the date of the value estimate be specified. The principle of change is constantly at work, influencing values daily.

Therefore, any value estimate is valid only at the time that it is formulated and can change from one day to the next. In most instances, appraisal assignments involve current value estimates; however, assignments involving value estimates as of some date in the past are not uncommon.

5. *Define the type of value to be estimated.* To avoid any misunderstanding later, the type of value estimated and reported should be clearly established before the appraisal process begins. This is important because the kinds of data collected depend to a large extent upon the type of value to be estimated. In addition, estimates of market value, investment value, insurable value, or salvage value all involve different methods and techniques in data analysis. The amount of weight or emphasis placed on all types of data varies, and there are differences in the methods and techniques used in interpreting the data to arrive at the desired value estimate.

Step 2—Preliminary Study

The second step consists of a study of the contemplated task. It includes the following considerations:

1. *Data needed.* The data to be gathered are determined by the type of property and the objective of the appraisal. The information gathered should include general market data as well as data about the specific property.

2. *Data sources.* All sources from which the primary and secondary data are to be obtained must be identified at this time.

3. *Personnel needed.* Identify the number and nature of any specialized help needed to carry out the appraisal. Such help may include cost estimators, engineers, or architects.

4. *Time needed.* The time required from start to completion of the assignment should be estimated. If the assignment is complex, a work schedule or flow chart should be developed.

5. *Determine fee.* Once the data, personnel, and time estimates have been established, a fee can be set. A description of the effort and the fee should be stated in writing and agreed to by both the client and the appraiser before further work takes place.

Step 3—Market Research and Analysis

The third step includes collecting and analyzing the data. The data may be broken down into the two main categories of external and internal data.

1. External or **macromarket data** describe the governmental, economic, social, and physical forces affecting value. National, regional, city, and neighborhood data that influence value should be compiled and analyzed. Factors such as local population trends, employment outlook, mortgage terms available, rental rates, and taxes should be considered. The neighborhood factors that influence value include:

Zoning controls
Availability of utilities
Transportation facilities
Street pattern and traffic
General appeal
Price range of area housing

Income and social status of neighborhood
Proximity to schools and churches
Recreation facilities
Percent built up in the immediate area
Types of construction in area
Stage in life cycle of the neighborhood
Nuisances

2. Internal or *micromarket data* relate to the forces within the property itself that create or destroy value. These data include the specific site, its improvements, and any constraints on usage. Some of the factors influencing site value are:

Private deed restriction
Lot or site frontage, size, and shape
Landscaping
Topography
Soil and subsoil
Available utilities
Sidewalks
Traffic

Some of the factors influencing the value of the improvements are:

Age of improvements
Size of improvements
Interior condition
Exterior condition
Heating system
Air conditioning
Plumbing
Electricity
Quality of construction
Amenities
Number of bathrooms
Number of bedrooms
Floor plan
Kitchen design
Storage

Appraisers generally use a checklist during their inspection of the site and improvements to make sure they do not miss anything important. Figure 19–3 illustrates a FNMA/FHLMC single-family residence appraisal form. In addition to collecting and analyzing the site and improvement data, appraisers must collect specific sales data, rental data, and income data on properties that are reasonably comparable to the property being appraised. This will be discussed at length later in this chapter under the market approach to value.

Step 4—Estimate Value Using the Three Approaches

Whenever possible, the fourth step should entail the use of all three approaches to value, namely, the cost approach, the market or sales comparison approach, and the

Property Description & Analysis **UNIFORM RESIDENTIAL APPRAISAL REPORT** File No.

SUBJECT

Property Address	Census Tract	LENDER DISCRETIONARY USE

City	County	State	Zip Code	Sale Price $

Legal Description — Date

Owner/Occupant — Map Reference — Mortgage Amount $

Sale Price $ — Date of Sale — PROPERTY RIGHTS APPRAISED — Mortgage Type

Loan charges/concessions to be paid by seller $ — ☐ Fee Simple — Discount Points and Other Concessions

R.E. Taxes $ — Tax Year — HOA $/Mo. — ☐ Leasehold — Paid by Seller $

Lender/Client — ☐ Condominium (HUD/VA)

☐ De Minimis PUD — Source

NEIGHBORHOOD

LOCATION	☐ Urban	☐ Suburban	☐ Rural	NEIGHBORHOOD ANALYSIS	Good	Avg.	Fair	Poor
BUILT UP	☐ Over 75%	☐ 25-75%	☐ Under 25%	Employment Stability	☐	☐	☐	☐
GROWTH RATE	☐ Rapid	☐ Stable	☐ Slow	Convenience to Employment	☐	☐	☐	☐
PROPERTY VALUES	☐ Increasing	☐ Stable	☐ Declining	Convenience to Shopping	☐	☐	☐	☐
DEMAND/SUPPLY	☐ Shortage	☐ In Balance	☐ Over Supply	Convenience to Schools	☐	☐	☐	☐
MARKETING TIME	☐ Under 3 Mos.	☐ 3-6 Mos.	☐ Over 6 Mos.	Adequacy of Public Transportation	☐	☐	☐	☐

PRESENT LAND USE %	LAND USE CHANGE	PREDOMINANT	SINGLE FAMILY HOUSING	Recreation Facilities	☐	☐	☐	☐
			PRICE $ (000) — AGE (yrs)					
Single Family ___	Not Likely	OCCUPANCY		Adequacy of Utilities	☐	☐	☐	☐
2-4 Family ___	Likely	☐ Owner		Property Compatibility	☐	☐	☐	☐
Multi-family ___	In process	☐ Tenant	Low	Protection from Detrimental Cond.	☐	☐	☐	☐
Commercial ___	To:	☐ Vacant (0-5%)	High	Police & Fire Protection	☐	☐	☐	☐
Industrial ___		☐ Vacant (over 5%)	Predominant	General Appearance of Properties	☐	☐	☐	☐
Vacant ___			—	Appeal to Market	☐	☐	☐	☐

Note: Race or the racial composition of the neighborhood are not considered reliable appraisal factors.
COMMENTS: _____

SITE

Dimensions _____ — Topography _____

Site Area _____ — ☐ Corner Lot — Size _____

Zoning Classification _____ — Zoning Compliance _____ — Shape _____

HIGHEST & BEST USE: Present Use _____ — Other Use _____ — Drainage _____

UTILITIES	Public	Other	SITE IMPROVEMENTS	Type	Public	Private	View _____
Electricity	☐		Street		☐	☐	Landscaping _____
Gas	☐		Curb/Gutter		☐	☐	Driveway _____
Water	☐		Sidewalk		☐	☐	Apparent Easements _____
Sanitary Sewer	☐		Street Lights		☐	☐	FEMA Flood Hazard Yes* ___ No ___
Storm Sewer	☐		Alley		☐	☐	FEMA* Map/Zone _____

COMMENTS (Apparent adverse easements, encroachments, special assessments, slide areas, etc.): _____

IMPROVEMENTS

GENERAL DESCRIPTION	EXTERIOR DESCRIPTION	FOUNDATION	BASEMENT	INSULATION
Units _____	Foundation _____	Slab _____	Area Sq. Ft. _____	Roof ☐
Stories _____	Exterior Walls _____	Crawl Space _____	% Finished _____	Ceiling ☐
Type (Det./Att.) _____	Roof Surface _____	Basement _____	Ceiling _____	Walls ☐
Design (Style) _____	Gutters & Dwnspts. _____	Sump Pump _____	Walls _____	Floor ☐
Existing _____	Window Type _____	Dampness _____	Floor _____	None ☐
Proposed _____	Storm Sash _____	Settlement _____	Outside Entry _____	Adequacy _____
Under Construction _____	Screens _____	Infestation _____		Energy Efficient Items:
Age (Yrs.) _____	Manufactured House _____			
Effective Age (Yrs.) _____				

ROOM LIST

ROOMS	Foyer	Living	Dining	Kitchen	Den	Family Rm.	Rec. Rm.	Bedrooms	# Baths	Laundry	Other	Area Sq. Ft.
Basement												
Level 1												
Level 2												

Finished area **above** grade contains: Rooms; Bedroom(s); Bath(s); Square Feet of Gross Living Area

INTERIOR

SURFACES	Materials/Condition	HEATING		KITCHEN EQUIP.	ATTIC	IMPROVEMENT ANALYSIS	Good	Avg.	Fair	Poor
Floors		Type		Refrigerator	None	Quality of Construction	☐	☐	☐	☐
Walls		Fuel		Range/Oven	Stairs	Condition of Improvements	☐	☐	☐	☐
Trim/Finish		Condition		Disposal	Drop Stair	Room Sizes/Layout	☐	☐	☐	☐
Bath Floor		Adequacy		Dishwasher	Scuttle	Closets and Storage	☐	☐	☐	☐
Bath Wainscot		COOLING		Fan/Hood	Floor	Energy Efficiency	☐	☐	☐	☐
Doors		Central		Compactor	Heated	Plumbing-Adequacy & Condition	☐	☐	☐	☐
		Other		Washer/Dryer	Finished	Electrical-Adequacy & Condition	☐	☐	☐	☐
		Condition		Microwave		Kitchen Cabinets-Adequacy & Cond.	☐	☐	☐	☐
Fireplace(s) #		Adequacy		Intercom		Compatibility to Neighborhood	☐	☐	☐	☐

AUTOS

CAR STORAGE:	Garage	Attached ☐	Adequate ☐	House Entry ☐	Appeal & Marketability	☐	☐	☐	☐
No. Cars ___	Carport	Detached ☐	Inadequate ☐	Outside Entry ☐	Estimated Remaining Economic Life				___ Yrs.
Condition ___	None	Built-In ☐	Electric Door ☐	Basement Entry ☐	Estimated Remaining Physical Life				___ Yrs.

Additional features: _____

COMMENTS

Depreciation (Physical, functional and external inadequacies, repairs needed, modernization, etc.): _____

General market conditions and prevalence and impact in subject/market area regarding loan discounts, interest buydowns and concessions: _____

Freddie Mac Form 70 10/86 **12Ch.** AD Forms and Worms Inc.,® 315 Whitney Ave., New Haven, CT 06511 1(800) 243-4545 Item #130960 Fannie Mae Form 1004 10/86

Figure 19–3 Uniform residential appraisal report

UNIFORM RESIDENTIAL APPRAISAL REPORT   File No.

Purpose of Appraisal is to estimate Market Value as defined in the Certification & Statement of Limiting Conditions.

COST APPROACH

BUILDING SKETCH (SHOW GROSS LIVING AREA ABOVE GRADE)
If for Freddie Mac or Fannie Mae, show only square foot calculations and cost approach comments in this space.

ESTIMATED REPRODUCTION COST – NEW – OF IMPROVEMENTS:

Dwelling _____ Sq. Ft. @ $ _____	= $ _____
_____ Sq. Ft. @ $ _____	= _____
Extras _____	= _____
	= _____
Special Energy Efficient Items _____	= _____
Porches, Patios, etc. _____	= _____
Garage/Carport _____ Sq. Ft. @ $ _____	= _____
Total Estimated Cost New	= $ _____

	Physical	Functional	External
Less			
Depreciation			= $ _____

Depreciated Value of Improvements	= $ _____
Site Imp. "as is" (driveway, landscaping, etc.)	= $ _____
ESTIMATED SITE VALUE	= $ _____
(If leasehold, show only leasehold value.)	
INDICATED VALUE BY COST APPROACH	= $ _____

(Not Required by Freddie Mac and Fannie Mae)
Does property conform to applicable HUD/VA property standards? ☐ Yes ☐ No
If No, explain:

Construction Warranty ☐ Yes ☐ No
Name of Warranty Program _____
Warranty Coverage Expires _____

SALES COMPARISON ANALYSIS

The undersigned has recited three recent sales of properties most similar and proximate to subject and has considered these in the market analysis. The description includes a dollar adjustment, reflecting market reaction to those items of significant variation between the subject and comparable properties. If a significant item in the comparable property is superior to, or more favorable than, the subject property, a minus (–) adjustment is made, thus reducing the indicated value of subject; if a significant item in the comparable is inferior to, or less favorable than, the subject property, a plus (+) adjustment is made, thus increasing the indicated value of the subject.

ITEM	SUBJECT	COMPARABLE NO. 1		COMPARABLE NO. 2		COMPARABLE NO. 3	
Address							
Proximity to Subject							
Sales Price	$	$		$		$	
Price/Gross Liv. Area	$	$		$		$	
Data Source							
VALUE ADJUSTMENTS	DESCRIPTION	DESCRIPTION	+ (–) $ Adjustment	DESCRIPTION	+ (–) $ Adjustment	DESCRIPTION	+ (–) $ Adjustment
Sales or Financing Concessions							
Date of Sale/Time							
Location							
Site/View							
Design and Appeal							
Quality of Construction							
Age							
Condition							
Above Grade	Total ¦ Bdrms ¦ Baths	Total ¦ Bdrms ¦ Baths		Total ¦ Bdrms ¦ Baths		Total ¦ Bdrms ¦ Baths	
Room Count							
Gross Living Area	Sq. Ft.	Sq. Ft.		Sq. Ft.		Sq. Ft.	
Basement & Finished Rooms Below Grade							
Functional Utility							
Heating/Cooling							
Garage/Carport							
Porches, Patio, Pools, etc.							
Special Energy Efficient Items							
Fireplace(s)							
Other (e.g. kitchen equip., remodeling)							
Net Adj. (total)		☐ + ☐ – $		☐ + ☐ – $		☐ + ☐ – $	
Indicated Value of Subject		$		$		$	

Comments on Sales Comparison: _____

INDICATED VALUE BY SALES COMPARISON APPROACH .... $ _____

INDICATED VALUE BY INCOME APPROACH (If Applicable) Estimated Market Rent $ _____ /Mo. x Gross Rent Multiplier _____ = $ _____

This appraisal is made ☐ "as is" ☐ subject to the repairs, alterations, inspections or conditions listed below ☐ completion per plans and specifications.

Comments and Conditions of Appraisal: _____

RECONCILIATION

Final Reconciliation: _____

This appraisal is based upon the above requirements, the certification, contingent and limiting conditions, and Market Value definition that are stated in
☐ FmHA, HUD &/or VA instructions.
☐ Freddie Mac Form 439 (Rev. 7/86)/Fannie Mae Form 1004B (Rev. 7/86) filed with client _____ 19 _____ ☐ attached.
I (WE) ESTIMATE THE MARKET VALUE, AS DEFINED, OF THE SUBJECT PROPERTY AS OF _____ 19 _____ to be $ _____

I (We) certify: that to the best of my (our) knowledge and belief the facts and data used herein are true and correct; that I (we) personally inspected the subject property, both inside and out, and have made an exterior inspection of all comparable sales cited in this report; and that I (we) have no undisclosed interest, present or prospective therein.

Appraiser(s) SIGNATURE _____	Review Appraiser SIGNATURE _____ ☐ Did ☐ Did Not
NAME _____	(if applicable) NAME _____ Inspect Property

Freddie Mac Form 70 10/86 **12Ch.** **AD** Forms and Worms Inc.,® 315 Whitney Ave., New Haven, CT 06511 1(800) 243-4545   Item #130960 Fannie Mae Form 1004 10/86

Figure 19–3 *continued*

income approach. The three different approaches serve as checks against one another.

COST APPROACH TO VALUE

The *cost approach to value,* or the *replacement cost approach* as it is sometimes called, is based on the idea that total property value is equal to the value of the land plus the current value of the improvement. The value is derived systematically in five steps as outlined here and described in detail in the following sections.

STEPS IN THE COST APPROACH TO VALUE

1. Estimate the value of the land as if vacant (using the sales comparison approach).
2. Estimate the cost to reproduce the improvements at the present time.
3. Estimate property depreciation.
4. Deduct depreciation from reproduction cost to arrive at the present depreciated value of improvements.
5. Add the land value to the depreciated value of improvements to arrive at the total estimate of value.

Estimate Land Value

Estimating land value as if the land were vacant is done, if sufficient data are available, by using the sales comparison or market approach. This approach involves collecting data on recent sales of similar land. Similarities to and differences from the subject property are identified and weighed. We discuss the market approach more fully later in this chapter.

Estimate Current Reproduction Cost

Reproduction cost is estimated by one of four methods.

Square Foot Method
The *square foot method* is the most common and easiest to apply. The square foot reproduction cost can be derived from local builders and contractors or from appraisal cost manuals. Some sources of these data are given in the supplementary readings at the end of this chapter. The reproduction cost per square foot is multiplied by the number of square feet in the subject building; the result gives an estimate of the reproduction cost. The square foot method of estimating reproduction cost is prevalent in single-family home appraisals.

Cubic Foot Method
The *cubic foot method* is similar to the square foot method, except that the building volume is used as the basis for evaluation. The cubic foot costs are derived from contractor estimates or appraisal cost manuals. The cost per cubic foot is then multiplied by the number of cubic feet in the building being appraised to arrive at the reproduction cost estimate.

Quantity Survey Method

The *quantity survey method* is the third and most detailed of the reproduction cost procedures. It involves a detailed breakdown and pricing of all materials, labor, architectural and engineering services, insurance, and contractor's overhead and profit. This method is seldom used because of the time and costs involved. It may be necessary, however, to use this method for unusual structures or where other valid data are not available.

Units-in-Place Method

This fourth method involves the pricing of various *units-in-place,* such as the roof, walls, or floors. It then considers the installed costs of each unit, such as plumbing, heating, electricity, and air conditioning. This method is also time-consuming and is, therefore, used infrequently. (See Figure 19–4.)

Estimate Depreciation

Depreciation, as it relates to appraising, is defined as loss in value from all causes. There are three basic types of depreciation: physical deterioration, functional obsolescence, and economic obsolescence. Each must be considered to determine its effect on the property value.

Physical Deterioration

Physical deterioration is the loss in value due to exposure to rain, wind, and other elements, combined with deferred maintenance. This depreciation can be either *curable* or *incurable.* If the cost of curing the problem is less than the dollar increase in value afterward, the deterioration is considered curable. Painting and new roofing are usually considered economically feasible, and hence, curable. Incurable physical deterioration includes factors such as sagging or structural deterioration. Physically curable deterioration is measured by estimating the **cost to cure** the deterioration. Physically incurable deterioration is measured by "capitalizing the rent loss" resulting from the incurable deterioration. (See Example 19–1.)

Functional Obsolescence

Functional obsolescence refers to the loss in value due to loss of utility within a structure. It also can be further classified as either *curable* or *incurable.* Whether curable or incurable, the obsolescence may be caused by either a deficiency or an

---

Example 19–1 Measuring Physical Incurable Deterioration by Capitalizing the Rent Loss

Assume that the property being appraised is a large, older home with sagging floors and a faulty foundation. In the appraiser's opinion, this condition is "incurable" and results in a monthly rent loss of $100. To estimate the amount of physical, incurable deterioration, the appraiser multiplies the rent loss of $100 by the gross monthly rent multiplier (GMRM), which is derived from recent sales of rental properties. (See Example 19–3 for an illustration of the GMRM.)

$$\text{Physical incurable deterioration} = \text{Monthly rent loss} \times \text{GMRM}$$

SEGREGATED COMPONENTS

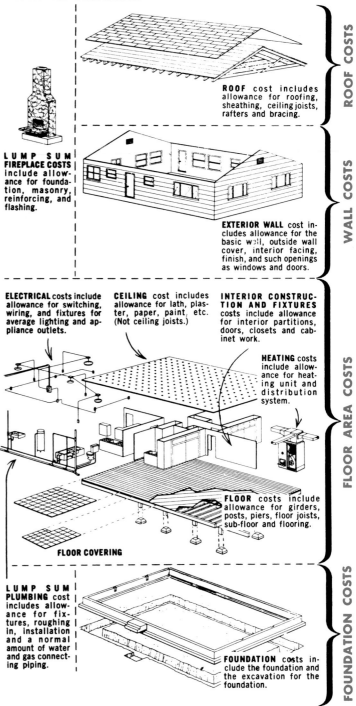

ROOF COSTS

ROOF cost includes allowance for roofing, sheathing, ceiling joists, rafters and bracing.

LUMP SUM FIREPLACE COSTS include allowance for foundation, masonry, reinforcing, and flashing.

WALL COSTS

EXTERIOR WALL cost includes allowance for the basic wall, outside wall cover, interior facing, finish, and such openings as windows and doors.

ELECTRICAL costs include allowance for switching, wiring, and fixtures for average lighting and appliance outlets.

CEILING cost includes allowance for lath, plaster, paper, paint, etc. (Not ceiling joists.)

INTERIOR CONSTRUCTION AND FIXTURES costs include allowance for interior partitions, doors, closets and cabinet work.

HEATING costs include allowance for heating unit and distribution system.

FLOOR AREA COSTS

FLOOR costs include allowance for girders, posts, piers, floor joists, sub-floor and flooring.

FLOOR COVERING

LUMP SUM PLUMBING cost includes allowance for fixtures, roughing in, installation and a normal amount of water and gas connecting piping.

FOUNDATION COSTS

FOUNDATION costs include the foundation and the excavation for the foundation.

Figure 19–4   Units-in-place

excess *(superadequacy)*. If the cost to cure the obsolescence or inutility is less than the dollar increase in value of the property after the cure, the obsolescence is considered curable. Replacement of old bathroom fixtures with new ones and replacing old electrical wires with new wiring are examples of curable obsolescence. *Incurable obsolescence* occurs when the cost to cure the inutility is not economically feasible. A poor floor plan that creates traffic through one bedroom to get to another might be considered functional incurable obsolescence. Functional curable obsolescence is measured by the ***cost to cure*** the obsolescence. Functional incurable obsolescence can be measured by ***capitalizing the rent loss*** attributed to the obsolescence.

Economic Obsolescence

Economic obsolescence (sometimes called external or environmental obsolescence) refers to the loss in value due to adverse environmental factors external to the subject property. It is generally incurable because the property owner has little or no control over these factors and, therefore, cannot cure the problem. A property owner could not, for example, change the traffic pattern in a commercial area. A factory constructed across the street from a residential block or railroad tracks located in a residential area are other causes of economic or environmental obsolescence.

When the property being appraised is of a type such that no rental market exists, it may be necessary to use *matched pairs* of sales to estimate economic obsolescence. In brief, this method involves finding several matched pairs of sales. Each pair must consist of one sale that was affected by the factor or factors causing economic obsolescence and another sale of a similar property that was not affected by that same economic obsolescence. After adjustments have been made between the two sales for all other differences, the remaining difference can be attributed to total economic obsolescence. The total economic obsolescence must then be reduced to reflect the allocation between land and improvements. Remember, you are measuring loss in value to the improvements only. Economic obsolescence can also be measured by "capitalizing the rent loss" attributed to the obsolescence. See example 19–2.

Example 19–2 Measuring Economic Obsolescence by Capitalizing the Rent Loss

Assume that the presence of a gas station across the street from a single-family rental property causes a monthly rent loss of $25. To calculate what effect this economic obsolescence has on the value of the property, we derive and apply the gross monthly rent multiplier (GMRM) to the monthly rent loss as follows:

$25 × 125 (GMRM) = $3,125 Value loss due to economic obsolescence

Since we are measuring the value loss in the building only, we must multiply the total economic obsolescence by the building ratio of the total investment. Assuming a land-to-building ratio of 20 percent land to 80 percent building, we proceed as follows:

$3,125 × .80 = $2,500 Economic obsolescence attributed to the building

The gross monthly rent multiplier (GMRM) is a factor derived from the market by dividing the current gross monthly rent of comparable properties into their selling prices.

Measuring Total Depreciation

Several methods of measuring each of the specific types of depreciation (physical, functional, and economic) have been mentioned. This discussion will be limited to one simple but widely used method of measuring total depreciation. Since it is difficult to measure depreciation by any scientific process, this method is substantially subjective. The estimate of depreciation and the method used are tempered by the knowledge, experience, and judgment of the appraiser.

The *effective age/economic life* concept of measuring total depreciation (physical, functional, and economic) uses a ratio of effective age to economic life. ***Effective age*** is estimated by observation, that is, estimating the age from appearance. It may be more than, equal to, or less than the actual age, depending on how well the property has been maintained.

Economic life means the total estimated time the property will be economically useful. The *remaining economic life* is the estimated number of useful years left in the property as of the date of the appraisal. This concept is illustrated by the following example:

Estimated reproduction cost new (today) of buildings	$47,082
Estimated effective age (by observation)	2 years
Estimated remaining economic life	38 years
Estimated total economic life	40 years

$$\frac{\text{Effective age}}{\text{Total economic life}} \quad \frac{2}{40} = .05 \text{ (or 5\%)}$$

$$\text{Total depreciation} = \$47{,}082 \times .05 = \$2{,}354$$

Deduct Depreciation and Add Back Land Value

After the depreciation has been estimated, subtract it from the reproduction cost, new, of the subject building and other improvements; then add land value to arrive at the estimate of total property value. Figure 19–5 illustrates the cost approach.

The major weakness of the cost approach is the time and money involved in gathering information to estimate reproduction costs and depreciation accurately. These weaknesses become more magnified in the appraisal of older buildings. Such

Valuation Section **UNIFORM RESIDENTIAL APPRAISAL REPORT** **File No.**

COST APPROACH

Purpose of Appraisal is to estimate Market Value as defined in the Certification & Statement of Limiting Conditions.

BUILDING SKETCH (SHOW GROSS LIVING AREA ABOVE GRADE)
If for Freddie Mac or Fannie Mae, show only square foot calculations and cost approach comments in this space

ESTIMATED REPRODUCTION COST-NEW-OF IMPROVEMENTS:	
Dwelling 1120 Sq. Ft. @ $ 34	= $ 38,080
Basement 980 Sq. Ft. @ $ 3	= 2,940
Extras Rec Room/Bsmt 140@$10	= 1,400
	=
Special Energy Efficient Items ----	=
Porches, Patios, etc. Deck	= 500
Garage/Carport 364 Sq. Ft. @ $8	= 2,912
Total Estimated Cost New	= $ 45,832
Less Depreciation (Physical | Functional | External)	= $ 2,354
Depreciated Value of Improvements	= $ 43,478
Site Imp. "as is" (driveway, landscaping, etc.)	= $ 1,250
ESTIMATED SITE VALUE	= $ 8,000
(If leasehold, show only leasehold value.)	
INDICATED VALUE BY COST APPROACH	= $ 52,728

Figure 19–5 The cost approach portion of the FHLMC/FNMA appraisal form

appraisals should be supported, if possible, by the other two approaches. When churches or other special-purpose buildings are appraised, the cost approach is given considerable weight. Often it is the only feasible approach because of a lack of market or income information.

MARKET APPROACH TO VALUE

The *market approach to value* entails comparing the property being appraised with similar properties that have sold recently. It is also referred to as the *comparative approach* or the *sales comparison approach.* Given a sufficient number of recent and comparable sales, the market approach provides a good measure for estimating value. In this approach, the appraiser must gather sales data for similar properties, compare the merits of each property in relation to the subject property, and adjust the price data for time, location, physical characteristics, and terms of sale in arriving at an estimate of value. These steps are summarized here and spelled out as shown.

STEPS INVOLVED IN THE MARKET APPROACH TO VALUE

1. Gather data on comparable sales.
2. Analyze data.
3. Compare the comparable sales with the subject property.
4. Adjust for differences.
5. Correlate to arrive at value estimate.

Gathering Data

Sufficient sales data for comparable properties are gathered from such sources as the appraiser's own files, public records, attorneys, multiple listing services, brokers, banks, and lending institutions. The appraiser should collect data from as many comparable sales as possible, since some of them will have to be discarded for one reason or another.

Analyzing Data

Once a sufficient number of sales figures have been gathered, the data must be analyzed to determine comparability. A preliminary physical inspection of each property is recommended. These are some characteristics of good comparable sales:

1. The comparable sales should be recent. In residential appraising, no more than one year should have elapsed since the sale.
2. The comparable sales should be arm's length, that is, not between relatives or in situations where other factors may have influenced the selling price.
3. The comparable sales should have been purchased using typical market financing. A sale involving a contract for deed is usually considered atypical and should not be used unless absolutely necessary, and then only after making the necessary adjustments.
4. The comparable sales should have been voluntary. Foreclosure sales would not represent valid comparisons.

5. The comparable sales should be in close proximity to the subject property and in similar environments.
6. The comparable sales should be physically similar to the subject property.

Comparing

In analyzing comparable sales, some will be rejected for not meeting one or more of the above characteristics. The appraiser should begin the comparison process with seven to ten good comparable sales. The ideal *comparable* (an appraiser's dream) is an exact replica of the subject property that sold today under typical market conditions. Unfortunately, such ideal comparables are seldom found. The appraiser must use the comparables available and make the necessary adjustments.

Adjusting

After selecting the comparable properties and making an analysis and comparison, it is necessary to adjust for differences in *time of sale, location, physical, and financial characteristics.* If comparable sales with atypical financing must be used, adjustments should be made for terms of sale. Figure 19–6 illustrates the adjustment process.

As can be seen, the specific items or factors to be compared between the three comparable properties and the subject property are itemized in the left column. Moving from left to right on the table, the next column describes information on the subject property. The next three columns provide room for the same descriptive information for each of the three comparable sales. Each of these three columns has one space for the item description and another space to indicate the amount of adjustment to make (if any) for any differences in that item between the subject property being appraised and the comparable sale. The descriptive column was marked "similar" in the example because the appraiser recognized no difference between the subject property and the comparable sale on that particular item and, consequently, made no adjustment.

Further, when comparing each item of the subject property that is being appraised to the comparable sales, the item of comparison was labeled either *similar, superior,* or *inferior* for each comparable sale. In all cases, the appraiser has compared and adjusted *from the comparable property to the subject property.* In other words, an item rated as "superior" indicates that the comparable property's item is superior to that same item of the subject property. Consequently, the selling price of the comparable property must be adjusted downward to reflect this difference so that, after all adjustments have been made, the adjusted selling prices of the comparable sales will accurately reflect what the subject property would sell for if it were on the market. This adjustment process is a difficult concept for many students to comprehend and can be made easier by following these guidelines:

1. Always compare and adjust from the comparable sale to the subject property.
2. When comparing the comparable property to the subject property, if the comparable property is *superior,* the comparable selling price should be adjusted downward.

The undersigned has recited three recent sales of properties most similar and proximate to subject and has considered these in the market analysis. The description includes a dollar adjustment, reflecting market reaction to those items of significant variation between the subject and comparable properties. If a significant item in the comparable property is superior to, or more favorable than, the subject property, a minus (–) adjustment is made, thus reducing the indicated value of subject; if a significant item in the comparable is inferior to, or less favorable than, the subject property, a plus (+) adjustment is made, thus increasing the indicated value of the subject.

ITEM	SUBJECT	COMPARABLE NO. 1		COMPARABLE NO. 2		COMPARABLE NO. 3	
Address	300 E. Fifth Mackinaw, Il	106 Giles Makckinaw, I		Lot 54 Heritage Lake RR Mackinaw, Il.		404 S. Eastern Ave. Minier, Il.	
Proximity to Subject		4 Blks. East		1 Mi. West		2 Blks. North	
Sales Price	$ ----		$ 49,300		$ 50,900		$ 54,900
Price/Gross Liv. Area	$	$ 31.80		$ 33.38		$ 35.42	
Data Source							
VALUE ADJUSTMENTS	DESCRIPTION	DESCRIPTION	+ (–) $ Adjustment	DESCRIPTION	+ (–) $ Adjustment	DESCRIPTION	+ (–) $ Adjustment
Sales or Financing Concessions							
Date of Sale/Time	----	Aug. 1988	--	Aug.1988	--	April 1988	---
Location	Good	Similar	--	Similar	--	Similar	---
Site/View	1/3 Acre/Gd	84x120/Infer	+500	107x275/sim	--	90x140/Infer	+500
Design and Appeal	Good	Similar	--	Similar	--	Similar	---
Quality of Construction	Good	Similar	--	Similar	--	Similar	---
Age	3 years	Similar	--	Similar	--	Similar	---
Condition	Good	Similar	--	Similar	--	Similar	---
Above Grade Room Count	Total 6 / Bdrms 3 / Baths 1	Total 6 / Bdrms 3 / Baths 1		Total 6 / Bdrms 3 / Baths 1½		Total 6 / Bdrms 3 / Baths 2	
Gross Living Area	1500 Sq. Ft.	1550 Sq. Ft.	-1000	1525 Sq. Ft.	-750	1550 Sq. Ft.	-1000
Basement & Finished Rooms Below Grade	Full Part.Finish	Similar	--	Full Unfinished	+500	None Inferior	+1500
Functional Utility	Good	Similar	--	Similar	--	Similar	--
Heating/Cooling	FWA/Central	Similar	--	FWA/No Air	+1000	Similar	--
Garage/Carport	1½ attached	1car attached	+500	2car attached	-500	2car attached	-500
Porches, Patio, Pools, etc.	Deck	Inferior	+500	Inferior	+500	Inferior	+500
Special Energy Efficient Items	None	Similar	--	Similar	--	Similar	--
Fireplace(s)	None	Fireplace	-750				
Other (e.g. kitchen equip., remodeling)	Kitchen remodeled	Similar	--	Inferior	+500	Inferior	+500
Net Adj. (total)		+ X –	$ 250	X +	$ 1,250	X +	$ 1,500
Indicated Value of Subject			$49,050		$ 52,150		$56,400

Comments on Sales Comparison: Comp #1 $49,050 x .50 = $24,525
Comp #2 $52,150 x .40 = $20,860
Comp #3 $56,400 x .10 = $ 5,640

INDICATED VALUE BY SALES COMPARISON APPROACH .... $ 51,025

INDICATED VALUE BY INCOME APPROACH (If Applicable) Estimated Market Rent $ _____ /Mo. x Gross Rent Multiplier _____ = $ _____

This appraisal is made ☐ "as is" ☐ subject to the repairs, alterations, inspections or conditions listed below ☐ completion per plans and specifications.

Comments and Conditions of Appraisal: _____

Final Reconciliation: _____

This appraisal is based upon the above requirements, the certification, contingent and limiting conditions, and Market Value definition that are stated in
☐ FmHA, HUD &/or VA instructions.
☐ Freddie Mac Form 439 (Rev. 7/86)/Fannie Mae Form 1004B (Rev. 7/86) filed with client _____ 19___ ☐ attached.
I (WE) ESTIMATE THE MARKET VALUE, AS DEFINED, OF THE SUBJECT PROPERTY AS OF _____ 19___ to be $ _____

I (We) certify: that to the best of my (our) knowledge and belief the facts and data used herein are true and correct; that I (we) personally inspected the subject property, both inside and out, and have made an exterior inspection of all comparable sales cited in this report; and that I (we) have no undisclosed interest, present or prospective therein.

Appraiser(s) SIGNATURE _____   Review Appraiser SIGNATURE _____ (if applicable) ☐ Did ☐ Did Not
NAME _____   NAME _____   Inspect Property

Freddie Mac Form 70 10/86 12Ch. AD Forms and Worms Inc.,® 315 Whitney Ave., New Haven, CT 06511 1(800) 243-4545   Item #130960 Fannie Mae Form 1004 10/86

Figure 19–6 Market approach portion of FHLMC/FNMA appraisal form

3. If the comparable property is *inferior* to the subject property, the comparable selling price should be adjusted upward.

In making the adjustments, the appraiser must avoid the temptation of inserting personal opinions on how much and when to adjust. An appraisal is made to interpret the premiums or discounts that the *market* places on the elements and report them accordingly. The appraiser should neither influence nor determine value, but rather estimate it.

Adjusting for Financing

Whenever one of the comparable sales sold with atypical financing, the comparable selling price must be adjusted to reflect such financing. For instance, if the comparable property was purchased for $90,000 with 90 percent, 10 percent interest, thirty-

---

STEPS IN ADJUSTING FOR FAVORABLE FINANCING

1. Compute the principal and interest payment for market financing:*
   $90,000 at 12%, 30 years—monthly P&I payment of $926.10
2. Compute the monthly principal and interest payment for the favorable financing:
   $90,000 at 10%, 30 years—monthly P&I payment of $790.20
3. Calculate the difference in the monthly payment:
   $926.10 − 790.20 = $135.90
4. Multiply the difference by 12 to get the annual difference:
   $135.90 × 12 = $1,630.80
5. Discount the annual difference derived in step 4 to present value (15 percent annuity factor, 3 years) to arrive at the adjustment for the interest rate differential:

   $1,630.80 × 2.283225 = $3,723.48
6. Adjust for the difference in loan fee points:
   1% on $90,000 or $900 vs. 3% on $90,000 or $2,700 = $1,800

   Step 6 requires no discounting since the $1,800 is immediate savings realized on the day the sale closes.
7. Add the interest rate differential adjustment ($3,723.48) to the loan fee adjustment (if any) ($1,800) to derive the total financing adjustment:
   Total adjustment $5,523.48—rounded to $5,500

*Assumes a 3-year holding period and 15% discount rate.

---

year, fixed rate financing, and a 1 percentage loan fee while prevailing market financing terms are 90 percent, 12 percent interest, and a 3 percentage loan fee, the comparable sale should be adjusted downward to reflect the favorable financing.

How Much to Adjust

There are several cash-equivalency models that are currently being used by appraisers to calculate the dollar amount of any adjustments for financing. Each of the models makes certain assumptions regarding market behavior and holding periods. The biggest mistake made in recent years has not been selection of the wrong cash-equivalency model to calculate the adjustment for financing, but rather, totally disregarding any needed financing adjustment. This failure to recognize and adjust for favorable financing was probably the single biggest reason for inflated appraisals during the early and mid-1980s. Recently, however, appraisal organizations and leaders in the primary and secondary mortgage market are espousing various cash-equivalency models to make the needed adjustments for financing. In our example, we used the cash-equivalency model to calculate the needed adjustment.

After all upward and downward adjustments have been made, their total provides a net adjustment (see bottom of Figure 19–6). This net adjustment is either added to or subtracted from the comparable property's selling price to arrive at the "indicated value" of the subject property (see last item of Figure 19–6).

Correlation

The last step in the market approach is to correlate and weight the three indications of value and arrive at a single estimate of value for the subject property using the market approach. In Figure 19–6 Comparable No. 1 is weighted the heaviest (.50) and No. 3 the least (.10), resulting in an estimate of value of $51,025 by use of the market approach.

Note on Usage

The market approach cannot be effectively used when there are few or no comparable sales available. It would carry little weight in determining the final estimate if there were only one or two comparable sales. When sufficient market data are available, however, the market approach is given considerable weight because it reflects value taken directly from the marketplace.

INCOME APPROACH TO VALUE— RESIDENTIAL SINGLE-FAMILY UNITS

The third approach to value, the *income approach,* is based on the idea that value is the present worth of expected future benefits arising from property ownership. This approach has its greatest application in the appraisal of income-producing properties. The function of the appraiser is to determine the present value of the expected future income stream of the subject property.

In residential appraising, a gross monthly rent multiplier *(GMRM)* is used to estimate value. These steps are followed in determining and applying the GMRM:

STEPS OF THE INCOME APPROACH FOR RESIDENTIAL PROPERTY

1. Locate and verify residential sales that are comparable to the subject property and that were renting at the time of sale.
2. Divide the selling price of each comparable sale by its gross monthly rental to obtain the GMRM.
3. Analyze and weigh the various multipliers obtained in step 2 and reconcile them into a single multiplier. The reconciliation process does not imply the simple averaging of the three GMRMs, but rather placing greater weight or emphasis on the GMRMs that best reflect the subject property.
4. Derive the market rent of the subject property from the marketplace by verifying rental data from similar rental properties and making necessary adjustments for any differences between the subject property and the rentals.
5. Multiply the weighted GMRM by the estimated economic rent of the subject property to arrive at the estimate of value for the subject property.

Example 19–3 Estimating Value of Single-Family Property—The Income Approach

The subject property's economic (market) rent has been derived from the market and estimated to be $450 per month. Recent sales of comparable rental property follow:

Sale #	Selling Price	÷	Monthly Rent	=	GMRM
1	$60,000	÷	$475	=	126.3
2	$65,000	÷	$500	=	130
3	$70,000	÷	$525	=	133.3

The indicated range of GMRMs is 126 to 133. Analysis of the GMRMs indicates that sales 1 and 2 should be given the most weight. Calculations of the weighting follow:

$$\text{Weighted GMRM} = (126 \times .40) + (130 \times .40) + (133 \times .20) = 129$$

The indicated value of the subject property is, therefore,

$$\text{Value} = \text{Rent} \times \text{GMRM}$$
$$= \$450 \times 129$$
$$= \$58,000 \text{ (rounded)}$$

INCOME APPROACH TO VALUE— INCOME-PRODUCING PROPERTIES

As we saw before, the concept behind the income approach is that value is the present worth of future income. The application of the income approach involves three steps listed here and explained at length below.

STEPS OF THE INCOME APPROACH TO VALUE FOR INCOME-PRODUCING PROPERTIES

1. Estimate the subject property's anticipated (future) net income
2. Select an appropriate capitalization rate
3. Translate the projected net income into an estimate of value by the process of capitalization

---

Estimating Income

All *capitalization* methods start with the subject property's net income and work toward arriving at an estimate of value. If the appraiser works with an inflated estimate of income, the result is an inflated estimate of value. It is, therefore, imperative that the appraiser obtain accurate income and expense information for the property being evaluated. If possible, the appraiser should obtain a three- to five-year operating history of the property that includes all income and expenses of the property.

Total income from the property being appraised should be identified. In an apartment building, this may include such items as rental income, income from coin-operated laundry facilities, and parking income. The expenses should be broken down into three categories: (a) fixed, (b) operating, and (c) reserve for replacement. *Fixed expenses* remain unchanged, regardless of the occupancy level of the building. Typical fixed expenses include taxes and insurance. *Operating expenses* vary with the occupancy level of the building and include, but are not limited to, the following: maintenance expenses, management expense, utility expense, lawn care, snow removal, legal and accounting expense, and others. Finally, the *reserve for replacement* is an allowance in the annual operating statement to provide for the systematic replacement of items within a building (e.g., stoves, refrigerators, carpeting, water heaters, window air conditioning units) whose useful life is less than that of the building itself. The planned replacement of these items is necessary to sustain the anticipated net income.

The amount of allowance for each replacement item is usually calculated as the cost to replace the item divided by the item's remaining useful life. For example, if all the refrigerators in a four-unit apartment building under appraisal are seven years old and the appraiser estimates a total useful life of ten years, a reserve must be set aside to replace the refrigerators in three years. Assuming each refrigerator costs $400, the total annual reserve for replacement for all refrigerators in the four units would be calculated as follows:

$$\text{Total annual reserve} = \frac{\$400 \times 4}{3}$$

$$= \$533 \text{ (rounded)}$$

The appraiser may increase or decrease the owner's reported income and expenses if market data justify such action. If the owner has included depreciation, debt service, and income taxes in the operating statements, the appraiser should eliminate them in the reconstructed operating statement because they represent owner expenses rather than property expenses. Such expenses would vary from owner to owner, depending on how each financed the purchase, the owner's tax bracket, and the depreciation technique used.

The analysis ends with a reconstructed operating statement as illustrated in Figure 19–7. The appraiser then takes the projected net income from the operating statement and capitalizes, or converts, it into an estimate of value using the appropriate capitalization method.

Capitalization Formulas

Capitalization formulas involve the three elements of income, rate, and value.

$$\text{Income} = \text{Rate times value}$$

$$\text{Rate} = \text{Income divided by value}$$

$$\text{Value} = \text{Income divided by rate}$$

If any two of the three components in the capitalization formulas are available or can be derived from the market data, the third component can be calculated. In economic theory, *rate* is a ratio between income and value expressed as a percentage:

$$\text{Rate} = \frac{\text{Income}}{\text{Value}}$$

RECONSTRUCTED OPERATING STATEMENT

Potential Gross Income Estimate Assuming Economic Rent
100% Occupancy

Scheduled Rental Income	$24,000	
Other Income	0	
Total Potential Gross Income		$24,000
Less: Vacancy and Collection Losses		−1,680
Effective Gross Income		22,320
Less Expenses:		
Fixed Expenses:		
Taxes	$2,700	
Insurance	1,000	3,700
Operating Expenses:		
Management	1,440	
Maintenance	2,400	
Utilities	1,380	
Ground Maintenance	450	
Legal & Accounting	300	
Other		5,970
Reserve for Replacement:		
Appliances	250	
Furnace	250	500
Total Estimated Expenses		−10,170
Net Income Before Recapture (NIBR)		$12,150

Figure 19–7 A format for reconstructing the operating statement

Example 19–4   Recapturing a Real Estate Investment—An Apartment House

If a given building has a remaining economic life of twenty-five years, the annual recapture rate necessary to recapture or recover the total building investment over its remaining economic life is 1/25 or 4 percent. Thus, the recapture rate reflects the annual rate at which the building portion of the investment must be recaptured to recover it fully over the period of its estimated economic life.

A $10,000 return on a $100,000 deposit in a savings and loan represents a 10 percent return on investment; however, this is not the case in a real estate investment since the real estate is composed, in part, of depreciable improvements. If we assume a $100,000 investment in an apartment building with a remaining economic life of 25 years, the investment must generate more than $10,000 to earn a 10 percent return. The difference lies in the recapture of the investment. The investor who invests $100,000 in a certificate of deposit is guaranteed the return of that $100,000, whereas the apartment owner has no such guarantee. The building portion of the investment is assumed to depreciate. Therefore, the property investment must generate $13,200 to provide for recapture or recovery of the investment together with a 10 percent return on investment. This amount is determined as follows:

Investment Composed of:	Requires:		Total Rate	Return Dollars
	Return on	Return of		
Building value $80,000 (25-yr economic life)	.10	.04	.14	$11,200
Land value $20,000	.10	—	.10	2,000
Land and building				$13,200

Any rate used to capitalize or convert an estimated net income stream into value is called the *capitalization rate*. The term **building capitalization rate** means the sum of the interest rate plus the recapture rate. In our example,

Interest rate	.10
Recapture rate	.04 (25-year life)
Building capitalization rate	.14

This *rate of* **return on investment** or the *capitalization (interest) rate* applies to both the land and building. The greater the risk, the higher the rate; conversely, a safer investment will have a lower rate of return. The *rate of* **return of investment**, or **recapture rate**, applies to buildings only and allows for their future depreciation. It does not apply to land. The recapture rate for a building is the reciprocal of its remaining economic life.

$$\text{Recapture rate} = \frac{1}{\text{Remaining economic life in years}}$$

Determining the Interest Rate

There are a number of ways to arrive at the appropriate interest rate. Three of the most common methods are (a) the built-up, or summation method; (b) the band of investments method; and (c) extracting the interest rate from market sales.

Built-up, or Summation, Method

The **built-up**, or **summation**, method begins with a riskless or safe rate and then modifies it to reflect the nature of the investment. The following example illustrates the built-up method of deriving a basic interest rate.

The Built-Up Method

Riskless rate (Interest earned on riskless investment)	8%
Risk rate (Interest rate earned due to increased risk of this investment)	3%
Illiquidity (Interest rate earned due to nonliquid nature of this investment)	2%
Management (Interest rate earned due to management required for investment)	2%
Indicated basic interest (risk) rate	18%

This method is useful in understanding the composition of an interest rate; however, it is of little practical value.

Table 19–2   Band of investments method of determining an interest rate

Suppliers of capital in band of investments	Portion of total investment		Risk rate		Weighted rate
First mortgagee	.70	×	.15	=	.105
Second mortgagee	.20	×	.18	=	.036
Equity investor	.10	×	.20	=	.020
Indicated interest rate					.161

Band of Investments Method

The second method, called **band of investments,** is frequently used. This method recognizes that, in most real estate investments, several different firms and individuals supply the capital. Each supplier of capital is exposed to varying degrees of risk; therefore, each charges a different interest rate. The band of investments method is nothing more than a weighted average of the total cost of investment capital for a given investment under market conditions. Table 19–2 illustrates how the band of investments method is used to derive an interest rate.

Extracting the Interest Rate Directly from Market Sales

The appraiser can extract an interest rate directly from market sales if there have been a sufficient number of recent sales comparable in quality with similar anticipated declining income streams. The information needed includes the selling price, the net income, and the estimated remaining useful life of the improvements. Example 19–5 illustrates how to extract the interest rate from the market.

Example 19–5   Extracting the Interest Rate from Market Sales

Let's assume that recently sold investment property comparable to the subject property being appraised yields the following amounts of return. An interest rate can be extracted from this market sale as follows:

Net income to land and building		$40,000
Sales price	$360,000	
Less land value (from the market)	− 72,000	
Building value	$288,000	
Estimated remaining life of building (25 years)		
Indicated recapture rate is 4% (1/25)		
Less "return of" building value ($288,000 × .04)		− 11,520
"Return on" land and building		$28,480
Interest rate = ($28,480 ÷ $360,000) =		.079

Income Capitalization

Capitalization is a discounting process that converts a projected income stream into an estimate of present value. The essential variables in the capitalization formula are the projected net income and the proper rate at which the income stream should be discounted to arrive at the present value. Again, the discount, or interest rate, used in the formula is called the *capitalization rate.*

Several capitalization methods are used to discount or convert net income into value. Each method has certain built-up assumptions about the nature of the income stream, the economic life of the improvements, and the division of value between land and improvements. Also, capitalization rates vary from period to period and from building to building, depending on the type of building, the age of the building, interest rates, and risks.

Capitalization in Perpetuity

Capitalization in perpetuity is the basic capitalization method used when there is no time limit put on the receipt of the income stream and no provision for capital recapture. This method is used in valuing unimproved farm ground. It assumes that land does not depreciate and will be capable of generating an income indefinitely. Furthermore, upon resale, the proceeds will provide the seller with complete capital recovery. In essence, the income is being capitalized at a discount rate that will provide a *return on* the investment, but no *return of* investment. The basic capitalization formula is this:

$$\text{Present value of property} = \frac{\text{Net income}}{\text{Capitalization rate}}$$

The basic capitalization formula is sometimes presented as follows:

$$\frac{I}{R/V}$$

$$\text{where} \quad I = \text{Net income}$$
$$R = \text{Capitalization rate}$$
$$V = \text{Value}$$

If any two of the three components in the capitalization formula are known or can be derived from the market data, the third component can be calculated.

For example, assume a property generates a net income of $12,000 and similar properties are selling at a capitalization rate of 9.5 percent. By applying the basic capitalization formula, we can capitalize the $12,000 income stream into an estimate of value as follows:

$$V = \frac{I}{R} = \frac{\$12,000}{.095} = \$126,316 \text{ (rounded)}$$

Direct Capitalization

In *direct capitalization,* an overall capitalization rate is extracted directly from market sales and applied to the net income of the subject property in the capitalization formula to arrive at the present value of the property.

The overall capitalization rate is composed of two rates:

1. Risk (interest) rate to provide a *return on* investment in both land and building.
2. Recapture (recovery) rate to provide a *return of* investment in the building portion of the investment.

There is a recapture provision inherent in the overall capitalization rate. Neither a specific time limit for recapture nor a remaining useful life of the building components is implied.

Derivation of overall capitalization rate. The **overall capitalization rate** is derived from the market by analyzing the relationship between the net income and selling prices of recently sold comparable properties as follows:

Sale number	Net income	÷	Selling price	=	Overall cap. rate
1	$12,000	÷	$126,000	=	.0952
2	14,000	÷	150,000	=	.0933
3	15,500	÷	158,000	=	.0981

As can be seen, similar properties are selling at an overall capitalization rate (or cap. rate, as it is sometimes called) of approximately 9.5 percent. This rate merely shows the current market relationship between net income and selling price and expresses it as a percentage. The overall (cap.) rate is similar to the price/earnings ratio in the stock market. The logic behind this method of capitalization is merely that if, in the past, investors have been buying and selling similar properties at a cap. rate of 9.5 percent, it is reasonable to assume that the net income of the subject property being appraised can be capitalized or converted into an estimate of value by using the same rate.

Application of the overall capitalization rate. Once the range of the overall capitalization rates has been determined, the appraiser analyzes and weighs the various rates and reconciles them into a single cap. rate *(R)* to be applied to the net income of the subject property to arrive at an estimate of value as follows:

$$\text{Subject property's net income} = \$12,000$$
$$\text{Overall rate (from the market)} = 9.5\%$$
$$\text{Income} \div \text{Rate} = \text{Value}$$
$$\$12,000 \div .0950 = \underline{\$126,300} \text{ (rounded)}$$

This method is used when there are enough market transactions of comparable properties to derive an accurate overall rate. The comparable sales should be similar as to age, operating expense ratios, and land-to-building ratios. The primary difficulty with this method of capitalization is the inability to obtain accurate net income estimates from the comparable sales. In many cases, parties to the transaction consider such information to be confidential.

Straight Line Method—Land Residual Technique

The *land residual technique* assumes a declining income stream and implies a specific period of time over which the capital is to be recaptured in the building portion of the investment. This method of capitalization is appropriate under these conditions:

1. The improvements are new, or relatively new, and represent the highest and best use of the land.
2. The appraiser is confident of the building value.
3. The income stream is projected to decline.
4. The appraiser tests to determine the highest and best use of a site.

Straight Line Method—Building Residual Technique

The *building residual technique* also assumes a declining income stream and implies a specific period of time over which the capital is to be recaptured on the building portion of the investment. As with the land residual technique, this method of capitalization also provides a *return on* land and building investment as well as a *return of* the building portion of the investment. This method of capitalization is appropriate under these conditions:

1. The buildings are old.
2. Land value can readily be determined.

Example 19–6   Land Residual Technique Illustrated

Assume the subject property is a new apartment building with a remaining economic life of 50 years and that it generates a net income of $16,000. The structure cost $120,000 to build, and this represents current market value. Applying the capitalization formula and an 8 percent interest rate, we can capitalize the net income into value as follows:

Net income to land and building	$16,000
Less: Income attributable to the building	
Building requirements are:	
"Return on" investment .08 (interest rate)	
"Return of" investment .02 (recapture rate)	
Building capitalization rate .10	

Apply the basic capitalization formula $\dfrac{I}{R/V}$ and the building capitalization rate to solve for I:

Income attributable to building ($120,000 × .10)	− 12,000
Residual or remaining income attributable to land	$ 4,000

Now apply the basic capitalization formula $\dfrac{I}{R/V}$ and the capitalization (interest) rate to solve for V:

Land value ($4,000 ÷ .08)	$ 50,000
Building value	120,000
Property value	$170,000

Example 19–7 Building Residual Technique Illustrated

The subject property is an older office building with a remaining economic life of ten years that generates a net income of $12,000. Recent land sales indicate the land value to be $15,000. Applying an 8 percent interest rate, we can convert the net income of the subject property into an estimate of value as follows:

Net income to land and building	$12,000
Less: Income attributed to land	
Calculated as follows:	
Land requirements are:	
"Return on" investment only (8% interest rate)	

Apply the basic capitalization formula $\dfrac{I}{R/V}$ to solve for I:

Income attributable to land = $15,000 × .08 =	−1,200
Residual or remaining income attributable to building	$10,800

Now apply the same basic capitalization formula $\dfrac{I}{R/V}$ to solve for building value:

Building value = $I \div R$	
= $10,800 ÷ .18* =	$60,000 Building value
Add back land value	15,000 Land value
Property value	$75,000 Property value

*Note: The building cap. rate consists of:

"Return on" investment (cap. or interest rate)	.08
"Return of" investment (recapture rate)	.10
Building cap. rate	.18

Annuity Capitalization

All of the previously described methods of capitalization assume a declining income stream and use rates in the capitalization formula to convert the net income into an estimate of value. *Annuity capitalization* assumes a net, level income stream and uses present worth factors to discount a projected net income stream into an estimate of present value. The reader should be familiar with these three present value tables in order to understand annuity capitalization:

1. Compound amount of $1.00, column 1, Appendix D.
2. Present worth of $1.00 (reversionary table), column 4, Appendix D.
3. Present worth of $1.00/year (annuity table), column 5, Appendix D.

Compound amount of $1.00. Table 19–3 represents the growth of one dollar at compound interest, calculated without the aid of the tables in the appendix.

Note that the addition of 10 percent interest every year is the same as multiplying the amount by 1.10. Hence, to calculate the value of $1.00 at the end of five years at 10 percent interest, the formula is $(\$1.10)^5$. As can be seen, the present value tables in Appendix D are based on end-of-year payments.

Year	Interest at 10%	Amount
0	0	1
1	.10	1.10
2	.11	1.21
3	.121	1.331
4	.1331	1.4641
5	.14641	1.61051

Table 19–3   Compound amount of $1.00

APPRAISAL AND
VALUE

Present worth of $1.00 (reversionary factors).   The present worth function is the reciprocal of the compound amount of $1.00 from Table 19–3. As can be seen from Table 19–3, $1.00 will grow to $1.10 in one year. It follows then that .909091 will grow to $1.00 in one year. The present worth of $1.00 to be received at the end of year one discounted at 10 percent is calculated by dividing the Table 19–3 amount of $1.10 into $1.00. The present worth of $1.00 to be received at the end of two years is calculated by dividing the Table 19–3 year two amount of $1.21 into $1.00. Five-year calculations are shown in Table 19–4.

Income to be received in the future is worth less than the same amount of money in hand today, since the money in hand now can earn interest. Therefore, future earnings must be discounted to arrive at their present value.

The present value of future income can be calculated by determining how much money would have to be invested today at a specific compound interest (discount) rate for today's investment to grow to the future payment in the given number of years. The amount of money that would have to be invested today is called the present value (PV) of the future payment or payments. *Present value,* or present worth, is the current value of income to be received at some specified future time, discounted by a given rate of interest, using present worth of $1.00 factors.

Precomputed present worth of $1.00 (reversionary) factors for various rates of interest and periods of time are found in Appendix D, column 4. These factors are used to convert a single lump sum payment to be received at some time in the future into an estimate of present value. These tables are used to estimate the present worth of the property reversion.

	10% interest (discount) rate	
Year	1/amount of $1	Present worth of $1
1	1/1.10	.909091
2	1/1.21	.826446
3	1/1.331	.751315
4	1/1.4641	.683013
5	1/1.61051	.620921

Table 19–4   Present worth of $1.00 (reversionary factors)

Table 19–5   Present worth of $1.00 per year (annuity factors)

	10% interest (discount) rate	
Year	Present worth of $1	Present worth of $1/year
1	.909091	.909091
2	.826446	1.735537
3	.751315	2.486852
4	.683013	3.169865
5	.620921	3.790786

Present worth of $1.00 per year (annuity factors).   The present worth of a series of payments (annuity) is the total of the present values of all the payments. The present worth of $1.00 per year received for five years, then, is an accumulation of the present worth of $1.00 figures for years one through five as shown in Table 19–5.

Column 5 in Appendix D shows the precomputed present worth of $1.00 per year annuity factors. The tables in Appendix D are used to convert an income stream into an estimate of present value. The **annuity factors** have a provision for capital recapture built into them, so there is no need to add a separate recapture rate.

Annuity capitalization is used when the projected income stream of the subject property has the characteristics of an annuity, that is, income expected at regular intervals in predictable amounts. This condition exists when the property being appraised is under long-term lease with a tenant of good credit standing.

Annuity Capitalization Method—Property Residual Technique

Although the annuity capitalization method can be used in conjunction with all the residual techniques—land residual, building residual, and property residual—the **property residual technique** is the most popular method and is used when the subject property is under a long-term lease with readily ascertainable rents. The leased fee value (lessor's interest) of leased property consists of two components:

1. *The present value of the income stream.* The income stream is discounted at an appropriate rate to reflect the risk involved.
2. *The present value of the property reversion to be received at the expiration of the lease.* The property reversion is discounted at a somewhat higher rate to reflect the additional risk involved in ownership of the property once the lease has expired.

MORTGAGE-EQUITY (ELLWOOD) TECHNIQUE

All previously discussed methods of capitalization disregard mortgage terms and assume the property being appraised is "free and clear." Many appraiser/analysts feel this assumption is unrealistic in light of actual investor behavior. The typical investor seeks to borrow most of the investment capital in order to maximize the yield on his equity through financial leverage. The mortgage-equity technique gives weight to the availability and cost of borrowed funds in arriving at the appropriate overall rate. Also, the mortgage-equity formula takes into account the equity yield

Example 19–8 Property Residual Technique Illustrated

Assume the subject property is a new office building costing $400,000 to build on a $100,000 site and under a long-term twenty-year net lease of $46,000 per year to a tenant with a Triple A credit rating. The risk inherent in such an investment is small, and a discount rate of 9 percent is considered reasonable. The building has an estimated economic life of forty years. The value of the property, as leased, is calculated as follows:

1. Present value of the 20-year income stream
   discounted at 9 percent ($46,000 × 9.1285*) $419,911
2. Present value of the property reversion in 20 years.
   The property reversion consists of:
   The land (value remains stable) $100,000
   The building
   $\dfrac{20 \text{ (years)}}{40 \text{ (years)}}$ × $400,000 $200,000
   Total property reversion $300,000
   Present value of property reversion
   ($300,000 × .1486**)   44,580
   Present value of leased fee interest $464,491

The leased fee value of $464,489 (usually rounded to $464,500) is considerably lower than the unleased value of $500,000. These figures indicate that the property is either being rented below economic (market) rent, thereby creating a positive leasehold interest in favor of the lessee, or that the building does not represent the highest and best use of the land.

*From Appendix D, Table D–2, Column 5, annuity factor, 20 years, 9%
**From Appendix D, Table D–3, Column 4, reversionary factor 20 years, 10% (higher discount rate used because of increased ri in unleased property).

---

demanded by prudent investment of capital. Mortgage equity also includes a provision to adjust for property appreciation or depreciation over the holding period. In projecting a net income stream, the mortgage-equity technique assumes short-term holding periods of five or ten years, rather than trying to "guesstimate" the economic life of the improvements and the size and shape of the income stream over thirty to fifty years. This seems to be more in line with actual investor behavior than the thirty- to fifty-year assumptions and projections called for in other capitalization techniques. Finally, mortgage equity aids the investor in determining the yield on his cash down payment (equity); all the other techniques ignore this important issue.

L. L. (Pete) Ellwood, a pioneer in the ***mortgage-equity (Ellwood) technique,*** has developed an algebraic formula and a set of precomputed tables to assist the appraiser/analyst in computing the overall rate by use of this technique. Several other publications on the mortgage-equity technique are now available and are listed at the end of this chapter. The student is encouraged to read further on this contemporary appraisal technique.

CORRELATION AND FINAL ESTIMATE

At this point, the appraiser has applied the cost approach, the market approach, and the income approach and has derived three different estimates of value. Having developed a value range, he must now establish a final estimate of value by reviewing all of the three approaches for accuracy. The next step is to evaluate the applicability of each approach relative to the purpose of the appraisal and the type of property being appraised.

If the property is being appraised for mortgage-lending purposes, its income-generating capacity takes precedence, and the income approach should be given greatest weight. If the property is being appraised for tax, condemnation, or sale purposes, the market approach should be given greater emphasis. If the appraisal is made for insurance purposes, the cost approach should be given greatest weight.

The type of property being appraised also determines which approach should be given the greatest weight. The cost approach should be emphasized on a special purpose property, such as a church or a factory, because of the lack of comparable sales and income data. The market approach should be given the greatest weight in appraising a home because the marketplace is filled with purchases and sales that constantly generate up-to-the-minute indications of market value. The market approach may be the only feasible approach on old, depreciated buildings with little or no dependable income data. Finally, when appraising income-producing properties, the appraiser should give greatest weight to the income approach because typical investors evaluate alternative investments similarly. The final estimate of value should be broken down between land and improvements.

If the appraiser carefully exercises skill, experience, and judgment in correlating the estimates, the results should indicate a valid final estimate of value. The results are then compiled and presented in a written report to the client.

APPRAISAL REPORT FORMATS

Letter Appraisal

Upon occasion, the client may not require a complete narrative report or even a form report. In this case, a one- to three-page letter appraisal may be used. The appraiser still performs all of the applicable approaches to value; however, the field notes and rough drafts of the indicators of value remain in the appraisal files. The letter appraisal merely contains a brief description of the property, the value estimate, and other selected data.

Form Appraisal

A form appraisal is reported on a preprinted form. The most popular residential appraisal form is the Uniform Residential Appraisal Report (URAR), which was developed jointly by the Federal National Mortgage Association and the Federal Home Loan Mortgage Corporation in 1986. This form has been adopted for use by HUD, the VA, and the Farmers Home Administration, as well as "Fannie Mae" and "Freddie Mac" lenders. It has all of the elements of a narrative appraisal. Recently, both FNMA and FHLMC began requiring neighborhood maps, floor plans of the subject property, and pictures of both the subject property and all comparable sales as part of the form report. Figure 19–3 provides a copy of the Uniform Residential Appraisal Report.

Narrative Appraisal

The narrative appraisal report provides the most in-depth information regarding the subject property, the real estate market, the applicable approaches to value, and the analysis of the appraiser's findings. In addition, the addenda to the report generally contain a wealth of supporting data. The report may be from 15 to 150 pages in length and sometimes longer. The major appraisal organizations have developed recommended narrative appraisal report formats. Since this type report is most time-consuming, it is also somewhat expensive. Such reports are generally required by out-of-state investors, eminent domain proceedings, and major financial institutions to assist them in their decision making.

SUMMARY

The purpose of an appraisal is to estimate value. Most appraisal assignments require an estimation of market value. However, the appraiser may be asked to estimate other types of value, depending on the client's needs. Other values commonly estimated include insurable value and investment value.

Major governmental, economic, social, and physical factors are constantly at work influencing value. The appraiser must observe, analyze, and interpret the effect of these factors on the value estimate.

Appraising is a systematic process. Prior to starting, the property must be clearly identified and the client's problem understood. Then the appraiser lays out a careful plan to determine how to conduct the appraisal. When the client and the appraiser agree on the plan, purpose, and fee, the appraiser proceeds to collect data and perform the analysis. The appraiser may apply the cost approach, market approach, or income approach; however, using a combination of all three usually gives the best results.

The cost approach to value is based on the estimated value of the land, plus the cost of replacing the improvements, minus any depreciation caused by physical deterioration, functional obsolescence, or economic obsolescence. The cost approach is best suited to special purpose properties, such as a church or factory, that lack income data or comparable sales. This approach is most reliable when the improvement is new or nearly new and the land is being utilized at its highest and best use. The cost approach is less reliable on older buildings.

The income approach takes the actual or estimated net income from the property and, through the process of capitalization, converts it into a property value. This approach is given the most weight for income-producing properties.

When applying the income approach to single-family homes and duplexes, a factor (GMRM) is derived from the market and applied to estimated gross monthly rent of the appraised property to arrive at an estimate of value. This approach usually sets the lower limit of value in single-family residential appraising because it does not reflect many of the nonmonetary benefits of home ownership that accrue to the homeowner. Consequently, this approach is given little weight in most higher priced single-family homes. However, if the home being appraised is in the lower value range and an active rental market exists for the property, the income approach is more reliable and should be given more weight.

The market approach compares the subject property being appraised to recent sales of similar properties. Differences between the subject property and the comparable properties are noted and dollar or percentage adjustments are made to the selling price of the comparable properties in arriving at a preliminary market value for the subject property. The market approach should be given considerable weight when sufficient market data are available.

Once all applicable approaches to value have provided indications of value, they are reconciled into a final estimate of value and presented in an appraisal report.

TERMS AND CONCEPTS

You can check your understanding of these terms against the glossary or by review in this chapter.

Annuity capitalization	Effective demand	Principle of contribution
Annuity factor	GMRM	Principles of increasing
Appraisal	Highest and best use	and decreasing
Building capitalization	Insurable value	returns
rate	Investment value	Principle of substitution
Building residual	Land residual technique	Property residual
technique	MAI	technique
Capitalization	Market value	Rate
Capitalization rate	Mortgage-equity	Reserve for replacement
Capitalizing the rent loss	(Ellwood) technique	RM
Comparable	Overall capitalization	Scarcity
Cost to cure	rate	SREA
Depreciation	Physical deterioration	Transferability
Economic life	Plottage value	Units-in-place
Effective age	Present value	Utility

What are the differences or relationships, if any, between the following?

Built-up (summation) method and Band of investments method	Cost approach to value, Market approach to value, and Income approach to value	Macromarket data and Micromarket data
Capitalization in perpetuity and Direct capitalization	Fixed expenses and Operating expenses	Recapture rate and Overall capitalization rate
Capitalization rate and Overall capitalization rate	Functional obsolescence and Economic obsolescence	Replacement cost, insurable, and Insurable value, depreciated
Comparative approach to value and Market approach to value	Function of appraisal and Purpose of appraisal	Return on investment and Return of investment
Cost approach to value and Market approach to value	Income approach to value and Capitalization	Square foot method, Cubic foot method, and Quantity survey method

Table 19–6

	Subject property	A	B	C	D
Price:	—	$40,000	$35,000	$38,000	$31,000
Date:	Now	this year	2 yr ago	1 yr ago	3 yr ago
Lot:	—	Equal	Equal	Equal	Double lot
Architecture:	—	Poorer	Better	Equal	Equal
Rooms:	7	6	7	6	7
Baths:	1½	1	1	1½	1
Condition:	—	Poorer	Better	Equal	Equal

19-1. What are the three approaches to appraising? Explain the steps involved in each approach.

19-2. Differentiate between market value and investment value.

19-3. Differentiate between effective age and actual age.

19-4. In appraising a residence, you find the four comparative sales in the block shown in Table 19–6. Assuming that the double lot for D was responsible for $1,000 additional price, that each room is worth $500, that the market increases 5 percent per year, and that other plus and minus adjustments average $500 apiece, what is the indicated value range for the subject property?

19-5. You have completed both the market and cost approaches on a single-family house appraisal assignment, both of which result in a value indication of $36,000. Five sales comparable to the subject property are shown in Table 19–7. Rental differences are due to the physical conditions of

the homes. All sales are in the same neighborhood. Using the GMRM, find the income approach to value. The subject property's estimated rental is $300.

19-6. An apartment building produces an annual net operating income of $50,000. The interest rate for the property has been estimated at 10.25 percent, and the economic life of the improvement is estimated to be 25 years. Three highly similar and competitive apartment buildings within two blocks of the subject property, offering essentially the same service and improvements as the subject, have sold in the past month. Comparable sales data and net operating income are shown in Table 19–8.

Table 19–7

Sale	Sale price	Monthly rent
1	$37,500	$320
2	$36,000	$310
3	$35,500	$300
4	$35,900	$310
5	$34,800	$300

Table 19–8

Comparable sales	Selling price	Net operating income
1	$400,000	$53,500
2	$450,000	$62,000
3	$325,000	$45,000

Using direct capitalization, capitalize or convert the subject property's net income into an estimate of value.

19-7. Use the information provided below for Comparables No. 1, No. 2, and No. 3 to arrive at an appraised value for a subject property in Rockingham County. Use the format of Figure 19–3. The subject property was appraised in March 1989.

Comparable No. 1 sold for $62,500 in May 1988. Since the prices of homes have increased, use a time adjustment of $1,500. Comparable No. 2 sold for $62,500 in March 1989, and no time adjustment is necessary. Comparable No. 3 sold for $53,600 in August 1988, so a time adjustment of $1,000 is to be used. The locations of all four properties are similar.

The subject property and No. 1 each have 2 acres. No. 2 has ½ acre (adjustment + $2,000), and No. 3 has ⅓ acre (adjustment + $2,500). The appeal and quality of construction are good on all four properties.

The subject property is twenty-seven years old, and older properties are considered of lower value. No. 1 is six years old (adjustment $2,000), and Nos. 2 and 3 are thirteen years old (adjustment $1,000). All four properties are in good condition.

The subject property has the largest living area (1,982 square feet), which is valued greater than No. 1 (1,706 square feet) by $2,000, greater than No. 2 (1,463 square feet) by $3,500 and greater than No. 3 (1,528 square feet) by $2,800.

The subject property has a full basement. No. 3 is inferior as it has no basement. A $5,000 adjustment is required. The other two have full basements; however, No. 1 is better than the subject by $3,000, and No. 2 is better than the subject by $2,000. The functional utility of No. 1 is valued at $2,000 more than any of the other three properties. Comparable sale No. 3 has a 1-car garage. Neither the subject nor the other two comparables have a garage. Make a $2,000 adjustment for the garage

Comparable No. 1 has a pool worth $6,000. No. 2 has a pool worth $2,000. Neither the subject property nor No. 3 has a pool.

The kitchen equipment for the subject property and No. 1 are rated good. No. 2 is poorer by $500, and No. 3 is poorer than the subject property by $2,500.

Weigh all comparable properties equally to arrive at an appraised value.

19-8. If houses in one particular suburb have a GMRM of 116, what is the difference in value between a house on Foxbough that has a gross rental income of $6,600 per year and a house on Woodvine Drive with a gross rental income of $5,240 per year?

19-9. The property being appraised is a twenty-five-year-old apartment building producing a yearly net income of $60,000. Assuming a twenty-year economic life for the building, determine the property value at a 9.5 percent interest rate and an estimated land value of $100,000. Use the appropriate residual method of capitalization.

![SUPPLEMENTARY READINGS]

SUPPLEMENTARY READINGS

American Institute of Real Estate Appraisers. *American Institute of Real Estate Appraisers Financial Tables.* Chicago, 1981.

American Institute of Real Estate Appraisers. *The Appraisal of Real Estate,* 9th ed. Chicago, 1987.

American Institute of Real Estate Appraisers. *The Appraisal of Rural Property.* Chicago, 1983.

American Institute of Real Estate Appraisers. *Appraising Residential Properties.* Chicago, 1988.

American Institute of Real Estate Appraisers. *Capitalization Theory and Techniques: Study Guide.* Chicago, 1984.

American Institute of Real Estate Appraisers. *The Dictionary of Real Estate Appraisal,* 2nd ed. Chicago, 1989.

Bloom, George F., and Harrison, Henry S. *Appraising the Single Family Residence.* Chicago: American Institute of Real Estate Appraisers, 1978.

Burton, James. *Evolution of the Income Approach.* Chicago: American Institute of Real Estate Appraisers, 1982.

Friedman, Jack P., and Ordway, Nicholas. *Income Property Appraisal and Analysis.* Reston, Va.: Reston, 1981.

Johnson, Irwin E. *The Instant Mortgage-Equity Technique.* Lexington, Mass.: D. C. Heath & Co., 1971.

Johnson, Irwin E. *Selling Real Estate by Morgage-Equity Analysis.* Lexington, Mass.: D. C. Heath & Co., 1976.

Kahn, Sanders A., and Case, Frederick E. *Real Estate Appraisal and Investment.* New York: Wiley, 1977.

Kinnard, William N. *Income Property Valuation.* Lexington, Mass.: Heath Lexington Books, 1971.

Kinnard, William, N., Jr. *An Introduction to Appraising Real Property.* Chicago: Society of Real Estate Appraisers, 1968.

Miles, Martin J. *Encyclopedia of Real Estate Formulas and Tables.* Englewood Cliffs, N.J.: Prentice-Hall, 1978. Chapters 7–10.

Pratt, Shannon P. *Valuing Small Business and Professional Practices.* Homewood, Ill.: Dow Jones-Irwin, 1986.

Shenkel, William M. *Modern Real Estate Appraisal.* New York: McGraw-Hill, 1978.

Society of Real Estate Appraisers. *The Appraiser's Guide to the Uniform Residential Appraisal Report,* 2nd ed. Chicago, 1989.

Ventolo, William L., Jr., and Williams, Martha R. *Fundamentals of Real Estate Appraisal,* 4th ed. Chicago: Real Estate Education Company, 1987.

CHAPTER 20
Property Management

A large number of families and commercial enterprises in the United States are housed in large, multistoried buildings. These buildings represent the bulk of the total invested capital in the country, and their rental income is a substantial portion of the total national income. The large amount of money involved, the complexity of the task, the necessity for specialized knowledge, and the frequency of absentee ownership cause owners of buildings to employ professional property managers. Properties must be attended to and maintained. Full occupancy is important. Rents must be maximized, but at a marketable amount. Problems arise continually and tenants must be satisfied. Many property owners do have competence in this area, however, and manage their own property. Whether the owner or someone else manages the property, the concepts discussed in this chapter apply to their business.

Property management has become recognized as a special field of its own. Community colleges and universities offer courses in property management as part of their real estate programs. In addition, many schools offer special courses in hotel management, country club management, and other specialized fields. The NATIONAL ASSOCIATION OF REALTORS® has established the Institute of Real Estate Management *(IREM)* for specialists in property management. Members of this institute can earn the professional designation of Certified Property Manager *(CPM)*. On-site managers can earn the designation Accredited Resident Manager (ARM), and firms that qualify can receive the Accredited Management Organization (AMO) designation. The Building Owners and Managers Association *(BOMA)* offers the professional designation of Real Property Administrator (RPA). Professional property managers require a comprehensive understanding of property value based on income and its potential value in the future. They must be knowledgeable in marketing, consumer behavior, maintenance, accounting and the legal aspects of property management.

SCOPE OF PROPERTY MANAGEMENT

Property management encompasses the management of all types of properties. Some multistory buildings house only one large organization, whereas others house several tenants who lease smaller units of space. The full scope of the property manager's job is apparent in the management of large buildings. Even when there is only one tenant, someone has to supervise the service and maintenance tasks. These tasks comprise part of the property manager's job. Some important types of buildings and the related property management tasks are discussed below.

Office Buildings

Prior to 1950, the majority of large office buildings were in the central business districts of larger cities. The buildings were concentrated there near transportation centers and other commercial activities. Since the 1950s, office building construction has gradually expanded both in central areas and in outlying areas. This continued demand for office space has grown because of the expansion of service establishments involving office workers. In addition, those using office space have demanded improvements in the quality of their facilities.

Hotels and Motels

Hotel management, a specialized endeavor, has its own unique problems. The primary difference is that hotel clients are mostly transients. The resort hotel falls into this category but deals with vacationing transients who often stay for a longer period of time.

Industrial Buildings

Industrial buildings contain space that is suitable for manufacturing or warehousing. The buildings are usually not finished or carpeted inside. In the earlier part of this century, multistory buildings were constructed primarily near central business areas or where rail transportation was available. Recently, the trend has been to locate one- or two-floor structures in industrial parks. In either case, the functions of managing industrial buildings include leasing space, maintenance, and providing the associated services.

Store Properties

Store properties take the form of department stores, shopping centers, or buildings housing retail establishments. Frequently, stores are located in the lower floors of buildings that have residential units or office space in the upper floors. Selection of generative tenants (Chapter 18) is especially important to maximize pedestrian traffic.

Residential Buildings

Several types of residential properties must be managed:

1. *Apartment buildings.* Large apartment buildings and complexes comprise a substantial portion of the nation's housing. These apartments may be (a) owned by private owners such as insurance companies who have invested their funds for income, (b) built as public housing and operated with assistance from the federal government, or (c) owned by the residents either as a cooperative or as a condominium. Each category requires a full scope of property management services.
2. *Single-family units.* Although the tendency is toward home ownership, a number of families still rent single-family dwellings. Homes that have been foreclosed by mortgage holders frequently end up as rental units, especially during slow sales periods in the market. The leasing of rental units makes up a substantial area of property management.
3. *Duplexes.* A home designed for two families is called a *duplex.* These homes, and others designed for three or four families, make up a large part of the rental income market. This type of structure allows a greater return from the land investment than a single-family home. Duplexes are often managed by the owners, who often live in one of the units.

APPROACHES TO PROPERTY MANAGEMENT

Property management involves a wide variety of tasks and responsibilities. These responsibilities can be handled by one of three basic approaches:

1. *A firm that deals exclusively in property management.* This type of company will usually be headed by one or more Certified Property Managers. The sole function of the business is to manage property for others.
2. *A real estate brokerage firm with a department set up to manage property.* In this case, property management is only part of the firm's total business. Other functions may include buying and selling real estate, performing appraisals, or subdividing and developing. In this case, one person would probably act as head of the property management department. She would be responsible for all aspects of managing the properties.
3. *A property manager who has responsibility for a specific building.* Many apartment and office buildings have a property manager's office set up on the premises for the manager and other management personnel. The property manager may work directly for the owner and be responsible for only that property. If the management of one property is not a full-time job, the person may also manage other buildings.

OBJECTIVES IN PROPERTY MANAGEMENT

Before describing the tasks of the property manager, it is important to consider ways of measuring how successful a property manager's job is being carried out. The following can be identified as objectives:

- Profits to the owner
- Fewer vacancies (high occupancy rate)
- Lower rate of turnover of units
- Low delinquencies
- Fewer complaints and repairs
- Low turnover of employees
- Good relations with owners and tenants

The property manager or the owner should have quantitative goals for each of these objectives. Figures from competitive units are always helpful in evaluating the performance of a property manager.

THE PROPERTY MANAGER

A property manager is a real estate professional hired to maintain the property and ensure the profitability of the owner's investment. Property managers must have a number of important qualifications. A broad knowledge of the technical aspects of real estate is, of course, basic. Understanding urban analysis and the economic forces affecting the properties is also mandatory. Business experience and courses in business administration are also important. Since property managers hire and supervise other people, experience in handling people is another valuable asset.

As part of the task of keeping the rental space filled, property managers need to make marketing analyses of the competition and of other external factors affecting the demand for and occupancy of the space. They must be able to establish rents and adjust them to economic and market conditions so that the operation will be profitable. Property managers must also know the many financial aspects of business and of real estate in particular. They should operate their properties so as to yield a satisfactory net income after all expenses and overhead have been paid.

Property managers should be familiar with the local area. Business contacts with banks, financial institutions, and professional associations provide important sources of clients. Knowledge of local economic forces helps them formulate pricing and marketing strategies.

Recently there has been a trend toward specialization in property management. The skills of the apartment house manager can be somewhat different from those of the office building manager, the shopping center manager, or the industrial park manager. Farm management requires still other skills.

Certified Property Manager (CPM)

Members of the NATIONAL ASSOCIATION OF REALTORS® who specialize in property management are able to further their professional interests through membership in the Institute of Real Estate Management (IREM). The institute confers the title of Certified Property Manager (CPM) to each individual who meets the following requirements:

1. Is a member of the NATIONAL ASSOCIATION OF REALTORS® or a local real estate board
2. Has been actively engaged in real estate management for at least three years
3. Demonstrates the ability to manage real estate
4. Meets minimum educational requirements
5. Subscribes to the institute bylaws and pledge
6. Provides evidence of honesty and integrity
7. Passes written examinations administered by the IREM, which may waive an examination if proof is given of fifteen years active property management experience

The Management Contract

A management contract is an agreement between a property owner and the person hired as the property manager. The contract describes the rights and duties of the manager as well as the rights and obligations of the owner. Standard property management forms are available from IREM. The following items are important and should be clearly covered in the contract agreement:

1. Exact description of property to be managed
2. Term during which the contract runs, showing the starting date and termination date
3. Names of the owner and the manager and a description of the duties of the manager; manager is usually defined as the agent of the owner who can act in the owner's behalf
4. Compensation of the manager, usually based on a percentage of gross collections, with a typical range being 5 to 8 percent.
5. Responsibility of the property manager to collect rents, hire employees, and pay expenses; agreement to explain how funds collected in excess of expenses are to be handled, as well as what happens if the collected funds are not sufficient to meet expenditures
6. Reports to be furnished to the owner and other persons
7. Extent to which the manager can make repairs and alterations or spend funds without the owner's consent
8. Obligations of the owner to furnish documents and funds needed

The initial effort to clarify the owner-manager relationship will help to alleviate problems in the future. The property management contract need not be on a particular form; however, the form published by the IREM provides a convenient basis for agreement. The term of the contract should depend upon the desires of both the owner and the manager. It need not necessarily be long-term. The continuance of a contract relationship should be based upon the owner's satisfaction with the work being performed as well as the manager's satisfaction with the relationship.

Functions of Property Managers

The overall function of property managers is to act for owners. In this capacity, they are responsible for all aspects of managing the property. They may be given this responsibility because some owners (a) do not want to be bothered with the effort,

(b) live at a distance, or (c) are willing to pay for this service because the property manager can do a much better job of management. The functions of property managers can be divided into the following groups:

1. *Generating income by securing and keeping tenants for the property*
   (a) Promotion and advertising of rental units
   (b) Negotiating leases or rental contracts
   (c) Modifying facilities to meet tenants' needs
   (d) Acting as liaison with tenants and handling complaints
   (e) Public relations
2. *Providing financial controls, records, and accounts*
   (a) Preparing management plans, financial analyses, budgets, and reports for owner
   (b) Controlling expenses
   (c) Rent collection
   (d) Payment of operating expenses and mortgage payments
   (e) Keeping records of receipts and disbursements
3. *Preserving the value of the property by providing upkeep and maintenance*
   (a) Hiring employees or securing outside services
   (b) Security, parking
   (c) Cleaning

The extensive and varied functions of the property manager cannot be executed solely by one person, especially not for a large building or where several properties are handled. The manager should explain to the owners the workings of the management organization and the different responsibilities carried out by the subordinate personnel. Most owners understand that this delegation of tasks is necessary, as in any other business. A clear understanding initially will help to prevent future problems.

The manager should also discuss uncertainties of the business with the owner. Although the manager may put out a top-quality effort, local business conditions and economic cycles may result in periods of high vacancy rates, causing decreased net income. It is important that the owner understand these uncertainties; it is just as important that the manager not make promises that it may be impossible to keep.

ORGANIZATION FOR PROPERTY MANAGEMENT

As in any business, the form of the property management organization and the way in which responsibilities are delegated have much to do with the operation's success.

Consider a property management firm or a department in a brokerage firm. How should it be organized? The operation depends on demonstrated competence for its survival. Many of those who try to handle property management on a part-time basis end up in failure. Some brokers regard property management as a secondary function to supplement the brokerage business, and this concept can lead to failure. It is important that the persons involved understand their full responsibility and their need for commitment.

Two general approaches to organization can be applied to property management: *functional management* and *project management*. These approaches are consis-

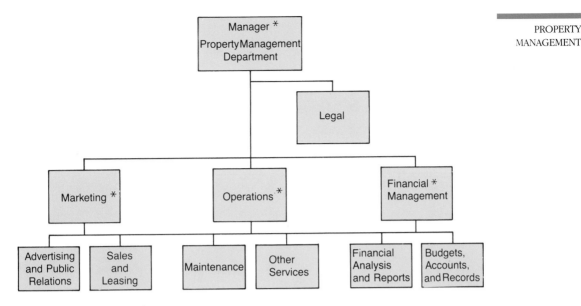

Figure 20–1   Functional organization

tent with general management theory and can be applied to any organization. Figure 20–1 shows a functional organization where people are delegated responsibility for one or more specialized functions. This chart may be more suitable for a larger property management firm. A smaller firm might have only four people (those marked *) with managerial responsibility. A very small organization may have only the property manager plus other specialists working directly for the manager to perform the many varied tasks.

The diagram in Figure 20–1 shows the various functions that must be performed. Almost any of these functions could be subcontracted to an outside agency. Independent agencies are available to handle accounts, advertising, maintenance, security, cleaning, or almost any of the needed services. An advantage to functional organization is that the functions are specialized, and well-trained people can be hired to perform each special function.

Figure 20–2 shows a diagram of a project organization. In the project organization, one person is delegated the complete responsibility for one or more buildings and is responsible for obtaining all personnel and services needed for buildings under his responsibility, whether the services be performed by hired personnel or subcontracted to others. The primary advantage of this organization is that one person can be held responsible for the operation and profitability of a particular building, development, or project.

The functional organization and the project organization each have their advantages. Figure 20–3 shows an organization chart that combines both concepts. In this case, one person is responsible for each building or project, but most of the services are also centralized for efficiency. Each property manager can then draw upon the central group for the services he needs. This organization has some of the advantages of each of the others. The company executive can hold one person responsible for the profitable operation of a unit and, at the same time, can make more efficient use of specialists.

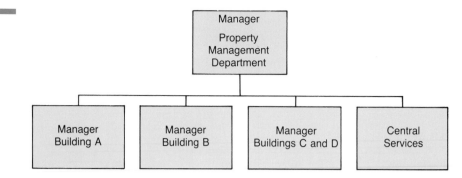

Figure 20–2   Project organization

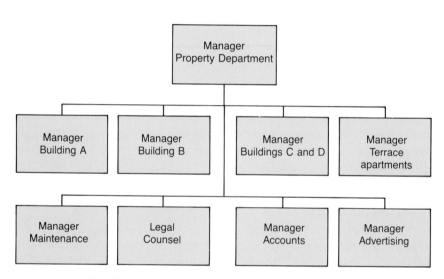

Figure 20–3   Combination functional and project organization

MARKETING OF INCOME PROPERTY

If the functions of a property manager are considered in the order in which they occur, the first element is to find qualified tenants to lease or rent the available units. This function is equivalent to marketing in any business. In this case, the product is building space. As with most products, marketing involves market research, product and space evaluation, formulation of a marketing strategy, advertising, and the ability to sell.

The marketing research function includes evaluating the particular property and comparing it to competitive properties. What are the specific advantages of this property? Who are its potential users? What price should be set to make it competitive? Analyzing the available competitive properties, their proximities, prices, number of existing vacancies, and other assets will provide information on the market situation and the current demand. In comparing it with other properties, it is necessary to consider their respective locations, ages, sizes of units, and the nature of existing users. Forms are available to use in describing a residential apartment unit. A good strategy is to inspect a sample of the competing properties and compare their attributes item by item with the subject property. This procedure will help determine if the price of the subject property is competitive. It can also be used as sales promotion data.

Having evaluated the property, the property manager must now identify its potential market. Consider a residential apartment unit. What do tenants look for when selecting apartments? Why do people select apartments instead of individual homes? Who are the potential tenants, and where are they now? Here are some possible answers to the last question: (a) They live in lower priced units now and want to improve their living standard; (b) they are newly married or planning marriage; (c) they are single and highly mobile; (d) their family size has increased or decreased recently; or (e) they presently live in the property and may or may not renew their lease. This type of analysis is important since it will identify the potential renters. The next logical step is to decide what promotion or advertising media will be most successful in reaching that market segment. If most of the potential customers are expected to move in from outside the community, the advertising strategy would be much different than if the potential market consisted of local people who want to upgrade their living standards. The following are some possible advertising media or other approaches to reach the market:

- Newspapers
- Radio and television
- Direct mail advertising
- Billboards
- Company, community, church, or other bulletins
- Personal visits to prospects
- Displays in commercial establishments or motels
- Other real estate brokers
- Information included with rental billings

The next step is sales promotion and selling, much of which is personal contact with present or potential clients. The data collected regarding the property, the competition, and the potential users will be useful in presenting an effective sales approach.

The final step is the preparation and signing of the lease. Leases may include various combinations of provisions and may include an escalator clause. A typical rent escalator clause could provide that the rent increase with an increase in property taxes. An increase in the cost-of-living index or wage increases granted to employees resulting from a union contract might also call for a change in the rent under an escalator clause.

The property management business, like most other businesses, is competitive. Sometimes a manager will make concessions to a prospective tenant to secure a lease. Typically, the property manager might agree to remodel the space, pay a portion of the tenant's moving expenses, or give free rent for the first month. The practice of giving a concession is more prevalent in times when vacancy rates are high. Concessions might also be used to induce a tenant to move from an existing location into a new building. Other possible lease provisions were discussed in Chapter 6.

Commercial Property

The marketing of commercial property brings up a number of additional important factors. Location is very important to commercial establishments. Customer traffic is very important to retail businesses; however, the types of people who comprise the traffic should be considered as well as the traffic count. In promoting commercial real estate, data on the amount and type of pedestrian traffic are vital for the potential tenant. It is not always easy to collect valid data. Companies specializing in conducting traffic surveys can be hired. Usually, they obtain very reliable results. Pedestrian traffic, however, is of little significance to physicians, dentists, or lawyers who look to other factors such as parking facilities, public transportation, and appearance of the property.

Pricing commercial property usually differs from pricing residential space. Residential properties are usually priced on a per-unit basis, such as a one-bedroom apartment at $200 per month or a three-bedroom apartment at $360 per month. Commercial property is often rented (a) on a percentage of gross sales basis; (b) by the front footage on the street or mall; or (c) by square footage of floor area. Consider the retail store in Figure 20–4 to compute rent by the three different methods:

1. The rent is charged as 2 percent of gross sales. Consider the gross sales for the month of March as $37,500. With this method, the rent would be 0.02 × $37,500, or $750 per month.
2. Consider the same property with the rent computed as $200 per front foot per year. Since the length along the street runs 36 feet, the rent would be

$$\$200 \times 36 \text{ ft} = \$7,200 \text{ per yr, or}$$

$$\frac{\$7,200}{12} = \$600 \text{ per mo}$$

3. On a square-foot basis, the area of the store is calculated as

$$140 \text{ ft} \times 36 \text{ ft} = 5,040 \text{ sq ft}$$

If the yearly rate is $1.50 per square foot, the rent would be

$$\$1.50 \times 5,040 \text{ sq ft} = \$7,560 \text{ per yr, or}$$

$$\frac{\$7,560}{12} = \$630 \text{ per mo}$$

Managing Condominiums

The condominium manager performs many tasks similar to those of an apartment manager, but there are some differences. She would collect monthly assessments, keep records, and pay bills for services, taxes, and insurance. She would have the responsibility for maintenance of common elements but not for maintenance related to the individual condominium units. She normally would not be responsible for legal proceedings to collect delinquent charges.

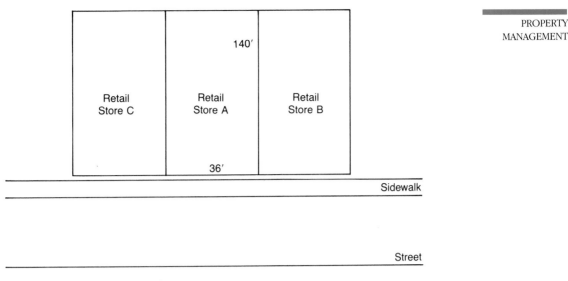

Figure 20–4   Retail store configuration

The property manager would serve as an agent of the condominium board of directors. The board, in turn, would agree to indemnify the agent or hold her harmless from adverse claims arising from the job of property manager.

OPERATIONS

The property manager is responsible for maintaining the structure and grounds, heating, trash disposal, operating equipment, and other items of common use by the tenants. Downs[1] separates the maintenance tasks into four basic categories:

1. Maintenance activities that protect the physical integrity of the building structure (e.g., repairs to foundations, roofs, exterior walls, stairways, driveways, and walks)
2. Maintenance associated with continued functional operation of a building and use by the occupants (e.g., heating, air conditioning, plumbing, electrical systems, elevators, laundry facilities, and swimming pools)
3. Standard housekeeping and cleaning operations
4. Maintenance operations related to improving the appearance or otherwise improving the competitive appeal of the property (decorating, landscaping, carpeting, mowing lawns, and similar items)

Services

Services offered to the tenants affect the rental rates of units; however, these services can often be supplied by the landlord more efficiently for all tenants than if each tenant were to secure her own. The following services add to the expenses of property operation but are frequently provided.

---

[1] James C. Downs, *Principles of Real Estate Management*. Chicago: Institute of Real Estate Management, 1980. Chapter 28.

Remodeling

Especially in the case of commercial properties, a tenant may require changes in layout or remodeling to suit particular business needs. It is often more efficient and economical for the manager to furnish this service. The cost could either be included in the rental rates or be levied as a separate charge. Property owners often maintain their own crew for this purpose or have subcontracts with outside agencies.

Cleaning

The manager is usually responsible for furnishing some cleaning services. In apartment buildings, cleaning services are generally restricted to the halls and other public areas. In office buildings, cleaning services are frequently provided for tenant-rented areas also. The cleaning crews can be employed directly, or the cleaning can be subcontracted to an outside agency.

Security

Some residential and many commercial buildings furnish one or more security guards. Security can be handled by guards hired by the property manager or by a professional security agency.

Parking Facilities

In suburban areas it is usually sufficient to provide unmonitored parking areas for tenant or customer parking. In areas where parking space is scarce, it is often necessary to provide either an attendant or automatic entrance control equipment to restrict parking facilities to authorized persons.

Managing Services

Providing services that meet the tenants' needs and desires is important to retain present tenants and secure new tenants. At the same time, the cost of the services must permit a satisfactory net income to the property owner.

When services are to be subcontracted, the manager should first seek a competitive bid for each service. Competitive bidding is also used in procuring maintenance supplies, especially when large amounts are involved. The first step in competitive bidding is to prepare a specification defining exactly what services or materials are required. Bidders can then quote their prices to furnish the specified services or materials. It is also usually desirable to allow bidders to submit auxiliary bids for performing the services in a way that differs from the specification. In some cases, suggestions of the bidders could provide adequate service, save money, and result in lower prices to the manager.

If contracts with service agencies can be made for long periods and the expenses budgeted in advance, cost control becomes easier. A contract to cover all maintenance and repairs to heating, electrical, and plumbing facilities removes the risk that unexpected breakdown will cause higher than planned expenses. This resembles an insurance policy in that the risks are transferred to the maintenance subcontractor. A maintenance subcontractor who has responsibility for all repairs at a fixed price may take more care in performing preventive maintenance.

If the management firm hires its own employees to provide the maintenance, security, or cleaning, it will need experience in many aspects of personnel management. Wage scales must be formulated. Potential employees must be found and their qualifications evaluated. Careful initial selection of employees pays off in the long run. The selection process should be followed by a training program if the new employees do not have adequate experience.

Many aspects of personnel management should be outlined in written policies and procedures. Employee insurance, work schedules, sick leave, holidays, pay increases, and vacations should all be covered so that employees can understand the policies and management can administer them with consistency and fairness.

House Rules

The property manager should establish a pleasant living atmosphere and provide for the welfare of the tenants. House rules and regulations can help. The following matters should be covered by rules if they apply to the particular building:

1. Swimming pools—who can use them, hours, safety regulations
2. Maximum number of occupants per apartment
3. Trash facilities—where to put trash, collection schedules
4. Use of playgrounds—who is allowed, responsibility for injuries
5. Activities permitted and prohibited in halls or front areas of the building and premises
6. Moving in or out—advance notice is required, restriction to weekdays or to particular daytime hours
7. Radio and television aerials—restrictions on installation
8. Loud playing of radios and television after specified hours
9. Pets
10. Clothes washing and drying—facilities available
11. Parking rules and restrictions, identification stickers
12. Night activities that may disturb other tenants and therefore are prohibited
13. Use of electrical appliances in apartments
14. Failure of electricity or landlord-maintained appliances—how to obtain maintenance service
15. Car washing—areas where it is permitted
16. Fire regulations
17. Storage facilities available—their cost, accessibility

FINANCIAL CONTROL

The primary objective in managing income property is to attain the highest net return. The long-term net profit must be considered along with the short-term goals. In addition, the management strategy must consider the risks involved. The risk from fire or other similar hazards can be alleviated by purchasing insurance. The manager must also deal with the risk that a larger than predicted number of units will remain vacant. This situation might result from changes in the general economy or from increased competition. High occupancy rates of office buildings in the 1960s encouraged excess construction of new office space. The resulting surplus was aggravated by the economic situation and produced unfavorable vacancy rates in the

1970s. Another risk that must be considered is that operating expenses can increase during a one- or two-year period over which the lease specifies a fixed rent. These and other risks must be identified, evaluated, and controlled.

These factors and risks must be considered when establishing rental schedules. The income from rent less the costs of services and overhead should yield the desired net income. At the same time, the rental rates must compete with other rental rates in the local area, or the vacancy rate will be too high.

Income Management

Since rents are the primary source of income, the timely payment of rents is very important. This begins with procedures for selecting tenants and for writing valid lease contract terms. Each tenant's credit, business position, and other qualifications should be obtained from the local credit bureaus. Checking prior landlords or other references also helps to evaluate potential tenants and avoid future problems. If a business property is involved, the terms given to a tenant may reflect that tenant's business position. Sometimes rents are lower at first to accommodate a business just getting started.

Adherence to a firm rental collection policy is vital. The tenant should understand that rents are due on the specified date whether or not she receives a notice. Payment of rents by the first day of the month is the policy recommended. Penalties for late payment should be clearly specified in the lease agreement. It is also important to enforce these terms so that tenants do not assume that the terms are unimportant. Although there may be a few extenuating circumstances, it does not pay to try to be nice to everyone who has a problem. If a property manager has not enforced rental payment terms in the past, it may lead to difficulty in enforcing them legally. Past practices provide implied consent to disregard the terms. If tenants do not pay rents on time, the manager must pursue a rigid follow-up system of notices and legal action. At the time rents are paid, the tenants should be given receipts even if they pay by check; receipts provide accurate bookkeeping records.

Expense Control and Accountability

The property manager must account for all money received, as well as money due but not received. Rents provide the main source of incoming funds; however, security deposits must also be handled.

A record must be kept of all expenses related to the property. If there are employees, payroll records including payroll taxes and social security records must also be kept.

The property manager should provide periodic reports showing the financial status of the property. These should be prepared for the property owner whether she had demanded them or not. It is important that the owner be kept current on all matters and not be surprised at the end of the year. A typical report would include income, expenditures, and net income for the period and for the year to date. Each piece of property should be evaluated separately so as to identify profitable and unprofitable endeavors. Unprofitable properties should be carefully scrutinized for changes that could improve their profit status. These same records and reports should also be used to project future expenses, prepare next year's budget, and set rental schedules for new or renewed leases covering future periods.

Many forms and methods are available for keeping accounting records and for reporting to the owner. The supplementary readings at the end of the chapter go into detail on these subjects (see especially Downs and Schwachter).

CONSULTING SERVICES

Property managers also provide consulting services to property owners or developers who are considering conversion, rehabilitation, or modernization of an existing property. A person who wants to buy, sell, or develop a property also often needs an advisory service.

The property manager's function as a consultant is to make recommendations that will enhance the income-producing capability of the property through a variety of alternatives. The *rehabilitation* of a property involves restoring a structure for its current use. *Modernization* involves replacing equipment, painting, or other operations that would improve the property in its present use.

Property Conversions

The property consultant may recommend *conversion* of the property into a different use. For example, an old mansion might be converted into business offices. This often happens where areas change and are rezoned. The experienced property manager is often asked to recommend the best usage or layout or the most suitable tenants for a property being evaluated. In this process of evaluation, a rental schedule would be drawn up to show the potential return on the investment. This schedule should include the property value, a market analysis, a neighborhood evaluation, and an income and expense analysis. In some cases, alternative plans would be considered. Consultants will often contract to manage the property in addition to making recommendations.

Conversions to Condominiums

Although we usually visualize a condominium as a newly constructed property, an owner often converts an existing property into a condominium. Conversion to a condominium may yield a high profit within a short period of time. However, since all properties are not easily converted, the property manager's advice is often sought. The success of a conversion to a condominium depends on the property's structure and location, the availability of financing at attractive interest rates, and the possible displacement of existing tenants. A variety of problems may occur when an existing property is to be converted to condominium units. Conversions have been criticized because of past abuses involving unethical conduct by developers. Most of these result from the displacement of existing tenants. The tenant must either find other rental property or purchase a condominium unit in the converted property. The tenant often does not have the financial capability to make the purchase. In some cases the tenants have purchased the structure to meet the conversion. In addition, some local governments have issued moratoriums on conversions or passed laws requiring four to six months relocation time before eviction.

Advocates of conversions to condominiums view them as revitalizing central city areas. They allow ownership for more persons. Moreover, condominiums tend to be better cared for and maintained than rental properties. They also increase the tax base by the increased value of the converted buildings.

SUMMARY

The task of managing apartments, office buildings, and other real estate involves many complexities. Thus, the need has evolved for professional property managers who work for a fee or salary. Generally, the terms and conditions of the manager's job are provided in a written contract between the manager and the owner. A manager might work as an independent, or with a property management firm, or in a department of a brokerage firm.

The manager's job can be broken down into three main categories. The marketing function deals with securing and keeping tenants to occupy the space and provide income. Next, the manager must provide services such as security, maintenance, and cleaning. Third, the manager must maintain financial control over income and expenses and keep adequate accounts and records.

Property managers also serve as consultants to property owners or potential buyers of investment properties. In that capacity, they evaluate property for potential modernization, rehabilitation, or conversion into income-producing property or for condominiums. The property manager's advice is usually sought for securing the highest net income from a parcel of property.

TERMS AND CONCEPTS

You can check your understanding of these terms and concepts against the glossary or by review in this chapter.

BOMA	Functional management	Project management
CPM	IREM	Rehabilitation
Duplex	Modernization	

PROBLEMS

20-1. Assume that you are a broker who manages a real estate office of ten salespersons. You plan to start managing property. Write a position description defining the property manager's responsibilities and authority.

20-2. List the important elements that should be in a contract between an owner of an apartment building and a person hired by the owner to manage the building.

20-3. Assume you are the manager of an apartment building and want to subcontract lawn care and external and internal housekeeping of all areas except inside the apartments. Prepare a specification to be sent out for bids.

20-4. An investor paid $371,000 for an industrial building with 11,000 square feet. If the investor wants a 12 percent annual return on the investment, what should be the rent per square foot?

20-5. A merchant signs a lease that sets a monthly rental of $700 or 6 percent of gross sales, whichever is less. If gross sales in February were $11,000, what is the merchant's rent?

20-6. What are the significant differences in maintenance of office buildings as compared to residential properties?

20-7. A property management firm manages eight apartment buildings. List the functions that could be better centralized and those that would be better decentralized to each building.

20-8. A commercial property containing 40,000

square feet is rented at $7.00 per square foot. If receipts last year were $172,000, what was the occupancy rate?

20-9. Make a list of questions to be asked at a tenant exit interview for tenants who do not renew their lease.

20-10. Assume you are asked to evaluate a property manager of a residential apartment building. What data would you collect on competitive units in the area to use as comparisons to evaluate the manager?

20-11. Prepare a list of questions a property manager should ask of prospective new tenants for an apartment complex. State why each question is important.

20-12. You are going to talk with tenants in an apartment building to determine how satisfied they are. Prepare a list of questions to ask.

20-13. A yearly financial summary is to be prepared for the owner of a large apartment building. List important figures to be supplied to the owner so she can compare the current year with past years.

SUPPLEMENTARY READINGS

Brauer, William; Sachar, Roger; Shepard, Reba; and Walters, William. *The Resident Manager.* Chicago: Institute of Real Estate Management, 1973.

Downs, James C. *Principles of Real Estate Management,* 12th ed. Chicago: Institute of Real Estate Management, 1980.

Glassmann, Sidney. *A Guide to Residential Management.* Washington, D.C.: National Association of Home Builders, 1978.

Hanford, Lloyd D., Sr. *The Property Management Process.* Chicago: Institute of Real Estate Management, 1972.

Kelley, Edward N. *Practical Apartment Management.* Chicago: Institute of Real Estate Management, 1981.

Kyle, Robert C., and Kennehan, Ann M. *Property Management,* 2nd ed. Chicago: Real Estate Education Company, 1984.

The Property Manager's Guide to Forms and Letters. Chicago: Institute of Real Estate Management, 1971.

The Real Estate Management Department. Chicago: Institute of Real Estate Management, 1967.

Schwachter, Robert S. *How to Make Money Developing and Managing Income Producing Property.* Englewood Cliffs, N.J.: Executive Reports Corporation, 1973.

Shenkel, William M. *Modern Real Estate Management.* New York: McGraw-Hill, 1979.

CHAPTER 21
Real Estate Investments

Real estate investments have several unique characteristics that make them very attractive for many people. The enduring quality and relative scarcity of real estate enhance its value, thereby making it good security for a loan.

The investor may generally borrow up to 80 or 90 percent of the purchase price of real estate investments. This use of borrowed funds to purchase an investment is not unique to real estate; however, few other investments provide such high percentage financing. The use of other people's money (OPM) to finance an investment—*leverage*—may provide the investor a much greater return on equity investment than he could realize in an unleveraged or low-leveraged investment.

Historically, the increasing value of real estate investments has kept pace with or exceeded the general rate of inflation. This capital appreciation makes real estate investments an effective hedge against inflation.

The real estate investor is able to deduct the interest expense on his loan and the depreciation allowances on his investment from the operating income. These combined deductions usually result in a substantial sheltering of income from taxes. Finally, the investor may exchange his investment with a "like-kind" property and defer some, if not all the taxes on the gain.

CHARACTERISTICS OF REAL ESTATE INVESTMENTS

Cash Outlay

Real estate investments usually involve much larger initial outlays of cash than do other forms of investments. Whereas stocks and bonds can be purchased for as little as $5 or $10, real estate investments, even with 90 percent financing, require initial cash outlays of hundreds and, more often, thousands of dollars.

Liquidity

Liquidity refers to the speed with which an investment can be converted to cash without substantial financial loss. Real estate investments generally involve a long-term commitment of investment funds. The principal reasons for most real estate investments being illiquid (not readily convertible to cash) are these:

1. *The heterogeneous nature of the product.* Since no two real estate investments are alike, one investment cannot readily be substituted for another. Consequently, the real estate market is more sluggish than the stock or bond market, where the stocks or bonds of a specific company are homogeneous (similar) in nature and are therefore readily substitutable between and among various investors.
2. *Lack of formal market.* Unlike the stock market, no formal real estate market exists to expedite the buying, selling, or trading of real estate investments or investment information. The advent of the computer has begun to alleviate this problem somewhat by creating national referral and exchange networks. However, the localized nature of the real estate market itself and the unique nature of each parcel of real estate act to perpetuate its illiquid nature.

Although the illiquidity of real estate investments is an obvious disadvantage, the real estate investor who would like to convert his investment to cash, without having to sell it first, may do so by refinancing. Although he does not take out all of the equity investment when refinancing, it may provide enough cash to satisfy his needs. Refinancing is illustrated later in the chapter.

Management

Unlike stocks and bonds, real estate investments must be managed. This function can be performed by the investor himself or by a professional real property management firm. In either case, the investor must recognize the added cost. Professional management firms normally charge a percentage of the gross income from the investment as a management fee. The fees charged range from five to ten percent of the gross income, depending on the type of building, age of building, type of tenants, location of the building, and the manager's duties and responsibilities stipulated in the property management agreement.

Risk

In *investment properties* (properties purchased primarily for capital appreciation with little or no cash flow during the investment holding period), *risk* refers to the chance of loss on the capital investment. The chance of a decrease in property value is always present. The prudent investor will consider this and demand a higher return to compensate for any increased risk. The investor compensates for the increased risk by reducing the amount he's willing to pay for the investment.

On *income-producing properties* (properties purchased primarily for cash flow), investors must also examine the quantity, quality, and durability of the income stream as another measure of risk. The *quantity of the income stream* obviously refers to the amount; the *quality of the income stream* refers to the assuredness of its receipt. The investor would anticipate little or no risk in the collection of rent from a major, financially responsible tenant. Conversely, the investor may expect greater risk of collection from a tenant who is less financially secure. The *durability of the income stream* refers to the anticipated duration or length of time the investment will generate an income. A property having only three years remaining on its lease may not be as valuable as a similar property with ten years on the lease. *Durability* also refers to the remaining economic life of the property. *Economic (useful) life* is the period of time over which the property will be useful to a particular taxpayer in his business or in the production of income.

Risk Versus Return

A direct relationship exists between the *risk* an investor perceives in any given investment and the *return* anticipated for accepting the risk. The higher the perceived risk of an investment, the higher the anticipated return by the investor. The investor reflects perceived risk in the marketplace by discounting the income stream or the asking price of the investment in negotiations with the seller.

The investment dollar is sought after by many different investment media throughout the world. Whenever one specific investment medium experiences a higher return than competing investments of similar risk, investment capital will be diverted to it. In time, with more and more investment funds being diverted to that higher yielding investment, the return from that investment will tend to decline. In essence, the economic principle of supply and demand operates in the capital market. In the long run, rates of return that are higher than normal probably result from the special analytical or management skills of the investor, the acceptance of an investment with a higher risk, or just plain luck.

INVESTMENT RETURNS

Investment returns generally come in one of two forms: a current return or a deferred return. Some investments experience a combination of both current return and deferred return.

Income that is generated by the investment periodically during the term of the investment holding period is called *current return* (sometimes referred to as *cash flow* or *cash on cash*). The current rate of return is usually expressed in one of two ways:

1. The relationship between the total investment value (purchase price) and the current return, that is,

$$\frac{\text{Current return}}{\text{Total investment value}} = \frac{\text{Rate of return on}}{\text{total investment}}$$

2. The relationship between the equity investment (down payment) and the current return, that is,

$$\frac{\text{Current return}}{\text{Equity investment}} = \frac{\text{Rate of return on}}{\text{equity investment}}$$

The rates of return may be used to reflect either "before tax" or "after tax" yields. Examples of investments that usually generate current return are apartment buildings, office buildings, mobile home parks, and parking lots. These same *income-producing properties* may also realize some deferred return on resale.

Income not received until the investment property is sold is called **deferred return**. The deferred return is the realized profit on resale. This deferred gain is the result of property appreciation and/or mortgage amortization.

Most *investment properties* realize deferred returns only and receive no current returns during the period of investment ownership, called the **holding period**. The investor, meanwhile, may incur expenses of ownership, called **ripening expenses** (e.g., real estate taxes and maintenance costs) during the holding period. His return on investment is completely deferred until resale. In the meantime, he may experience a negative cash flow on his investment.

An example of an investment that usually shows a deferred return only is rolling timberland on the perimeter of a city. The investor anticipates that the property will ripen into prime land for future subdividing and developing.

Measuring Investment Returns

The investor invests his money today in anticipation of receiving future benefits—current return (cash flow) and/or deferred return. In order to be able to make intelligent investment decisions, the investor must have a valid method of measuring the returns offered by various real estate investments. This requires an understanding of the time value of money.

Time Value of Money

Assume that an investor is presented with three different investments, all with the same purchase price. Each of the investments will generate a $15,000 *return on* investment as shown below, and a *return of* the investment at the end of five years.

Year	A	B	C
1	0	$3,000	$15,000
2	0	3,000	0
3	0	3,000	0
4	0	3,000	0
5	$15,000	3,000	0
	$15,000	$15,000	$15,000

Which investment would he choose? Investment C is obviously the best choice since all of the *return on* this investment is received in the first year, allowing the investor the ability to reinvest the money in another investment.

If investment A were chosen, the investor would miss the opportunity of reinvesting the $15,000 for the next four years, since he does not receive it until the fifth year. This loss of interest is called the *opportunity cost* of the investment. In summary, money to be received at some time in the future will not earn interest in the current year. Conversely, a dollar received today is worth more than a dollar received one year from today, since it can earn interest. Money has *time value.*

Present Value

The present worth of future benefits can be determined by *discounting* those benefits at an interest rate that is acceptable to the investor. Most real estate investments can be visualized as a series of cash inflows and outflows over the holding period. For instance, assume that an income-producing investment generates a positive cash flow of $15,000 per year for four years and that the property can be sold for $165,000 at the end of the four years.

Applying the time value of money theory, we know that no prudent investor will pay $225,000 today for the right to receive a total stream of income totaling $225,000 over a four-year period. To determine how much an investor would pay, the income stream must be discounted to present value at a rate acceptable to the investor. Assuming a rate of 14 percent, the present value of the future benefits can be calculated (using the present value tables found in Appendix D) as shown in Table 21–1.

As can be seen, the $225,000 in cash flows discounted at 14 percent has a *present value (PV)* of $141,398.89. This, then, is what the investor should pay for the property in order to yield a return of 14 percent on his investment.

Net Present Value

Net present value is one of the methods of measuring the acceptability of an investment. The concept involves discounting all cash *inflows* and *outflows* by the investor's desired return. The present value of the cash outflows are then subtracted from the present value of the cash inflows to determine the *net present value (NPV)* of the investment. A positive net present value indicates an acceptable investment. A negative net present value indicates an unacceptable investment. Let's apply the net present value concept to the preceding example. If the proposed investment were offered for sale at $150,000, would the investment be acceptable to our investor desiring a 14 percent return?

Since the net present value is negative, the investment should be rejected.

Table 21–1   Present value (PV) of $1 (at 14%)

Year	Cash flow		Discount factor		PV of cash flows		
1	$15,000	×	.877193	=	$ 13,157.90		
2	$15,000	×	.769468	=	$ 11,542.02		
3	$15,000	×	.674971	=	$ 10,124.57		
4	$15,000	×	.592080	=	$ 8,881.20	P.V. of inflows	$141,398.89
4	(sale) $165,000	×	.592080	=	$ 97,693.20	P.V. of outflows	− 150,000.00
	$225,000				$141,398.89	Negative net present value	8,601.11

Internal Rate of Return

The **internal rate of return (IRR)** is another commonly used method of measuring investment returns. It can measure and compare returns on both a "before-" and "after-tax" basis. If the cash flows are "before tax," the IRR will be before tax. If the cash flows are "after tax," the IRR will be after tax. Also, the IRR can be used to measure either return on *total investment* or return on *equity investment*. Finally, the IRR allows the investor to ask many "What if?" questions. Typical questions might include

- What if the sale price increases?
- What if the sale price decreases?
- What if the annual cash flow drops $1,000 per year?
- What if the tax rate on capital gains changes?

The IRR itself is the discount rate that equates the present value of all the cash inflows with the present value of all the outflows. The IRR method is more complicated than net present value because it involves a "trial and error" procedure along with mathematical interpolation to arrive at the rate.

In the preceding example, we found the net present value (NPV) was a negative $8601.11. Using the IRR, we are looking for a rate that would make the NPV zero. Obviously, the rate is less than 14 percent.

The IRR procedure begins by selecting a first guess or starting point. The cash flows are then discounted at the selected rate. If the present value of the cash inflows is larger than the initial cash outflow (down payment), the procedure is repeated using a higher interest rate. Conversely, if the present value of the cash inflows is smaller than the initial cash outflow (down payment), the procedure is repeated using a lower interest rate. This procedure of "bracketing" is continued until the discounted present value of the cash inflows is exactly equal to the initial cash outflow or down payment.

Although such procedures can be time-consuming, once a starting point (first guess) is determined, the process of bracketing in on the IRR is easy. The starting point can be determined by the summation of the average annual cash-flow rate and the average annual appreciation rate for the investment.

Example 21–1 illustrates the process.

FINANCIAL LEVERAGE

The use of borrowed funds to magnify the return on an equity investment is called **positive financial leverage.** Almost all real estate can be financed or leveraged up to 70 or 80 percent, and it is not uncommon to get 90 to 95 percent financing. Hence, a real estate investor may be able to buy and control $100,000 worth of real estate with little more than $5,000 or $10,000 of his own funds.

To illustrate, let us assume that investor A is considering the purchase of an investment with a selling price of $100,000. The investment generates a net income of $16,000 annually. The investor has the option of paying all cash for the investment or using borrowed funds at the rate of 14 percent interest to leverage the invest-

Example 21–1   Computing the IRR

An income-producing property generates an after-tax cash flow of $5,000 per year for five years and $4,000 per year for the next five years, after which the property can be sold for $40,000 (after taxes). The investment requires an initial cash investment of $35,000. What is the "after tax" IRR for the investment?

First, let's calculate our starting point.
1. *Average annual cash flow rate*

$$\frac{\$45,000}{10 \text{ years}} = \$4,500 \text{ per year} \qquad \frac{\$4,500}{\$35,000 \text{ investment}} = .1286$$

2. *Average annual appreciation (depreciation) rate*

Initial investment	$35,000
Resale price	40,000
Total appreciation	$5,000
Annual appreciation	500

$$\text{Average annual appreciation rate} \quad \frac{\$500}{\$35,000} = \qquad +.0143$$

Approximate starting point .1429

The average annual appreciation (or depreciation) is added to (or subtracted from) the average annual cash flow rate. The starting point used should be somewhat less than .1429 because the return from the property appreciation is deferred ten years. Let's use 14 percent.

Starting at 14 percent, the results are:

Year	Cash flow		Discount factor (14%)		PV (at 14%)
1	$ 5,000	×	.877193	=	$ 4,385.97
2	5,000	×	.769468	=	3,847.34
3	5,000	×	.674971	=	3,374.86
4	5,000	×	.592080	=	2,960.40
5	5,000	×	.519368	=	2,596.84
6	4,000	×	.455587	=	1,822.35
7	4,000	×	.399637	=	1,598.55
8	4,000	×	.350559	=	1,402.24
9	4,000	×	.307508	=	1,230.03
10	4,000	×	.269744	=	1,078.98
Subtotal	$45,000				
10 (sale)	$40,000	×	.269744	=	$10,789.76
					$35,087.32

Present value of inflows	$35,087.32
Less: Present value of outflow (down payment)	35,000
Net present value	+ $87.32

Since the net present value is slightly positive, we know that the true IRR is somewhat higher than 14 percent. We can repeat the procedure using a slightly higher interest rate—say, 15 percent.

Year	Cash flow		Discount factor		PV (at 15%)
1	$ 5,000	×	.869565	=	$ 4,347.83
2	5,000	×	.756144	=	3,780.72
3	5,000	×	.657516	=	3,287.58
4	5,000	×	.571753	=	2,858.77
5	5,000	×	.497177	=	2,485.89
6	4,000	×	.432328	=	1,729.31
7	4,000	×	.375937	=	1,503.75
8	4,000	×	.326902	=	1,307.61
9	4,000	×	.284262	=	1,137.05
10	4,000	×	.247185	=	988.74
10 (sale)	$40,000	×	.247185	=	9,887.40
					$33,314.65

Present value of inflows	$33,314.65
Less: Present value of outflows	$35,000.00
Net present value	(−$ 1,685.35)

Since the net present value is negative, we can conclude that the IRR is somewhere between 14 percent and 15 percent.

To find the exact IRR, a process known as interpolation is used. The interpolation formula is:

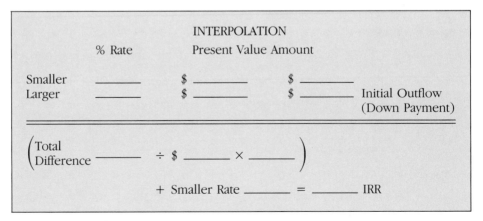

Let's interpolate to determine the exact IRR in our example.

As can be seen in the following box, .14049 is the IRR for this example. Although the procedures involved in calculating the IRR manually are very time consuming, IRR worksheets and computer programs are readily available to greatly reduce the time required.

	INTERPOLATION		
	% Rate	Present Value Amount	
Smaller	.14	$ 35,087.32	$ 35,087.32
Larger	.15	$ 33,314.65	$ 35,000.00 Initial Outflow (Down Payment)

$$\left(\text{Total Difference} \quad .01 \quad \div \quad 1,772.67 \quad \times \quad 87.32 \right)$$

$$+ \text{ Smaller Rate } \underline{.14} = \underline{.14049} \text{ IRR}$$

ment. Table 21–2 shows the effect of the use of borrowed funds on the equity return.

As can be seen, the use of borrowed funds has a very favorable effect on the investor's equity return. The use of 50 percent borrowed funds (Option 2) has increased the equity return from 16 to 18 percent. The use of 80 percent borrowed funds (Option 3) increases the equity return from 16 to 24 percent, a whopping 50 percent increase.

Although financial leverage is generally discussed in a positive sense, leverage sometimes works against the investor. Whenever the cost of borrowing is more than

Table 21–2   Positive financial leverage

	OPTION 1 All-cash purchase (100% equity)	OPTION 2 1:1 Leverage (50% borrowed/ 50% equity)	OPTION 3 4:1 Leverage (80% borrowed/ 20% equity)
Selling price	$100,000	$100,000	$100,000
Equity investment	100,000	50,000	20,000
Net income	16,000	16,000	16,000
Less: Cost of borrowing at 14% interest	0	−7,000	−11,200
Cash return	16,000	9,000	4,800
$\dfrac{\text{Cash return}}{\text{Equity investment}} =$	$\dfrac{16,000}{100,000}$ = 16% free and clear return	$\dfrac{9,000}{50,000}$ = 18%	$\dfrac{4,800}{20,000}$ = 24%

the free and clear return on an investment, the use of borrowed funds will magnify the loss to the equity investor. This is called **negative** (or reverse) **financial leverage.** In the previous example demonstrating the favorable effects of positive financial leverage, the cost of borrowing was 14 percent and the *free-and-clear* return was 16 percent. To demonstrate the adverse effects of negative financial leverage, let us ssume the cost of borrowing increases to 18 percent. Examine Table 21–3 to see the effect.

As can be seen, when the cost of borrowing exceeds the free and clear return, the return on equity will be reduced. In this example, the use of financial leverage reduced the equity return from 16 to 14 percent (Option 2) and finally (Option 3), down to a dismal 8 percent return. You must remember that financial leverage is a double-edged sword. It magnifies both gains and losses.

EQUITY GROWTH THROUGH FINANCIAL LEVERAGE

When an investor uses borrowed funds to purchase a real estate investment, any increase in property value (capital appreciation) accrues entirely to the equity investor, even though he may have an equity investment of only 5 or 10 percent of the total property value. As a result of this benefit, the investor's equity grows substantially even with just a modest increase in overall property value. An illustration will demonstrate this point (Example 21–2).

DEPRECIATION ALLOWANCES

Depreciation allowance is a noncash flow, deductible expense used in calculating taxable income. This depreciation for taxes is an accounting concept and is not associated with the realities of the market value of the property; that is, even though an investment's market value actually appreciates, the depreciation expense for tax purposes is unaffected.

Table 21–3 Negative financial leverage

	OPTION 1 All-cash purchase (100% equity)		OPTION 2 1:1 Leverage (50% borrowed/ 50% equity)	OPTION 3 4:1 Leverage (80% borrowed/ 20% equity)
Selling price	$100,000		$100,000	$100,000
Equity investment	100,000		50,000	20,000
Net income	16,000		16,000	16,000
Less: Cost of borrowing at 18% interest	0		−9,000	−14,400
Cash return	16,000		7,000	1,600
$\dfrac{\text{Cash return}}{\text{Equity investment}} =$	$\dfrac{16,000}{100,000} =$	16% free and clear return	$\dfrac{7,000}{50,000} = 14\%$	$\dfrac{1,600}{20,000} = 8\%$

Example 21–2 Equity Increase from Appreciation—Leveraged Versus All-Cash Investment

An investor is considering the alternatives of purchasing a $100,000 investment on either an all-cash basis or by using 90 percent financing. Assume that the investor will hold the investment for 10 years and the investment is expected to increase $40,000 over the holding period. Let us compare the equity growth from capital appreciation on an all-cash basis versus 90 percent financing.

	All-cash purchase	90% Financing
Purchase price	$100,000	$100,000
Equity investment	100,000	10,000
(4% appreciation/year) 10 years later		
Investment value	$140,000	$140,000
Increase in equity (from appreciation)	40,000	40,000
Percentage increase in equity growth	$\dfrac{\text{Equity growth}}{\text{Original equity}} = 40\%$	$\dfrac{\text{Equity growth}}{\text{Original equity}} = 400\%$

Rationale for Depreciation Allowances

The Internal Revenue Service (IRS) classifies the building portion of a real estate investment as a wasting asset. It is assumed that, given enough time, any building will eventually lose value. As such, any investor who invests capital in a wasting asset is allowed to recapture or recover his capital over a predetermined period of time.

Real estate that qualifies for the depreciation allowance must be used in the taxpayer's trade or business or for the production of income. Nonincome-producing property such as a single-family owner-occupied residence cannot be depreciated.

Steps in Calculating Depreciation Deductions

1. *Allocate purchase price between land and building.* When depreciating a real estate investment, the total investment value is allocated between the land and building since only the building portion of the investment can be depreciated. *Land does not depreciate.* There are four acceptable methods of making such an allocation. The investor should be cautioned, however, that regardless of the method used, if the allocation is not "reasonable," the IRS may contest it.

(a) Tax assessor's ratio—This method involves the use of a ratio derived from the tax assessor's assessment of the property. This same ratio is applied to the purchase price of the investment, thus giving an allocation between land and building for depreciation purposes. For example, assume a tax assessor has assessed property at $75,000, with $50,000 for the building and $25,000 for the land. This 2:1 building-to-land ratio is applied to the purchase price of $120,000, resulting in an $80,000 building value and a $40,000 land value.

(b) The value allocation may be stipulated in the sales contract between the buyer and seller.

(c) The value allocation may be made simply on the basis of a qualified appraiser's estimate.

(d) The investor may make the allocation himself.

2. *Determine the applicable recovery period.* Once the value has been allocated between the land and building, next we determine the period of time over which the asset can be depreciated. For properties purchased after December 31, 1986, the recovery periods are 27.5 years for residential rental property and 31.5 years for commercial and industrial property.

3. *Determine the method of depreciation that can be used.* For real estate purchased after December 31, 1986, the investor is limited to using straight-line depreciation. Of course, investors who purchased their properties at an earlier time are allowed to continue using the method of depreciation that was available to them at the time of their purchase.

Straight-Line Depreciation

To calculate the annual straight-line depreciation allowance, the *depreciable basis* of the property is divided by the recovery period. The *depreciable basis* of an asset is its cost plus any capital improvements and minus any depreciation already taken. This annual depreciation allowance remains fixed throughout the appropriate recovery period.

The amount of annual depreciation can also be calculated by dividing the appropriate recovery period into 100 percent to find the annual depreciation or recovery rate to be applied to the asset. The recovery rate is always the reciprocal of the recovery period; that is, one over the recovery period.

For example, consider a building having a value of $300,000 depreciated over a 27.5-year recovery period. The structure has an annual depreciation allowance of $10,909 calculated as follows:

$$\frac{\text{Annual}}{\text{depreciation}} = \frac{\text{Depreciable basis}}{\text{Recovery period}} = \frac{300,000}{27.5}$$
$$= \$10,909$$
$$\text{(rounded)}$$

$$\frac{\text{Annual}}{\text{depreciation}} = \frac{1}{27.5} = .0364 \times \$300,000$$
$$= \$10,909 \text{ (rounded)}$$

The annual depreciation allowance remains the same over the entire recovery period.

TAX CONSIDERATIONS

The Tax Reform Act (**TRA**) of 1986 has had a significant impact on real estate. This section will discuss the general aspects of the 1986 TRA as well as other tax matters that affect the real estate investor.

Classification of Real Estate Investments for Tax Purposes

The Internal Revenue Service considers four classes of real estate investments. Different tax rules have an impact on each of the four classifications. The property categories are:

1. Personal residences
2. Property held for sale by dealers
3. Property held for use in a trade or business
4. Property held for the production of income or investment property

Personal Residences

An individual's personal residence, though not considered an investment by the IRS, has certain tax implications. The owner is allowed to deduct the interest on his mortgage (up to $1 million) from his federal income tax. In addition, the real estate taxes are deductible. However, none of the maintenance or repair costs are deductible, and the homeowner is not allowed to depreciate his residence for tax purposes. As discussed in Chapter 11, the owner-occupant may defer all the gain on the sale of his residence if he purchases a new residence within twenty-four months before or after the sale of his former residence and the purchase price equals or exceeds the adjusted selling price of the former residence. Finally, the owner-occupant is entitled to a $125,000, once-in-a-lifetime exemption from capital gains tax once he reaches age fifty-five. (See Chapter 11 for details.) Any loss incurred on the sale of a primary residence is not deductible.

Property Held for Sale by Dealers

Property held primarily for sale in the ordinary course of business is considered inventory and the owner of such real estate is considered a *dealer* rather than an *investor*. As such, he is not allowed to depreciate such property. Any gain from the sale of such inventory is considered ordinary income and taxed accordingly. There is no particular set of criteria that the IRS uses in determining whether or not the taxpayer is a dealer or an investor. However, some of the things that may cause the unfavorable *dealer* classification are:

- An occupation in real estate
- Frequent buying and selling of property
- Subdividing
- Short-term holding of investments

Property Held for Use in a Trade or Business

Properties that are held for use in a trade or business are considered factors of production, not inventory, and are therefore depreciable. In addition, the owner may deduct the operating expenses and interest expense associated with the property. The IRS classifies such property as *1231 assets*. Although such properties are not considered capital assets, a special provision in the law allows their sale to be treated as long-term capital gain if held for over six months and sold at a gain. If sold at a loss, 1231 assets may be treated as an ordinary loss. Since the 1986 TRA eliminated the favorable treatment of long-term capital gain, all gains are taxed as ordinary income regardless of the holding period. Consequently, the taxpayer's ability to declare any gain on the sale of 1231 assets as "long-term capital gain" and any loss as an "ordinary loss" no longer provides a tax advantage. However, should the favorable long-term capital gains tax be reinstituted, the taxpayer would regain the benefit. The Internal Revenue Service and the tax courts both agree that investors who spend a substantial amount of time in the management of rental units are engaged in a trade or business. Hence, most real estate investments will be classified as such.

Property Held for the Production of Income or As Investment Property

Tax courts disagree on what differentiates trade or business property from investment property. "Trade or business" is not defined in the code. However, if the property is raw land held for speculation or income-producing property under a triple-net lease, it will most likely be classified as investment property. Although the investor holding investment property is able to deduct operating expenses from such investments, his interest deduction is limited. Most investors will seek to obtain the more favorable "trade or business" classification for tax purposes.

TRA 1986—Income Classifications

The Tax Reform Act of 1986 established three different income classifications for the taxpayer, namely:

1. *Active income* (salaries and wages)
2. *Portfolio income* (interest and dividends)
3. *Passive income* (limited partnerships, trade or business in which the investor does not "materially participate," rental activity)

As can be seen, the tax code specifically classifies real estate that is owned and operated to derive rental income as a "passive activity." Hotels and motels are specifically excluded from the passive activity category. Generally speaking, any losses generated by passive income activities cannot be used to shelter or offset income from either active or portfolio income. Passive losses may be used to shelter passive income only. Any unused passive losses may be carried forward indefinitely (referred to as "suspended losses") to offset passive income in later years.

Transition Rules

The passive loss rules disallow using 100 percent of the losses to shelter any active or portfolio income on properties acquired after October 22, 1986. For passive losses incurred on properties purchased before October 23, 1986, the passive loss rule is phased in over five years as follows:

Year	Losses and credits allowed	Losses and credits disallowed
1987	65%	35%
1988	40%	60%
1989	20%	80%
1990	10%	90%
1991	0	100%

In other words, if an investor experiences a $10,000 loss in 1990 on a passive activity acquired before October 23, 1986, he can deduct 10 percent of the loss

($1,000) against active and/or portfolio income that year. The remaining $9,000 loss can be carried forward and used to shelter passive income in later years. If the passive activity had been purchased after October 22, 1986, none of the loss would have been allowed in 1990 and the entire $10,000 loss would be carried forward. As another example involving transition rules, assume that an investor owns two passive activity investments. One of the investments was purchased before October 23, 1986, and one was purchased after October 22, 1986. In 1988, one of the investments produced a loss and the other one showed a gain. In this instance, the transition percentage (40 percent) is applied to the lesser of (1) net passive loss from the investments or (2) the pre–October 23, 1988, passive activity loss. The allowable deduction against active or portfolio income in 1988 is $2,000. The remaining $3,000 is carried forward. Calculations follow.

Passive Activity Investment #1	*Passive Activity Investment #2*
Purchased pre-October 23, 1986	Purchased January 1, 1987
Produced a $15,000 loss	Produced a $10,000 gain

* Net passive loss: $5,000 × .40 = $2,000 loss allowed
* Pre-October 23, 1986
  Passive activity loss: $15,000

When a passive loss activity is ultimately sold, any losses carried forward and any current losses in the year of sale may be used in the following sequence:

First, to offset any gain from the sale of other passive activity investments.
Second, to offset any income from other passive activity investments.
Finally, any remaining loss may be used to offset or shelter active or portfolio income. This is the one time that the tax code allows the investor to use losses from a passive activity to shelter active or portfolio income.

"Active Participation" Versus "Passive Participation"
The fact that an investor "actively participates" in a "rental real estate activity" does not change the classification of income or loss derived from such an investment from "passive" to "active." However, an "exception" to the *passive loss rules* is provided to those investors who "actively participate" in rental real estate and hold at least a 10 percent interest in the investment. For such investors, if their income is $100,000 or less, they are allowed to deduct up to $25,000 of "passive losses" against "active" and/or portfolio income. This $25,000 exception is reduced fifty cents for every dollar the investor's income exceeds $100,000. Consequently, the exception is phased out entirely for those investors earning $150,000 or more.

1986 Tax Reform Act—Depreciation

Prior to the passage of the 1986 Tax Reform Act (TRA), the real estate investor was allowed to recapture his investment in a depreciable asset over nineteen years. In addition, accelerated methods of depreciation enabled the investor to enhance his depreciation allowance in the early years of the investment holding period. The combined effect of short write-off periods, accelerated methods of depreciation and interest expense deductions generally produced massive "tax losses" in the early years of the investment, which were used to shelter the investor's other income. A tax loss of $20,000 to an investor in the 50 percent tax bracket saved the investor $10,000 in federal income tax. Many investors were evaluating the merits of an investment on the basis of its tax effect on them rather than the economic merits of the property itself. Consequently, many investors in the higher tax brackets were paying inflated prices to buy a "tax shelter." The TRA of 1986 changed all that.

New Tax Rules—Straight-Line Depreciation

For real properties placed into service on or after January 1, 1987, the real estate investor is limited to the use of straight-line depreciation. Certain personal property may still use accelerated methods of depreciation.

The recovery periods over which the investor can depreciate his real estate investment have also been lengthened as follows:

	Recovery Period
Residential rental property	27.5 years
Nonresidential rental property	31.5 years

The combined effects of eliminating the accelerated methods of depreciation in favor of straight-line depreciation and lengthening the time period over which the investment in the wasting asset may be recaptured has greatly reduced depreciation deductions. This substantial reduction in noncash flow depreciation deductions has considerably weakened real estate as a tax shelter and has caused real estate values to decrease considerably in the short run.

Tax Rates Reduced

Individual Income Tax

The TRA of 1986 lowered both the individual and the corporate income tax rates. For 1988 and beyond, there are only two tax rates for the individual, 15 percent and 28 percent. However, the 15 percent bracket is being phased out for taxpayers above a certain income level. This phase-out is carried out by charging an additional tax (surtax) of 5 percent on taxable income within specified ranges (see Table 21–4).

Let's assume that a married taxpayer filing jointly has a taxable income of $95,000. The federal income taxes are calculated as follows:

Taxes on first $29,750 at 15%	$4,462
Taxes on balance	
$95,000 − $29,750 = $65,250 at 28%	$18,270
Surtax	
$95,000 − $71,900 = $23,100 at 5%	$1,155
Total taxes due	$23,887

Corporate Tax Rates

The corporate tax rates have also been reduced. Remember, however, that income from a corporation is subject to double taxation: individual income tax and the corporate tax. This can be solved by forming a Subchapter S corporation. Then, provided all requirements are met, the corporate income will flow through to the shareholder and be taxed as individual income. The corporate tax rates for 1988 are shown in Table 21–5.

Table 21–4   Federal income tax rates for individuals—1988

Filing status	Tax rate
Single taxpayers	
0–$17,850	15%
Over $17,850	28%
Surtax of 5% on income between $43,145 and $89,560	
Head of household	
0–$23,900	15%
Over $23,900	28%
Surtax of 5% on income between $61,650 and $123,790	
Married, filing jointly	
0–$14,875	15%
Over $29,750	28%
Surtax of 5% on income between $71,900 and $149,250	
Married, filing separately	
0–$14,875	15%
Over $14,875	28%
Surtax of 5% on income between $35,960 and $113,300	

"At Risk" Rules

Historically, investors have been able to purchase sizable investments using "nonrecourse" loans, that is, loans whereby the investor is not personally liable for repayment. These highly leveraged investments generated large tax shelters for investors who were risking little or no personal liability. Several years ago, the first *at risk* rules were passed, but real estate investments were exempt. The TRA of 1986

Table 21–5   Corporate tax rates

Income level	Tax rate
0–$50,000	15%
$50,000 to $75,000	25%
Over $75,000	34%
In addition, a surtax of 5% is levied on income between $100,000 and $335,000.	

changed all that. The law now limits the losses that are deductible for real estate investments to the investor's actual economic interest. In other words, the investor's deductible losses are limited to the amount he has "at risk." This "at risk" amount, or the amount the investor could actually lose, generally consists of his down payment and loans for which he is personally liable (recourse loans). Seller financing is not considered when determining the amount "at risk." Losses disallowed by the "at risk" rules for any given year may be carried forward.

Installment Sales

It is not uncommon for the typical real estate investor who has held an investment for a period of time to be faced with a considerable tax burden when he goes to sell the property. One way to reduce this tax burden is to sell the investment on an installment basis. In so doing, the investor spreads the receipt of the gain, and hence the tax liability, over several years. In addition, any attractive terms offered by the seller will facilitate the sale of the property.

The formula used to calculate the recognized (taxable) gain for the period is as follows:

$$\text{Recognized (taxable) gain} = \frac{\text{Total gain}}{\text{Contract price}} \times \text{Payments received}$$

Where:

Total gain = selling price − selling expenses − adjusted basis
Contract price = selling price − seller's mortgage assumed by buyer (if any)
+ excess of seller's mortgage over basis
Payments received = down payment + principal payments + boot (other property or notes) + excess of seller's mortgage over basis

For example, assume an investor sells a property on the installment basis at a sales price of $150,000 in December 1989. He receives a cash down payment of $10,000 as his only payment that year. The buyer assumes the seller's mortgage in the amount of $50,000. The selling expenses were $5,000. The seller's adjusted basis was $105,000. The gain recognized in the year of sale is calculated as follows:

Sales price		$150,000
Less:		
Selling expenses	5,000	
Adjusted basis	100,000	
		− 105,000
Total gain		$ 45,000
Sales price		$150,000
Less:		
Mortgage assumed by buyer		− 50,000
Total contract price		$100,000

Payments received	$ 10,000

Recognized gain in year of
sale = $\dfrac{\$\ 45,000}{\$100,000} \times \$10,000$

= $\$\ 4,500$ gain recognized in the year of the sale

Note that if the sum of the adjusted basis and selling expenses are less than the loan assumed by the buyer, the difference is added to the contract price and to the payment received. In subsequent years, the recognized (taxable) gain is calculated as follows:

$$\text{Payment received} \times \text{gross profit percentage}$$

Where:

$$\text{Gross profit percentage} = \frac{\text{total gain}}{\text{contract price}}$$

In the preceding example, the gross profit percentage was

$$\frac{\$45,000}{\$100,000}\ \text{or}\ 45\%.$$

Certain sales are not eligible for installment reporting.

Rehabilitation Tax Credits

The Tax Reform Act of 1986 still provides investors a tax credit for expenditures to rehabilitate certain commercial, industrial, and residential properties. The allowable tax credits are as follows:

Nonresidential properties placed in service before 1936 that are not certified historic improvements	10%
Residential properties	20%
Nonresidential certified historic improvements	20%

For example, assume an investor bought a commercial property that was constructed prior to 1936 for $100,000 and spent another $50,000 on rehabilitation expenditures. The investor is entitled to a 10 percent *rehabilitation tax credit* on the $50,000 rehabilitation expenditure or $5,000. The $5,000 credit reduced the investor's tax liability by $5,000. The federal government offers the tax credit as an incentive to encourage the rehabilitation of existing structures. In order to qualify for the credit, the investor must depreciate the structure using straight-line depreciation. The depreciable basis of the building must be reduced by the amount of the credit taken. The rehabilitation expenditures must exceed the greater of $5,000 or the adjusted basis of the property in order to qualify for the credit. Investors who hold rehabilitation properties less than five years are subject to recapture of a portion of the credit.

Low-Income Housing Credit

In an attempt to stimulate investment in low-income housing, Congress passed the Low-Income Housing Credit Act of 1986. For a housing project to qualify, a specified portion of the property must be occupied by low-income tenants. This is known as the "minimum set-aside requirement." The investor may satisfy this requirement in one of two ways:

1. 20 percent of the units in the project must be set aside for rental by tenants whose income is 50 percent or less of the area's median gross income; OR
2. 40 percent of the units in the project must be set aside for rental by tenants whose income is 60 percent or less of the area's median gross income.

The low-income housing credit may be taken each year for ten years and varies as follows:

1. The investor is entitled to a 4 percent tax credit if he purchases an existing investment that will be used as a low-income project.
2. If an investor builds or rehabilitates a low-income project that involves other federal subsidies, he is entitled to a 4 percent tax credit.
3. Investors who construct a new low-income project are entitled to a 9 percent tax credit.

For example, if an investor builds a new low-income housing project in 1990 for $300,000, he is entitled to a $27,000 tax credit in that year and for the next nine years provided it meets the other requirements.

Capital Gains

The favorable long-term capital gains tax was eliminated by the TRA of 1986. Any gain on the sale of a real estate investment will now be included and taxed as ordinary income.

ANALYZING A REAL ESTATE INVESTMENT

In analyzing a real estate investment, the investor should conduct (a) a detailed analysis of the location; (b) a thorough inspection of the physical condition of the investment; and (c) a financial analysis. These steps are discussed in detail.

Location Analysis

It has been said many times that "the three most important factors influencing value are location, location, and location." The various factors and amenities that affect the neighborhood of the specific investment should be thoroughly analyzed. For instance, an investor who is considering the purchase of an apartment complex should consider location factors such as these:

1. Convenience to shopping, employment, recreation, schools, and public transportation
2. Existing vacancy rates and turnover
3. Proximity of competing apartment complexes
4. Type of tenants in the neighborhood

5. Existence of unimproved apartment sites
6. Composition, age, and condition of neighborhood buildings
7. Reputation of the neighborhood as a place to live
8. Population growth
9. Existence of sidewalks and street lights
10. Condition of streets
11. Availability of parking, snow removal, and trash collection

The above list represents only a sampling of some of the factors that should be considered in evaluating the merits of a particular location. A wise investor will develop a checklist to ensure that he does not overlook any important factors.

Physical Analysis

The physical condition of the property will reflect the degree of care the present owners have exercised during their period of ownership. If the inspection reveals considerable needed maintenance, the new owners will soon be required to make considerable, and sometimes untimely, cash outlays.

In addition to deferring necessary maintenance, the seller may have delayed investing in needed capital improvements, such as repaving the parking lot or installing a new roof or furnace. These factors may make the property difficult or impossible to rent. The prudent investor would be wise to consider the cost of the necessary expenditures and deduct it from the price he is willing to pay.

It should be clear that the physical condition of the building has a very definite influence on the quality, quantity, and durability of the subject investment's projected net income stream. Consequently, a detailed physical inspection of the building by a competent engineer is necessary to minimize the risk of purchasing an unwise investment.

Financial Analysis

Many of the concepts needed to analyze the property from a financial standpoint have been presented earlier in the chapter. These concepts, along with other relevant factors, are explained via the step-by-step analysis of the hypothetical investment in Example 21–3.

Example 21–3   Detailed Financial Analysis of a Typical Real Estate Investment

In January of 1990, a middle-aged investor asked you to analyze a property for him. The property is a one-year-old brick four-unit apartment with an asking price of $100,000. The investment can be financed with an 80 percent, thirty-year fully amortized mortgage at an interest rate of 11 percent with annual payments.

The building portion of the investment is considered as 80 percent of the total. The investment is expected to appreciate 20 percent over the holding period. Straight-line depreciation is applied, using a 27.5-year recovery period. For ease in analysis, all income and expenses, including the mortgage payment, are annualized. The investor files a separate return and is in the 28 percent tax bracket. He wants to earn a 13 percent return on his equity investment. How much should he pay for the property?

Step 1: Reconstruct an Operating Statement

Essentially, the investor in an income-producing property is purchasing an anticipated *net income stream*. The accuracy of any financial analysis begins with a realistic projection of the property's net income. The investor begins by obtaining the owner's existing income and expense records. He should be cautioned, however, that the records furnished by the owner should be examined with a jaundiced eye. The current owner's vested interest is sometimes sufficient motivation to distort, misrepresent, or conveniently forget vital information concerning the property's past income and expenses.

In addition, in verifying the past income and expense records, the potential investor should be aware of any pending increases in expenses and reflect them in the projected operating statement. Finally, the investor should compare the projected operating statement of the investment being analyzed to the income and expense records of similar investments in the area. Local property owner associations or professional property managers are excellent sources for such information. In addition, several organizations publish operating cost information. The Institute of Real Estate Management (IREM) publishes an analysis of income and expenses for apartment buildings, cooperatives, and condominiums. The New York State College of Agriculture analyzes rental costs for variety stores and food chains. The Building Owners and Managers Association (BOMA) is also a valuable reference for office building expenses. The Urban Land Institute collects income and expense information on shopping centers. Most of these sources break the information down geographically and by size and age of buildings. Figure 21–1 shows the reconstructed operating statement for the investment being analyzed. As can be seen, the investment generates a projected net income of $12,731. Our financial analysis continues, then, with Step 2.

Step 2: Calculate Taxable Income (Loss)—Year One

NET INCOME	$12,731 (from operating statement)
Less:	
Interest expense	$8,800 (11% on an $80,000 mortgage)
Depreciation deduction	$2,909 (using straight-line depreciation, 27.5 years)
Total deductions	$11,709
TAXABLE INCOME (LOSS)	$ 1,022

As can be seen, the investment will generate a taxable income of $1,022 in the first year using straight-line depreciation over 27.5 years.

Step 3: Calculate Before-Tax Cash Flow—Year One

NET INCOME	$12,731
Less: Debt service	−9,139 (Table E–1 Appendix E)
BEFORE-TAX CASH FLOW	$ 3,592

The investment generates a positive *before-tax cash flow* (sometimes called *gross spendable income*) of $3,592. In other words, before the investor pays any income taxes that might be due on the property, he has $3,592 in his pocket after paying all operating

```
          PROJECTED (ACTUAL) INCOME AND EXPENSE ANALYSIS

                                                              Dollar Amount
                                                              ─────────────

GROSS INCOME POTENTIAL
   4units at $400/month                                           19,200
   Less vacancy and collection loss                             − 1,344
EFFECTIVE GROSS RENTAL INCOME                                    17,856
   Less expenses
      Fixed expenses
         Taxes                            1,600
         Insurance                          450
                                        ────────

                                        ────────
Total fixed expenses                                    2,050
Operating expenses
   Utilities (paid by tenant)
   Maintenance                              800
   Management                             1,600
   Advertising                              250
   Supplies                                 200
   Legal and accounting                     225
                                        ────────

                                        ────────
Total operating expenses                                3,075
Total expenses                                                  − 5,125
NET OPERATING INCOME                                            12,731
```

Figure 21–1   Operating statement

expenses and after making his mortgage payment. As our calculations show in step 4, the investor pays $286 in incomes taxes on the property in the first year.

Step 4: Calculate the Tax Effect—Year One

TAXABLE INCOME (LOSS)	$1,022
× Investor's tax bracket	.28
TAXES PAYABLE (SAVED)	$ 286 Payable

Two of the most important criteria real estate investors use in evaluating a real estate investment are the amount of *after-tax cash flow* (sometimes called *net spendable income*) generated by the investment and the tax shelter the investment provides. The amount of after-tax cash flow is influenced by the type of financing available to the investor, the depreciation method, and the investor's tax bracket. After-tax cash flow is the amount of cash left over after the investor pays all operating expenses, the debt service (principal and interest) on his mortgage, and any income tax due on the property. Step 5 calculates the after-tax cash flow.

Step 5: Calculate After-Tax Cash Flow—Year One

BEFORE-TAX CASH FLOW	$3,592 (from Step 3)
Less: Taxes payable or	
Plus: Taxes saved	− 286 (from Step 4)
AFTER-TAX CASH FLOW	$3,306

Table 21–6 shows a seven-year projected cash flow for the preceding investment. The columns are as follows:

1. Column D is net operating income (from the reconstructed operating statement).
2. Column E1 + E2 is debt service (principal plus interest)—in our example, $9,139.
3. Column F is before-tax cash flow.
4. Column G is annual depreciation (using the specified depreciation technique).
5. Column H is Column E1 + G (interest expense plus depreciation expense).
6. Column I is taxable income (Column D minus Column H, if positive).
7. Column J is tax loss (Column D minus Column H, if negative).
8. Column K is taxes payable (Column I times tax rate).
9. Column L is tax savings (Column J times tax rate).
10. Column M is after-tax cash flow plus the value of the tax loss (Column F minus K or Column F plus L).
11. Column N is Column M plus equity build-up (Column E2).

In the first year, the property generates a $12,731 net income (column D). The interest deduction of $8,800 (column E1), plus first-year depreciation of $2,909 (column G) provides a total deduction of $11,709 (column H). When the total deductions are subtracted from the investment's net income, a taxable income of $1,022 results (column I).

In the 28 percent tax bracket, the investor experiences a $286 tax liability (column K) in year one. When the tax liability (a cash outflow) of $286 is subtracted from the before-tax cash flow of $3,592 (column F), it results in an after-tax cash flow of $3,306 (column M) in year one. The after-tax cash flow yield on equity in year one is:

$$\frac{\text{After-tax cash flow}}{\text{Equity}} = \frac{\$3,306}{\$20,000} = .1653$$

This after-tax equity yield is only one measure of investment return. The total after-tax yield on an investment may be more or less than .1653, depending on whether or not the investor experiences any after-tax deferred return or yield created by property appreciation. In order to determine after-tax equity return, we must first calculate the after-tax proceeds (net proceeds) on sale.

Calculating Net Proceeds on Sale

When the investor decides to sell, he is faced with several expenses that must be paid out of the sale proceeds. The typical expenses involved in the sale of an investment property include the sales commission expense, attorney fees, the tax liability, and the payment of any remaining mortgage balance. Figure 21–2 demonstrates the procedure in arriving at the net proceeds on the sale of the case study investment. Assuming the property is sold after six years, as can be seen, the net proceeds after taxes are $26,197.

Application of Net Present Value (NPV)

Table 21–7 shows the present value of the after-tax inflow generated by the investment. The after-tax cash flow figures were taken from Column M of Table 21–6. The *after-tax sale*

TABLE 21–6 Cash flow and tax benefits of investment property ownership—straight-line depreciation, 27.5-year recovery

Purchase price		Mortgage terms	
Land Allocation	20,000	Length of Loan	30 years
Building Allocation	80,000	Interest Rate	11%
Total Value	100,000	Annual Payment (Prin. Int.)	$9,139
Financed Percentage	.80	DEPRECIATION	
Mortgage Amount	80,000	Recovery Period	27.5 Years
Cash Equity	20,000	Method Used	Straight-Line
NET OPERATING INCOME	12,731		
TAX BRACKET	28%		

Year	(D) Net operating income	(E1) Interest	(E2) Principal	(F) Before-tax cash flow	(G) Depreciation	(H) Deducts for tax purposes	(I) Taxable income	(J) Taxable loss	(K) Tax payable	(L) Tax savings	(M) After-tax cash flow	(N) Total benefit after tax
1	$12,731	8,800	339	3,592	2,909	11,709	1,022		286		3,306	3,645
2	12,731	8,763	376	3,592	2,909	11,672	1,059		297		3,295	3,671
3	12,731	8,721	418	3,592	2,909	11,630	1,101		308		3,284	3,702
4	12,731	8,675	464	3,592	2,909	11,584	1,147		321		3,271	3,735
5	12,731	8,624	515	3,592	2,909	11,533	1,198		335		3,257	3,772
6	12,731	8,568	571	3,592	2,909	11,477	1,254		351		3,241	3,812
7	$11,386	52,151	2,683	21,552	17,454	69,605	6,781		1,898		19,654	22,337

	Adjusted basis	
	Original basis	$100,000
Plus	Capital improvements	0
Plus	Costs of sale (7%)	8,400
Equals	Subtotal	$108,400
Minus	Depreciation	−17,280
Minus	Partial sales	0
Equals	Adjusted basis at sale	$ 91,120
	Gain	
	Sales price	$120,000
Minus	Adjusted basis	−91,120
Equals	Gain	28,880
	Tax liability	
	Gain	$28,880
Times	Tax bracket	× .28
Equals	Tax liability	$8,086
	Net sale proceeds	
	Sales price	$120,000
Minus	Sales costs	−8,400
Minus	Mortgage balance (after 6 years)	−77,317
Minus	Tax liability	−8,086
Equals	Net proceeds on sale (after tax)	$26,197

Figure 21–2   Calculations of net proceeds on sale—equity reversion

proceeds were taken from Figure 21–2. Since the net present value is positive, the investor requiring a 13 percent return should accept the investment. The property obviously generates a return higher than 13 percent. To determine the exact amount of after-tax yield, we shall employ the internal rate of return (IRR) method.

Application of the IRR

First, we must determine the starting point as follows:

1. *Average annual cash flow rate*

    Year
    1   3,306
    2   3,295
    3   3,284
    4   3,271
    5   3,257
    6   3,241

$$\$19,654 \div 6 = \frac{\$3,276 \text{ Average}}{\$20,000 \text{ Equity}} = .1638$$

Table 21–7 Application of net present value at 13%

Year	After-tax cash flow		Present value (PV) factor at 13% (See Appendix D, Table D-6)		After-tax cash flow discounted to present value at a 13% rate
1	3,306	×	.884956	=	$ 2,926
2	3,295	×	.783147	=	2,580
3	3,284	×	.693050	=	2,276
4	3,271	×	.613319	=	2,006
5	3,257	×	.542760	=	1,768
6	3,241	×	.480319	=	1,557
6 (sale)	26,197	×	.480319	=	12,583
			PV of cash inflows		$25,698
			Less: PV of cash outflows		20,000
			Net present value		$ 5,698

2. *Average annual appreciation (depreciation) rate*

Initial investment	$20,000
Resale proceeds	26,197

$$\text{Total appreciation} \quad \$ 6,197 \div 6 = \frac{\$1,033}{\$20,000} = .0516$$

$$\text{Equity } .2154$$

Since the return from property appreciation is deferred six years, we will begin with a starting point slightly less than .2154, say, 20 percent.

The REALTORS® National Marketing Institute of the NATIONAL ASSOCIATION OF REALTORS® has developed convenient IRR worksheets to facilitate the IRR process. Figure 21–3 shows such a worksheet. Remember, the IRR procedure involves a trial and error approach to determine the discount rate that will equate the present value of the inflows with the present value of the outflows, in this case $20,000 (the down payment). In essence, then, our target is the outflow of $20,000. Discounting the cash inflows by 20 percent resulted in a present value of $19,680. This figure is slightly lower than our *target,* the investment amount of $20,000; therefore, the discounting process must be repeated at a slightly lower rate—19 percent. Discounting the inflows at 19 percent results in a present value of $20,416, slightly over the present value of the cash outflow of $20,000. Therefore, we know the true IRR falls somewhere between 19 and 20 percent. By interpolating, the exact IRR was calculated at .1957.

Tax-Deferred Exchange

Our investor could, through proper planning, preserve his equity by using an exchange rather than paying the tax liability due on sale. A thumbnail sketch of *tax-deferred exchanges* follows.

General requirements. Under Section 1031 of the Internal Revenue Code, no gain or loss is recognized "if property held for productive use in trade or business or for investment is

Internal Rate of Return Worksheet

Date _____

Name _____ Property _____

Net Sale Proceeds $ 26,197 _____ Investment Amount $ 20,000 (Target) _____

End of Year	Cash Flow	Discount at 20 %		Discount at ____ %		Discount at 19 %		Discount at ____ %	
		P.V. of 1	Amount	P.V. of 1	Amount	P.V. of 1	Amount	P.V. of 1	Amount
1	3306	.833333	2755			.840336	2778		
2	3295	.694444	2281			.706165	2327		
3	3284	.578704	1900			.593416	1949		
4	3271	.482253	1577			.498669	1631		
5	3257	.401878	1309			.419049	1365		
6	3241	.334898	1085			.352142	1141		
7									
8									
9									
10									
11									
12									
13									
14									
15									
16									
17									
18									
19									
20									
Reversion Year 6	26,197	.334898	8773			.352142	9225		
Reversion Year ___									
Reversion Year ___									
TOTALS			19,680				20,416		

INTERPOLATION

% Rate		$ Present Value Amount	
Smaller	.19	$ 20,416	→ $ 20,416
Larger	.20	$ 19,680	Investment Amount $ 20,000

[Absolute Difference .01 + $ 736] x $ 416] + Smaller Rate .19 = .1957 %

Prepared by _____

Figure 21–3   Internal rate of return worksheet

exchanged solely for property of 'like kind' which is to be held either for productive use in trade or business or for investment." Inventory held primarily for sale does not qualify for a nontaxable exchange. Although the IRS does not publish specific guidelines concerning the necessary holding period to qualify for a nontaxable exchange, clearly a home built by a contractor does not qualify. Another classification that does not qualify is the primary residence (Chapter 11 discussed other techniques to defer the gain on primary residences). The requirement that the property be of **like kind** refers to the distinction between personal property and real property. In essence, personal property may be exchanged for personal property, and real property may be exchanged for real property. Real property may not be exchanged for personal property.

Boot. Very few exchanges are made that do not involve a tax liability to one of the participants. This occurs because of the value differences between properties exchanged and the resultant need for one of the parties to pay some *boot.* **Boot** is considered any "unlike kind property" received and may include any of these:

- Relief from indebtedness
- Personal property for real estate
- Money
- Note, mortgage, and so forth

In order for our investor to structure a completely tax-deferred exchange on a property that shows a gain, he must receive property with an equal or greater equity and a higher market value than the property he transferred. In other words, our investor must pay boot and assume a larger loan. The following section shows how an exchange might look to our investor.

The possibilities for a tax-deferred exchange are almost endless and should be given careful consideration as a means of preserving equity, increasing financial leverage, pyramiding investments, maximizing depreciation deductions, increasing cash flow, and accomplishing dozens of other investment objectives. The prudent investor should spend time researching the intricacies of tax-deferred exchanges and dispel the theory that such techniques are too complicated to understand and apply.

The Tax Reform Act of 1986 eliminated the favorable long-term capital gains tax. This will most likely foster renewed interest in exchanging rather than selling in order to defer taxes.

Sample Exchange

After five years our investor's four-unit apartment is worth $150,000 and has a loan balance of $96,270. His basis is $89,280. He may exchange for an office complex valued at $250,000 with a first mortgage of $125,000 and a basis of $100,000. This exchange would be completely tax-free for him, thereby preserving the equity he would otherwise have to pay out in taxes if he were to sell. The three steps used to calculate his recognized gain follow.

Step 1: Balancing equities

	4-Unit Investor	Office Complex Investor
Market value	$150,000	$250,000
Loans	− 96,270	− 125,000
Equity	$ 53,730	$125,000
Boot paid	+ 71,270	0
Balance	$125,000	$125,000

Our investor must pay an additional $71,270 in boot to balance the equities of the properties.

Step 2: Computing realized gain

	4-Unit Investor	Office Complex Investor
Real estate received	$250,000	$150,000
Boot received	0	71,270
Loan on property transferred	+96,270	+125,000
Total consideration	346,270	346,270
Less: Adjusted basis of property transferred	−89,280	−100,000
Less: Loans on property received	−125,000	−96,270
Realized gain	$131,990	292,490

Step 3: Computing recognized gain

	4-Unit Investor	Office Complex Investor
Loans on property transferred	$ 96,270	$ 125,000
Less: Loans on property received	−125,000	−96,270
Equals mortgage boot	0	28,730
Plus cash boot	0	+71,270
Equals total boot received	0	100,000
Recognized gain*		$ 100,000

---

*Recognized gain is the lesser of either (a) realized gain or (b) boot received. As can be seen, our four-unit investor has realized a gain of $131,990. However, none of this gain is recognized (taxable) in the year of sale. The entire gain of $131,990 is deferred. The second party to the exchange has a realized gain of $292,490 and a $100,000 recognized (taxable) gain in the year of the sale. He defers $192,490 of his gain. The deferred gain is subtracted from the basis of the newly acquired investments for both parties to the exchange, thereby resulting in an adjusted basis for the new investment.

ALTERNATIVE INVESTMENT MEDIA

Although this chapter focused primarily on an apartment building investment in its discussion of various principles and concepts, many other types of real estate investments offer the same benefits and share the same or similar risks.

Over the last ten years, the number of new real estate investment media available to the investor has increased considerably. With the advent of joint ventures, syndications, and limited partnerships, the investor may participate jointly in ski resorts, motel condominiums, medicos or medical condominiums, recreational land development, miniwarehouses, camping resorts, office buildings, subdivisions, indoor tennis clubs, long-term leases, and hundreds of other investments. The Real Estate Investment Trust *(REIT),* sometimes called "the mutual funds of real estate," is also available to the small investor who could not otherwise invest in real estate. Real estate investment trust certificates are sold in small denominations through the organized stock exchanges. They are not subject to corporate federal income tax so long as 90 percent of the profits are distributed to the investors. The REIT, in turn, reinvests the money in construction and development loans, other long-term mortgages, and real property investments.

Historically, investing in real estate has produced rewarding returns to the prudent investor. The interplay of depreciation and interest expense deductions coupled with the investor's use of financial leverage and long-term property appreciation are key elements to the attractiveness of such investments.

Most active investors use one of several methods to measure the profitability of an investment. Discounted cash flow analysis and internal rate of return (IRR) have gained wide acceptance over the years.

The Tax Reform Act (TRA) of 1986 had a significant impact on real estate investments. The act reduced the maximum tax rate on individual income to 28 percent. Congress estimated that this tax reduction cost the federal government over $200 billion in lost revenue. In an attempt to maintain "revenue neutrality," the loss in revenue created by the individual tax rate reduction was offset by reducing or eliminating many of the long-standing tax benefits the real estate investor has enjoyed over the years.

The most significant features of the Tax Reform Act of 1986 affecting real estate investments are:

- Requiring investors to use straight-line depreciation rather than accelerated methods
- Increasing the recovery periods for depreciating real estate investments to 27.5 years for residential investments and 31.5 years for nonresidential investments
- Eliminating the favorable long-term capital gains tax and taxing all gains from real estate investments at the ordinary income rates
- Eliminating the investment tax credit
- Implementing "passive loss" rules that limit the investor's ability to deduct losses from real estate investments
- Expanding the "at risk" rules to real estate investments
- Reducing the rehabilitation tax credit
- Modifying the low-income housing benefits

It has been estimated that the new tax laws have reduced real estate values by as much as 20 percent in some parts of the country. The use of tax-deferred exchanges to avoid paying ordinary income tax rates on any gains will most likely increase in the years to come.

TERMS AND CONCEPTS

You can check your understanding of these terms against the glossary or by review in this chapter.

After-tax cash flow (Net spendable income)	Depreciable basis	Liquidity
	Depreciation	Net present value (NPV)
"At risk" rules	Durability	Rehabilitation tax credit
Before-tax cash flow (Gross spendable income)	Economic (useful) life	REIT
	Holding period	Ripening expense
	Internal rate of return (IRR)	Straight-line depreciation
Boot	Leverage	Tax-deferred exchange
Capital gain	Like kind property	TRA
Cash flow		1231 Assets

What are the differences or relationship, if any, between the following:

Active income and	Investment property and	Positive financial
Passive income	Income-producing	leverage and Negative
Before-tax cash flow and	property	financial leverage
After-tax cash flow	IRR and NPV	Risk and Return
Current return and	Nonresidential and	1231 Assets and Capital
Deferred return	Residential tax credit	Assets

PROBLEMS

21-1. Calculate the present value of each of the three income streams using a 12 percent discount rate.

Year	A	B	C
1	$5,000	$7,000	$6,000
2	4,000	2,500	4,000
3	1,000	500	0

21-2. Assume the cost to purchase each of the income streams from problem 21-1 above is $8,000. You desire to earn a 14 percent return on your investment. Calculate the net present value of each of the income streams.

21-3. An income-producing property on a five-year lease generates an after-tax cash flow of $15,000 for the first three years and $16,000 for the remaining two years. At the end of the lease, it is estimated that the property would net $20,000 after taxes to the investor. The property can be purchased with an equity investment of $40,000. Calculate the IRR for the investment.

21-4. Discuss the depreciation method and recovery periods available to the real estate investor who purchases property today.

21-5. Discuss the methods of allocating an investment's purchase price between the land and building components.

21-6. Discuss the tax consequences of being classified as a dealer rather than an investor.

21-7. Explain the transition rules as they apply to passive losses on investments purchased before October 23, 1986.

21-8. Discuss the "exception" to the passive loss rules as they apply to real estate investors. At what point is the exception phased out?

21-9. In 1989, an investor bought a six-unit apartment building for $150,000. The land portion of the investment comprised 20 percent of the total investment. What is the first year depreciation deduction?

21-10. Discuss the "at risk" rules as they apply to real estate investments.

21-11. In December 1989, investor Adams sold a property on the installment basis at a sales price of $300,000. He received a cash down payment of 10 percent in the year of sale. The buyer assumed the seller's mortgage in the amount of $175,000. The selling expenses were $24,000. The seller's adjusted basis was $200,000. Calculate the recognized gain in the year of sale. What was the gross profit percentage?

21-12. What are the rehabilitation tax credits for residential and nonresidential properties? Nonresidential certified historic improvements?

21-13. What is the tax credit on a low-income housing project built in 1990 at a cost of $200,000?

21-14. Investor Johnson purchased a ten-unit apartment building in 1990 at a cost of $200,000. The land comprised 20 percent of the investment. The purchase was financed with an 80 percent, thirty-year fixed rate mortgage at an interest rate of 10 percent. The property generated a gross annual income of $48,000. Vacancy and collection losses were 10 percent of gross income. The operating expense ratio was 38 percent of effective gross income. Investor's tax bracket was 28 percent and the monthly payment factor at 10 percent for thirty years was equal to $8.78 per $1,000. Calculate the before- and after-tax cash flow in year one.

Allen, Roger H. *Real Estate Investment Strategy,* 3rd ed. Cincinnati, Ohio: South-Western Publishing Co., 1989.

Case, Frederick E. *Investing in Real Estate,* 2nd ed. Englewood Cliffs, N.J.: Prentice-Hall, 1988.

Casey, William J. *Real Estate Investment Planning.* New York: Institute for Business Planning.

Jaffe, Austin J., and Sirmans, C. F. *Fundamentals of Real Estate Investment.* Englewood Cliffs, N.J.: Prentice-Hall, 1989.

Plattner, Robert H. *Real Estate Investment Analysis and Management.* Columbus, Ohio: Merrill Publishing Co., 1988.

Realtors National Marketing Institute. *Marketing Investment Real Estate: Finance, Taxation, Techniques,* 3rd ed. Chicago, 1987.

Swesnik, Richard H. *Acquiring and Developing Income-Producing Real Estate,* 2nd ed. Reston, Va.: Reston, 1985.

Wiedemer, John P. *Real Estate Investment,* 3rd ed. Reston, Va.: Reston Publishing Co., 1985.

APPENDIXES

APPENDIX A
Glossary

A

Abatement The termination of an offensive activity.

Abstract of title A summary, arranged in chronological order, of the essential provisions of every recorded document pertaining to a particular parcel of land.

Abut To be next to or touch another property or body of water.

Accelerated cost recovery systems (ACRS) A provision in the Economic Recovery Tax Act of 1981 that specifies a period for accelerated depreciation of income-producing real property. It also provides for three-, five-, and ten-year depreciation for personal property groups.

Accelerated depreciation A method for calculating depreciation that provides for greater deductions in the earlier years of the life of the property improvement.

Acceleration clause A provision in a note such that, if payments are in default, the owner of the note can declare the entire balance due and payable earlier than the stated due date.

Acceptance An expression by one to whom an offer is made (the offeree) of his assent to the terms set forth in the offer, which is communicated to the one who makes the offer (the offeror).

Access The right of a property owner to have a means of entry and exit from her property to a public street.

Accretion The process by which the area of a parcel of land bounded by a river, lake, or waters is gradually increased by the deposit of soil due to the natural action of water.

Accrued depreciation The actual depreciation in a property that has already accrued as of a given date; past depreciation.

Acknowledgment A certification by a notary public or other public officer of a statement by a person that he executed a particular document as a free and voluntary act.

Acre A measure of land area equal to 43,560 sq. ft.

Action A court process to enforce a right.

Actual age The number of years a building has been in existence; the chronological age.

Actual agency An agency relationship where authority is delegated by the principal.

Actual notice Knowledge of a fact acquired by a person who is expressly told of the fact, or who personally observes the fact.

Add-on interest A method of interest computation whereby interest is charged on the entire principal amount for the term, regardless of periodic repayments.

Adjustable mortgage loan (AML) A type of variable-rate mortgage used by national banks.

Adjustable-rate mortgage loan (ARM) A type of variable-rate loan used by federally chartered savings and loan associations.

Administrator A person appointed by a probate court to handle the estate of a deceased person who left no will.

Ad valorem According to value.

Ad valorem **tax** A real property tax based on the value of the property.

Adverse possession When real property is possessed for a statutorily prescribed period of time so the owner's title is lost and the title is vested in the possessor.

Adverse user When a trespasser enters upon and uses the land of another and by continuing her wrongful use of the property for a period of time specified by statute, acquires a right to use the property.

After acquired title A doctrine under which a prior grantee automatically obtains title to real estate acquired by a grantor who previously attempted to convey title that he did not in fact own.

Agency The relationship between a principal and agent whereby the agent represents the principal in dealing with third parties.

Agent A person who has authority to act for another.

Agreement for deed See installment contract.

Air rights A landowner's right to the use and enjoyment of the space above her land to the extent that she can effectively occupy it.

Alienate To transfer an interest or interests in real property.

Alienation clause (due-on-sale) Gives lender the right to call the entire balance due if property is sold.

Alligator Investment property with a negative cash flow.

Alluvion Soil that is deposited on land bounded by a river, lake, or tidal waters as a result of current, wave, or tidal action.

ALTA American Land Title Association.

ALTA title insurance policy A broad form of title insurance policy that includes unusual risks such as factors that could be disclosed by inspection of the land or by a survey.

Amenities Pleasing and agreeable qualities; intangible benefits of property ownership such as pride of ownership or scenic beauty.

Amortization The payment of a debt in periodic installments over a prescribed term.

Annexation The act of attaching or adding personal property to land so it becomes a part of the real property.

Annual loan constant The annual debt service over the amount borrowed expressed as a ratio.

Annual percentage rate (APR) The effective interest rate as required under the Truth-in-Lending Act.

Annuity A series of payments as receipts over a period of years.

Appraisal An estimate of value of a parcel of property.

Appraisement See appraisal.

Appraiser A person qualified by experience and education to make value estimates or appraisals of real property.

Appreciation An increase in property value.

Appurtenance Anything part of or transferred with the land when it is conveyed.

Assemblage Process of joining several contiguous parcels of property together under single ownership.

Assess Estimate property value as a basis for taxation.

Assessed value See assessment.

Assessment A valuation placed on real property as a basis to set the amount of tax levied. (See also special assessment.)

Assessor A person who officially makes property assessments.

Assignee The person to whom an assignment is made.

Assignment The transfer of a right.

Assignment of mortgage Transfer of a mortgage and the lender's rights to another party.

Assignor The person who assigns or transfers a right or legal interest to another.

Assumption An agreement whereby one person assumes the obligation of another, such as the assumption of a mortgage.

Attachment Same as lien.

Attestation The act of a witness signing his name to an instrument, deed, or other document as a means of establishing its validity.

Aviation easement The right to control use of space at a set height and distance from airport runways.

B

Balloon payment The unpaid balance of a long-term loan that is paid off in a lump sum at the end of the loan term.

Baseline A reference line running east and west in the government survey system.

Basis point One-hundredth of 1 percent.

Bench mark A permanent marker used by surveyors.

Beneficiary The lender in a deed of trust.

Bequest A gift of personal property by will.

Bilateral contract A contract of mutual exchange of promises by the parties.

Bill of sale An instrument in writing that transfers ownership of tangible personal property, such as furniture.

Bill to quiet title A legal proceeding to determine the condition of title to real estate.

Binder Same as offer and acceptance.

Blanket mortgage A single mortgage covering more than one piece of real estate.

Bona fide In good faith.

Bona fide purchaser One who purchases something in good faith and for value without knowledge of any adverse rights or claims of persons other than the seller.

Bond A security issued to raise funds, with the promise to pay a certain amount to the landholder on a specified date. Interest is payable in installments over the term of the bond.

Boot Cash or unlike property.

Breach of contract The unjustified or unexcused failure of a party to perform her stated obligations or performance of obligations not in conformance with the terms of the contract.

Broker A person who acts as the agent of another in the process of buying or selling property.

Building codes Regulations concerning the quality of building materials and methods having the objective of preventing fire, injury, or spread of disease.

Bundle of rights The group of interests and rights of a person who owns real property.

Buy-down A third party puts up money to reduce the borrower's monthly payments.

C

Capitalization The process of converting net income into a value estimate.

Capitalization rate Ratio of income to value.

Capitalize the rent cost A discounting process that converts a monthly rent loss into an estimate of value loss due to obsolescence.

Caveat emptor Let the buyer beware.

Certificate of deposit (CD) A savings instrument of usually 2–10 years; earns a higher interest than a passbook account.

Chain A unit of measure equal to 66 feet.

Chain of title The recorded history of all transactions involving title to a given parcel of land beginning with the patent or deed from the government or other original owner to the present time.

Chattel Personal property.

Chattel mortgage A mortgage on personal property.

Civil action A court action involving civil laws (rather than criminal law).

Claim of title Also known as *claim of right*. When an adverse possessor, without any actual right or title, enters upon and occupies another person's real estate with the intent to make it his own.

Closing Meeting or arrangement when all payments are settled and title is transferred.

Closing statement A statement prepared for the settlement of a sale of real property that includes the computations and adjustments of money for buyer, seller, and sometimes the broker.

Cloud on title An adverse claim against title to a parcel of land that appears from the public records to be valid but which in fact is invalid or barred for reasons that must be proved by evidence outside the public records.

Codicil An amendment or addition to an existing will.

Coinsurance A clause that has the insured carry a proportion of the risk of underinsured property.

Collateral Real or personal property pledged as security on a promise to pay.

Collateral heirs Persons not lineally related to a decedent (e.g., an uncle, niece, or nephew).

Color of title When an occupant wrongfully possesses another person's property on the basis of an instrument or judicial decree that appears to give her title to the property but which in fact does not.

Commercial property Real property, including retail stores, office buildings, shopping centers, motels, and restaurants.

Commingle To mix funds of a client with the funds of the broker or agent.

Commission The payment the broker receives for rendering a service, usually expressed as a percentage of the property sale price.

Commitment When used by a mortgage institution, a promise to give a loan to the applicant.

Common elements Those areas within a condominium that each unit owner has the right to use in common with each other owner.

Common law The body of law based on custom and usage and created by the courts.

Community property Co-ownership of property between husband and wife in which each spouse owns half of all property acquired during marriage by joint efforts.

Competency The ability of a person to acquire rights and incur liabilities and thereby alter his legal status.

Compound interest The interest paid on the principal and the accrued interest.

Concurrent ownership Ownership where two or more persons possess simultaneous estates on the same property.

Condemnation The legal proceedings by which the right of eminent domain is exercised and private property is taken for a public use.

Condition An act or event that either creates *(condition precedent)* or extinguishes *(condition subsequent)* a duty by a promisor.

Condition precedent An act or event that must occur before a promisor's duty to perform arises.

Condition subsequent An act or event that extinguishes a duty owed by a promisor.

Conditional acceptance When an offeree indicates her agreement providing or on the condition that the offeror do something more or different than he promised to do in the offer. (See also counteroffer.)

Condominium A form of ownership in which each unit in a multiunit building is individually owned and all common areas (land, halls, exterior walls, recreational facilities, etc.) are co-owned by the unit owners in common.

Consequential losses Indirect losses that may be covered by insurance, such as loss of profits of a business as a result of a fire.

Conservator Someone appointed by a court to take legal charge of a person incapable of managing his own affairs. This also includes taking charge of that person's property.

Consideration Something a promisor bargains for and receives in exchange for her promise that results in a legal benefit to the promisor or a legal detriment to the promisee.

Construction loan A mortgage loan, usually for a short period, that allows the borrower to construct an improvement on a property.

Constructive eviction When wrongful acts by a landlord, or someone acting under her authority, deprive a tenant of his beneficial use and enjoyment of leased premises.

Constructive notice (public notice) Knowledge of a fact attributed to an individual by operation of law even though she has no actual knowledge of the fact.

Consummate dower After the death of a husband, the dower interest the wife has in her husband's estate.

Contiguous Next to and in actual contact.

Contingencies Contractual conditions that must be satisfied before the contract is in effect.

Contingent Dependent upon an uncertain future event.

Contingent remainder Delay of possession and enjoyment of an estate until the preceding estate is terminated and conditions are met.

Contour Surface shape of land.

Contract An agreement that the law will enforce. For an agreement to be a contract, the following elements must be present: mutual assent, consideration, reality of consent, competent parties, legality of subject matter, and in writing when required by statute.

Contract for deed See installment sale contract.

Contract of sale A binding agreement between a buyer and a seller of real estate.

Conventional mortgage A mortgage other than one guaranteed by FHA or VA.

Convey To transfer a legal interest or interests in real property.

Conveyance The transfer of a legal interest or interests in real property.

Cooperative An apartment or multifamily building owned by several persons through a corporation, such that each owner is a stockholder and also leases a portion of the building.

Co-owner Also known as a *cotenant*. Any one of two or more owners of simultaneous interests in the same property.

Co-ownership Also known as *cotenancy*. Ownership of a legal interest in property by two or more persons at the same time.

Corporation An artificial entity created by and under the authority of a state or other government for private or public purposes.

Cost approach A property appraisal process in which the appraiser estimates building value as replacement cost minus depreciation and then adds land value.

Cost to cure An expenditure required to remedy a physical or functional obsolescence in a structure.

Cotenancy See co-ownership.

Cotenant See co-owner.

Counteroffer A counter proposal by an offeree to an offeror that impliedly manifests the offeree's unwillingness to assent to the terms of the original offer. (See also conditional acceptance.)

Covenant (warranty) A covenant in a deed is a promise by the grantor that certain conditions exist and that something is true. Covenants in deeds and leases may also restrict the use that may be made of property; commonly known as "restrictive covenants."

Covenant of seizin (covenant of title) A promise or assurance by a grantor that he owns the estate or interest that he purports to convey by the deed.

Covenant of title A promise or assurance by a grantor that she is the owner of the property being transferred, that she has the right to convey it, and that it is free of encumbrances of claims of other persons.

Covenant running with the land When both the benefit and the burden created by the covenant attach to or become appurtenant to the lands of the covenantor (promisor) and the covenantee (promisee).

CPM Certified Property Manager.

Cul-de-sac A circular turn-around street in a property development.

Curtesy The right acquired by a husband in real property owned by his wife.

D

Damages Indemnity or compensation for loss or injury to a person or property resulting from a breach of contract or other wrongful act.

Datum A known elevation from which heights and depths are measured.

Decedent A deceased person.

Declaration of restrictions An instrument other than a deed containing restrictive covenants incorporated by reference and made part of a deed.

Decree A court order as a result of a judicial proceeding.

Dedication The gift of an interest in real property to a government for public use.

Deed A written instrument that, when legally delivered and accepted, transfers title to real property from one person to another.

Deed of trust Also known as a *trust deed*. A written instrument by which a debtor (trustor) transfers title to real estate to a trustee who holds it in trust for a creditor (beneficiary) to secure performance of an obligation owed by the debtor to the creditor.

Default The failure of a person to fulfill a duty.

Default risk The possibility that a lender is not able to obtain loan repayment.

Defeasance clause The clause in a mortgage note that allows the mortgagor to redeem his property after all payments due the mortgagee are paid.

Deficiency judgment A personal judgment against a mortgagor-debtor for the amount of the defaulted debt not met by the proceeds of the foreclosure sale of mortgaged property.

Delinquency Late in payment (or nonpayment) of amount due on a loan.

Delivery of a deed Also known as *legal delivery*. An informal act essential to the transfer of title. The intent is determined from the grantor's words and conduct and all circumstances surrounding the transaction.

Demise The transfer of land by the owner to another person.

Deposit receipt A printed form offer that constitutes a receipt for a deposit made by a prospective purchaser of real estate; it becomes a contract when properly signed by the purchaser and accepted and signed by the seller.

Depository Institutions Deregulation and Monetary Control Act of 1980 Federal law covering deregulation of banks and savings and loan institutions.

Depreciation A loss of real property value due to physical deterioration, functional obsolescence, and/or economic obsolescence. Also, a tax-deductible, non-cash flow expense.

Deterioration Loss of utility due to wear and tear, usage, action of the elements, or disintegration.

Devise The transfer of real property by will.

Devisee A person to whom real property is transferred by will.

Discount Difference between the face amount of a note or mortgage and the cash received from the instrument.

Discount points A one-time charge (1 point equals 1 percent) for mortgages issued below market interest rate.

Discount rate The rate of interest a bank must pay to borrow from a Federal Reserve bank.

Disintermediation When the public withdraws or refrains from placing funds in financial institutions, and instead makes direct investments, such as money market funds.

Divided interest Ownership of a portion of a larger parcel of property.

Domicile The legal residence of a person.

Dominant estate The parcel of land that benefits from an easement appurtenant.

Donee One who receives a gift.

Donor One who makes a gift.

Dower In common law, the wife's rights in property owned by the husband.

Due-on-sale clause A mortgage clause that stipulates that the entire balance becomes due if the property is sold.

Due process of law A constitutional guarantee that provides protection of rights of individuals in two ways. The first, *procedural due process,* requires that a person be given notice of the intention to deprive him of his life, liberty, or property and that he be afforded a hearing in which to defend himself. The second, *substantive due process,* guarantees an individual that she shall not be unreasonably or arbitrarily deprived of life, liberty, or property.

Duress A threat to do, or the actual doing of, a wrongful act that compels another person to enter into a contract through fear.

E

Earnest money Money given by a purchaser to show intent to perform the terms of a contract.

Easement A legal interest that one person has in land belonging to or in the possession of another person entitling the owner of the easement to use the other person's land.

Easement appurtenant An easement that burdens one parcel of land (the servient estate) for the benefit of another parcel (the dominant estate).

Easement by necessity An easement that is created by operation of law when a grantor conveys a portion of a larger parcel of land and in doing so landlocks either the portion that is transferred or the part that is retained.

Easement by prescription An easement that is acquired by adverse use for a statutory period of time.

Easement in gross A right to use the land of another, where no dominant estate is involved.

Economic life The period of time over which the property is estimated to be profitably utilized.

Economic obsolescence Loss in property value caused by conditions external to the property.

Economic rent The rent that a property could generate if it were available today; market rent.

Effective age The apparent age of a property based on its appearance; may be more than, the same as, or less than the actual or chronological age.

Egress A means of exit from a parcel of land.

Emblements Annual crops, legally considered personal property.

Eminent domain The power by which government can take private property for public use upon payment of a just compensation.

Enabling acts State laws permitting municipalities to establish planning agencies.

Encroachment The projection of a building or structure on the land of one owner beyond the common boundary line onto the land or into the airspace of an adjoining owner.

Encumber To burden a parcel of land with an adverse legal interest.

Encumbrance Anything that imposes a legal burden on title to land such as liens for security purposes, easements, and restrictive covenants.

Environment The totality of human surroundings—

the natural and artificial physical, biological, and cultural factors that affect health, senses, and intellect.

EOY End of year.

Equal Credit Opportunity Act (ECOA) Federal Reserve Board regulation prohibiting discrimination in lending.

Equity The value of a property owner's interest above the amount of the outstanding mortgage debt.

Equity financing Use of buyer's or owner's funds to finance property.

Equity of redemption The right of a defaulting mortgagor-debtor to prevent foreclosure and have the encumbrance of the mortgage removed from his title by paying the full amount of the outstanding debt plus interest and any expenses incurred by the mortgagee-creditor.

Equity participation mortgage A mortgage whereby the lender obtains an equity in the pledged property in addition to interest.

Erosion The loss of land by wearing action of water or wind.

Escalator clause A contract clause that provides for an upward or downward adjustment in interest, rent, or other factors to cover specified contingencies.

Escheat The passing of title to property to the state, or a county of a state, when a property owner dies without leaving a will and without heirs.

Escrow A legal arrangement for closing or completing a real estate transaction. Also, a written instrument or item of value deposited with an escrow agent to be delivered by her to another person upon the fulfillment of a condition.

Escrow account Same as *impound.*

Escrow agent (escrowee) A person or corporation employed by parties to a real estate transaction to receive documents and money and deliver them in accordance with their instructions.

Escrow agreement (escrow instructions) A contract between the parties to a real estate transaction to effect a settlement of the transaction in escrow.

Escrow instructions (escrow agreement) Instructions given by parties to a real estate transaction to an escrow agent concerning things to be done by him to complete the transaction.

Estate The nature, quantity, and quality of an ownership interest in real estate that is presently possessory or may become possessory in the future.

Estate at sufferance (tenancy at sufferance) An interest in real property that exists when a tenant (lessee) or mortgagor remains in possession of leased premises or "holds over" after her right to possession has ended.

Estate at will (tenancy at will) An interest in real property that has no fixed period of duration and is terminable at the desire of the owner or the tenant.

Estate for life See life estate.

Estate for years (for a term) A legal interest in real property measured by a fixed or definite period of time.

Estate from year-to-year (from period-to-period) A legal interest in real property that continues from week-to-week, month-to-month, or year-to-year.

Estate of inheritance An estate that may descend to heirs by will or intestate succession.

Estoppel A doctrine of law that prevents a person from asserting rights inconsistent with his prior words or conduct.

Ethics Duties of a member of a profession toward clients, the public, or others in the profession.

Eviction The physical dispossession by a landlord of a tenant from leased premises.

Exception A right or portion of property reserved for the grantor in a conveyance by deed.

Exclusive agency listing A listing agreement between a seller and a broker in which either has a right to sell the property; if sold by the broker, a commission will be due.

Exclusive right to sell A listing agreement between a seller and a broker whereby the broker receives a commission, regardless of who sells the property.

Exculpatory clause A clause in an agreement that attempts to absolve one party from liability for personal injury or property damage resulting from her own negligent conduct.

Execute To sign and deliver an instrument, such as a deed.

Executor A person specified in a will to carry out its provisions.

Express contract A contract in which the promises of the parties are revealed in either written or oral words.

Express easement An easement that comes into being by written language that reflects an intent to create it.

F

Fee simple absolute estate The largest property estate an owner can own, including inherited estates, estates of indefinite duration, and estates with no restrictions.

Fee simple determinable estate An estate in fee simple that terminates automatically upon the happening of a condition.

Fee subject to a condition subsequent estate An estate in fee simple that may be terminated by the holder of a right of entry upon the happening of a condition.

FHA (Federal Housing Administration) A federal agency that insures home mortgages.

FHLB (Federal Home Loan Bank System) An agency that serves and regulates savings and loan associations.

FHLMC (Federal Home Loan Mortgage Corporation) An agency that provides a secondary market for mortgages.

Fiduciary A relationship of trust and confidence between a principal and an agent.

Financing statement An instrument filed with the recorder or register of deeds indicating that personal property is encumbered.

Fixed-rate mortgage (FRM) A loan in which the interest rate is constant over the life of the loan.

Fixture Anything that originally was personal property but which has been attached to real property in such a manner to be regarded by law as part of the real property.

Flashing Sheet metal or other material used around chimneys or other places to prevent water seepage.

FNMA (Federal National Mortgage Association) An agency that provides a secondary market for mortgages.

Footing The base on which a home foundation stands.

Forbearance The giving up of a right to which a person is entitled.

Foreclosure A legal process by which property serving as security for an obligation is sold when a default occurs.

Forfeiture The loss of money or right due to default or failure to perform in accord with a contract.

Foundation The portion of a structure that supports the first floor and construction above it.

Franchise An arrangement whereby a local broker is affiliated with a larger organization, usually national.

Fraud A false representation or concealment of a material fact, made with knowledge of its falsity and with the intent to mislead, which results in injury to another party.

Freddie Mac Same as FHLMC.

Freehold estate An ownership interest in real property that lasts for an uncertain period of time.

Front foot A measure of property by which the distance is measured along the street, highway, stream, or other body of water.

FSLIC (Federal Savings and Loan Insurance Corporation) An agency that provides insurance for deposits in savings and loan associations.

Functional obsolescence Outdated design, fixtures, and other factors within the structure itself that detract from a building's value.

Future interest A legal interest in real property that postpones an owner's right of possession and enjoyment of the property.

G

General lien A lien effective against a person's real and personal property.

Ginnie Mae Same as GNMA.

Grade The level of the ground at the structure foundation.

Graduated lease A lease providing for a variable rate of rent depending upon some future event.

Grant To transfer or convey a legal interest in property.

Grantee The person to whom title to real estate is transferred by a deed.

Grantor The person who transfers title to real estate by a deed.

Gross income Income from a property before expenses are deducted.

Gross lease A lease agreement whereby the property owner pays taxes, insurance, repairs, and other costs.

Ground lease An agreement for rental of land only.

Ground rent The portion of property income attributed to the ground value itself; in a few states a person can own a structure and rent the ground.

Growing equity mortgage (GEM) Long-term loan with fixed interest rate; monthly payments increased by predetermined amount to accelerate payoff.

Guardian A person granted power by a court to take care of and manage the property of another person who has been declared legally incapable of administering his own affairs.

H

Habendum A provision in a deed that defines the extent of the ownership to be granted to and enjoyed by the grantee.

Heirs The persons designated by statute to receive an estate where there is no will.

Hereditaments Any property that can be inherited.

Highest and best use The use of a property that will yield the greatest return on the property.

Holographic will A will written, dated, and signed in the testator's handwriting, but not witnessed.

Homestead Any real estate where the owner resides that is exempt from creditor's claims to an amount specified by state law.

HUD Department of Housing and Urban Development.

Hypothecate To give something as security without giving up its possession.

I

Implied contract A contract in which no promises are expressly stated orally or in writing by the parties, but the existence of the contract and its terms are manifested by the conduct of the parties.

Impound Account where funds are set aside to pay taxes, insurance, and other debts when due.

Improvement Structure on real property.

Incapacity See incompetency.

Inchoate Not complete, such as a wife's dower interest while the husband is living.

Income approach A valuation method that capitalizes or converts the current benefits of the property into an estimate of value.

Incompetent A person who is not legally able to enter into binding contracts due to insanity, senility, insufficient age, or mental infirmity.

Incorporeal Rights, such as an easement, that are intangible and without physical existence.

Industrial revenue bonds Bonds issued to raise funds for developing commercial buildings for lease or industrial parks.

Infant (minor) A person who lacks the legal capacity or competency to alter his legal status by incurring liabilities or acquiring rights because of youthfulness. Depending upon the statutory provisions in a state, a person is a minor if under eighteen or twenty-one years of age.

Ingress A means of entry to a property.

Inheritance tax A tax on the right to receive property from a decedent either by will or by intestate succession.

Injunction An order by a court instructing a person to do or not to do something.

Installment sale contract (land contract, installment contract, and contract for deed) A contract in which a seller of real estate promises to deliver a deed to the buyer at some time in the future after the buyer has, in an agreed-upon number of payments of principal and interest, paid the purchase price in full.

Instrument A written legal document.

Insurable interest A person's interest in property such that an occurrence of a peril would cause financial loss to that person.

Insurance A contractual agreement where the insurer agrees to reimburse the insured for financial loss.

Interest A share or right in property ownership.

Interest escalation clause Provides for variable rate of interest according to a standard index.

Interim financing Same as construction loan.

Intermediary Financial institution, including banks and savings and loan associations.

Intermediation The process whereby persons place their savings in financial institutions who then lend the funds to others.

Inter vivos Among the living.

Intestate Dies leaving no will.

Intestate succession The distribution of the assets of one who dies leaving no will among heirs in accordance with the provisions of a state statute.

Involuntary lien. A lien such as taxes or mechanic's lien imposed without consent of the property owner.

J

Joint tenancy Co-ownership of property by two or more persons (joint tenants) in equal shares. When the co-owner dies, his interest in the property passes to the surviving co-owners.

Joint tenant One who co-owns property in joint tenancy with another person or persons.

Joint venture An equity participation in which a lender puts up funds and others, such as developers, contribute expertise.

Joists Wood beams in a house to which the floor is nailed and the ceiling lath of the floor below is nailed.

Judgment A court determination of a legal dispute.

Judgment lien A lien on real property created by the recording of a court judgment.

Just compensation A term used in connection with the taking of property by eminent domain that refers to the damages awarded to an owner whose property is taken. The damages are measured by the value of the property.

K

Kicker A benefit to the lender beyond ordinary interest, such as the increased appreciation of the property.

L

Land Land consists of the surface of the earth, the airspace above, and the subsurface below the surface. Also synonymous with real estate and real property.

Land contract See installment sale contract.

Landlocked Surrounded by adjacent land with no means of access.

Landlord A property owner who leases to another person.

Land trust When a trustee receives record title to real estate restricted by an ancillary agreement whereby the beneficiary of the trust retains full control and management.

Latent defect Concealed defect not easily determined from an inspection of the property.

Lease A contract between the property owner and another person to use or occupy the land for a set period of time.

Leased fee The landlord's interest.

Leasehold A possessory legal interest in real property acquired by a tenant (lessee) when she enters into a rental agreement with the owner of the property (landlord or lessor).

Leasehold estate The interest of a tenant.

Legal capacity The legal ability to enter into contracts or to convey title to property.

Legal description A property description sufficient for use in a deed or other instrument.

Legatee A person who receives personal property in a will.

Lessee The tenant in a lease agreement.

Lessor The landlord in a lease agreement.

Leverage The use of borrowed funds to increase the effective rate of return on an investment.

Levy To place a tax on a person or property.

License A permission granted to use the land of another; also a right granted by the state to engage in a business.

Lien An encumbrance in which the land serves as security for the payment of debt or discharge of an obligation.

Life estate An ownership interest in real property the duration of which is measured by the life or lives of one or more persons.

Life estate *pur autre vie* When the duration of a life estate is measured by a lifetime of someone other than its owner.

Life tenant The owner of a life estate.

Lineal heirs Direct line descendants (i.e., children and grandchildren).

Liquid assets Cash or other assets that can be quickly converted to cash with little or no sacrifice in value.

Liquidated damages A specified sum of money agreed upon by contracting parties that will be received by the other or others if one of the parties commits a breach of the contract.

Lis pendens A notice recorded to indicate that a lawsuit is pending.

Listing (agreement) A contract of employment between an owner (seller) of real estate and a real estate broker that authorizes the latter, as an agent, to find a buyer who is ready, willing, and able to purchase the owner's property.

Loan commitment A promise by a lender to provide a loan at a future date against a particular property.

Loan origination The process whereby a lender initiates a loan with a borrower.

Loan servicing Collecting loan payments, keeping records, following up on delinquencies, and taking foreclosure actions relating to a mortgage loan.

Loan-to-value ratio The ratio of amount borrowed to the property market value, usually expressed as a percentage.

Loan underwriting The process of evaluating the risks in a particular loan related to value of property and deciding whether or not to extend a loan to the borrower.

M

MAI A professional designation earned by a member of the American Institute of Real Estate Appraisers.

Marginal land Land in use that barely pays the cost of working it.

Marketable title (merchantable title) A title to real estate so free from defects and encumbrances that there can be no doubt as to its validity or any reasonable apprehension of danger of litigation.

Market approach The process of comparing the subject property to equivalent properties sold recently to arrive at an estimate of value for a property being appraised.

Market interest rate Interest rate currently demanded by lenders and investors.

Market rent The current rent that real estate would bring if available for rent.

Market value The price that property would be expected to bring in the open market under normal conditions.

Master limited partnership (MLP) A term used to describe a large partnership with ownership interests that are publicly registered and freely traded in the marketplace.

Maturity The date a note or mortgage must be paid in full.

Meandered Area such as a lake on which taxes are not paid.

Meander line The approximate border of a natural body of water.

Mechanic's lien A lien that can be filed by mechanics or material suppliers; it is against real property created by statute for the purpose of securing payments for services performed or materials furnished in the construction or repair of buildings or making other improvements to land.

Meridian Map lines running north and south to locate land under the governmental survey system.

Metes and bounds A method of legal description using measurements, boundaries, and directions.

MGIC (Mortgage Guaranty Insurance Corporation) An agency that provides insurance for the top 5–30 percent of a loan.

Mineral rights A legal interest in land that includes the right to remove minerals from land.

Minor A person not of legal age. (See infant.)

Modernization Replacement of outmoded fixtures, equipment, and other improvements with modern features.

Monetary Control Act of 1980 An act that allows savings and loan associations to operate like banks.

Money market The markets where funds are lent or borrowed for less than one year.

Monument A natural or artificial fixed object.

Moral suasion Efforts to change regulations or interest rates; Federal Reserve efforts to restrict banks from excess lending.

Moratorium A period of time when a lender may waive interest and/or principal payment on a loan.

Mortgage A written instrument in which real estate is used as security for repayment of a debt or obligation.

Mortgage-backed security (MBS) Bond or other security secured by a pool of mortgages.

Mortgage banker A person or organization using funds to originate loans with the expectation of reselling them.

Mortgage broker An organization or person who seeks and originates mortgages for a fee for another lender.

Mortgage company An organization acting primarily as a mortgage banker.

Mortgage market The overall market where mortgages are originated, bought, and sold.

Mortgage note A promissory note with a mortgage as security.

Mortgagee The party who lends money for the mortgage.

Mortgagor The party who borrows money with property as security.

Multiple listing A service whereby other brokers in an organization are allowed to sell a listed property.

Mutual assent An offer to contract made by one party (offeror) and an acceptance given by the party to whom it is made (offeree).

Mutual mistake When both parties enter into an agreement under a mistaken assumption concerning a material fact.

Mutual savings bank A financial intermediary accepting and investing savings primarily in residential mortgages.

N

Navigable water A waterway capable of passage by watercraft; navigable if so designated on a U.S. or state map.

Negative amortization Mortgage where the loan balance increases owing to payments less than interest due.

Negative leverage Situation where the cost of funds exceeds the rate of return on the real estate.

Negligence The failure to exercise reasonable care under the circumstances.

Net lease A lease agreement in which the tenant pays rent plus all taxes, insurance, repairs, and other costs.

Net listing A listing agreement whereby the owner receives a set amount if the property is sold and the broker receives the money above that amount.

Net operating income (NOI) The property gross earnings less the operating expenses, but before interest and depreciation expenses are deducted.

Nominal consideration Consideration having no relationship to the actual value of the contract or property conveyed.

Nominal interest rate The interest rate stipulated in an agreement.

Nonconforming use A use of land that lawfully existed before a zoning ordinance that is legally continued after the effective date of the ordinance, even though the use no longer conforms to the new zoning regulations.

Nonfreehold estate Any estate in land other than a fee simple and a life estate.

Notice To have knowledge of something. Notice may be either actual or constructive (public).

Novation When a property purchaser assumes a mortgage debt and the original borrower is released by the lender from further obligation.

NOW (negotiated order of withdrawal) accounts Checking accounts paying interest.

Nuisance The wrongful interference by one person with the use and enjoyment of real estate owned by another.

O

Obsolescence Loss in value due to obsolete or out-of-date design or construction.

Offer A promise made by one person (the offeror) to another person (the offeree) which by its terms invites the formation of a contract.

Omnibus Reconciliation Act of 1980 An act that places federal limitations on use of tax-exempt bonds to finance home ownership.

Open-end mortgage A mortgage agreement that allows the mortgagor to borrow additional funds in the future without rewriting the mortgage.

Open listing A listing agreement whereby either the owner or the broker can sell the property; if the broker is the procuring cause, a commission is due.

Operating ratio Ratio of operating expenses to effective gross income.

Option A contract in which one party obligates herself to hold an offer open for a stated period of time.

Optionee A person who holds an option.

Optionor An owner who gives an option to another person.

Ordinance A law passed by the legislative body.

Origination fee Fee for processing a mortgage application.

Overhang The portion of a roof extending beyond the walls.

P

Package mortgage A mortgage that includes personal property as part of the security.

Partial release clause A clause in a blanket mortgage whereby the lender agrees to release individual parcels of property upon payment of a specified portion of the loan.

Participation mortgage A loan in which two or more lenders participate.

Partition An action seeking to have property owned by two or more persons sold and the proceeds divided between the parties or to have the property divided into two or more portions.

Partnership An association of two or more persons to carry on a business for profit as co-owners.

Party wall A wall erected on the line between two adjacent properties for the use of both parties.

Pass-through security Mortgage-backed securities in which the payments received are passed through to the holders of the securities.

Patent A grant of title to land by a government or sovereign of a country to one or more individuals.

Percentage lease A lease whereby the fee paid is a percentage of the income from business done on the premises.

Personal property Same as chattel. Tangible and intangible things capable of being owned that are not real property.

Physical depreciation Physical deterioration and concurrent loss in property value caused by wear, tear, and decay.

PITI Payments covering principal, interest, taxes, and insurance.

Plat A map showing how a property is subdivided into lots.

Plottage In the process of combining two or more plots of ground together (see assemblage), plottage is the resulting greater utility and value than when held separately.

Point A charge of 1 percent of the loan amount made at origination of mortgage.

Point of beginning The starting point in a metes and bounds legal description.

Police power The inherent power of the state to enact legislation to promote the health, safety, morals, and general welfare of society by reasonable regulation of individual rights.

Possession Actual, or the right to, control.

Possibility of reverter A legal interest in real property that causes title to automatically vest in the owner of the interest when a fee simple determinable comes to an end.

Power of attorney A written instrument in which one person authorizes another to act in his behalf.

Prefabricated home Home built or partially assembled prior to delivery to the building site.

Premium Amount above the face value of a loan.

Prepayment penalty A penalty for payment of a mortgage balance before it is due.

Prepayment privilege The right of a borrower to pay a mortgage ahead of the scheduled due date without penalty.

Prescription Acquiring a right in property by adverse use of the property continuous for the period established by statute.

Prescriptive easement An easement obtained by adverse use.

Present value The current value of future benefits or the discounted value of future payments.

Primary lender A lender who originates loans.

Prime rates The interest rate charged by lenders to their best rated customers.

Principal The person who employs an agent. Also, the amount of a loan.

Principal meridian One of the north and south survey lines established to locate property.

Private mortgage insurance Insurance issued by a private insurer that insures the lender for loss on a loan up to a certain percentage of the loan.

Probate To establish the authenticity of a will in an appropriate court. Probate refers to all matters pertaining to the estates of deceased persons over which probate courts have jurisdiction.

Procuring cause The broker or other person who was the prime factor in bringing about the sale of a property.

Profit Also known as *profit à prendre*. The right of a person to enter upon the land of another person and remove something from it.

Promise An assurance by a person (promisor) that she will conduct herself in a certain way or bring about a specified result in the future, which is communicated to another person (promisee).

Promissory note A written promise of a person (maker) to pay a specified sum of money to another person (payee) in accordance with terms and conditions agreed upon by the parties.

Property Used in two senses: to refer to rights that a person has in something that is owned; and to refer to the object itself in which such rights exist.

Property brief A folder containing information on a particular property.

Proration A division of taxes, interest, and insurance so that the seller and the buyer pay the portion covering his period of ownership.

Publication A formal declaration made by a testator at the time of signing a will saying it is her last will and testament.

Purchase money mortgage A mortgage taken by the seller as part of the purchase price.

Pyramiding A process of acquiring additional properties by refinancing existing properties.

Q

Qualify To determine a person's financial status and ability to purchase property.

Quasi Similar to but not actually.

Quiet enjoyment Right of property owner to use his property without adverse claims of another to title or interest.

Quitclaim deed A deed that conveys title or interest, if any, that the grantor has in the property.

R

Rafter A board that supports the roof of a house.

Raw land Land with no improvements.

Real estate Real property; land and improvements to the land.

Real estate investment trust (REIT) An organization operating much like a mutual fund, where funds are invested in real property.

Real Estate Mortgage Trust (REMT) or Real Estate Mortgage Conduit (REMIC) A type of REIT that buys and sells mortgages rather than real property.

Real property Real estate.

REALTOR® A registered trademark for use of active members of the NATIONAL ASSOCIATION OF REALTORS®.

Recasting Changing terms of a loan while retaining the same loan.

Receiver clause A provision in a mortgage loan allowing the mortgagee to appoint a receiver to look after the lender's interests if the borrower defaults.

Recordation The process by which instruments relating to legal interests in real estate are reproduced in official records and are available to the public.

Recovery fund A fund established in some states by fees from licensed brokers and salespeople to reimburse individuals for actual unrecoverable losses due to wrongful acts of licensees.

Rectangular survey system A system for legal description of property based on principal meridians, baselines, and a grid system.

Redemption Buying back one's property subsequent to a court sale.

Redlining Lending or insurance practices that discriminate against certain areas of a community.

Refinance To obtain a new loan, usually larger, against a currently financed property.

Regulation B Implementation of the Equal Credit Opportunity Act.

Regulation X Implementation of RESPA.

Regulation Z Implementation of Truth-in-Lending Act.

Rehabilitation Restoration of existing structure without changing its floor plan or style.

Release The act of relinquishing, conceding, or giving up a right, claim, or privilege by the person in whom it exists or to whom it accrues to the person against whom it might have been demanded or enforced.

Release of mortgage An instrument that states that a mortgage has been satisfied.

Remainder An estate where the right of possession and enjoyment of the property is postponed until after the termination of a life estate.

Remainderman A person designated as being entitled to own an estate after the life estate has terminated.

Remedy Legal relief available through court action to redress a wrong.

Renegotiable rate mortgages (RRM) A mortgage where the interest rate is renegotiated at intervals, usually every three to five years.

Rent Consideration paid for use of property.

Replacement cost The cost incurred in replacing one property with another of similar utility, using modernized equipment, materials, and techniques.

Reproduction costs The cost of reproducing an exact replica property based on current prices.

Rescind To void a contract and restore the contracting parties to their prior legal and monetary positions.

Reservation A right kept by a grantor when conveying property.

Reserve requirements Levels of bank reserves specified by the Federal Reserve.

RESPA Real Estate Settlement Procedures Act.

Restriction An encumbrance created by deed or special agreement that limits use of the property.

Reverse-annuity mortgage (RAM) An agreement in which the borrower receives monthly payments from the lender with real property for the security.

Reversion The portion of an estate remaining with the original grantor after the termination of a leasehold or life estate.

Revocation The withdrawal of an offer by the offeror before it has been accepted by the offeree.

Right A legal interest protected by the law.

Right of entry The right to bring legal action to terminate a fee subject to a condition subsequent upon the happening of a prohibited condition.

Right of first refusal A provision that allows a party to purchase the property at the terms offered to any other party.

Right of redemption A person's right by law to buy back property taken by forced sale for a period of time.

Right of severance The right of a joint tenant to terminate his co-ownership interest in property by transferring that interest to another person with or without the consent of the other tenants.

Right of survivorship When a deceased co-owner's interest in property passes to the surviving co-owner rather than to the decedent's estate.

Right-of-way The right to cross over or under another person's property for ingress, egress, utility lines, or sewers.

Riparian rights Rights of an owner of property abutting water to use the water and have uninterrupted flow.

Rod A measure of length equal to 16½ feet.

Rollover mortgage A loan having a call date earlier than the full amortization period.

Run with the land When easements or restrictions do not expire when ownership is transferred.

Rural Pertaining to the country, rather than urban.

S

Satisfaction Discharge of lien upon payment of debt.

Savings and loan association (S&L) Federal or state chartered thrift institution.

Seal An impression made to attest to the execution of a written instrument; also the word *seal* typed in to form a sealed document.

Secondary lender A person or organization purchasing loans that have been originated by a primary lender.

Secondary mortgage market The market in which originators of mortgages can sell the mortgage to others.

Second mortgage A mortgage having a lien against the property subservient to the first mortgage.

Section A unit of land measure one mile square containing 640 acres.

Section 203(b) Refers to the standard FHA insured loan.

Section 245/203 Same as 203(b), except mortgage loan has graduated payments.

Security deposit Deposit given by lessee to landlord to protect against property damage.

Seizin The possession of land under a claim of freehold estate.

Senior mortgage A mortgage, usually a first mortgage, having priority over another.

Separate property In states recognizing community property, separate property is any property owned by either spouse before marriage or property acquired by either spouse by gift or inheritance.

Septic tank An underground tank used for sewage treatment where city sewerage is not available.

Servicing fee Fee charged to mortgage holder for collecting payments and payment of taxes and insurance.

Servient estate Land that carries the burden of an easement.

Servient owner The owner of a parcel of land (servient estate) burdened by an easement.

Setback A distance from the curb to the building. Often a minimum setback is specified by ordinance.

Settlement The process of completing the sale of real property. Same as closing.

Settlement statement A statement showing all charges and credits to property buyer and property seller. Same as closing statement.

Severalty Sole ownership; by one person.

Severance Take from the land, such as minerals or timber.

Shared appreciation mortgage (SAM) A mortgage loan agreement in which the lender shares in the appreciation of the real property.

Sheriff's deed A deed given as a result of a court order to sell property in satisfaction of a judgment.

Signature The act of writing a person's name or making a mark or symbol with the intent that it attest the validity of a written instrument.

Simple interest Interest charged only on the outstanding principal.

Site A plot of ground upon which anything is, has been, or will be located.

Situs Location.

Sole security clause A mortgage clause that allows the lender, in case of default, to take action only against the pledged property; there is no personal liability by borrower.

Special agent Agent authorized by a principal to handle one particular transaction.

Special assessment An assessment against real estate to pay for improvements such as sidewalks, curbs, street lights, or other items that benefit certain property owners.

Special warranty deed A form of deed whereby the grantor warrants the title only against claims generated while the grantor owned the property.

Specification A document describing requirements for a house, subdivision, or other project.

Specific lien A lien that affects only a single parcel of property.

Specific performance A legal action to compel the performance of the terms of an agreement, such as the sale of a home.

Spot zoning Zoning that sets aside certain areas for purposes different from the general area requirements.

Standby commitment A commitment by a lender to make a mortgage loan within a certain time period.

Statement of record A statement that must be filed with HUD for lot sales subject to the Interstate Land Sales Full Disclosure Act.

Statute State or federal legislative law.

Statute of Frauds The state law that requires that certain contracts, including those for the sale of real property, must be in writing.

Statutory lien Liens defined by state law.

Statutory right of redemption A right given to a mortgagor-debtor in some states that enables her to buy back her property from the bidder who purchased it at a foreclosure sale.

Straight-line depreciation Computation of depreciation assuming a level wear-out period.

Strawman One who purchases property for another to conceal the identity of the real purchaser.

Strict foreclosure A court decree vesting title to mortgaged property in the mortgagee upon the default of the mortgagor without any sale of the property.

Stud Vertical timber in a house wall.

Subchapter S corporation A corporation that, for federal income tax purposes, can elect to be taxed as an individual proprietorship.

Subdivision A tract of land divided into lots suitable for residential purposes.

Subject property The property under analysis or appraisal.

Subject to The purchase of real property subject to a mortgage, whereby the original holder remains personally liable for the mortgage.

Sublease The transfer of a legal interest in leased premises by a tenant to another person that is less than the tenant's leasehold interest.

Subordinate To make a mortgage subservient to another mortgage.

Subrogation clause In an insurance policy, a clause permitting the insurer to sue in the name of the insured a third party accused of negligence.

Subsequent purchaser for value A purchaser for value in good faith and without notice of any adverse interest in the property purchased.

Substitution principle The principle that property cannot be worth more than its replacement cost.

Surrender Reconveyance of property or lease to mortgagee or landlord.

Survey The process that determines the shape, area, and position of a parcel of land by locating its boundaries.

Sweat equity An individual's equity in property due to physical effort expended.

Syndicate A group of persons joining together to deal in real property for profit.

T

Takeout commitment Promise by a lender to provide a permanent loan to pay off a construction loan.

Tandem plan GNMA loan subsidization plan for housing projects whereby GNMA buys below-market-rate mortgages at close to par and resells them at a discount.

Tangible Existing physically; that which can be touched.

Tax A levy for governmental purposes.

Tax deed A deed to real estate executed and delivered by a county officer to the successful purchaser at a tax foreclosure sale.

Tax-free exchange A trade of like properties allowing taxes to be deferred.

Tax lien A charge against property that makes it security for unpaid taxes.

Tax sale Sale of property as a result of nonpayment of taxes.

Tax shelter A loss that can be used to offset taxable income.

Tenancy at sufferance (estate at sufferance) An interest in real property that exists when a tenant (lessee) or mortgagor remains in possession of leased premises or holds over after his right to possession has ended.

Tenancy at will An interest in real property that has no fixed period of duration and is terminable at the desire of the landlord or the tenant.

Tenancy by the entirety A form of co-ownership of property between husband and wife, each having an equal undivided interest and the right of survivorship.

Tenancy for a term (estate for years) An ownership interest in property created by a lease, the duration of which is measured by a fixed or definite period of time.

Tenancy from period-to-period See estate from year-to-year.

Tenancy in common Co-ownership of property by two or more persons whose shares may be unequal and with no right of survivorship.

Tenements Rights in real property that pass with conveyance of the property.

Termites Antlike insects that eat wood and cause destruction.

Term loan A loan having the entire principal due at maturity.

Testamentary disposition A transfer of property by will at death.

Testate Having a will.

Testator One who makes a will.

Tideland Land covered by water at high tide and uncovered at low tide.

Time is of the essence A contract clause that makes it essential that the provisions be carried out at the specified time.

Timesharing Ownership of property for a specified period of each year.

Time value of money Relation of value at one time to value at another through discounting or compounding at a certain interest rate.

Title Used in two ways: ownership—all the rights an owner may have with respect to land—and the evidence upon which ownership is based.

Title defect An adverse right of one person to an interest in another person's title.

Title insurance policy A contract according to the terms of which a title insurance company obligates itself to indemnify a buyer or a lender against losses resulting from defects in the title to a specified parcel of land.

Title of record Title as revealed in public records.

Title search An examination of public records pertaining to a parcel of land to determine the status of ownership.

Title theory Mortgage law theory that the lender holds legal title to property, whereas the borrower holds equitable rights.

Topography The nature of the surface of land, such as level, rolling, and so forth.

Torrens system A system of land title registration that makes the status of title to land ascertainable from a certificate issued by a public official.

Tort A civil wrong against a person or his property.

Tort liability The responsibility of one who commits a tort to pay damages to one who sustains injury or property damage as a result of her wrongful conduct.

Township A unit in the governmental survey system six miles square.

Tract An area of land.

Trade fixture An item of personal property attached to leased premises by a tenant for purposes of use in his trade or business.

Transaction A business deal.

Transfer development rights (TDR) Transfer of zoning rights from one parcel of property to another.

Trespass The unlawful entry upon another's land or interference with an occupant's right of possession.

Trust Real or personal title to property held by a trustee for a beneficiary.

Trust deed See deed of trust.

Trustee A person who receives property or a title under an agreement to hold it for the benefit of another (beneficiary).

Trustee's deed A deed by a trustee to convey land held in trust.

Trustor The owner-borrower in a deed of trust.

Truth-in-Lending Act Federal law requiring that a lender disclose an effective interest rate (APR) in a lending transaction.

U

Underimprovement A property not being used to its fullest and best potential.

Underwriting Evaluating borrower creditworthiness and cash value and ascertaining risks involved prior to deciding whether or not to make a loan.

Undue influence When one person is under the domination of another and is induced to do something she would not otherwise have done had it not been for the unfair persuasion by the dominant party.

Unenforceable contract An otherwise valid contract

that fails to meet the requirement of some particular statute or rule of law and thus is not entitled to a legal remedy when breached.

Unilateral contract A contract in which one of the parties has made a promise in exchange for an act or forbearance.

Unilateral mistake When only one party enters the agreement under an erroneous assumption concerning a material fact.

Universal agent An agent authorized to do any or all acts for the principal.

Urban Pertaining to a city or heavily settled area.

Usury Interest on a loan at a rate higher than allowed by law.

V

VA Veterans Administration.

VA mortgage A loan partially guaranteed by the Veterans Administration.

Valuable consideration A right, interest, profit, or benefit accrued to one party or some forbearance, detriment, loss, or responsibility given or suffered by a party to a deed or contract.

Value The dollar amount that property will bring in the open market.

Variable-rate mortgage (VRM) A mortgage loan for which the interest varies according to an index.

Variance The right to deviate from the use of land prescribed by an existing zoning ordinance.

Vendee The buyer.

Vendor The seller.

Vest To give an interest in property.

Vested remainder An estate in land, the possession and enjoyment of which is delayed only until the termination of a preceding estate.

Void Having no legal or binding effect.

Voidable Subject to being rescinded.

Voidable contract An agreement that is binding on all parties until one exercises her rights and elects to rescind the agreement.

Voidable deed A deed that transfers voidable title until the grantor or his legal representative has the transfer rescinded or voided because of fraud, undue influence, infancy, duress, mental infirmity, or other legal reason.

Voluntary lien A lien created by an agreement, such as a mortgage, that results in a debt.

W

Waiver of defense clause A loan clause stating the borrower has a right to notice before the lender can obtain a judgment.

Ward An infant or other legally incompetent person placed by the court under the care of a guardian or conservator.

Warehousing Making a guarantee, for a fee and for a set time, that funds will be available under specified terms.

Warranty See covenant.

Warranty deed A deed that includes covenants of seizin, right of quiet enjoyment, freedom from encumbrances, further assurance, and warranty forever.

Waste The neglect, misuse, alteration, or destruction of land by a person rightfully in possession that causes a substantial and permanent decrease in its value to the estate or legal interest owned by another person.

Water rights Rights associated with the use of water adjacent to, in, or underneath property.

Will An oral or written declaration by an owner to make a disposition of her property effective upon her death.

Witnessed will (formal will) A written will signed by the maker (testator) whose signature is witnessed or attested to by witnesses whose signatures must also appear on the will.

Wrap-around mortgage A junior mortgage that includes an existing senior mortgage.

Y

Yield Return on an investment or loan.

Z

Zoning The division of an area or community by a government into districts or zones with regulations as to the use of land varying from one zone to another.

APPENDIX B
Residential Construction Nomenclature

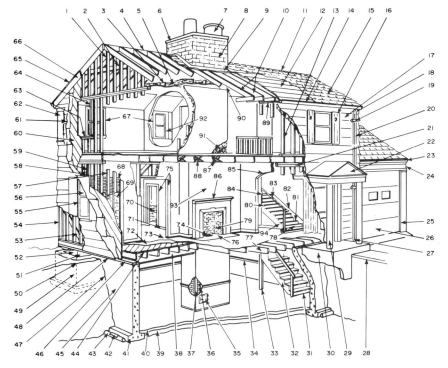

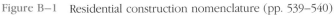

Figure B–1   Residential construction nomenclature (pp. 539–540)

1 GABLE STUD	31 BASEMENT STAIR RISER	63 ROUGH HEADER
2 COLLAR BEAM	32 STAIR STRINGER	64 WINDOW STUD
3 CEILING JOIST	33 GIRDER POST	65 CORNICE MOULDING
4 RIDGE BOARD	34 CHAIR RAIL	66 FRIEZE OR BARGE BOARD
5 INSULATION	35 CLEANOUT DOOR	67 WINDOW CASING
6 CHIMNEY CAP	36 FURRING STRIPS	68 LATH
7 CHIMNEY POTS	37 CORNER STUD	69 INSULATION
8 CHIMNEY	38 GIRDER	70 WAINSCOTING
9 CHIMNEY FLASHING	39 CINDER OR GRAVEL FILL	71 BASEBOARD
10 RAFTERS	40 CONCRETE BASEMENT FLOOR	72 BUILDING PAPER
11 RIDGE	41 FOOTING FOR FOUNDATION WALL	73 FINISH FLOOR
12 ROOF BOARDS	42 PAPER STRIP	74 ASH DUMP
13 STUD	43 FOUNDATION DRAIN TILE	75 DOOR TRIM
14 EAVE TROUGH OR GUTTER	44 DIAGONAL SUBFLOORING	76 FIREPLACE HEARTH
15 ROOFING	45 FOUNDATION WALL	77 FLOOR JOISTS
16 BLIND OR SHUTTER	46 SILL	78 STAIR RISER
17 BEVEL SIDING	47 BACKFILL	79 FIRE BRICK
18 DOWNSPOUT OR LEADER GOOSENECK	48 TERMITE SHIELD	80 NEWEL CAP
19 DOWNSPOUT OR LEADER STRAP	49 AREAWAY WALL	81 STAIR TREAD
20 DOWNSPOUT OR LEADER CONDUCTOR	50 GRADE LINE	82 FINISH STRINGER
21 DOUBLE PLATE	51 BASEMENT SASH	83 STAIR RAIL
22 ENTRANCE CANOPY	52 AREAWAY	84 BALUSTERS
23 GARAGE CORNICE	53 CORNER BRACE	85 PLASTER ARCH
24 FRIEZE	54 CORNER STUDS	86 MANTEL
25 DOOR JAMB	55 WINDOW FRAME	87 FLOOR PLATE
26 GARAGE DOOR	56 WINDOW LIGHT	88 BRIDGING
27 DOWNSPOUT OR LEADER SHOE	57 WALL STUDS	89 LOOKOUT
28 SIDEWALK	58 HEADER	90 ATTIC SPACE
29 ENTRANCE POST	59 WINDOW CRIPPLE	91 METAL LATH
30 ENTRANCE PLATFORM	60 WALL SHEATHING	92 WINDOW SASH
	61 BUILDING PAPER	93 CHIMNEY BREAST
	62 PILASTER	94 NEWEL

Figure B–1   (continued)

APPENDIX C
State Commissions and Their Publications

Alabama
Alabama Real Estate Commission
750 Washington St.
Montgomery, AL 36130
Alabama Real Estate Law
Update (Newsletter)

Alaska
Department of Commerce and Economic
    Development
Division of Occupational Licensing
Real Estate Commission
P.O. Box D-LIC
Juneau, AK 99811–0800
Real Estate Brokers and Salesmen
    Centralized Licensing Statutes

Arizona
Department of Real Estate
1645 W. Jefferson
Phoenix, AZ 85007
Instructions to License Applicants

Arkansas
Authority of Arkansas Real Estate Commission
One River Front Place, Suite 660
North Little Rock, AR 72114
Real Estate License Law and Regulations
Arkansas Real Estate Examinations

California
California Department of Real Estate
P.O. Box 187001
Attention: Licensing Dept.
Sacramento, CA 95818–7001
Instructions to License Applicants
Real Estate Law
Real Estate Education in California
(several others)

Colorado
Colorado Real Estate Commission
1776 Logan, 4th Floor
Denver, CO 80203
Colorado Real Estate Reference Guide

Connecticut
State of Connecticut
Department of Consumer Protection
State Office Building
Hartford, CT 06106
Real Estate Licensing, Law and Regulations
    Concerning the Conduct of Real Estate Brokers
    and Salesmen

Delaware
Delaware Real Estate Commission
Department of Administrative Services, Division of
    Business and Occupational Regulation
Margaret O'Neill Building
P.O. Box 1401
Dover, DE 19901
Real Estate License Act and Primer
Newsletter

District of Columbia
Real Estate Commission
614 H Street N.W.
Washington, DC 20001

Florida
Florida Real Estate Commission
State Office Building
400 W. Robinson St.
Orlando, FL 32802
Florida Licensing Requirements
Florida Real Estate License Law

Georgia
Real Estate Commission
3200 Presidential Drive
Presidential Park
Atlanta, GA 30340
Georgia Real Estate Manual ($5.50 charge)

Hawaii
State of Hawaii
Professional and Vocational Licensing Division
Dept. of Commerce and Consumer Affairs
P.O. Box 3469
Honolulu, HI 96801
Hawaii Revised Statutes: Real Estate Brokers and Salesmen
Hawaii Administrative Rules: Real Estate Brokers and Salesmen

Idaho
Real Estate Commission
State Capitol Building
Boise, ID 83720
Idaho Real Estate Brokers Law

Illinois
Department of Professional Regulation
320 West Washington, 3rd Floor
Springfield, IL 62786
The Real Estate License Act of 1983

Indiana
Indiana Real Estate Commission
State Office Building, Room 1021
100 N. Senate Ave
Indianapolis, IN 46204–2246
Real Estate License Laws

Iowa
Iowa Real Estate Commission
1918 S.E. Hulsizer Ave.
Ankeny, IA 50021
Real Estate License Law
Real Estate Rules and Regulations

Kansas
Kansas Real Estate Commission
Landon State Office Bldg.
900 Jackson St., Room 501
Topeka, KS 66612–1220
Kansas Real Estate Broker's License Law

Kentucky
Kentucky State Real Estate Commission
222 South First Street, Suite 300
Louisville, KY 40202
Law Governing Real Estate in Kentucky
Kentucky Real Estate Newsletter
Real Estate Assessment for Licensure

Louisiana
Real Estate Commission
P.O. Box 14785
Baton Rouge, LA 70898
Louisiana Real Estate License Law of 1920
Louisiana Real Estate Commission Rules and Regulations
Real Estate Assessment for Licensure
Requirements for Louisiana Salesperson License

Maine
Maine Real Estate Commission
State House Station 35
Augusta, ME 04333
License Law, Rules and Regulations

Maryland
Maryland Real Estate Commission
501 St. Paul Place, Suite 804
Baltimore, MD 21202
Real Estate Law

Massachusetts
Board of Registration of Real Estate Brokers and Salesmen
Leverett Saltonstall Building, Room 1520
100 Cambridge St.
Boston, MA 02202
Real Estate License Law and Regulations

Michigan
Department of Licensing and Regulation
P.O. Box 30018
Lansing, MI 48909
Real Estate Red Book, Real Estate License Laws and Rules
Requirements for Real Estate Licensure

Minnesota
Department of Administration
St. Paul, MN 55155
Minnesota Law, Real Estate Regulations

Mississippi
Mississippi Real Estate Commission
1920 Dunbarton Street
Jackson, MS 39216
Real Estate Brokers License Act
Rules and Regulations, Code of Ethics

Missouri
Missouri Real Estate Commission
3523 North Ten Mile Drive, P.O. Box 1339
Jefferson City, MO 65102
Missouri Real Estate Commission, Rules and Regulations

Montana
Board of Realty Regulation
Department of Commerce
1424 9th Avenue
Helena, MT 59620–0407
Real Estate Act

Nebraska
Nebraska Real Estate Commission
301 Centennial Mall South, P.O. Box 94667
Lincoln, NE 68509–4667
*Nebraska Real Estate License Act and Rules and
    Regulations*
Nebraska Real Estate Appraiser License Act
Consumer Guide to Buying and Selling Homes

Nevada
Real Estate Division, Department of Commerce
201 South Fall St.
Carson City, NV 89710
Nevada Handbook for Real Estate Licensees

New Hampshire
NH Real Estate Commission
Johnson Hall
State Office Park South
107 Pleasant St.
Concord, NH 03301
NH Code of Administrative Rules

New Jersey
Division of the New Jersey Real Estate Commission
201 East State St., P.O. Box 1510
Trenton, NJ 08625
*The New Jersey Real Estate License Act and Rules and
    Regulations*

New Mexico
The New Mexico Real Estate Commission
4125 Carlisle N.E.
Albuquerque, NM 87107
*State of New Mexico Real Estate Law and Rules and
    Regulations*

New York
Department of State, Division of Licensing Services
162 Washington Ave.
Albany, NY 12231–0001
Real Estate Salespersons License Law
Real Estate Brokers License Law

North Carolina
North Carolina Real Estate Licensing Board
P.O. Box 17100
Raleigh, NC 27619–7100
*North Carolina Real Estate Licensing Board Rules
    and Regulations*

Real Estate Licensing in North Carolina
*Your Place at the Beach: A Buyer's Guide to Vacation
    Real Estate*

North Dakota
North Dakota Real Estate Commission
P.O. Box 727
314 East Thayer Ave.
Bismarck, ND 58502
*Real Estate License Law and Commission Rules and
    Regulations*

Ohio
Ohio Division of Real Estate and Ohio Real Estate
    Commission
Two Nationwide Plaza
Columbus, OH 43266–0547
Real Estate License Law and Commerce Rules
    ($7.00 charge)

Oklahoma
The Oklahoma Real Estate Institute
4040 Lincoln Blvd., Suite 100
Oklahoma City, OK 73105
*Oklahoma Real Estate License Code and Rules and
    Regulations*

Oregon
Department of Commerce, Real Estate Division
158 12th St. N.E.
Salem, OR 97310–0240
Real Estate and Escrow Activities 1987
Oregon Administrative Rules—Real Estate Division
Property Management Rules

Pennsylvania
Bureau of Professional and Occupational Affairs
State Real Estate Commission
P.O. Box 2649
Harrisburg, PA 17105–2649
*Rules and Regulations of the State Real Estate
    Commission*
Real Estate Licensing and Registration Act

Rhode Island
Rhode Island Real Estate Division
Department of Business Regulation
233 Richmond St., Suite 230
Providence, RI 02903–4230
Real Estate Licensing Laws and Rules and Regulations

South Carolina
South Carolina Real Estate Commission
Capitol Center—AT&T Bldg.
1201 Main St., Suite 1500
Columbia, SC 29201
License Law and Regulations

South Dakota

South Dakota State Real Estate Commission
P.O. Box 490
Pierre, SD 57501–0490
South Dakota Real Estate License Laws and Rules and Regulations ($3.00 charge)

Tennessee

The Tennessee Real Estate Commission
1808 West End Bldg., 11th Floor
Nashville, TN 37219–5322
Real Estate Official Manual

Texas

Texas Real Estate Commission
P.O. Box 12188, Capitol Station
Austin, TX 78711
The Real Estate License Act
Rules of the Texas Real Estate Commission

Utah

Department of Business Regulation, Division of Real Estate
160 East 300 South, P.O. Box 45802
Salt Lake City, UT 84145–0802
Real Estate License Law
Utah Real Estate News (quarterly)
Division of Real Estate, Acts, Rules, etc.

Vermont

Vermont Real Estate Commission
Office of the Secretary of State
Montpelier, VT 05602
Vermont Laws and Rules Relating to Real Estate

Virginia

Department of Commerce
3600 West Broad Street
Richmond, VA 23230–4917
Virginia Real Estate Board Regulations
Real Estate License Laws
Fair Housing Laws

Washington

Department of Licensing, Real Estate Division
P.O. Box 247
Olympia, WA 98504–8001
Law Governing Licensing of Real Estate Brokers and Salesmen
Real Estate Practice in the State of Washington

West Virginia

West Virginia Real Estate Commission
1033 Quarrier St., Suite 400
Charleston, WV 25301
West Virginia Real Estate License Law and Administrative Regulations

Wisconsin

Real Estate Examining Board
P.O. Box 8935
Madison, WI 53708
Wisconsin Real Estate Law

Wyoming

Wyoming Real Estate Commission
4301 Herschler Bldg.
Cheyenne, WY 82002
Wyoming Real Estate Laws and Regulations

APPENDIX D
Present Value Tables

FORMULAS

Column 1—

Value of $1 at compound interest $= (1 + i)^n$

Column 2—

Accumulation of $1 per period $= \dfrac{(1 + i)^n - 1}{i}$

Column 3—

Sinking fund factor $= \dfrac{i}{(1 + i)^n - 1}$

Column 4—

Present value of $1 $= \dfrac{1}{(1 + i)^n}$

Column 5—

Present value of annuity $1 per period $= \dfrac{1 - (1 + i)^{-n}}{i}$

Column 6—

Installment to amortize $1 $= \dfrac{i}{1 - (1 + i)^{-n}}$

Table D–1   8% annual compound interest

Years	1 Value of $1 at compound interest	2 Accumulation of $1 per period	3 Sinking fund factor	4 Present value of $1	5 Present value of annuity $1 per period	6 Installment to amortize $1
1	1.0800	1.0000	1.0000	0.9259	0.9259	1.0800
2	1.1664	2.0800	0.4808	0.8573	1.7833	0.5608
3	1.2597	3.2464	0.3080	0.7938	2.5771	0.3880
4	1.3605	4.5061	0.2219	0.7350	3.3121	0.3019
5	1.4693	5.8666	0.1705	0.6806	3.9927	0.2505
6	1.5869	7.3359	0.1363	0.6302	4.6229	0.2163
7	1.7138	8.9228	0.1121	0.5835	5.2064	0.1921
8	1.8509	10.6366	0.0940	0.5403	5.7466	0.1740
9	1.9990	12.4876	0.0801	0.5002	6.2469	0.1601
10	2.1589	14.4866	0.0690	0.4632	6.7101	0.1490
11	2.3316	16.6455	0.0601	0.4289	7.1390	0.1401
12	2.5182	18.9771	0.0527	0.3971	7.5361	0.1327
13	2.7196	21.4953	0.0465	0.3677	7.9038	0.1265
14	2.9372	24.2149	0.0413	0.3405	8.2442	0.1213
15	3.1722	27.1521	0.0368	0.3152	8.5595	0.1168
16	3.4259	30.3243	0.0330	0.2919	8.8514	0.1130
17	3.7000	33.7503	0.0296	0.2703	9.1216	0.1096
18	3.9960	37.4503	0.0267	0.2502	9.3719	0.1067
19	4.3157	41.4463	0.0241	0.2317	9.6036	0.1041
20	4.6610	45.7620	0.0219	0.2145	9.8181	0.1019
21	5.0338	50.4230	0.0198	0.1987	10.0168	0.0998
22	5.4365	55.4568	0.0180	0.1839	10.2007	0.0980
23	5.8715	60.8933	0.0164	0.1703	10.3711	0.0964
24	6.3412	66.7648	0.0150	0.1577	10.5288	0.0950
25	6.8485	73.1060	0.0137	0.1460	10.6748	0.0937

Years	1 Value of $1 at compound interest	2 Accumulation of $1 per period	3 Sinking fund factor	4 Present value of $1	5 Present value of annuity $1 per period	6 Installment to amortize $1
26	7.3964	79.9545	0.0125	0.1352	10.8100	0.0925
27	7.9881	87.3509	0.0114	0.1252	10.9352	0.0914
28	8.6271	95.3389	0.0105	0.1159	11.0511	0.0905
29	9.3173	103.9660	0.0096	0.1073	11.1584	0.0896
30	10.0627	113.2833	0.0088	0.0994	11.2578	0.0888
31	10.8677	123.3460	0.0081	0.0920	11.3498	0.0881
32	11.7371	134.2137	0.0075	0.0852	11.4350	0.0875
33	12.6761	145.9508	0.0069	0.0789	11.5139	0.0869
34	13.6901	158.6269	0.0063	0.0730	11.5869	0.0863
35	14.7854	172.3170	0.0058	0.0676	11.6546	0.0858
36	15.9682	187.1024	0.0053	0.0626	11.7172	0.0853
37	17.2456	203.0706	0.0049	0.0580	11.7752	0.0849
38	18.6253	220.3162	0.0045	0.0537	11.8289	0.0845
39	20.1153	238.9415	0.0042	0.0497	11.8786	0.0842
40	21.7245	259.0569	0.0039	0.0460	11.9246	0.0839
41	23.4625	280.7814	0.0036	0.0426	11.9672	0.0836
42	25.3395	304.2440	0.0033	0.0395	12.0067	0.0833
43	27.3667	329.5835	0.0030	0.0365	12.0432	0.0830
44	29.5560	356.9502	0.0028	0.0338	12.0771	0.0828
45	31.9205	386.5062	0.0026	0.0313	12.1084	0.0826
46	34.4741	418.4267	0.0024	0.0290	12.1374	0.0824
47	37.2321	452.9008	0.0022	0.0269	12.1643	0.0822
48	40.2106	490.1329	0.0020	0.0249	12.1891	0.0820
49	43.4275	530.3436	0.0019	0.0230	12.2122	0.0819
50	46.9017	573.7711	0.0017	0.0213	12.2335	0.0817

Table D-2   9% annual compound interest

Years	1 Value of $1 at compound interest	2 Accumulation of $1 per period	3 Sinking fund factor	4 Present value of $1	5 Present value of annuity $1 per period	6 Installment to amortize $1
1	1.0900	1.0000	1.0000	0.9174	0.9174	1.0900
2	1.1881	2.0900	0.4785	0.8417	1.7591	0.5685
3	1.2950	3.2781	0.3051	0.7722	2.5313	0.3951
4	1.4116	4.5731	0.2187	0.7084	3.2397	0.3087
5	1.5386	5.9847	0.1671	0.6499	3.8897	0.2571
6	1.6771	7.5233	0.1329	0.5963	4.4859	0.2229
7	1.8280	9.2004	0.1087	0.5470	5.0330	0.1987
8	1.9926	11.0285	0.0907	0.5019	5.5348	0.1807
9	2.1719	13.0210	0.0768	0.4604	5.9952	0.1668
10	2.3674	15.1929	0.0658	0.4224	6.4177	0.1558
11	2.5804	17.5603	0.0569	0.3875	6.8052	0.1469
12	2.8127	20.1407	0.0497	0.3555	7.1607	0.1397
13	3.0658	22.9534	0.0436	0.3262	7.4869	0.1336
14	3.3417	26.0192	0.0384	0.2992	7.7862	0.1284
15	3.6425	29.3609	0.0341	0.2745	8.0607	0.1241
16	3.9703	33.0034	0.0303	0.2519	8.3126	0.1203
17	4.3276	36.9737	0.0270	0.2311	8.5436	0.1170
18	4.7171	41.3014	0.0242	0.2120	8.7556	0.1142
19	5.1417	46.0185	0.0217	0.1945	8.9501	0.1117
20	5.6044	51.1602	0.0195	0.1784	9.1285	0.1095
21	6.1088	56.7646	0.0176	0.1637	9.2922	0.1076
22	6.6586	62.8734	0.0159	0.1502	9.4424	0.1059
23	7.2579	69.5320	0.0144	0.1378	9.5802	0.1044
24	7.9111	76.7899	0.0130	0.1264	9.7066	0.1030
25	8.6231	84.7010	0.0118	0.1160	9.8226	0.1018

Years	1 Value of $1 at compound interest	2 Accumulation of $1 per period	3 Sinking fund factor	4 Present value of $1	5 Present value of annuity $1 per period	6 Installment to amortize $1
26	9.3992	93.3241	0.0107	0.1064	9.9290	0.1007
27	10.2451	102.7233	0.0097	0.0976	10.0226	0.0997
28	11.1672	112.9684	0.0089	0.0895	10.1161	0.0989
29	12.1722	124.1355	0.0081	0.0822	10.1983	0.0981
30	13.2677	136.3077	0.0073	0.0754	10.2737	0.0973
31	14.4618	149.5754	0.0067	0.0691	10.3428	0.0967
32	15.7634	164.0372	0.0061	0.0634	10.4062	0.0961
33	17.1821	179.8006	0.0056	0.0582	10.4644	0.0956
34	18.7284	196.9827	0.0051	0.0534	10.5178	0.0951
35	20.4140	215.7111	0.0046	0.0490	10.5668	0.0946
36	22.2513	236.1251	0.0042	0.0449	10.6118	0.0942
37	24.2539	258.3764	0.0039	0.0412	10.6530	0.0939
38	26.4367	282.6303	0.0035	0.0378	10.6908	0.0935
39	28.8160	309.0670	0.0032	0.0347	10.7255	0.0932
40	31.4095	337.8831	0.0030	0.0318	10.7574	0.0930
41	34.2363	369.2925	0.0027	0.0292	10.7866	0.0927
42	37.3176	403.5289	0.0025	0.0268	10.8134	0.0925
43	40.6762	440.8465	0.0023	0.0246	10.8380	0.0923
44	44.3370	481.5227	0.0021	0.0226	10.8605	0.0921
45	48.3274	525.8598	0.0019	0.0207	10.8812	0.0919
46	52.6768	574.1872	0.0017	0.0190	10.9002	0.0917
47	57.4178	626.8641	0.0016	0.0174	10.9176	0.0916
48	62.5854	684.2819	0.0015	0.0160	10.9336	0.0915
49	68.2181	746.8672	0.0013	0.0147	10.9482	0.0913
50	74.3577	815.0854	0.0012	0.0134	10.9617	0.0912

Table D–3   10% annual compound interest

Years	1 Value of $1 at compound interest	2 Accumulation of $1 per period	3 Sinking fund factor	4 Present value of $1	5 Present value of annuity $1 per period	6 Installment to amortize $1
1	1.1000	1.0000	1.0000	0.9091	0.9091	1.1000
2	1.2100	2.1000	0.4762	0.8264	1.7355	0.5762
3	1.3310	3.3100	0.3021	0.7513	2.4869	0.4021
4	1.4641	4.6410	0.2155	0.6830	3.1699	0.3155
5	1.6105	6.1051	0.1638	0.6209	3.7908	0.2638
6	1.7716	7.7156	0.1296	0.5645	4.3553	0.2296
7	1.9487	9.4872	0.1054	0.5132	4.8684	0.2054
8	2.1436	11.4359	0.0874	0.4665	5.3349	0.1874
9	2.3579	13.5795	0.0736	0.4241	5.7590	0.1736
10	2.5937	15.9374	0.0627	0.3855	6.1446	0.1627
11	2.8531	18.5312	0.0540	0.3505	6.4951	0.1540
12	3.1384	21.3843	0.0468	0.3186	6.8137	0.1468
13	3.4523	24.5227	0.0408	0.2897	7.1034	0.1408
14	3.7975	27.9750	0.0357	0.2633	7.3667	0.1357
15	4.1772	31.7725	0.0315	0.2394	7.6061	0.1315
16	4.5950	35.9497	0.0278	0.2176	7.8237	0.1278
17	5.0545	40.5447	0.0247	0.1978	8.0216	0.1247
18	5.5599	45.5992	0.0219	0.1799	8.2014	0.1219
19	6.1159	51.1591	0.0195	0.1635	8.3649	0.1195
20	6.7275	57.2750	0.0175	0.1486	8.5136	0.1175
21	7.4003	64.0025	0.0156	0.1351	8.6487	0.1156
22	8.1403	71.4028	0.0140	0.1228	8.7715	0.1140
23	8.9543	79.5431	0.0126	0.1117	8.8832	0.1126
24	9.8497	88.4974	0.0113	0.1015	8.9847	0.1113
25	10.8347	98.3471	0.0102	0.0923	9.0770	0.1102

Years	1 Value of $1 at compound interest	2 Accumulation of $1 per period	3 Sinking fund factor	4 Present value of $1	5 Present value of annuity $1 per period	6 Installment to amortize $1
26	11.9182	109.1818	0.0092	0.0839	9.1609	0.1092
27	13.1100	121.1000	0.0083	0.0763	9.2372	0.1083
28	14.4210	134.2100	0.0075	0.0693	9.3066	0.1075
29	15.8631	148.6310	0.0067	0.0630	9.3696	0.1067
30	17.4494	164.4942	0.0061	0.0573	9.4269	0.1061
31	19.1944	181.9436	0.0055	0.0521	9.4790	0.1055
32	21.1138	201.1379	0.0050	0.0474	9.5264	0.1050
33	23.2252	222.2517	0.0045	0.0431	0.5694	0.1045
34	25.5477	245.4769	0.0041	0.0391	9.6086	0.1041
35	28.1025	271.0246	0.0037	0.0356	9.6442	0.1037
36	30.9127	299.1271	0.0033	0.0323	9.6765	0.1033
37	34.0040	330.0398	0.0030	0.0294	9.7059	0.1030
38	37.4044	364.0438	0.0027	0.0267	9.7327	0.1027
39	41.1448	401.4482	0.0025	0.0243	9.7570	0.1025
40	45.2593	442.5930	0.0023	0.0221	9.7791	0.1023
41	49.7852	487.8524	0.0020	0.0201	9.7991	0.1020
42	54.7638	537.6376	0.0019	0.0183	9.8174	0.1019
43	60.2401	592.4014	0.0017	0.0166	9.8340	0.1017
44	66.2642	652.6415	0.0015	0.0151	9.8491	0.1015
45	72.8906	718.9056	0.0014	0.0137	9.8628	0.1014
46	80.1796	791.7962	0.0013	0.0125	9.8753	0.1013
47	88.1976	871.9758	0.0011	0.0113	9.8866	0.1011
48	97.0174	960.1736	0.0010	0.0103	9.8969	0.1010
49	106.7191	1057.1909	0.0009	0.0094	9.9063	0.1009
50	117.3910	1163.9100	0.0009	0.0085	9.9148	0.1009

Table D–4   11% annual compound interest

Years	1 Value of $1 at compound interest	2 Accumulation of $1 per period	3 Sinking fund factor	4 Present value of $1	5 Present value of annuity $1 per period	6 Installment to amortize $1
1	1.1100	1.0000	1.0000	0.9009	0.9009	1.1100
2	1.2321	2.1100	0.4739	0.8116	1.7125	0.5839
3	1.3676	3.3421	0.2992	0.7312	2.4437	0.4092
4	1.5181	4.7097	0.2123	0.6587	3.1024	0.3223
5	1.6851	6.2278	0.1606	0.5935	3.6959	0.2706
6	1.8704	7.9129	0.1264	0.5346	4.2305	0.2364
7	2.0762	9.7833	0.1022	0.4817	4.7122	0.2122
8	2.3045	11.8594	0.0843	0.4339	5.1461	0.1943
9	2.5580	14.1640	0.0706	0.3909	5.5370	0.1806
10	2.8394	16.7220	0.0598	0.3522	5.8892	0.1698
11	3.1518	19.5614	0.0511	0.3173	6.2065	0.1611
12	3.4985	22.7132	0.0440	0.2858	6.4924	0.1540
13	3.8833	26.2116	0.0382	0.2575	6.7499	0.1482
14	4.3104	30.0949	0.0332	0.2320	6.9819	0.1432
15	4.7846	34.4054	0.0291	0.2090	7.1909	0.1391
16	5.3109	39.1900	0.0255	0.1883	7.3792	0.1355
17	5.8951	44.5009	0.0225	0.1696	7.5488	0.1325
18	6.5436	50.3960	0.0198	0.1528	7.7016	0.1298
19	7.2633	56.9395	0.0176	0.1377	7.8393	0.1276
20	8.0623	64.2029	0.0156	0.1240	7.9633	0.1256
21	8.9492	72.2652	0.0138	0.1117	8.0751	0.1238
22	9.9336	81.2143	0.0123	0.1007	8.1757	0.1223
23	11.0263	91.1479	0.0110	0.0907	8.2664	0.1210
24	12.2392	102.1742	0.0098	0.0817	8.3481	0.1198
25	13.5855	114.4133	0.0087	0.0736	8.4217	0.1187

Years	1 Value of $1 at compound interest	2 Accumulation of $1 per period	3 Sinking fund factor	4 Present value of $1	5 Present value of annuity $1 per period	6 Installment to amortize $1
26	15.0799	127.9988	0.0078	0.0663	8.4881	0.1178
27	16.7387	143.0787	0.0070	0.0597	8.5478	0.1170
28	18.5799	159.8174	0.0063	0.0538	8.6016	0.1163
29	20.6237	178.3972	0.0056	0.0485	8.6501	0.1156
30	22.8923	199.0209	0.0050	0.0437	8.6938	0.1150
31	25.4105	221.9133	0.0045	0.0394	8.7331	0.1145
32	28.2056	247.3237	0.0040	0.0355	8.7686	0.1140
33	31.3082	275.5294	0.0036	0.0319	8.8005	0.1136
34	34.7521	306.8376	0.0033	0.0288	8.8293	0.1133
35	38.5749	341.5898	0.0029	0.0259	8.8552	0.1129
36	42.8181	380.1646	0.0026	0.0234	8.8786	0.1126
37	47.5281	422.9827	0.0024	0.0210	8.8996	0.1124
38	52.7562	470.5108	0.0021	0.0190	8.9186	0.1121
39	58.5594	523.2670	0.0019	0.0171	8.9357	0.1119
40	65.0009	581.8264	0.0017	0.0154	8.9511	0.1117
41	72.1510	646.8273	0.0015	0.0139	8.9649	0.1115
42	80.0876	718.9783	0.0014	0.0125	8.9774	0.1114
43	88.8972	799.0659	0.0013	0.0112	8.9886	0.1113
44	98.6759	887.9632	0.0011	0.0101	8.9988	0.1111
45	109.5303	986.6392	0.0010	0.0091	9.0079	0.1110
46	121.5786	1096.1694	0.0009	0.0082	9.0161	0.1109
47	134.9523	1217.7482	0.0008	0.0074	9.0235	0.1108
48	149.7970	1352.7004	0.0007	0.0067	9.0302	0.1107
49	166.2747	1502.4974	0.0007	0.0060	9.0362	0.1107
50	184.5649	1668.7722	0.0006	0.0054	9.0417	0.1106

Table D–5 12% annual compound interest

Years	1 Value of $1 at compound interest	2 Accumulation of $1 per period	3 Sinking fund factor	4 Present value of $1	5 Present value of annuity $1 per period	6 Installment to amortize $1
1	1.1200	1.0000	1.0000	0.8929	0.8929	1.1200
2	1.2544	2.1200	0.4717	0.7972	1.6901	0.5917
3	1.4049	3.3744	0.2963	0.7118	2.4018	0.4163
4	1.5735	4.7793	0.2092	0.6355	3.0373	0.3292
5	1.7623	6.3528	0.1574	0.5674	3.6048	0.2774
6	1.9738	8.1152	0.1232	0.5066	4.1114	0.2432
7	2.2107	10.0890	0.0991	0.4523	4.5638	0.2191
8	2.4760	12.2997	0.0813	0.4039	4.9676	0.2013
9	2.7731	14.7757	0.0677	0.3606	5.3282	0.1877
10	3.1058	17.5487	0.0570	0.3220	5.6502	0.1770
11	3.4785	20.6546	0.0484	0.2875	5.9377	0.1684
12	3.8960	24.1331	0.0414	0.2567	6.1944	0.1614
13	4.3635	28.0291	0.0357	0.2292	6.4235	0.1557
14	4.8871	32.3926	0.0309	0.2046	6.6282	0.1509
15	5.4736	37.2797	0.0268	0.1827	6.8109	0.1468
16	6.1304	42.7533	0.0234	0.1631	6.9740	0.1434
17	6.8660	48.8837	0.0205	0.1456	7.1196	0.1405
18	7.6900	55.7497	0.0179	0.1300	7.2497	0.1379
19	8.6128	63.4397	0.0158	0.1161	7.3658	0.1358
20	9.6463	72.0524	0.0139	0.1037	7.4694	0.1339
21	10.8038	81.6987	0.0122	0.0926	7.5620	0.1322
22	12.1003	92.5026	0.0108	0.0826	7.6446	0.1308
23	13.5523	104.6029	0.0096	0.0738	7.7184	0.1296
24	15.1786	118.1552	0.0085	0.0659	7.7843	0.1285
25	17.0001	133.3339	0.0075	0.0588	7.8431	0.1275

Years	1 Value of $1 at compound interest	2 Accumulation of $1 per period	3 Sinking fund factor	4 Present value of $1	5 Present value of annuity $1 per period	6 Installment to amortize $1
26	19.0401	150.3339	0.0067	0.0525	7.8957	0.1267
27	21.3249	169.3740	0.0059	0.0469	7.9426	0.1259
28	23.8839	190.6989	0.0052	0.0419	7.9844	0.1252
29	26.7499	214.5827	0.0047	0.0374	8.0218	0.1247
30	29.9599	241.3327	0.0041	0.0334	8.0552	0.1241
31	33.5551	271.2926	0.0037	0.0298	8.0850	0.1237
32	37.5817	304.8477	0.0033	0.0266	8.1116	0.1233
33	42.0915	342.4294	0.0029	0.0238	8.1354	0.1229
34	47.1425	384.5210	0.0026	0.0212	8.1566	0.1226
35	52.7996	431.6635	0.0023	0.0189	8.1755	0.1223
36	59.1356	484.4631	0.0021	0.0169	8.1924	0.1221
37	66.2318	543.5987	0.0018	0.0151	8.2075	0.1218
38	74.1797	609.8306	0.0016	0.0135	8.2210	0.1216
39	83.0812	684.0102	0.0015	0.0120	8.2330	0.1215
40	93.0510	767.0914	0.0013	0.0107	8.2438	0.1213
41	104.2171	860.1424	0.0012	0.0096	8.2534	0.1212
42	116.7231	964.3594	0.0010	0.0086	8.2619	0.1210
43	130.7299	1081.0825	0.0009	0.0076	8.2696	0.1209
44	146.4175	1211.8125	0.0008	0.0068	8.2764	0.1208
45	163.9876	1358.2300	0.0007	0.0061	8.2825	0.1207
46	183.6661	1522.2177	0.0007	0.0054	8.2880	0.1207
47	205.7060	1705.8837	0.0006	0.0049	8.2928	0.1206
48	230.3908	1911.5897	0.0005	0.0043	8.2972	0.1205
49	258.0377	2141.9805	0.0005	0.0039	8.3010	0.1205
50	289.0022	2400.0183	0.0004	0.0035	8.3045	0.1204

Years	1 Value of $1 at compound interest	2 Accumulation of $1 per period	3 Sinking fund factor	4 Present value of $1	5 Present value of annuity $1 per period	6 Installment to amortize $1
1	1.1300	1.0000	1.0000	0.8850	0.8850	1.1300
2	1.2769	2.1300	0.4695	0.7831	1.6681	0.5995
3	1.4429	3.4069	0.2935	0.6931	2.3612	0.4235
4	1.6305	4.8498	0.2062	0.6133	2.9745	0.3362
5	1.8424	6.4803	0.1543	0.5428	3.5172	0.2843
6	2.0820	8.3227	0.1202	0.4803	3.9975	0.2502
7	2.3526	10.4047	0.0961	0.4251	4.4226	0.2261
8	2.6584	12.7573	0.0784	0.3762	4.7988	0.2084
9	3.0040	15.4157	0.0649	0.3329	5.1317	0.1949
10	3.3946	18.4197	0.0543	0.2946	5.4262	0.1843
11	3.8359	21.8143	0.0458	0.2607	5.6869	0.1758
12	4.3345	25.6502	0.0390	0.2307	5.9176	0.1690
13	4.8980	29.9847	0.0334	0.2042	6.1218	0.1634
14	5.5348	34.8827	0.0287	0.1807	6.3025	0.1587
15	6.2543	40.4175	0.0247	0.1599	6.4624	0.1547
16	7.0673	46.6717	0.0214	0.1415	6.6039	0.1514
17	7.9861	53.7391	0.0186	0.1252	6.7291	0.1486
18	9.0243	61.7251	0.0162	0.1108	6.8399	0.1462
19	10.1974	70.7494	0.0141	0.0981	6.9380	0.1441
20	11.5231	80.9468	0.0124	0.0868	7.0248	0.1424
21	13.0211	92.4699	0.0108	0.0768	7.1016	0.1408
22	14.7138	105.4910	0.0095	0.0680	7.1695	0.1395
23	16.6266	120.2048	0.0083	0.0601	7.2297	0.1383
24	18.7881	136.8314	0.0073	0.0532	7.2829	0.1373
25	21.2305	155.6195	0.0064	0.0471	7.3300	0.1364

Years	1 Value of $1 at compound interest	2 Accumulation of $1 per period	3 Sinking fund factor	4 Present value of $1	5 Present value of annuity $1 per period	6 Installment to amortize $1
26	23.9905	176.8500	0.0057	0.0417	7.3717	0.1357
27	27.1093	200.8406	0.0050	0.0369	7.4086	0.1350
28	30.6335	227.9498	0.0044	0.0326	7.4412	0.1344
29	34.6158	258.5833	0.0039	0.0289	7.4701	0.1339
30	39.1159	293.1991	0.0034	0.0256	7.4957	0.1334
31	44.2010	332.3150	0.0030	0.0226	7.5183	0.1330
32	49.9471	376.5159	0.0027	0.0200	7.5383	0.1327
33	56.4402	426.4630	0.0023	0.0177	7.5560	0.1323
34	63.7774	482.9032	0.0021	0.0157	7.5717	0.1321
35	72.0685	546.6806	0.0018	0.0139	7.5856	0.1318
36	81.4374	618.7491	0.0016	0.0123	7.5979	0.1316
37	92.0242	700.1864	0.0014	0.0109	7.6087	0.1314
38	103.9874	792.2106	0.0013	0.0096	7.6183	0.1313
39	117.5057	896.1981	0.0011	0.0085	7.6268	0.1311
40	132.7815	1013.7039	0.0010	0.0075	7.6344	0.1310
41	150.0431	1146.4852	0.0009	0.0067	7.6410	0.1309
42	169.5487	1296.5283	0.0008	0.0059	7.6469	0.1308
43	191.5900	1466.0770	0.0007	0.0052	7.6522	0.1307
44	216.4967	1657.6669	0.0006	0.0046	7.6568	0.1306
45	244.6413	1874.1637	0.0005	0.0041	7.6609	0.1305
46	276.4446	2118.8047	0.0005	0.0036	7.6645	0.1305
47	312.3824	2395.2498	0.0004	0.0032	7.6677	0.1304
48	352.9922	2707.6321	0.0004	0.0028	7.6705	0.1304
49	398.8811	3060.6243	0.0003	0.0025	7.6730	0.1303
50	450.7356	3459.5049	0.0003	0.0022	7.6752	0.1303

Table D–7   14% annual compound interest

Years	1 Value of $1 at compound interest	2 Accumulation of $1 per period	3 Sinking fund factor	4 Present value of $1	5 Present value of annuity $1 per period	6 Installment to amortize $1
1	1.1400	1.0000	1.0000	0.8772	0.8772	1.1400
2	1.2996	2.1400	0.4673	0.7695	1.6467	0.6073
3	1.4815	3.4396	0.2907	0.6750	2.3216	0.4307
4	1.6890	4.9211	0.2032	0.5921	2.9137	0.3432
5	1.9254	6.6101	0.1513	0.5194	3.4331	0.2913
6	2.1950	8.5355	0.1172	0.4556	3.8887	0.2572
7	2.5023	10.7305	0.0932	0.3996	4.2883	0.2332
8	2.8526	13.2328	0.0756	0.3506	4.6389	0.2156
9	3.2519	16.0853	0.0622	0.3075	4.9464	0.2022
10	3.7072	19.3373	0.0517	0.2697	5.2161	0.1917
11	4.2262	23.0445	0.0434	0.2366	5.4527	0.1834
12	4.8179	27.2708	0.0367	0.2076	5.6603	0.1767
13	5.4924	32.0887	0.0312	0.1821	5.8424	0.1712
14	6.2613	37.5811	0.0266	0.1597	6.0021	0.1666
15	7.1379	43.8424	0.0228	0.1401	6.1422	0.1628
16	8.1372	50.9804	0.0196	0.1229	6.2651	0.1596
17	9.2765	59.1176	0.0169	0.1078	6.3729	0.1569
18	10.5752	68.3941	0.0146	0.0946	6.4674	0.1546
19	12.0557	78.9692	0.0127	0.0829	6.5504	0.1527
20	13.7435	91.0249	0.0110	0.0728	6.6231	0.1510
21	15.6676	104.7684	0.0095	0.0638	6.6870	0.1495
22	17.8610	120.4360	0.0083	0.0560	6.7429	0.1483
23	20.3616	138.2971	0.0072	0.0491	6.7921	0.1472
24	23.2122	158.6586	0.0063	0.0431	6.8351	0.1463
25	26.4619	181.8708	0.0055	0.0378	6.8729	0.1455

Years	1 Value of $1 at compound interest	2 Accumulation of $1 per period	3 Sinking fund factor	4 Present value of $1	5 Present value of annuity $1 per period	6 Installment to amortize $1
26	30.1666	208.3328	0.0048	0.0331	6.9061	0.1448
27	34.3899	238.4994	0.0042	0.0291	6.9352	0.1442
28	39.2045	272.8893	0.0037	0.0255	6.9607	0.1437
29	44.6931	312.0938	0.0032	0.0224	6.9830	0.1432
30	50.9502	356.7869	0.0028	0.0196	7.0027	0.1428
31	58.0832	407.7371	0.0025	0.0172	7.0199	0.1425
32	66.2148	465.8203	0.0021	0.0151	7.0350	0.1421
33	75.4849	532.0350	0.0019	0.0132	7.0482	0.1419
34	86.0528	607.5200	0.0016	0.0116	7.0599	0.1416
35	98.1002	693.5728	0.0014	0.0102	7.0700	0.1414
36	111.8342	791.6730	0.0013	0.0089	7.0790	0.1413
37	127.4910	903.5072	0.0011	0.0078	7.0868	0.1411
38	145.3398	1030.9983	0.0010	0.0069	7.0937	0.1410
39	165.6873	1176.3380	0.0009	0.0060	7.0997	0.1409
40	188.8835	1342.0253	0.0007	0.0053	7.1050	0.1407
41	215.3272	1530.9088	0.0007	0.0046	7.1097	0.1407
42	245.4731	1746.2362	0.0006	0.0041	7.1138	0.1406
43	279.8393	1991.7092	0.0005	0.0036	7.1173	0.1405
44	319.0168	2271.5483	0.0004	0.0031	7.1205	0.1404
45	363.6791	2590.5652	0.0004	0.0027	7.1232	0.1404
46	414.5942	2954.2446	0.0003	0.0024	7.1256	0.1403
47	472.6374	3368.8384	0.0003	0.0021	7.1277	0.1403
48	538.8067	3841.4763	0.0003	0.0019	7.1296	0.1403
49	614.2396	4380.2827	0.0002	0.0016	7.1312	0.1402
50	700.2332	4994.5225	0.0002	0.0014	7.1327	0.1402

Table D–8   15% annual compound interest

Years	1 Value of $1 at compound interest	2 Accumulation of $1 per period	3 Sinking fund factor	4 Present value of $1	5 Present value of annuity $1 per period	6 Installment to amortize $1
1	1.1500	1.0000	1.0000	0.8696	0.8696	1.1500
2	1.3225	2.1500	0.4651	0.7561	1.6257	0.6151
3	1.5209	3.4725	0.2880	0.6575	2.2832	0.4380
4	1.7490	4.9934	0.2003	0.5718	2.8550	0.3503
5	2.0114	6.7424	0.1483	0.4972	3.3522	0.2983
6	2.3131	8.7537	0.1142	0.4323	3.7845	0.2642
7	2.6600	11.0668	0.0904	0.3759	4.1604	0.2404
8	3.0590	13.7268	0.0729	0.3269	4.4873	0.2229
9	3.5179	16.7858	0.0596	0.2843	4.7716	0.2096
10	4.0456	20.3037	0.0493	0.2472	5.0188	0.1993
11	4.6524	24.3493	0.0411	0.2149	5.2337	0.1911
12	5.3503	29.0017	0.0345	0.1869	5.4206	0.1845
13	6.1528	34.3519	0.0291	0.1625	5.5831	0.1791
14	7.0757	40.5047	0.0247	0.1413	5.7245	0.1747
15	8.1371	47.5804	0.0210	0.1229	5.8474	0.1710
16	9.3576	55.7175	0.0179	0.1069	5.9542	0.1679
17	10.7613	65.0751	0.0154	0.0929	6.0472	0.1654
18	12.3755	75.8364	0.0132	0.0808	6.1280	0.1632
19	14.2318	88.2118	0.0113	0.0703	6.1982	0.1613
20	16.3665	102.4436	0.0098	0.0611	6.2593	0.1598
21	18.8215	118.8101	0.0084	0.0531	6.3125	0.1584
22	21.6447	137.6316	0.0073	0.0462	6.3587	0.1573
23	24.8915	159.2764	0.0063	0.0402	6.3988	0.1563
24	28.6252	184.1678	0.0054	0.0349	6.4338	0.1554
25	32.9190	212.7930	0.0047	0.0304	6.4641	0.1547

Years	1 Value of $1 at compound interest	2 Accumulation of $1 per period	3 Sinking fund factor	4 Present value of $1	5 Present value of annuity $1 per period	6 Installment to amortize $1
26	37.8568	245.7120	0.0041	0.0264	6.4906	0.1541
27	43.5353	283.5688	0.0035	0.0230	6.5135	0.1535
28	50.0656	327.1041	0.0031	0.0200	6.5335	0.1531
29	57.5755	377.1696	0.0027	0.0174	6.5509	0.1527
30	66.2118	434.7451	0.0023	0.0151	6.5660	0.1523
31	76.1435	500.9570	0.0020	0.0131	6.5791	0.1520
32	87.5651	577.1005	0.0017	0.0114	6.5905	0.1517
33	100.6998	664.6655	0.0015	0.0099	6.6005	0.1515
34	115.8048	765.3653	0.0013	0.0086	6.6091	0.1513
35	133.1755	881.1701	0.0011	0.0075	6.6166	0.1511
36	153.1519	1014.3456	0.0010	0.0065	6.6231	0.1510
37	176.1246	1167.4974	0.0009	0.0057	6.6288	0.1509
38	202.5433	1343.6222	0.0007	0.0049	6.6338	0.1507
39	232.9248	1546.1655	0.0006	0.0043	6.6380	0.1506
40	267.8636	1779.0903	0.0006	0.0037	6.6418	0.1506
41	308.0431	2046.9536	0.0005	0.0032	6.6450	0.1505
42	354.2496	2354.9971	0.0004	0.0028	6.6478	0.1504
43	407.3870	2709.2466	0.0004	0.0025	6.6503	0.1504
44	468.4951	3116.6335	0.0003	0.0021	6.6524	0.1503
45	538.7692	3585.1279	0.0003	0.0019	6.6543	0.1503
46	619.5847	4123.8979	0.0002	0.0016	6.6559	0.1502
47	712.5224	4743.4824	0.0002	0.0014	6.6573	0.1502
48	819.4008	5456.0049	0.0002	0.0012	6.6585	0.1502
49	942.3109	6275.4053	0.0002	0.0011	6.6596	0.1502
50	1083.6575	7217.7163	0.0001	0.0009	6.6605	0.1501

Table D–9   16% annual compound interest

Years	1 Value of $1 at compound interest	2 Accumulation of $1 per period	3 Sinking fund factor	4 Present value of $1	5 Present value of annuity $1 per period	6 Installment to amortize $1
1	1.1600	1.0000	1.0000	0.8621	0.8621	1.1600
2	1.3456	2.1600	0.4630	0.7432	1.6052	0.6230
3	1.5609	3.5056	0.2853	0.6407	2.2459	0.4453
4	1.8106	5.0665	0.1974	0.5523	2.7982	0.3574
5	2.1003	6.8771	0.1454	0.4761	3.2743	0.3054
6	2.4364	8.9775	0.1114	0.4104	3.6847	0.2714
7	2.8262	11.4139	0.0876	0.3538	4.0386	0.2476
8	3.2784	14.2401	0.0702	0.3050	4.3436	0.2302
9	3.8030	17.5185	0.0571	0.2630	4.6065	0.2171
10	4.4114	21.3215	0.0469	0.2267	4.8332	0.2069
11	5.1173	25.7329	0.0389	0.1954	5.0286	0.1989
12	5.9360	30.8501	0.0324	0.1685	5.1971	0.1924
13	6.8858	36.7862	0.0272	0.1452	5.3423	0.1872
14	7.9875	43.6720	0.0229	0.1252	5.4675	0.1829
15	9.2655	51.6595	0.0194	0.1079	5.5755	0.1794
16	10.7480	60.9250	0.0164	0.0930	5.6685	0.1764
17	12.4677	71.6730	0.0140	0.0802	5.7487	0.1740
18	14.4625	84.1407	0.0119	0.0691	5.8178	0.1719
19	16.7765	98.6032	0.0101	0.0596	5.8775	0.1701
20	19.4607	115.3796	0.0087	0.0514	5.9288	0.1687
21	22.5745	134.8404	0.0074	0.0443	5.9731	0.1674
22	26.1864	157.4148	0.0064	0.0382	6.0113	0.1664
23	30.3762	183.6012	0.0054	0.0329	6.0442	0.1654
24	35.2364	213.9774	0.0047	0.0284	6.0726	0.1647
25	40.8742	249.2138	0.0040	0.0245	6.0971	0.1640

Years	1 Value of $1 at compound interest	2 Accumulation of $1 per period	3 Sinking fund factor	4 Present value of $1	5 Present value of annuity $1 per period	6 Installment to amortize $1
26	47.4141	290.0880	0.0034	0.0211	6.1182	0.1634
27	55.0003	337.5020	0.0030	0.0182	6.1364	0.1630
28	63.8004	392.5023	0.0025	0.0157	6.1520	0.1625
29	74.0084	456.3027	0.0022	0.0135	6.1656	0.1622
30	85.8498	530.3111	0.0019	0.0116	6.1772	0.1619
31	99.5857	616.1608	0.0016	0.0100	6.1872	0.1616
32	115.5194	715.7466	0.0014	0.0087	6.1959	0.1614
33	134.0025	831.2659	0.0012	0.0075	6.2034	0.1612
34	155.4430	965.2686	0.0010	0.0064	6.2098	0.1610
35	180.3138	1120.7114	0.0009	0.0055	6.2153	0.1609
36	209.1640	1301.0251	0.0008	0.0048	6.2201	0.1608
37	242.6303	1510.1892	0.0007	0.0041	6.2242	0.1607
38	281.4511	1752.8193	0.0006	0.0036	6.2278	0.1606
39	326.4832	2034.2704	0.0005	0.0031	6.2309	0.1605
40	378.7206	2360.7534	0.0004	0.0026	6.2335	0.1604
41	439.3158	2739.4739	0.0004	0.0023	6.2358	0.1604
42	509.6063	3178.7896	0.0003	0.0020	6.2377	0.1603
43	591.1433	3688.3958	0.0003	0.0017	6.2394	0.1603
44	685.7262	4279.5391	0.0002	0.0015	6.2409	0.1602
45	795.4424	4965.2656	0.0002	0.0013	6.2421	0.1602
46	922.7131	5760.7070	0.0002	0.0011	6.2432	0.1602
47	1070.3470	6683.4189	0.0001	0.0009	6.2442	0.1601
48	1241.6027	7753.7666	0.0001	0.0008	6.2450	0.1601
49	1440.2590	8995.3691	0.0001	0.0007	6.2457	0.1601
50	1670.7006	10435.6289	0.0001	0.0006	6.2463	0.1601

APPENDIX E
Amortization Tables: Monthly and Annually

Table E–1   Monthly payment to amortize a $1,000 loan

Interest years	8%	9%	10%	11%	12%	13%	14%	15%	16%	17%	18%	19%	20%
1	86.99	87.45	87.92	88.38	88.85	89.32	89.79	90.26	90.73	91.21	91.68	92.16	92.63
2	45.23	45.68	46.14	46.61	47.07	47.54	48.01	48.49	48.96	49.44	49.92	50.41	50.90
3	31.34	31.80	32.27	32.74	33.21	33.69	34.18	34.67	35.16	35.65	36.15	36.66	37.16
4	24.41	24.89	25.36	25.85	26.33	26.83	27.33	27.83	28.34	28.86	29.37	29.90	30.43
5	20.28	20.76	21.25	21.74	22.24	22.75	23.27	23.79	24.32	24.85	25.39	25.94	26.49
6	17.53	18.03	18.53	19.03	19.55	20.07	20.61	21.15	21.69	22.25	22.81	23.38	23.95
7	15.59	16.09	16.60	17.12	17.65	18.19	18.74	19.30	19.86	20.44	21.02	21.61	22.21
8	14.14	14.65	15.17	15.71	16.25	16.81	17.37	17.95	18.53	19.12	19.72	20.33	20.95
9	13.02	13.54	14.08	14.63	15.18	15.75	16.33	16.92	17.53	18.14	18.76	19.39	20.03
10	12.13	12.67	13.22	13.77	14.35	14.93	15.53	16.13	16.75	17.38	18.02	18.67	19.33
11	11.42	11.96	12.52	13.09	13.68	14.28	14.89	15.51	16.14	16.79	17.44	18.11	18.79
12	10.82	11.38	11.95	12.54	13.13	13.75	14.37	15.01	15.66	16.32	16.99	17.67	18.37
13	10.33	10.90	11.48	12.08	12.69	13.31	13.95	14.60	15.27	15.94	16.63	17.33	18.04
14	9.91	10.49	11.08	11.69	12.31	12.95	13.60	14.27	14.95	15.64	16.34	17.05	17.77
15	9.56	10.14	10.75	11.37	12.00	12.65	13.32	14.00	14.69	15.39	16.10	16.83	17.56
16	9.25	9.85	10.46	11.09	11.74	12.40	13.08	13.77	14.47	15.19	15.91	16.65	17.39
17	8.98	9.59	10.21	10.85	11.51	12.19	12.87	13.58	14.29	15.02	15.76	16.50	17.26
18	8.75	9.36	10.00	10.65	11.32	12.00	12.70	13.42	14.14	14.88	15.63	16.38	17.15
19	8.55	9.17	9.81	10.47	11.15	11.85	12.56	13.28	14.02	14.76	15.52	16.29	17.06
20	8.36	9.00	9.65	10.32	11.01	11.72	12.44	13.17	13.91	14.67	15.43	16.21	16.99

Interest years	8%	9%	10%	11%	12%	13%	14%	15%	16%	17%	18%	19%	20%
21	8.20	8.85	9.51	10.19	10.89	11.60	12.33	13.07	13.82	14.59	15.36	16.14	16.93
22	8.06	8.71	9.38	10.07	10.78	11.50	12.24	12.99	13.75	14.52	15.30	16.09	16.88
23	7.93	8.59	9.27	9.97	10.69	11.42	12.16	12.92	13.69	14.46	15.25	16.04	16.84
24	7.82	8.49	9.17	9.88	10.60	11.34	12.10	12.86	13.63	14.42	15.21	16.01	16.81
25	7.72	8.39	9.09	9.80	10.53	11.28	12.04	12.81	13.59	14.38	15.17	15.98	16.78
26	7.63	8.31	9.01	9.73	10.47	11.22	11.99	12.76	13.55	14.34	15.15	15.95	16.76
27	7.54	8.23	8.94	9.67	10.41	11.17	11.95	12.73	13.52	14.32	15.12	15.93	16.75
28	7.47	8.16	8.88	9.61	10.37	11.13	11.91	12.70	13.49	14.29	15.10	15.91	16.73
29	7.40	8.10	8.82	9.57	10.32	11.09	11.88	12.67	13.47	14.27	15.08	15.90	16.72
30	7.34	8.05	8.78	9.52	10.29	11.06	11.85	12.64	13.45	14.26	15.07	15.89	16.71
31	7.28	8.00	8.73	9.48	10.25	11.03	11.82	12.62	13.43	14.24	15.06	15.88	16.70
32	7.23	7.95	8.69	9.45	10.22	11.01	11.80	12.61	13.42	14.23	15.05	15.87	16.70
33	7.18	7.91	8.66	9.42	10.20	10.99	11.79	12.59	13.40	14.22	15.04	15.86	16.69
34	7.14	7.87	8.63	9.39	10.18	10.97	11.77	12.58	13.39	14.21	15.03	15.86	16.69
35	7.10	7.84	8.60	9.37	10.16	10.95	11.76	12.57	13.38	14.21	15.03	15.85	16.68
36	7.07	7.81	8.57	9.35	10.14	10.94	11.74	12.56	13.38	14.20	15.02	15.85	16.68
37	7.03	7.78	8.55	9.33	10.12	10.92	11.73	12.55	13.37	14.19	15.02	15.85	16.68
38	7.01	7.76	8.53	9.31	10.11	10.91	11.73	12.54	13.37	14.19	15.02	15.85	16.68
39	6.98	7.73	8.51	9.30	10.10	10.90	11.72	12.54	13.36	14.19	15.01	15.84	16.67
40	6.95	7.71	8.49	9.28	10.09	10.90	11.71	12.53	13.36	14.18	15.01	15.84	16.67

Table E–2 Annual payment to amortize a $1,000 loan

Interest years	8%	9%	10%	11%	12%	13%	14%	15%	16%	17%	18%	19%	20%
1	1080.00	1090.00	1100.00	1110.00	1120.00	1130.00	1140.00	1150.00	1160.00	1170.00	1180.00	1190.00	1200.00
2	560.77	568.47	576.19	583.93	591.70	599.48	607.29	615.12	622.96	630.83	638.72	646.62	654.55
3	388.03	395.06	402.12	409.21	416.35	423.52	430.73	437.98	445.26	452.57	459.92	467.31	474.73
4	301.92	308.67	315.47	322.33	329.23	336.19	343.20	350.27	357.38	364.53	371.74	378.99	386.29
5	250.46	257.09	263.80	270.57	277.41	284.31	291.28	298.32	305.41	312.56	319.78	327.05	334.38
6	216.32	222.92	229.61	236.38	243.23	250.15	257.16	264.24	271.39	278.61	285.91	293.27	300.71
7	192.07	198.69	205.41	212.22	219.12	226.11	233.19	240.36	247.61	254.95	262.36	269.85	277.42
8	174.01	180.67	187.44	194.32	201.30	208.39	215.57	222.85	230.22	237.69	245.24	252.89	260.61
9	160.08	166.80	173.64	180.60	187.68	194.87	202.17	209.57	217.08	224.69	232.39	240.19	248.08
10	149.03	155.82	162.75	169.80	176.98	184.29	191.71	199.25	206.90	214.66	222.51	230.47	238.52
11	140.08	146.95	153.96	161.12	168.42	175.84	183.39	191.07	198.86	206.76	214.78	222.89	231.10
12	132.70	139.65	146.76	154.03	161.44	168.99	176.67	184.48	192.41	200.47	208.63	216.90	225.26
13	126.52	133.57	140.78	148.15	155.68	163.35	171.16	179.11	187.18	195.38	203.69	212.10	220.62
14	121.30	128.43	135.75	143.23	150.87	158.67	166.61	174.69	182.90	191.23	199.68	208.23	216.89
15	116.83	124.06	131.47	139.07	146.82	154.74	162.81	171.02	179.36	187.82	196.40	205.09	213.88
16	112.98	120.30	127.82	135.52	143.39	151.43	159.62	167.95	176.41	185.00	193.71	202.52	211.44
17	109.63	117.05	124.66	132.47	140.46	148.61	156.92	165.37	173.95	182.66	191.49	200.41	209.44
18	106.70	114.21	121.93	129.84	137.94	146.20	154.62	163.19	171.88	180.71	189.64	198.68	207.81

19	104.13	111.73	119.55	127.56	135.76	144.13	152.66	161.34	170.14	179.07	188.10	197.24	206.46
20	101.85	109.55	117.46	125.58	133.88	142.35	150.99	159.76	168.67	177.69	186.82	196.05	205.36
21	99.83	107.62	115.62	123.84	132.24	140.81	149.54	158.42	167.42	176.53	185.75	195.05	204.44
22	98.03	105.91	114.01	122.31	130.81	139.48	148.30	157.27	166.35	175.55	184.85	194.23	203.69
23	96.42	104.38	112.57	120.97	129.56	138.32	147.23	156.28	165.45	174.72	184.09	193.54	203.07
24	94.98	103.02	111.30	119.79	128.46	137.31	146.30	155.43	164.67	174.02	183.45	192.97	202.55
25	93.68	101.81	110.17	118.74	127.50	136.43	145.50	154.70	164.01	173.42	182.92	192.49	202.12
26	92.51	100.72	109.16	117.81	126.65	135.65	144.80	154.07	163.45	172.92	182.47	192.09	201.76
27	91.45	99.73	108.26	116.99	125.90	134.98	144.19	153.53	162.96	172.49	182.09	191.75	201.47
28	90.49	98.85	107.45	116.26	125.24	134.39	143.66	153.06	162.55	172.12	181.77	191.47	201.22
29	89.62	98.06	106.73	115.61	124.66	133.87	143.20	152.65	162.19	171.81	181.49	191.23	201.02
30	88.83	97.34	106.08	115.02	124.14	133.41	142.80	152.30	161.89	171.54	181.26	191.03	200.85
31	88.11	96.69	105.50	114.51	123.69	133.01	142.45	152.00	161.62	171.32	181.07	190.87	200.70
32	87.45	96.10	104.97	114.04	123.28	132.66	142.15	151.73	161.40	171.13	180.91	190.73	200.59
33	86.85	95.56	104.50	113.63	122.92	132.34	141.88	151.50	161.20	170.96	180.77	190.61	200.49
34	86.30	95.08	104.07	113.26	122.60	132.07	141.65	151.31	161.04	170.82	180.65	190.51	200.41
35	85.80	94.64	103.69	112.93	122.32	131.83	141.44	151.13	160.89	170.70	180.55	190.43	200.34
36	85.34	94.24	103.34	112.63	122.06	131.62	141.26	150.99	160.77	170.60	180.47	190.36	200.28
37	84.92	93.87	103.03	112.36	121.84	131.43	141.11	150.86	160.66	170.51	180.39	190.30	200.24
38	84.54	93.54	102.75	112.13	121.64	131.26	140.97	150.74	160.57	170.44	180.33	190.26	200.20
39	84.19	93.24	102.49	111.91	121.46	131.12	140.85	150.65	160.49	170.37	180.28	190.22	200.16
40	83.86	92.96	102.26	111.72	121.30	130.99	140.75	150.56	160.42	170.32	180.24	190.18	200.14

APPENDIX F
Remaining Mortgage Balance Tables

These tables may be used to determine the percentage of the original loan that remains unpaid as of a given point in time. There may be slight errors due to rounding.

Example:

What is the unpaid balance on an $80,000, thirty-year mortgage at 8 percent interest after five years?

Solution: Find the thirty-year column headed "Original Term in Years." Then follow the "Age of Loan" column down to five years. The number 95.07 is located where the two columns intersect. This represents the percentage loan balance remaining on the loan. This figure is then multiplied by the original loan amount to arrive at the dollar amount of the remaining loan balance. For example,

$$\text{Unpaid balance} = .9507 \times \$80,000 = \$76,056$$

Table F–1 Remaining balance at 8.00% interest amortized monthly

Age of loan	Original term in years						
	10	15	20	25	30	35	40
1	93.19	96.40	97.89	98.69	99.16	99.46	99.64
2	85.82	92.51	95.60	97.27	98.26	98.87	99.26
3	77.84	88.29	93.12	95.74	97.28	98.23	98.84
4	69.20	83.72	90.43	94.07	96.22	97.54	98.39
5	59.84	78.77	87.53	92.27	95.07	96.80	97.90
6	49.70	73.41	84.38	90.32	93.83	95.99	97.36
7	38.72	67.60	80.97	88.21	92.48	95.11	96.79
8	26.83	61.31	77.27	85.92	91.02	94.16	96.17
9	13.95	54.51	73.27	83.45	89.44	93.14	95.49
10	.00	47.13	68.94	80.76	87.72	92.02	94.76
11		39.15	64.25	77.86	85.87	90.82	93.97
12		30.50	59.17	74.71	83.86	89.52	93.11
13		21.13	53.67	71.30	81.69	88.10	92.18
14		10.99	47.71	67.61	79.33	86.57	91.18
15		.00	41.25	63.61	76.78	84.91	90.09
16			34.26	59.29	74.02	83.12	88.91
17			26.69	54.60	71.03	81.18	87.63
18			18.49	49.52	67.79	79.07	86.25
19			9.62	44.02	64.28	76.79	84.75
20			.00	38.06	60.48	74.32	83.13
21				31.61	56.36	71.65	81.37
22				24.63	51.90	68.75	79.47
23				17.07	47.08	65.62	77.41
24				8.87	41.85	62.22	75.17
25				.00	36.19	58.54	72.76
26					30.06	54.56	70.14
27					23.42	50.24	67.31
28					16.22	45.57	64.23
29					8.44	40.51	60.91
30					.00	35.03	57.31
31						29.09	53.41
32						22.67	49.18
33						15.70	44.61
34						8.16	39.66
35						.00	34.29
36							28.48
37							22.19
38							15.37
39							7.99
40							.00

Table F–2 Remaining balance at 8.50% interest amortized monthly

Age of loan	Original term in years						
	10	15	20	25	30	35	40
1	93.37	96.55	98.01	98.79	99.24	99.52	99.69
2	86.15	92.80	95.84	97.47	98.42	99.00	99.35
3	78.29	88.71	93.49	96.04	97.53	98.43	98.99
4	69.74	84.26	90.92	94.48	96.55	97.81	98.59
5	60.43	79.42	88.13	92.79	95.49	97.13	98.16
6	50.30	74.16	85.09	90.94	94.34	96.40	97.68
7	39.28	68.42	81.78	88.93	93.08	95.60	97.17
8	27.28	62.18	78.18	86.74	91.71	94.73	96.61
9	14.22	55.39	74.26	84.36	90.22	93.78	96.00
10	.00	48.00	69.99	81.77	88.60	92.75	95.34
11		39.95	65.35	78.95	86.84	91.63	94.62
12		31.19	60.30	75.88	84.92	90.41	93.84
13		21.66	54.80	72.54	82.83	89.08	92.98
14		11.29	48.81	68.90	80.56	87.64	92.05
15		.00	42.30	64.95	78.08	86.06	91.04
16			35.21	60.64	75.39	84.35	89.94
17			27.49	55.95	72.46	82.48	88.74
18			19.09	50.85	69.27	80.46	87.44
19			9.95	45.29	65.80	78.25	86.02
20			.00	39.25	62.02	75.84	84.48
21				32.67	57.90	73.23	82.79
22				25.51	53.43	70.38	80.96
23				17.71	48.55	67.28	78.97
24				9.23	43.25	63.91	76.80
25				.00	37.48	60.24	74.45
26					31.20	56.24	71.88
27					24.36	51.89	69.08
28					16.92	47.16	66.04
29					8.82	42.01	62.73
30					.00	36.40	59.13
31						30.30	55.21
32						23.66	50.94
33						16.43	46.29
34						8.56	41.24
35						.00	35.73
36							29.74
37							23.22
38							16.13
39							8.41
40							.00

Table F–3   Remaining balance at 9.00% interest amortized monthly

Age of loan	Original term in years						
	10	15	20	25	30	35	40
1	93.54	96.69	98.13	98.88	99.32	99.57	99.73
2	86.47	93.08	96.08	97.66	98.57	99.11	99.44
3	78.73	89.12	93.84	96.33	97.75	98.60	99.12
4	70.28	84.80	91.39	94.87	96.86	98.04	98.77
5	61.02	80.07	88.71	93.27	95.88	97.44	98.39
6	50.90	74.89	85.77	91.53	94.81	96.77	97.97
7	39.84	69.23	82.57	89.62	93.64	96.04	97.51
8	27.73	63.04	79.06	87.53	92.36	95.25	97.01
9	14.49	56.27	75.22	85.24	90.96	94.37	96.46
10	.00	48.86	71.03	82.74	89.43	93.42	95.87
11		40.76	66.44	80.00	87.75	92.38	95.21
12		31.90	61.41	77.01	85.92	91.24	94.49
13		22.20	55.92	73.74	83.92	89.99	93.71
14		11.60	49.91	70.16	81.73	88.63	92.85
15		.00	43.34	66.25	79.33	87.14	91.92
16			36.16	61.97	76.71	85.50	90.89
17			28.29	57.28	73.84	83.72	89.77
18			19.69	52.16	70.70	81.77	88.54
19			10.29	46.56	67.27	79.63	87.20
20			.00	40.43	63.52	77.30	85.73
21				33.72	59.41	74.74	84.13
22				26.39	54.92	71.95	82.37
23				18.37	50.01	68.89	80.45
24				9.60	44.64	65.55	78.35
25				.00	38.76	61.89	76.05
26					32.33	57.89	73.54
27					25.30	53.51	70.79
28					17.61	48.73	67.78
29					9.20	43.49	64.49
30					.00	37.77	60.89
31						31.50	56.96
32						24.65	52.65
33						17.16	47.94
34						8.96	42.79
35						.00	37.16
36							31.00
37							24.26
38							16.88
39							8.82
40							.00

Table F–4   Remaining balance at 9.50% interest amortized monthly

Age of loan	Original term in years						
	10	15	20	25	30	35	40
1	93.70	96.83	98.24	98.97	99.38	99.62	99.77
2	86.78	93.35	96.30	97.84	98.71	99.21	99.52
3	79.17	89.53	94.18	96.60	97.96	98.76	99.24
4	70.81	85.32	91.84	95.23	97.14	98.26	98.93
5	61.61	80.70	89.27	93.73	96.24	97.71	98.59
6	51.51	75.62	86.44	92.08	95.25	97.11	98.22
7	40.40	70.03	83.33	90.27	94.16	96.45	97.82
8	28.18	63.89	79.92	88.27	92.97	95.72	97.37
9	14.76	57.14	76.16	86.08	91.65	94.92	96.88
10	.00	49.72	72.04	83.67	90.21	94.04	96.34
11		41.56	67.50	81.02	88.62	93.07	95.74
12		32.60	62.51	78.11	86.87	92.01	95.09
13		22.74	57.03	74.91	84.95	90.84	94.37
14		11.91	51.01	71.39	82.84	89.56	93.58
15		.00	44.38	67.52	80.52	88.14	92.72
16			37.10	63.27	77.97	86.59	91.76
17			29.10	58.59	75.17	84.89	90.72
18			20.30	53.46	72.09	83.01	89.56
19			10.63	47.81	68.71	80.95	88.30
20			.00	41.60	64.98	78.68	86.90
21				34.78	60.89	76.19	85.37
22				27.28	56.39	73.45	83.69
23				19.03	51.45	70.44	81.84
24				9.96	46.01	67.13	79.81
25				.00	40.04	63.50	77.58
26					33.47	59.50	75.12
27					26.25	55.10	72.42
28					18.31	50.27	69.45
29					9.59	44.96	66.19
30					.00	39.12	62.60
31						32.70	58.66
32						25.65	54.33
33						17.89	49.56
34						9.37	44.33
35						.00	38.57
36							32.24
37							25.29
38							17.64
39							9.24
40							.00

Table F–5   Remaining balance at 10.00% interest amortized monthly

Age of loan	Original term in years						
	10	15	20	25	30	35	40
1	93.87	96.97	98.35	99.05	99.44	99.67	99.80
2	87.09	93.62	96.52	98.01	98.83	99.30	99.58
3	79.60	89.92	94.50	96.85	98.15	98.90	99.34
4	71.33	85.83	92.27	95.57	97.40	98.45	99.07
5	62.20	81.32	89.80	94.16	96.57	97.96	98.78
6	52.10	76.33	87.08	92.61	95.66	97.42	98.45
7	40.96	70.82	84.07	90.88	94.65	96.81	98.09
8	28.64	64.73	80.75	88.98	93.53	96.15	97.69
9	15.03	58.01	77.08	86.88	92.30	95.42	97.25
10	.00	50.58	73.02	84.56	90.94	94.60	96.76
11		42.37	68.55	82.00	89.43	93.71	96.22
12		33.30	63.60	79.17	87.77	92.72	95.63
13		23.29	58.13	76.04	85.93	91.63	94.97
14		12.22	52.09	72.58	83.91	90.42	94.25
15		.00	45.42	68.76	81.66	89.08	93.45
16			38.05	64.54	79.19	87.61	92.56
17			29.91	59.88	76.45	85.98	91.58
18			20.91	54.74	73.43	84.18	90.50
19			10.98	49.05	70.09	82.19	89.31
20			.00	42.77	66.41	80.00	87.99
21				35.83	62.33	77.57	86.54
22				28.16	57.83	74.89	84.93
23				19.69	52.86	71.93	83.15
24				10.34	47.37	68.66	81.19
25				.00	41.30	65.05	79.02
26					34.60	61.06	76.62
27					27.20	56.65	73.98
28					19.02	51.78	71.05
29					9.98	46.40	67.82
30					.00	40.46	64.26
31						33.90	60.31
32						26.64	55.96
33						18.63	51.15
34						9.78	45.84
35						.00	39.97
36							33.48
37							26.32
38							18.40
39							9.66
40							.00

Table F–6   Remaining balance at 10.50% interest amortized monthly

Age of loan	Original term in years						
	10	15	20	25	30	35	40
1	94.03	97.10	98.45	99.13	99.50	99.71	99.83
2	87.39	93.88	96.72	98.16	98.94	99.39	99.64
3	80.03	90.30	94.81	97.09	98.33	99.03	99.43
4	71.85	86.33	92.68	95.90	97.64	98.63	99.19
5	62.78	81.92	90.32	94.57	96.88	98.18	98.94
6	52.70	77.03	87.70	93.10	96.04	97.69	98.65
7	41.52	71.59	84.79	91.47	95.10	97.15	98.33
8	29.10	65.56	81.56	89.66	94.06	96.54	97.97
9	15.31	58.86	77.97	87.65	92.90	95.87	97.58
10	.00	51.43	73.99	85.42	91.62	95.12	97.14
11		43.17	69.57	82.94	90.20	94.29	96.65
12		34.01	64.66	80.19	88.62	93.37	96.11
13		23.84	59.21	77.13	86.86	92.35	95.51
14		12.54	53.16	73.74	84.91	91.22	94.85
15		.00	46.45	69.97	82.75	89.96	94.11
16			38.99	65.79	80.35	88.56	93.29
17			30.72	61.15	77.68	87.01	92.38
18			21.53	56.00	74.72	85.29	91.37
19			11.33	50.28	71.44	83.37	90.25
20			.00	43.93	67.79	81.25	89.00
21				36.88	63.74	78.89	87.62
22				29.05	59.24	76.27	86.08
23				20.36	54.25	73.37	84.38
24				10.71	48.71	70.14	82.49
25				.00	42.56	66.56	80.38
26					35.73	62.58	78.05
27					28.14	58.17	75.46
28					19.72	53.27	72.59
29					10.38	47.83	69.40
30					.00	41.79	65.85
31						35.08	61.92
32						27.63	57.55
33						19.37	52.70
34						10.19	47.32
35						.00	41.34
36							34.71
37							27.34
38							19.16
39							10.08
40							.00

Table F–7 Remaining balance at 11.00% interest amortized monthly

Age of loan	Original term in years						
	10	15	20	25	30	35	40
1	94.18	97.22	98.54	99.20	99.55	99.74	99.85
2	87.69	94.13	96.91	98.31	99.05	99.46	99.69
3	80.45	90.67	95.10	97.31	98.49	99.14	99.51
4	72.37	86.81	93.07	96.20	97.86	98.78	99.30
5	63.36	82.51	90.81	94.95	97.16	98.39	99.08
6	53.30	77.71	88.29	93.57	96.39	97.94	98.82
7	42.08	72.36	85.48	92.03	95.52	97.45	98.54
8	29.56	66.38	82.34	90.30	94.55	96.90	98.22
9	15.59	59.71	78.84	88.38	93.47	96.28	97.87
10	.00	52.28	74.93	86.23	92.26	95.60	97.48
11		43.98	70.57	83.84	90.92	94.83	97.04
12		34.72	65.71	81.17	89.42	93.98	96.55
13		24.39	60.28	78.19	87.74	93.02	96.00
14		12.86	54.23	74.86	85.87	91.96	95.39
15		.00	47.47	71.15	83.79	90.77	94.71
16			39.94	67.01	81.46	89.45	93.95
17			31.53	62.39	78.87	87.97	93.11
18			22.15	57.24	75.97	86.33	92.16
19			11.68	51.49	72.74	84.49	91.11
20			.00	45.08	69.13	82.44	89.93
21				37.92	65.11	80.15	88.62
22				29.94	60.63	77.59	87.16
23				21.03	55.62	74.74	85.53
24				1.09	50.03	71.57	83.71
25				.00	43.80	68.02	81.67
26					36.85	64.06	79.41
27					29.09	59.65	76.88
28					20.43	54.72	74.05
29					10.78	49.23	70.90
30					.00	43.09	67.39
31						36.25	63.47
32						28.62	59.10
33						20.10	54.22
34						10.60	48.77
35						.00	42.70
36							35.92
37							28.35
38							19.92
39							10.50
40							.00

Table F–8 Remaining balance at 11.50% interest amortized monthly

Age of loan	Original term in years						
	10	15	20	25	30	35	40
1	94.34	97.34	98.63	99.26	99.60	99.78	99.87
2	87.99	94.37	97.10	98.44	99.14	99.52	99.73
3	80.86	91.03	95.38	97.51	98.63	99.24	99.57
4	72.88	87.29	93.45	96.48	98.06	98.92	99.40
5	63.93	83.09	91.29	95.32	97.42	98.57	99.20
6	53.89	78.38	88.86	94.01	96.71	98.17	98.98
7	42.64	73.11	86.15	92.55	95.90	97.72	98.73
8	30.02	67.19	83.10	90.91	95.00	97.22	98.44
9	15.87	60.56	79.68	89.07	93.99	96.66	98.13
10	.00	53.12	75.85	87.01	92.86	96.03	97.78
11		44.78	71.55	84.70	91.59	95.32	97.38
12		35.43	66.74	82.11	90.17	94.53	96.94
13		24.94	61.34	79.21	88.57	93.64	96.44
14		13.18	55.28	75.95	86.78	92.65	95.88
15		00	48.49	72.30	84.77	91.53	95.26
16			40.88	68.20	82.52	90.28	94.56
17			32.34	63.61	80.00	88.87	93.77
18			22.77	58.46	77.17	87.30	92.89
19			12.03	52.69	73.99	85.54	91.90
20			.00	46.22	70.44	83.56	90.80
21				38.96	66.45	81.34	89.55
22				30.82	61.97	78.85	88.16
23				21.70	56.96	76.06	86.60
24				11.47	51.33	72.93	84.85
25				.00	45.03	69.43	82.89
26					37.96	65.49	80.69
27					30.03	61.09	78.22
28					21.14	56.14	75.45
29					11.18	50.60	72.35
30					.00	44.38	68.87
31						37.41	64.97
32						29.60	60.60
33						20.84	55.69
34						11.02	50.19
35						.00	44.03
36							37.11
37							29.36
38							20.67
39							10.93
40							.00

Table F–9   Remaining balance at 12.00% interest amortized monthly

Age of loan	Original term in years						
	10	15	20	25	30	35	40
1	94.49	97.46	98.72	99.32	99.64	99.80	99.89
2	88.27	94.60	97.27	98.56	99.23	99.58	99.77
3	81.27	91.38	95.65	97.71	98.77	99.33	99.63
4	73.39	87.75	93.81	96.74	98.25	99.05	99.48
5	64.50	83.65	91.74	95.65	97.66	98.73	99.31
6	54.48	79.04	89.42	94.43	97.00	98.37	99.11
7	43.20	73.84	86.79	93.05	96.26	97.97	98.89
8	30.48	67.99	83.83	91.49	95.42	97.51	98.64
9	16.15	61.39	80.50	89.73	94.48	97.00	98.36
10	.00	53.95	76.75	87.76	93.42	96.42	98.04
11		45.58	72.52	85.53	92.22	95.77	97.69
12		36.13	67.75	83.02	90.87	95.04	97.29
13		25.50	62.37	80.19	89.35	94.21	96.84
14		13.51	56.32	77.00	87.64	93.28	96.33
15		.00	49.50	73.41	85.71	92.23	95.75
16			41.81	69.36	83.53	91.05	95.11
17			33.15	64.80	81.08	89.72	94.38
18			23.39	59.66	78.32	88.22	93.56
19			12.39	53.87	75.20	86.52	92.63
20			.00	47.35	71.69	84.62	91.59
21				40.00	67.74	82.47	90.42
22				31.71	63.29	80.05	89.09
23				22.37	58.27	77.32	87.60
24				11.85	52.61	74.25	85.92
25				.00	46.24	70.78	84.03
26					39.06	66.88	81.90
27					30.97	62.48	79.49
28					21.85	57.53	76.78
29					11.58	51.95	73.73
30					.00	45.65	70.29
31						38.56	66.42
32						30.58	62.05
33						21.57	57.13
34						11.43	51.59
35						.00	45.34
36							38.30
37							30.36
38							21.42
39							11.35
40							.00

Table F-10 Remaining balance at 12.50% interest amortized monthly

Age of loan	Original term in years						
	10	15	20	25	30	35	40
1	94.63	97.57	98.80	99.38	99.67	99.83	99.91
2	88.56	94.83	97.44	98.68	99.31	99.63	99.80
3	81.68	91.72	95.90	97.89	98.89	99.41	99.69
4	73.89	88.19	94.16	96.99	98.42	99.16	99.55
5	65.06	84.20	92.18	95.97	97.88	98.88	99.40
6	55.07	79.68	89.94	94.82	97.28	98.55	99.23
7	43.76	74.57	87.41	93.51	96.59	98.19	99.03
8	30.94	68.77	84.54	92.03	95.81	97.78	98.81
9	16.43	62.21	81.30	90.36	94.93	97.31	98.56
10	.00	54.78	77.62	88.47	93.94	96.78	98.28
11		46.37	73.45	86.32	92.81	96.18	97.96
12		36.84	68.74	83.89	91.53	95.50	97.60
13		26.05	63.40	81.14	90.08	94.74	97.19
14		13.84	57.35	78.02	88.45	93.87	96.73
15		.00	50.50	74.49	86.59	92.88	96.20
16			42.74	70.49	84.49	91.77	95.60
17			33.96	65.97	82.11	90.50	94.93
18			24.02	60.84	79.42	89.07	94.17
19			12.75	55.04	76.37	87.45	93.30
20			.00	48.46	72.91	85.62	92.32
21				41.02	69.00	83.54	91.21
22				32.59	64.57	81.19	89.96
23				23.05	59.55	78.52	88.54
24				12.24	53.87	75.51	86.93
25				.00	47.44	72.09	85.10
26					40.15	68.22	83.04
27					31.90	63.84	80.70
28					22.56	58.88	78.05
29					11.98	53.27	75.05
30					.00	46.90	71.66
31						39.70	67.81
32						31.54	63.46
33						22.31	58.53
34						11.85	52.95
35						.00	46.62
36							39.46
37							31.35
38							22.17
39							11.77
40							.00

Table F–11   Remaining balance at 13.00% interest amortized monthly

Age of loan	Original term in years						
	10	15	20	25	30	35	40
1	94.78	97.68	98.88	99.43	99.71	99.85	99.92
2	88.84	95.04	97.60	98.79	99.38	99.68	99.83
3	82.08	92.04	96.14	98.05	99.00	99.48	99.73
4	74.38	88.63	94.48	97.22	98.57	99.26	99.61
5	65.62	84.74	92.60	96.27	98.08	99.01	99.48
6	55.66	80.31	90.45	95.18	97.53	98.72	99.33
7	44.31	75.28	88.01	93.95	96.89	98.39	99.16
8	31.41	69.55	85.23	92.55	96.17	98.01	98.97
9	16.72	63.03	82.07	90.96	95.35	97.59	98.74
10	.00	55.61	78.47	89.14	94.42	97.11	98.49
11		47.16	74.37	87.07	93.36	96.56	98.20
12		37.55	69.71	84.72	92.15	95.93	97.88
13		26.61	64.40	82.05	90.78	95.22	97.51
14		14.17	58.36	79.00	89.21	94.40	97.08
15		.00	51.49	75.54	87.43	93.48	96.60
16			43.67	71.59	85.40	92.43	96.05
17			34.77	67.10	83.10	91.23	95.43
18			24.64	62.00	80.47	89.87	94.72
19			13.12	56.18	77.49	88.32	93.91
20			.00	49.57	74.09	86.56	93.00
21				42.04	70.22	84.55	91.95
22				33.47	65.82	82.27	90.76
23				23.72	60.81	79.67	89.41
24				12.63	55.11	76.71	87.86
25				.00	48.62	73.35	86.11
26					41.23	69.52	84.11
27					32.83	65.16	81.84
28					23.27	60.20	79.26
29					12.38	54.56	76.32
30					.00	48.13	72.97
31						40.82	69.16
32						32.50	64.82
33						23.04	59.89
34						12.26	54.27
35						.00	47.88
36							40.61
37							32.34
38							22.92
39							12.20
40							.00

Table F–12   Remaining balance at 13.50% interest amortized monthly

Age of loan	Original term in years						
	10	15	20	25	30	35	40
1	94.92	97.79	98.95	99.48	99.74	99.87	99.93
2	89.11	95.26	97.74	98.89	99.44	99.72	99.86
3	82.47	92.36	96.37	98.21	99.10	99.54	99.77
4	74.87	89.05	94.80	97.43	98.71	99.35	99.67
5	66.18	85.26	93.00	96.54	98.26	99.12	99.55
6	56.24	80.93	90.94	95.53	97.75	98.86	99.42
7	44.87	75.98	88.58	94.37	97.17	98.57	99.27
8	31.87	70.31	85.89	93.04	96.50	98.23	99.10
9	17.00	63.83	82.81	91.52	95.74	97.84	98.90
10	.00	56.42	79.29	89.78	94.87	97.40	98.68
11		47.95	75.26	87.79	93.87	96.89	98.42
12		38.26	70.66	85.52	92.73	96.32	98.13
13		27.17	65.39	82.92	91.42	95.66	97.79
14		14.50	59.36	79.95	89.93	94.90	97.40
15		.00	52.47	76.55	88.22	94.03	96.96
16			44.59	72.66	86.27	93.04	96.46
17			35.58	68.21	84.04	91.91	95.89
18			25.27	63.13	81.48	90.62	95.23
19			13.48	57.31	78.56	89.14	94.47
20			.00	50.66	75.22	87.45	93.61
21				43.05	71.40	85.51	92.63
22				34.35	67.03	83.30	91.50
23				24.40	62.03	80.77	90.21
24				13.02	56.32	77.87	88.74
25				.00	49.78	74.56	87.06
26					42.30	70.77	85.13
27					33.75	66.44	82.93
28					23.97	61.49	80.40
29					12.79	55.82	77.52
30					.00	49.34	74.23
31						41.93	70.46
32						33.46	66.14
33						23.76	61.21
34						12.68	55.57
35						.00	49.12
36							41.74
37							33.31
38							23.66
39							12.62
40							.00

Table F–13 Remaining balance at 14.00% interest amortized monthly

Age of loan	Original term in years						
	10	15	20	25	30	35	40
1	95.06	97.89	99.02	99.53	99.77	99.88	99.94
2	89.38	95.46	97.89	98.98	99.50	99.75	99.88
3	82.85	92.67	96.59	98.35	99.19	99.60	99.80
4	75.35	89.46	95.09	97.63	98.84	99.42	99.71
5	66.73	85.77	93.38	96.80	98.43	99.22	99.61
6	56.82	81.53	91.40	95.85	97.96	98.99	99.50
7	45.43	76.66	89.13	94.76	97.43	98.73	99.37
8	32.34	71.06	86.53	93.50	96.81	98.42	99.22
9	17.29	64.63	83.53	92.05	96.10	98.07	99.04
10	.00	57.23	80.09	90.39	95.28	97.67	98.84
11		48.73	76.13	88.48	94.35	97.20	98.61
12		38.97	71.58	86.28	93.27	96.67	98.35
13		27.74	66.36	83.76	92.03	96.06	98.04
14		14.83	60.35	80.86	90.61	95.35	97.69
15		.00	53.44	77.53	88.97	94.54	97.29
16			45.51	73.70	87.09	93.61	96.83
17			36.38	69.30	84.93	92.54	96.30
18			25.90	64.24	82.45	91.32	95.69
19			13.85	58.42	79.59	89.90	94.99
20			.00	51.73	76.31	88.28	94.18
21				44.05	72.54	86.42	93.25
22				35.22	68.21	84.27	92.19
23				25.07	63.23	81.81	90.96
24				13.41	57.50	78.98	89.56
25				.00	50.92	75.72	87.94
26					43.36	71.98	86.08
27					34.67	67.68	83.95
28					24.68	62.74	81.49
29					13.20	57.06	78.67
30					.00	50.53	75.43
31						43.02	71.70
32						34.40	67.42
33						24.49	62.49
34						13.09	56.84
35						.00	50.33
36							42.86
37							34.27
38							24.39
39							13.04
40							.00

Table F–14 Remaining balance at 14.50% interest amortized monthly

Age of loan	Original term in years						
	10	15	20	25	30	35	40
1	95.19	97.98	99.08	99.57	99.79	99.90	99.95
2	89.64	95.65	98.02	99.06	99.55	99.78	99.89
3	83.23	92.96	96.79	98.49	99.27	99.65	99.83
4	75.83	89.86	95.37	97.82	98.95	99.49	99.75
5	67.27	86.27	93.74	97.04	98.58	99.32	99.67
6	57.40	82.12	91.85	96.15	98.15	99.11	99.57
7	45.99	77.33	89.66	95.12	97.66	98.87	99.45
8	32.81	71.80	87.14	93.93	97.09	98.59	99.32
9	17.58	65.41	84.23	92.56	96.43	98.28	99.16
10	.00	58.04	80.87	90.97	95.67	97.91	98.99
11		49.51	76.98	89.13	94.79	97.48	98.78
12		39.67	72.49	87.01	93.77	96.99	98.54
13		28.30	67.31	84.57	92.60	96.42	98.27
14		15.17	61.32	81.74	91.24	95.77	97.95
15		.00	54.40	78.48	89.68	95.01	97.58
16			46.41	74.70	87.87	94.14	97.16
17			37.19	70.35	85.78	93.13	96.67
18			26.53	65.32	83.37	91.97	96.10
19			14.22	59.51	80.58	90.62	95.45
20			.00	52.79	77.36	89.06	94.70
21				45.04	73.65	87.27	93.83
22				36.09	69.35	85.19	92.82
23				25.74	64.39	82.80	91.66
24				13.80	58.66	80.03	90.32
25				.00	52.05	76.83	88.77
26					44.40	73.14	86.98
27					35.58	68.88	84.91
28					25.38	63.95	82.52
29					13.60	58.26	79.76
30					.00	51.69	76.58
31						44.10	72.90
32						35.33	68.65
33						25.21	63.74
34						13.51	58.07
35						.00	51.52
36							43.95
37							35.21
38							25.12
39							13.46
40							.00

Table F–15　　Remaining balance at 15.00% interest amortized monthly

Age of loan	Original term in years						
	10	15	20	25	30	35	40
1	95.33	98.08	99.14	99.60	99.81	99.91	99.96
2	89.90	95.84	98.14	99.14	99.60	99.81	99.91
3	83.61	93.25	96.99	98.61	99.35	99.69	99.85
4	76.30	90.24	95.64	97.99	99.06	99.56	99.79
5	67.82	86.75	94.08	97.27	98.72	99.40	99.71
6	57.97	82.70	92.27	96.43	98.33	99.21	99.63
7	46.54	77.99	90.17	95.46	97.87	99.00	99.53
8	33.27	72.53	87.73	94.34	97.35	98.75	99.41
9	17.87	66.19	84.90	93.03	96.74	98.46	99.27
10	.00	58.83	81.62	91.51	96.02	98.12	99.11
11		50.29	77.80	89.75	95.20	97.74	98.93
12		40.37	73.38	87.71	94.24	97.28	98.71
13		28.87	68.24	85.34	93.13	96.76	98.47
14		15.51	62.27	82.59	91.84	96.15	98.18
15		.00	55.35	79.39	90.34	95.45	97.84
16			47.31	75.68	88.61	94.63	97.46
17			37.99	71.37	86.59	93.67	97.01
18			27.16	66.38	84.25	92.57	96.48
19			14.59	60.57	81.53	91.29	95.88
20			.00	53.84	78.37	89.80	95.17
21				46.02	74.71	88.07	94.36
22				36.95	70.46	86.07	93.41
23				26.42	65.53	83.74	92.30
24				14.19	59.80	81.04	91.03
25				.00	53.15	77.90	89.54
26					45.43	74.26	87.82
27					36.48	70.04	85.82
28					26.08	65.13	83.50
29					14.01	59.44	80.81
30					.00	52.83	77.68
31						45.16	74.05
32						36.26	69.84
33						25.92	64.94
34						13.92	59.27
35						.00	52.68
36							45.03
37							36.15
38							25.85
39							13.88
40							.00

Table F–16   Remaining balance at 15.50% interest amortized monthly

Age of loan	Original term in years						
	10	15	20	25	30	35	40
1	95.46	98.17	99.20	99.64	99.83	99.92	99.96
2	90.16	96.03	98.26	99.22	99.64	99.83	99.92
3	83.98	93.53	97.17	98.72	99.42	99.73	99.88
4	76.76	90.62	95.90	98.15	99.15	99.61	99.82
5	68.35	87.22	94.41	97.48	98.85	99.47	99.75
6	58.54	83.26	92.68	96.70	98.49	99.30	99.68
7	47.09	78.64	90.66	95.78	98.07	99.11	99.59
8	33.74	73.24	88.30	94.72	97.58	98.89	99.49
9	18.17	66.95	85.55	93.48	97.02	98.63	99.37
10	.00	59.62	82.35	92.03	96.35	98.32	99.22
11		51.06	78.61	90.34	95.58	97.96	99.06
12		41.08	74.24	88.37	94.68	97.55	98.87
13		29.43	69.15	86.08	93.63	97.07	98.64
14		15.85	63.21	83.40	92.40	96.50	98.38
15		.00	56.29	80.27	90.97	95.84	98.08
16			48.21	76.62	89.30	95.07	97.72
17			38.78	72.37	87.36	94.18	97.31
18			27.79	67.41	85.08	93.13	96.83
19			14.96	61.62	82.44	91.91	96.26
20			.00	54.87	79.34	90.49	95.61
21				46.99	75.74	88.83	94.84
22				37.80	71.54	86.89	93.95
23				27.09	66.63	84.63	92.90
24				14.58	60.91	82.00	91.69
25				.00	54.23	78.92	90.27
26					46.45	75.34	88.61
27					37.37	71.16	86.68
28					26.77	66.28	84.42
29					14.42	60.59	81.80
30					.00	53.95	78.73
31						46.20	75.15
32						37.17	70.98
33						26.63	66.11
34						14.34	60.44
35						.00	53.81
36							46.09
37							37.08
38							26.57
39							14.30
40							.00

Table F–17   Remaining balance at 16.00% interest amortized monthly

Age of loan	Original term in years						
	10	15	20	25	30	35	40
1	95.58	98.25	99.25	99.67	99.85	99.93	99.97
2	90.41	96.20	98.37	99.28	99.68	99.86	99.94
3	84.34	93.80	97.35	98.83	99.48	99.76	99.89
4	77.22	90.98	96.14	98.30	99.24	99.66	99.85
5	68.88	87.68	94.73	97.67	98.96	99.53	99.79
6	59.11	83.80	93.07	96.94	98.63	99.39	99.72
7	47.65	79.27	91.13	96.09	98.25	99.21	99.65
8	34.21	73.95	88.85	95.08	97.80	99.01	99.55
9	18.46	67.71	86.18	93.90	97.27	98.77	99.45
10	.00	60.40	83.05	92.52	96.66	98.50	99.32
11		51.82	79.39	90.91	95.93	98.17	99.18
12		41.78	75.09	89.01	95.09	97.79	99.00
13		30.00	70.05	86.78	94.09	97.34	98.80
14		16.19	64.14	84.18	92.93	96.82	98.57
15		.00	57.21	81.12	91.56	96.21	98.29
16			49.09	77.54	89.96	95.49	97.97
17			39.57	73.34	88.08	94.64	97.58
18			28.41	68.42	85.88	93.65	97.14
19			15.33	62.65	83.30	92.49	96.62
20			.00	55.88	80.28	91.13	96.00
21				47.95	76.73	89.54	95.28
22				38.65	72.58	87.67	94.44
23				27.75	67.70	85.48	93.46
24				14.98	61.99	82.91	92.30
25				.00	55.30	79.90	90.94
26					47.45	76.37	89.35
27					38.25	72.24	87.49
28					27.46	67.39	85.30
29					14.82	61.70	82.74
30					.00	55.04	79.73
31						47.23	76.21
32						38.07	72.09
33						27.34	67.25
34						14.75	61.57
35						.00	54.92
36							47.13
37							37.99
38							27.28
39							14.72
40							.00

Table F–18 Remaining balance at 16.50% interest amortized monthly

Age of loan	Original term in years						
	10	15	20	25	30	35	40
1	95.71	98.33	99.30	99.70	99.87	99.94	99.97
2	90.65	96.37	98.48	99.34	99.71	99.87	99.94
3	84.69	94.06	97.51	98.93	99.53	99.79	99.91
4	77.68	91.33	96.37	98.43	99.32	99.70	99.87
5	69.41	88.12	95.03	97.85	99.06	99.59	99.82
6	59.67	84.34	93.44	97.17	98.77	99.46	99.76
7	48.20	79.88	91.58	96.37	98.41	99.30	99.69
8	34.68	74.63	89.38	95.42	98.00	99.12	99.61
9	18.76	68.45	86.79	94.30	97.51	98.91	99.52
10	.00	61.17	83.74	92.99	96.94	98.66	99.41
11		52.58	80.14	91.44	96.26	98.36	99.28
12		42.47	75.91	89.61	95.46	98.01	99.12
13		30.56	70.92	87.46	94.53	97.60	98.94
14		16.53	65.04	84.93	93.42	97.11	98.73
15		.00	58.12	81.94	92.12	96.54	98.48
16			49.97	78.42	90.58	95.87	98.18
17			40.36	74.28	88.77	95.07	97.83
18			29.04	69.40	86.64	94.14	97.42
19			15.71	63.65	84.13	93.03	96.94
20			.00	56.88	81.17	91.74	96.37
21				48.90	77.69	90.21	95.69
22				39.49	73.58	88.41	94.90
23				28.42	68.75	86.28	93.97
24				15.37	63.05	83.78	92.87
25				.00	56.34	80.84	91.57
26					48.44	77.37	90.04
27					39.12	73.28	88.25
28					28.15	68.47	86.13
29					15.23	62.79	83.63
30					.00	56.11	80.69
31						48.24	77.23
32						38.96	73.15
33						28.04	68.34
34						15.16	62.68
35						.00	56.01
36							48.15
37							38.89
38							27.99
39							15.14
40							.00

Table F–19 Remaining balance at 17.00% interest amortized monthly

Age of loan	Original term in years						
	10	15	20	25	30	35	40
1	95.83	98.41	99.35	99.73	99.88	99.95	99.98
2	90.89	96.53	98.58	99.40	99.74	99.89	99.95
3	85.05	94.31	97.67	99.02	99.58	99.82	99.92
4	78.12	91.67	96.59	98.56	99.39	99.74	99.89
5	69.93	88.55	95.31	98.02	99.16	99.64	99.84
6	60.23	84.86	93.79	97.38	98.88	99.52	99.79
7	48.75	80.49	92.00	96.63	98.56	99.38	99.74
8	35.15	75.31	89.88	95.74	98.18	99.22	99.67
9	19.06	69.18	87.37	94.68	97.73	99.03	99.58
10	.00	61.93	84.40	93.42	97.20	98.80	99.48
11		53.34	80.88	91.94	96.56	98.53	99.37
12		43.17	76.71	90.18	95.81	98.21	99.23
13		31.13	71.78	88.10	94.93	97.83	99.07
14		16.87	65.93	85.64	93.88	97.38	98.87
15		.00	59.02	82.73	92.64	96.85	98.65
16			50.83	79.28	91.17	96.21	98.38
17			41.14	75.19	89.42	95.47	98.05
18			29.67	70.36	87.36	94.59	97.68
19			16.08	64.63	84.92	93.54	97.23
20			.00	57.85	82.03	92.30	96.70
21				49.83	78.61	90.84	96.07
22				40.33	74.56	89.10	95.32
23				29.08	69.76	87.05	94.44
24				15.76	64.09	84.61	93.39
25				.00	57.37	81.73	92.16
26					49.41	78.33	90.69
27					39.99	74.29	88.96
28					28.84	69.51	86.91
29					15.63	63.85	84.48
30					.00	57.16	81.61
31						49.23	78.20
32						39.84	74.17
33						28.73	69.40
34						15.58	63.76
35						.00	57.07
36							49.15
37							39.78
38							28.69
39							15.55
40							.00

Table F–20   Remaining balance at 17.50% interest amortized monthly

Age of loan	Original term in years						
	10	15	20	25	30	35	40
1	95.95	98.49	99.39	99.75	99.90	99.96	99.98
2	91.13	96.69	98.67	99.45	99.77	99.90	99.96
3	85.39	94.55	97.81	99.10	99.63	99.84	99.93
4	78.57	92.00	96.79	98.68	99.45	99.77	99.90
5	70.45	88.97	95.58	98.18	99.24	99.68	99.87
6	60.79	85.36	94.13	97.58	98.99	99.58	99.82
7	49.29	81.08	92.41	96.87	98.70	99.46	99.77
8	35.62	75.97	90.37	96.03	98.35	99.31	99.71
9	19.35	69.90	87.93	95.03	97.93	99.13	99.64
10	.00	62.68	85.04	93.84	97.43	98.93	99.55
11		54.08	81.59	92.42	96.84	98.68	99.45
12		43.86	77.49	90.73	96.14	98.39	99.32
13		31.69	72.61	88.72	95.30	98.04	99.18
14		17.22	66.81	86.33	94.31	97.62	99.00
15		.00	59.90	83.49	93.12	97.13	98.80
16			51.69	80.10	91.72	96.54	98.55
17			41.92	76.08	90.04	95.84	98.26
18			30.29	71.29	88.05	95.00	97.91
19			16.46	65.59	85.68	94.01	97.49
20			.00	58.81	82.85	92.83	97.00
21				50.75	79.50	91.43	96.41
22				41.15	75.50	89.76	95.71
23				29.74	70.75	87.77	94.88
24				16.16	65.09	85.40	93.88
25				.00	58.37	82.59	92.71
26					50.36	79.24	91.30
27					40.84	75.26	89.64
28					29.51	70.52	87.65
29					16.04	64.89	85.29
30					.00	58.18	82.48
31						50.20	79.14
32						40.71	75.16
33						29.42	70.43
34						15.98	64.80
35						.00	58.11
36							50.14
37							40.66
38							29.38
39							15.96
40							.00

APPENDIX G
FHA Schedule
of Closing Costs

Table G–1   FHA schedule of closing costs (Dallas, TX)

Sales price of property	Total closing costs	Sales price of property	Total closing costs
$10,000	$700	$35,000	$ 950
$11,000	$700	$36,000	$ 950
$12,000	$700	$37,000	$ 950
$13,000	$750	$38,000	$ 950
$14,000	$750	$39,000	$1000
$15,000	$750	$40,000	$1000
$16,000	$750	$41,000	$1000
$17,000	$750	$42,000	$1000
$18,000	$800	$43,000	$1000
$19,000	$800	$44,000	$1050
$20,000	$800	$45,000	$1050
$21,000	$800	$46,000	$1050
$22,000	$800	$47,000	$1050
$23,000	$50	$48,000	$1050
$24,000	$850	$49,000	$1050
$25,000	$850	$50,000	$1100
$26,000	$850	$51,000	$1100
$27,000	$850	$52,000	$1100
$28,000	$900	$53,000	$1100
$29,000	$900	$54,000	$1150
$30,000	$900	$55,000	$1150
$31,000	$900	$56,000	$1150
$32,000	$900	$57,000	$1150
$33,000	$900	$58,000	$1150
$34,000	$950	$59,000	$1200

Table G–1 (continued)

Sales price of property	Total closing costs	Sales price of property	Total closing costs
$60,000	$1200	$ 85,000	$1400
$61,000	$1200	$ 86,000	$1400
$62,000	$1200	$ 87,000	$1450
$63,000	$1200	$ 88,000	$1450
$64,000	$1250	$ 89,000	$1450
$65,000	$1250	$ 90,000	$1450
$66,000	$1250	$ 91,000	$1450
$67,000	$1250	$ 92,000	$1500
$68,000	$1250	$ 93,000	$1500
$69,000	$1250	$ 94,000	$1500
$70,000	$1250	$ 95,000	$1500
$71,000	$1300	$ 96,000	$1500
$72,000	$1300	$ 97,000	$1550
$73,000	$1300	$ 98,000	$1550
$74,000	$1300	$ 99,000	$1550
$75,000	$1300	$100,000	$1550
$76,000	$1350	$101,000	$1550
$77,000	$1350	$102,000	$1600
$78,000	$1350	$103,000	$1600
$79,000	$1350	$104,000	$1600
$80,000	$1350	$105,000	$1600
$81,000	$1400	$106,000	$1600
$82,000	$1400	$107,000	$1600
$83,000	$1400	$108,000	$1650
$84,000	$1400	$109,000	$1650

Sales price of property	Total closing costs	Sales price of property	Total closing costs
$110,000	$1650	$136,000	$1900
$111,000	$1650	$137,000	$1900
$112,000	$1650	$138,000	$1900
$113,000	$1700	$139,000	$1950
$114,000	$1700	$140,000	$1950
$115,000	$1700	$141,000	$1950
$116,000	$1700	$142,000	$1950
$117,000	$1700	$143,000	$1950
$118,000	$1750	$144,000	$2000
$119,000	$1750	$145,000	$2000
$120,000	$1750	$146,000	$2000
$121,000	$1750	$147,000	$2000
$122,000	$1750	$148,000	$2000
$123,000	$1800	$149,000	$2000
$124,000	$1800	$150,000	$2050
$125,000	$1800	$151,000	$2050
$126,000	$1800	$152,000	$2050
$127,000	$1800	$153,000	$2050
$128,000	$1800	$154,000	$2050
$129,000	$1850	$155,000	$2100
$130,000	$1850	$156,000	$2100
$131,000	$1850	$157,000	$2100
$132,000	$1850	$158,000	$2100
$133,000	$1850	$159,000	$2100
$134,000	$1900	$160,000	$2150
$135,000	$1900		

APPENDIX H
Professional, Trade, and Other Real Estate Associations

American Chapter, International Real Estate Federation (AC/IREF)
777 14th St. NW
Washington, DC 20005
202-383-1032

American Conference of Real Estate Investment Trusts
608 13th St. NW
Washington, DC 20005
202-347-9464

American Institute of Real Estate Appraisers (AIREA)
430 N. Michigan
Chicago, IL 60611
312-329-8559
This group, also known as the Appraisal Institute, formulates and enforces standards of professional conduct for its members, promotes research, and publishes materials related to appraisal of real property. The institute confers the MAI (Member, Appraisal Institute) designation upon persons who meet requirements for experience, education, and examinations. It also awards the RM (Residential Member) to those who specialize in the appraisal of single-family homes and apartments of up to four units. With ASREC, it sponsors the Annual Congress of Real Estate Appraisers, Valuers, and Counselors. AIREA publishes *The Appraisal Journal and Appraiser.*

American Land Title Association (ALTA)
1828 L St. NW Suite 705
Washington, DC 20036
209-296-3671
Abstracters, title insurance companies, title insurance agents, and attorneys belong to this organization. It provides information and services to legislators, regulators, users of title services, its members, and the public.

American Real Estate and Urban Economics Association (AREUEA)
School of Business
Indiana University
Bloomington, IN 47405
812-335-3297

American Society of Home Inspectors
3299 K St. NW 7th Fl.
Washington, DC 20007
202-842-3096
A nonprofit organization of professional home inspectors. The society's Standards of Practice has been developed to cover the basic elements of a home inspection.

American Society of Real Estate Counselors (ASREC)
430 N. Michigan Ave.
Chicago, IL 60611
312-329-8427
The American Society of Real Estate Counselors (ASREC) is an affiliate of the NATIONAL ASSOCIATION OF REALTORS®. The organization was formed in 1953 to meet a growing need for competent, independent real estate advice and guidance from qualified experts whose services are offered to the public on a fee basis. Members subscribe to a rigidly enforced Code of Ethics and Standards of Professional Practice and are qualified to use the designation CRE (Counselor of Real Estate).

Institute of Real Estate Management (IREM)
430 N. Michigan Ave.
Chicago, IL 60611
312-661-1930

This group was organized to recognize persons who have demonstrated qualifications in real property management. The CPM (Certified Property Manager) designation is awarded to persons with experience, courses, and qualifications in property management. The institute also awards the AMO (Accredited Management Organization) to firms that specialize in property management, provided the firm is under the responsibility of a CPM and has all employees bonded.

National Association of Home Builders of the United States (NAHB)
15th and M Sts. NW
Washington, DC 20005
202-822-0200
The association is concerned with adequate housing in the United States, improvement of home building materials and techniques, and holding to high professional standards and ethics. It was formerly associated with NAREB as the Home Builders Institute.

National Association of Real Estate Appraisers (NAREA)
8383 East Evans Rd.
Scottsdale, AZ 85260–3614

National Association of Real Estate Brokers
P.O. Box 56483
Washington, DC 20041
202-289-6655

National Association of Real Estate Investment Trusts (NAREIT)
1129 20th St. NW
Washington, DC 20036
202-785-8717
The national trade association for the real estate investment trust (REIT) industry, holding $10 billion in assets. With membership of publicly held real estate investment trusts, corporations, and former REITs and Associate Members, the association is the primary industry voice on matters involving its members in both governmental and public affairs. Established in 1960, the association is the only source of industry-wide statistics and analysis based on historical, current-market, and quarterly-report data from all REITs, and it functions as the central source and clearinghouse for its members.

National Association of Real Estate License Law Officials (NARELLO)
P.O. Box 129
Centreville, UT 84104
801-531-8202

Membership includes officials involved with the administration and enforcement of real estate sales and brokerage license laws in the various states. The objective of the organization is to raise standards of competency and provide uniformity in licensing for the protection of the public and the betterment of the real estate profession.

NATIONAL ASSOCIATION OF REALTORS® (NAR)
430 N. Michigan Ave.
Chicago, IL 60611
312-329-8200
(See Appendix I.)

National Association of Review Appraisers and Mortgage Underwriters
8715 Via De Commancio
Scottsdale, AZ 85258
602-998-3000
Members include appraisers, review appraisers, and others with responsibilities relating to the appraisal review process. The association provides seminars and awards designations to members. Objectives include the establishment of standard procedures and ethical guidelines.

Real Estate Educators Association
230 N. Michigan Ave., Suite 1200
Chicago, IL 60601
312-372-9800
Members of the association can be involved in any aspect of real estate education. The organization promotes educational and professional standards of competence and performance.

REALTORS® Land Institute
430 N. Michigan Ave.
Chicago, IL 60611
312-329-8440
This is composed of REALTORS® who specialize in land, including agricultural and urban land, subdivision and shopping center development, and recreational facilities. The institute awards the AFLM (Accredited Farm and Land Member) designation to those with advanced education, experience, and professional service contributions.

REALTORS® National Marketing Institute
430 N. Michigan Ave.
Chicago, IL 60611
312-670-3780
This institute serves specialists in commercial investment brokerage, residential sales, and real estate office administration. It awards the designation CRB (Certified Real Estate Brokerage Manager), the CRS (Certified Residential

Specialist), and the CCIM (Certified Commercial Investment Member).

Society of Industrial and Office REALTORS® (SIOR)
777 14th St. NW, Suite 400
Washington, DC 20005
202-383-1150
Real estate brokers who are involved in industrial property transactions or public utilities or who work in financial institutions belong to this organization. The SIOR designations of Salesman Affiliate or Firm Affiliate are granted to qualified members.

Society of Real Estate Appraisers (SREA)
225 N. Michigan Ave., Suite 724
Chicago, IL 60601
312-819-2400
The society provides courses and conferences related to real property appraisal. Prior to 1963, the name was Society of Residential Appraisers. The award SREA (Senior Real Estate Appraiser) is given to those completing specified requirements.

Urban Land Institute (ULI)
1090 Vermont Ave., NW
Washington, DC 20005
202-289-8500

The membership is comprised of individuals, firms, corporations, and associations to promote better planning and development of urban areas. The institute performs studies and prepares reports on trends that affect the development and use of land. ULI is an independent, nonprofit, research and educational organization incorporated in 1936 to improve the quality and standards of land use and development. The institute conducts practical research in various fields of real estate knowledge; identifies and interprets land use trends in relation to changing economic, social and civic needs; and disseminates pertinent information leading to orderly and more efficient use and development of land.

Women's Council of REALTORS® (WCR)
430 N. Michigan Ave.
Chicago, IL 60611
312-329-8483
This group was formed in 1939 to provide guidance to women in the real estate field. It offers specialized programs, training, and publications, including *The Communique,* the official magazine of WCR, and the *Referral Roster,* a listing of members by locale.

APPENDIX I
NATIONAL ASSOCIATION OF REALTORS® and Its Code of Ethics

The National Association of Real Estate Boards (NAREB) was organized in 1908. It changed its name to the NATIONAL ASSOCIATION OF REALTORS® (NAR) in 1974. It acts as a parent organization for local real estate groups. Members of local real estate boards who are affiliated with the national organization are called REALTORS®. Thus, the word REALTOR® is a registered trade name and is not correctly used to identify any real estate broker unless a member of the NATIONAL ASSOCIATION OF REALTORS®.

To promote ethical practices, the NATIONAL ASSOCIATION OF REALTORS® developed and adopted a code of ethics in 1913. All members of the NATIONAL ASSOCIATION OF REALTORS® and local affiliated boards subscribe to this code. The code has been significant in elevating the real estate business to a position of public respect. It also provides a helpful guide to all engaged in the real estate business. The code is broken down into articles dealing with relations to the public, relations to the client, and relations to the fellow REALTOR®. It has frequently been amended to reflect necessary changes in the business as it relates to society.

The professional organization functions at three levels—national, state, and local. Real estate brokers who belong to the local board also belong to the state and national organizations.

Policy Objectives

The NATIONAL ASSOCIATION OF REALTORS® lists the following policy objectives.

1. To encourage rehabilitation and construction with emphasis on private housing, through the use of tax incentives, subsidies for low-income families, code enforcement, and expanded mortgage financing.
2. To discourage restrictive practices that increase costs of construction and inhibit employment.

Note: Where the word REALTOR® is used in this Code and Preamble, it shall be deemed to include REALTOR-ASSOCIATE®. Pronouns shall be considered to include REALTORS® and REALTOR-ASSOCIATES® of both genders.

3. To exempt government-backed loans from state usury laws.
4. To allow accelerated depreciation and capital gains credits.
5. To replace public housing with interest-subsidized home ownership for low-income families.
6. To eliminate slums.
7. To encourage mass transportation systems.
8. To limit property taxes to reasonable rates.
9. To promote free-market and free-enterprise farms.
10. To discourage banking industry expansion into real estate operations.

The *GRI* (Graduate Realtors Institute) designation is awarded to persons who have completed a specified GRI course study in aspects of real estate such as appraisal, law, finance, property management, or related topics.

Membership Categories

Full membership in the NATIONAL ASSOCIATION OF REALTORS® is open to licensed real estate brokers, whereas others can obtain membership in other categories.

1. *Active Members* are licensed real estate brokers actively engaged in the real estate business in the territory covered by the local board. They often control activities of their associates or employees and are called *REALTORS®*.
2. *Associate Members* are licensed real estate salespeople holding either a broker's or a salesperson's license and are associated with a REALTOR®.
3. *Affiliate Members* are individuals in the community or members of local firms interested in the affairs of the local board. They do not vote or hold office on the board.
4. *Honorary Members* are retired former active members who meet local eligibility requirements.

Special Institutes

The main function of the NATIONAL ASSOCIATION OF REALTORS® is to raise professional standards. The association sponsors special institutes to disseminate published information and promote professional education. These special institutes and their member designations are listed in Appendix H.

Code of Ethics*

Preamble . . .

Under all is the land. Upon its wise utilization and widely allocated ownership depend the survival and growth of free institutions and of our civilization. The REAL-

---

*The code was adopted in 1913 and was amended or revised in 1924, 1928, 1950, 1951, 1952, 1956, 1961, 1962, 1974, 1982, 1986, and 1987.

Published with the consent of the NATIONAL ASSOCIATION OF REALTORS®, author of and owner of all rights in the Code of Ethics of the NATIONAL ASSOCIATION OF REALTORS®, © NATIONAL ASSOCIATION OF REALTORS®—All Rights Reserved.

The NATIONAL ASSOCIATION OF REALTORS® reserves exclusively unto itself the right to comment on and interpret the CODE and particular provisions thereof. For the NATIONAL ASSOCIATION's official interpretations of the CODE, see INTERPRETATIONS OF THE CODE OF ETHICS; NATIONAL ASSOCIATION OF REALTORS®.

TOR® should recognize that the interests of the nation and its citizens require the highest and best use of the land and the widest distribution of land ownership. They require the creation of adequate housing, the building of functioning cities, the development of productive industries and farms, and the preservation of a healthful environment.

Such interests impose obligations beyond those of ordinary commerce. They impose grave social responsibility and a patriotic duty to which the REALTOR® should dedicate himself, and for which he should be diligent in preparing himself. The REALTOR®, therefore, is zealous to maintain and improve the standards of his calling and shares with his fellow REALTORS® a common responsibility for its integrity and honor. The term REALTOR® has come to connote competency, fairness, and high integrity resulting from adherence to a lofty ideal of moral conduct in business relations. No inducement of profit and no instruction from clients ever can justify departure from this ideal.

In the interpretation of his obligation, a REALTOR® can take no safer guide than that which has been handed down through the centuries, embodied in the Golden Rule, "Whatsoever ye would that men should do to you, do ye even so to them."

Accepting this standard as his own, every REALTOR® pledges himself to observe its spirit in all of his activities and to conduct his business in accordance with the tenets set forth below.

Article 1
The REALTOR® should keep himself informed on matters affecting real estate in his community, the state, and nation so that he may be able to contribute responsibly to public thinking on such matters.

Article 2
In justice to those who place their interests in his care, the REALTOR® should endeavor always to be informed regarding laws, proposed legislation, governmental regulations, public policies and current market conditions in order to be in a position to advise his clients properly.

Article 3
The REALTOR® should endeavor to eliminate in his community any practices which could be damaging to the public or bring discredit to the real estate profession. The REALTOR® should assist the government agency charged with regulating the practices of brokers and salesmen in his state.

Article 4
To prevent dissension and misunderstanding and to assure better service to the owner, the REALTOR® should urge the exclusive listing of property unless contrary to the best interest of the owner.

Article 5
In the best interests of society, of his associates, and his own business, the REALTOR® should willingly share with other REALTORS® the lessons of his experience and study for the benefit of the public, and should be loyal to the Board of REALTORS® of his community and active in its work.

Article 6

The REALTOR® should seek no unfair advantage over other REALTORS® and should conduct his business so as to avoid controversies with other REALTORS®.

Article 7

In accepting employment as an agent, the REALTOR® pledges himself to protect and promote the interests of the client. This obligation of absolute fidelity to the client's interest is primary, but it does not relieve the REALTOR® of the obligation to treat fairly all parties to the transaction.

Article 8

The REALTOR® shall not accept compensation from more than one party, even if permitted by law, without full knowledge of all parties to the transaction.

Article 9

The REALTOR® shall avoid exaggeration, misrepresentation, or concealment of pertinent facts. He has an affirmative obligation to discover adverse factors that a reasonably competent and diligent investigation would disclose.

Article 10

The REALTOR® shall not deny equal professional services to any person for reasons of race, creed, sex, or country of national origin. The REALTOR® shall not be a party to any plan or agreement to discriminate against a person or persons on the basis of race, creed, sex, or country of national origin.

Article 11

A REALTOR® is expected to provide a level of competent service in keeping with the Standards of Practice in those fields in which the REALTOR® customarily engages.

The REALTOR® shall not undertake to provide specialized professional services concerning a type of property or service that is outside his field of competence unless he engages the assistance of one who is competent on such types of property or service, or unless the facts are fully disclosed to the client. Any person engaged to provide such assistance shall be so identified to the client and his contribution to the assignment should be set forth.

The REALTOR® shall refer to the Standards of Practice of the National Association as to the degree of competence that a client has a right to expect the REALTOR® to possess, taking into consideration the complexity of the problem, the availability of expert assistance, and the opportunities for experience available to the REALTOR.®

Article 12

The REALTOR® shall not undertake to provide professional services concerning a property or its value where he has a present or contemplated interest unless such interest is specifically disclosed to all affected parties.

Article 13

The REALTOR® shall not acquire an interest in or buy for himself, any member of his immediate family, his firm or any member thereof, or any entity in which he has a substantial ownership interest, property listed with him, without making the true position known to the listing owner. In selling property owned by himself, or in which he has an interest, the REALTOR® shall reveal the facts of his ownership or interest to the purchaser.

Article 14

In the event of a controversy between REALTORS® associated with different firms, arising out of their relationship as REALTORS®, the REALTORS® shall submit the dispute to arbitration in accordance with the regulations of their board or boards rather than litigate the matter.

Article 15

If a REALTOR® is charged with unethical practice or is asked to present evidence in any disciplinary proceeding or investigation, he shall place all pertinent facts before the proper tribunal of the member board or affiliated institute, society, or council of which he is a member.

Article 16

When acting as agent, the REALTOR® shall not accept any commission, rebate, or profit on expenditures made for his principal-owner, without the principal's knowledge and consent.

Article 17

The REALTOR® shall not engage in activities that constitute the unauthorized practice of law and shall recommend that legal counsel be obtained when the interest of any party to the transaction requires it.

Article 18

The REALTOR® shall keep in a special account in an appropriate financial institution, separated from his own funds, monies coming into his possession in trust for other persons, such as escrows, trust funds, clients' monies and other like items.

Article 19

The REALTOR® shall be careful at all times to present a true picture in his advertising and representations to the public. He shall neither advertise without disclosing his name nor permit any person associated with him to use individual names or telephone numbers, unless such person's connection with the REALTOR® is obvious in the advertisement.

Article 20

The REALTOR®, for the protection of all parties, shall see that financial obligations and commitments regarding real estate transactions are in writing, expressing the exact agreement of the parties. A copy of each agreement shall be furnished to each party upon his signing such agreement.

Article 21

The REALTOR® shall not engage in any practice or take any action inconsistent with the agency of another REALTOR®.

Article 22

In the sale of property which is exclusively listed with a REALTOR®, the REALTOR® shall utilize the services of other brokers upon mutually agreed upon terms when it is in the best interests of the client.

Negotiations concerning property which is listed exclusively shall be carried on with the listing broker, not with the owner, except with the consent of the listing broker.

Article 23

The REALTOR® shall not publicly disparage the business practice of a competitor nor volunteer an opinion of a competitor's transaction. If his opinion is sought and if the REALTOR® deems it appropriate to respond, such opinion shall be rendered with strict professional integrity and courtesy.

APPENDIX J
Section of Land Showing Acreage and Distances

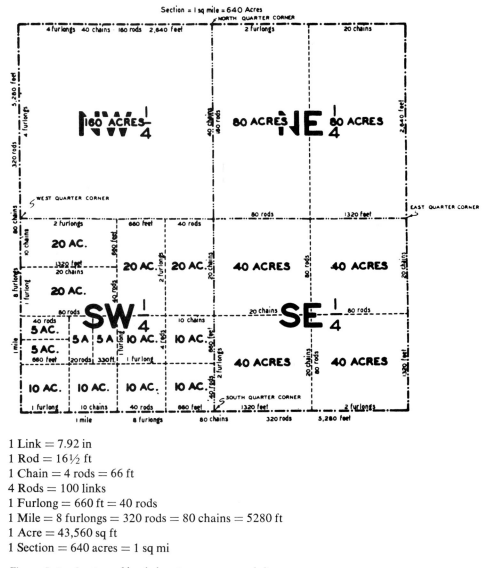

1 Link = 7.92 in
1 Rod = 16½ ft
1 Chain = 4 rods = 66 ft
4 Rods = 100 links
1 Furlong = 660 ft = 40 rods
1 Mile = 8 furlongs = 320 rods = 80 chains = 5280 ft
1 Acre = 43,560 sq ft
1 Section = 640 acres = 1 sq mi

Figure J–1   Section of land showing acreage and distances

Source: John S. Hoag. *Fundamentals of Land Measurement*. Chicago: Chicago Title and Trust Co.

APPENDIX K
FNMA and FHLMC Documents

These following documents are the most widely used and include the residential loan application, mortgage, deed of trust, and adjustable rate loan rider.

CHAMPION FEDERAL SAVINGS AND LOAN ASSOCIATION

Branch No. _____

RESIDENTIAL LOAN APPLICATION

Loan Officer No. _____

MORTGAGE APPLIED FOR	☐ Conventional ☐ FHA	Amount	Interest Rate	No. of Months	Monthly Payment Principal & Interest	Escrow Impounds (to be collected monthly)
	☐ VA ☐ _____	$	%			☐ Taxes ☐ Hazard Ins. ☐ Mtg. Ins. ☐

Prepayment Option

SUBJECT PROPERTY

Property Street Address	City	County	State	Zip	No. Units

Legal Description (Attach description if necessary)	Year Built

Purpose of Loan ☐ Purchase ☐ Construction Permanent ☐ Construction ☐ Refinance ☐ Other (Explain)

Complete this line if Construction Permanent or Construction Loan

	Lot Value Data	Original Cost	Present Value (a)	Cost of Imps. (b)	Total (a + b)	ENTER TOTAL AS PURCHASE PRICE IN DETAILS OF PURCHASE
Year Acquired						

Complete this line if a Refinance Loan

Year Acquired	Original Cost	Amt. Existing Liens	Purpose of Refinance	Describe Improvements ☐ made ☐ to be made

Cost $ _____

Title Will Be Held In What Name(s)	Manner In Which Title Will Be Held

Source of Down Payment and Settlement Charges

This application is designed to be completed by the borrower(s) with the lender's assistance. The Co-Borrower Section and all other Co-Borrower questions must be completed and the appropriate box(es) checked if ☐ another person will be jointly obligated with the Borrower on the loan, or ☐ the Borrower is relying on income from alimony, child support or separate maintenance or on the income or assets of another person as a basis for repayment of the loan, or ☐ the Borrower is married and resides, or the property is located, in a community property state.

BORROWER			CO-BORROWER		
Name	Age	School Yrs. ___	Name	Age	School Yrs. ___

Present Address No. Years ___ ☐ Own ☐ Rent	Present Address No. Years ___ ☐ Own ☐ Rent
Street	Street
City/State/Zip	City/State/Zip
Former address if less than 2 years at present address	Former address if less than 2 years at present address
Street	Street
City/State/Zip	City/State/Zip
Years at former address ☐ Own ☐ Rent	Years at former address ☐ Own ☐ Rent

Marital Status	☐ Married ☐ Separated ☐ Unmarried (incl. single, divorced widowed)	DEPENDENTS OTHER THAN LISTED BY CO-BORROWER NO. / AGES	Marital Status	☐ Married ☐ Separated ☐ Unmarried (incl. single, divorced widowed)	DEPENDENTS OTHER THAN LISTED BY CO-BORROWER NO. / AGES

Name and Address of Employer	Years employed in this line of work or profession? ___ years	Name and Address of Employer	Years employed in this line of work or profession? ___ years
	Years on this job ___ ☐ Self Employed*		Years on this job ___ ☐ Self Employed*

Position/Title	Type of Business	Position/Title	Type of Business

Social Security Number***	Home Phone	Business Phone	Social Security Number***	Home Phone	Business Phone

---

GROSS MONTHLY INCOME				MONTHLY HOUSING EXPENSE**			DETAILS OF PURCHASE	
Item	Borrower	Co-Borrower	Total		Present	Proposed	Do Not Complete If Refinance	
Base Empl. Income	$	$	$	Rent	$		a. Purchase Price	$
Overtime				First Mortgage (P&I)		$	b. Total Closing Costs (Est.)	
Bonuses				Other Financing (P&I)			c. Prepaid Escrows (Est.)	
Commissions				Hazard Insurance			d. Total (a + b + c)	$
Dividends/Interest				Real Estate Taxes			e. Amount This Mortgage	( )
Net Rental Income				Mortgage Insurance			f. Other Financing	( )
Other ✝ (Before completing, see notice under Describe Other Income below)				Homeowner Assn. Dues			g. Other Equity	( )
				Other			h. Amount of Cash Deposit	( )
				Total Monthly Pmt.	$	$	i. Closing Costs Paid by Seller	( )
				Utilities			j. Cash Reqd. For Closing (Est.)	$
Total	$	$	$	Total	$	$		

DESCRIBE OTHER INCOME

NOTICE ✝

☐ B. Borrower ☐ C. Co-Borrower   Alimony, child support, or separate maintenance income need not be revealed if the Borrower or Co-Borrower does not choose to have it considered as a basis for repaying this loan.

Monthly Amount
$

IF EMPLOYED IN CURRENT POSITION FOR LESS THAN TWO YEARS COMPLETE THE FOLLOWING

B/C	Previous Employer/School	City/State	Type of Business	Position/Title	Dates From/To	Monthly Income
						$

THESE QUESTIONS APPLY TO BOTH BORROWER AND CO-BORROWER

If a "yes" answer is given to a question in this column, please explain on an attached sheet.

	Borrower Yes or No	Co-Borrower Yes or No
Are there any outstanding judgments against you?	___	___
Have you been declared bankrupt within the past 7 years?	___	___
Have you had property foreclosed upon or given title or deed in lieu thereof in the last 7 years?	___	___
Are you a party to a law suit?	___	___
Are you obligated to pay alimony, child support, or separate maintenance?	___	___
Is any part of the down payment borrowed?	___	___
Are you a co-maker or endorser on a note?	___	___

	Borrower Yes or No	Co-Borrower Yes or No
Are you a U.S. citizen?	___	___
If "no," are you a resident alien?	___	___
If "no," are you a non-resident alien?	___	___
Explain Other Financing or Other Equity (if any).		

*FHLMC/FNMA require business credit report, signed Federal Income Tax returns for last two years; and, if available, audited Profit and Loss Statement plus balance sheet for same period.
**All Present Monthly Housing Expenses of Borrower and Co-Borrower should be listed on a combined basis.
***Optional for FHLMC

FHLMC 65 Rev. 10/86

Fannie Mae Form 1003 Rev. 10/86

Figure K–1   Residential loan application

This Statement and any applicable supporting schedules may be completed jointly by both married and unmarried co-borrowers if their assets and liabilities are sufficiently joined so that the Statement can be meaningfully and fairly presented on a combined basis; otherwise separate Statements and Schedules are required (FHLMC 65A/FNMA 1003A). If the co-borrower section was completed about a spouse, this statement and supporting schedules must be completed about that spouse also.

☐ Completed Jointly   ☐ Not Completed Jointly

Assets			Liabilities and Pledged Assets			

Indicate by (*) those liabilities or pledged assets which will be satisfied upon sale of real estate owned or upon refinancing of subject property.

Description	Cash or Market Value	Creditors' Name, Address and Account Number		Acct. Name if Not Borrower's	Mo. Pmt. and Mos. Left to Pay	Unpaid Balance
Cash Deposit Toward Purchase Held By	$	Installment Debts (include "revolving" charge accounts)			$ Pmt./Mos.	$
Checking and Savings Accounts (Show Names of Institutions (Account Numbers) Bank, S & L or Credit Union		Co.	Acct. No.			
		Addr			/	
		City				
Addr		Co.	Acct. No.			
City		Addr			/	
Acct. No.		City				
Bank, S & L or Credit Union		Co.	Acct. No.			
		Addr				
		City			/	
Addr		Co.	Acct. No.			
City		Addr				
Acct. No.		City			/	
Bank, S & L or Credit Union		Co.	Acct. No.			
		Addr				
Addr		City			/	
City		Other Debts including Stock Pledges				
Acct. No.						
Stocks and Bonds (No./Description)					/	
		Real Estate Loans Co.	Acct. No.			
		Addr			╳	
		City				
Life Insurance Net Cash Value Face Amount $		Co.	Acct. No.		╳	
		Addr				
Subtotal Liquid Assets		City				
Real Estate Owned (Enter Market Value from Schedule of Real Estate Owned)		Automobile Loans Co.	Acct. No.			
Vested Interest in Retirement Fund		Addr				
Net Worth of Business Owned (ATTACH FINANCIAL STATEMENT)		City				
		Co.	Acct. No.			
Automobiles Owned (Make and Year)						
		City				
Furniture and Personal Property		Alimony/Child Support/Separate Maintenance Payments Owed to			/	╳
Other Assets (Itemize)						
		Total Monthly Payments			$	
Total Assets	A $	Net Worth (A minus B) $			Total Liabilities	B $

SCHEDULE OF REAL ESTATE OWNED (If Additional Properties Owned Attach Separate Schedule)

Address of Property (Indicate S if Sold, PS if Pending Sale or R if Rental being held for income)		Type of Property	Present Market Value	Amount of Mortgages & Liens	Gross Rental Income	Mortgage Payments	Taxes, Ins Maintenance, and Misc.	Net Rental Income
	▽		$	$	$	$	$	$
		TOTALS →	$	$	$	$	$	$

List Previous Credit References

▽	B–Borrower C–Co-Borrower	Creditor's Name and Address	Account Number	Purpose	Highest Balance	Date Paid
					$	

List any additional names under which credit has previously been received _____

AGREEMENT: The undersigned applies for the loan indicated in this application to be secured by a first mortgage or deed of trust on the property described herein, and represents that the property will not be used for any illegal or restricted purpose, and that all statements made in this application are true and are made for the purpose of obtaining the loan. Verification may be obtained from any source named in this application. The original or a copy of this application will be retained by the lender, even if the loan is not granted. The undersigned ☐ intend or ☐ do not intend to occupy the property as their primary residence.

I/we fully understand that it is a federal crime punishable by fine or imprisonment, or both, to knowingly make any false statements concerning any of the above facts as applicable under the provisions of Title 18, United States Code, Section 1014.

_____ Date _____   _____ Date _____
Borrower's Signature   Co-Borrower's Signature

Information for Government Monitoring Purposes

The following information is requested by the Federal Government for certain types of loans related to a dwelling, in order to monitor the lender's compliance with equal credit opportunity and fair housing laws. You are not required to furnish this information, but are encouraged to do so. The law provides that a lender may neither discriminate on the basis of this information, nor on whether you choose to furnish it. However, if you choose not to furnish it, under Federal regulations this lender is required to note race and sex on the basis of visual observation or surname. If you do not wish to furnish the above information, please check the box below. (Lender must review the above material to assure that the disclosures satisfy all requirements to which the Lender is subject under applicable state law for the particular type of loan applied for.)

Borrower: ☐ I do not wish to furnish this information   Co-Borrower: ☐ I do not wish to furnish this information
Race/National Origin: Race/National Origin:
☐ American Indian, Alaskan Native ☐ Asian, Pacific Islander   ☐ American Indian, Alaskan Native ☐ Asian, Pacific Islander
☐ Black ☐ Hispanic ☐ White   ☐ Black ☐ Hispanic ☐ White
☐ Other (specify) _____   ☐ Other (specify) _____
Sex: ☐ Female ☐ Male   Sex: ☐ Female ☐ Male

To Be Completed by Interviewer

This application was taken by:
☐ face to face interview
☐ by mail
☐ by telephone

_____   _____
Interviewer   Name of Interviewer's Employer

_____   _____
Interviewer's Phone Number   Address of Interviewer's Employer

FHLMC Form 65 Rev. 10/86   **REVERSE**   Fannie Mae Form 1003 Rev. 10/86
                                F.31219 Rev. 4/86

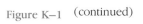

Figure K–1   (continued)

MORTGAGE

THIS MORTGAGE ("Security Instrument") is given on ...., 19......... The mortgagor is .... ("Borrower"). This Security Instrument is given to ....CHAMPION FEDERAL SAVINGS AND LOAN ASSOCIATION................................., which is organized and existing under the laws of ...., and whose address is ....115 East Washington Street — Bloomington, Illinois 61701.. ("Lender"). Borrower owes Lender the principal sum of .... Dollars (U.S. $...............................). This debt is evidenced by Borrower's note dated the same date as this Security Instrument ("Note"), which provides for monthly payments, with the full debt, if not paid earlier, due and payable on .... This Security Instrument secures to Lender: (a) the repayment of the debt evidenced by the Note, with interest, and all renewals, extensions and modifications; (b) the payment of all other sums, with interest, advanced under paragraph 7 to protect the security of this Security Instrument; and (c) the performance of Borrower's covenants and agreements under this Security Instrument and the Note. For this purpose, Borrower does hereby mortgage, grant and convey to Lender the following described property located in .... County, Illinois:

which has the address of ...., ...,
                                     [Street]   [City]

Illinois .... ("Property Address");
             [Zip Code]

TOGETHER WITH all the improvements now or hereafter erected on the property, and all easements, rights, appurtenances, rents, royalties, mineral, oil and gas rights and profits, water rights and stock and all fixtures now or hereafter a part of the property. All replacements and additions shall also be covered by this Security Instrument. All of the foregoing is referred to in this Security Instrument as the "Property."

BORROWER COVENANTS that Borrower is lawfully seised of the estate hereby conveyed and has the right to mortgage, grant and convey the Property and that the Property is unencumbered, except for encumbrances of record. Borrower warrants and will defend generally the title to the Property against all claims and demands, subject to any encumbrances of record.

THIS SECURITY INSTRUMENT combines uniform covenants for national use and non-uniform covenants with limited variations by jurisdiction to constitute a uniform security instrument covering real property.

ILLINOIS—Single Family—FNMA/FHLMC UNIFORM INSTRUMENT   Form 3014 12/83
                                                      44713 SAF SYSTEMS AND FORMS
                                                            CHICAGO, IL

Figure K–2   Mortgage

UNIFORM COVENANTS. Borrower and Lender covenant and agree as follows:

1. Payment of Principal and Interest; Prepayment and Late Charges. Borrower shall promptly pay when due the principal of and interest on the debt evidenced by the Note and any prepayment and late charges due under the Note.

2. Funds for Taxes and Insurance. Subject to applicable law or to a written waiver by Lender, Borrower shall pay to Lender on the day monthly payments are due under the Note, until the Note is paid in full, a sum ("Funds") equal to one-twelfth of: (a) yearly taxes and assessments which may attain priority over this Security Instrument; (b) yearly leasehold payments or ground rents on the Property, if any; (c) yearly hazard insurance premiums; and (d) yearly mortgage insurance premiums, if any. These items are called "escrow items." Lender may estimate the Funds due on the basis of current data and reasonable estimates of future escrow items.

The Funds shall be held in an institution the deposits or accounts of which are insured or guaranteed by a federal or state agency (including Lender if Lender is such an institution). Lender shall apply the Funds to pay the escrow items. Lender may not charge for holding and applying the Funds, analyzing the account or verifying the escrow items, unless Lender pays Borrower interest on the Funds and applicable law permits Lender to make such a charge. Borrower and Lender may agree in writing that interest shall be paid on the Funds. Unless an agreement is made or applicable law requires interest to be paid, Lender shall not be required to pay Borrower any interest or earnings on the Funds. Lender shall give to Borrower, without charge, an annual accounting of the Funds showing credits and debits to the Funds and the purpose for which each debit to the Funds was made. The Funds are pledged as additional security for the sums secured by this Security Instrument.

If the amount of the Funds held by Lender, together with the future monthly payments of Funds payable prior to the due dates of the escrow items, shall exceed the amount required to pay the escrow items when due, the excess shall be, at Borrower's option, either promptly repaid to Borrower or credited to Borrower on monthly payments of Funds. If the amount of the Funds held by Lender is not sufficient to pay the escrow items when due, Borrower shall pay to Lender any amount necessary to make up the deficiency in one or more payments as required by Lender.

Upon payment in full of all sums secured by this Security Instrument, Lender shall promptly refund to Borrower any Funds held by Lender. If under paragraph 19 the Property is sold or acquired by Lender, Lender shall apply, no later than immediately prior to the sale of the Property or its acquisition by Lender, any Funds held by Lender at the time of application as a credit against the sums secured by this Security Instrument.

3. Application of Payments. Unless applicable law provides otherwise, all payments received by Lender under paragraphs 1 and 2 shall be applied: first, to late charges due under the Note; second, to prepayment charges due under the Note; third, to amounts payable under paragraph 2; fourth, to interest due; and last, to principal due.

4. Charges; Liens. Borrower shall pay all taxes, assessments, charges, fines and impositions attributable to the Property which may attain priority over this Security Instrument, and leasehold payments or ground rents, if any. Borrower shall pay these obligations in the manner provided in paragraph 2, or if not paid in that manner, Borrower shall pay them on time directly to the person owed payment. Borrower shall promptly furnish to Lender all notices of amounts to be paid under this paragraph. If Borrower makes these payments directly, Borrower shall promptly furnish to Lender receipts evidencing the payments.

Borrower shall promptly discharge any lien which has priority over this Security Instrument unless Borrower: (a) agrees in writing to the payment of the obligation secured by the lien in a manner acceptable to Lender; (b) contests in good faith the lien by, or defends against enforcement of the lien in, legal proceedings which in the Lender's opinion operate to prevent the enforcement of the lien or forfeiture of any part of the Property; or (c) secures from the holder of the lien an agreement satisfactory to Lender subordinating the lien to this Security Instrument. If Lender determines that any part of the Property is subject to a lien which may attain priority over this Security Instrument, Lender may give Borrower a notice identifying the lien. Borrower shall satisfy the lien or take one or more of the actions set forth above within 10 days of the giving of notice.

5. Hazard Insurance. Borrower shall keep the improvements now existing or hereafter erected on the Property insured against loss by fire, hazards included within the term "extended coverage" and any other hazards for which Lender requires insurance. This insurance shall be maintained in the amounts and for the periods that Lender requires. The insurance carrier providing the insurance shall be chosen by Borrower subject to Lender's approval which shall not be unreasonably withheld.

All insurance policies and renewals shall be acceptable to Lender and shall include a standard mortgage clause. Lender shall have the right to hold the policies and renewals. If Lender requires, Borrower shall promptly give to Lender all receipts of paid premiums and renewal notices. In the event of loss, Borrower shall give prompt notice to the insurance carrier and Lender. Lender may make proof of loss if not made promptly by Borrower.

Unless Lender and Borrower otherwise agree in writing, insurance proceeds shall be applied to restoration or repair of the Property damaged, if the restoration or repair is economically feasible and Lender's security is not lessened. If the restoration or repair is not economically feasible or Lender's security would be lessened, the insurance proceeds shall be applied to the sums secured by this Security Instrument, whether or not then due, with any excess paid to Borrower. If Borrower abandons the Property, or does not answer within 30 days a notice from Lender that the insurance carrier has offered to settle a claim, then Lender may collect the insurance proceeds. Lender may use the proceeds to repair or restore the Property or to pay sums secured by this Security Instrument, whether or not then due. The 30-day period will begin when the notice is given.

Unless Lender and Borrower otherwise agree in writing, any application of proceeds to principal shall not extend or postpone the due date of the monthly payments referred to in paragraphs 1 and 2 or change the amount of the payments. If under paragraph 19 the Property is acquired by Lender, Borrower's right to any insurance policies and proceeds resulting from damage to the Property prior to the acquisition shall pass to Lender to the extent of the sums secured by this Security Instrument immediately prior to the acquisition.

6. Preservation and Maintenance of Property; Leaseholds. Borrower shall not destroy, damage or substantially change the Property, allow the Property to deteriorate or commit waste. If this Security Instrument is on a leasehold, Borrower shall comply with the provisions of the lease, and if Borrower acquires fee title to the Property, the leasehold and fee title shall not merge unless Lender agrees to the merger in writing.

7. Protection of Lender's Rights in the Property; Mortgage Insurance. If Borrower fails to perform the covenants and agreements contained in this Security Instrument, or there is a legal proceeding that may significantly affect Lender's rights in the Property (such as a proceeding in bankruptcy, probate, for condemnation or to enforce laws or regulations), then Lender may do and pay for whatever is necessary to protect the value of the Property and Lender's rights in the Property. Lender's actions may include paying any sums secured by a lien which has priority over this Security Instrument, appearing in court, paying reasonable attorneys' fees and entering on the Property to make repairs. Although Lender may take action under this paragraph 7, Lender does not have to do so.

Any amounts disbursed by Lender under this paragraph 7 shall become additional debt of Borrower secured by this Security Instrument. Unless Borrower and Lender agree to other terms of payment, these amounts shall bear interest from the date of disbursement at the Note rate and shall be payable, with interest, upon notice from Lender to Borrower requesting payment.

Figure K–2   (continued)

If Lender required mortgage insurance as a condition of making the loan secured by this Security Instrument, Borrower shall pay the premiums required to maintain the insurance in effect until such time as the requirement for the insurance terminates in accordance with Borrower's and Lender's written agreement or applicable law.

8. Inspection. Lender or its agent may make reasonable entries upon and inspections of the Property. Lender shall give Borrower notice at the time of or prior to an inspection specifying reasonable cause for the inspection.

9. Condemnation. The proceeds of any award or claim for damages, direct or consequential, in connection with any condemnation or other taking of any part of the Property, or for conveyance in lieu of condemnation, are hereby assigned and shall be paid to Lender.

In the event of a total taking of the Property, the proceeds shall be applied to the sums secured by this Security Instrument, whether or not then due, with any excess paid to Borrower. In the event of a partial taking of the Property, unless Borrower and Lender otherwise agree in writing, the sums secured by this Security Instrument shall be reduced by the amount of the proceeds multiplied by the following fraction: (a) the total amount of the sums secured immediately before the taking, divided by (b) the fair market value of the Property immediately before the taking. Any balance shall be paid to Borrower.

If the Property is abandoned by Borrower, or if, after notice by Lender to Borrower that the condemnor offers to make an award or settle a claim for damages, Borrower fails to respond to Lender within 30 days after the date the notice is given, Lender is authorized to collect and apply the proceeds, at its option, either to restoration or repair of the Property or to the sums secured by this Security Instrument, whether or not then due.

Unless Lender and Borrower otherwise agree in writing, any application of proceeds to principal shall not extend or postpone the due date of the monthly payments referred to in paragraphs 1 and 2 or change the amount of such payments.

10. Borrower Not Released; Forbearance By Lender Not a Waiver. Extension of the time for payment or modification of amortization of the sums secured by this Security Instrument granted by Lender to any successor in interest of Borrower shall not operate to release the liability of the original Borrower or Borrower's successors in interest. Lender shall not be required to commence proceedings against any successor in interest or refuse to extend time for payment or otherwise modify amortization of the sums secured by this Security Instrument by reason of any demand made by the original Borrower or Borrower's successors in interest. Any forbearance by Lender in exercising any right or remedy shall not be a waiver of or preclude the exercise of any right or remedy.

11. Successors and Assigns Bound; Joint and Several Liability; Co-signers. The covenants and agreements of this Security Instrument shall bind and benefit the successors and assigns of Lender and Borrower, subject to the provisions of paragraph 17. Borrower's covenants and agreements shall be joint and several. Any Borrower who co-signs this Security Instrument but does not execute the Note: (a) is co-signing this Security Instrument only to mortgage, grant and convey that Borrower's interest in the Property under the terms of this Security Instrument; (b) is not personally obligated to pay the sums secured by this Security Instrument; and (c) agrees that Lender and any other Borrower may agree to extend, modify, forbear or make any accommodations with regard to the terms of this Security Instrument or the Note without that Borrower's consent.

12. Loan Charges. If the loan secured by this Security Instrument is subject to a law which sets maximum loan charges, and that law is finally interpreted so that the interest or other loan charges collected or to be collected in connection with the loan exceed the permitted limits, then: (a) any such loan charge shall be reduced by the amount necessary to reduce the charge to the permitted limit; and (b) any sums already collected from Borrower which exceeded permitted limits will be refunded to Borrower. Lender may choose to make this refund by reducing the principal owed under the Note or by making a direct payment to Borrower. If a refund reduces principal, the reduction will be treated as a partial prepayment without any prepayment charge under the Note.

13. Legislation Affecting Lender's Rights. If enactment or expiration of applicable laws has the effect of rendering any provision of the Note or this Security Instrument unenforceable according to its terms, Lender, at its option, may require immediate payment in full of all sums secured by this Security Instrument and may invoke any remedies permitted by paragraph 19. If Lender exercises this option, Lender shall take the steps specified in the second paragraph of paragraph 17.

14. Notices. Any notice to Borrower provided for in this Security Instrument shall be given by delivering it or by mailing it by first class mail unless applicable law requires use of another method. The notice shall be directed to the Property Address or any other address Borrower designates by notice to Lender. Any notice to Lender shall be given by first class mail to Lender's address stated herein or any other address Lender designates by notice to Borrower. Any notice provided for in this Security Instrument shall be deemed to have been given to Borrower or Lender when given as provided in this paragraph.

15. Governing Law; Severability. This Security Instrument shall be governed by federal law and the law of the jurisdiction in which the Property is located. In the event that any provision or clause of this Security Instrument or the Note conflicts with applicable law, such conflict shall not affect other provisions of this Security Instrument or the Note which can be given effect without the conflicting provision. To this end the provisions of this Security Instrument and the Note are declared to be severable.

16. Borrower's Copy. Borrower shall be given one conformed copy of the Note and of this Security Instrument.

17. Transfer of the Property or a Beneficial Interest in Borrower. If all or any part of the Property or any interest in it is sold or transferred (or if a beneficial interest in Borrower is sold or transferred and Borrower is not a natural person) without Lender's prior written consent, Lender may, at its option, require immediate payment in full of all sums secured by this Security Instrument. However, this option shall not be exercised by Lender if exercise is prohibited by federal law as of the date of this Security Instrument.

If Lender exercises this option, Lender shall give Borrower notice of acceleration. The notice shall provide a period of not less than 30 days from the date the notice is delivered or mailed within which Borrower must pay all sums secured by this Security Instrument. If Borrower fails to pay these sums prior to the expiration of this period, Lender may invoke any remedies permitted by this Security Instrument without further notice or demand on Borrower.

18. Borrower's Right to Reinstate. If Borrower meets certain conditions, Borrower shall have the right to have enforcement of this Security Instrument discontinued at any time prior to the earlier of: (a) 5 days (or such other period as applicable law may specify for reinstatement) before sale of the Property pursuant to any power of sale contained in this Security Instrument; or (b) entry of a judgment enforcing this Security Instrument. Those conditions are that Borrower: (a) pays Lender all sums which then would be due under this Security Instrument and the Note had no acceleration occurred; (b) cures any default of any other covenants or agreements; (c) pays all expenses incurred in enforcing this Security Instrument, including, but not limited to, reasonable attorneys' fees; and (d) takes such action as Lender may reasonably require to assure that the lien of this Security Instrument, Lender's rights in the Property and Borrower's obligation to pay the sums secured by this Security Instrument shall continue unchanged. Upon reinstatement by Borrower, this Security Instrument and the obligations secured hereby shall remain fully effective as if no acceleration had occurred. However, this right to reinstate shall not apply in the case of acceleration under paragraphs 13 or 17.

Figure K–2   (continued)

NON-UNIFORM COVENANTS. Borrower and Lender further covenant and agree as follows:

19. Acceleration; Remedies. Lender shall give notice to Borrower prior to acceleration following Borrower's breach of any covenant or agreement in this Security Instrument (but not prior to acceleration under paragraphs 13 and 17 unless applicable law provides otherwise). The notice shall specify: (a) the default; (b) the action required to cure the default; (c) a date, not less than 30 days from the date the notice is given to Borrower, by which the default must be cured; and (d) that failure to cure the default on or before the date specified in the notice may result in acceleration of the sums secured by this Security Instrument, foreclosure by judicial proceeding and sale of the Property. The notice shall further inform Borrower of the right to reinstate after acceleration and the right to assert in the foreclosure proceeding the non-existence of a default or any other defense of Borrower to acceleration and foreclosure. If the default is not cured on or before the date specified in the notice, Lender at its option may require immediate payment in full of all sums secured by this Security Instrument without further demand and may foreclose this Security Instrument by judicial proceeding. Lender shall be entitled to collect all expenses incurred in pursuing the remedies provided in this paragraph 19, including, but not limited to, reasonable attorneys' fees and costs of title evidence.

20. Lender in Possession. Upon acceleration under paragraph 19 or abandonment of the Property and at any time prior to the expiration of any period of redemption following judicial sale, Lender (in person, by agent or by judicially appointed receiver) shall be entitled to enter upon, take possession of and manage the Property and to collect the rents of the Property including those past due. Any rents collected by Lender or the receiver shall be applied first to payment of the costs of management of the Property and collection of rents, including, but not limited to, receiver's fees, premiums on receiver's bonds and reasonable attorneys' fees, and then to the sums secured by this Security Instrument.

21. Release. Upon payment of all sums secured by this Security Instrument, Lender shall release this Security Instrument without charge to Borrower. Borrower shall pay any recordation costs.

22. Waiver of Homestead. Borrower waives all right of homestead exemption in the Property.

23. Riders to this Security Instrument. If one or more riders are executed by Borrower and recorded together with this Security Instrument, the covenants and agreements of each such rider shall be incorporated into and shall amend and supplement the covenants and agreements of this Security Instrument as if the rider(s) were a part of this Security Instrument. [Check applicable box(es)]

☐ Adjustable Rate Rider   ☐ Condominium Rider   ☐ 2–4 Family Rider

☐ Graduated Payment Rider   ☐ Planned Unit Development Rider

☐ Other(s) [specify]

BY SIGNING BELOW, Borrower accepts and agrees to the terms and covenants contained in this Security Instrument and in any rider(s) executed by Borrower and recorded with it.

....(Seal)
—Borrower

....(Seal)
—Borrower

———————————————————— [Space Below This Line For Acknowledgment] ————————————————————

STATE OF   .... ⎫
                                 ⎬ SS:
COUNTY OF   .... ⎭

I,..., a Notary Public in and for said county and state, do hereby certify that
...., personally appeared before me and is (are) known or proved to me to be the person(s) who, being informed of the contents of the foregoing instrument, have executed same, and acknowledged said instrument to be .... free and voluntary act and deed and that
(his, her, their)
.... executed said instrument for the purposes and uses therein set forth.
(he, she, they)

Witness my hand and official seal this........................... day of ...., 19......

My Commission Expires:

....(SEAL)
Notary Public

This instrument was prepared by..
44771

Figure K–2   (continued)

NOTE

...., 19.........   ...., ...
                                                                                   [City]   [State]

....
                                               [Property Address]

1. BORROWER'S PROMISE TO PAY

In return for a loan that I have received, I promise to pay U.S. $.. (this amount is called "principal"), plus interest, to the order of the Lender. The Lender is .... I understand that the Lender may transfer this Note. The Lender or anyone who takes this Note by transfer and who is entitled to receive payments under this Note is called the "Note Holder."

2. INTEREST

Interest will be charged on unpaid principal until the full amount of principal has been paid. I will pay interest at a yearly rate of ....%.

The interest rate required by this Section 2 is the rate I will pay both before and after any default described in Section 6(B) of this Note.

3. PAYMENTS

(A) Time and Place of Payments

I will pay principal and interest by making payments every month.

I will make my monthly payments on the .... day of each month beginning on ...., 19......... I will make these payments every month until I have paid all of the principal and interest and any other charges described below that I may owe under this Note. My monthly payments will be applied to interest before principal. If, on ...., ..., I still owe amounts under this Note, I will pay those amounts in full on that date, which is called the "maturity date."

I will make my monthly payments at ....
.... or at a different place if required by the Note Holder.

(B) Amount of Monthly Payments

My monthly payment will be in the amount of U.S. $..

4. BORROWER'S RIGHT TO PREPAY

I have the right to make payments of principal at any time before they are due. A payment of principal only is known as a "prepayment." When I make a prepayment, I will tell the Note Holder in writing that I am doing so.

I may make a full prepayment or partial prepayments without paying any prepayment charge. The Note Holder will use all of my prepayments to reduce the amount of principal that I owe under this Note. If I make a partial prepayment, there will be no changes in the due date or in the amount of my monthly payment unless the Note Holder agrees in writing to those changes.

5. LOAN CHARGES

If a law, which applies to this loan and which sets maximum loan charges, is finally interpreted so that the interest or other loan charges collected or to be collected in connection with this loan exceed the permitted limits, then: (i) any such loan charge shall be reduced by the amount necessary to reduce the charge to the permitted limit; and (ii) any sums already collected from me which exceeded permitted limits will be refunded to me. The Note Holder may choose to make this refund by reducing the principal I owe under this Note or by making a direct payment to me. If a refund reduces principal, the reduction will be treated as a partial prepayment.

6. BORROWER'S FAILURE TO PAY AS REQUIRED

(A) Late Charge for Overdue Payments

If the Note Holder has not received the full amount of any monthly payment by the end of .... calendar days after the date it is due, I will pay a late charge to the Note Holder. The amount of the charge will be ....% of my overdue payment of principal and interest. I will pay this late charge promptly but only once on each late payment.

(B) Default

If I do not pay the full amount of each monthly payment on the date it is due, I will be in default.

(C) Notice of Default

If I am in default, the Note Holder may send me a written notice telling me that if I do not pay the overdue amount by a certain date, the Note Holder may require me to pay immediately the full amount of principal which has not been paid and all the interest that I owe on that amount. That date must be at least 30 days after the date on which the notice is delivered or mailed to me.

(D) No Waiver By Note Holder

Even if, at a time when I am in default, the Note Holder does not require me to pay immediately in full as described above, the Note Holder will still have the right to do so if I am in default at a later time.

(E) Payment of Note Holder's Costs and Expenses

If the Note Holder has required me to pay immediately in full as described above, the Note Holder will have the right to be paid back by me for all of its costs and expenses in enforcing this Note to the extent not prohibited by applicable law. Those expenses include, for example, reasonable attorneys' fees.

7. GIVING OF NOTICES

Unless applicable law requires a different method, any notice that must be given to me under this Note will be given by delivering it or by mailing it by first class mail to me at the Property Address above or at a different address if I give the Note Holder a notice of my different address.

Any notice that must be given to the Note Holder under this Note will be given by mailing it by first class mail to the Note Holder at the address stated in Section 3(A) above or at a different address if I am given a notice of that different address.

MULTISTATE FIXED RATE NOTE—Single Family—**FNMA/FHLMC UNIFORM INSTRUMENT**   Form 3200 12/83

Figure K–3   Note

8. OBLIGATIONS OF PERSONS UNDER THIS NOTE

If more than one person signs this Note, each person is fully and personally obligated to keep all of the promises made in this Note, including the promise to pay the full amount owed. Any person who is a guarantor, surety or endorser of this Note is also obligated to do these things. Any person who takes over these obligations, including the obligations of a guarantor, surety or endorser of this Note, is also obligated to keep all of the promises made in this Note. The Note Holder may enforce its rights under this Note against each person individually or against all of us together. This means that any one of us may be required to pay all of the amounts owed under this Note.

9. WAIVERS

I and any other person who has obligations under this Note waive the rights of presentment and notice of dishonor. "Presentment" means the right to require the Note Holder to demand payment of amounts due. "Notice of dishonor" means the right to require the Note Holder to give notice to other persons that amounts due have not been paid.

10. UNIFORM SECURED NOTE

This Note is a uniform instrument with limited variations in some jurisdictions. In addition to the protections given to the Note Holder under this Note, a Mortgage, Deed of Trust or Security Deed (the "Security Instrument"), dated the same date as this Note, protects the Note Holder from possible losses which might result if I do not keep the promises which I make in this Note. That Security Instrument describes how and under what conditions I may be required to make immediate payment in full of all amounts I owe under this Note. Some of those conditions are described as follows:

Transfer of the Property or a Beneficial Interest in Borrower. If all or any part of the Property or any interest in it is sold or transferred (or if a beneficial interest in Borrower is sold or transferred and Borrower is not a natural person) without Lender's prior written consent, Lender may, at its option, require immediate payment in full of all sums secured by this Security Instrument. However, this option shall not be exercised by Lender if exercise is prohibited by federal law as of the date of this Security Instrument.

If Lender exercises this option, Lender shall give Borrower notice of acceleration. The notice shall provide a period of not less than 30 days from the date the notice is delivered or mailed within which Borrower must pay all sums secured by this Security Instrument. If Borrower fails to pay these sums prior to the expiration of this period, Lender may invoke any remedies permitted by this Security Instrument without further notice or demand on Borrower.

WITNESS THE HAND(S) AND SEAL(S) OF THE UNDERSIGNED.

....(Seal)
-Borrower

....(Seal)
-Borrower

....(Seal)
Borrower

[Sign Original Only]

Figure K–3   (continued)

DEED OF TRUST

THIS DEED OF TRUST is made this........................day of........................,
19...., among the Grantor,..
....................................(herein "Borrower"),....................................
...., of.........................., Virginia, and....................
........................, of.................................., Virginia, trustees (any one of whom may act
and who are referred to herein as "Trustee"), and the Beneficiary,....................................
...., a corporation organized and existing under the laws of
......................................, whose address is....................................
....(herein "Lender").

BORROWER, in consideration of the indebtedness herein recited and the trust herein created, irrevocably grants
and conveys to Trustee, in trust, with power of sale, the following described property located in the............
...., State of Virginia:

which has the address of ....,..............,
_____[Street]_____[City]
..........................(herein "Property Address");
[State and Zip Code]

TOGETHER with all the improvements now or hereafter erected on the property, and all easements, rights,
appurtenances, rents (subject however to the rights and authorities given herein to Lender to collect and apply such
rents), royalties, mineral, oil and gas rights and profits, water, water rights, and water stock, and all fixtures now or
hereafter attached to the property, all of which, including replacements and additions thereto, shall be deemed to be
and remain a part of the property covered by this Deed of Trust; and all of the foregoing, together with said property
(or the leasehold estate if this Deed of Trust is on a leasehold) are herein referred to as the "Property";

To SECURE to Lender (a) the repayment of the indebtedness evidenced by Borrower's note dated...........
..........................(herein "Note"), in the principal sum of....................................
....Dollars, with interest thereon, providing for monthly
installments of principal and interest, with the balance of the indebtedness, if not sooner paid, due and payable on
....................................; the payment of all other sums, with
interest thereon, advanced in accordance herewith to protect the security of this Deed of Trust; and the performance of
the covenants and agreements of Borrower herein contained; and (b) the repayment of any future advances, with
interest thereon, made to Borrower by Lender pursuant to paragraph 21 hereof (herein "Future Advances").

Borrower covenants that Borrower is lawfully seised of the estate hereby conveyed and has the right to grant
and convey the Property, that the Property is unencumbered, and that Borrower will warrant and defend generally
the title to the Property against all claims and demands, subject to any declarations, easements or restrictions listed
in a schedule of exceptions to coverage in any title insurance policy insuring Lender's interest in the Property.

Figure K–4   Deed of trust

UNIFORM COVENANTS. Borrower and Lender covenant and agree as follows:

1. Payment of Principal and Interest. Borrower shall promptly pay when due the principal of and interest on the indebtedness evidenced by the Note, prepayment and late charges as provided in the Note, and the principal of and interest on any Future Advances secured by this Deed of Trust.

2. Funds for Taxes and Insurance. Subject to applicable law or to a written waiver by Lender, Borrower shall pay to Lender on the day monthly installments of principal and interest are payable under the Note, until the Note is paid in full, a sum (herein "Funds") equal to one-twelfth of the yearly taxes and assessments which may attain priority over this Deed of Trust, and ground rents on the Property, if any, plus one-twelfth of yearly premium installments for hazard insurance, plus one-twelfth of yearly premium installments for mortgage insurance, if any, all as reasonably estimated initially and from time to time by Lender on the basis of assessments and bills and reasonable estimates thereof.

The Funds shall be held in an institution the deposits or accounts of which are insured or guaranteed by a Federal or state agency (including Lender if Lender is such an institution). Lender shall apply the Funds to pay said taxes, assessments, insurance premiums and ground rents. Lender may not charge for so holding and applying the Funds, analyzing said account or verifying and compiling said assessments and bills, unless Lender pays Borrower interest on the Funds and applicable law permits Lender to make such a charge. Borrower and Lender may agree in writing at the time of execution of this Deed of Trust that interest on the Funds shall be paid to Borrower, and unless such agreement is made or applicable law requires such interest to be paid, Lender shall not be required to pay Borrower any interest or earnings on the Funds. Lender shall give to Borrower, without charge, an annual accounting of the Funds showing credits and debits to the Funds and the purpose for which each debit to the Funds was made. The Funds are pledged as additional security for the sums secured by this Deed of Trust.

If the amount of the Funds held by Lender, together with the future monthly installments of Funds payable prior to the due dates of taxes, assessments, insurance premiums and ground rents, shall exceed the amount required to pay said taxes, assessments, insurance premiums and ground rents as they fall due, such excess shall be, at Borrower's option, either promptly repaid to Borrower or credited to Borrower on monthly installments of Funds. If the amount of the Funds held by Lender shall not be sufficient to pay taxes, assessments, insurance premiums and ground rents as they fall due, Borrower shall pay to Lender any amount necessary to make up the deficiency within 30 days from the date notice is mailed by Lender to Borrower requesting payment thereof.

Upon payment in full of all sums secured by this Deed of Trust, Lender shall promptly refund to Borrower any Funds held by Lender. If under paragraph 18 hereof the Property is sold or the Property is otherwise acquired by Lender, Lender shall apply, no later than immediately prior to the sale of the Property or its acquisition by Lender, any Funds held by Lender at the time of application as a credit against the sums secured by this Deed of Trust.

3. Application of Payments. Unless applicable law provides otherwise, all payments received by Lender under the Note and paragraphs 1 and 2 hereof shall be applied by Lender first in payment of amounts payable to Lender by Borrower under paragraph 2 hereof, then to interest payable on the Note, then to the principal of the Note, and then to interest and principal on any Future Advances.

4. Charges; Liens. Borrower shall pay all taxes, assessments and other charges, fines and impositions attributable to the Property which may attain a priority over this Deed of Trust, and leasehold payments or ground rents, if any, in the manner provided under paragraph 2 hereof or, if not paid in such manner, by Borrower making payment, when due, directly to the payee thereof. Borrower shall promptly furnish to Lender all notices of amounts due under this paragraph, and in the event Borrower shall make payment directly, Borrower shall promptly furnish to Lender receipts evidencing such payments. Borrower shall promptly discharge any lien which has priority over this Deed of Trust; provided, that Borrower shall not be required to discharge any such lien so long as Borrower shall agree in writing to the payment of the obligation secured by such lien in a manner acceptable to Lender, or shall in good faith contest such lien by, or defend enforcement of such lien in, legal proceedings which operate to prevent the enforcement of the lien or forfeiture of the Property or any part thereof.

5. Hazard Insurance. Borrower shall keep the improvements now existing or hereafter erected on the Property insured against loss by fire, hazards included within the term "extended coverage", and such other hazards as Lender may require and in such amounts and for such periods as Lender may require; provided, that Lender shall not require that the amount of such coverage exceed that amount of coverage required to pay the sums secured by this Deed of Trust.

The insurance carrier providing the insurance shall be chosen by Borrower subject to approval by Lender; provided, that such approval shall not be unreasonably withheld. All premiums on insurance policies shall be paid in the manner provided under paragraph 2 hereof or, if not paid in such manner, by Borrower making payment, when due, directly to the insurance carrier.

All insurance policies and renewals thereof shall be in form acceptable to Lender and shall include a standard mortgage clause in favor of and in form acceptable to Lender. Lender shall have the right to hold the policies and renewals thereof, and Borrower shall promptly furnish to Lender all renewal notices and all receipts of paid premiums. In the event of loss, Borrower shall give prompt notice to the insurance carrier and Lender. Lender may make proof of loss if not made promptly by Borrower.

Unless Lender and Borrower otherwise agree in writing, insurance proceeds shall be applied to restoration or repair of the Property damaged, provided such restoration or repair is economically feasible and the security of this Deed of Trust is not thereby impaired. If such restoration or repair is not economically feasible or if the security of this Deed of Trust would be impaired, the insurance proceeds shall be applied to the sums secured by this Deed of Trust, with the excess, if any, paid to Borrower. If the Property is abandoned by Borrower, or if Borrower fails to respond to Lender within 30 days from the date notice is mailed by Lender to Borrower that the insurance carrier offers to settle a claim for insurance benefits, Lender is authorized to collect and apply the insurance proceeds at Lender's option either to restoration or repair of the Property or to the sums secured by this Deed of Trust.

Unless Lender and Borrower otherwise agree in writing, any such application of proceeds to principal shall not extend or postpone the due date of the monthly installments referred to in paragraphs 1 and 2 hereof or change the amount of such installments. If under paragraph 18 hereof the Property is acquired by Lender, all right, title and interest of Borrower in and to any insurance policies and in and to the proceeds thereof resulting from damage to the Property prior to the sale or acquisition shall pass to Lender to the extent of the sums secured by this Deed of Trust immediately prior to such sale or acquisition.

6. Preservation and Maintenance of Property; Leaseholds; Condominiums; Planned Unit Developments. Borrower shall keep the Property in good repair and shall not commit waste or permit impairment or deterioration of the Property and shall comply with the provisions of any lease if this Deed of Trust is on a leasehold. If this Deed of Trust is on a unit in a condominium or a planned unit development, Borrower shall perform all of Borrower's obligations under the declaration or covenants creating or governing the condominium or planned unit development, the by-laws and regulations of the condominium or planned unit development, and constituent documents. If a condominium or planned unit development rider is executed by Borrower and recorded together with this Deed of Trust, the covenants and agreements of such rider shall be incorporated into and shall amend and supplement the covenants and agreements of this Deed of Trust as if the rider were a part hereof.

7. Protection of Lender's Security. If Borrower fails to perform the covenants and agreements contained in this Deed of Trust, or if any action or proceeding is commenced which materially affects Lender's interest in the Property, including, but not limited to, eminent domain, insolvency, code enforcement, or arrangements or proceedings involving a bankrupt or decedent, then Lender at Lender's option, upon notice to Borrower, may make such appearances, disburse such sums and take such action as is necessary to protect Lender's interest, including, but not limited to, disbursement of reasonable attorney's fees and entry upon the Property to make repairs. If Lender required mortgage insurance as a condition of making the loan secured by this Deed of Trust, Borrower shall pay the premiums required to maintain such insurance in effect until such time as the requirement for such insurance terminates in accordance with Borrower's and Lender's written agreement or applicable law. Borrower shall pay the amount of all mortgage insurance premiums in the manner provided under paragraph 2 hereof.

Any amounts disbursed by Lender pursuant to this paragraph 7, with interest thereon, shall become additional indebtedness of Borrower secured by this Deed of Trust. Unless Borrower and Lender agree to other terms of payment, such amounts shall be payable upon notice from Lender to Borrower requesting payment thereof, and shall bear interest from the date of disbursement at the rate payable from time to time on outstanding principal under the Note unless payment of interest at such rate would be contrary to applicable law, in which event such amounts shall bear interest at the highest rate permissible under applicable law. Nothing contained in this paragraph 7 shall require Lender to incur any expense or take any action hereunder.

8. Inspection. Lender may make or cause to be made reasonable entries upon and inspections of the Property, provided that Lender shall give Borrower notice prior to any such inspection specifying reasonable cause therefor related to Lender's interest in the Property.

Figure K–4   (continued)

9. Condemnation. The proceeds of any award or claim for damages, direct or consequential, in connection with any condemnation or other taking of the Property, or part thereof, or for conveyance in lieu of condemnation, are hereby assigned and shall be paid to Lender.

In the event of a total taking of the Property, the proceeds shall be applied to the sums secured by this Deed of Trust, with the excess, if any, paid to Borrower. In the event of a partial taking of the Property, unless Borrower and Lender otherwise agree in writing, there shall be applied to the sums secured by this Deed of Trust such proportion of the proceeds as is equal to that proportion which the amount of the sums secured by this Deed of Trust immediately prior to the date of taking bears to the fair market value of the Property immediately prior to the date of taking, with the balance of the proceeds paid to Borrower.

If the Property is abandoned by Borrower, or if, after notice by Lender to Borrower that the condemnor offers to make an award or settle a claim for damages, Borrower fails to respond to Lender within 30 days after the date such notice is mailed, Lender is authorized to collect and apply the proceeds, at Lender's option, either to restoration or repair of the Property or to the sums secured by this Deed of Trust.

Unless Lender and Borrower otherwise agree in writing, any such application of proceeds to principal shall not extend or postpone the due date of the monthly installments referred to in paragraphs 1 and 2 hereof or change the amount of such installments.

10. Borrower Not Released. Extension of the time for payment or modification of amortization of the sums secured by this Deed of Trust granted by Lender to any successor in interest of Borrower shall not operate to release, in any manner, the liability of the original Borrower and Borrower's successors in interest. Lender shall not be required to commence proceedings against such successor or refuse to extend time for payment or otherwise modify amortization of the sums secured by this Deed of Trust by reason of any demand made by the original Borrower and Borrower's successors in interest.

11. Forbearance by Lender Not a Waiver. Any forbearance by Lender in exercising any right or remedy hereunder, or otherwise afforded by applicable law, shall not be a waiver of or preclude the exercise of any such right or remedy. The procurement of insurance or the payment of taxes or other liens or charges by Lender shall not be a waiver of Lender's right to accelerate the maturity of the indebtedness secured by this Deed of Trust.

12. Remedies Cumulative. All remedies provided in this Deed of Trust are distinct and cumulative to any other right or remedy under this Deed of Trust or afforded by law or equity, and may be exercised concurrently, independently or successively.

13. Successors and Assigns Bound; Joint and Several Liability; Captions. The covenants and agreements herein contained shall bind, and the rights hereunder shall inure to, the respective successors and assigns of Lender and Borrower, subject to the provisions of paragraph 17 hereof. All covenants and agreements of Borrower shall be joint and several. The captions and headings of the paragraphs of this Deed of Trust are for convenience only and are not to be used to interpret or define the provisions hereof.

14. Notice. Except for any notice required under applicable law to be given in another manner, (a) any notice to Borrower provided for in this Deed of Trust shall be given by mailing such notice by certified mail addressed to Borrower at the Property Address or at such other address as Borrower may designate by notice to Lender as provided herein, and (b) any notice to Lender shall be given by certified mail, return receipt requested, to Lender's address stated herein or to such other address as Lender may designate by notice to Borrower as provided herein. Any notice provided for in this Deed of Trust shall be deemed to have been given to Borrower or Lender when given in the manner designated herein.

15. Uniform Deed of Trust; Governing Law; Severability. This form of deed of trust combines uniform covenants for national use and non-uniform covenants with limited variations by jurisdiction to constitute a uniform security instrument covering real property. This Deed of Trust shall be governed by the law of the jurisdiction in which the Property is located. In the event that any provision or clause of this Deed of Trust or the Note conflicts with applicable law, such conflict shall not affect other provisions of this Deed of Trust or the Note which can be given effect without the conflicting provision, and to this end the provisions of the Deed of Trust and the Note are declared to be severable.

16. Borrower's Copy. Borrower shall be furnished a conformed copy of the Note and of this Deed of Trust at the time of execution or after recordation hereof.

17. Transfer of the Property; Assumption. If all or any part of the Property or an interest therein is sold or transferred by Borrower without Lender's prior written consent, excluding (a) the creation of a lien or encumbrance subordinate to this Deed of Trust, (b) the creation of a purchase money security interest for household appliances, (c) a transfer by devise, descent or by operation of law upon the death of a joint tenant or (d) the grant of any leasehold interest of three years or less not containing an option to purchase, Lender may, at Lender's option, declare all the sums secured by this Deed of Trust to be immediately due and payable. Lender shall have waived such option to accelerate if, prior to the sale or transfer, Lender and the person to whom the Property is to be sold or transferred reach agreement in writing that the credit of such person is satisfactory to Lender and that the interest payable on the sums secured by this Deed of Trust shall be at such rate as Lender shall request. If Lender has waived the option to accelerate provided in this paragraph 17, and if Borrower's successor in interest has executed a written assumption agreement accepted in writing by Lender, Lender shall release Borrower from all obligations under this Deed of Trust and the Note.

If Lender exercises such option to accelerate, Lender shall mail Borrower notice of acceleration in accordance with paragraph 14 hereof. Such notice shall provide a period of not less than 30 days from the date the notice is mailed within which Borrower may pay the sums declared due. If Borrower fails to pay such sums prior to the expiration of such period, Lender may, without further notice or demand on Borrower, invoke any remedies permitted by paragraph 18 hereof.

Non-Uniform Covenants. Borrower and Lender further covenant and agree as follows:

18. Acceleration; Remedies. Except as provided in paragraph 17 hereof, upon Borrower's breach of any covenant or agreement of Borrower in this Deed of Trust, including the covenants to pay when due any sums secured by this Deed of Trust, Lender prior to acceleration shall mail notice to Borrower as provided in paragraph 14 hereof specifying: (1) the breach; (2) the action required to cure such breach; (3) a date, not less than 30 days from the date the notice is mailed to Borrower, by which such breach must be cured; and (4) that failure to cure such breach on or before the date specified in the notice may result in acceleration of the sums secured by this Deed of Trust and sale of the Property. The notice shall further inform Borrower of the right to reinstate after acceleration and the right to bring a court action to assert the non-existence of a default or any other defense of Borrower to acceleration and sale. If the breach is not cured on or before the date specified in the notice, Lender at Lender's option may declare all of the sums secured by this Deed of Trust to be immediately due and payable without further demand and may invoke the power of sale and any other remedies permitted by applicable law. Lender shall be entitled to collect all reasonable costs and expenses incurred in pursuing the remedies provided in this paragraph 18, including, but not limited to, reasonable attorney's fees.

If Lender invokes the power of sale, Lender or Trustee shall give to Borrower a copy of a notice of sale in the manner prescribed by applicable law. Trustee shall give public notice of sale by advertising, in accordance with applicable law, once a week for four successive weeks in a newspaper published or having general circulation in the county or city in which the Property or some portion thereof is located, and by such additional or different form of advertisement as the Trustee may deem advisable, if any. Trustee may sell the Property on the twenty-second day after the first advertisement or any day thereafter. Trustee, without demand on Borrower, shall sell the Property at public auction to the highest bidder at the time and place and under the terms designated in the notice of sale in one or more parcels and in such order as Trustee may determine. Trustee may postpone sale of all or any parcel of the Property by public announcement at the time and place of any previously scheduled sale or by advertising in accordance with applicable law. Lender or Lender's designee may purchase the Property at any sale.

Trustee shall deliver to the purchaser Trustee's deed conveying the Property so sold with special warranty of title. The recitals in Trustee's deed shall be prima facie evidence of the truth of the statements made therein. Trustee shall apply the proceeds of the sale in the following order: (a) to all reasonable costs and expenses of the sale, including, but not limited to, Trustee's fees of . . . .% of the gross sale price, reasonable attorney's fees and costs of title evidence; (b) to the discharge of all taxes, levies and assessments on the Property, if any, as provided by applicable law; (c) to all sums secured by this Deed of Trust; and (d) the excess, if any, to the person or persons legally entitled thereto, including, if any, holders of liens inferior to this Deed of Trust in order of their priority, provided that Trustee has actual notice of such liens. Trustee shall not be required to take possession of the Property prior to the sale thereof or to deliver possession of the Property to the purchaser at such sale.

19. Borrower's Right to Reinstate. Notwithstanding Lender's acceleration of the sums secured by this Deed of Trust, Borrower shall have the right to have any proceedings begun by Lender to enforce this Deed of Trust discontinued at any time prior to the earlier to occur of (i) the fifth day before sale of the Property pursuant to the power of sale contained in this Deed of Trust or (ii) entry of a judgment enforcing this Deed of Trust if: (a) Borrower pays Lender all sums which would be then due under this Deed of Trust, the Note and notes securing Future Advances, if any, had no acceleration occurred; (b) Borrower cures all breaches of any other covenants or agreements of Borrower contained in this Deed of Trust; (c)

Figure K–4 (continued)

Borrower pays all reasonable expenses incurred by Lender and Trustee in enforcing the covenants and agreements of Borrower contained in this Deed of Trust and in enforcing Lender's and Trustee's remedies as provided in paragraph 18 hereof, including, but not limited to, reasonable attorney's fees; and (d) Borrower takes such action as Lender may reasonably require to assure that the lien of this Deed of Trust, Lender's interest in the Property and Borrower's obligation to pay the sums secured by this Deed of Trust shall continue unimpaired. Upon such payment and cure by Borrower, this Deed of Trust and the obligations secured hereby shall remain in full force and effect as if no acceleration had occurred.

20. Assignment of Rents; Appointment of Receiver; Lender in Possession. As additional security hereunder, Borrower hereby assigns to Lender the rents of the Property, provided that Borrower shall, prior to acceleration under paragraph 18 hereof or abandonment of the Property, have the right to collect and retain such rents as they become due and payable.

Upon acceleration under paragraph 18 hereof or abandonment of the Property, Lender, in person, by agent or by judicially appointed receiver, shall be entitled to enter upon, take possession of and manage the Property and to collect the rents of the Property, including those past due. All rents collected by Lender or the receiver shall be applied first to payment of the costs of management of the Property and collection of rents, including, but not limited to, receiver's fees, premiums on receiver's bonds and reasonable attorney's fees, and then to the sums secured by this Deed of Trust. Lender and the receiver shall be liable to account only for those rents actually received.

21. Future Advances. Upon request of Borrower, Lender, at Lender's option prior to release of this Deed of Trust, may make Future Advances to Borrower. Such Future Advances, with interest thereon, shall be secured by this Deed of Trust when evidenced by promissory notes stating that said notes are secured hereby. At no time shall the principal amount of the indebtedness secured by this Deed of Trust, not including sums advanced in accordance herewith to protect the security of this Deed of Trust, exceed the original amount of the Note plus US $..................................

22. Release. Upon payment of all sums secured by this Deed of Trust, Lender shall request Trustee to release this Deed of Trust and shall surrender all notes evidencing indebtedness secured by this Deed of Trust to Trustee. Trustee shall release this Deed of Trust without charge to Borrower. Borrower shall pay all costs of recordation, if any.

23. Substitute Trustee. Lender may from time to time in Lender's discretion remove Trustee and appoint a successor trustee to any Trustee appointed hereunder. Without conveyance of the Property, the successor trustee shall succeed to all the title, power and duties conferred upon the Trustee herein and by applicable law.

24. Identification of Note. The Note is identified by a certificate on the Note executed by any Notary Public who certifies an acknowledgement hereto.

In Witness Whereof, Borrower has executed and sealed this Deed of Trust.

....(Seal)
—Borrower

....(Seal)
—Borrower

State of Virginia,.......................................County ss:

The foregoing instrument was acknowledged before me this...................................
(date)

by ....
(person acknowledging)

My Commission expires:

....
Notary Public

————————————— (Space Below This Line Reserved For Lender and Recorder) —————————————

Figure K–4   (continued)

NOTE

US $..........................   ...., Virginia
City

.........................., 19....

FOR VALUE RECEIVED, the undersigned ("Borrower") promise(s) to pay..........................
...., or order, the principal sum of
....Dollars, with interest on the unpaid principal balance from the date of this Note, until paid, at the rate of....................
.....................percent per annum. Principal and interest shall be payable at.....................
...., or such other place as the Note holder may designate, in consecutive monthly installments of..
......................Dollars (US $..........................), on the..................
.............day of each month beginning..........................., 19..... Such monthly installments shall continue until the entire indebtedness evidenced by this Note is fully paid, except that any remaining indebtedness, if not sooner paid, shall be due and payable on...

If any monthly installment under this Note is not paid when due and remains unpaid after a date specified by a notice to Borrower, the entire principal amount outstanding and accrued interest thereon shall at once become due and payable at the option of the Note holder. The date specified shall not be less than thirty days from the date such notice is mailed. The Note holder may exercise this option to accelerate during any default by Borrower regardless of any prior forbearance. If suit is brought to collect this Note, the Note holder shall be entitled to collect all reasonable costs and expenses of suit, including, but not limited to, reasonable attorney's fees.

Borrower shall pay to the Note holder a late charge of..........................percent of any monthly installment not received by the Note holder within..........................days after the installment is due.

Borrower may prepay the principal amount outstanding in whole or in part. The Note holder may require that any partial prepayments (i) be made on the date monthly installments are due and (ii) be in the amount of that part of one or more monthly installments which would be applicable to principal. Any partial prepayment shall be applied against the principal amount outstanding and shall not postpone the due date of any subsequent monthly installments or change the amount of such installments, unless the Note holder shall otherwise agree in writing.

Presentment, notice of dishonor, and protest are hereby waived by all makers, sureties, guarantors and endorsers hereof. This Note shall be the joint and several obligation of all makers, sureties, guarantors and endorsers, and shall be binding upon them and their successors and assigns.

Any notice to Borrower provided for in this Note shall be given by mailing such notice by certified mail addressed to Borrower at the Property Address stated below, or to such other address as Borrower may designate by notice to the Note holder. Any notice to the Note holder shall be given by mailing such notice by certified mail, return receipt requested, to the Note holder at the address stated in the first paragraph of this Note, or at such other address as may have been designated by notice to Borrower.

The indebtedness evidenced by this Note is secured by a Deed of Trust, dated..........................
...................., and reference is made to the Deed of Trust for rights as to acceleration of the indebtedness evidenced by this Note.

....(Seal)

....(Seal)

....(Seal)
         Property Address   *(Execute Original Only)*

This is to certify that this is the Note described in and secured by a Deed of Trust dated..................
....................on property located in..., Virginia.
My commission expires:

....
                               Notary Public

Figure K–5   Note

ADJUSTABLE RATE LOAN RIDER

NOTICE: THE SECURITY INSTRUMENT SECURES A NOTE WHICH CONTAINS A PROVISION ALLOWING FOR CHANGES IN THE INTEREST RATE. INCREASES IN THE INTEREST RATE WILL RESULT IN HIGHER PAYMENTS. DECREASES IN THE INTEREST RATE WILL RESULT IN LOWER PAYMENTS.

This Rider is made this . . . . day of . . . . , 19 . . . . . , and is incorporated into and shall be deemed to amend and supplement the Mortgage, Deed of Trust, or Deed to Secure Debt (the "Security Instrument") of the same date given by the undersigned (the "Borrower") to secure Borrower's Note to . . . .
. . . .
(the "Lender") of the same date (the "Note") and covering the property described in the Security Instrument and located at . . . .

Property Address

Modifications. In addition to the covenants and agreements made in the Security Instrument, Borrower and Lender further covenant and agree as follows:

A. INTEREST RATE AND MONTHLY PAYMENT CHANGES

The Note has an "Initial Interest Rate" of . . . . . %. The Note interest rate may be increased or decreased on the . . . . . day of the month beginning on . . . . , 19 . . . . . and on that day of the month every . . . . . months thereafter.

Changes in the interest rate are governed by changes in an interest rate index called the "Index". The Index is the:

[Check one box to indicate Index.]

(1) ☐* "Contract Interest Rate, Purchase of Previously Occupied Homes, National Average for all Major Types of Lenders" published by the Federal Home Loan Bank Board.

(2) ☐* . . . .
. . . .

[Check one box to indicate whether there is any maximum limit on changes in the interest rate on each Change Date; if no box is checked there will be no maximum limit on changes.]

(1) ☐ There is no maximum limit on changes in the interest rate at any Change Date.

(2) ☐ The interest rate cannot be changed by more than . . . . . percentage points at any Change Date.

If the interest rate changes, the amount of Borrower's monthly payments will change as provided in the Note. Increases in the interest rate will result in higher payments. Decreases in the interest rate will result in lower payments.

B. LOAN CHARGES

It could be that the loan secured by the Security Instrument is subject to a law which sets maximum loan charges and that law is interpreted so that the interest or other loan charges collected or to be collected in connection with the loan would exceed permitted limits. If this is the case, then: (A) any such loan charge shall be reduced by the amount necessary to reduce the charge to the permitted limit; and (B) any sums already collected from Borrower which exceeded permitted limits will be refunded to Borrower. Lender may choose to make this refund by reducing the principal owed under the Note or by making a direct payment to Borrower.

C. PRIOR LIENS

If Lender determines that all or any part of the sums secured by this Security Instrument are subject to a lien which has priority over this Security Instrument, Lender may send Borrower a notice identifying that lien. Borrower shall promptly act with regard to that lien as provided in paragraph 4 of the Security Instrument or shall promptly secure an agreement in a form satisfactory to Lender subordinating that lien to this Security Instrument.

D. TRANSFER OF THE PROPERTY

If there is a transfer of the Property subject to paragraph 17 of the Security Instrument, Lender may require (1) an increase in the current Note interest rate, or (2) an increase in (or removal of) the limit on the amount of any one interest rate change (if there is a limit), or (3) a change in the Base Index figure, or all of these, as a condition of Lender's waiving the option to accelerate provided in paragraph 17.

By signing this, Borrower agrees to all of the above.

. . . .(Seal)
—Borrower

. . . .(Seal)
—Borrower

* *If more than one box is checked or if no box is checked, and Lender and Borrower do not otherwise agree in writing, the first Index named will apply.*

Figure K–6 Adjustable rate loan rider

INDEX

WE VALUE YOUR OPINION—PLEASE SHARE IT WITH US

Merrill Publishing and our authors are most interested in your reactions to this textbook. Did it serve you well in the course? If it did, what aspects of the text were most helpful? If not, what didn't you like about it? Your comments will help us to write and develop better textbooks. We value your opinions and thank you for your help.

Text Title _____ Edition _____

Author(s) _____

Your Name (optional) _____

Address _____

City _____ State _____ Zip _____

School _____

Course Title _____

Instructor's Name _____

Your Major _____

Your Class Rank _____ Freshman _____ Sophomore _____ Junior _____ Senior

_____ Graduate Student

Were you required to take this course? _____ Required _____ Elective

Length of Course? _____ Quarter _____ Semester

1. Overall, how does this text compare to other texts you've used?

_____ Superior _____ Better Than Most _____ Average _____ Poor

2. Please rate the text in the following areas:

	Superior	Better Than Most	Average	Poor
Author's Writing Style	_____	_____	_____	_____
Readability	_____	_____	_____	_____
Organization	_____	_____	_____	_____
Accuracy	_____	_____	_____	_____
Layout and Design	_____	_____	_____	_____
Illustrations/Photos/Tables	_____	_____	_____	_____
Examples	_____	_____	_____	_____
Problems/Exercises	_____	_____	_____	_____
Topic Selection	_____	_____	_____	_____
Currentness of Coverage	_____	_____	_____	_____
Explanation of Difficult Concepts	_____	_____	_____	_____
Match-up with Course Coverage	_____	_____	_____	_____
Applications to Real Life	_____	_____	_____	_____

3. Circle those chapters you especially liked:
   1 2 3 4 5 6 7 8 9 10 11 12 13 14 15 16 17 18 19 20
   What was your favorite chapter? _____
   Comments:

4. Circle those chapters you liked least:
   1 2 3 4 5 6 7 8 9 10 11 12 13 14 15 16 17 18 19 20
   What was your least favorite chapter? _____
   Comments:

5. List any chapters your instructor did not assign. _____

6. What topics did your instructor discuss that were not covered in the text?_____

   _____

7. Were you required to buy this book? _____ Yes _____ No

   Did you buy this book new or used? _____ New _____ Used

   If used, how much did you pay? _____

   Do you plan to keep or sell this book? _____ Keep _____ Sell

   If you plan to sell the book, how much do you expect to receive? _____

   Should the instructor continue to assign this book? _____ Yes _____ No

8. Please list any other learning materials you purchased to help you in this course (e.g., study guide, lab manual).

   _____

9. What did you like most about this text? _____

   _____

10. What did you like least about this text? _____

    _____

11. General comments:

    May we quote you in our advertising? _____ Yes _____ No

    Please mail to: Boyd Lane
                      College Division Research Department
                      P. O. Box 508
                      Columbus, Ohio 43216-0508

    Thank you!